Presidential Chronicles

Volume VI:
Progressivism and Prosperity

BOOKS BY DAVID FISHER

Presidential Chronicles – Volume I: The Founders
(The Lives of George Washington, John Adams, Thomas Jefferson, James Madison, and James Monroe) (2021)

Presidential Chronicles – Volume II: Democracy Expands
(The Lives of John Quincy Adams, Andrew Jackson, Martin Van Buren, William Henry Harrison, and John Tyler) (2021)

Presidential Chronicles – Volume III: The Path to National Fracture
(The Lives of James Polk, Zachary Taylor, Millard Fillmore, Franklin Pierce, and James Buchanan) (2021)

Presidential Chronicles – Volume IV: War and Its Aftermath
(The Lives of Abraham Lincoln, Andrew Johnson, Ulysses Grant, Rutherford Hayes, and James Garfield) (2022)

Presidential Chronicles – Volume V: Dawn of a New Century
(The Lives of Chester Arthur, Grover Cleveland, Benjamin Harrison, William McKinley, and Theodore Roosevelt) (2022)

Presidential Chronicles – Volume VI: Progressivism and Prosperity
(The Lives of William Taft, Woodrow Wilson, Warren Harding, and Calvin Coolidge) (2023)

Optimize Now (or else!): How to Leverage Processes and Information to Achieve Enterprise Optimization (and Avoid Enterprise Extinction) (2003)

Presidential Chronicles

Volume VI:

Progressivism and Prosperity

THE LIVES OF:

William Taft

Woodrow Wilson

Warren Harding

Calvin Coolidge

David Fisher

2023

ISBN: 9798393699345

Imprint: Independently published

For Helene, Robin, and Brian

Table of Contents

Author's Forward

Welcome to **Volume VI** of ***Presidential Chronicles***, the series of books and videos on American history as seen through the lives of the Presidents of the United States. I initiated this series with the concept of providing *robust yet concise* biographies of every U.S. President. Using the vast content available from my personal library of more than 1,100 first edition presidential biographies, my goal is to distill the essence of these stories into compact form for those with either a serious or casual interest in my subjects. I lean heavily on direct quotes from the principal characters, as well as period-based images that seek to further bring these unique individuals to life. There are two notable changes with the introduction of Volume VI. While I remain committed to delivering robust yet concise biographies, the sheer volume of material available for our 20th Century Presidents had led to a slight increase in the length of each of these portrayals. As such, I am only able to incorporate four biographies in this particular volume, instead of the five that have appeared in each of the first five volumes in this series. I anticipate this approach will continue in subsequent volumes. As the biographies have each gotten a bit longer, I have incorporated chapters to help navigate through the stories of these presidential lives.

Volume VI: ***Progressivism and Prosperity*** tells the life stories of the following four American Presidents who shepherded their country through a dynamic period of change and growth:

William Taft
Woodrow Wilson
Warren Harding
Calvin Coolidge

As Theodore Roosevelt passed the torch to his successors, the dynamic spirit of progressivism continued to reign supreme, bringing increased reforms that sought to utilize the authority of the Federal government to directly enhance the lives of the American people. These changes corresponded to a rise in international prominence that eventually witnessed the impact of American might in helping to conclude the devastation of World War I. In the wake of that victory, many Americans turned inward, rejecting participation in Woodrow Wilson's vision of a League of Nations that they viewed as an infringement on American sovereignty. Instead, they embraced Warren Harding's pitch for a "Return to Normalcy," that was dominated by an "America First" agenda. Harding and his successor Calvin Coolidge cut taxes, reduced spending, paid down the debt, curtailed immigration, and pursued policies that led to the greatest decade of prosperity in American history. As told in ***Progressivism and Prosperity***, the Twenties did indeed "Roar" for the American people, before giving way to an unprecedented economic crash as these Presidents passed the torch to the next batch of American leaders.

As noted, the primary sources for all the books in the ***Presidential Chronicles*** series come from my personal collection of presidential biographies. I am deeply indebted to the authors of these books for their passion and depth of research that help bring our Presidents to life. The Primary Sources listed after each individual biography in this volume contributed the vast majority of my understanding of the President covered in that section. All direct quotations are noted in the text and referenced in the Notes section at the back of each biography. The vast majority of these quotations come from these primary sources, although additional references are noted in detail as well. I have not edited these quotations, including obvious misspellings or grammar mistakes, as I believe the original language provides the best insight into the essence of these individuals.

In terms of images, my strong preference is also to leverage the artistry provided in the biographies from my personal library. Many come from the Primary Sources which contributed to my understanding of each subject as reflected in the book's narrative. In some instances, I also utilize images from other biographies in my library, which are noted in the section entitled "Primary Sources Specifically for Illustrations." Additional images come from online research, with particular gratitude to the collections from the Library of Congress and the Smithsonian Institution, including the careful manner in which these images are sourced.

All images, from any of these sources, are referenced in detail in the section entitled "Illustrations and Their Sources." I have striven to identify each artist as well, sometimes getting out a magnifying glass to pull an artist's name from a signed work in one of the books from my personal collection. Unfortunately, many images from 19th Century and early 20th Century biographies are not credited to the artist, in which case I have identified that the artist is unknown. To the best of my knowledge, 100% of these images are available in the public domain. I'm happy to correct any instance in which my assessment of public domain status is incorrect.

As the sole contributor to ***Presidential Chronicles***, I have worked hard to ensure accuracy, appropriate sourcing, and fair representations of the facts and circumstances which led the rise (and at times falls) of the Presidents of the United States. Any errors along these lines, from substance to indexing to typos, is both unintentional and regrettable.

David Fisher
Bethesda, Maryland
September 2023

PRESIDENTIAL CHRONICLES
VOLUME VI: PROGRESSIVISM AND PROSPERITY
I: THE LIFE OF WILLIAM TAFT
DAVID FISHER

I: The Life of William Taft

Preface

William Taft had the loftiest goals growing up. He aspired to the highest office his country had to offer. No, not the presidency of the United States. Taft bought into the vision best articulated in the family by his father, who once told him, "To be Chief Justice of the United States is more than to be President in my estimation."[1] Taft wholeheartedly agreed and charted a path to reach that ultimate plateau. After finishing second in his class at Yale, the young attorney landed his first job on the Bench at the tender age of 29 when he was appointed to the Superior Court of his home state of Ohio. After transitioning to the nation's capital as his country's youngest Solicitor General, he subsequently felt himself blessed to be named by President Benjamin Harrison to the newly created Federal judgeship on the U.S. Circuit Court of Appeals back in his hometown of Cincinnati. Taft now had a lifetime appointment that was just a step removed from his ultimate dream job, and he was still only 34 years old. Life couldn't be better.

But Taft's career trajectory took an unexpected turn when another president, William McKinley, called him to Washington to offer him a different kind of job. This was a shocker – an opportunity that would require him to step down from the Bench and move halfway around the world. The United States had recently acquired the Philippines at the conclusion of its war with Spain, and McKinley wanted Taft to set up a new civil government. Taft was torn, forced to choose between his lifelong pursuit of judicial prominence and the call to duty by his national leader. In the end, duty won out, and Taft's career path became muddled. As he thrived in his role as Governor-General of the archipelago, bringing a non-imperialist mindset to establish "the Philippines for the Filipinos,"[2] he also found himself trapped. Not once but twice during this tenure, he was offered a spot on his beloved Supreme Court, but both times felt compelled to decline. He was committed to the people of the Philippines, and even fervent personal desire couldn't compel him to desert his current calling.

Taft's executive responsibilities eventually landed him in the Cabinet of President Theodore Roosevelt as Secretary of War. Not only would he continue to oversee the Philippines (now from a distance), but he also became Roosevelt's jack-of-all-trades, representing him in crises around the globe. In addition to running the War Department, Taft was put in charge of the monumental task of getting the Panama Canal built. He helped forestall a revolution in Cuba. He went on a world tour of diplomatic significance, all at the behest of his close friend, President Roosevelt. And when the President once again offered him his dream job on the Court, he turned it down again, as his own chance at the presidency was dangling before his eyes. Taft didn't want to be President. He knew he probably wouldn't be very good at it. But Roosevelt was essentially ready to anoint him as his heir apparent, and Taft's wife, Nellie, and the rest of his family, pushed him to reluctantly follow along. The normally jolly and effective public servant was thus thrust into the worst four years of his life.

Taft was never suited to the toils of the presidency, and he certainly struggled across the demands of the job. But, what truly derailed Taft was the simple fact that he wasn't Theodore Roosevelt. Roosevelt's ardent followers complained incessantly about their chief's successor, helping to lead Roosevelt to personally conclude that the selection of Taft had been a mistake. Once that decision was made, Roosevelt moved out to correct his error by taking on Taft, both personally and professionally, crushing Taft's soul while completely fracturing the Republican Party. Roosevelt's selfish ploy proved disastrous, handing the presidency back to the Democrats on a silver platter.

Fortunately for Taft (and the United States), this was not the end of his story. His sorrowful stint as President was merely an unfortunate interlude. Less than a decade later, the Republicans recaptured the presidency in the form of Warren Harding, who early in his tenure offered Taft his fourth opportunity to join the Supreme Court. This time, nothing would stand in his way, as he not only rose to join the nation's highest tribunal, but he would do so as its Chief. In becoming the only person in American history to serve as both President and on the Supreme Court, Taft jumped into the role with gusto, not only overseeing some landmark decisions in his nearly nine-year tenure but also remaking many aspects of the entire Federal judiciary. He was finally in his dream job, and he didn't disappoint – himself or his country. In the end, William Taft's lifelong service to his country was indeed remarkable by any estimation, as long as you forget those awful four years in the presidency.

1. Lofty Expectations

The first of the Tafts to arrive in the New World was Robert, a carpenter, who made the journey from England in the late 1600s. Robert Taft settled in the Massachusetts colony, where his patriotic family would eventually volunteer to fight for independence from the Mother Country during the Revolutionary War. The family tradition of judicial service came along when William's grandfather, Peter, moved to Vermont and put on the robes of a county judge. His son took this a step further. Alphonso Taft, the father of the future President, journeyed from his home in Vermont to New Haven, Connecticut, for his education at Yale. Alphonso finished #3 in the class of 1833 and then stayed on to complete his studies at Yale Law School. From there, Alphonso Taft headed west to set up shop in the city of Cincinnati, which was growing by leaps and bounds after the introduction of the Miami and Erie Canal. Alphonso was a successful attorney who became a leading member of the community, helping to attract the first railroads, which fueled even further growth. Alphonso established his roots in Cincinnati with his bride, Fanny Phelps, and their two young children, Charles and Peter. But the marriage abruptly ended when Fanny died in 1852 at the tender age of 29. Alphonso did not stay single long, tying the knot with Louisa Torrey just a year and a half after the passing of his first wife. Louisa had a similar background to Alphonso, having grown up in New England,

I-1: Taft's parents, Alphonso and Louisa, circa 1859

and spent time in New Haven, where she and her sister, Delia, often attended lectures at Yale. Louisa was a strong, independent woman, who sought intellectual pursuits with the menfolk in town, often much to her preference than traditional socializing with their wives.

The new couple would add four children to their family, beginning with a son, Sammie, who died shortly after his first birthday after being inflicted with whooping cough. Next came William Howard, born September 15, 1857. He was a big boy from the very beginning. Just seven weeks after his birth, Taft's mother remarked, "He is very large of his age and grows fat every day. ... He spreads his hands to any one who will take him and his face is wreathed with smiles at the slightest provocation."[3] Taft dealt with obesity his entire life but didn't let that take away from his genial personality – at least most of the time. The Taft household was a serious one, where high expectations were set by both parents. The most attention, and the most pressure, came from Louisa, who supported her children but pushed them to succeed. Taft got more of his loveable personality from his father, but Alphonso could also be quite demanding. If the children started to slip in school, they were called lazy, and corrections were required. Taft's future bride, Nellie, once wrote favorably of her husband's upbringing, "The two, the father and mother, had created a family atmosphere in which the children breathed in the highest ideals, and were stimulated to sustained and strenuous intellectual and moral effort in order to conform to the family standard." In most all respects, Taft exceeded these admittedly high expectations.

Will Taft, as he was most commonly known, was only four years old when the Civil War erupted, but he was mostly immune from the national calamity. He and his family were sufficiently removed from the fight that the war had little impact on him. His youth was filled with schoolwork but also featured plenty of outdoor activities, including many team sports. Baseball was his passion, along with swimming and wrestling. But his education was always number one. Taft entered Woodward High School at the age of 13, making the mile-long walk each way to engage in the city's most serious educational

I-2: Taft, circa 1863 (age ~6)

institute for young men. Extracurricular activities were non-existent at Woodward. It was schooling during the day, with more study at night. And Taft thrived. He was a popular student, reflecting his outgoing and amiable personality, and also respected as his own work ethic (and constant urgings of his parents) led him to the second spot in his graduating class. Taft was honored with the salutatorian address during commencement ceremonies in 1874, where his topic was women's suffrage.

I-3: Taft, 1868 (age 11)

Throughout this period, Taft became enamored with the law. His father had been appointed to the Superior Court of Ohio, and Taft couldn't get enough of hearing about this honored posting. He looked forward to visits to his father's courtroom, and enjoyed breaks in his own studies during the evenings at home when his father would not only tell him stories of the cases under his purview, but also imbued a fascination with the history and traditions of the legal profession. Early

I-4: Taft's childhood home, Cincinnati, OH

on, Taft had his heart set. He would become a lawyer, then a judge, and if all went well, he'd reach the pinnacle – a spot on the U.S. Supreme Court.

The first real step on this journey was a foregone conclusion. His father had attended Yale, his mother sat in on classes at Yale, and both his older brothers had thrived at Yale. The path to New Haven was clear, and Taft enrolled in 1874 at the age of 17. The freshman surely stood out in a crowd, topping six feet in height and tipping the scales at 225 pounds. He also stood out in the classroom, where hard work combined with his natural smarts to take him to the top of his class. That standing was important to him and his family back home, and he tracked the scores regularly. To be sure, Taft had other interests as well, but he kept many of them in check. While he was a champion wrestler on campus, and a standout rower, his father wouldn't permit playing in any team sports. Tafts didn't go to Yale for baseball or football; they went for an education, with high expectations for academic excellence. Taft didn't disappoint. While known for procrastinating and then crashing to complete his assignments on time, Taft excelled year after year with the demanding academic curriculum at Yale.

As Taft progressed at Yale, his father moved up in the world as well, becoming the first in the family to achieve national prominence. Toward the latter portion of the scandal-ridden second term of President Ulysses Grant, Alphonso Taft was appointed Secretary of War upon the resignation of William Belknap in March 1876. As the scandals continued, Alphonso was quickly on the move. Just three months into his tenure in Grant's Cabinet, he was shifted to Attorney General, after Edwards Pierrepont became Minister to Great Britain. This national recognition was a boost to the Taft name and certainly helped the prospects of Bill Taft (as he was now commonly called).

I-5: Taft at Yale, 1875 (age ~18)

Taft wasn't entirely all work and no play at Yale. He was very social, and his hearty laugh and good humor added to his popularity. He also made lifelong friends, including those associated with the Skull & Bones society, to which he was granted admission in his senior year. When he was running for President in 1908, Taft gave a speech at the University of Wisconsin in which he reflected on the relationships he had made during his own college days. "The friendships that you then form [in college] are friendships you can never form again. In this four years of life there is an epitome of the life to come, it is true, but it is life with a higher standard, with purer ideals than any life that is to come in the whirlwind you are to meet hereafter. It is to this that I call your attention, and tell you to enjoy it to the full."[4] Bill Taft had certainly followed that advice during his tenure at Yale, and it paid him dividends for the rest of his life.

The end at Yale came in 1875. Taft narrowly missed his goal of the top of his class, finishing second (out of 132 graduates), just a couple of points shy of his friend, Clarence Kelsey. His commencement address was entitled "The Professional and Political Prospects of the College Graduate." His sights remained high, and his fondness for Yale remained strong. "I love Yale as I love my mother,"[5] he would say some thirty years later. Nevertheless, when choosing where he would study the law, it wouldn't be in New Haven, but rather back home in Cincinnati.

Taft chose Cincinnati Law School to further the pursuit of his chosen profession, which would take place in the comfortable, yet demanding

I-6: Pike's Opera House in Cincinnati, circa 1875

surroundings of family. The path to the Bar in the United States was transitioning during this era. While many continued to "read the law" in apprenticeship mode with existing attorneys, law schools were increasingly becoming more prevalent on the path to the legal profession. The students at Cincinnati would get the best of both, as all 60 students were required to gain practical experience in a local firm to round out their course of study. For Taft, this meant signing on with his father's old law firm. It was a busy time for Taft, which included a stint as a local reporter for the *Cincinnati Commercial* on the courtroom beat. Taft had a talent for the press, leading to a full-time job offer if he would give up the law. This was a non-starter for William Taft.

During this period, Taft did not shy away from the social opportunities available in Cincinnati. He enjoyed dating a number of young women, often with trips to the theater or the city's best restaurants. According to Taft, "nowhere … will you find girls as pretty, as interesting, as stylish, and as fresh."[6] But he had to be careful, always under the watchful eyes of his demanding parents. At one point, his father rebuked him for taking too much time away from his legal training with these more frivolous pursuits. "I do not think that you have accomplished this past year as much as you ought," his father admonished. "Our anxiety for your success is very great and I know that there is but one way to attain it, and that is by self-denial and enthusiastic hard work in the profession. … This gratifying your fondness for society is fruitless."[7] Taft did his best to balance all these competing interests and, for the most part, thrived in everything he touched.

Politics first entered Taft's life in earnest with the 1880 election cycle, coinciding with his graduation from law school and his admittance to the Bar. Taft committed himself to his father's Republican Party and stumped a bit here and there for the party's nominee, James Garfield. He also earned his first political appointment. When Miller Outcalt was named Prosecutor for Hamilton County in January 1881, he sought out Taft as his top assistant. Taft accepted the post, providing what his future bride described as "the most valuable experience he could possibly have in fitting him for trial work at the bar."[8] Taft also began to make political connections of his own, benefitting from his father's stature as well as his own growing reputation.

Both Tafts were about to move up in the political world. After Garfield's election and subsequent assassination, the new President,

I-7: President Chester Arthur

Chester Arthur, called Alphonso Taft to Washington to offer him the post of minister to Austria-Hungary. During their meeting, the President also mentioned a new opportunity for his son, if he wanted it. William Taft was appointed the Collector of Internal Revenue for the First District, headquartered in Cincinnati. Taft took over the position in March 1882, upon which he quickly discovered how much he disliked the job. The position was pure drudgery, forcing him to spend long hours at his desk dealing with mounds of minutiae. Moreover, he detested the political aspects of the job. President Arthur had been a career spoilsman at a time when political patronage was the primary currency that fueled the machines from one election cycle to the next. In the wake of Garfield's murder by a deranged office-seeker, Arthur would eventually transform into a true advocate for civil service reform, but for now, he was still in his traditional mode when Taft was told to make room for new appointees in his shop. Throwing out good workers for bad for purely political reasons was anathema to Taft. He informed his father, that to get rid of "perhaps the best men in the service so far as reliability, knowledge of duty, and energy" because of politics would "cause a very big stink [and] I do not want to have a hand in it. ... I would rather resign [than] do the dirty work."[9] So, resign he did.

Meanwhile, Taft had other things on his mind – namely, one Helen Herron. The Herrons and Tafts were family friends, and Taft had known Nellie (everyone called her Nellie) since their youths. Nellie was an exceptional student, having attended Miami University in Oxford, Ohio. She was incredibly well-rounded, with a love for music, reading, literature, philosophy, and many other subjects. She was also fiercely independent and longed for meaningful engagement in society, which for her often meant seeking encounters with learned men. She was also ambitious – seriously ambitious. This drive was sparked as a young girl with an extended stay in the White House of Rutherford and Lucy Hayes. The Herrons were close with the Hayeses, including a short stint as law partners. The Hayeses enjoyed out-of-town guests, and that included the Herrons in his first year in office (1877). Nellie later admitted to a reporter that from that White House experience, she had vowed to marry a man "destined to be President of the United States."[10] Indeed she would.

Taft started courting Nellie Herron in 1884 while she was working as a teacher and he was establishing himself as an attorney. They shared a love of the theater, and both joined a theatrical group in which each appeared in several plays. When Nellie and a couple of friends began hosting a weekly gathering for intellectually stimulating conversation, Taft was among the invited participants. "We called it a 'salon,'" Nellie recalled, "because we planned to receive a company who were to engage in what we considered brilliant discussion of topics intellectual and economic."[11] The attraction was mutual, but Taft was the more aggressive of the pair in pursuing the match. He proposed marriage in April 1885, and while Nellie provided a tentative acceptance the following month, he still had his work cut out for him to keep her in the fold. He was relentless in his offers of affection, telling her, "Oh Nellie, do say that you will try to love me. Oh, how I will work and strive to be better and do better. Oh Nellie, you must love me."[12] His persistence paid off. A little over a year later, the couple tied the knot in the home of

I-8: Nellie Herron's "Salon" with Taft in the center and Nellie to his right, 1884

I-9: William and Nellie Taft at the time of their wedding, 1886

Nellie's parents. From there, it was off to Europe for a glorious honeymoon of cathedrals, museums, and plenty of shopping. When the newlyweds returned home, they moved into their new house in suburban Walnut Hills overlooking the Ohio River, just on the outskirts of Cincinnati.

Nellie Taft was the most influential person in the life of William Taft (with Theodore Roosevelt being a close second). Unfortunately, her ambition was often at odds with his. She thought her husband's longing for the Bench was short-sighted. He had so much going for him, he could do better. She wanted to be First Lady, and felt if he played his cards right, there was no reason her husband couldn't bring her all the way to the White House. She pushed him every step of the way, like his parents, but with a different end game in mind. Alphonso and Louisa Taft were aligned with their son on a path to a judgeship, and perhaps all the way to the Supreme Court. Taft's natural instincts knew this was what he was meant to do. Nellie Taft thought otherwise and was never shy in saying so.

2. Judge Taft

Given the different perspectives of the newlyweds on career trajectories for Taft, it was an interesting turn of events when his first opportunity to don a judicial robe came just a couple of years into their marriage. Early in 1887, the practicing attorney arrived at home with news that he was being offered a place on the Superior Court of Ohio, the same post that had launched his father onto a career of national prominence. Taft was only 29 years old, seven years out of law school, which may have been the reason that his wife responded, "Oh, don't try to be funny. That's perfectly impossible."[13] In fact, the offer was perfectly legitimate. Judge Judson Harmon had decided to retire from his elected position. That gave Governor Joseph Foraker the opportunity to select anyone he wanted to serve the final 14 months of his term. Foraker and Taft had not exactly been politically aligned, but Foraker knew Taft "well enough to know that he had a strong intellectual endowment, a keen, logical, analytical mind, and that all the essential foundations for a good judge had been well and securely laid."[14] Taft was effusive in his appreciation for his dream opportunity, telling Foraker, "Considering the opportunity so honorable a position offers to a young man of my age and circumstances, my debt to you is very great. The responsibility you assume for me in making this appointment will always be an incentive to an industrious and conscientious discharge of my duties."[15] There was only one problem. Nellie Taft was opposed to the whole thing. According to Taft's spouse, the opportunity

> was not a matter for such warm congratulation after all. … I dreaded to see him settled for good in the judiciary and missing all the youthful enthusiasms and exhilarating difficulties which a more general contact with the world would have given him. In other words, I began even then to fear the narrowing effects of the Bench and to prefer for him a diverse experience which would give him an all-round professional development.

In this instance, Taft had the final say, gratefully accepting his first judicial appointment. But this fundamental disagreement would never really go away, with Nellie ultimately winning more than she lost.

Taff's relatively brief stint on the Superior Court brought him a reputation on one of the most contentious topics across the country –

battles between management and labor. With the rise of big cities and the migration of workers from farms to factories, all the rules favored big business. The supply of labor far exceeded demand, enabling the bosses to make big profits on the backs of their employees. They kept wages low, working conditions were poor, and there wasn't much the workers could do about it. Labor unions began to rise to counter this treatment, but the unions often ran into governmental barriers. The laws as passed by the legislatures, enforced by the executives, and adjudicated by the courts almost always favored management. Judge William Taft fell squarely into this pattern as he donned his judicial robe.

The most prominent cases in Taft's courtroom were conflicts between management and labor. The most significant of these was *Moores & Company v. Bricklayers Union No. 1*, which came to Taft in 1889 after just a few months on the job. The bricklayers were in a dispute with Parker Brothers, a local builder, and decided to go on strike. To put pressure on management, the bricklayers threatened action against Moores & Company, a supplier of limestone to Parker Brothers. Moores sued and got a favorable ruling from a lower court, which was appealed to Judge Taft. Taft took his customary exhaustive review of the case and ultimately sided with Moores. In a theme that would repeat in future cases for Taft, he determined that the action against Moores was an unlawful boycott. Since the bricklayers were not in a dispute with Moores, they had no legal right to refuse to do business with the company. According to Taft, motive mattered. The judge ruled that under common law, "there are losses wilfully caused to one by another in the exercise of what otherwise would be a lawful right, from simple motives of malice."[16] Taft issued an injunction to halt the boycott, initiating his anti-union, pro-business reputation.

When Taft's appointed term came to an end, he successfully ran to succeed himself, capturing just shy of 60% of the vote. But he would complete only a short portion of his elected term as another opportunity came along that pulled him from his beloved Bench. In 1889, an opening appeared on the U.S. Supreme Court. The selection would be made by the new President, Benjamin Harrison, of nearby Indiana, and many of Taft's friends were lobbying for him to get the job. Taft was just 32 years old with extremely limited judicial experience. He thought the talk was pure nonsense. "My chances of going to the moon and of donning a silk gown at the hands of President Harrison are about equal,"[17] Taft wrote

I-10: President Benjamin Harrison

his father. President Harrison agreed, giving the promotion to David Brewer from the Eighth Circuit. But Harrison was moved by all the talk in favor of Taft, leading him to a different offer that would place him in the Supreme Court on a regular basis – not as a judge, but as an advocate. Harrison wanted Taft to be the nation's sixth Solicitor General.

The position of Solicitor General was formally introduced in the United States in the administration of Ulysses Grant in 1870. The role was to be the primary representative of the Federal government in cases before the Supreme Court. As a direct report to the Attorney General, the Solicitor was also tasked with preparing legal briefs for the President and the Cabinet. This was a tall task for anyone, let alone someone with virtually no experience in Federal law. Plus, this meant leaving the Bench, which Taft was loath to do. The greatest proponent for his acceptance, though, was right by his side – Taft's wife, Nellie. Mrs. Taft felt her husband was being held back as a state judge in Ohio compared to a leading member of the Federal executive branch in the nation's capital. Her goal for Taft remained the presidency, not the Supreme Court, and this executive position and the political connections it would offer within the top ranks of the Republican Party was an ideal step for her husband to take. The Washington social scene had a powerful attraction for Nellie as well. With the strong push from within his home, Taft agreed to accept the position. The previous Solicitor Generals entered office at an average age of 48. At the time he accepted the post, Taft had just turned 33.

This was not an easy transition for Taft and one for which he was initially quite discouraged. While Nellie was setting up shop in their small home on DuPont Circle, Taft was being escorted to his tiny office in the bowels of the Justice Department. His staff consisted of one secretary, who he had to share with others. His caseload was backlogged as his post had been vacant for the past two months. He was also learning on the fly with his first practical exposure to the kind of Federal disputes

I-11: Taft as Solicitor General, 1890 (age 33)

that play out in front of the Supreme Court. Fortunately, his work ethic and natural talents kicked in as he dove into his work. The job turned out to be a phenomenal crash course throughout which he performed admirably, even though it took him a few cases to start finding his footing in his own mind as an effective advocate. He was self-deprecating in a note to his father about his early performances in the courtroom, explaining that his biggest challenge was "in holding the attention of the Supreme Court justices. They seem to think when I begin to talk that is a good chance to ... read ... letters, to eat lunch, and to devote their attention to correcting proof."[18] These sentiments aside, the results were excellent, as Taft won 15 of 18 cases in his first year on the job.

The happiest in this venture was clearly Nellie Taft. She reveled being in the nation's capital and all that came with it. This meant hobnobbing with the political elites. Taft made friends quickly, and that meant nights on the town with members of the Supreme Court, Attorney General W.H. Miller, and leading members of Congress, including the likes of Senator Henry Cabot Lodge and Speaker of the House Thomas Reed. Taft's most notable new connection, though, was a reformer from New York who had a seat on the Civil Service Commission. His name was Theodore Roosevelt. In many ways, the two were complete opposites. Roosevelt was fiery, pugnacious, and impulsive, while Taft was typically calm, deliberate, and judicial in every sense of the word. But despite these personality differences, they were aligned around many of the same topics, and they truly enjoyed each other's company. They lived near each other, often walked to work together, regularly met for lunch, and essentially became fast friends. Next to his wife, Theodore Roosevelt would have the greatest influence on the life and career of William Taft – most often for the better, but in some cases, absolutely for the worst.

I-12: Theodore Roosevelt, member of the Civil Service Commission

There were additional family developments for the Tafts at this point about five years into their marriage, on both ends of the circle of life. Taft's older brother, Peter, was dying of tuberculosis, and his father was also fading fast. Alphonso Taft had gone to California to see if the better climate might help improve his heart and lung troubles, but it wasn't working. As things deteriorated, Taft raced to the coast to be with his father for his final few days. While his father was unconscious most of that time, at one point he awakened, and with a clear mind, Taft recalled, "he looked up at me in the sweetest way imaginable and said to me, 'Will, I love you beyond expression.'"[19] Taft owed a lot to his father, who had played such an important part in the first half of his life, and this was a comforting way for that relationship to come to an end. At the other end of the spectrum, Taft became a father himself for the first time. Nellie gave birth on September 8, 1889, to a baby boy they named Robert Alphonso. According to the proud papa, "I have been accused of the unjudicial conduct of rushing out into the street after the boy came and yelling, 'Hurrah! For a man is born unto me!'"[20] This would be the first of three children the Tafts would bring into the

I-13: Nellie Taft (center) with the couple's first two children, Helen and Robert

world, with Helen arriving in 1891, and Charles following six years later. The Tafts also began a family tradition of escaping to a spot overlooking the St. Lawrence River in Canada for their regular summer vacations. Murray Bay offered a beautiful rustic setting, "simple as a camp in the woods,"[21] where the Taft family would venture most summers for the next twenty years.

Once again, William Taft wouldn't be in the job of Solicitor General for very long. This time, the U.S. Congress opened up the opportunity of a lifetime with the expansion of the Federal court system. In Harrison's final year in office, Congress created the U.S. Circuit Court of Appeals to take the pressure off the overloaded Federal judiciary. This meant 12 new openings on the Federal Bench, with the Sixth Circuit housed in Taft's hometown of Cincinnati. In his understated fashion, Taft declared his interest. "I like judicial life," Taft wrote, "and there is only one higher judicial position in the country than that in the line of promotion to the Supreme Court."[22] Taft pulled out all the stops to capture the position and got a boost from many of his friends in both Washington and Ohio. The members of the Cincinnati Bar telegraphed President Harrison: "We earnestly recommend the appointment of Solicitor General Taft to the new judgeship for the Ohio Circuit. His service on the Superior bench here has shown that he possesses judicial qualities of the highest order. The Cincinnati Bar is practically unanimous in urging his appointment."[23] Of course, there was one prominent naysayer in the bunch, and that was Nellie Taft. Once again, contrary to her husband's ambitions, she thought a lifetime appointment to the Bench would be self-defeating. She warned her husband, "If you get your heart's desire ... it will put an end to all the opportunities you now have of being thrown with the bigwigs."[24] When the appointment came, though, Taft accepted on the spot. Nellie would later admit that "I think he enjoyed the work of the following eight years more than any he has ever undertaken."[25]

Taft could not have been happier, settling back into his home life in Cincinnati with a lifetime appointment as a Federal judge still at the young age of 34. The Sixth Circuit covered all or parts of four states, including Ohio, Kentucky, Tennessee, and Michigan. While he spent most of his time in Cincinnati, he also 'rode the circuit,' traveling to other locations in his region to hear cases as well. It was not long before Taft was widely recognized for his conservative views from the Bench. He was diligent in his reviews and detailed in his decisions. And he enjoyed every minute of it, despite some of the controversial cases that came before him. Once again, labor-management issues were at the heart of a number of those most challenging legal actions.

I-14: Judge Taft, circa 1894 (age ~37)

Three cases in particular provide notable insights into Taft's judicial determinations during his tenure as a Federal judge. The first related to a union strike in the case of *Toledo, Ann Arbor, and North Michigan Railway Company v. Brotherhood of Locomotive Engineers*. The case echoed the same kinds of issues Taft had encountered at the state level in the *Moores* case. The Brotherhood went on strike against the Toledo line in 1893. Per "Rule 12" of their bylaws, all members were expected to strike not only Toledo but also any other rail line that did business with the prime instigator of union disgruntlement. This created secondary, or "sympathetic" strikes, which led to the lawsuit against the engineers. While Judge Taft conceded in his ruling that everyone had "an inalienable right to bestow his labor as he will, and to withhold his labor where he will. … [But] generally speaking this is true, not absolutely."[26] Since the strikers had no grievance against these other railroads, their actions were unlawful. According to Taft, "… the existence and enforcement of Rule 12, under their organic law, make the whole Brotherhood a criminal conspiracy against the laws of their country."[27] This boycott was a violation of the property rights of the employer and contrary to the nation's interstate commerce laws. Taft issued an injunction against any strike related to this case that was against a railway where the workers did not have a direct grievance against the employer other than its relationship with the Toledo line. Chalk one up for management, and just the beginning of Taft accumulating a reputation as an anti-labor, injunction-happy jurist.

As worker unrest continued to mount, so did the violence associated with some of these disputes. In the case of a strike in Chicago against the Pullman Palace Car Company in 1894, President Grover Cleveland called in the military to quell a violent state of unrest. This work stoppage had long tentacles, eventually shutting down nearly all rail travel across 27 states. The assessment of Cleveland's Attorney General Richard Olney was that this strike was a violation of Federal law as it impacted both interstate commerce and the delivery of the U.S. mail. Based on this analysis, Cleveland felt justified in using armed soldiers to end the work stoppage once and for all. Chicago was outside the jurisdiction of Judge William Taft, but his court became engaged when one of the leaders of the American Railway Union that was leading the strike against Pullman showed up in Cincinnati to recruit railway workers to honor the walkout and try to bring Pullman to be bargaining table. Frank Phelan set his sights on the workers of the Cincinnati Southern Railroad, which happened to be in receivership, and, therefore, under the auspices of Taft's court. When the receiver complained to the Court about Phelan's actions, Taft intervened with another injunction, which Phelan quickly brushed aside. "I don't care if I am violating injunctions," he told his union colleagues. "No matter what the result may be to-morrow, if I go to jail for sixteen generations I want you to do as you have done."[28] With that, Phelan was arrested and hauled into Judge Taft's court.

To no one's surprise, Taft once again determined that this secondary strike against the railroad in his jurisdiction and under Federal receivership was simply unlawful. With a courtroom packed with animated laborers and tensions running particularly high, Judge Taft calmly issued his ruling. While first affirming the union's legal right to organize, collectively bargain, raise money, and strike against employers with which they had legitimate grievances, as he had ruled before, these secondary strikes were simply unlawful. According to Judge Taft:

> His [Phelan's] coming here, and his advice to the Southern Railway employees, or to the employees of the other roads, to quit, has nothing to do with the terms of their employment. They were not dissatisfied with their service or their pay. Phelan came to Cincinnati to carry out the purpose of a combination of men, and his act in inciting the employees of all Cincinnati roads to quit service was part of that combination. If the combination was unlawful, then every act

> in pursuance of it was unlawful, and his instigation of the strike would be an unlawful wrong done by him to every railway company in the city, for which they can recover damages, and for which, so far as his acts affected the Southern Railway, he is in contempt of court.[29]

Taft's injunction stood, and Phelan was sent to prison for six months. Taft noted in the closing portion of his ruling that "The punishment for a contempt is the most disagreeable duty a court has to perform, but it is one from which the court cannot shrink. If the orders of the court are not obeyed the next step is unto anarchy."[30] Taft's line of reasoning was consistently applied through each of these cases, much to the discontent of the unions.

The final case of note in Taft's tenure on the Federal bench took on a different flavor. This one related to the still relatively new antitrust statute that Congress approved and President Harrison signed into law. The statute had been on the books for nearly a decade, but very few antitrust suits had been brought by the government under the Sherman Antitrust Act. With so few precedents, judges were very much on the hot seat in terms of being among the first to interpret the law in a real-world setting. One such case found its way to the Sixth Circuit and Judge William Taft in 1898.

The Addyston Pipe & Steel Company of Cincinnati was formed with five other pipe companies from the states of Kentucky, Alabama, and Tennessee. The government claimed this combination violated the Sherman Act and should be dismantled. The company admitted coming together to avoid the ruinous competition amongst themselves. However, it argued before the court that even after joining forces, the company still controlled only 30% of the national pipe market, which could hardly be considered a monopoly given the need to compete for prices against the remaining competition. Judge Taft disagreed. "Where the sole object of both parties in making the contract as expressed therein, is merely to restrain competition, and enhance or maintain prices," Taft wrote in his ruling, "it would seem that there was nothing to justify or excuse the restraint, that it would necessarily have a tendency to monopoly, and therefore would be void."[31] This was a shot across the bow against big business, with Addyston quick to file an appeal with the Supreme Court. That Court's ruling was unanimous, sustaining the decision by Judge Taft. For one of the first times, the judiciary sided with the government in an antitrust case, with William Taft's exhaustive opinion carrying the day, not only in his court, but in the nation's capital as well.

Taft loved the law and went by the book regardless of any personal interests he might have in a particular matter. For example, he ruled in a banking case against his father-in-law, John Herron, who was angered by the result. Herron believed Taft went overboard in trying to appear neutral, and that his ultimate decision was unfair. Taft heard him out and suggested he appeal to the Supreme Court. Herron did, and lost again. In another case, Taft ruled against a buddy from his days at Yale in a dispute with an Assistant Secretary of State. His friend lost his job in the process, and Taft lost a friend, but that was simply the price to pay for being entrusted as a Federal judge. Even former President Benjamin Harrison, the man who put Taft on the Bench, received no special favors from Taft. After leaving the presidency, Harrison returned to the practice of law and had a case pending before Judge Taft. Thinking he needed more time to prepare, he sought an extension for the trial date. Taft denied the request. He thought the time was ample, and no one deserved special treatment, even a man to whom Taft owed so much.

Taft was on top of the world during his tenure on the Federal bench. He was doing exactly the kind of work he had longed to do, and he was confident in his abilities to mete out justice in a thorough and fair manner. He was often invited to make speeches throughout his circuit. It was a task he didn't enjoy, but he accepted many, often at the urging of Nellie, who continued to want to expand his exposure in case a political opportunity might come along. Taft also remained deeply committed to the legal profession itself. Throughout most of his tenure in the Sixth Circuit, he did double duty as the dean of his alma mater, the Cincinnati Law School, where he also taught classes twice a week in the area of real property law. When his other alma mater came calling, however, he declined its entreaties. The presidency at Yale opened up in 1898, and Taft was approached about the opportunity, but he turned it down flat. First, he had no interest in leaving the Federal Bench, but he also felt that despite his love for the institution, it wasn't the right fit. He didn't believe he had the depth of education or experience to take on the responsibility. "A man like myself who ... is necessarily lacking in the wide culture, breadth of learning, and technical preparation in the science of education which are needed to discharge the duties that I have attempted to describe," Taft concluded it "would make a great mistake, and injure both the University and himself were he to assume the high obligations of the office of President. ... For these reasons, I have no hesitation in saying definitely that were the Corporation of Yale to invite me to become President, I should decline the great honor."[32] Taft wanted to be right where he was, serving out his lifetime judicial appointment, with only one job that would entice him away – a spot on the Supreme Court. But then came a telegram from the President of the United States, sending those best laid plans right out the window.

3. The Philippines

While Taft was hearing cases in his Cincinnati courthouse over the past couple of years, his country had been at war. The conflict was with Spain, emanating from a rebellion in Spanish-held Cuba. President William McKinley sought negotiations for months to ease the path to Cuban independence, but the Spanish were reluctant to accede to McKinley's demands. This ultimately led to a declaration of war in June 1898. The battles lasted just a few months as the Americans trounced the Spanish on land and on the sea. This included destroying Spanish fleets in both the Caribbean and in the faraway Philippines. When the Treaty of Paris was finally signed, the Americans had new equities in Cuba, and new titles to the Philippines, Guam, and Puerto Rico. The U.S. was becoming a colonial power for the first time in its history.

While the Filipinos were happy to see their Spanish overlords ousted, they initially didn't see much improvement with the Americans. The U.S. military had taken charge of the islands and found themselves fighting an ongoing insurgency led by rebel Emilio Aguinaldo. The Americans had all the firepower, but the rebel Filipinos knew the land and were settling into a rhythm of timely raids and overall guerilla warfare. The rebels initiated most of the battles, which the Americans always ended, but typically without much in the way of real victories. The Filipinos simply disappeared back into the jungles and then resumed their lives until the next opportunity to attack.

I-15: President William McKinley in the Cabinet Room in the White House

President McKinley had choices as to what to do with the Philippines. He rejected most of the available options. He decided that granting independence was out of the question, as the Filipinos were largely uneducated and had never participated in any form of government before. McKinley reasoned that such a move would simply result in anarchy. The President concluded that any such independence would be short-lived, likely resulting in colonization by one of the other European powers. Alternatively, McKinley could have lived the life of the typical imperialist, welcoming the new colony with no expectation other than the people of the archipelago largely serving the interests of the mother country for generations to come. The President rejected this approach as being un-American. He ultimately concluded, "there was nothing left for us to do but to take them all, and to educate the Filipinos, and uplift and civilize and Christianize them, and by God's grace do the very best we could by them, as our fellow-men for whom Christ also died."[33] President McKinley continued to insist there was nothing imperialistic in the actions of the Americans. In remarks at the Home Market Club in Boston, the President affirmed his intent to afford the Filipinos "every opportunity to prosecute their lawful pursuits; encouraging them in thrift and industry; making them feel and know that we are their friends, not their enemies, that their good is our aim, that their welfare is our welfare."[34] Bringing that vision to life was an unprecedented step for the United States, and the President needed to find the right man to lead that effort. In talking things over with his Secretary of State, William Day, McKinley asserted, "I want a man to head the commission, who is strong, honest and tactful; a man of education and executive ability; a man who is fearless, but conservative, and who will get along with the army people." Day replied, "That sounds like Bill Taft."[35]

Day, who was McKinley's closest adviser in Washington, had gotten to know Taft when both served as judges in Ohio. The fact that Taft had never done anything remotely like this assignment didn't matter. In Day's judgment, he had all the qualifications the President was seeking. In short order, the President agreed, upon which he sent the following telegram to the Federal judge in the Sixth Circuit: "I would like to see you in Washington in important business within the next few days. On Thursday if possible."[36] When Taft read the telegram he was utterly confused. He had known McKinley over the years but had not been in touch with him recently. As he talked over the message with Nellie, all he could think of was that this might relate to an opening on the Supreme Court, which everyone knew was Taft's primary ambition in life. But there had been no indication of an opening on the Court, so Taft remained perplexed as he planned his trip to the nation's capital. When he arrived and met with the President, he was in for the surprise of his life.

"Judge, I would like to have you go to the Philippines," McKinley told Taft in their one-on-one meeting. "We must establish a government out there and I would like you to help me do it."[37] Taft was completely taken aback. The only thing he knew about the Philippines was that he thought it had been a mistake for the Americans to take possession of the islands. This was the basis for his initial denial of interest in the opportunity. "Why, Mr. President," Taft exclaimed, "that would be impossible. I am not in sympathy with your policy. I don't think we ought to take the Philippines. They are sure to entail a great deal of trouble and expense." The President countered, "Neither do I, but that isn't the question. We've got them. What I want you to do is to go there and establish a civil government."[38] Taft was thinking as fast as he could, trying to assess the personal sacrifice his President was asking him to make. Agreeing to this appointment would require him to resign from the Federal Bench, tossing aside his lifetime appointment and likely derailing any chance he'd have to eventually rise to the Supreme Court. After expressing those very real concerns, McKinley tried to reassure him. "If you give up this judicial office at my request you shall not suffer," the President informed Taft. "If I last, and the opportunity comes, I shall appoint you. ... If I am here, you will be here."[39] Taft undoubtedly appreciated the sentiment, but was savvy enough to realize that such assurances were subject to so many variables that it was certainly nothing he could count on.

The President was fixed on Taft as his man, and he brought in his big guns to try to close the deal. Under the President's proposal, Taft would lead a Commission to the Philippines, with the expectation that he would eventually become Governor-General whenever the situation in the islands enabled the removal of the military, which remained in command at this time. Taft would report to Secretary of War Elihu Root, who would have oversight over both the military and civilian operations in the Philippines. Root put the pressure on Taft to accept, appealing to his sense of patriotism, with a little guilt tossed into the mix.

> Here is a field that calls for risk and sacrifice. Your country is confronted with one of the greatest problems in its history and you, Judge Taft, are asked to take immediate charge of the solution of that problem seven thousand miles away from

> home. You are at the parting of the ways. Will you take the easier course, the way of least resistance, with the thought that you had the opportunity to serve your country and declined it because of the possible sacrifice, or will you take the more courageous course and risking much, achieve much? This work in the Philippines will give you an invaluable experience in building up a government and in the study of laws needed to govern a people, and such experience cannot but make you a broader, better judge, should you be called upon to serve your country in that capacity.[40]

Taft left Washington bewildered, uncertain about what to do. But none of those closest to him had any doubts. He had no choice but to accept.

Nellie Taft, who continued to have the greatest influence on Taft's decision-making, had no hesitation in encouraging her husband to jump at the opportunity being offered by the President. She admitted that she was "very glad because it gave Mr. Taft an opportunity for exactly the kind of work I wished him to do."[41] She wanted him off the Bench and welcomed the chance for him to show the people in the political class just what he could do. Plus, she was excited about the prospects of a wonderful experience for her and her family. "I wasn't sure what it meant," Nellie later admitted, "but I knew instantly that I didn't want to miss a big and novel experience. I have never shrunk before any obstacles when I had an opportunity to see a new country and I must say I have never regretted any adventure."[42] Taft's brother Horace also got into the act of prodding Taft to accept. He told his brother, "You can do more good in that position in a year than you could on the bench in a dozen."[43] Taft hemmed and hawed for over a week while the President awaited his decision. For his own sake, he wanted nothing but to forget the whole thing and get back to presiding over cases in the friendly confines of the Cincinnati courthouse. But the pressure from all sides to accept was overwhelming, so he eventually did. As his wife later wrote, "So he resigned from the Bench; the hardest thing he ever did."[44]

Taft and his fellow commissioners knew virtually nothing of the Philippines at the time they accepted their assignment. The archipelago now in possession of the United States was a collection of more than seven million people spread across more than 7,500 islands located southeast of China and due east of Vietnam across the South China Sea. Ninety-five percent of the total land area concentrated on the largest 11

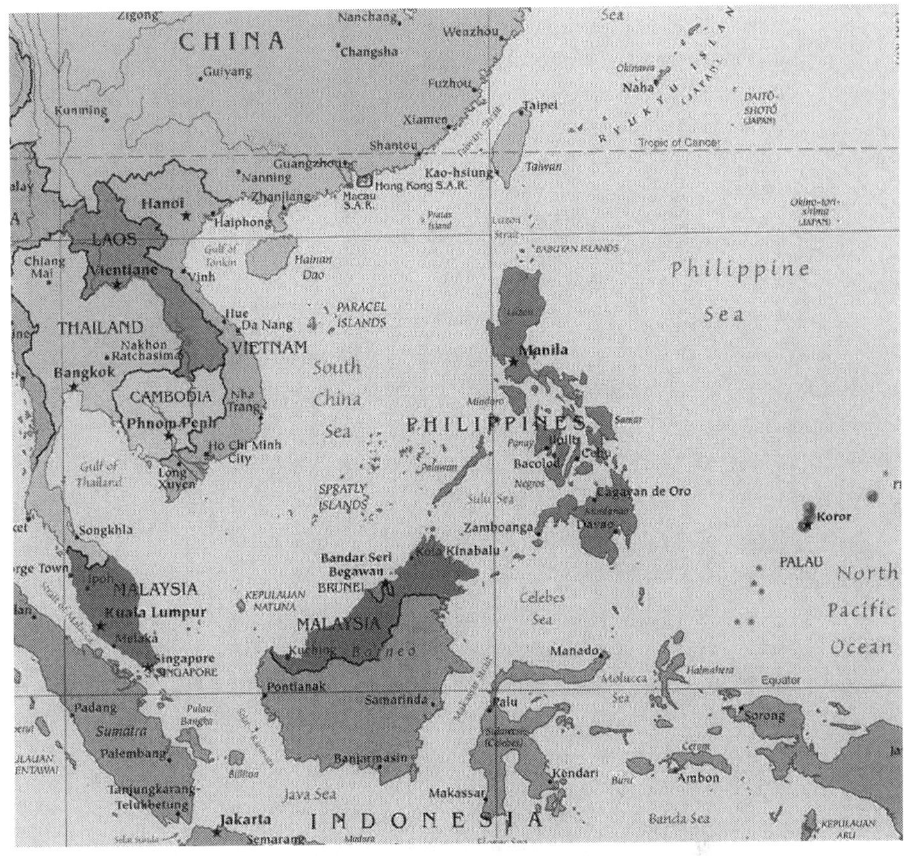

I-16: Map of the Philippines and its nearest Asian neighbors

islands. Luzon was the biggest and housed the capital of Manila, with Mindanao a slightly smaller second in size. The mostly uneducated population consisted of 30 races and dialects, although the two dominant tribes were the Tagalogs and the Visayans. The natives had never had any role in the government, which had been controlled entirely by Spain for the past three centuries. For the past two years, the American military had been in charge, dealing with the ongoing insurrection under rebel leader Emilio Aguinaldo. From this, the new commissioners were charged with putting the islands on the ultimate path to self-government and independence. There was no blueprint for this kind of activity, no model for Taft to follow. Taft had plenty of doubts about the ability for himself, or anyone, to succeed under these conditions. President McKinley, however, was certainly optimistic, as was his future Vice President, Taft's old friend, Theodore Roosevelt, who wrote:

> A few more difficult tasks have devolved upon any man of our nationality during our century and a quarter of public life than the handling of the Philippine Islands just at this time; and it may be doubted, whether among men now living, another could be found as well fitted as Judge Taft to do this incredibly difficult work.[45]

The faith of these leaders in Washington was about to be tested halfway around the world.

After Taft officially stepped down from the Federal Bench, he not only had to get his own affairs in order, but he also had to prepare to transplant his family some 8,400 miles from Cincinnati to the Philippines. All of the commissioners would be bringing their families with them for this extended assignment abroad. Two of Taft's colleagues were academics, including Dean Worcester from the University of Michigan and Bernard Moses from the University of California. Judge Henry Ide joined General Luke Wright to round out the commission. All met in San Francisco in April 1900 before boarding the army transport *Hancock* on their journey largely into the unknown. They got down to work right away, holding regular conferences on the ship while the families settled in, getting to know each other at the outset of this new venture. The

I-17: The Second Philippine Commission (L to R): Dean Worcester, Henry Ide, Taft, Bernard Moses, and Luke Wright, circa 1900

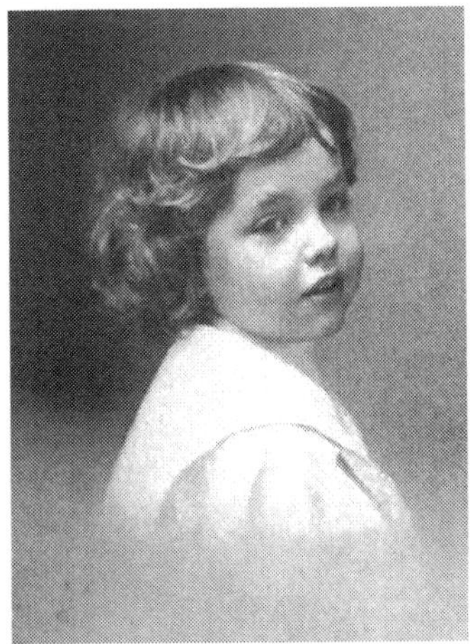

I-18: Charlie Taft, circa 1900 (age ~4)

youngest of the bunch was four-year-old Charles Taft, who caught everyone's attention. "Charlie continues to be as full of spirits and as determined to have his own way as ever," wrote his father. "We call him 'the tornado'; he creates such a sensation when he lands in the midst of the children on board the ship."[46] There were additional light-hearted moments as the travelers enjoyed stopovers in Honolulu and Yokohama, Japan. The latter included an official meeting with the Emperor, along with a number of diplomatic receptions. Taft's weight proved a bit problematic for the Japanese. In one instance, the obese leader of the American contingent was simply unable to accommodate the eating patterns of the Japanese to sit on the floor during their meal. The hosts eventually found a small, padded stool to accommodate their oversized guest. Similarly, transportation on a rickshaw required a double-seater for Taft. Nellie and the other wives and children enjoyed an extended stay in Japan while the commissioners got back on their transport and headed to their final destination to try to figure out how to start the Filipinos on the path to self-government.

The situation at the time of their arrival was indeed daunting. The Filipinos had hardly embraced their new American overlords. The Aguinaldo-led insurrection continued unabated, fueling the antagonistic relationship with the U.S. military. General Arthur MacArthur, who had recently taken over for Elwell Otis, was in command as the Military Governor over the entire archipelago. MacArthur, who sent an aide to greet the new civilian commission rather than welcome them himself, wasted little time in communicating his displeasure at their arrival when they met

I-19: The leader of the Philippine insurrection, Emilio Aguinaldo

in person the day after their arrival. The general informed Taft "that he regarded our coming as a personal reflection on him and that while he was, of course, obliged to submit to our presence there, resented it nevertheless."[47] MacArthur had as much contempt for the new commission as he had for the Filipino people, whom he felt still needed to be tamed, and would likely never be able to govern themselves. The mission of the commission, in MacArthur's mind, was pure folly, and he had no intention of diverting from his military's focus to bring the rebellion to its knees and force the Filipinos into submission.

I-20: Military Governor of the Philippines Arthur MacArthur

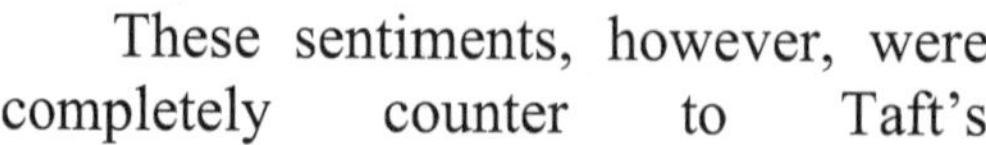

These sentiments, however, were completely counter to Taft's instructions. According to his Commander-in-Chief, Taft and his commission were charged with creating a new government that was to be "designed not for our satisfaction, or for the expression of our theoretical views, but for the happiness, peace and prosperity of the people of the Philippine Islands, and the measures adopted should be made to conform to their customs, their habits, and even to their prejudices, to the fullest extent consistent with the accomplishment of ... just and effective government."[48] While the American actions in the Philippines to date differed little from a traditional colonizing power, Taft was about to turn that approach on its head. He became the embodiment of McKinley's approach of "benevolent assimilation,"[49] the complete opposite of the imperialist epithets being hurled in the direction of the administration. "Indeed, he [Taft] was the most active anti-imperialist of them all," according to Nellie. "He was doing the work of carrying out a thoroughly anti-imperialistic policy, but he recognised the difference between abandoning the Philippines to a certain unhappy fate and guiding them to substantial independence founded on self-dependence."[50] Taft drew the distinction between his plans and these more traditional imperialist powerhouses.

> If we assume control over a people merely in the spirit of conquest and merely to extend our control and merely from the lust of power, then we may be properly denounced as imperialists; but if we assume control over a people for the benefit of that people and with the purpose of developing them to a self-governing capacity, and with the intention of giving them the right to become independent when they shall show themselves fit, then the charge that we are imperialists is utterly without foundation.[51]

Taft was committed to this latter approach, despite the long odds, and even the antagonism toward the notion from those currently entrusted with command of the operation.

Make no mistake, Taft was not blind to the long odds confronting his commission. He shared some early insights into his views of the Filipino people in a letter to Nellie, who was still exploring the island of Japan. "About two per cent were fairly well educated," Taft wrote, "while all the rest were ignorant, quiet, polite people, ordinarily inoffensive and light-hearted, of an artistic temperament, easily subject to immoral influences, quite superstitious and inclined, under the direction of others, to great cruelty."[52] He was frank in his initial assessment of the Filipinos' "utter incapacity … to found and maintain a decent government by themselves."[53] But he was committed to trying, knowing the onus would be on his commission to overcome these inherent limitations. As he later testified to Congress, "Self-government does not come by nature. … It must be taught even to the educated who are used to a different system."[54] But even in this regard, Taft started cautiously. The most important thing he felt he could do at the time was to listen.

Taft initially set out on a three-month period of pure fact-finding. This included an intense education of his own about the history and culture of the Filipino people. He intended to meet not just with the leaders and elites of the islands but also with the members of the working and lower classes. Taft worked 12-hour days, including numerous public hearings that could inform his plans for the establishment of civil government and the foundational legislation that would accompany that evolution. The Filipino people quickly moved past their caution about Taft and his commission. In particular, they appreciated the earnestness of his intent, which was fundamentally different than the military rulers they had seen to date. The fact that Taft was clearly at odds with the American generals was actually a boon to his popularity with the Filipinos. As important was Taft's entire persona. He was calm and patient, willing to listen for hours on end to nearly any one of the Filipinos who cared to offer him context or opinions. Even when his American counterparts grew tired of these sessions, Taft never cut them off. "Let 'em go on," Taft would say. "For once the Filipinos shall have a chance to say all they want to."[55] This was all part of Taft's so-called "policy of attraction,"[56] which sought to reassure the Filipinos that he believed in a future of "the Philippines for the Filipinos,"[57] despite the odds against them.

There was yet another piece of Taft's emerging credibility and acceptance by the Filipinos. He told them the truth. While he remained committed to his optimistic vision, he did not paint a panacea that would materialize overnight. He was frank in his assessments while always maintaining his optimistic outlook. When he made tough decisions, he deviated from the imposition of posted edicts to which the Filipinos had become so accustomed. Rather, he always took the time to explain his determinations to the Filipino people. His use of humor, which was typically accompanied by his hearty laugh, was another reassuring touch that helped convince the Filipinos that he truly had their best interest at heart. It was these very human qualities that set Taft apart, making him the perfect person at this point in time for this perilous mission. As Roosevelt later said:

> I think that almost all men who have been brought in close contact, personally and officially, with Judge Taft are agreed that he combines, as very, very few men ever can combine, a standard of absolutely unflinching rectitude on every point of public duty, and a literally dauntless courage and willingness to bear responsibility, with a knowledge of men, and a far-reaching tact and kindliness, which enable his great abilities and high principles to be of use in a way that would be impossible were he not thus gifted with the capacity to work hand in hand with his fellows.[58]

Newspaperman Mark Sullivan similarly wrote, "From the beginning, a relation of affection and confidence existed between this jovial fat man from Cincinnati and the heterogeneous tribes of little brown men of the Archipelago. … He encouraged them to call on him and Mrs. Taft, he disarmed them by the openness and freedom of his talk, charmed them by his simplicity."[59] This was the man in whom the Filipino people began to place their trust.

As the fact-finding continued, Taft and his fellow commissioners got down to the tasks at hand. New legislation would be needed to account for nearly all aspects of civil society. This meant a whole new criminal code, a new court system, an Internal Revenue Act, districting for the legislative assembly, regulations for the settlement and sale of land, and the initial formation of local governments to be run by the Filipinos themselves. Eight months of detailed hearings preceded the passage of the Judiciary Act and the Code of Criminal Procedure. A Supreme Court was established, with a balanced set of associate justices (three Americans and three Filipinos), but, importantly, run by a Filipino Chief Justice. Fourteen judicial districts were established, requiring the importation of some jurists while always seeking opportunities to insert qualified Filipinos into these roles once convinced of their competence to perform the task at hand. Investments were initiated for improvements in roads, harbors, and schools, while government bureaus were created for forestry, mining, and statistics. Some of the commission's biggest obstacles came from other Americans, particularly those in the uniform of the U.S. military, who were technically still in charge. According to Nellie Taft, "The tone [MacArthur] adopted in his correspondence with the Commission kept them in a constant state of controlled anger. … The General objected to almost every suggestion put forward by them and did

I-21: Taft (center) with fellow commissioners Luke Wright (left) and Henry Ide (right)

not hesitate to tell them in plain words that he did not welcome advice from them concerning military or any other matters. It was really a very difficult situation."[60] Yet Taft remained undeterred.

In fact, his next step was to hit the road and meet the people where they were. With Nellie and the children having recently arrived, they all set forth on another grand adventure. They took the first of numerous trips deep into the islands. Fortunately, the positive reputation the commission had begun to receive preceded most of these visits. As such, they were welcomed with open arms at nearly every stop. "Everywhere we go," Taft wrote to Secretary of War Root, "we find arches, flowers, with lanterns and flags crowning our path and everywhere we find every evidence of real rejoicing of the people at our coming."[61] Nellie added the following description on the commission's first tour of Bulanga, the capital of the province of Bataan: "Bunting and paper flowers of every hue were mixed with long palm leaves and branches of bamboo and everything in the nature of an ornament that could possibly be used, while from every angle and at every point fluttered small American flags, some of them home-made."[62] More important than the aesthetics, of course, was the direct engagement with the Filipino people. The commission held hearings in every town, patiently listening to the input from the locals and using the opportunities to further its objectives of educating the Filipinos on what self-government was all about.

I-22: Democratic candidate for President, William Jennings Bryan, 1900

If things weren't difficult enough, though, it was an election year back home, and the Philippines were front and center in the campaign. The contest was a rematch between President McKinley and the Democratic nominee, William Jennings Bryan. Bryan had ditched his emotive advocacy for bimetallism that had been prominent in the previous canvass to focus on his charges of imperialism against the current administration. "We condemn and denounce the Philippine policy of the present administration," the Democratic platform read. "The Filipinos cannot be made citizens without endangering our civilization; we favor an immediate declaration of the nation's purpose to give the Filipinos first, a stable form of government; second, independence; third, protection from outside influence or rather interference."[63] The ripple effect of this rhetoric was profound in the Philippines, giving hope to the insurrectionists that if they could hold out a little longer, and if Bryan could claim the presidency, then independence may be just around the corner. Taft continued to think such a move would be disastrous for a people so unprepared for such autonomy. Times were tense as the Americans went to the polls. But there was actually little cause for concern. The American people had strongly supported the war with Spain, McKinley was more popular than ever, and the incumbent cruised to reelection in November 1900, expanding on his victorious margins in both the electoral count and the popular vote when compared to four years before. The American people had spoken clearly, setting up for the next stage of development in the Philippines.

There was one additional catalyst that would shortly lead to the transition from military to civilian control of the archipelago. Just a month into McKinley's second term, Emilio Aguinaldo was finally captured, thanks to a daring raid led by American General Frederick Funston. From his prison cell, Aguinaldo brought the insurrection to a definitive end with the following statement to his people:

> The complete termination of hostilities and a lasting peace are not only desirable but absolutely essential to the welfare of the Philippines. ... Enough of blood, enough of tears and desolation. ... By acknowledging and accepting the sovereignty of the United States throughout the entire archipelago, as I now do without any reservation whatsoever, I believe that I am serving thee, my beloved country.[64]

With the fighting now over, Taft prepared to take control of the islands from General MacArthur. Just a couple of months later, on July 4, 1901, he was formally sworn in as the first Governor-General of the Philippines.

This was a definitive moment in the evolution of McKinley's vision and very much a cause for celebration. The Filipino people had gotten to know Taft and trusted him far more than the American military. They showed up in force at the Cathedral Plaza in the heart of Manila to

I-23: Taft being sworn in as the first Governor-General of the Philippines, July 4, 1901

celebrate the transition. "American flags covered the canopied platforms and floated from every possible point of vantage," wrote Nellie Taft. "Americans and Filipinos, all in gala attire, were pressed close together in the spectators' stands which extended on either side of the central pavilion; the plaza below was thronged with Filipinos of every rank and condition, in all manner of bright jusis and calicos."[65] In his inaugural remarks, Taft reiterated his commitment to building the foundation for civil government, as well as his pledge to slowly but surely integrate the Filipino people into that government as soon as they demonstrated the ability to do so.

If anything, Taft worked even harder now that he was fully in charge. He expanded his commission by adding three Filipinos to the effort. He established the Department of Instruction to take on the hard work of figuring out how to implement some form of universal education. To this end, more than 600 teachers were imported from the United States to begin this monumental task. The commission formalized both the Municipal Government Act and Provincial Government Law, upon which Taft hit the road again to fully explain these foundational principles directly to the Filipino people. Once again, the commissioners were welcomed with grand celebrations wherever they went across the 30 provinces they would eventually visit. At each stop, Taft held public hearings, where he not only shared his views but also continued to extend these sessions to listen to what the locals had to say. As he periodically incorporated some of these suggestions into future laws, his popularity soared all the more. Most importantly was his willingness to trust the Filipino people with actual positions of responsibility. The surest sign that Taft meant what he said was his placement of local leaders into the machinery of government. He was proving each day that the prospects of self-government were real, and with mutual trust and cooperation, such a transition could perhaps take place sooner than anyone ever imagined.

Throughout this period, perhaps the happiest person throughout the archipelago was the First Lady of the islands, Nellie Taft. She was exultant over her husband's position of leadership, a role that not only exceeded his rather pedestrian post on the Federal Bench but also one that augured well for future political prospects back home. As significant was her own joy at being the center of attention. Nellie was celebrated as royalty wherever she went, and her social events were the talk of the islands. Immediately after the inauguration of the Governor-General, the Tafts replaced the MacArthurs as the residents of the Malacanan Palace. Nellie quickly made their new home a social centerpiece. "It has historic associations which give it an atmosphere that I found to be quite thrilling," Nellie later wrote of her new home. "On clear evenings it [the verandah] was the most delightful spot I have ever seen. I began to love the tropical nights and to feel that I never before had known what nights

I-24: Malacanan Palace, Manila, The Philippines

can be like."[66] Taft was a social creature himself, and while he was swamped with his primary duties, he was not blind to the social responsibilities that come with being the leader of the Filipino people. He happily followed Nellie's lead in engaging with the local community in groups small and large throughout his tenure as Governor-General.

The entire operation was thrust into temporary chaos when word arrived that President McKinley had been shot. An anarchist by the name of Leon Czolgosz had fired two rounds into the President's midsection in a receiving line at the Pan-American Exposition in Buffalo on September 6, 1901. Taft and the Filipino people were united in monitoring the condition of the man whose vision had given them all so much hope. When McKinley succumbed to his wounds a couple of weeks later, sadness engulfed the islands, along with a fear of the unknown. Nellie Taft spoke for the family when she wrote that "the extraordinary sweetness of his nature inspired in every one with whom he came in close contact a strong personal affection, and we had reason to feel this more than most people. Truly, it was as if the foundations of our world had crumbled under us."[67] The Filipinos had to once again deal with the fear of the unknown. All eyes shifted to Taft's friend, Theodore Roosevelt, who had joined McKinley's ticket in the recent campaign, and now found himself as the youngest President in the history of the United States.

I-25: Rendering of the assassination of President McKinley by Leon Czolgosz, September 6, 1901

I-26: President Theodore Roosevelt

Roosevelt had caught the imagination of his countrymen with his heroics alongside his fellow Rough Riders in the victorious battle in capturing the San Juan Heights in Cuba during the recent war. Shortly after the hostilities ceased, Roosevelt was entrusted with the governorship of his home state of New York. A year later, he was nominated as McKinley's VP, and now he was the President of the United States. Roosevelt was also one of the nation's leading expansionists and a proponent of a dominant position for the United States in world affairs. He was adamantly pro-annexation when it came to the Philippines, and he was also completely on board with the path that McKinley and Taft had embarked upon. The brief panic that materialized after McKinley's death quickly dissipated thanks in part to reassuring remarks from Roosevelt, but even more so from the trust the Filipinos continued to place in their Governor-General.

Many Filipinos were, therefore, even more concerned when Governor Taft was diagnosed with a serious illness just a little more than a month later. Nellie was on vacation in China when Taft reported being under the weather. The initial diagnosis was dengue fever, but when things didn't improve, the doctors looked for another cause. They found it in the form of an abdominal abscess that had reached a point where emergency surgery was needed. Taft was taken from the Malacanan Palace on a stretcher and rushed to the First Reserve Army hospital, where he underwent the first of two surgeries. Things were touch-and-go for the first 24 hours as the doctors were concerned about blood poisoning. After the second surgery, the patient began to stabilize, but he was still pretty weak. President Roosevelt was among those who was particularly concerned. Taft wanted to recover right where he was, but Roosevelt ordered him home for an extended rest. The House and Senate were both planning hearings on the state of affairs in the Philippines, and Roosevelt thought a return to the States could be doubly productive – a better environment for which Taft could recover, as well as provide the most credible testimony to any doubters in Congress about the administration's Philippines policy. Taft's heart was deeply embedded in his mission, so while he was loath to leave the Filipino people, he thought he could do some good by meeting with Congress in person. After placing General Luke Wright temporarily in charge, the Tafts left for home on Christmas Eve, 1901.

Taft spent most of his time in Cincinnati, where he made excellent progress in gaining back his strength. He needed all the energy he could muster for those congressional hearings, which continued off-and-on for nearly three weeks. Congress was sharply divided on the mission in the Philippines. Some questioned the American role at all, while others were direct with their inquiries about what they perceived as limited progress. Sure enough, Taft was the best advocate the administration or the Filipinos could have put forward. He downplayed the negative stories as completely overblown while sharing numerous accounts and statistics about the very real progress that was being made. He also tried to set expectations, trying to get the members of Congress to realize what a huge undertaking the Americans had signed up for. Taft was deeply committed to his program to establish

> a government suited to the present possibilities of the people, which shall gradually change, conferring more and more right upon the people to govern themselves, thus educating them in self-government, until their knowledge of government, their knowledge of liberty, shall be such that further action may be taken either by giving them statehood or by making them a quasi-independent government like Canada or Australia or, if they desire it, independence.[68]

With support and patience, the prospects were excellent, according to Taft. There was no question that Taft won over some converts with his heartfelt advocacy.

While Taft was completing his recovery in Cincinnati (a third surgery was required), the administration was becoming increasingly concerned about one of the thorniest issues the Americans and Filipinos faced. Catholicism was the dominant religion throughout the islands and had been for centuries. The Church registry listed more than 6.5 million Catholics across the archipelago, with more than a thousand monks in place as well. The Spanish friars had dominated virtually all local communities for decades, essentially serving as the de facto representatives of the Spanish government with significant authority over their local domains. "He [the friar] was simply everything in his parish," noted Nellie Taft. "By law, he came to discharge many civil functions and to supervise, correct or veto everything which was done, or was sought to be done in the pueblo. … In a word, he was the government of the parish."[69] In general, the Filipinos loved being Catholic, but they despised these friars, who had accumulated all the best land for themselves, paid no taxes, and often ruled in an exploitative manner. During the recent insurrection, hundreds of friars were killed, while the rest either fled the islands or sought refuge in Manila. The Americans were now faced with two challenges – what to do with the remaining friars, and how to get the land away from the Church so they could return it to the Filipino people.

Everyone knew William Taft was a stickler for the law. The Treaty of Paris, which ended the Spanish-American War, had been explicit that property rights would be honored by the Americans. Since the ownership of those 400,000 acres of prime farmland was clearly in the hands of the Spanish friars, he needed some legal means to get it back. After numerous discussions with President Roosevelt, the decision was made for Taft to go to the Vatican to try to buy the land from the Church. This was going to be a delicate mission, particularly since the United States did not recognize the Vatican at the time. Roosevelt made it clear that "Your errand will not be in any sense or degree diplomatic in its nature, but will be purely a business matter of negotiation by you as Governor of the Philippines for the purchase of property from the owners thereof, and the settlement of land titles in such a manner as to contribute to the best interests of the people of the Islands."[70] Taft continued to get tasked with one unprecedented challenge after another.

At first, it appeared Taft would sail for Rome alone. Nellie was unable to go since Robert had come down with Scarlet Fever and needed her care. But in stepped Louisa Taft to fill that potential void. When Taft's mother heard that Nellie couldn't make the trip, she invited herself to go instead. "Well, Will," Louisa told her son, "I don't think you ought to make such a trip alone when you are so far from strong, so I just think I'll go with you in Nellie's place."[71] And she did just that, ultimately having the time of her life, in all settings – social, shopping, sightseeing, and business. Her presence was clearly a comfort to Taft, who had his work cut out for him.

Taft and his mother arrived in Rome in May 1902. A cordial meeting took place with Pope Leo XIII, who indicated an openness to the prospect of the Americans acquiring the Church's land in the Philippines. He established a committee of Cardinals to further the negotiations. The talks progressed slowly, with lots of details to be ironed out. Taft patiently tried to address all concerns, as well as establish a reasonable purchase price. By late July, after Nellie and the rest of the family had finally arrived, Taft felt he had done as much as he could in person and needed to get back to the Philippines. The entire family went for a farewell greeting with the Pope, which was memorable for all. At one point, the Pope asked young Robert "what he expected to be when he grew up." Nellie later wrote that "my self-confident son replied that he intended to be the Chief Justice of the Supreme Court."[72] Like father like son. The negotiations would eventually take more than a year but ultimately yielded a satisfactory conclusion. The Americans purchased the Church lands for approximately $7.5 million. These prime farmlands were then carved into small parcels and sold to the Filipino people to recoup the upfront American investment. It was also agreed that the friars would not return to their parishes. It was a difficult, elongated negotiation but represented another major accomplishment for William Taft on behalf of the Filipino people.

I-27: Pope Leo XIII, 1900

Things didn't get any easier for Taft as he returned to the Philippines. A near perfect storm of strife had overcome the islands. A cholera outbreak was spreading widely, domestic cattle were dying by the thousands due to a rinderpest infestation, crops were failing, and fears of famine were widespread. The Filipinos' lone hope lay with the large man from America. So, when Taft once again set foot on Philippine soil, he was cheered from one end of Manila to the other. "Wherever his eyes rested he saw people, crowding windows, roofs, river banks and city walls, all of them cheering wildly and waving hats or handkerchiefs," Nellie Taft later wrote. "And the thing which moved him most was the fact that the welcoming throng was not just representative of the wealthy and educated class, but included thousands of the people, barefooted and in calicoes, who had come in from the neighbouring and even the far provinces to greet him."[73] Taft appreciated the adulation but also realized the high expectations that came with it. So, he rolled up his sleeves and got right back to work.

Building on his previous efforts, Taft tried to accelerate the welcoming of Filipinos into positions of civil government. While he understood the importance of such a move as much as anyone, he was still cautious, reluctant to take the risk of moving too quickly and setting the people up for failure. As such, the lower levels of government began to be filled more and more by the Filipinos, but the more senior positions were still largely staffed by Americans. This caused some frustration, but Taft communicated the need for the Filipino people to be patient with him, just as he was being patient with them. From a policy standpoint, Taft focused primarily on expanding the educational system, increasing economic development (to include more exports of raw materials to the United States), as well as infrastructure, such as the building of highways and rail lines. All of these efforts were part of Taft's plan to slowly but surely increase the economic viability of the Philippines while incrementally turning over more and more responsibilities to the Filipino people. Despite the tough conditions, all signs indicated steady and meaningful progress. And just like that, Taft got another one of those telegrams that threatened to completely disrupt his world.

4. Duty Calls, Dream Denied

The notice Taft received reflected the offer he had been hoping for his entire life. Out of the blue, President Roosevelt cabled: "Taft, Manila. On January first there will be a vacancy on the Supreme Court to which I earnestly desire to appoint you. … I feel that your duty is on the Court unless you have decided not to adopt a judicial career. I greatly hope you will accept. Would appreciate early answer. Roosevelt."[74] Instead of jumping up and down for joy, though, Taft was distraught. He had become completely committed to his mission in the Philippines. He saw how much of a difference he was making and how much the Filipino people were counting on him. He just couldn't see how he could leave with so much work still undone. So, Taft made the heart-rending decision to turn down the opportunity he had always craved. "Great honour deeply appreciated but must decline," Taft wrote to the President. "Situation here most critical from economic standpoint. Change proposed would create much disappointment and lack of confidence among people. Two years now to follow of greater importance to development of islands than previous two years. … Look forward to the time when I can accept such an offer, but even if it is certain that it can never be repeated I must now decline."[75] Roosevelt acceded to Taft's wishes, telling his friend that "if possible, your refusal on the ground you give makes me admire you and believe in you more than ever."[76] But this was not the end of the story.

Just a month later, Roosevelt came back to Taft again. "I am sorry, old man," the President wrote, "but after faithful effort for a month to try to arrange matters on the basis you wanted I find that I shall have to bring you home and put you on the Supreme Court. I am very sorry, I have the greatest confidence in your judgment; but, after all, old fellow, if you will permit me to say so, I am President and see the whole field. The responsibility for any error must ultimately come upon me, and therefore I cannot shirk this responsibility or in the last resort yield to anyone else's decision if my judgment is against it."[77] Now, what was Taft to do? The President was insistent, and it was, after all, Taft's dream job. Nevertheless, he remained torn. This time, however, he concluded he served at the pleasure of the President, and his Commander-in-Chief was calling him home. "Recognise soldier's duty to obey orders," Taft cabled. "If your judgment is unshaken I bow to it and shall earnestly and enthusiastically labour to settle [the] question [of] friars' lands before I leave, and to convince the people that no change of policy is at hand; that Wright is their warm friend as sincere as they think me, and that we both are but exponents of the sincere good will toward them of yourself and the American people."[78] With that, he announced his intent to leave, and began making plans to do just that.

But the Filipino people were not going to let Taft go without a fight. He was their future, the lone man who was truly committed to their cause. While General Wright was well regarded, he wasn't Taft, and the Filipinos were not ready to accept this highly disruptive change. According to Nellie Taft, who strongly opposed the move as she never wanted her husband to go back to the Bench – even the Supreme Court – "Within two days the whole city of Manila was placarded, in all the necessary languages, with the simple and uniform sentiment: 'Queremos Taft,' 'We Want Taft.'"[79] Next was a grand rally at the Malacanan Palace. On January 10, 1903, columns of citizens marched on the palace with bands playing and flags flying. Speaker after speaker, from all manner of society, stood to praise Taft and request that he reconsider his decision to leave. "The climax came when Pedro A. Paterno began by comparing Mr. Taft with Jesus Christ," Nellie later wrote, "saying that as Christ had converted the cross into a symbol of glory and triumph, so had Governor Taft turned a dying people to the light and life of modern liberties."[80] The protest extended all the way to the White House, which was inundated with telegrams, begging President Roosevelt to change course and allow Governor Taft to remain in place. This included cables from fellow commissioners Worcester,

I-28: Governor-General Taft in the Philippines, circa 1902 (age ~45)

Ide, and James Smith, the latter of whom had recently joined the commission. They conveyed the serious risk that would be associated with Taft's withdrawal. Moreover, the American President heard from some of the Filipino members of the commission, who remarked, "We solemnly affirm that feelings [of the] Philippine people would be deeply hurt by the departure of Taft."[81] The President was moved by all the entreaties, particularly those from the Filipinos themselves. He concluded, "as long as this is the tack on which the native mind is working it would be inadvisable to take him away."[82] The only thing left was to communicate the decision to the Governor-General. "Taft, Manila, All right, stay where you are," the President wrote tersely. "I shall appoint some one else to the Court."[83] Taft knew what he was passing up, but his current commitment overrode all other considerations as he accepted Roosevelt's final decision. He would later write, "In my view, a duty is an entirety, and it is not fulfilled until it is entirely fulfilled."[84] In this case, he had signed up for a mission that was not yet complete. It was his duty to remain, and he was ready to get back to work on behalf of a people who had touched his heart with their emotional pleas, despite the cost to his own ambition. There was widespread relief among the Filipino people at this turn of events, even though this reprieve turned out to only be short-lived.

President Roosevelt's right-hand man in Washington was his Secretary of War Elihu Root. Root, who was one of the nation's top legal minds, had joined the McKinley administration shortly after the Spanish-American War concluded and had carried through into the Roosevelt administration after McKinley's assassination. He had been reluctant to enter government service in the first place, and while he had become committed to his responsibilities, he had decided it was time to return to his private station. Root informed Roosevelt of his decision just about six months after Taft had turned down the appointment to the Court. Now, Roosevelt came back, requesting Taft to return to Washington to fill the void at the War Department upon Root's planned departure. The key to Roosevelt's entreaty was that as the Secretary of War, Taft

> will still have the ultimate control of the Philippine situation and whatever was done would be under your immediate supervision. It seems to me that from the standpoint of the interests of the Islands alone you could well afford to take the place, which involves the general regulation, supervision and

> control of the Philippine Government. I need not say what an immense help you would be to me. … If only there were three of you. Then I would have one of you on the Supreme Court, as the Ohio member, in place of Day; one of you in Root's place as Secretary of War, when he goes out, and one of you permanently Governor of the Philippines. No one can quite take your place as Governor; but no one of whom I can think save only you can at all take Root's place as Secretary.[85]

For Taft, this offer was different, mainly because this role would retain direct involvement in the mission in the Philippines, perhaps with the opportunity to do even more good from Washington with someone like his trusted companion, Luke Wright, taking over on the islands. It didn't hurt that Nellie was thrilled by this turn of events. Nellie still longed for the presidency for her husband, and this kind of move was precisely the kind of political spot she thought could realistically be a springboard to the White House. A position in Roosevelt's Cabinet was "in line with … the kind of career I wanted for him and expected him to have," she wrote.[86] But Taft still waffled on the decision, consumed with the thought he might be perceived as abandoning the Filipino people and a mission he fervently believed in. After six weeks of indecision, he finally relented, and signaled an acceptance of the offer from the President. This time, there would be no turning back.

The Tafts had a few months before they needed to report to Washington, and it was a busy time for the Governor-General to plan and execute his transition. Wright had been his partner from the beginning, so that portion of the transition was pretty straightforward, but there were countless odds and ends, particularly in the areas of foundational legislation, that Taft wanted to bring to closure before he handed over the reins. Of course, William Taft wasn't the only member of the family departing the Philippines. For his wife and three children, this had been their home (and lifestyle) for nearly four years. They had their own relationships to end, and Nellie, for one, had plans to go out in style. She wanted one more party – one that would be remembered. After extended deliberations, she settled on a costume party with a Venetian theme, with her husband at center stage. Getting an appropriate costume that fit the large American was one of the last obstacles for Taft to overcome on his Philippine mission.

> So it is settled that I must assume the robes and headgear of the husband of the Adriatic, the Doge of Venice. The question is whether the robe can be made historically accurate and at the same time so conceal my nether extremities as to make it unnecessary for me to dye my nether undergarments to a proper color, for the entire Orient cannot produce tights of a sufficient size. The Council of War, meaning Nellie, has not advised me on the subject, but tights or no tights we shall have a Doge of Venice that never was on land or sea.[87]

The costume-makers came through, and the event was a grand success. "It will linger in my memory as one of the most entrancing evenings of my life,"[88] recalled Nellie Taft.

I-29: The Tafts, along with family and friends, dressed up for the Venetian Carnival, 1903

The Tafts left for home on December 12, 1903, with time to reflect on the past four years. The Federal Judge had dropped everything to travel halfway across the world at the behest of his President to bring civil government to a land that had little concept of what that even meant. While others (both military and civilian) were content to occupy a conquered land and get what they could from this largely uneducated mass of island inhabitants, Taft saw nothing but opportunity – opportunity to lift the Filipinos out of their generations of subjugation and put them on a path to competently managing their own society in an orderly manner for their own mutual benefit. The United States had never attempted such an undertaking before, and all indications are that William

Taft was the primary catalyst to making as much progress as was witnessed over the course of these four years. He cast aside the naysayers and patiently waded into the mass of details needed to establish a civil society essentially from scratch. The foundational laws were established, the courts were up and running, locals were beginning to be welcomed into positions of trust, educational reform was taking root, and economic measures (including investment in infrastructure) were starting to take shape. The Philippines still had a long way to go, but by most accounts they had already made more progress than almost anyone had imagined possible. And most of that credit went to William Taft. President Roosevelt was among those singing the praises of the outgoing Governor-General, telling an audience at the University of California that:

> Not only have peace and material well being come to those Islands to a degree never before known in their recorded history, and to a degree infinitely greater than had ever been dreamed possible by those who knew them best, but more than that, a greater measure of self government has been given to them than is now given to any other Asiatic people under alien rule, than to any other Asiatic people under their own rulers, save Japan alone.[89]

William Taft would continue to oversee American activity in the Philippines for most of the next decade, first as Secretary of War and then as President of the United States. He would visit the islands a couple more times and was actively involved in trying to further their prospects for eventually meriting full independence. But that progress was admittedly slow, glacially slow in the eyes of many Filipinos. Despite the warmth the locals felt toward Taft and the Americans for the initiation of a path to a new and better life, the frustrations would mount, and eventually turn to anger, as American leaders continued to refuse to leave their ward and grant the independence that the Filipinos would come to feel was long overdue. That freedom would come, but not for nearly half a century. Only in the wake of the Second World War would independence finally be granted to the Philippines, on July 4, 1946. William Taft should surely be credited with an earnest and credible effort to start that process at the end of the 19th Century. It wasn't his fault that it would be nearly the middle of the 20th Century before full independence would finally come to fruition.

5. Roosevelt's Jack-of-all-Trades

William Taft was going to be a different kind of War Secretary for a different kind of President. Theodore Roosevelt was a born reformer with a moral compass that pushed him to do right as he saw fit, offering a "square deal" for all. He believed in using the powers of the presidency to the fullest extent, following in the mode of an Andrew Jackson or Abraham Lincoln. According to Roosevelt, "Occasionally great national crises arise which call for immediate and vigorous executive action, and in such cases it is the duty of the President to act upon the theory that he is the steward of the people [who] has the legal right to do whatever the needs of the people demand unless the Constitution or the laws explicitly forbid him to do it."[90] Roosevelt would take this bold approach to his entire agenda, both foreign and domestic. For the next five years, his right hand in implementing many of those policies, particularly those outside the boundaries of the United States, would be Secretary William Taft.

Taft's diplomatic duties began right away. A stop in Japan on the way home included another meeting with the Emperor, principally to discuss that country's tensions with Russia that would soon lead to war. Once in Washington, Nellie settled on a home at 16th and K Street, just a few blocks from the War Department and the White House. It was a far cry from the Malacanan Palace and all the domestic servants to which she had become so accustomed. Still, she was thrilled to have her husband in the thick of running this administration and the possibilities for his future prospects staring them in the face. The Tafts were not well-off financially, but fortunately, older brother Charles had more money than he knew what to do with, having married one of Ohio's richest heiresses. Charles passed along some investment income to help Nellie afford to take on the social aspects expected of the wife of the War Secretary.

William Taft was far more than the typical Secretary of War for his President. Whenever he wasn't traveling the world on behalf of his chief, Taft was at Roosevelt's side as a jack-of-all-trades. He was Roosevelt's most trusted advisor on almost any topic, including wise legal counsel on numerous thorny issues for a President who always pushing the envelope on presidential authority. Taft even assisted in the 1904 election, writing speeches and occasionally stumping for the campaign. He loathed these

I-30: Taft as Secretary of War, circa 1905 (age ~48)

particular duties, but he was all-in with Roosevelt, regardless of the ask. According to biographer Arthur Dunn, "Roosevelt loaded tons of work upon his secretary of war and the harder he was pushed the better work he did."[91] Whenever Roosevelt would leave town, he did so comfortably with the knowledge that he had Taft holding down the fort. "Things will be all right in Washington," President Roosevelt would say, "I have left Taft sitting on the lid."[92] The relationship became incredibly close and trusting. "I love my chief and … I admire him from top to toe,"[93] Taft once said while serving as Roosevelt's War Secretary. The affection was genuine, and it was mutual, as evidenced by the uproarious laughter that so often emanated from their get togethers.

The first major mission for the new Secretary of War took place in Panama. Thanks to some unofficial assistance from Roosevelt and the American Navy, Panama had declared its independence from Colombia the previous year, and treaties had already been concluded for the building of the long-desired canal to connect the Atlantic and the Pacific. But the work was completely stalled, and the President was growing increasingly frustrated. In November 1904, he sent Secretary Taft to investigate. Technically, the role was to take over the lead of the seven-man Isthmian Canal Commission that was responsible for overseeing the construction of the canal. Upon arriving in the Canal Zone, the new chair of the commission saw nothing but a complete mess, a "sorry sight" of convoluted logistics. Taft noted that "such conditions of general unhealthiness prevailed as made it seem almost too much to expect that any kind of clean-up program could be made effectual."[94] The previous attempt by the French to build a canal in a similar location had been bogged down by engineering challenges leading to high cost overruns, while operating in a lethal environment of rampant yellow fever and malaria which killed thousands of workers. Upon arrival, Taft immediately began a series of meetings with Panamanian President Manuel Amador. Negotiations cut through the bureaucratic snarl that had brought the work to a standstill. Fortunately, the host nation conceded the establishment of free trade between Panama and the designated Canal Zone. Moreover, agreements were reached for the construction of docks and railroads, housing for the imported workers, and all manner of logistical necessities without which construction could barely begin, let alone progress on Roosevelt's timetable.

I-31: Secretary Taft at the trainmaster's office in Panama, circa 1904

Disease was the other seemingly intractable matter which needed to be solved. For this, Taft turned to Colonel William Gorgas of the Army Medical Corps. Gorgas had been focusing on mosquitos as the prime culprit in spreading these deadly diseases while serving in Cuba. He found that drying out the swamps in Cuba, which served as breeding grounds for the mosquitos, had a dramatic effect on the prominence of these tropical diseases. Taft bought into the strategy and imported Gorgas to Panama to replicate his feat. The success was nothing short of a medical miracle, making it far easier to recruit workers to the Canal Zone and make them much more productive once they got there.

Taft also lost confidence in the civilian engineers who had been leading the project prior to his engagement. He wanted more discipline in the force and more control over their efforts. Fortunately, he had one

I-32: Secretary Taft and George Goethals, Panama

of the finest groups of engineers on the planet at his disposal in the form of the U.S. Army Corps of Engineers. Taft put Major George Goethals in charge as another catalyst to spur progress in the construction of the canal. Once he had these fundamentals in place, Taft returned to Washington, but the situation in Panama was always on his mind. He would make a total of seven trips to the Canal Zone over the course of seven years, and retained personal oversight of the project through much of its development. He would no longer be in office when the long-awaited engineering marvel opened for business in 1914. Nevertheless, it was clear to most involved in those dicey early years, that Taft played a critical role in breaking down barriers to get the effort underway and on the path to success when others had been far less effective in trying to do just that.

Meanwhile, the Philippines continued to be a focal point for Taft. His point of advocacy had shifted to Capitol Hill, where he was constantly lobbying members of Congress to do more for the Filipino people. This included requests for appropriations to support investments in education and infrastructure, along with a tireless effort to get the legislature to drop all tariffs between the Philippines and the United States to help spur the Filipino economy. However, for every success Taft notched he seemed to encounter even more obstacles. The Secretary believed the best way to overcome the intransigence was to get the members of Congress to see the progress being made for themselves. To this end, he organized a trip to the archipelago for 30 members of Congress. Before they embarked on the journey, the traveling party swelled to 80, including a number of guests. The most prominent in the group was the President's highly independent, free-wheeling, and

I-33: President Roosevelt's daughter, Alice Longworth (front, center) joined Secretary Taft (second row, center) on the fact-finding mission to the Philippines

popular oldest daughter, Alice Longworth. The two-month voyage in the summer of 1905 was a tremendous success. Taft and his family were received as returning heroes, and the Filipinos put on impressive displays for their guests. It was still an uphill battle to free up appropriations for the cause, but this goodwill visit did leave a positive impression on many of the traveling members on the real progress being made, and that their investments to date were having a positive impact. All-in-all, it was another productive contribution from Taft, who appeared exhausted by the end of the tour, even though he was doing the kind of beneficent work he had come to relish. To persevere through the stress and fatigue, Taft did what he often did – he ate. Taft returned from the Philippines tipping the scale at 320 pounds. His perennial struggle with obesity would continue with wide fluctuations. Within six months, he was back down to about 250 pounds.

Roosevelt's Cabinet suffered a setback with the passing of Secretary of State John Hay on July 1, 1905. Roosevelt had been accustomed to counting on two men more than any other – Elihu Root and William Taft. Root's return to private practice had opened the door to bring Taft into the Cabinet. Now with the top spot open, Roosevelt went straight back to Root to fill it. Root was reluctant after having just left the year before, but it wasn't in him to turn down his close friend, who also happened to be the President of the United States. For the balance of Roosevelt's administration, the threesome of Roosevelt, Root, and Taft ran the country. They were so close that some started referring to them as the Three Musketeers. Roosevelt was D'Artagnan, Root was Athos, and Taft became Porthos. At times they even referred to each other by these nicknames in their correspondence. Root and Taft played very different roles in the top echelon of Roosevelt's supporting cast. Root was the intellectual truthteller, unwavering in his support for his chief but also unafraid to speak his mind, even when it ran counter to the views of the President. Taft was more of a "yes-man," seemingly always in agreement with Roosevelt, typically with a grand smile or hearty laugh to correspond with his customary concurrences. Roosevelt continued to build on his progressive agenda, with Root and Taft constantly at his side and the American people in broad support.

I-34: Secretary Taft with Secretary of State Elihu Root, circa 1905

While Taft was more than a half dozen years removed from his beloved Federal Bench, he still longed for the day when he could return to the judiciary with a placement on the Supreme Court. For the third time, he was presented with just such an opportunity by Theodore

Roosevelt. Henry Brown's resignation in 1906 opened up the coveted spot, and Roosevelt again offered it to Taft. For the third time, he turned it down. Nellie Taft once again inserted herself into the decision-making over her husband's career moves, and once again it was visions of the presidency that guided her thinking. Roosevelt had already announced on the night he won reelection that "Under no circumstances will I be a candidate for or accept another nomination."[95] Roosevelt remained extremely popular and could undoubtedly have won another term, but he remained committed to this pledge, which opened the floodgates to speculate on a potential successor. Most Republicans felt Root or Taft would be Roosevelt's preferred replacement, and whoever he endorsed would likely get the nomination. Nellie could see the object of her ambition nearly within her grasp, and she wasn't about to let her husband throw that all away. Nellie was "bitterly opposed to my accepting the (Court) position," Taft confided with the President, and had warned him he would be making "the mistake of my life" if he accepted the appointment.[96] Charlie, still not yet ten years old, stated the case as plain as anyone: "Ma wants him to wait and be President."[97]

President Roosevelt tried to be understanding while putting the decision into perspective. "It is not a light thing to cast aside the chance of the Presidency," he wrote to Taft. "It is well to remember that the shadow of the Presidency falls on no man twice, save in most exceptional circumstances." He concluded, "Now, my dear Will ... it is a hard choice to make, and you yourself have to make it."[98] If it were just up to Taft, the decision was obvious. "I would prefer to go on the Supreme Bench for life than to run for the Presidency," he wrote, "and that in twenty years of judicial service I could make myself more useful to the country than as President, even if my election should come about."[99] He could have added that he would have been a lot happier following the judicial path as well. But his closest family, friends, and advisers (with the exception of his mother) all came down on the side of pursuing the presidency. So, he relented and turned down the Court – a decision that brought him nothing but misery.

While the presidential buzz was growing in Washington, Taft had more immediate crises to deal with. For the second time, he was about to be pulled into a mess that had emanated from the results of the Spanish-American War. This time, the trouble was much closer to American shores, as the prospects of a revolution in Cuba had caught the attention of the Roosevelt administration. U.S.-Cuban policy had been governed in large part by two pieces of legislation passed by Congress. The first was the so-called Teller Amendment, named for its sponsor, Henry Teller from Colorado. President McKinley signed the statute into law just prior to the declaration of war against Spain, codifying the position that the United States "hereby disclaims any disposition of intention to exercise sovereignty, jurisdiction, or control over said island [Cuba] except for pacification thereof, and asserts its determination, when that is accomplished, to leave the government and control of the island to its people."[100] Pretty straightforward. But after the war, the Americans were not confident that the Cubans were ready for self-government (not too dissimilar to the sentiments over the Philippines), so Elihu Root, then serving as McKinley's Secretary of War, drafted the language that became known as the Platt Amendment (named for Senator Orville Platt of Connecticut). Per this latest statute, a total of seven conditions were imposed on Cuban governance, beginning with limitations on Cuba's rights to make treaties with other nations and restrictions on their engagement in international commerce. The U.S. also insisted that the Cubans agree "that the United States may exercise the right to intervene for the preservation of Cuban independence, the maintenance of a government adequate for the protection of life, property, and individual liberty, and for discharging the obligations with respect to Cuba imposed by the Treaty of Paris on the United States."[101] The Cubans were given no choice but to accept this language into their new constitution. While the Americans formally granted Cuban independence in 1902, it remained under the watchful eye of the United States.

I-35: Cuban President Tomás Palma

Tomás Palma was elected President of Cuba, but there were charges of malfeasance in the election. There was also discontent across wide swaths of the Cuban population, dissatisfied with Palma's leadership. By mid-1906, a real crisis was at hand. The American Consul-General in Cuba reported that "devastating and paralysing civil strife" was rampant.[102] Palma himself concluded that he could no longer hold back the rebels, who were massing on the outskirts of Havana with 20,000 armed men. A bloody revolution might be only a few days away. Palma reached out to President Roosevelt for American assistance to prevent chaos and bloodshed in his country. Roosevelt agreed to intervene. Naturally, he turned to his most reliable subordinate to handle yet another international crisis. William Taft was on the road again.

Taft arrived in Havana on September 21, 1906. He found the island as advertised, near a state of open rebellion. There was an uneasy truce in place as Taft disembarked his transport, but the American War Secretary saw virtual anarchy everywhere he looked. He followed his instincts, which always began with fact-finding. Against the wishes of the Palma government, Taft immediately began hosting discussions with leaders on both sides of the conflict. He went deeper into society as well to gain the perspectives of laborers, bankers, lawyers, and merchants, in addition to the rival politicians. It only took a few days for Taft to begin to draw some conclusions. While he found Palma to be personally beyond reproach, he did conclude that there had been irregularities in the recent election. He also faulted the rebels, deriding the "irresponsible character of the men in arms."[103] He decided to try a compromise to lower tensions that could pave the way for productive negotiations.

Taft refused to call for Palma's ouster but did propose changes in his Cabinet. According to Taft's proposal, Palma would disband the current set of advisers and reconstitute the Cabinet to include at least some members from the rival Liberal Party. To this, Palma outright refused. Instead, he and his entire government resigned, leaving no one in charge. Taft stated, "I have never known a more disgusting situation," with real danger in his midst. "Our reports show that the insurgent commanders have lost control of their forces which are now lawless bands. The situation seems to demand the use of force."[104] Or at least a *show* of force.

Taft took two steps that diffused the situation, preventing the clash of arms from erupting. First, he took control of the Cuban government. Taft issued a proclamation in which he said:

> The failure of [the Cuban] Congress to act on the irrevocable resignation of the President of the Republic of Cuba or to elect a successor leaves the country without a Government at a time when great disorder prevails, and requires that, pursuant to the request of Mr. Palma, the necessary steps be taken in the name and authority of the President of the United States to restore

> order and protect life and property in the Island of Cuba and the islands and keys adjacent thereto, and for this purpose to establish therein a provisional government.[105]

Taft named himself as the temporary head of that government, effective immediately. To lend credibility to the American takeover required the second step that Taft initiated and President Roosevelt approved – sending in the marines. Within hours, the members of the American military who were in naval vessels near Cuban waters waiting for orders came ashore in what Taft called the Army of Cuban Pacification. This initial force was quickly supplemented by U.S. army soldiers, at which point all sides laid down their arms. To ease the minds of the Cubans, Taft made it clear that "the Provisional Government hereby established will be maintained only long enough to restore order, peace and public confidence."[106] He insisted that no Cuban officials outside of the very top ranks would be dismissed, and that the Cuban flag (and not the American flag) would continue to fly over government buildings.

Taft had succeeded in his first task, which was to avoid bloodshed, but resolving what appeared to be intransigence on both sides of the conflict was not going to be so straightforward. And while he would continue to oversee the effort the Americans would play in those negotiations, he would not be the man on the ground in the midst of these debates. For that, President Roosevelt tapped Charles Magoon, whom Taft had gotten to know as the Governor of the Panama Canal Zone and ultimately the American Minister to Panama. On October 13, 1906, Taft transitioned his new authority to Magoon as Cuba's provisional governor. The American military presence would remain in Cuba for two-and-a-half years, departing when a new Cuban government emerged to power in February 1909 at the very end of the Roosevelt administration.

Taft's venture to Cuba was short (what he later described as "those awful twenty days"[107]) but highly impactful. His calm yet decisive intervention prevented Cubans from fighting Cubans in the streets. In this instance, American intervention was a source of immediate good, consistent with Roosevelt's vision for the United States throughout the Western Hemisphere. He was effusive in his praise for Taft. "I doubt whether you have ever rendered our country a greater service than the one you are now rendering,"[108] Roosevelt wrote as he authorized Taft's return to the States. Talk of the presidency continued to heat up across Republican political circles.

The one person who didn't want to talk at all about these future prospects was William Taft. He still expressed little interest in running for the office. In truth, he was more than happy continuing to be part of the Three Musketeers, taking on his President's greatest challenges, and continuing to deliver for the American people, including those newly acquired. In the meantime, Roosevelt continued to see how valuable Taft was in these foreign arenas, so he decided on yet another mission for his War Secretary, who was more akin these days to the "Secretary of Peace."[109] Taft had previously committed to the people of the Philippines that he would personally return for the opening of the first Philippine National Assembly. Roosevelt decided to expand the mission into a veritable world tour. In total, the Tafts would travel to eight countries, covering 24,000 miles, throughout 1907. The first stops were in Japan and China. There were some ill feelings in Japan over Roosevelt's role in helping to bring the recent Russo-Japanese war to a conclusion. Roosevelt received global plaudits for his efforts, including the recently introduced Nobel Peace Prize, but many in Japan felt they were shorted in the outcome. Taft went to see the Emperor and Foreign Minister to soothe over any lingering discontent. The China discussions were mostly focused on economics, as the Americans were continuing to try to increase trade with the Chinese, with heavy competition from the European powers.

I-36: Secretary Taft speaking at the opening of the Philippine National Assembly, October 1907

The most joyous part of the journey took place in the Philippines, where Taft was once again welcomed with open arms. Just about every day throughout their stay, there were "dinners, luncheons, teas, receptions, balls, meetings, celebrations, trips of inspection, and business conferences."[110] Taft had many discussions with the leaders who were emerging to advance the cause of self-rule and, as always, offered his true thoughts on the most challenging topic when he spoke to the Assembly.

> How long this process of political preparation of the Filipino people is likely to be is a question which no one can certainly answer. When I was in the Islands the last time, I ventured the opinion that it would take considerably longer than a generation. I have not changed my view upon this point; but the issue is one upon which opinions differ. … We are engaged in working out a great experiment. No other nation has attempted it, and for us to fix a certain number of years in which the experiment must become a success and be completely realized would be, in my judgment, unwise. As I premised, however, this is a question for settlement by the Congress of the United States.[111]

As noted earlier, it would be nearly four more decades before independence was finally granted to the people of the Philippines.

Taft continued with more high-level diplomacy on the way back to the United States. Most notably were visits with the leaders in Russia (more discussions over the recent war settlement) and then off to Europe for meetings in Germany. It was here that Taft learned of the death of his mother, Louisa. Taft knew that she was in failing health and had broached the subject of postponing his trip, but Louisa would have none of it. She would not be the reason her son wouldn't live up to his promise to be present at the opening of the National Assembly in the Philippines, even if it meant she would be gone before his return. By the time the Tafts landed on the U.S. mainland in late December, Louisa Taft had already been in her grave for a couple of weeks, alongside her husband at the Spring Grove Cemetery in Cincinnati.

With the presidential election about to take center stage for William Taft, it is worth noting his tremendous accomplishments as Secretary of War. He continued his oversight and advocacy for the Filipino people, he brought order out of chaos to put the Panama Canal project on track, he averted a revolution in Cuba, and he did countless other tasks, both within his official purview and beyond, on behalf of a grateful President. And he did it all with good cheer, nary a complaint, and a consistent track record of success. He may have been the most productive War Secretary in American history who didn't actually oversee a war. The *New York Sun* was the periodical that heaped praise on Taft more than any other, both before and during his presidency. Therefore, the following editorial should be taken with at least a notion of skepticism. Yet, beyond the hyperbole, there's a lot of truth behind the following characterization of Taft's tenure at the War Department.

> Merely to record the movements and missions of the Secretary of War requires a nimble mind. He journeys from Washington to Manila to reassure ten millions of natives restive under an experimental scheme of civil government and turns up in Panama to speed the digging of the Isthmian Canal. To give a fillip to a campaign for reform in some western State, or direct the southern Republicans in the way they should go, or enlighten the people Down East as to the President's home policy, or illuminate the recesses of a problem in jurisdiction for the benefit of a bar association, is only a matter of grabbing a time table and throwing a change of clothing into a travelling bag. Such are mere relaxations and holiday jaunts for the Hon. William H. Taft. A Cuban revolution would be a poser to most statesmen, and to an ordinary Secretary of War a labour of Hercules; but to the business of bringing peace with honour to a distracted land, deposing one government and setting up another, meanwhile gratifying everybody and winning the esteem of the fiercest warrior, Mr. Taft devotes only one page of the Calendar and takes ship for the States to resume his routine duties as if he had done nothing out of the common. … No emergency, no exigency can put the Hon. William H. Taft down. With a heart for any fate, buoyant as hope, versatile as the kaleidoscope, indefatigable as fate and indomitable as victory, he is a most amazing and effective Secretary of War. 'Cabinet help' when William H. Taft is the instrument and medium, is tantamount to the energy and force of a whole Administration.[112]

And now, the entire nation was talking about Taft's future, his next undertaking, which seemed on target for the presidency.

6. President Taft: Whether He Wants It or Not

I-37: President Theodore Roosevelt

The man who would ultimately decide who would become the next President of the United States was the current incumbent. Theodore Roosevelt's first decision was whether or not to walk back his campaign pledge and simply run again himself. Victory was virtually certain, but he refused to consider the entreaties coming his way. With the name Roosevelt left off the ballot, all eyes turned to the President for his preferred successor, the man he considered most likely to continue his policies on behalf of the American people. The only two names that popped into his head were Elihu Root and William Taft. It turns out that neither man wanted to make the run, but Root was more emphatic in his refusal. "I would rather see Elihu Root in the White House than any other man and would walk on my hands and knees from the White House to the Capitol to see Root made president," Roosevelt wrote. "But I know it cannot be done. Wild horses couldn't drag him into making a public campaign."[113] That left only Taft, who by now had little choice in the matter. After turning down the Court in 1906, he had signaled his willingness to make the race, as much as it went against his personal feelings. With the two most important and influential people in his life (his wife and his President) pushing the campaign on him with all the vigor they could muster, he reluctantly resigned himself to run. It would make for a miserable 1908, and an even more dismal four years to follow, but at this point his fate was sealed. William Taft was going to become the President of the United States whether he wanted to or not.

While Nellie Taft remained thrilled at the tantalizing prospect of realizing her dream to become the First Lady of the United States, she felt little joy during the 1908 campaign. In fact, she devoted just two pages of her 400-page memoirs to the contest, opening with the remark, "I cannot go into the details of the preliminary convention fight."[114] Her distrust of President Roosevelt, as well as her own husband's lack of interest and poor performance as a campaigner, undoubtedly contributed to her being ill at ease over the subject. Taft's brother Charlie opened up campaign offices in both Cincinnati and Washington, but Roosevelt was always going to be the prime mover of the effort. The President came out four-square in favor of Taft for the Republican nomination with remarks on January 27, 1908. "I believe with all my soul Taft, far more than any other public man of prominence, represents the principles for which I stand," Roosevelt declared, "and I should hold myself false to my duty if I sat supine and let the men who have taken such joy in my refusal to run again select some candidate whose success would mean the undoing of what I have sought to achieve."[115] Roosevelt's theme, which would become a great source of conflict, was that Taft was the right man to succeed him because he was fully committed to continuing all that *he* stood for. "If we can elect him President," Roosevelt concluded, "we achieve all that could be achieved by continuing me in the office, and yet we avoid all the objections, all the risk of creating a bad precedent."[116] These comments should have been a warning signal to all, but they caused nary a blip. Taft also saw his ascension to be a call to continue to deliver on the Roosevelt agenda. Little did he know that no one could live up to that standard in Roosevelt's eyes, a fact which would play out with devastating consequences throughout much of Taft's term in office.

Roosevelt pushed Taft nearly every day to get out on the campaign trail and make aggressive speeches that would rally their fellow Republicans to his mantle. Taft just didn't have it in him. He had been elected to office just once in his lifetime (as a judge in the state of Ohio), and despite his gregarious personality, he loathed the notion of campaigning for votes for himself. He knew he didn't have the style to whip up voters into the kind of frenzy that Roosevelt was so naturally good at. Instead, he tended to bore his audiences with lawyerly treatises filled with legislative proposals backed up by mounds of statistics. But all of this mattered little, as the people loved Roosevelt, and Roosevelt had selected his man. Taft's ambivalence remained on display as he declared on the eve of the Republican National Convention, "I'd rather not say what I think of happenings in Chicago. Besides I am the man least interested."[117] But his sentiments, frankly, no longer mattered. The party was lining up behind Taft regardless of whether he wanted its nomination or not.

Nellie Taft remained on edge as the convention was gearing up at the Chicago Coliseum in June 1908. She was convinced that Roosevelt was going to change his mind and decide at the last minute to run himself. While monitoring the gathering from Washington, she cringed for the entirety of the 49-minute ovation that Roosevelt received when his administration was recognized early in the event. She ignored the fact that her husband's claim to the presidency was almost entirely based on Roosevelt's endorsement. Instead, she jealously focused on the incumbent who was soaking in the adoration while her husband's nomination was quietly waiting in the wings. When the roll call of the states started, Taft's moment of ascendancy had finally arrived. Seven names were put forward, but Taft was the clear choice of the delegates. He recorded 702 votes on the first ballot to capture the nomination. Senator Philander Knox was a distant second with only 68 votes. With a strong push from his home delegation of New York, Congressman James Sherman came away with the nomination for Vice President on the first

I-38: Republican Campaign Banner, Taft and VP candidate James Sherman, 1908

ballot. Nellie Taft was with her husband in his office when word of the nomination came in. While pleased with the result, she remained petty in her views of her husband's current boss. "I only want it [the celebration] to last more than forty-nine minutes," she exclaimed. "I want to get even for the scare that Roosevelt's cheer of forty-nine minutes gave me yesterday." Taft merely smiled and said, "Oh, my dear, my dear!"[118]

After receiving the Republican nomination, Taft resigned his post as Secretary of War, and the couple immediately left for some downtime at The Homestead, a resort in Hot Springs, Virginia. In the meantime, the Democrats trotted out William Jennings Bryan for the third time in the last four electoral cycles. Bryan found his charges of imperialism against Roosevelt and Taft to be falling flat, so he shifted the focus of his powerful oratory to Taft's reputation as anti-labor from his days on the Bench. Roosevelt implored Taft to get on the campaign trail himself, to rigorously defend his record, and to take Bryan's meager political profile to task. "Do not answer Bryan; attack him!" Roosevelt urged. "Don't let him make the issues."[119] But Taft was slow to respond.

I-39: Taft during the 1908 presidential campaign

When he did make a public statement, he did little to elicit any excitement. Despite Nellie's encouragement to break from the Roosevelt hold on him and the party and make clear his own bona fides as a candidate, Taft knew that his electoral prospects hinged squarely on his commitment to the Roosevelt agenda. His pitch – his added value – was to take Roosevelt's grand ideas and ensure they secured the formal backing of law. "The chief function of the next Administration, in my judgment, is … a progressive development of that which has been performed by President Roosevelt," Taft wrote, "to complete and perfect the machinery by which these standards may be maintained, by which the lawbreakers may be promptly restrained and punished, but which shall operate with sufficient accuracy and dispatch to interfere with legitimate business as little as possible."[120] Such rhetoric excited no one.

Roosevelt continued to be Taft's biggest supporter while also serving as his most profound critic. "I am not very much pleased with the way Taft's campaign is being handled," Roosevelt lamented. "I do wish that Taft would put more energy and fight into the matter."[121] "Oh Lord, I do get angry now and then over the campaign," he added later. "Of course I suppose everyone always feels that he would manage things a little differently if he had the doing of them; but certainly I would like to put more snap into the business."[122] Urging more aggressive tactics, Roosevelt informed Taft that "Prize fights are won by knocking out the other man when he is groggy."[123] Secretary of State Root chimed in as well. "For reasons which I am absolutely unable to fathom," Root wrote to Roosevelt, "Taft does not arouse the enthusiasm which his record and personality warrant us in believing he ought to arouse."[124] But none of this should have been a surprise. Taft had been forecasting his aversion to the campaign for months (if not years). In the midst of the criticism, Taft meekly admitted:

> I am sorry, but I cannot be more aggressive than my nature makes me. That is the advantage and disadvantage of having been on the Bench. I can't call names and I can't use adjectives when I don't think the case calls for them, so you will have to get along with that kind of a candidate. I realize what you say of the strength that the President has by reason of those qualities which are the antithesis of the judicial, but so it is with me, and if the people don't like that kind of a man then they have got to take another.[125]

There was no longer any time for substitutions on this menu. Taft was the candidate, and the American people were seemingly going to have to take him as he was.

The reverence for Theodore Roosevelt carried the day in 1908, and that meant the election of his hand-picked successor, William Taft, as the 27th President of the United States. The results were not close. Taft captured 29 states to 17 for Bryan. The count in the Electoral College was a dominating 321 to 162. His edge in the popular tally was more than 1.2 million votes, a thoroughly convincing margin of 8.5%. The numbers weren't quite as strong as Roosevelt's from the previous canvass, but they easily surpassed all other winners since Ulysses Grant. Roosevelt's joy was the one that overflowed at the result. "We have beaten them to a frazzle," Roosevelt exulted. Publicly, the President proclaimed, "The nomination of Mr. Taft was a triumph over reactionary conservatism, and his election was a triumph over unwise and improper radicalism."[126] Taft himself was mostly muted in the wake of victory. His bride, on the other hand, was thrilled. "I was never so happy in my life," was Nellie's simple response.[127] Taft did one thing in the immediate aftermath of his victory – he wrote a thank you note to his former boss. "The first letter that I wish to write is to you," Taft conveyed to Roosevelt, "because you have always been the chief agent in working out the present state of affairs and my selection and election are chiefly your work. You and my brother Charlie made that possible which in all probability would not have occurred otherwise."[128] Little did Taft know that the hypersensitive Roosevelt was irked by Taft's attempt at gratitude. His brother Charlie? Roosevelt subsequently analogized that such a remark was like saying, "Abraham Lincoln and the bond seller Jay Cooke saved the Union."[129] This was just the beginning of the resentment that would only continue to grow.

I-40: Taft, the golfer, Hot Springs, VA, December 1908

Presidents-elect have two primary tasks to complete during the interregnum; select a Cabinet and draft an Inaugural Address. Taft was slow to start on both. Mainly, he played golf. Taft had recently picked up the game, and it now became a daily obsession that persisted throughout his presidency. He claimed the exercise was needed to help keep his weight down, but mostly it was an opportunity to get away from all things presidential. The Tafts ensconced themselves at the Terrett Cottage near Augusta National in Georgia, where he played golf while Nellie contemplated how she planned to run the White House as First Lady. When he could procrastinate no longer, Taft finally started charting out his Cabinet, and he quickly ran into problems. He had recently told Roosevelt that he intended to retain those in the current Cabinet who wanted to remain and continue to pursue Roosevelt's progressive agenda. "I wish you would tell the boys I have been working with that I want to continue all of them," Taft confided to the President. "They are all fine fellows and they have been mighty good to me. I want them all to stay just as they are."[130] Roosevelt was thrilled. But, now, Taft started to backtrack. Taft's focus was more on law than policy. "Mr. Roosevelt's function has been to preach a crusade against certain evils," Taft commented. "He has aroused the public to demand reform. … It becomes my business to put that reform into legal execution."[131] And for that, Taft wanted lawyers, not ideological policy advocates as his chief advisers. That meant changes, creating yet another mini-fracture in the Taft-Roosevelt relationship.

In the end, only two holdovers remained from Roosevelt's final Cabinet. James Wilson continued as the Secretary of Agriculture for his third consecutive President, and George von L. Meyer shifted from Postmaster General to the Department of the Navy. And then in came the attorneys. President McKinley's former Attorney General, Philander Knox, was tabbed as Secretary of State. The more controversial appointments included two Democrats – Jacob Dickinson at the War Department and Franklin MacVeagh at Treasury. And then there was Richard Ballinger at the Department of the Interior. This one may have hurt Roosevelt most of all. Conservation was at the top of Roosevelt's domestic agenda, and he had put people in place throughout Interior to aggressively push actions consistent with the progressive philosophy. Secretary James Garfield, the son of the former President, was an outdoorsman like Roosevelt and close to the outgoing President. He had also just signed an extension to his lease in Washington under the impression that he would be retained. Taft tried to let Garfield down easily with his decision. "It means that I cannot retain in my Cabinet a good many who served Mr. Roosevelt in that capacity, although I have for them a warmth of affection and a great respect," Taft said. "The truth is that in the selection of my Cabinet I have tried to act as judicially as

I-41: President Taft and his Cabinet

(Left to Right): Secretary of the Interior Richard Ballinger, Secretary of the Navy George Meyer, Secretary of State Philander Knox, Personal Secretary Charles Norton, Taft (seated) Postmaster General Frank Hitchcock, Secretary of Agriculture James Wilson, Treasury Secretary Franklin MacVeagh, Attorney General George Wickersham, and Secretary of Commerce and Labor Charles Nagel (not pictured, Secretary of War Jacob Dickinson)

possible and to free myself altogether from the personal aspect, which has embarrassed me not only with respect to you, but with respect to the members of the body of which we both formed a part."[132] He was clearly aware of the ripple effect some of these decisions might have, but he knew first-hand how important it was for a President to have the right advisers in place. If feelings were ruffled in the process, then so be it. Taft's Cabinet would indeed be loyal to the chief. All but Ballinger and Dickinson would serve all four years. Taft got plenty of legal advice from his crew, but the bunch fell far short of expectations in the eyes of the Roosevelt progressives – yet another strike against the hand-picked successor.

Roosevelt decided to upend tradition and invite William and Nellie Taft to spend the night before the transfer of power in the White House. Taft was happy to accept. He continued to insist that some of the noise percolating about Taft deviating from the Roosevelt agenda was all nonsense. In accepting the invitation, he shared his thoughts with Roosevelt that, "People have attempted to represent that you and I were in some way at odds during the last three months, whereas you and I know that there has not been the slightest difference between us, and I welcome the opportunity to stay the last night of your administration under the White House roof to make as emphatic as possible the refutation of any such suggestion."[133] Relations were cordial the evening of March 3, but a little stiff, as all parties tread a bit lightly in their conversation. There were still many in the Roosevelt camp who thought the whole thing to be a mistake and that Roosevelt should be the one taking another oath the following day. Roosevelt already shared some of those concerns himself. The next day, as he was preparing to leave, Roosevelt told Mark Sullivan that Taft's "all right. He means well and he'll do his best. But he's weak. They'll get around him. They'll—" Roosevelt put his shoulder against Sullivan's shoulder and pushed, "they'll lean against him."[134]

For those who believe in ominous signs, the weatherman offered a beauty on the day of Taft's inauguration as President of the United States. Conditions were simply atrocious. For the first time in more than 75 years, the presidential inauguration was forced indoors. Taft and Roosevelt were good-natured about the turn of events. "I knew there'd be a blizzard when I went out," Roosevelt declared when the pair met for breakfast on the day of the inauguration. "You're wrong," Taft replied with a chuckle, "it is my storm. I always said it would be a cold day when I got to be President of the United States."[135] Taft waited for the last minute to make the call to cancel the outdoor portion of the festivities, hating to disappoint the thousands who had shown up to take in the ceremonies, but the blizzard-like conditions made an outdoor event impossible. Taft

I-42: Outgoing President Roosevelt with Incoming President Taft, Inauguration Day, March 4, 1909

opted to place his hand on the century-old Bible of the Supreme Court as he took his oath from Chief Justice Melville Fuller. He then gave a methodical policy-filled address that was more like an Annual Message to Congress. Taft went topic by topic and gave his views on how his administration would handle subjects such as the trusts, the tariff, conservation, the building of the Panama Canal, and on and on and on. There was no fiery rhetoric, merely policy statements in plain language. At the end, Taft left his audience with these final thoughts:

> Having thus reviewed the questions likely to recur during my administration, and having expressed in a summary way the position which I expect to take in recommendations to Congress and in my conduct as an Executive, I invoke the considerate sympathy and support of my fellow-citizens and the aid of the Almighty God in the discharge of my responsible duties.[136]

Many of those in attendance had come more to say goodbye to Roosevelt than to celebrate Taft's rise to the presidency. For his part, Roosevelt tried to stay out of the limelight and pass the torch to Taft. He had already announced he was going to get as far away from the Washington scene as possible, signing on for an African safari that was due to last at least a year. "Down at the bottom," Roosevelt had written William Allen White the previous August, "my main reason for wishing to go to Africa for a year is so that I can get where no one can accuse me of running, nor do Taft the injustice of accusing him of permitting me to run, the job."[137] True to his word, Roosevelt left Washington as soon as the formal transition was complete, and within a few days he was bound for Africa. Such a distance would hardly lessen the Rooseveltian cloud that hung over the Taft presidency from the very beginning.

The one ray of sunshine that inauguration day was the one hovering over the nation's new First Lady, Helen (Nellie) Taft. She was dressed to the nines for the day she had dreamed about since she was a young girl. And she started out in style. For the first time in American history, the new President traveled back to the Executive Mansion from his inaugural with his wife by his side. "I see no reason," Nellie later remarked, "why the president's wife may not now come into some rights on that day also."[138] She continued:

I-43: President Taft was joined by First Lady Nellie Taft on the ride from the Capitol to the White House after being sworn in as President, March 4, 1909

> For me that drive was the proudest and happiest event of Inauguration Day. Perhaps I had a little secret elation in thinking that I was doing something which no woman had ever done before. I forgot the anxieties of the preceding night; the consternation caused by the fearful weather; and every trouble seemed swept aside. My responsibilities had not yet begun to worry me, and I was able to enjoy, almost to the full, the realisation that my husband was actually President of the United States and that it was this fact which the cheering crowds were acclaiming.[139]

The Tafts were center stage that evening at the Inaugural Ball at the Pension Building. Some 10,000 guests crowded the large hall for the celebration, which Nellie likely enjoyed more than anyone. She had finally achieved her lifelong ambition, even if her husband was reticent about the next day, and, for that matter, for the next four years.

I-44: The White House as it looked on March 4, 1909

The other key person alongside for the bulk of the Taft presidency was his military aide, Captain Archibald Butt. Archie Butt had first encountered Taft in the Philippines when he was put in charge of Taft's social calendar. The pair hit it off, and Butt became not only one of Taft's closest companions but also a personal confidante on almost any subject. Butt had moved on from the Philippines for service in Cuba, but he found his way to the White House as the military aide to President Roosevelt beginning the previous March. The two bonded instantly, and Butt became a regular presence at Roosevelt's side. Butt was athletic and an outdoorsman like Roosevelt, and the two often engaged in

I-45: President Taft with his military aide, Captain Archibald Butt, circa 1909

physical activities. When Taft succeeded Roosevelt, he asked Butt to stay on and continue in his role as military aide. He had an unusual spot in history, as one of the closest colleagues to two American Presidents who started out as best friends and then transitioned into bitter rivals over the course of just a couple of years. It was heart-wrenching work for Butt, who loved both men, to watch the relationship collapse before his (and everyone else's) eyes. Butt realized at the very outset of Taft's term that this presidency would be very different from the prior one. "President Taft is one of the finest human engines I ever knew," he said during Taft's first month in office, "but like every other engine, is not very effective without a fire under the boiler. Roosevelt used to be constantly building the fire."[140] After attending a Gridiron dinner, one of the social events of the season in Washington, Butt concluded that "Nothing shows what a hold Theodore has on the public mind more than the dinner this evening. Even when he is away and in no way interfering in politics, such is the personality of the man that almost the entire evening was wit and humor devoted to him, while the president [and] most of the cabinet present … were hardly mentioned."[141] This was the aura hanging over the new President of the United States.

Presidents usually had a bit of a honeymoon to settle into their new role. After the Senate confirmed the top nominations for the new administration, Congress traditionally went into recess until the following December. But that was not going to be the case for the presidency of William Taft. The tariff had always been a politically charged issue that tended to divide parties into sectional factions, making it nearly impossible to pass legislation that didn't offend large blocks of constituencies. Since there was still no income tax in the United States at the time of Taft's inauguration, the tariff (i.e., a tax on imports) remained the principal means of funding the Federal government. William McKinley had been a leader in the protectionist movement that favored high tariffs that made foreign products less competitive in U.S. domestic markets. But even he had started to look at the topic through a different lens. In fact, in the last speech he ever gave, which took place the day before he was assassinated, McKinley advocated for increased usage of reciprocity agreements for mutual free trade to help the growing business for U.S. exports. Theodore Roosevelt essentially ignored the tariff during his terms in office, mostly because of the no-win volatility of the issue. For the 1908 election cycle, however, the Republican Party took a stand on the issue. Not only did the party's platform advocate for reductions in the tariff, which currently stood at historically high levels, but it also encouraged the next President to call for a special session of Congress to enact these changes immediately after the inauguration.

Roosevelt had warned Taft to be wary of the tariff, but Taft was not about to begin his administration by turning his back on a core plank of the party platform that was particularly appealing to the progressive wing of the party. Taft had embraced lower tariffs during the campaign. "It is my judgment that a revision of the tariff in accordance with the pledge [of the] Republican platform will be, on the whole, a substantial revision downward,"[142] he had announced. The expectations were now high for him to deliver on that commitment. When the session convened, however, just a couple of weeks into his term, the new President surprised nearly all observers with a terse opening statement that was nearly void of any form of advocacy. In just 329 words, Taft initiated the session by calling for "immediate consideration to the revision of the Dingley tariff act,"[143] but failed to mention his expectations as to whether that revision should be upward or downward. Some in Congress, particularly in the Senate, took this as a license to counterbalance any potential reductions (which had been the thrust of the Republican platform) with *increases* on many items of import. When the progressives pounced on what they perceived as backsliding against the commitments from the campaign, Taft fell back on the need to adhere to the separation of powers and provide the opportunity for the legislature to do what it thought was best. He told Nelson Aldrich, a leader in the Senate, that "I have no disposition to exert any other influence than that which it is my function under the Constitution to exercise."[144] This was a far cry from Roosevelt's regular usage of the Presidential "Bully Pulpit" to drive the national agenda in the direction he supported. Taft, rather naively, put his faith in the Republican leadership to follow the dictates of the party from the campaign. "I have not found [Senator] Aldrich or [Speaker of the House Joe] Cannon in any way deceptive in the dealings that I have had with them, and I believe they are acting in good faith," he wrote.[145] All Taft would commit to was re-engaging at the time of a conference committee between the two houses if he believed the proposed legislation wasn't sufficient in bringing the tariff rates down. The only piece of advocacy emanating from the White House was a narrow one. It was the reiteration of a longstanding plea from Taft to finally provide the Philippines with

I-46: Speaker of the House Joe Cannon and Senator Nelson Aldrich

free trade with the United States. Beyond that, he was content to remain quiet and await the legislative process to work itself out.

Congressman Sereno Payne of New York took the lead in the House of Representatives, which passed a reduction measure that encompassed a broad range of items, except for luxury goods. This was good news for the progressives. But conflict immediately ensued in the Senate. Aldrich did have the lead, but he was aligned with the conservatives in the party, many of whom wanted *more* protection, not less. The Senate bill essentially turned the House measure upside down. The conference committee would have to resolve these broad discrepancies before anything could be sent to the President for his consideration.

At this point, Taft did engage and tried to push for unity on tariff reductions. He invited 19 legislators, conservatives and progressives, to the White House for dinner to push his views and try to forge a compromise. The leading progressives, such as Robert La Follette of Wisconsin, were adamant that Taft needed to make it clear he would veto any measure that didn't bring most rates down. The President remained non-committal. And then the congressional leadership betrayed him. Cannon and Aldrich stacked the conference committee with protectionists, instantly generating distrust in the relatively small but extremely vocal progressive caucus. In the end, the Payne-Aldrich Tariff that emerged from the conference committee did lower rates on 654 products, but also raised rates on 220 items, and left in place the already high rates for the remaining 1,150 items. The progressives felt betrayed. They expected no increases of any kind and reductions generally across the board. This effort fell far short of what they were convinced the President had promised during the campaign.

President Taft now had the first important decision to make of his presidency. It would clearly set the tone as to his alignment with the conservative or progressive wings of his party. There were other considerations as Taft weighed his options on a potential veto. There were additional elements of this bill that appealed to him. First, the free trade measures for the Philippines were included for everything except a limitation on tobacco imports. This was something for which Taft had been advocating throughout the past decade. "It has been a long, hard fight," Taft wrote to Nellie, "and the possibility of great improvement arising from this feature of the present tariff bill is one of the reasons why I should be very reluctant to veto the bill."[146] This was not lost on the legislators who decided to include it in the first place. Second, Taft had asked for, and received, a provision to establish an independent Tariff Board that would try to take politics out of this messy process in the future by empowering the Board to study the economic trends and make rate recommendations to Congress commensurate with those fluctuations. The Board would only be temporary at first but could be made permanent down the road. Lastly, Congress included a provision for a 1% corporate tax on net income of corporations whose earnings topped $5,000 per year. Taft was opposed to congressional action on a *personal* income tax since he didn't want to sign something that the Supreme Court had previously ruled to be unconstitutional. Taft favored a personal income tax but advocated for that via a constitutional amendment so as to not create a direct challenge to the Court. In this case, Congress followed suit, including the corporate tax provision as an immediate alternative, and shortly thereafter sending the 16th Amendment to authorize the personal income tax to the states for consideration. But these additional provisions were mostly just noise to the progressives. This was a test of whether or not William Taft was really going to continue the policies of their hero, Theodore Roosevelt, or fall back on traditional conservative principles.

Taft weighed his options carefully, with political ramifications very much on his mind.

> The vetoing of the bill, of course, would throw me out of the leaders in the Senate and the House, and would make me almost hopeless in respect to effecting my reforms of next year, so you see how much more hangs on the question than the mere subject of the rates in the tariff bill. Of course, the position I have taken in respect to the tariff bill and downward revision may open me to a charge of inconsistency, and not standing to my promises, if I were to sign a bill that was distinctly at variance with those promises, and that is the only thing that puts me in a position where I can contemplate a possibility of a veto.[147]

"Charges of inconsistency" was a mild interpretation of the reaction Taft would encounter if he signed the bill, which he was about to find out after placing his name on the legislation on August 5, 1909.

The progressive press was unabashed in its condemnation of the betrayal by the President on the first major effort of his administration. While Roosevelt had always shied away from the politics of the tariff, his supporters were convinced that if TR was still in the White House, the result would have been completely different. The prevailing view was that Taft was clearly aligned with the Republican old guard, and the progressive movement was in trouble. Taft thought all of this was a complete overreaction. He recognized how difficult tariff legislation was and how the results always left people upset. He thought the right move was to get on the road and take that message directly to the American people, who would surely understand his position. The trip spanned more than two months and

I-47: President Taft, circa 1909 (age ~52)

included more than 250 speeches, but the only one that really mattered took place on September 17 at the Opera House in Winona, Minnesota. Taft reverted to form, engaging in a lengthy legalistic set of remarks on why tariff legislation is so difficult, and that people may have built in their own minds unrealistic expectations. "I did not promise that everything should go downward," Taft said. "What I promised was, that there should be many decreases, and that in some things increases would be found to be necessary; but that on the whole I conceived that the change of conditions would make the revision necessarily downward, and that, I contend, under the showing which I have made, has been the result of the Payne Bill."[148] The only line that anyone paid attention to, though, was the President's conclusion that "On the whole, therefore, I am bound to say that I think the Payne-Tariff Bill is the best tariff bill that the Republican party ever passed."[149] The progressives were appalled, and made their opinions known loud and clear. If this was the "best" they could expect, then they had the wrong man in charge. This misstep would be difficult for Taft to overcome.

And then he ran headfirst into the conservationists. Conservation was another of Roosevelt's signature topics, having worked with his team to set aside an unprecedented 150 million acres of western land into protected status, more than three times his four predecessors combined. While Roosevelt favorite James Garfield had been replaced by Richard Ballinger as Secretary for the Department of the Interior, much of the remaining staff hailed from the progressive wing of the party. Their leader was Gifford Pinchot, an independently wealthy man who was on a personal crusade to advance the cause of conservation from his perch as the Chief of the U.S. Forest Service. Ballinger and Pinchot

I-48: Conservationist and leading progressive, Gifford Pinchot

I-49: Secretary of the Interior Richard Ballinger

clashed from the outset, as the corporate lawyer now in the Cabinet believed his job was to promote conservation in "a safe, sane, and conservative way without impeding the development of the great West and without hysteria in one direction or another."[150] To the progressives, this approach was clearly a step back, which became even more pronounced when Ballinger decided to nullify one of Garfield's last moves in office that had set aside for conservation purposes millions of acres of public land that sat alongside the nation's waterways. Ballinger convinced the President that some of these actions may have exceeded the authorizations provided by Congress and that they should be held back until such time as Congress updated the statute. Such reasoning was perfectly aligned with Taft's vision for codifying Roosevelt's executive actions in law so they could be sustained over time. Pinchot and the progressives simply saw a sellout. And they said so. Pinchot jumped the chain of command and complained directly to the President, with other criticisms about Ballinger reaching his desk about the same time.

Louis Glavis was a little-known field agent in the General Land Office and a close associate of Pinchot. Glavis uncovered evidence that he believed implicated Secretary Ballinger in a fraudulent attempt to seize federal coal lands in Alaska prior to joining the Cabinet. Pinchot complained again to Taft, who investigated, and decided to back his Secretary. In fact, the only one to be ousted as a result of the investigation was Glavis. Plus, Taft admonished Pinchot for operating outside of the chain of command. "The heads of the Departments are the persons through whom I must act," Taft wrote at the time, "and unless the bureau chiefs are subordinate to the heads it makes government of an efficient character impossible."[151] At this point, the gloves came off as far as Pinchot was concerned. He started making public utterances that were critical of the President. Taft was angered by the insubordination but was reluctant to fire his forestry chief because of how it might play in the mind of Theodore Roosevelt. "I am beginning to think that is just what he [Pinchot] wants to force me to do, and I will not do it," Taft noted in a letter to his brother, Charlie.

> If the whole contention is the result of some sort of conspiracy, Pinchot's dismissal would only bring about what they are trying to do, an open rupture between Roosevelt and myself, and I am determined [if] such a rupture is ever brought about that it shall not be through any action of mine. Theodore may not approve of all I have done and I don't expect him to do so, but I shall try not to do anything which he might regard as a challenge to him. No, Charlie, I am going to give Pinchot as much rope as he wants, and I think you will find that he will hang himself.[152]

And he certainly did. Pinchot kept up the pressure on the administration, accentuated by a public letter to Senator Jonathan Dollinger in December 1909 that was highly critical of both Taft and Ballinger. At this point, Taft held back no longer. He informed Pinchot, "Your letter was in effect an improper appeal to Congress and the public to excuse in advance the guilt of your subordinates before I could act and against my decision in the Glavis case. ... By your own conduct you have destroyed your usefulness as a helpful subordinate."[153] Pinchot was formally terminated on January 7, 1910. Within a couple of months, he was on his way to Europe to meet with Roosevelt, who was wrapping up his African safari and planned some touring on the Continent before returning to the States. Pinchot had a long list of complaints at the ready to share with his former chief, the beginning of the process to turn Roosevelt against his successor and get back in the game himself.

The widespread criticism was definitely affecting the President. He continued a presidential tradition by railing in private about his unfair treatment in the press. But this was yet another area in which he refused to help himself. Roosevelt had been the master at cozying up to the press, contributing to the generally positive coverage he received. Taft thought such action was beneath the dignity of the President of the United States.

Around this same time, he aired his views on the topic with the editor of *Everybody's Magazine:*

> I am going to do what I think is best for the country, within my jurisdiction and power, and then let the rest take care of itself. I am not looking for a second term, and I am not going to subject myself to the worry involved in establishing a publicity bureau, or attempting to set myself right before the people in any different way from that which is involved in the ordinary publication of what is done. The misrepresentations which are made by the muckraking correspondents I cannot neutralize, and I don't intend to.[154]

As the bad press mounted, Taft chose to ignore it. He told Butt to no longer bring him any newspapers that were critical of him. Butt thought this to be a mistake, and that it would give Taft a false sense of security, but Taft stuck with the order.

Taft's challenges with the press extended into the realm of presidential policies. Publishers and editors across the country were miffed over the tariff Taft signed that only partially reduced the rates for print paper and wood pulp. Their ire was similarly raised when Taft sought to increase the rates of second class mail, which were discounted from first class for newspapers, magazines, and other periodicals. The President was confident in his deliberative decision-making process, telling Otto Bannard:

> The truth is that the present magazines are getting about fifty millions of dollars out of the Government that they are not entitled to, and I am going to fight that thing through. I do not care anything about them. They have shown themselves just exactly as selfish as the interests which they have attacked, and I propose to have justice done. If we wish to contribute a subsidy of fifty millions to the education of the country, I can find a good deal of better method of doing it than by the circulation of *Collier's Weekly* and *Everybody's Magazine*.[155]

What may have sounded like a decent policy in a vacuum, ignored the anger it would generate in the nation's press. Very few papers would go out of their way to say anything good about President William Taft.

So, what did Taft do in the midst of this maelstrom? He exhibited bursts of anger, constant frustration, and his formerly ever-present smile virtually vanished from the scene. "I feel dreadfully sorry for him," noted

Archie Butt. "He gets so low in spirits that it is impossible to cheer him. [He] just sits silently by … and grows morose."[156] Deep lines started to appear on Taft's face, and he was diagnosed with gout in one of his feet. This was not all that surprising since during this stressful period, Taft did what he often did – he ate – a lot, typically starting his day with a 12-ounce steak and moving on from there. Despite an extensive exercise regimen, which included his daily golf game, the weight kept piling on, now topping 350 pounds. For those who thought he should play less golf because it distracted him from his official duties, Taft simply scoffed. While he claimed the exercise was essential, more importantly, the golf course was a rare escape for Taft from the painful grind of the trials of the presidency. "The beauty of golf to me," Taft confessed to Butt, "is that you cannot play if you permit yourself to think of anything else." This was precisely what Taft craved, to *not* think about the presidency. His testiness on the topic was in evidence when Taft was urged to change his golf plans so he could meet with the President of Chile. "I'll be damned if I will give up my game of golf to see this fellow," Taft angrily remarked.[157] Taft's obesity led to more embarrassing moments as he often fell asleep in meetings and at events, often right in the middle when other people of prominence were talking. Butt and Nellie were constantly popping into meetings just to see if Taft had nodded off. They would often use a loud cough to try to wake him when this happened.

I-50: President Taft as "Golfer in Chief"

Taft's home life was also challenging in his first year as President. From the very beginning, Nellie Taft had jumped into her role of managing the White House with gusto. This was a point of inflection for Nellie, who admittedly became less involved in her husband's activities, and primarily focused on running her new home and the social responsibilities that came with being the First Lady.

> My very active participation in my husband's career came to an end when he became President. I had always had the satisfaction of knowing almost as much as he about the politics and the intricacies of any situation in which he found himself, and my life was filled with interests of a most unusual kind. But in the White House I found my own duties too engrossing to permit me to follow him long or very far into the governmental maze which soon enveloped him.[158]

Nellie made a number of changes shortly after moving into the White House. She replaced the traditional male steward with a female housekeeper, feeling the staff "need a woman's guidance and control."[159] Elizabeth Jaffrey was abrasive and often a turn-off to the staff, but she had the full confidence of the First Lady in executing her vision for the running of the executive mansion. Nellie often held court in the Red Room, welcoming guests on a regular basis from the elites across the Washington establishment. She also helped oversee the completion of the renovation of the West Wing that had been initiated under Roosevelt. This included the completion of the Oval Office, for which Taft was the first presidential occupant.

I-51: The original Oval Office used by President Taft, 1909

Nellie Taft moved quickly to redecorate her new home in her

I-52: First Lady Helen ("Nellie") Taft

own image. This included an oriental style in the living quarters reflecting their long stay in Asia. Along these lines, she remarked once on how much she loved the cherry trees that were unique to Japan. When the mayor of Tokyo heard the remark, as a gesture of goodwill, he sent 2,000 of the trees to Washington as a gift. The First Lady had them planted just off the National Mall, surrounding the Tidal Basin. "I wonder if any of them will ever attain the magnificent growth of the ancient and dearly loved cherry trees of Japan," she remarked. She would be extremely pleased to know how popular the annual Cherry Blossom Festival has become in the spring every year. She was also especially proud of her garden parties, which were held approximately four times per year. Overall, the very social First Couple entertained more than any of their predecessors in recent memory.

But in the midst of this flurry of activity, Nellie Taft's dream job took a sharp turn when she fell ill on a cruise on the presidential yacht on the Potomac River near George Washington's home at Mount Vernon. The President wrote his son, Robert, that the First Lady had suffered "a very severe nervous attack, in which ... she lost all muscular control of her right arm and her right leg and of the vocal cords and the muscles governing her speech."[160] Nellie Taft had suffered a stroke just a few months into her husband's presidency. Archie Butt observed that "The President looked like a great stricken animal. … I have never seen greater suffering or pain on a man's face."[161] Despite the political challenges swirling around him, Taft pushed the work aside to tend to his wife. The lingering effects were partial paralysis of some of the muscles in Nellie's face, as well as difficulty regaining the power of speech. According to

Mrs. More, one of the housekeepers, the President did everything he could to create a low-stress, positive environment for his wife. "He never permits himself to appear serious for a minute when he is in her room," she said. "He laughs all the time and tries to amuse her."[162] This was a tall task given how much grief he was feeling during the course of his day job, but his wife's health had quickly eclipsed his presidential concerns. Taft's dedication to Nellie's recovery included patiently helping her regain command of her speech. He was heard saying on one occasion, "Now please, darling, try and say 'the' -that's it, 'the.' That's pretty good, but now try it again."[163] Nellie's sisters (Emily, Jane, Francis, and Maria) all helped out while the First Lady slowly made her recovery. After three intense months, she started to resemble her old self, but it would take about a year before she was truly herself again and back in the full swing of being First Lady of the United States. Nellie's eventual recovery was certainly the best news her husband had during that first year, which was clearly a struggle on almost every front.

There were some successes for Taft in the early portion of his presidency, but they were typically in areas that garnered little attention from the press or the public. Civil Service Reform had been a prominent issue in the 1880s and 1890s, but by 1909 the topic was no longer front page news. Taft did further this cause in a material way, adding 35,000 fourth class postmasters to the protected list, along with 20,000 skilled workers in the Navy Yard. These classifications continued the drive to replace political patronage with demonstrated competence as the means to fill the roster of civil servants. "Reforms of this kind are the result of the hardest kind of work in the closet," said the President. "They cannot be exploited in the

I-53: President Taft, circa 1910 (age ~53)

headlines. They tire the audience. Those who effect them must generally be contented with a consciousness of good service rendered, and must not look for the reward of popular approval."[164] Treasury Secretary MacVeagh put it this way: "I know of no Presidential record with respect to civil service reform, that equals that of President Taft; and yet nothing is said about and little is known about it by the public at large."[165] These reforms were a credit to the administration, but they did little to enhance Taft's sagging reputation.

The same could be said for one of the most significant reforms introduced by President Taft that shifted the locus of power in Washington. Prior to Taft, there was no unified budget process for the Federal government. Congress worked directly with each Cabinet agency to craft discrete budgets that were translated into appropriations to be presented to the President for his signature. As the constitutional leader of the executive branch, Taft felt this approach was missing a critical step. He believed that the nation's chief executive should pull together a single budget, making trade-offs across his Cabinet agencies to prioritize those programs that he believed would be most impactful for the American people. Congress was not terribly interested in Taft's proposed innovation, as it inserted the President into a process it had previously performed without him as a middleman. But Taft was determined to pursue this reform. "In my opinion, it is entirely competent for the President to submit a budget, and Congress can not forbid or prevent it," Taft proclaimed. "It is quite within his duty and power to have prepared and to submit to Congress and the country, a statement of resources, obligations, revenues, expenditures and estimates, in the form he deems advisable. And this power I propose to exercise."[166] So, Taft started creating annual unified budgets and submitting them to Congress, which promptly ignored them while continuing to execute the old budget process. But Taft was able to get Congress to authorize a Commission on Economy and Efficiency to assess the situation, as well as to make other recommendations that would improve the administration of the executive branch. The commission's final report in 1912 was entitled "The Need for a National Budget," and essentially sanctioned Taft's original proposal. The next few Congresses let the recommendations sit on the shelf, but they didn't disappear. In 1921, the Budget and Accounting Act was passed, which established the Bureau of the Budget, and required the President to submit a single proposed budget to Congress on an annual basis. The essence of that process continues to the present day. This was a significant accomplishment that was initiated by Taft in his role as the nation's "chief administrator," but it still didn't move the needle on his popularity.

Taft knew it had been a rough year. He felt it personally, and it continued to affect his moods. He simply had no answer on how to remain committed to his own convictions and personality while also trying to stay true to the legacy of Theodore Roosevelt. At the heart of the matter, these two goals were increasingly proving to be incompatible. Taft wasn't as progressive as Roosevelt, but, frankly, no one would compare favorably to the former President to his supporters (or him). All of this angst and disappointment weighed on Taft every day. Shortly after his first anniversary in the White House, Taft found himself in friendly territory, giving a speech to a Yale fraternity dinner at the Raleigh Hotel. "Brother Bridgeman [the toastmaster] offers me a recipe for acquiring twenty-five successive terms," Taft remarked.

> I thank Mr. Bridgeman, but the first term is enough for me. Judging from the trouble and the worry of getting through the first year of my first term, the contemplation of twenty-five terms, or more than one, is more than I can stand. It will require all the energy, philosophy, strength of character, and every other thing which the Psi U fraternity teaches to carry me through one term.[167]

This was just one year into his term. And things were about to get worse.

7. He's Not TR

Theodore Roosevelt had been true to his word. He left on Inauguration Day and got about as far away from American politics as he could. His African safari had been a big success, as was his barnstorming through Europe, where he gave rousing speeches and hobnobbed with royalty. And even though his presence hung over virtually every decision Taft made in that first year, at least it was a figurative presence, not a physical one. That was about to change. Theodore and Edith Roosevelt stepped foot on New York soil on June 18, 1910, to the booming sound of a 21-gun salute from the more than 100 boats escorting their return in the harbor. Hundreds of thousands lined Broadway for a parade celebrating the former President's return. Taft sent their mutual friend, Captain Butt, to welcome Roosevelt back and offer his best wishes. Butt was side-by-side with Roosevelt, in awe of the massive display of affection. "I have never witnessed anything like it," Butt recalled, "and

I-54: Former President Theodore Roosevelt being welcomed upon his return to New York, June 18, 1910

it was to see just one man in a frock suit, it was simply marvelous."[168] Despite the prodding he had already received from his hardcore progressive followers, Roosevelt still attempted to show deference to Taft and stay out of the limelight. "I shall keep my mind open while I keep my mouth shut,"[169] he said to friends urging him to speak out on behalf of their cause. But this was Theodore Roosevelt, and he wasn't going to stay silent for long. It wasn't in his DNA.

The initial attempts to reunite Taft and Roosevelt were awkward. When the President sent an invitation for his predecessor to join him at the White House, Roosevelt declined. "Now, my dear Mr. President," Roosevelt replied, "your invitation to the White House touches me greatly, and also what Mrs. Taft wrote to Mrs. Roosevelt. But I don't think it well for an ex-President to go to the White House, or indeed to go to Washington, except when he cannot help it."[170] Not many people turn down an invitation from the President of the United States, and the incumbent was hurt. Within a few weeks, an alternative meeting site was approved by both parties. The Tafts felt summer vacations in Canada were inappropriate for a U.S. President, so they opted for a change from their longstanding visits to Murray Bay. They chose in its place a cottage in Beverly, Massachusetts, near their close friends John and Natalie Hammond, to be their summer retreat for these presidential years. Roosevelt's daughter, Alice, lived nearby, and he had plans to visit her.

I-55: President Taft's vacation cottage at Beverly, Massachusetts

Given the proximity, a visit to see the Tafts was also arranged, with Roosevelt bringing Senator Henry Cabot Lodge along for the ride. The greeting between the old friends was rather clumsy, breaking down initially over what to call each other. As Nellie Taft recalled, "Colonel Roosevelt took both hands of the President, and said, 'Mr. President, it is fine to see you looking so well.' 'But why 'Mr. President'?' laughed the President. 'Because,' replied Colonel Roosevelt, 'it used to be 'Mr. President' and 'Will,' now it must be 'Mr. President' and 'Theodore.'"[171] But Taft continued to call his guest "Mr. President" throughout the two-hour visit. The pair stayed away from topics of substance, with much of the discussion recounting Roosevelt's recent trip. The First Lady was relieved that the get together was generally positive for all concerned. "I was present at this interview and remember it as being remarkably pleasant and entertaining," she noted.

> I was glad on this occasion to find the spirit of sympathetic comradship still paramount. … I dwell on the memory of this agreeable meeting with Mr. Roosevelt and the entertainment it afforded me, because by his manner he succeeded in convincing me that he still held my husband in the highest esteem and reposed in him the utmost confidence, and that the rumours of his antagonism were wholly unfounded.[172]

Nevertheless, Nellie concluded, "I was not destined to enjoy this faith and assurance for very long."[173] Indeed.

Roosevelt spent the summer at his home at Oyster Bay, welcoming his progressive friends who railed against the current administration. They were upset about the tariff, angry about the dismissal of Pinchot, dismayed about the backtracking on conservation, let down by the lack of patronage afforded to the progressives, and concerned about Taft's seemingly close relations with the old guard Republicans in Congress. What they were really saying, though, is that Taft simply wasn't their hero. Taft wasn't TR. They wanted Roosevelt, and not a cheap imitation. All of this played into Roosevelt's ego, and his own political juices started to flow. Theodore Roosevelt was back in town, and he wasn't capable of just sitting on the sidelines. Just a couple of months after his return, Roosevelt hit the road and started making speeches – wildly popular speeches that began to push the progressive mantra further than ever before.

Roosevelt traveled to the American West, where he was always welcomed with open arms. He gave more than 100 speeches to large, cheering crowds in what felt like a campaign atmosphere. Most of the remarks fed off the speech of August 31 in Osawatomie, Kansas, where Roosevelt introduced his theme of "New Nationalism." According to Taft biographer Judith Anderson, Roosevelt's "New Nationalism" included "such measures as the elimination of special interests from politics, more publicity about corporate affairs, laws prohibiting the use of corporate funds in politics, the revision of the tariff schedule, graduated income and inheritance taxes, direct primaries, the publication of campaign contributions, and the use of national resources to benefit all the people."[174] This was progressivism on steroids, bringing Rooseveltian morality into national policy. The crowds (and the press) loved it.

And what about the current President, Roosevelt's close friend and hand-picked successor? William Taft was barely mentioned in any of Roosevelt's barnstorming addresses, and the omission was clearly noticed at the White House. Taft complained to his brother, Charlie, "I am bound to say that his speeches are fuller of the ego now than they ever were, and he allows himself to fall into a style that makes one think he considers himself still the President of the United States. In most of these speeches he has utterly ignored me."[175] This was undoubtedly by design, as Roosevelt was increasingly convinced that Taft was no longer the man to carry his agenda forward. He wasn't ready for a formal break, or to announce a bid to win the presidency back, but his actions gave every indication that that was exactly what he was thinking.

Taft had plenty of reasons to be depressed. During the summer of 1910, he had the unpleasant duty to name a new Chief Justice of the Supreme Court. With the passing of Melville Fuller after nearly 22 years as Chief Justice, Taft needed to fill the slot that he had so longed for himself. "There is nothing I would have loved more than being Chief Justice of the United States," he said at the time. "I cannot help seeing the irony of the fact that I, who desired that office so much, should now be signing the commission of another man."[176] One has to wonder if Taft considered appointing himself and stepping down from the presidency once he was confirmed by the Senate. But even if the thought crossed his mind, he didn't act on it. At one point, Taft had virtually promised the promotion to Charles Evans Hughes, whom he had appointed to be an

I-56: Chief Justice Edward White

Associate Justice on the Court earlier in his term. Upon reflection, however, the President concluded that the 48-year-old Hughes was a bit too inexperienced to take over as Chief Justice, so he went in a very different direction. Edward White was a Southern Democrat who had served the Confederacy during the Civil War. He was elevated to the Court by Grover Cleveland in 1894, and Taft crossed party lines to nominate him to be the Chief Justice. The move surprised and angered many Republicans, many of whom were already at odds with the administration. Taft would go on to appoint five additional justices to the Court during his term as President, each one a reminder of what might have been if his own career had taken a different path.

Taft also had to deal with rejection at the polls as the Republicans were routed in the midterm congressional elections. The fracturing between the conservatives and the progressives in the party opened the door for a big swing for the Democrats. The rival party picked up 58 seats in the House to gain control of a chamber in Congress for the first time since 1894. The Democratic pickup of seven seats in the Senate wasn't enough to take the majority, but since many progressive Republicans in that chamber were more aligned with the Democrats than the conservatives in their own party, at least on certain issues, the party of the administration was unlikely to be able to get its way on legislation in either the Upper or Lower House. Taft's domestic agenda had already struggled, and the prospects for any positive movement forward seemed likely to be dead on arrival.

It was with this in mind that Taft's next move was considered highly controversial. The latest piece of legislation for which the President was advocating was for a reciprocity (free trade) deal with Canada. He promoted the concept in his Annual Message in December 1910, signed the agreement with Canada the following month, and then worked hard

I-57: U.S. Capitol, circa 1910

with the Lame Duck Congress to achieve passage before the even more oppositional legislators would be seated. He was unsuccessful. The surprise was what happened next. Taft decided to immediately call the new Democratic-led Congress into a special session for April 1911 to continue consideration of the Canadian trade agreement. This was a risky move, as it gave the Democrats the opportunity to get a several-months head start on whatever legislation they wanted. Taft didn't care. He wanted the reciprocity deal, and if it meant working with the Democrats in the majority, then so be it. "I do not care a tinker's dam whether it injures my political prospects or not," Taft announced when the wisdom of his approach was questioned. "It may be economically rotten. But I regard it as good statesmanship."[177] He even did some personal lobbying, inviting a number of Democrats to join him on the golf course to urge acceptance of the treaty in a very personal way. "I am determined to leave no stone unturned in an effort to secure the approval of the reciprocity measure," Taft declared in the midst of the legislative battle. "It is one of the most important pieces of legislation that has been under consideration in a decade, and the opportunity to make this favorable trade agreement will have passed, probably forever, if we do not strike at this time."[178] All these efforts paid off, with the measure passing the Senate in July 1911, mostly behind the votes of Democrats and progressive Republicans. And then even this victory all fell apart.

A comment by the new House Speaker, Champ Clark from Missouri, was the primary catalyst to kill the deal in Canada. Clark was advocating for the agreement when he remarked, "I am for this Bill, because I hope to see the day when the American flag will float over every square foot of the British North American possessions clear to the North Pole. They are people of our blood: They speak our language. Their institutions are much like ours. They are trained in the difficult art of self-government."[179] To all of Canada, this sounded much more like an attempt at annexation, not merely the establishment of free trade. The liberal government in Canada, which had been supporting the trade pact, fell as a result of the backlash against these comments, and when the new legislature took its seats, it voted to reject the reciprocity agreement that Taft had fought so hard to achieve. While many trade deals with Canada would follow over the years, the first taste of true free trade was not established between these North American neighbors for another 77 years.

All of these setbacks continued to contribute to Taft's misery in the White House, but nothing was more devastating to the incumbent President than the increasing antagonism emanating from the mouth of Theodore Roosevelt. Roosevelt continued to aggressively push his New Nationalism and was no longer doing much to hide his disdain for Taft and the mistake he had made in handing him the presidency. His negative views of the Taft administration were reaching the President through public and private channels on a continuous basis. Taft was stuck walking the halls of the White House trying to figure out how this rupture had come about. At one point, Taft blamed others for turning Roosevelt against him. "I have doubted up to the present time," he told Archie Butt, "whether he really intended to fight my administration or not, but he sees no one but

I-58: President Taft, circa 1910 (age ~53)

my enemies, and if by chance he sees any supporters of the administration, he does not talk intimately with any of them."[180] The impact of those intruding busybodies was severe. "Somehow people have convinced the Colonel that I have gone back on him and he does not seem to be able to get that out of his mind. But it distresses me very deeply, more deeply than anyone can know."[181] Taft reached out to newspaper publisher Charles Kohlsaat to express his grief. "You are a great friend of Colonel Roosevelt's," Taft began. "Through some misunderstanding he feels hurt with me. I must have done something that displeases him very much. Knowingly I have done nothing to hurt his feelings. I may have been tactless, but not intentionally did I do anything to displease him. I owe him everything. He is responsible for my being president. I am so disturbed it keeps me awake nights."[182] At times, though, the President went from anguish to anger. "The other day," Archie Butt noted, "he [Taft] swore a terrific oath and threw his [golf] club twenty-five yards from him in anger. This was so unlike him that even the caddies looked astonished. It makes me think he is losing just a little bit of command of himself."[183] Butt may have been in the toughest position of all throughout this ordeal. He loved both men yet couldn't get out of his front row seat to the disintegration of the relationship between his past and current Presidents.

Amidst all this personal and political swirl, President Taft still had a job to do, which included challenges beyond these domestic heartaches. Taft's term in office was surrounded by Presidents (McKinley, Roosevelt, and Wilson) who had extensive dealings in foreign affairs, including taking the country into two wars. Taft may have come to the White House with an extensive resume of foreign engagement, but his international activities were rather tepid compared to his peers during this era. Taft's efforts in the area of international trade policy have already been covered, with limited results to his credit. Taft gave Secretary of State Philander Knox a fair amount of autonomy over his portfolio, with a handful of accomplishments and some

I-59: Secretary of State Philander Knox

other near misses. On the positive side of the scale, Knox did lead the administration to satisfactory results via arbitration with England over longstanding issues related to the New England fisheries. He also settled a border dispute between Maine and New Brunswick (Canada) that had dragged on for years.

President Roosevelt had introduced a twist to the Monroe Doctrine, moving that policy into more of an interventionist mode. During his 1904 Annual Message, Roosevelt declared that "Chronic wrongdoing, or an impotence which results in a general loosening of the ties of civilized society ... may force the United States, however reluctantly, in flagrant cases of such wrongdoing or impotence, to the exercise of an international police power"[184] anywhere in the Western Hemisphere. Roosevelt employed this new policy in the Dominican Republic during his presidential tenure, and Taft used it as well. The instability of note manifested in Nicaragua in December 1909, with a clash of arms feared between the supporters of President José Santos Zelaya and Conservative Party leader José Estrada. With American lives and property on the line, Taft sent in a small contingent of U.S. Marines to try to maintain the peace. Knox and the Americans aligned themselves with Estrada, who eventually rose to the presidency the following year, and along with it, recognition from the United States, which had been withdrawn during the previous intense period.

Taft and Knox sought to maintain positive relationships with the new regime, particularly with high U.S. interest in the region due to the ongoing construction of the cross-Isthmian canal in neighboring Panama. The path they pursued was economic, so-called "Dollar Diplomacy," providing extensive, high-risk loans to the Estrada government to maintain positive relationships that helped American trade while keeping the Europeans at bay. The results were poor, and Estrada was forced to resign in 1912. He was replaced by conservative Adolfo Díaz, whose position was highly tenuous. In fact, in relatively short order, he signaled to Knox that he could not guarantee the safety of Americans within his borders and asked for military assistance to help stabilize his country. Following the Roosevelt Corollary, Taft complied with the request. Ongoing instability led the Americans to keep troops in Nicaragua for nearly 20 years.

The closest the Americans came to a full-scale war during the administration of William Taft was over ongoing conflicts on the southern border with Mexico. This was another country trying to hold itself together, with rebellion seemingly on the cusp in March 1911. American Ambassador Henry Wilson traveled to Washington to brief President Taft on the seriously deteriorating conditions. Widespread disorder, including violent riots, were spreading throughout Mexico in protest over the government of Porfirio Díaz, actions that were being spurred on by rival Francisco Madero, who was in exile in San Antonio, Texas. Taft moved quickly, but prudently. He dispatched 20,000 American soldiers along the U.S.-Mexico border but gave strict orders not to intervene unless directed from Washington. The move caused panic in some circles in the United States, fearful of a Roosevelt disciple taking advantage of a poor neighbor in chaos to further imperialistic aspirations. But Taft's presidential temperament was hardly Rooseveltian. He made it clear that he would follow the Constitution when it came to anything that might amount to an act of war. "The assumption by the press that I contemplate intervention on Mexican soil to protect American lives or property is of course gratuitous," Taft said, "because I seriously doubt whether I have such authority under any circumstances, and if I had, I would not exercise it without express Congressional approval."[185] When two Americans were killed in fighting near Douglas, Arizona, the push came from the other direction, with demands to intervene and protect American lives. Taft held his fire. He determined that sending in the U.S. military would likely create even more risk for the 40,000 American citizens in Mexico at the time. He watched as the Díaz government fell and Madero was elected, but the situation remained tenuous. Just a month before Taft left office, Madero was arrested and assassinated, leaving Taft's successor to deal with the ongoing instability on the Southern border.

The area of foreign affairs that garnered Taft's attention more than any other than the failed trade deal with Canada, was how to solve international disputes short of going to war. With his judicial bearings guiding his thought process, Taft came to believe that arbitration that leveraged neutral third-party jurists was a far more sensible approach to problem solving than force of arms. In a speech in March 1910 to the American Arbitration and Peace League in New York, Taft suggested an expanded use of arbitration to settle such matters. He boldly told this audience, "If we do not have arbitration, we shall have war."[186] It turned out that the representatives from Britain and France who were in attendance were intrigued. The United States had already negotiated some arbitration treaties in the previous administration, but most of those had significant limitations that required the U.S. Senate to approve the use of arbitration on a case-by-case basis based on the issue involved in the dispute. Taft wanted to revisit these limitations, to push the envelope to automatically apply the construct of arbitration even in the most sensitive matters. Secretary Knox led discussions with his British and French counterparts, and agreements to this effect were favorably completed. But the administration had a big hill to climb in the U.S. Senate to get them ratified, with the opposition led by Henry Cabot Lodge.

Senator Lodge's caucus was not inclined to hand over the most sensitive decisions a government might have to make to some third party. These senators started adding amendments to the agreement, particularly related to topics where "the honor, independence, and vital interests"[187] of the United States were concerned. So many scenarios were captured in these amendments that Taft could no longer support the treaty, which he felt was a shame, and a real missed opportunity. "It was not that those treaties would have abolished war; nobody said they would," Taft proclaimed, "but it was that they were a step in the right direction toward the practical ideal under which war might have been impossible. Other nations might have followed our lead with one another, and we would have an interlacing of treaties. The Senate has put so many amendments to the Treaty that it is doubtful whether the adoption of the same would be a step forward."[188] In fact, Taft declined to even pass along the amended treaty to the partner nations for consideration. Personally, this was one of Taft's biggest disappointments in a presidency that was filled with them.

The President found that getting away from the office was the best way to avoid the headaches associated with being President. "Out-of-sight, out-of-mind" isn't necessarily the best strategy for someone who happens to be President of the United States, but Taft increasingly put things off to the last minute, and sought refuge away from the White House as often as he could. In terms of his penchant for procrastination, Captain Butt had previously concluded that "if the president continues to transact business as he is transacting it now, he will be about three years behind when the fourth of March 1913 rolls around."[189] When in Washington, golf continued to be Taft's daily source of distraction, which often brought derision from the press. His home state's *Ohio State Journal* sarcastically noted that the President "hardly gets fairly settled down to golf" than duties of office begin to interfere.[190] He also now had a healthy First Lady by his side, who continued to plan social activities on a regular basis, as well as large parties as often as she could. The apex of the First Couple's entertaining came in June 1911. The occasion was their silver wedding anniversary, and Nellie pulled out all the stops. She described the scene in her memoirs:

> It was a night garden party with such illuminations as are quite beyond description. Every tree and bush was ablaze with myriads of tiny coloured lights, the whole stately mansion was outlined in a bright white glow; there were strings of bobbing, fantastic lanterns wherever a string would go; the great fountain was playing at its topmost height in every colour of the rainbow; while on the gleaming point of the Monument and on the flag stretched in the breeze from the staff on the top of the White House shone the steady gleam of two searchlights.[191]

I-60: President Taft and his family at the time of his 25th wedding anniversary, 1911 (L to R): Charlie, Nellie, Helen, President Taft, & Robert

I-61: First Lady Helen ("Nellie") Taft

More than 3,000 guests joined the Tafts in celebrating their 25 years of marriage at an event that lasted nearly to 2:00 am. It was indeed a highlight for both of them and yet another distraction from the duties of his office.

But what Taft seemed unable to get enough of were speaking opportunities that completely removed him from the nation's capital as frequently as possible. There was almost no request he was inclined to turn down, no matter how trivial. Taft affirmed embracing this sort of escapism. "When you are being hammered . . . not only by the press, but by members of your own party in Washington," Taft rationalized one day, "and one feels that there isn't anything quite right that he can do, the pleasure of going out into the country, of going into a city that hasn't seen a president for twenty years and then makes a big fuss over him, in order to prove to him that there is somebody that does not know of his defects, is a pleasure that I don't like to forego."[192] And away he went, on trips short and long, near and far – almost anything to get away from the toils of the presidency.

Unfortunately, Taft wasn't very effective in these speaking engagements, which in 1911 included one of the longest trips in presidential history. Taft was on the road for two months, journeying some 18,000 miles across 28 states, delivering nearly 400 speeches. While he was generally warmly received upon arrival, the reaction to his remarks was tepid at best. Even Archie Butt, who had recently been promoted to the rank of major, remarked that Taft's speeches were "dry and full of statistics, and we cannot get him away from figures. ... He gives too much detail and not enough general principles."[193] Taft returned from this particular trip feeling good about himself, calling the affair "a great success." "That trip, if it did not dispel and break up the whole insurgency movement which was aimed at me, at least demonstrated to the country how weak it was and that there was no substance for any of the claims which the leaders of it were making," the President concluded.[194] Here, Taft was taking dead aim at Roosevelt and the progressives, but his read was simply off. A more likely assessment was that Taft over-conflated the presence of large crowds and respectful receptions with changing attitudes more to his favor. In fact, there was little evidence that he was swaying his audiences much at all. On the contrary, it was Roosevelt's momentum that appeared to be continuing to increase throughout 1911.

The Roosevelt cloud continued to cast a shadow onto Taft's presidency, with the ultimate rupture right around the corner. One of the areas where the progressives had actually offered cheers to the Taft administration was in the aggressive posture of the Justice Department in pursuing antitrust cases against some of the largest businesses the nation had to offer. Taft had signaled his support for such cases back in his days as a Federal judge in the Addyston Trust trial in 1898 when successful cases related to the Sherman Antitrust Act were still few and far between. The progressives in the Roosevelt administration picked up the trustbusting mantle, but the Taft Justice Department actually took it to another level. In his single term in office, Taft's team tried more than twice as many antitrust cases (89) as Roosevelt's (43), including bringing to conclusion cases that led to the breakup of both Standard Oil and the American Tobacco Company. But one of these cases was hardly cheered by those closest to the Roosevelt camp. In fact, it was the case brought against U.S. Steel that drew the wrath of Roosevelt, serving as the final straw to sever relations between the two men.

In the latter stages of Roosevelt's presidency, the economy fell into a panic, and Wall Street suffered one of the biggest dips in the history of the U.S. stock market. Financier J.P. Morgan was called upon to help shore up the financial system with an infusion of cash from the banking community. Some large firms that were heavily leveraged were also in trouble, including one of the nation's primary steel producers, the Tennessee Coal and Iron Company. Morgan's U.S. Steel, the dominant player in the industry, offered to rescue Tennessee Coal but was reluctant to make the purchase out of concerns over the Sherman Antitrust Act. Adding Tennessee Coal to its operation would give the combined company 62% of the U.S. steel market. Morgan sought out President Roosevelt, looking for a guarantee that the government wouldn't file suit. Roosevelt gave them enough assurances to move forward, writing later, "I answered that while of course I could not advise them to take the action proposed, I felt it no public duty of mine to interpose any objection."[195] This was good enough for Morgan, who completed the transaction in a move that surely benefited U.S. Steel, but also helped shore up a struggling economy.

Four years later, along came the Justice Department of William Taft under Attorney General George Wickersham, who decided to file an antitrust suit against U.S. Steel, primarily based on its acquisition of

I-62: Attorney General George Wickersham

Tennessee Coal and Iron. Roosevelt was livid. He perceived the move as a personal attack against him. "Taft was a member of my Cabinet when I took that action," Roosevelt confided to James Garfield. "We went over it in full and in detail, not only at one but at two or three meetings. He was enthusiastic in his praise of what was done. It ill becomes him either by himself or through another afterwards to act as he is now acting."[196] He later reiterated, "We went over the whole transaction afterwards in the cabinet, and Mr. Taft was emphatic in his commendation. Of course it was one of those cases where the protest should have been made instantly, or else from every consideration of honorable obligation never under any circumstances afterwards."[197] Roosevelt's sister, Corrine Robinson, emphasized, "If it had not been for that Steel suit! I was talking with Theodore only last week, and he said that he could never forgive."[198] It was shortly after the filing of the Steel suit that Roosevelt went from simply making political speeches to talking seriously about running again for his old job. He confided with friends that if the party wanted him as the nominee, he would consider accepting. After Robert La Follette, who was seeking to challenge Taft from the progressive wing of the Republican Party, collapsed at a banquet on February 2, 1912, the door was wide open for Roosevelt to step into the race on behalf of his legion of progressive followers. Within a few days, Roosevelt proclaimed, "My hat is in the ring. The fight is on and I am stripped to the buff!"[199] A couple of weeks later, on February 21, he made it official. "I will accept the nomination for President if it is tendered to me," Roosevelt announced, "and I will adhere to this decision until the convention has expressed its preference."[200] And so began the worst year of William Taft's life.

8. Rock Bottom

Nellie Taft was certainly not surprised that Roosevelt got back into the game, regardless of the damage this signaled for the Republican Party or her husband, the President, and Roosevelt's former close friend. Many of Taft's supporters instantly claimed that Roosevelt had reneged on his promise back on election night in 1904 that "under no circumstances will I be a candidate for or accept another nomination." Roosevelt claimed no inconsistency. In his memoirs, he clarified the statement merely reflected his conviction that he would not seek another *consecutive* term.

> The third term tradition has no value whatever except as it applies to a third consecutive term. While it is well to keep it as a custom, it would be a mark of both weakness and unwisdom for the American people to embody it into a Constitutional provision which could not do them good and on some given occasion might work real harm.[201]

In other words, his pledge was old news and no longer applicable. Roosevelt immediately hit the stump, and hit hard at Taft. The move completely fractured the Republican party. The conservative old guard generally stuck with Taft, while the progressives leaped to embrace Roosevelt. The former President focused on the relatively new process some states had adopted to elect delegates to the national convention – popular electoral primaries rather than state conventions. After a slow start, Roosevelt ran the table, winning the last nine of these contests, including a convincing win in Taft's home state of Ohio.

Throughout this acrimonious race for the Republican nomination, poor Archie Butt continued to be caught in the middle of this dispute, and it was starting to overwhelm him. Butt was exhausted, both mentally and physically, and he and Taft both concluded that some kind of break was essential. Butt and a friend headed off to Europe for rest and recovery. He left in March with a plan to be away for two months and then return in time for the Republican Convention. After a relaxing month in Italy, he started to get anxious and decided to return early. He bought a ticket on a brand new ocean liner, the pride of the British passenger lines. It was called the RMS *Titanic*. The ship set sail for the United States with Butt aboard on April 10. Just before midnight on April 14, the ship struck an iceberg and started to sink. Only 20 lifeboats were available on this

I-63: Sinking of the Titanic, April 1912

maiden voyage, which accommodated only about a third of the passengers on board. Major Archibald Butt was among the 1,503 who perished that night as the *Titanic* sank to the bottom of the Atlantic.

President Taft was shocked and deeply saddened by the overall tragedy, but particularly about the personal loss of his aide and close friend. "He was like a member of my family, and I feel his loss as if he had been a younger brother," Taft said upon hearing the sad news. "I cannot refrain from saying that I miss him every minute, and that every house and every person suggests him. Every walk I take somehow is lacking in his presence, and every door that opens seems to be his coming."[202] Taft honored Butt and his travelling companion, Francis Millet, who also perished, with the building of a memorial fountain that was placed on the south grounds of the White House.

As Taft mourned the loss of Butt, his despondency increased as Roosevelt's aggressive push for the nomination continued. He didn't want to fight Roosevelt on anything, let alone for the Republican nomination for President of the United States. In many ways, Taft didn't want a second term. After all, he had been miserable throughout his presidency, and had said many times words to the effect of, "I am not very anxious for a second term as it is, and I certainly will not make any compromises to secure one. … A number of our best presidents have had only one term, and there is nothing disgraceful in not having two."[203] But then Roosevelt really started to get under his skin. In particular, he took on Taft's beloved judiciary, signaling his support for one of the mantras of the progressive movement, the proposition of judicial recall. When "a judge decides a constitutional question, when he decides what the people as a whole can or cannot do," Roosevelt said, "the people should have the right to recall that decision if they think it is wrong."[204] This notion was anathema to Taft, making court decisions, and possibly even judicial job security, subject to second-guessing by popular will. Taft had already not been quiet in objecting to the recall movement. In fact, he had vetoed the initial applications of both New Mexico and Arizona to become states in the Union due to the fact that recall provisions were included in their proposed state constitutions. Only after assurances that those would be removed did he authorize subsequent legislation to create the 47th and 48th states. As for Roosevelt's rhetoric, Taft believed it went beyond political posturing. This was an assault on the democratic system he fervently believed in. The President started to become more committed to the race, not so much in his mind to secure himself a second term, but more so to keep this new and dangerous Roosevelt out of a position of power. "One who so lightly regards constitutional principles and especially the independence of the judiciary," Taft proclaimed, "and who is so naturally impatient of legal restraints, and of due legal procedure, and who has so misunderstood what liberty regulated by law is, could not safely be entrusted with successive presidential terms. I say this sorrowfully, but I say it with the full conviction of truth."[205] He later commented to Charles Thompson of *The New York Times*, "Whether I win or lose is not important. I am in

I-64: President Taft signing the revised New Mexico Statehood Bill, 1912

this fight to perform a public duty – the duty of keeping Theodore Roosevelt out of the White House. I believe I represent a safer and saner view of our government and its Constitution."[206] Perhaps for the first time, William Taft was ready to fight to capture the Republican nomination.

The battle reached a climax as the Republicans were getting ready to meet in convention in Chicago in early June 1912. The convention was due to open on the 7th, but the outcome was essentially decided in administrative meetings in the week leading up to the formal gathering. Those meetings centered on the Credentials Committee, which had the unenviable task of resolving disputes over which delegates had been formally authorized to represent their states. More than 250 such disputes were presented to the committee, far more than in any previous party convention. The conflicts seemed to be exacerbated by the confusion over the new primary system used to select delegates by popular vote in a number of states in this election cycle. The Credentials Committee had a lot to sort out in a very short period of time.

I-65: Crowds arriving at the Chicago Coliseum for the 1912 Republican National Convention

In this case, the odds were stacked heavily in favor of Taft. The incumbent still enjoyed the support of the conservative old guard wing of the Republican Party, which, not surprisingly, controlled the apparatus of the convention. Nearly all of the members of the Credentials Committee supported the President, making their one-sided decisions quite predictable. Of the first 102 disputes decided, all but one favored Taft. Roosevelt, who was monitoring the situation closely from his home at Oyster Bay, smelled a rat. To no one's surprise, he was not inclined to sit idly by and let some bureaucrats, in his mind, take the nomination away from him before the convention even began. He hopped a train to

Chicago and arrived in a fighting spirit. To his cheering supporters, Roosevelt bellowed from his hotel window, "It is a fight against theft, and the thieves will not win!"[207] The night before the convention, as the disputes continued to go against him, Roosevelt spoke at a gathering of some twenty-thousand supporters at a nearby auditorium. "We fight in honorable fashion for the good of mankind; fearless of the future; unheeding of our individual fates; with unflinching hearts and undimmed eyes; we stand at Armageddon, and we battle for the Lord!"[208] But none of this grandstanding had any impact on the Credentials Committee. When the convention was gaveled to order by chairman Elihu Root, 235 of the disputes had been resolved in favor of Taft's delegates, to only 19 for Roosevelt. The nomination had essentially been decided before the festivities had officially begun.

Roosevelt was never one to go down without a fight, and the decisions he made over the next few days doomed the chances for the Republicans or their progressive offshoot to have any chance of winning the White House, essentially handing power to his political enemy, the Democratic nominee Woodrow Wilson. He also crushed the political career of his former friend, President William Taft. Roosevelt was so wrapped up in his righteous cause that he'd lost sight of the implications of his decisions, which proved highly destructive to the people and organizations with which he had been aligned throughout most of his career. Roosevelt's first decision was to play havoc with the Republican Convention itself. Since he no longer had any path to victory, he wanted it known that he considered the proceedings to be illegitimate. In Roosevelt's typical pugilistic fashion, he had Henry Allen of Kansas read the following statement to the convention delegates:

> A clear majority of the delegates honestly elected to this convention were chosen by the people to nominate me. Under the direction, and with the encouragement of Mr. Taft, the majority of the National Committee, by the so-called 'steam roller' methods, and with scandalous disregard of every principle of elementary honesty and decency stole eighty or ninety delegates, putting on the temporary roll call a sufficient number of fraudulent delegates to defeat the legally expressed will of the people, and to substitute a dishonest for an honest majority. ...

> I hope that the men elected as Roosevelt delegates will now decline to vote on any matter before the Convention. I do not release any delegate from his honorable obligation to vote for me if he votes at all; but under the actual conditions I hope that he will not vote at all. The Convention as now composed has no claim to represent the voters of the Republican Party. It represents nothing but successful fraud in overriding the will of the rank and file of the party. Any man nominated by the Convention as now constituted would be merely the beneficiary of this successful fraud; it would be deeply discreditable to any man to accept the Convention's nomination under these circumstances; and any man thus accepting it would have no claim to the support of any Republican on party grounds, and would have forfeited the right to ask the support of any honest man of any party on moral grounds.[209]

Most of Roosevelt's delegates that had been allowed their seats in the convention dutifully fell in line and refused to cast any votes when the roll was called. Officially, this made Taft's first ballot nomination a *fait accompli.* The final recording of the votes showed Taft with 561, Roosevelt with 187, and Robert La Follette with 41. But that clear victory hardly unified the party. In fact, it did exactly the opposite.

The very night of Taft's nominating vote, Roosevelt pulled together his zealous progressive devotees and initiated the launch of their own political party. Roosevelt told the raucous crowd that he was all in. "If you wish me to make the fight, I will make it even if only one State will support me,"[210] the progressive champion declared. The group committed to pull together its national caucus to meet in its own convention in less than 60 days to launch a third-party candidate for the presidency. To no one's surprise, when the representatives of the Progressive Party met for the first time, Roosevelt was elevated as their standard-bearer, with another leading progressive, California Governor Hiram Johnson, as the number two on the ticket. This solidified the fracture of the Republican Party, essentially guaranteeing victory for Wilson, who had overtaken House Speaker Champ Clark to capture the Democratic nomination on the 46th ballot. "Good old Teddy," Wilson noted as the Republican Party split. "What a help he is."[211]

So, where was William Taft while all this was going on? Primarily, he remained in Washington with very little comment. He played a lot of golf, an activity he simply refused to curtail despite the political swirl that surrounded him. "I have been told that I ought to do this, ought to do that, ought to do the other; that I ought to say this, ought to say that, ought to say the other; that I do not keep myself in the headlines; that there is this or that trick I might turn to my advantage. I know it, but I can't do it."[212] So, throughout the summer, he mostly stayed out of the limelight, playing lots of golf but doing virtually nothing to promote his own cause.

Of course, Taft's heart wasn't in the race to begin with. He had never wanted to be President, didn't like being President, and was looking forward to the time when he no longer had to be President. "The truth is," Taft said as things were unfolding that summer, "I am not very happy in this renomination and re-election business. … I am not going to squeal or run away. But after it is all over I shall be glad to retire and let another take the burden."[213] As long as that someone wasn't Theodore Roosevelt. More so than a victory for himself, Taft's only real goal was to keep Roosevelt from winning back the White House.

The campaign was nasty, with plenty of name-calling, including Roosevelt's reference of Taft as a "man with brains of about three guinea-pig power."[214] But mostly, TR took a different tact to try to belittle Taft. He chose to ignore him, trying to make the race entirely about him against Wilson. When someone at a campaign event shouted, "Tell us about Taft!" Roosevelt responded, "I never discuss dead issues."[215] The ripple effects of Roosevelt's run were felt throughout the Republican community. Even Cabinet members were divided, having their loyalty to both men now caught in a vice. Elihu Root, who was closer to Roosevelt than Taft, stayed out of the race completely, unwilling to choose sides in public. Roosevelt's sister, Corrine, expressed the

I-66: Theodore Roosevelt on the stump during the 1912 campaign

sadness so many in the inner circle were feeling.

> When I think of the old days at the White House and how these two men seemed to love one another it makes me very unhappy to think of the great chasm which lies between them now. How they would get together and talk and discuss matters! And I remember the way their laughs would mingle and reverberate through the corridors and rooms, and Edith [Roosevelt] would say: 'It is always that way when they are together.'[216]

The person most affected by all this divisiveness was clearly William Taft. In the stretch run, he got out on the road to campaign, but the effort was lackluster, partly because the rift with Roosevelt was personally devastating. He remained at a loss as to how it all fell apart. He was dismayed, for example, when he learned through others that the note of appreciation he sent at the time of his election that credited his brother, Charlie, as well as Roosevelt, had been so offensive to TR. During the campaign, he shared with his brother, "I learn directly, and I have heard it in so many different ways in addition to the direct statement from Griscom that he regarded this letter as an occasion for feeling bitterly toward me, because I dared to include you in the same class with him as assisting me in my canvas[s] for the Presidency. I venture to say that swelledheadedness could go no further than this."[217] He confided with a friend, "No one knows how deeply he has wounded me. I shall always be gratified for what he did for me, but since he has come back he has seared me to the very soul."[218] He said to another gathering, "I hope that somebody, sometime, will recognize the agony of spirit that I have undergone."[219] One of the most poignant scenes noted during the campaign was captured by Louis Seibold of the *New York World*. During transit on the presidential train between campaign addresses, "Taft 'slumped over with his head between his hands [and said] Roosevelt was my closest friend.' And then he bowed his head and covered his eyes and cried."[220]

With just a couple of weeks left before the vote, the campaign took an unexpected turn when an attempt was made on Roosevelt's life as he was getting ready to make a speech in Milwaukee. John Schrank fired a shot directly at Roosevelt from about 30 feet away, hitting him square in the chest. He was saved from serious injury by the thick wad of papers with his typed-out speech along with his glasses case, both of which were directly in the path of the bullet. He went down, but made a self-diagnosis that the wound wasn't fatal, so he insisted, against all advice, that he was "going to make that speech if I die doing it."[221] After struggling through those remarks, Roosevelt ended up in the hospital, where he stayed for most of the rest of the canvass. The Tafts wired their "heartfelt sympathy" to Roosevelt, but privately Taft was in a state of disbelief over the grandstanding by Roosevelt in giving the address. "I have never been so disgusted about anything he has done as at the speech he made to his audience after the shooting,"[222] Taft shared with his brother Horace. That's how far apart these two old friends had become.

The results of the election were a foregone conclusion. Roosevelt and Taft split their vote, easily handing the majority in the Electoral College to Wilson. Wilson captured 40 states and 435 electoral votes, compared with Roosevelt at six states and 88 electoral votes, while the incumbent, William Taft, was successful in just two states (Utah and Vermont), accumulating a measly eight electoral votes. While a number of incumbent Presidents had failed to win renomination by their parties, Taft's showing in 1912 was the worst in American history for an incumbent who had received the nomination of his party in a run for re-election. The popular vote numbers, though, were telling in terms of what might have been. Wilson won the presidency with only 41.8% of the popular vote. Since the popular vote expansion in the late 1820s, only Abraham Lincoln, who also ran against a fractured party in opposition in 1860, captured the presidency with a smaller percentage of the popular vote (39.8%). On the flip side, Roosevelt and Taft combined to receive 50.6% of the popular vote – nearly nine percentage points higher than Wilson. Roosevelt's foray into tearing apart the Republican Party in 1912 handed his real political opposition the White House in a result that became predictable months before voters went to the ballot box. But he was on the warpath, and nothing could hold him back, come what may.

One of the ironies of the awful election year of 1912 was that William Taft, in some ways, got the result he wanted, given the choices available. He didn't want another term, nor did he want Roosevelt to get another term, and both of those things happened. His true preference would have been the election of Charles Evans Hughes, the former Governor of New York, whom Taft had placed onto the Supreme Court in 1910. If his party could have unified around a candidate like Hughes, Taft would likely have been happy to stand down, and the presidency may well have remained with the Republicans. But, such an option never materialized. So, while Taft was by no means happy to be turning the White House over to a Democrat, at least it wasn't him anymore, and it wasn't Roosevelt either.

Taft held his head high when thinking back on his presidential term. He told the Lotos Club in New York ten days after the votes had been tallied, "I beg you to believe that in spite of the very emphatic verdict by which I leave the office, I cherish only the deepest gratitude to the American people for having given me the honour of having held the office, and I sincerely hope in looking back over what has been done that there is enough of progress made to warrant me in the belief that real good has been accomplished, even though I regret that it has not been greater."[223] To a different audience, he shared his views on some of the specifics. "I am content to retire from it with a consciousness that I have done the best l could. I have strengthened the Supreme Bench, have given them a good deal of new … legislation, have not interfered with business, have kept the peace, and on the whole have enabled people to pursue their various occupations without interruption." He admitted, however, that it was "a very humdrum, uninteresting administration, and it does not attract the attention or enthusiasm of anybody."[224] This was a fair assessment, even though it omitted the personal anguish he had suffered throughout his single term in office.

I-67: President-elect Woodrow Wilson and President Taft, Inauguration Day, March 4, 1913

Nellie Taft was the one in the family who was most distraught when March 4, 1913, rolled around, and Woodrow Wilson took his oath of office. She waited until the last minute, taking a final tour of the White House, before departing for the train station. Taft was actually in a buoyant mood, seemingly far less stressed than his successor. He even stuck around for the luncheon after the presidential party had returned from the Capitol. The weight of the world had been lifted off his shoulders, and unlike most Presidents when they leave office, Taft already had a soft landing spot lined up. He was extremely pleased to be heading back to Yale.

9. Professor, Rapprochement, and Peace

Taft had been the first President to receive the newly approved $75,000 annual salary during his term in office. While Nellie never scrimped on entertainment or clothes, she was naturally frugal in most other areas. She managed their finances such that they left the White House with about $100,000 of his presidential income in the bank. Still, Taft was only 55 years old when he left government service and was neither ready to retire nor financially able to do so. Fortunately, when his alma mater came calling at just the right time with an offer to teach, he jumped at the chance. In fact, he started his new job less than a month after exiting the White House, having been hired as the Kent Professor of Law for Yale College, as well as a Professor of Constitutional Law for Yale Law School. Upon accepting the position, he stated that he did so with "the earnest hope that from a somewhat extensive and varied experience I may have gleaned something which may be of use to the young men with whom I shall come in contact."[225] At first, though, his instruction was very much by the book, and it was not well received. His approach was deemed exceedingly dull, and to their credit, some of his students called him on it. They suggested that he teach them more from his personal experiences, helping them understand how government really worked in the context of the law using real-world reflections and anecdotes. The new approach was a big hit, and Taft became more comfortable as he settled into his new routine.

I-68: Yale University, 1906

Taft was also extremely pleased to no longer have to deal with the trials and tribulations of being President of the United States. "You don't know how much fun it is to sit back. . . and watch the playing of the game down there in Washington, without any responsibility of my own," he said.[226] He was much more relaxed, and in many ways back to his old genial self, with the big smile and the hearty laugh. The reduction in stress contributed to his ability to lose about 80 pounds over the course of eight months. He was content, having resigned himself to the fact that with a Democrat in the White House, his chances at his dream job on the Supreme Court had likely come and gone forever. He began telling friends that "I expect to live and die a professor,"[227] and he seemed OK with that.

Taft was plenty busy during his eight years in New Haven. In addition to teaching his classes, he also coached the freshman debate team, went to plenty of social events with Nellie, and the couple became active in a variety of activities throughout their new community. He also continued to travel. Speaking requests poured in from across the country, and he accepted as many as he could, pocketing anywhere from $400 to $1000 for each event, on top of the $5000 per year he earned at Yale. While he tailored each address to the specific audience, he always included some general themes about his beliefs in a sound, conservative, constitutional government as the proper foundation of the United States.

While Taft was very much at peace, the world during Woodrow Wilson's administration was most definitely not. World War I erupted in 1914, and the U.S. was deeply divided about whether or not to enter the conflict. President Wilson was adamantly opposed, seeking to keep his country neutral while the rest of the world was deep into ghastly trench warfare. At first, Taft was outspoken in support of his successor. "The task of the President is a heavy one," Taft proclaimed. "He is our President. He is acting for the whole country. He is anxious to find a way out of the present difficulty without war. Before party, before ourselves, we are for our country. That is what he is working for. … Let us stand by him in this juncture. Our honor is safe with him."[228] But over time, as the conflagration continued and American shipping was increasingly at risk due to the destructive force of the German submarines, Taft became more critical of the current administration. In fact, it was opposition to Wilson's policies that began to rekindle his relationship with Theodore Roosevelt.

The first meeting between Taft and Roosevelt after the horrific election year of 1912 came at the funeral of a mutual friend in 1915. The two were civil toward each other but not much more than that. "It was a bit stiff," according to Taft, "but it was all right. It was pleasant enough, but it was not cordial or intimate."[229] Throughout this time, Roosevelt was one of the most outspoken critics of Wilson's refusal to bring the Americans into the war. Both men were committed to making Wilson a one-term President, rallying around the Republican candidate, Charles Evans Hughes, in the 1916 race. They eventually found themselves on the same stage at the Union League Club in New York during the canvass. "Mr. Roosevelt and I are very anxious to secure the election of Mr. Hughes to the Presidency," Taft announced to the supportive crowd, "and to oust the present incompetent, meddling, muddling, opportunistic Administration."[230] The election was a nail-biter with a disappointing result for the Republicans, as Wilson won re-election 277-254 in the Electoral College.

While Wilson had run both his first term and his campaign on the premise of keeping America out of war, circumstances led to an about-face just a month after taking his oath of office for the second time. A couple of months prior, Germany had announced a policy of unrestricted submarine warfare, which was seen as a direct assault on the sovereignty of neutral nations like the United States. This turn of events finally led Wilson to seek a declaration of war on April 2, 1917. Young men from across the country signed up for the fight, including Taft's 20-year-old son, Charlie, who dropped out of Yale to volunteer for the cause. It was an emotional time for Taft, who sent his son off with the following words: "It is hard, my darling boy, to let you go. You are the apple of our eye.

I-69: Taft saying farewell to his son Charlie who was leaving for Europe in World War I, 1917

But we would not have it different. If sacrifice is to be made who are we that we should escape it? And now, Charlie my loving son, good-bye till we meet again. You are knight sans peur et sans reproche. God bless you and keep you."[231] Charlie Taft did his duty, survived the war unscathed, and then returned to New Haven to complete his undergraduate and law degrees.

William Taft did not exactly sit on the sideline when so many boys were putting their lives on the line in Europe. He was an aggressive advocate for the purchase of Liberty Bonds to fund the war effort. Moreover, he answered Wilson's call to join the Labor Conference Board, which was established to help the administration deal with labor disputes at a time when disruptions in the workplace could be devastating to the war effort. As per usual, Taft sought perspectives from all sides in seeking fairness in these duties while keeping the needs of the country prominent in his thoughts. In many cases, he surprised observers by siding with labor regarding work conditions and even wages. After Congress formally established a War Labor Board, Taft answered this call as well, taking a one-year leave of absence from his post at Yale to serve. By one account, Taft was credited with helping to avert some 138 work stoppages during his tenure. He was proud to be able to serve again and believed his contributions were meaningful.

Around this time, Taft had another contact with Theodore Roosevelt, and for the first time in a long time, this interaction actually featured a much more upbeat tone. Roosevelt was authoring a paper, and he reached out to Lodge, Root, and Taft to review the work and offer some advice – just like the old days. Taft responded with a couple of suggestions that immediately resonated with Roosevelt. In a letter beginning with the cordial greeting, "Dear Will," Roosevelt offered his appreciation. "I have embodied both these suggestions," he wrote. "I think them capital. I am rather ashamed I never thought of them myself, and I am malevolently pleased that neither Root nor Lodge thought of them!"[232] Relations had not been fully restored, but both men started to think that perhaps such a reconciliation might be possible. In fact, complete rapprochement took place just a couple of months later. Author Bill Severn captured the story:

> Taft happened to be in Chicago early in May, 1918, stopping by the Blackstone Hotel, and on his way up in the elevator he learned that Roosevelt was dining at the hotel. Impulsively, Taft took the elevator back down, walked into the dining room,

and crossed to the table where Roosevelt was seated alone. Other guests, already somewhat agog over the fact that Roosevelt was among them, recognized Taft and a hush came over the dining room. Taft said, 'Hello, Theodore.' Roosevelt looked up, surprised, and then grinned and clasped the hand Taft held out to him. As they shook hands heartily, the other diners rose from their tables and cheered. Taft and Roosevelt sat together and talked for more than half an hour. 'He was really much pleased,' Taft noted, 'and very cordial.'

I-70: Theodore Roosevelt, 1918

The timing of the chance encounter was important, as Roosevelt didn't have much time left. He had suffered greatly during a recent expedition in the jungles of the Amazon, and never recovered his youthful vitality. In fact, less than eight months after this meeting, Theodore Roosevelt was dead. Taft was one of the most somber attendees at Roosevelt's funeral, lingering with tears in his eyes long after most of the mourners had departed. A couple of years later, Taft shared with Roosevelt's sister Bamie, "I want to say to you how glad I am that Theodore and I came together after that long painful interval. Had he died in a hostile state of mind toward me, I would have mourned the fact all my life. I loved him always and cherish his memory."[233] Finally, a sense of peace after all that anguish.

Meanwhile, the global anguish on the battlefields of Europe was finally coming to an end, thanks in large part to the entry of the United States. Shortly after the armistice was declared on November 11, 1918, President Wilson announced his plans to personally attend the peace negotiations in Paris. Among the Fourteen Points that he planned to seek in the agreement was one with which William Taft was very much aligned – the establishment of a League of Nations with a goal of maintaining world peace through collective security and the settlement of disputes through negotiation and arbitration. Taft had been a vocal advocate for just such an alliance since the days of his presidency and had continued the push since leaving the White House. The group to which he had become aligned had called itself the League to Enforce Peace. Formally organized in June 1915 with Taft as President, this version of a global coalition to prevent wars had some of its genesis in the arbitration agreement Taft had sought to establish with Britain and France during his presidency. In February 1917, Taft had advocated for the League in an address to the National Chamber of Commerce in Washington:

> The purpose of the League to Enforce Peace is to organize the world's strength into an international police to enforce a procedure with respect to issues likely to lead to war, which will prevent all wars but those which nothing can prevent. The procedure to be enforced is the submission of questions of a legal nature, the decision of which must be guided by rules of law, to an international court for its judgment, and the submission of all other questions to an impartial commission to hear and decide, its decision to take the form of a recommendation of compromise. The judgment of the legal questions by the court will be legally and in honor binding on the parties. ... If every issue between nations is forced to arbitration or recommendations, it will compel deliberation by those who think of war.[234]

Other luminaries, such as Elihu Root, inventor Alexander Graham Bell, Harvard University President Abbott Lowell, and former Secretary of Commerce Oscar Strauss were just a few of the leading citizens who joined Taft in his advocacy. While Wilson's proposed League of Nations had some differences from Taft's League to Enforce Peace, many of the goals and methods were similar. This alignment yielded strong advocacy from Taft and his group when the Treaty of Versailles (which included the provision for the League of Nations) was submitted to the U.S. Senate for consideration.

Taft was dismayed when the debate in the Senate grew increasingly partisan and rancorous. The isolationist leader in the Senate, Henry Cabot Lodge, led the vocal opposition. When the group proposed a number of amendments that would limit the scope of the League, President Wilson balked. Both sides delved into a take-it-or-leave-it mindset, much to the dismay of William Taft. The former President came to Washington to personally lobby members of the Senate, telling Republicans who were objecting to the proposal on the table, “I don’t like Wilson any better than you do, but I think I can rise above my personal attitude in order to help along the world and the country. I don’t care who gets credit for the League of Nations, if it goes through.”[235] He later added, “I beg you, consider the consequences if you defeat the treaty. ... We are in sight of the promised land. Don’t prevent our reaching there.”[236] His words fell on deaf ears. Both sides stubbornly dug in, with the future of the League very much in doubt, at least as far as the United States was concerned. Taft was seething as he watched this golden opportunity falter before his eyes. He accused both Wilson and Lodge of putting “their personal prestige and the saving of their ugly faces above the welfare of the country and the world.”[237] But that’s what happened. The vote on the treaty received the support of a majority of senators, but not the two-thirds supermajority needed to affirm treaties. The League would be formed, but without the membership of the United States, much to the chagrin of William Taft.

10. Dreams Do Come True

Two Ohioans ran for the presidency in 1920 in what turned out to be a landslide election. Senator Warren Harding, who was calling for a "Return to Normalcy," ran more against the policies of the outgoing President, Woodrow Wilson, than against his actual opponent, Governor James Cox. Harding's message resonated with the electorate, handing him victories in 37 of the 48 states. His 26.2% margin of victory in the popular vote was the largest since the election of the nation's fifth President, James Monroe, exactly 100 years before. Taft knew Harding well. After all, Harding had the honor of placing Taft's name into nomination at the Republican Convention in 1908. As a courtesy, Taft ventured to Harding's home in Marion, Ohio, to chat with the President-elect and share some ideas on some potential presidential appointments. As their breakfast was coming to an end, Harding tossed in the following remark: "By the way, I want to ask you, would you accept a position on the Supreme Bench because if you would, I'll put you on the court."[238] Perhaps Taft wouldn't die a professor after all. Perhaps, William Taft's long-awaited dream might finally become reality.

Taft happily answered Harding's query in the positive, but he did narrow his chances a bit when he honestly shared that only the position of Chief Justice would be appropriate for a former President. There actually was no precedent in this area as no former President had ever been placed on the Court before in any capacity, but Taft felt strongly about the propriety of this condition. Little did Taft know that his golden opportunity was just around the corner. Just 76 days after Harding was sworn in as President, Chief Justice Edward White died. Harding didn't nominate Taft for the opening right away, as there were a couple of other considerations in play. But just over a month

I-71: President Warren Harding with Chief Justice Taft, circa 1921

after White's passing, the President did send Taft's nomination to the Senate. Taft was in Canada on business that day, but that didn't matter to the Senate, which immediately took up the nomination. After a few speeches, they voted, and Taft was confirmed just a few hours later as the 10th Chief Justice of the United States on June 30, 1921. The vote was 61-4. Despite many detours along the way, Taft's lifelong dream had finally come true.

I-72: Taft being sworn in as Chief Justice of the Supreme Court, 1921

Taft would leave a powerful imprint not only on his beloved Supreme Court but also on the entire Federal judiciary. Taft believed significant reform was needed to fix a deeply backlogged court system that was experiencing significant delays in meting out justice across the country and in the nation's highest tribunal. He would also oversee a strongly conservative Court that dealt with some of the nation's new complexities associated with the recently passed constitutional amendments related to the income tax and the establishment of prohibition, as well as ongoing challenges between management and labor. But his greatest contribution was arguably outside the courtroom, in the realm of structural judicial reform.

Under his own authority, Taft initiated changes at the Supreme Court itself. This ranged from proper attire for all who entered the Court to a reorganization of the support staff. No one worked harder than the Chief. He rose at 5:15 each morning and often finished the day working at home well into the night. He brought a cheerful mood to the office in the U.S. Capitol every day, with that joyous smile that had been all-too non-existent during his presidential years now back, reflecting his natural persona. Even his health was better, with his weight down to one of its lowest levels in years, falling below 260 pounds, and staying there. Taft loved the work and threw himself into every aspect of his responsibilities. "The prestige of this Court," Taft wrote, "next to my wife and my children, is the nearest thing to my heart in life."[239] And he was driven to live up to that high standard, eschewing non-Court related activities. He said after a few years into the job that he was "never free from the burden of feeling that whenever I attempt to do anything else I am taking time from my judicial work."[240] He still got in his daily exercise, usually by walking to and from work, often with his ideological rival on the Court, 80-year-old Oliver Wendell Holmes. However, golf was

I-73: A slimmed-down post-President Taft

mostly out. While the sport had been a welcome escape during his presidency, such a distraction was no longer needed or welcome.

What didn't seem to be a barrier to Taft was the concept of a strict separation of powers. Taft actively engaged with the Harding and Coolidge administrations on appointments to the Federal bench (some of which he favored, while others he essentially vetoed). He was also not shy about lobbying Congress for more funding, as well as pursuing some of the most significant reforms in the history of the Federal judiciary. Taft laid out his concerns in a speech to the American Bar Association in Chicago shortly after taking over the Court in October 1921. Taft called for three major reforms:

> First, an increase in the judicial force in the trial federal courts and an organization and effective distribution of the force by a council of judges; second, simplicity of procedure in the trial federal courts; and third, a reduction in the obligatory jurisdiction of the Supreme Court and an increase in the field of its discretionary jurisdiction by *certiorari*.[241]

All three proposals were groundbreaking. The first two were primarily administrative, while the third would completely upend the process that determined which cases would ever be heard by the Supreme Court. The latter change would take more time (and more convincing), but Taft didn't hesitate to jump in on the former. In another odd test of the separation of powers, Taft worked closely with Attorney General Harry Daugherty to craft legislation for consideration by Congress for what eventually would be called the Judges Act of 1922. The proposal had two primary objectives. First, it was to grant the authority for the Chief Justice to work with the leaders of the District Courts to rebalance the caseload across the Federal judiciary, as necessary, to alleviate the growing backlog in some districts with the aid of underworked judges from other districts. Second, Taft advocated for a "Council of Judges," to drive further administrative reforms throughout the Federal judiciary. If approved, this would align the Chief Justice with the senior judges from the nine Circuit Courts, who would all gather at an annual conference to discuss topics like caseloads, rules of procedure, improved libraries for District judges, the possible transferring of judges, and guidelines to expedite the throughput of cases. Nothing like this had ever been done before. Pretty much every Federal Judge operated his own fiefdom with little coordination. Importantly, this conference would not be about cases or constitutional interpretation. Those topics were strictly off the table. But Taft believed some form of administrative standards were necessary to enhance the efficiency of the Federal judiciary, which had been increasingly suffering without such a system in place.

While Taft received lots of support for these commonsense proposals, he encountered some strong opposition as well. The Chief Justice twice went to testify in front of the Senate Judiciary Committee to make his case. He emphasized that "the mere increase of courts or judges will not suffice. We must have machinery of a quasi-executive character. ... We must have teamwork and judges must be under some sort of disciplinary obligation."[242] One of his principal opponents in the matter was Senator John Shields from Tennessee, who thought the idea of the conference was simply a boondoggle, and that Taft was overstepping his authority in even making the proposal. "The judicial power is the power to try and determine controversies," according to Shields. "The power to establish courts and provide them with judges is a legislative power."[243] There was also a concern that the proposal was turning the Chief Justice into some form of executive over the entire Federal judiciary, which had never been the case before. The Chief Justice had historically led the Supreme Court, as called for in the Constitution, but that was the limit of his executive authority. Some were worried about centralizing too much power in the nationwide judicial system in one person, perhaps lessening the diversity of opinions in play with the more distributed model that had been around since the early days of the Republic. Taft was undeterred, knocking down these sideshow issues and maintaining his focus on the benefits of the organizational adjustment and the annual collaboration. In the end, Taft was triumphant. The Judges Act of 1922 passed both Houses of Congress by wide margins (36 to 16 in the Senate and 139 to 78 in the House). Just a few months later, Taft oversaw the first national conference for the Federal Judiciary. As advertised, it was a rather dull affair, focusing on the administrative reforms that Taft had been pushing. Mostly uncontroversial, it was also highly valuable, and became a staple of the Federal judiciary in various forms going forward.

The new Chief Justice was just getting started. The bigger transformation he was advocating was to give the Supreme Court complete discretion on which cases to hear and which ones to reject. In the current system, when the elevation of cases to the Court was automatic, the wait times had extended to two years in some cases, which Taft believed to be an affront to the administration of real justice. Taft thought the nation's highest court should only spend time on cases that raised significant constitutional issues. And he made it clear who was best positioned to decide which cases those would be. "[It] should be reserved to the discretion of the Supreme Court," he told members of the Chicago Bar, "to say whether the issue ... is of sufficient importance to justify a hearing of it."[244] This was the concept of *certiorari* – "a type of writ, meant for rare use, by which an appellate court decides to review a case at its discretion."[245] Taft was a tour de force in pushing for Congressional approval, getting both the executive branch and the American Bar Association to join the fight as well. In the end, the legislation passed easily. The vote in the Senate, in fact, was 76 to 1. Going forward, most petitions to the Court would be denied, leaving the final say in the hands of the appropriate District or Circuit Court. The Supreme Court would focus all of its attention on those cases its members deemed to be the most relevant for the nation's highest tribunal.

Taft continued to push reforms for the balance of his tenure on the Court, but this was about as far as he got in terms of success. He did get another 24 District judges added to the Federal roster to help further alleviate the backlog of cases, but his other reforms would have to wait another decade or so to come to reality. Most of these suggestions were related to an effort to unify the Federal rules of procedure in law and equity, similar to proposals he had made while serving as President and on the faculty at Yale. Many did come to fruition via the Federal Rules and Procedure Act of 1938, but that was several years after he had passed from the scene.

While Taft's greatest impact as Chief Justice was in these areas of administrative reforms, he certainly put his stamp on actual cases as well. And he was hardly just along for the ride. During his tenure, Taft wrote about 30 decisions a year, about 50% more than each of his colleagues. Almost all of these were for the majority, in part because he had a comfortable 7-2 or 6-3 conservative slant in the make-up of the Court throughout his tenure, but also because he saw the Chief Justice as a unifier of the institution, which could be disrupted if he wrote too many dissents. Over the course of his nearly nine years on the Bench, only 20 out of his 266 written opinions dissented with the majority.

I-74: The Taft Court, circa 1923
(Front Row, L to R): William Van Devanter, Joseph McKenna, Taft, Oliver Wendell Holmes, and James McReynolds
(Back Row, L to R): Pierce Butler, Louis Brandeis, George Sutherland, and Edward Sanford

There are far too many cases to cover from Taft's service on the Supreme Court, but a handful will suffice to give a flavor for the judicial leanings of the Chief Justice and his Court. For the most part, he favored property rights over the rights of organized labor and also consistently supported a broad interpretation of congressional authority in cases related to interstate commerce. Taft's idol was John Marshall, who served as Chief from 1801 to 1835. Taft had once said, "I would rather have been Marshall than any other American. ... He made this country."[246] Marshall brought to life many early constitutional principles with a strong bent toward the power of the national government, including cases related to the Commerce Clause. Taft was committed to maintaining that tradition. He supported the view that if goods were at all connected to other materials throughout the value chain, and if those connections spanned state lines, then Congress had the authority to regulate just about any aspect of that business enterprise. Such was the situation in *Stafford v. Wallace* (1922), in which the Court upheld the constitutionality of the Packers and Stockyards Act. The meat packers in Chicago filed suit against the Act, claiming they were a local operation and therefore exempt from congressional regulation related to *interstate* commerce. The Taft Court strongly disagreed.

> The stockyards are not a place of rest or final destination. … The stockyards are but a throat through which the current flows, and the transactions which occur therein are only incidents to this current from the West to the East, and from one state to another. ... The sales are not in this aspect merely local transactions. ... The stockyards and sales are necessary factors in the middle of the current of commerce.
>
> Whatever amounts to more or less constant practice, and threatens to obstruct or unduly burden the freedom of interstate commerce is within the regulatory power of Congress under the Commerce Clause, and it is primarily for Congress to consider and decide the fact of danger and meet it. This Court will certainly not substitute its judgment for that of Congress in such a matter unless the relation of the subject to interstate commerce and its effect upon it are clearly non-existent.[247]

Chalk up a resounding victory for the powers of the Federal government.

That same year, though, Taft was joined by seven of his colleagues (including the leading liberals, Holmes and Louis Brandeis) to curtail the scope of congressional authority. The case was *Bailey v. Drexel Furniture* (1922), in which the tax provision of the 1919 Child Labor Tax Law was at issue. The statute imposed a ten percent excise tax on companies that employed children (as specifically defined in the law). Notwithstanding the reasonable intent of the measure, the Court determined that Congress exceeded its authority by imposing a *penalty* disguised as a *tax*. "The good sought in

I-75: Chief Justice Taft, circa mid-1920s

unconstitutional legislation," Taft wrote for the majority, "is an insidious feature because it leads citizens and legislators of good purpose to promote it without thought of the serious breach it will make in the ark of our covenant or the harm which will come from breaking down ... the maintenance of local self government, on the one hand, and the national power on the other."[248] He concluded that "To give such magic to the word 'Tax' would be to break down all constitutional limitations of the power of Congress and completely wipe out the sovereignty of the states."[249] The case had implications early in the 21st Century when Chief Justice John Roberts ruled that the individual mandate clause in the Affordable Care Act (also called "Obamacare") did not meet the standards set by the Taft Court as a "penalty," but was, rather, a constitutionally permitted execution of the taxing power of the Federal government.

Taft's presidential roots were front and center in the case of *Myers v. United States* (1926). At issue was the dismissal of Frank Myers by the Wilson administration from his job as a postmaster in Portland, Oregon. The termination, which occurred when Myers was three years into his four-year term, was challenged based on a statute passed in 1876 that permitted such firings only "by and with the advice of the Senate."[250] Since senatorial consent was not given, Myers sued to get his job back. The government did not deny that the provisions of the statute were not followed. Rather, it argued that the requirement of senatorial consent was unconstitutional. Taft dove into this case, not just for the issue at hand, but also to address what many had deemed an unconstitutional effort by the Radical Republicans in the 40th Congress to deny President Andrew Johnson the right to fire members of his Cabinet – a right all previous Presidents had had at their disposal. The Tenure of Office Act of 1867, for the first time, required a President to get approval from the Senate before he could dismiss any member of his administration who had previously been confirmed by that body. The language of the Constitution leaves the question open to debate as to whether or not Congress could impose its will in this manner. Article II, Section 2 of the Constitution provides the President with the authority to "nominate, by and with the Advice and Consent of the Senate, shall appoint Ambassadors, other public Ministers and Consuls, Judges of the supreme Court, and all other Officers of the United States …"[251] But the founding document is silent on whether similar permission is needed for the inverse

I-76: President Andrew Johnson, circa 1868

action; i.e., the removal of an appointee who had previously been confirmed by the Senate. In the case of Andrew Johnson, he consciously violated the act when he dismissed Secretary of War Edwin Stanton with the intent to attack the constitutionality of the act in the courts. Unable to get his case into the judicial process, Congress impeached Johnson for the violation and came one vote away from removing him from office. Chief Justice Taft intended to settle once and for all whether any statute that denies the right of a President to fire an executive branch employee passed constitutional muster. His firm conclusion was that it did not.

Taft poured into the history of the topic, which had been debated from the earliest days of the Republic. He studied some of those debates, as well as clauses that had been both inserted and removed from proposed legislation in the very first Congress. But he went even further, taking a broad view of the authority of the executive based on a different clause in Article II. Taft focused on Section 3, which included the following responsibility of the President of the United States: "he shall take care that the Laws be faithfully executed."[252] As a former President, Taft could speak with confidence in his view that in order to fulfill this constitutional requirement, the executive must be able to compel his subordinates to adhere to his lawful dictates, as buttressed by an unrestricted power to terminate them at his will. According to Taft's opinion, "to hold otherwise would make it impossible for the President in case of political or other difference with the Senate or Congress to take care that the laws be faithfully executed."[253] Given that, not only was the current law before the courts unconstitutional, based on the same principle, so was the statute that almost brought down President Johnson.

> It therefore follows that the Tenure of Office Act of 1867, in so far as it attempted to prevent the President from removing executive officers who had been appointed by him and with the

> advice and consent of the Senate, was invalid and that subsequent legislation of the same effect was equally so. For the reasons given, we must therefore hold that the provision of the law of 1876 by which the unrestricted power of removal of first class postmasters is denied to the President is in violation of the situation and invalid.[254]

It may have come 60 years too late, but Andrew Johnson could posthumously take comfort in that the Supreme Court finally determined he was right all along. Moreover, the precedent became a fixture for Presidents going forward, a definitive gift from the only man to lead both of these branches of government. Taft himself noted, "I never wrote an opinion that I felt to be so important in its effect."[255]

One final case of note was one where Taft prevailed in the majority, but it was the minority opinion of Justice Louis Brandeis that eventually carried the day, with implications for modern jurisprudence. The case was *Olmstead v. United States* (1928), in which Ray Olmstead of Seattle was charged with bootlegging. The evidence in the case, which was overwhelming, was entirely obtained by a wiretap, which Olmstead claimed was an illegal search and seizure and, therefore, a violation of the Fourth Amendment. Taft and the majority disagreed. "The amendment does not forbid what was done here," wrote the Chief Justice. "There was no searching. There was no seizure. The evidence was secured by the use of hearing and that only. There was no entry of the house or offices of the defendant. … The language of the amendment can not be extended to include telephone wires reaching to the whole world from the defendant's home or office."[256] Without a statute banning such practice, the

I-77: Chief Justice Taft

Fourth Amendment alone was insufficient to toss out the evidence. Part of Taft's thinking was influenced by the understanding of common law at the time "that the admissibility of evidence is not affected by the illegality of the means by which it was obtained."[257] Oliver Holmes was one of three dissenters who claimed, "for my part I think it is a less evil that some criminal should escape than that the government should play an ignoble part."[258] But it was Justice Brandeis's powerful dissent that would eventually influence what would become the standard for modern rules of evidence. Speaking of the Founding Fathers, Brandeis wrote:

I-78: Associate Justice Louis Brandeis

> They conferred, as against the Government, the right to be let alone – the most comprehensive of rights and the right most valued by civilized men. To protect that right, every unjustifiable intrusion by the Government upon the privacy of the individual, whatever the means employed, must be deemed a violation of the Fourth Amendment. And the use, as evidence in a criminal proceeding, of facts ascertained by such intrusion must be deemed a violation of the Fifth. [It was] immaterial that the intrusion was in aid of law enforcement. … Experience should teach us to be most on our guard to protect liberty when the Government's purposes are beneficent. Men born to freedom are naturally alert to repel invasion of their liberty by evil-minded rulers. The greatest dangers to liberty lurk in insidious encroachments by men of zeal, well meaning but without understanding.[259]

It took another 40 years, but Brandeis's view would eventually become the guiding principle for law enforcement and the judicial system across the country.

As the 1920s began to wind down, so did William Taft. The Chief Justice had already suffered a pair of heart attacks in 1924, and five years

I-79: Chief Justice Taft administering the oath of office to Herbert Hoover, March 4, 1929

later, he was beginning to fade. He did have the honor to swear the nation's 31st President, Herbert Hoover, into office in 1929, just as he had with Calvin Coolidge four years before. Just a few months later, when Taft's brother, Charlie, died, Taft insisted, against his doctor's advice, to travel to Cincinnati for the funeral. He returned in a weakened state, both physically and emotionally. Friends and family counseled a trip to the hospital, where he was admitted to see if the doctors could facilitate some improvement. Little progress was made. The next recommendation was complete rest, and for that, he and Nellie traveled to Asheville, North Carolina, where they checked into the familiar Grove Park Inn. By January 1930, it was clear that Taft's recovery was unlikely and that he could no longer perform his duties. With great sadness, but with due consideration to the institution he so dearly loved, Taft sent his son, Robert, to the Court to announce his retirement effective on February 3. Justice Holmes authored a note of thanks that was signed by all the justices on the Court:

> We call you Chief Justice still – for we can not give up the title by which we have known you all these later years and which you have made dear to us. We can not let you leave us without trying to tell you how dear you have made it. You came to us from achievement in other fields and with the prestige of the illustrious place that you lately held and you showed us in new form your voluminous capacity for getting work done, your humor that smoothed the rough places, your golden heart that brought you love from every side and most of all from your brethren whose tasks you have made happy and light. We grieve at your illness, but your spirit has given life and impulse that will abide whether you are with us or away.[260]

Taft wasn't about to step away without offering opinions on who should take his place. As President, he had considered Charles Evans Hughes for Chief Justice but concluded he wasn't quite ready to lead the Court at that time. Now, there was no question in his mind that Hughes was the right man for the job. Hughes had stepped down from the Court in 1916 to run for President. He had recently served as Secretary of State to Presidents Warren Harding and Calvin Coolidge. As Taft was preparing to resign his seat, he was already lobbying President Hoover to put Hughes in his place. Hoover agreed, and Hughes took over as Chief Justice just a couple of weeks later.

I-80: Chief Justice Taft at Union Station, Washington, D.C., 1929 (age 72)

In the meantime, Taft knew the end was coming soon. He decided to return to his home in Washington. He took the train from Asheville to Union Station, where many saw the former President and Chief Justice rolled around in a wheelchair for the first time. For the next couple of weeks, Taft welcomed a small contingent of close family and friends to reminisce and say goodbye. The end came on March 8, 1930. President Hoover declared 30 days of national mourning. Adorned in his Chief Justice robe, Taft lay in state in the Capitol rotunda, the first President not to die in office to be afforded such an honor. Taft wanted a simple funeral, without sermons or eulogies. This was performed at the All Souls Unitarian Church, after which Taft's body was taken to Arlington National Cemetery, where the former Secretary of War was laid to rest. Nellie was placed at his side when she passed 13 years later.

Taft had one final gift to bestow upon his beloved Supreme Court. From earlier in his tenure, he had lobbied for a separate building for the Court, outside the confines of the Capitol. As an independent branch of government, Taft believed the Court deserved an independent structure in which to operate. Congress approved the concept in 1925, and Taft was named to the Building Commission overseeing the site selection and building design. The nearly $10 million in funding was appropriated in 1929, but Taft had passed away by the time the building was completed in 1935. When the cornerstone was laid in 1932, Chief Justice Hughes remarked, "For this enterprise now progressing to completion ... we are indebted to the late Chief Justice William Howard Taft more than anyone else. This building is the result of his intelligent persistence."[261]

I-81: Chief Justice Charles Evans Hughes speaking at the dedication of the new Supreme Court Building, 1932

This wasn't the only thing for which the country was indebted to William Taft – not by a long shot. The career public servant had thrived in some of the most challenging assignments his nation encountered throughout his adult life. He took on challenges from the Bench and disputes across the globe. He established the foundation for a new nation in the Philippines, guided the construction of the Panama Canal, and helped prevent a revolution in Cuba. And he selflessly turned down offers of his life's ambition to rise to the Supreme Court to tend to other duties. He performed all of these activities with enthusiasm and without complaint, happy to be of service. This is the kind of resume that gets one considered for the presidency, and when a popular incumbent endorses you, such a possibility can become inevitable, even for a man who really didn't want the job. Taft's daughter Helen once observed that her father's four years in the White House "were the only unhappy years of his entire life."[262] This was undoubtedly true. He didn't like the job, wasn't well-suited for it, and admittedly struggled with many elements that came with the high honor. Worst of all, with his performance he ended up alienating his predecessor, and ultimately became estranged from Theodore Roosevelt. When Roosevelt completed his about face on his former friend and ran against him in 1912, Taft hit rock bottom. Losing the office after one term was something of a relief, but the entire experience engendered significant anguish all along the way.

Fortunately, this tragic interlude in the life of William Taft gave way to a happy ending, when his dream job finally came to fruition in 1921. President Warren Harding touched Taft's soul with his appointment as Chief Justice of the Supreme Court, and Taft didn't disappoint in a performance marked by major institutional reforms as well as some noteworthy decisions from the Bench. Taft only got nine years on the Court as a result of turning down his previous offers, but they were extremely productive and happy years that left a lasting impression. William Taft's presidency was a bust that was filled with sadness. However, that can't take anything away from his heroic service to his nation beyond the confines of his four years in the White House. His gravestone properly highlights his two most prominent jobs as the only person to serve as both President and Chief Justice of the United States. But a more fitting epitaph might have followed the tradition of Thomas Jefferson, who eschewed the presidency for his tombstone as a painful period not to be highlighted for posterity. The masons who etched the memorial on Taft's tomb could have filled multiple headstones with his remarkable contributions to American society and just left off the presidency altogether, which would have left a much happier reflection for posterity on the life of William Taft.

20 Quotations from William Taft

Date	Context and Source	Quote
January 29, 1908	His views on the Philippines and imperialism; From a speech to the Tippecanoe Club in Cleveland (Davis. p. 89)	"If we assume control over a people merely in the spirit of conquest and merely to extend our control and merely from the lust of power, then we may be properly denounced as imperialists; but if we assume control over a people for the benefit of that people and with the purpose of developing them to a self-governing capacity, and with the intention of giving them the right to become independent when they shall show themselves fit, then the charge that we are imperialists is utterly without foundation."
~ 1900	Reflecting his patience in listening to the perspectives of the Filipino people; During hearings in the Philippines (Davis. p. 131)	"Let 'em go on. … For once the Filipinos shall have a chance to say all they want to."
October 1902	Turning down President Theodore Roosevelt for nomination to the Supreme Court (for the first time); From a letter to Roosevelt (Duffy. p. 155)	"Situation here most critical from economic standpoint. Change proposed would create much disappointment and lack of confidence among people. Two years now to follow of greater importance to development of islands than previous two years. ... Look forward to the time when I can accept such an offer, but even if it is certain that it can never be repeated I must now decline."
June 1908	On the prospects of receiving the Republican nomination for President; From comments to reporters (Anderson, J. p. 99)	"I'd rather not say what I think of happenings in Chicago. Besides I am the man least interested."
July 1908	Commits to maintaining (and codifying) Theodore Roosevelt's policies if he wins the presidency; From his official acceptance of the Republican nomination (Anderson, D. p. 60)	"The chief function of the next Administration, in my judgment, is distinct from, and a progressive development of that which has been performed by President Roosevelt. The chief function of the next Administration is to complete and perfect the machinery by which these standards may be maintained, by which the law- breakers may be promptly restrained and punished, but which shall operate with sufficient accuracy and

		dispatch to interfere with legitimate business as little as possible."
Summer 1908	His objections to people pushing him to campaign in ways uncomfortable to him; In response to a complaint from within the Republican Party (Anderson, D. p. 48)	"I am sorry, but I cannot be more aggressive than my nature makes me. That is the advantage and disadvantage of having been on the Bench. I can't call names and I can't use adjectives when I don't think the case calls for them, so you will have to get along with that kind of a candidate. I realize what you say of the strength that the President has by reason of those qualities which are the antithesis of the judicial, but so it is with me, and if the people don't like that kind of a man then they have got to take another."
November 1908	Offering thanks to Theodore Roosevelt for helping him become President; From a letter to Roosevelt after his electoral victory (Duffy. p. 219)	"I have just reached Hot Springs and have only now taken up my correspondence. The first letter that I wish to write is to you, because you have always been the chief agent in working out the present state of affairs and my selection and election are chiefly your work. You and my brother Charlie made that possible which in all probability would not have occurred otherwise."
September 17, 1909	Praise for the Payne-Aldrich Tariff; From a speech in Winona, Minnesota (Duffy. p. 240)	"On the whole, therefore, I am bound to say that I think the Payne-Tariff Bill is the best tariff bill that the Republican party ever passed."
December 1909	Refuses to court the press as President; From his response to a question from the editor of *Everybody's Magazine* (Anderson, D. p. 217)	"I am going to do what I think is best for the country, within my jurisdiction and power, and then let the rest take care of itself. I am not looking for a second term, and I am not going to subject myself to the worry involved in establishing a publicity bureau, or attempting to set myself right before the people in any different way from that which is involved in the ordinary publication of what is done. The misrepresentations which are made by the muckraking correspondents I cannot neutralize, and I don't intend to."
January 7, 1910	Terminating Gifford Pinchot as the Chief of the U.S. Forest Service; From a letter to Pinchot (Duffy. p. 249)	"Your letter was in effect an improper appeal to Congress and the public to excuse in advance the guilt of your subordinates before I could act and against my decision in the Glavis case. … By your own conduct you have destroyed your usefulness as a helpful subordinate."
~1910-1911	Lamenting the increasing rift with	"Through some misunderstanding he feels hurt with me. I must have done something

	Theodore Roosevelt; From a conversation with Charles Kohlsaat (Anderson, J. p. 224)	that displeases him very much. Knowingly I have done nothing to hurt his feelings. I may have been tactless, but not intentionally did I do anything to displease him. I owe him everything. He is responsible for my being president. I am so disturbed it keeps me awake nights."
1911	On why he liked to travel away from the White House so often as President; From remarks to an audience in Ohio (Anderson, J. p. 35)	"When you are being hammered . . . not only by the press, but by members of your own party in Washington, and one feels that there isn't anything quite right that he can do, the pleasure of going out into the country, of going into a city that hasn't seen a president for twenty years and then makes a big fuss over him, in order to prove to him that there is somebody that does not know of his defects, is a pleasure that I don't like to forego."
April 25, 1912	On his opposition to Theodore Roosevelt and the progressives who supported judicial recall; From a campaign speech in Boston (Manners. p. 226)	"One who so lightly regards constitutional principles and especially the independence of the judiciary, and who is so naturally impatient of legal restraints, and of due legal procedure, and who has so misunderstood what liberty regulated by law is, could not safely be entrusted with successive presidential terms. I say this sorrowfully, but I say it with the full conviction of truth."
June 1912	Views on his renomination; From comments to a friend (Anderson, J. p. 243)	"The truth is, I am not very happy in this renomination and re-election business. … I am not going to squeal or run away. But after it is all over I shall be glad to retire and let another take the burden."
Summer 1912	On his reaction to Theodore Roosevelt's treatment of him during the campaign (post-convention); From remarks to a friend (Manners. p. 179)	"No one knows how deeply he has wounded me. I shall always be gratified for what he did for me, but since he has come back he has seared me to the very soul."
1912 (late in the year)	Reflecting on his accomplishments as President; From a letter to his wife (Anderson, J. p. 249)	"I am content to retire from it with a consciousness that I have done the best l could. I have strengthened the Supreme Bench, have given them a good deal of new … legislation, have not interfered with business, have kept the peace, and on the whole have enabled people to pursue their various occupations without interruption." He admitted, however, that it was "a very humdrum, uninteresting administration, and it does not attract the attention or enthusiasm of anybody."

February 1917	Advocating for the League to Enforce Peace; From remarks to the National Chamber of Commerce (Duffy. p. 307)	"The purpose of the League to Enforce Peace is to organize the world's strength into an international police to enforce a procedure with respect to issues likely to lead to war, which will prevent all wars but those which nothing can prevent. The procedure to be enforced is the submission of questions of a legal nature, the decision of which must be guided by rules of law, to an international court for its judgment, and the submission of all other questions to an impartial commission to hear and decide, its decision to take the form of a recommendation of compromise. The judgment of the legal questions by the court will be legally and in honor binding on the parties. That is implied in the submission to the court. The recommendation of compromise, however, is not in law or in honor binding, unless the party accepts it. The League does not propose to enforce either. Sometime, if the League comes into successful operation it may be thought well to enforce judgments just as domestic judgments are enforced. … If every issue between nations is forced to arbitration or recommendations, it will compel deliberation by those who think of war."
1921	On his relief about his rapprochement with Theodore Roosevelt; From remarks to Roosevelt's sister, Bamie, after Roosevelt's death (Manners. p. 314)	"I want to say to you how glad I am that Theodore and I came together after that long painful interval. Had he died in a hostile state of mind toward me, I would have mourned the fact all my life. I loved him always and cherish his memory."
~1921-1922	His views on the Supreme Court; From comments at a Gridiron Club dinner (Severn. p. 162)	"The prestige of this Court, next to my wife and my children, is the nearest thing to my heart in life."
~1924	His advocacy to let the Supreme Court decide for itself which cases to hear - the concept of *certiorari*; From remarks to members of the Chicago Bar (Severn. p. 177)	"[It] should be reserved to the discretion of the Supreme Court to say whether the issue... is of sufficient importance to justify a hearing of it."

Primary Sources

Anderson, Donald.

William Howard Taft: A Conservative's Conception of the Presidency. Cornell University Press. Ithaca, NY. 1973.

Anderson, Judith.

William Howard Taft: An Intimate History. W.W. Norton & Company. New York, NY. 1981.

Burton, David.

William Howard Taft: In the Public Service. Robert E. Krieger Publishing Company. Malabar, FL. 1986.

Davis, Oscar.

William Howard Taft: The Man of the Hour. P.W. Ziegler Co. Philadelphia, PA. 1908.

Duffy, Herbert.

William Howard Taft: A Biography. Minton, Balch & Company. New York, NY. 1930.

Manners, William.

TR and Will: A Friendship that Split the Republican Party. Harcourt, Brace & World, Inc. New York, NY. 1969.

Severn, Bill.

William Howard Taft: The President Who Became Chief Justice. David McKay Company, Inc. New York, NY. 1970.

Taft, Helen.

Recollections of Full Years. Dodd, Mead & Company. New York, NY. 1914

Primary Sources Specifically for Illustrations

Dunn, Robert.

William Howard Taft: American. The Chapple Publishing Company, LTD. Boston, MA. 1908.

Illustrations and Their Sources

Cover: **William Taft** (Artist: Anders Zorn. 1911. White House Historical Association, White House History Collection. https://www.whitehousehistory.org/photos/president-william-howard-taft)

I-1 **Taft's parents, Alphonso and Louisa, circa 1859** (Artist: William Walcutt. Cincinnati, OH. circa 1859. Courtesy of the William Taft National Historic Site)

I-2: **Taft, circa 1863 (age ~6)** (Artist: Unknown. Circa 1863. Dunn. p. 209)

I-3: **Taft, 1868 (age 11)** (Artist: Unknown. 1868. Davis. p. 35)

I-4: **Taft's Childhood Home, Cincinnati, OH** (Author Photo)

I-5: **Taft at Yale, 1875 (age ~18)** (Artist: Unknown. 1875. Davis. p. 54)

I-6: **Pike's Opera House in Cincinnati, circa 1875** (Artist: D. J. Kenny. Original appeared in "Illustrated Cincinnati," published by Robert Clarke & Co. Digitized by the Public Library of Cincinnati and Hamilton County. Retrieved from *Cincinnati Magazine*. "Take the 1875 Tour of Cincinnati" by Greg Hand, posted March 22, 2016. https://www.cincinnatimagazine.com/citywiseblog/cincinnati-curiosities-illustrated-cincinnati/)

I-7: **President Chester Arthur** (Artist: C.M. Bell. 1882. Retrieved from the Library of Congress. https://www.loc.gov/item/96524270/)

I-8: **Nellie Herron's "Salon" with Taft in the center and Nellie to his right, 1884** (Artist: Unknown. H. Taft. p. 12)

I-9: **William and Nellie Taft at the time of their wedding, 1886** (Artist: Unknown. H. Taft. p. 16)

I-10: **President Benjamin Harrison** (Artist: Unknown. Retrieved from *The Life of Gen. Benjamin Harrison and Whitelaw Reid* by J.W. Shepp. Political Publishing Co. Chicago, IL. 1892. p. 10)

I-11: **Taft as Solicitor General, 1890 (age 33)** (Artist: Unknown. 1890. Courtesy of the William Taft National Historic Site)

I-12: **Theodore Roosevelt, member of the Civil Service Commission** (Artist: Unknown. Retrieved from *Theodore Roosevelt: The Boy and the Man* by James Morgan. The Macmillan Company. London. 1910. p. 78)

I-13: **Nellie Taft (center) with the couple's first two children, Helen and Robert** (Artist: Unknown. H. Taft. p. 26)

I-14: **Judge Taft, circa 1894 (age ~37)** (Artist: Brown Bros. Davis. p. 65)

I-15: **President William McKinley in the Cabinet Room in the White House** (Artist: Unknown. Retrieved from *The Life of William McKinley, Volume I, by Charles Olcott.* Houghton Mifflin Company. Boston, MA. 1916. p. 394)

I-16: **Map of the Philippines and its nearest Asian neighbors** (Prepared by the CIA. Originally appeared in the CIA World Factbook. Retrieved from *The South China Sea*. Southeast Asia Political Map. https://www.southchinasea.org/2011/08/19/southeast-asia-political-map-cia/)

I-17: **The Second Philippine Commission (L to R): Dean Worcester, Henry Ide, Taft, Bernard Moses, and Luke Wright, circa 1900** (Artist: Unknown. Retrieved from the Library of Congress. www.loc.gov/item/2003688480/)

I-18: **Charlie Taft, circa 1900 (age ~4)** (Artist: Unknown. H. Taft. p. 36)

I-19: **The leader of the Philippine insurrection, Emilio Aguinaldo** (From a photograph furnished by Felipe Aguincillo. Retrieved from the *History of the Philippines and the Life and Achievements of Admiral George Dewey* by Marshall Everett. J.S. Ziegler & Co. Chicago, IL. 1899. p. 37)

I-20: **Military Governor of the Philippines Arthur MacArthur** (Artist: Unknown. Late 19th Century. Retrieved from Wikipedia. https://en.wikipedia.org/wiki/Arthur_MacArthur_Jr.#/media/File:Arthur_MacArthur_Jr.jpg)

I-21: **Taft (center) with fellow commissioners Luke Wright (left) and Henry Ide (right)** (Artist: Unknown. circa 1901. Retrieved from the Library of Congress. www.loc.gov/item/00649513/)

I-22: **Democratic candidate for President, William Jennings Bryan, 1900** (Artist: Unknown. Retrieved from the Library of Congress. https://www.loc.gov/pictures/item/2003656987/)

I-23: **Taft being sworn in as the first Governor-General of the Philippines, July 4, 1901** (Artist: Unknown. H. Taft. p. 208)

I-24: **Malacanan Palace, Manila, The Philippines** (Artist: Unknown. H. Taft. p. 214)

I-25: **Rendering of the assassination of President McKinley by Leon Czolgosz, September 6, 1901** (Artist: Unknown. Retrieved from *McKinley and Men of Our Times* by Edward Pell, James Buel, and James Boyd. Historical Society of America. 1901. p. 50)

I-26: **President Theodore Roosevelt** (Artist: Harris & Ewing. 1907. Davis. p. 19)

I-27: **Pope Leo XIII, 1900** (Artist: Philip Alexius de Laszlo. 1900. Retrieved from the JSS Virtual Gallery. http://www.jssgallery.org/Other_Artists/Philip_Alexius_de_Laszlo/Pope_Leo_XIII.htm)

I-28: **Governor-General Taft in the Philippines, circa 1902 (age ~45)** (Artist: Unknown. circa 1902. Retrieved from the Library of Congress. www.loc.gov/item/2013649079/)

I-29: **The Tafts, along with family and friends, dressed up for the Venetian Carnival, 1903** (Artist: Unknown. H. Taft. p. 205)

I-30: **Taft as Secretary of War, circa 1905 (age ~48)** (Artist: Harris & Ewing. circa 1905. Retrieved from the Library of Congress. www.loc.gov/item/2016856193/).

I-31: **Secretary Taft at the trainmaster's office in Panama, circa 1904** (Artist: Brown Bros. Davis. p 185)

I-32: **Secretary Taft and George Goethals, Panama** (Artist: Unknown. H. Taft. p. 290)

I-33: **President Roosevelt's daughter, Alice Longworth (front, center) joined Secretary Taft (second row, center) on the fact-finding mission to the Philippines** (Artist:

Unknown. Retrieved from the Smithsonian Institution, National Museum of Asian Art. "Alice in Asia: The 1905 Taft Mission to Asia." https://asia.si.edu/essays/alice-in-asia/)

I-34: **Secretary Taft with Secretary of State Elihu Root, circa 1905** (Artist: B.M. Clinedinst. circa 1905. Retrieved from the Library of Congress. www.loc.gov/item/2003688477/)

I-35: **Cuban President Tomás Palma** (Artist: Unknown. Retrieved from "The World's Work" Volume III. February 1902. p. 1686. https://archive.org/details/worldswork03gard/page/1686/mode/2up?view=theater

I-36: **Secretary Taft speaking at the opening of the Philippine National Assembly, October 1907** (Artist: Unknown. October 1907. Dunn. p. 150)

I-37: **President Theodore Roosevelt** (Artist: C.M. Bell. circa 1904. Retrieved from *The Man Roosevelt: A Portrait Sketch* by Francis Leupp. D. Appleton and Company. New York, NY. 1904. Frontispiece)

I-38: **Republican Campaign Banner, Taft and VP candidate James Sherman, 1908** (Artist: Unknown. 1908. Courtesy of the William Taft National Historic Site)

I-39: **Taft during the 1908 presidential campaign** (Artist: Unknown. Dunn. p. 17)

I-40: **Taft, the golfer, Hot Springs, VA, December 1908** (Artist: Keystone View Company. Hot Springs, VA. December 1908. Retrieved from the Library of Congress, www.loc.gov/item/96522777/)

I-41: **President Taft and his Cabinet (Left to Right): Secretary of the Interior Richard Ballinger, Secretary of the Navy George Meyer, Secretary of State Philander Knox, Personal Secretary Charles Norton, Taft (seated), Postmaster General Frank Hitchcock, Secretary of Agriculture James Wilson, Treasury Secretary Franklin MacVeagh, Attorney General George Wickersham, and Secretary of Commerce and Labor Charles Nagel (not pictured, Secretary of War Jacob Dickinson)** (Artist: Unknown. Retrieved from *George von Lengerke Meyer: His Life and Public Services* by M.A. DeWolfe Howe. Dodd, Mead and Co. New York. NY. 1919. p. 426)

I-42: **Outgoing President Roosevelt with Incoming President Taft, Inauguration Day, March 4, 1909** (Artist: Brown Brothers. March 4, 1909. Retrieved from the Library of Congress. https://www.loc.gov/item/2013651501/)

I-43: **President Taft was joined by First Lady Nellie Taft on the ride from the Capitol to the White House after being sworn in as President, March 4, 1909** (Artist: Keystone View Company. March 4, 1909. Retrieved from the Library of Congress. www.loc.gov/item/00650959/)

I-44: **The White House as it looked on March 4, 1909** (Artist: Unknown. H. Taft. p. 324)

I-45: **President Taft with his military aide, Captain Archibald Butt, circa 1909** (Artist: Unknown. circa 1909. Retrieved from arlingtoncemetery.net. www.arlingtoncemetery.net/awbutt.htm)

I-46: **Speaker of the House Joe Cannon and Senator Nelson Aldrich** (Cannon: Artist: Harris & Ewing. 1908. Davis. p. 205.; Aldrich: Artist: Engraving from the Memorial Encyclopedia of the State of Rhode Island. 1916. Retrieved from Wikipedia.

https://en.wikipedia.org/wiki/Nelson_W._Aldrich#/media/File:Nelson_W._Aldrich_1841%E2%80%931915.jpg)

I-47: **President Taft, circa 1909 (age ~52)** (Artist: Moffett Studio. circa 1909. Davis. Frontispiece)

I-48: **Conservationist and leading progressive, Gifford Pinchot** (Artist: Underwood & Underwood. *Pinchot Autobiography*. New York, NY. p. 496)

I-49: **Secretary of the Interior Richard Ballinger** (Artist: Unknown. circa 1911. Retrieved from the Library of Congress. https://www.loc.gov/item/2002699144/)

I-50: **President Taft as "Golfer in Chief"** (Artist: George Grantham Bain. circa 1909. Retrieved from the Library of Congress. www.loc.gov/item/2003654860/)

I-51: **The original Oval Office used by President Taft, 1909** (Artist: Harris & Ewing. Library of Congress. Retrieved from Wikipedia. https://en.wikipedia.org/wiki/Oval_Office#/media/File:White_House,_President's_Office_LOC14832v_cropped.jpg)

I-52: **First Lady Helen ("Nellie") Taft** (Artist: Harris & Ewing. Davis. p. 55)

I-53: **President Taft, circa 1910 (age ~53)** (Artist: William Schevill. circa 1910. Retrieved from the National Portrait Gallery, Smithsonian Institution. https://npg.si.edu/object/npg_NPG.72.25?destination=edan-search/default_search%3Fpage%3D1%26edan_local%3D1%26edan_q%3Dwilliam%252Btaft)

I-54: **Former President Theodore Roosevelt being welcomed upon his return to New York, June 18, 1910** (Artist: Unknown. 1910. Retrieved from the Library of Congress. https://www.loc.gov/resource/ppmsca.35899/)

I-55: **President Taft's vacation cottage at Beverly, Massachusetts** (Artist: Unknown. H. Taft. p. 370)

I-56: **Chief Justice Edward White** (Artist: Harris & Ewing. Retrieved from the Library of Congress, https://www.loc.gov/item/2016857489/)

I-57: **U.S. Capitol, circa 1910** (Originally available from the Architect of the Capitol. Retrieved from Wikipedia. https://en.wikipedia.org/wiki/61st_United_States_Congress#/media/File:USCapitol1906.jpg)

I-58: **President Taft, circa 1910 (age ~53)** (Artist: Harris & Ewing. circa 1910. Retrieved from the Library of Congress. www.loc.gov/item/2016856219/)

I-59: **Secretary of State Philander Knox** (Artist: Harris & Ewing. 1908. Davis. p. 195)

I-60: **President Taft and his family at the time of his 25th wedding anniversary, 1911 (L to R): Charlie, Nellie, Helen, President Taft, & Robert** (Artist: Unknown. June 1911. Retrieved from the Library of Congress. www.loc.gov/item/97505479/)

I-61: **First Lady Helen ("Nellie") Taft** (Artist: Karl Kronstrand. 1910. Retrieved from Wikipedia. https://en.wikipedia.org/wiki/Helen_Herron_Taft#/media/File:Htaft.jpeg)

I-62: **Attorney General George Wickersham** (Artist: Underwood & Underwood. 1929. Retrieved from the Library of Congress. https://www.loc.gov/pictures/item/2002711675/)

I-63: **Sinking of the Titanic, April 1912** (Artist: Willie Stower. Originally appeared in Magazine *Die Gartenlaube*. 1912. Retrieved from Wikipedia. https://en.wikipedia.org/wiki/Sinking_of_the_Titanic#/media/File:St%C3%B6wer_Titanic.jpg)

I-64: **President Taft signing the revised New Mexico Statehood Bill, 1912** (Artist: Harris & Ewing. 1912. Retrieved from the Library of Congress. www.loc.gov/item/2016861539/)

I-65: **Crowds arriving at the Chicago Coliseum for the 1912 Republican National Convention** (Artist: Bain News Service. Chicago, IL. June 1912. Retrieved from the Library of Congress. https://www.loc.gov/pictures/item/2014690519/)

I-66: **Theodore Roosevelt on the stump during the 1912 campaign** (Artist: Underwood & Underwood. September 1912. Retrieved from the Library of Congress. https://www.loc.gov/pictures/item/2009633789/)

I-67: **President-elect Woodrow Wilson and President Taft, Inauguration Day, March 4, 1913** (Artist: Unknown. March 4, 1913. Retrieved from the Library of Congress. www.loc.gov/item/00650962/)

I-68: **Yale University, 1906** (Artist: Richard Rummell. 1906. Yale campus facing north. Retrieved from Wikipedia. https://en.wikipedia.org/wiki/Yale_University#/media/File:Rummell,_Richard_Yale_University_cropped.jpg)

I-69: **Taft saying farewell to his son Charlie who was leaving for Europe in World War I, 1917** (Artist: Unknown. 1917. Courtesy of the William Taft National Historic Site)

I-70: **Theodore Roosevelt, 1918, just a few months before he died** (Artist: Underwood & Underwood. 1918. Retrieved from *Theodore Roosevelt: An Intimate Biography* by William Thayer. Houghton Mifflin Company. Boston, MA. 1919. p. 318)

I-71: **President Warren Harding with Chief Justice Taft, circa 1921** (Artist: Harris & Ewing. circa 1921. Retrieved from the Library of Congress. www.loc.gov/item/2016885827/)

I-72: **Taft being sworn in as Chief Justice of the Supreme Court, 1921** (Artist: Unknown. 1921. Retrieved from *Smithsonian Magazine*. "Chief Justice, Not President, Was William Taft's Dream Job" by Erick Trickey. Posted December 5, 2016. https://www.smithsonianmag.com/history/chief-justice-not-president-was-william-howard-tafts-dream-job-180961279/)

I-73: **A slimmed-down post-President Taft** (Artist: Unknown. Retrieved from POTUS-Geeks. "Presidential Athletes: William Howard Taft's Wrestling Career." https://potus-geeks.livejournal.com/710210.html)

I-74: **The Taft Court, circa 1923 (Front Row, L to R): William Van Devanter, Joseph McKenna, Taft, Oliver Wendell Holmes, and James McReynolds; (Back Row, L to R): Pierce Butler, Louis Brandeis, George Sutherland, and Edward Sanford** (Artist: Harris & Ewing. circa 1923. Retrieved from the National Portrait Gallery, Smithsonian Institution. Gift of Aileen Conkey.

https://npg.si.edu/object/npg_S_NPG.84.307?destination=edan-search/default_search%3Fpage%3D1%26edan_local%3D1%26edan_q%3Dwilliam%252Btaft)

I-75: **Chief Justice Taft, circa mid-1920s** (Artist: Harris & Ewing. circa mid-1920s. Retrieved from the Library of Congress. www.loc.gov/item/2016856210/)

I-76: **President Andrew Johnson, circa 1868** (Artist: Unknown. Retrieved from *The Life and Public Services of Andrew Johnson* by John Savage. Derby & Miller. New York, NY. 1866. Frontispiece)

I-77: **Chief Justice Taft** (Artist: Emily Waite. circa 1923-1924. Retrieved from Heritage Auctions. https://historical.ha.com/itm/political/presidential-relics/william-howard-taft-oil-portrait-by-emily-burling-waite/a/6035-47150.s)

I-78: **Associate Justice Louis Brandeis** (Artist: Harris & Ewing. circa 1916. Retrieved from the Library of Congress. https://www.loc.gov/pictures/item/2004673443/)

I-79: **Chief Justice Taft administering the oath of office to Herbert Hoover, March 4, 1929** (Artist: National Photo Company. March 4, 1929. Retrieved from the Library of Congress. www.loc.gov/item/00650968/)

I-80: **Chief Justice Taft at Union Station, Washington, D.C., 1929 (age 72)** (Artist: Underwood & Underwood. 1929. Retrieved from the Library of Congress. www.loc.gov/item/96510829/)

I-81: **Chief Justice Charles Evans Hughes speaking at the dedication of the new Supreme Court Building, 1932** (Artist: Harris & Ewing. 1932. Retrieved from the Library of Congress. https://www.loc.gov/resource/hec.36986/)

Notes

[1] Severn. 1.
[2] Davis. 121.
[3] Severn. 2.
[4] Davis. 41.
[5] Severn. 9.
[6] Severn. 17.
[7] Anderson, J. 46.
[8] Taft, H. 9.
[9] Severn. 21.
[10] Anderson, J. 49.
[11] Taft, H. 10.
[12] Anderson, J. 54.
[13] Taft, H. 21.
[14] Duffy. 14.
[15] Duffy. 15.
[16] Burton. 16.
[17] Burton. 18.
[18] Anderson, J. 59.
[19] Severn. 42.
[20] Severn. 34.
[21] Taft, H. 309.
[22] Anderson, J. 60.
[23] Duffy. 33.
[24] Anderson, J. 61.
[25] Taft, H. 30.
[26] Burton. 21.
[27] Davis. 71.
[28] Davis. 73.
[29] Duffy. 43.
[30] Davis. 79.
[31] Davis. 91.
[32] Duffy. 54.
[33] Olcott, Charles. *The Life of William McKinley. Volume II.* Houghton Mifflin Company. Boston, MA. 1916. p. 110.
[34] Merry, Robert. *President McKinley: Architect of the American Century.* Simon & Schuster. New York, NY. 201. p. 364.
[35] Davis. 110.
[36] Taft, H., 32.
[37] Severn. 48.
[38] Duffy. 72.
[39] Severn. 50.
[40] Duffy. 73.
[41] Anderson, J. 80.
[42] Taft, H. 33.
[43] Duffy. 75.

[44] Taft, H. 35.
[45] Davis. 92.
[46] Taft, H. 54.
[47] Severn. 54.
[48] Severn. 52.
[49] Olcott, Charles. *The Life of William McKinley. Volume II.* Houghton Mifflin Company. Boston, MA. 1916. p. 172.
[50] Taft, H. 222.
[51] Davis. 189.
[52] Taft, H. 84.
[53] Anderson, J. 74.
[54] Davis. 147.
[55] Davis. 131.
[56] Davis. 119.
[57] Davis. 121.
[58] Duffy. 134.
[59] Anderson, J. 82.
[60] Taft, H. 110.
[61] Anderson, J. 72.
[62] Taft, H. 152.
[63] Duffy. 96.
[64] Merry, Robert. *President McKinley: Architect of the American Century.* Simon & Schuster. New York, NY. 201. p. 469.
[65] Taft, H. 207.
[66] Taft, H. 212.
[67] Taft, H. 224.
[68] Duffy. 141.
[69] Taft, H. 131.
[70] Taft, H. 239.
[71] Taft. H. 237.
[72] Taft, H. 247.
[73] Taft, H. 251.
[74] Taft, H. 262.
[75] Duffy. 155.
[76] Taft, H. 265.
[77] Duffy. 157.
[78] Taft, H. 266.
[79] Taft, H. 267.
[80] Taft. H. 268.
[81] Pringle, Henry. *The Life and Times of William Howard Taft: A Biography. Volume I.* Archon Books. Hamden, CT. 1964. p. 247.
[82] Pringle, Henry. *The Life and Times of William Howard Taft: A Biography. Volume I.* Archon Books. Hamden, CT. 1964. p. 247.
[83] Taft. H. 269.
[84] Davis. 37.
[85] Duffy. 163.
[86] Anderson, J. 84.
[87] Duffy. 165.

[88] Taft, H. 272.
[89] Duffy. 166.
[90] Miller, Nathan. *Theodore Roosevelt: A Life*. William Morrow and Company, Inc. New York, NY. 1992. p. 377.
[91] Anderson, J. 89.
[92] Severn. 70.
[93] Anderson, J. 89.
[94] Duffy. 170.
[95] Severn. 71.
[96] Severn. 81.
[97] Manners. 47.
[98] Severn. 82.
[99] Duffy. 181.
[100] Beede, Benjamin, *The War of 1898, and U.S. Interventions, 1898–1934: An Encyclopedia: Military History of the United States; v. 2. Garland reference library of the humanities; vol. 933*. Taylor & Francis. 1994. pp. 119–121.
[101] Duffy. 183.
[102] Taft, H. 294.
[103] Duffy. 188.
[104] Duffy. 191.
[105] Duffy. 193.
[106] Duffy. 193.
[107] Taft, H. 295.
[108] Duffy. 195.
[109] Duffy. 200.
[110] Taft, H. 315.
[111] Davis. 232.
[112] Taft, H. 303.
[113] Anderson, J. 91.
[114] Taft, H., 321.
[115] Anderson, D. 28.
[116] Anderson, D. 30.
[117] Anderson, J. 99.
[118] Anderson, J. 103.
[119] Anderson, D. 48.
[120] Anderson. D. 60.
[121] Manners. 60.
[122] Anderson, D. 43.
[123] Anderson, J. 108.
[124] Anderson, D. 48.
[125] Anderson, D. 48.
[126] Anderson, J. 114.
[127] Anderson, J. 114.
[128] Duffy. 219.
[129] Miller, Nathan. *Theodore Roosevelt: A Life*. William Morrow and Company, Inc. New York, NY. 1992. p. 492.
[130] Manners. 55.

[131] Severn. 95.
[132] Duffy. 244.
[133] Anderson, J. 119.
[134] Manners. 5.
[135] Manners. 17.
[136] *William Howard Taft Inaugural Address.* Originally delivered March 4, 1909. *Presidential Inaugural Addresses.* Word Cloud Classics. San Diego, CA. 2019. p. 244.
[137] Manners. 79.
[138] Anderson, J. 121.
[139] Taft, H. 332.
[140] Anderson, J. 124.
[141] Anderson, J. 128.
[142] Anderson, J. 169.
[143] Taft, William. *Message Regarding Tariff Legislation*. March 16, 1909. Presidential Speeches. Miller Center, University of Virginia. Retrieved August 30, 2022. https://millercenter.org/the-presidency/presidential-speeches/march-16-1909-message-regarding-tariff-legislation
[144] Anderson, J. 192.
[145] Anderson, D. 105.
[146] Anderson, D. 107.
[147] Anderson, D. 112.
[148] Duffy. 239.
[149] Duffy. 240.
[150] Anderson, J. 181.
[151] Anderson, D. 74.
[152] Manners. 118.
[153] Duffy. 249.
[154] Anderson, D. 217.
[155] Anderson, D. 210.
[156] Anderson, J. 25.
[157] Anderson, J. 33.
[158] Taft, H. 365.
[159] Taft, H. 349.
[160] Severn. 106.
[161] Anderson, J. 165.
[162] Anderson, J. 167.
[163] Anderson, J. 167.
[164] Anderson, D. 92.
[165] Anderson, D. 92.
[166] Anderson, D. 90.
[167] Anderson, J. 185.
[168] Manners. 164.
[169] Severn. 111.
[170] Manners. 169.
[171] Taft, H. 383.
[172] Taft, H. 383.
[173] Taft, H. 384.
[174] Anderson, J. 217.

[175] Manners. 177.
[176] Severn. 116.
[177] Anderson, D. 139.
[178] Anderson, D. 143.
[179] Duffy. 265.
[180] Anderson, J. 220.
[181] Manners. 188.
[182] Anderson, J. 224.
[183] Manners. 179.
[184] Millard, Candice. *The River of Doubt: Theodore Roosevelt's Darkest Journey*. Anchor Books. New York, NY. 2005. p. 39.
[185] Anderson, D. 267.
[186] Severn. 137.
[187] Anderson, D. 276.
[188] Duffy. 270.
[189] Anderson, J. 23.
[190] Anderson, J. 32.
[191] Taft, H. 391.
[192] Anderson, J. 35.
[193] Anderson, D. 224.
[194] Anderson, D. 225.
[195] Brands, H.W. *T.R.: The Last Romantic*. BasicBooks. New York, NY. 1997. p. 603.
[196] Manners. 201.
[197] Manners. 201.
[198] Anderson, J. 210.
[199] Severn. 122.
[200] Severn. 122.
[201] Roosevelt, Theodore. *An Autobiography*. Charles Scribner's Sons. New York, NY. 1899. p. 425.
[202] Anderson, J. 229.
[203] Anderson, J. 27.
[204] Severn. 122.
[205] Manners. 226.
[206] Anderson, J. 228.
[207] Severn. 125.
[208] Manners. 238.
[209] Manners. 261.
[210] Manners. 265.
[211] Manners. 266.
[212] Anderson, J. 246.
[213] Anderson, J. 243.
[214] Duffy. 283.
[215] Manners. 275.
[216] Manners. 212.
[217] Manners. 179.
[218] Manners. 179.
[219] Anderson, J. 231.

[220] Anderson, J. 231
[221] Manners. 281.
[222] Anderson, J. 247.
[223] Taft, H. 394.
[224] Anderson, J. 249.
[225] Severn. 129.
[226] Anderson, J. 255.
[227] Severn. 129.
[228] Severn. 140.
[229] Anderson, J. 257.
[230] Manners. 297.
[231] Manners. 300.
[232] Manners. 304.
[233] Manners. 314.
[234] Duffy. 307.
[235] Severn. 148.
[236] Severn. 152.
[237] Severn. 152.
[238] Burton. 122.
[239] Severn. 162.
[240] Severn. 159.
[241] Burton. 125.
[242] Severn. 173.
[243] Burton. 126.
[244] Severn. 177.
[245] "Writ of certiorari." Legal Information Institute. Cornell Law School. The word "certiorari" comes from Law Latin and means "to be fully informed." Retrieved on September 2, 2022. https://www.law.cornell.edu/wex/writ_of_certiorari#:~:text=See%3A%20certiorari,higher%20court%20may%20review%20it.
[246] Severn. 116.
[247] Severn. 189.
[248] Severn. 192.
[249] Burton. 135.
[250] Severn. 200.
[251] Constitution of the United States: A Transcription. Article II, Section 2. America's Founding Documents. National Archives. Retrieved on September 2, 2022. https://www.archives.gov/founding-docs/constitution-transcript
[252] Constitution of the United States: A Transcription. Article II, Section 3. America's Founding Documents. National Archives. Retrieved on September 2, 2022. https://www.archives.gov/founding-docs/constitution-transcript
[253] Duffy. 317.
[254] Duffy. 317.
[255] Burton. 137.
[256] Burton. 139.
[257] Burton. 139.
[258] Burton. 139.
[259] Severn. 208.
[260] Burton. 141.
[261] Severn. 184.
[262] Anderson, J. 255.

Index

PRESIDENTIAL CHRONICLES
VOLUME VI: PROGRESSIVISM AND PROSPERITY
II: THE LIFE OF WOODROW WILSON
DAVID FISHER

II: The Life of Woodrow Wilson

Preface

When Woodrow Wilson arrived in Paris in December 1918 for the post-World War I Peace Conference, he was a man sitting on top of the world. After finally bringing his country into the conflict on the side of the Allies, the American President mobilized the full power of the United States toward defeating the Central Powers and delivered on that promise in a little more than a year. Millions of grateful citizens showed up in France, England, and Italy to cheer at the top of their lungs the man who appeared to save western civilization as they knew it. Moreover, many of the revelers were enamored with his vision to create new structures, like his proposed League of Nations, to ensure no such conflagrations would ever happen again. Such was the apex in the life and career of Woodrow Wilson. It was also mostly downhill from there.

Wilson made many compromises that deviated from his original Fourteen Points, on which the peace talks were supposed to be based, to get the Allies to agree to his League, which was the most important part of the plan in the eyes of the American President. But many of those ideological concessions represented major disappointments to Wilson's adherents, and had devastating consequences when the punitive Treaty of Versailles was put into effect. Moreover, when Wilson returned home with the Treaty in hand, he ran into fervent opposition in a United States Senate that he had mostly ignored throughout the negotiations. Wilson badly misread the need to engage these legislators until it was too late. Both sides stubbornly locked into a take-it-or-leave-it mentality, which ultimately meant defeat for Wilson. His own country would never join his beloved League.

Wilson never gave up fighting for his vision, and that cost him as well. Always frail, and with a history of physical setbacks, Wilson took his case directly to the American people in a grueling campaign-style speaking tour for which he was not up to the task. His oratory was as brilliant as always as he rose to the occasion to speak, but after each address, his body continued to break down, eventually succumbing to a massive stroke. He spent the last year and a half of his presidency as an invalid, watching his precious League of Nations go down to defeat not once but twice in the Senate. In the meantime, his wife assumed the role of deciding which few items she would bring to Wilson's attention in the longest period in American history where the President was primarily unable to function.

Woodrow Wilson rose through the ranks of the academic community to become one of his nation's foremost political scientists. After returning to his alma mater, Princeton University, as both professor and university president, he eventually made the pivot he had longed for, going from academic to statesman, first as governor of New Jersey and then, almost immediately thereafter, as President of the United States. Wilson was cheered for his progressive agenda and active leadership in moving legislation through the system with acts intended to make a real difference in people's lives. When war came, he maintained American neutrality for as long as he could before changing circumstances convinced him the time was right to lead his nation into war. That decision, and the follow-on execution, made the difference in the Allied victory. This was a lifetime of success, leading to heights few human beings would ever experience. But from those great heights often come great falls. Wilson was ultimately unable to deliver on many of his most profound ideas. The fact that an even more devastating war materialized less than a generation into the future served as the ultimate repudiation of Woodrow Wilson's greatest efforts.

1. Professor Wilson

Both sides of Woodrow Wilson's lineage hailed from the United Kingdom. His fraternal grandfather, James, left the Irish town of Ulster in 1806, settling in Steubenville, Ohio, with his wife, Anne. James Wilson was a prominent man in his community, owning a pair of newspapers, along with serving one term in the Ohio state legislature. The couple's tenth child, Joseph, came along in 1822. He yearned to preach and pursued the ministry with his studies at the Theological Seminary in Alleghany, Pennsylvania, followed by a stint at the seminary in Princeton, New Jersey, in 1846. Joseph Wilson was an exceptional orator, able to move people with his words, both from the pulpit and in the classroom. He became a professor of rhetoric at the Steubenville Male Academy before committing to a career as a Presbyterian minister.

The ministry was also prominent in Wilson's maternal heritage. The Reverend Thomas Woodrow ventured from Scotland to England in 1820 before eventually sailing for New York in 1835. His daughter, Jessie, was 13 at the time of that journey, which eventually continued on to Ohio, where she fell in love with Joseph Wilson. She was 21 and he 27 when

II-1: The Rev. Dr. Joseph Wilson, Wilson's father

II-2: Jesse Wilson, Wilson's mother

the couple exchanged their vows. Just a couple of weeks later, Joseph was ordained as a Presbyterian minister, opening up new career opportunities. It turns out the brightest prospects were in the South, specifically Staunton, Virginia, whose First Presbyterian Church offered his first ministry. Making the couple feel right at home, the Church provided its 12-room manse as living quarters, where Joseph would craft his sermons on the back porch and where they would begin to raise their family.

II-3: Wilson's Birthplace, Staunton, VA

After two girls entered the Wilsons' world, they welcomed a boy on December 29, 1856. According to his mother, Thomas Woodrow Wilson "is a fine healthy fellow. He is much larger than either of the others, and just as fat as he can be. Everyone tells us he is a beautiful boy. What is best of all, he is just as good as he can be – as little trouble as it is possible for a baby to be."[1] Young Tommy would later admit to being a bit of a "mamma's boy," appreciating the nurturing his mother offered and the value of humility she instilled in him. But it was his father who had by far the greatest influence on Wilson, likely the greatest of his entire life.

The Wilsons didn't stay long in Staunton. Just a couple of years after young Tommy arrived on the scene, the family headed further south. The

II-4: First Presbyterian Church of Augusta, GA

First Presbyterian Church of Augusta, Georgia, offered its ministry to Joseph Wilson, along with a healthy $2,500 salary. It was here that Wilson experienced his earliest memory – the onset of the Civil War. "My earliest recollection is of standing at my father's gateway in Augusta when I was four years old," Wilson later recalled, "hearing some one pass and say that Mr. Lincoln was elected and there was to be war. … Catching the intense tones of [the stranger's] excited voice, I remember running in to ask my father what it meant."[2] The war had far greater implications for his father than for Wilson, as Augusta was largely spared from the horrors of the conflict. Joseph Wilson believed firmly in the Southern cause. Just a couple of weeks before Georgia announced its separation from the Union in January 1861, Joseph Wilson offered a sermon on the "Mutual Relation of Masters and Slaves as Taught in the Bible." He made clear his position on "how completely the Bible brings human slavery underneath the sanction of divine authority."[3] Joseph became an ardent spokesman for the prevailing sentiments in the South. In fact, he mirrored the efforts of the Southern states to secede from the Union by helping to lead the separation of the Presbyterian Church from all connections to the North. Joseph Wilson was elected the permanent clerk of the newly established Southern Presbyterian Church of the United States, a position he held for nearly four decades. These sentiments clearly impacted his son. A college friend, Robert McCarter, later recalled a conversation in which he found Wilson to be "very full of the South and quite a secessionist, … he taking the Southern side and getting quite bitter."[4] Throughout his life, Wilson tended to romanticize the South of his youth, and while eventually repudiating secession and the institution of slavery, he would often claim "that the only place in the country, the only place in the world, where nothing has to be explained to me is the South."[5]

While Wilson felt little impact during the war itself, he had a greater recollection of Reconstruction, particularly seeing Federal troops in the streets to enforce the new Constitutional amendments and national statutes designed to protect the freedmen. He was around 13 when he came face to face with former General Robert E. Lee. "I have only the delightful memory of standing, when a lad, for a moment by General Lee's side and looking up into his face," Wilson recalled some 40 years later. "Lee was an ideal combination of what a man inherits and what he may make of himself; he was a man who saw his duty, who conceived it in high terms, and who spent himself, not upon his own ambitions, but in the duty that lay before him."[6] Such reverence was not surprising, not only because of Wilson's affinity for the Southern cause but also for the profound sense of duty that Wilson would develop for himself over the years.

During the war and its immediate aftermath, Tommy Wilson experienced an unexceptional upbringing. Not surprisingly, he grew up in a religious household where his parents were both loving and stern. Wilson was often unwell as a child, regularly suffering from stomach ailments and headaches. He needed glasses from an early age to compensate for his poor eyesight. Wilson enjoyed the typical youthful activities, including outdoor sports, where baseball was his favorite. He had difficulty learning, almost assuredly because he suffered from what would later be understood as dyslexia. He struggled to learn the alphabet and didn't begin to read until around age 11 when he finally figured out on his own how to overcome his disability. But Wilson's early education was to be found more in the home and the church with his father than in any classroom.

Joseph Wilson's greatest gift to his community and his son came through his oratory. By all accounts, he was exceptional when speaking, either from the pulpit or in conversation. There was nothing casual in the way he expressed himself, from the words he chose to the manner in which they were delivered to make his points. Wilson didn't master this art just by observation. In fact, it was a constant point of emphasis.

> My father would not permit me to blurt things out, or stammer a half-way job of telling whatever I had to tell. If I became excited in explaining some boyish activity he always said,

> 'Steady, now Thomas; wait a minute. Think! Think what it is you wish to say, and then choose your words to say it.' As a young boy, therefore, even at the age of four or five, I was taught to think about what I was going to say, and then I was required to say it correctly. Before I was grown, it became a habit.[7]

This habit would become Wilson's calling card, one that would set him apart from his peers throughout his academic and political careers.

Within a couple of years of the war's end, the Wilsons were on the move again. The next stop was Columbia, South Carolina, where Joseph was appointed to the faculty of the local theological seminary. While the Wilsons enjoyed Columbia, the parish wasn't enamored with its new minister, so it wasn't long before another family move was in the works. Wilmington, North Carolina, became the new home at a time in the mid-1870s when the family was going through some significant changes. Marriage was on the way for both of Wilson's older sisters, and at the age of 16, he was ready to head off to college. The Presbyterian community of Davidson, North Carolina, had established Davidson College in 1837. Not surprisingly, a significant portion of the student body attended as preparation for a career in the ministry, which remained a consideration for Wilson at this time. It was at Davidson that Wilson became a serious student, finally figuring out how to overcome his dyslexia while pursuing his natural attraction to intellectual pursuits. His father's influence remained front and center as he pursued academic subjects that allowed him to demonstrate his prowess at public speaking. The highlight for Wilson in his one year at Davidson was his role with the Eumenean Literary Society. The ability to formulate his thoughts and present a compelling argument on the debate stage was the most natural thing for Wilson. Unfortunately, Wilson wasn't able to escape one of his other common tendencies – illness. He seemed to constantly be under the weather, with headaches, colds, and various intestinal issues – not to mention homesickness, which had enveloped him as well. After completing his freshman year at Davidson, Wilson went home and never returned.

By no means was Wilson planning to give up on his academic career, but he took some time to recalibrate and prepare to head in a different direction. He did some serious soul-searching as he headed to the family's new home in Wilmington. "I am now in my seventeenth year,"

Wilson noted at the time, "and it is sad, when looking over my past life, to see how few of those seventeen years I have spent in the fear of God and how much I have spent in the service of the Devil." For Wilson, it was time for that to change. "If God will give me the grace, I will try to serve Him from this time on."[8] He spent the next year studying on his own, while also continuing to master his oratorical skills. It was not uncommon for Tommy Wilson to stand at his father's pulpit during the week and offer some of the great speeches from history to the empty church. Whatever career he would ultimately pursue, he was confident that the arts of speaking and persuasion would be integral to his success.

The College of New Jersey is the fourth-oldest institution of higher learning in the United States. Chartered in 1746, the country's first Presbyterian college took its place alongside Harvard, William and Mary, and Yale as destinations for serious pre-Revolution academic study. Future President James Madison was one of the school's early attendees. The Reverend John Witherspoon, who signed the Declaration of Independence as a member of the Second Continental Congress, had served as the institution's President for more than 25 years. While many boys from wealthy families in the South matriculated to William and Mary, it was not uncommon for those like Madison to head north to the institution based in Princeton, New Jersey. The Civil War interrupted that path for a while, but southerners were slowly starting to find their way once again to Princeton. Tommy Wilson was one of them.

II-5: Nassau Hall, The College of New Jersey

The tall but slender Wilson found himself in a whole new world as he entered college in 1875 at the age of 18. Feeling like a fish out of water, he was initially aloof while trying to find his place on a campus that was dominated by northerners, many of whom were second or third generation attendees. Not surprisingly, his most natural fit was in the world of debate, becoming a member of the school's American Whig

Society early in his tenure. His classroom performance was nothing special. Wilson tended to thrive in the subjects which leaned on public speaking but did poorly in those that did not. He ended his freshman year ranked 26th out of 114 students.

Wilson didn't care much for the style of teaching at the College of New Jersey, which relied heavily on rote memorization and recitation. He yearned to pursue intellectual challenges on the path to real wisdom, which was largely absent from his classroom experience. Undeterred, he simply developed his own educational path. Wilson became a regular presence in the voluminous Chancellor Green Library. During this self-initiated study, he gravitated to the history and governmental structure of Britain, reading everything he could get his hands on that was authored by the likes of John Bright and Edmund Burke. Wilson was attracted to the politics of William Gladstone, who was in and out of office as the British Prime Minister during this era. He took this personal development seriously, taking detailed notes on what he read, sometimes capturing thoughts in the margins of books and transcribing them when he returned to his room. The lack of meaningful coursework was not going to stop Tommy Wilson from maximizing his educational opportunity.

If anyone was guiding Wilson's activities, it was his father. The pair looked forward to reuniting during breaks in the school calendar. One summer included a father-son trip to the Centennial Exposition in Philadelphia, the first World's Fair in the United States. But Joseph Wilson's influence on his son was hardly limited to their face-to-face encounters. Years of counsel had already permeated Wilson's worldview, which was centered on a religious-based call to service, a commitment to intellectual curiosity, and a passion to lead and inspire others through the power of words – both written and spoken. That guidance continued during Wilson's college years through a robust correspondence that was often instructive, at times critical, but always supportive. "You have talents – you have character, you

II-6: Wilson, circa 1873 (age ~17)

have a manly bearing," his father once wrote during these college years. "You have self-reliance. You have almost every advantage coupled I trust with genuine love for God. Do not allow yourself, then, to feed on dreams – daydreams though they be. … It is genius that usually gets to the highest tops – but, what is the secret heart of genius? the ability to work with painstaking self-denial."[9] Ray Baker served President Wilson during the post-war peace talks in Paris and later was hand-picked to write Wilson's official biography. Baker described the relationship and correspondence between father and son as follows: "His father was the greatest figure of his youth – perhaps the greatest of his whole life. The letters between the two can be called nothing but love letters."[10] Sometimes it was "tough love" from the pen of Joseph Wilson, but deep-seated love, nonetheless.

The influence of his father was most obvious when Tommy Wilson took the stage in the form of debate. The Whig Society proved insufficient to satisfy his thirst for intellectual dispute. Wilson decided to start his own literary society which he called the "Liberal Debating Club." The ten-member group met every Saturday night to consider the most prominent political questions of the day. Wilson's skills in this arena were evident to all, including one friend who later recalled rather nostalgically, "mere records cannot produce the appealing tones of his voice and the fire in his eyes as he exercised his remarkable skill in debate. He got as much fun out of it as a great many men now achieve in athletics."[11] Wilson's closest friend in college was Robert Bridges, who later noted:

> We soon found out that he had an eager mind. That is a rare quality among youngsters of eighteen. But there was not a touch of the pedant about him. He was as keen for the life of the college as any one of us; but we soon discovered that what he called 'the play of the mind' was as exhilarating to him as the play of the body to the athlete. … The thing he was most interested in (to which this play of words was accessory) was Government. Now that sounds abstract and dull. To him it meant the evolution of a method by which all kinds of people could live together in the same country and same world. For him it began in our little college world with its coteries.[12]

It was, indeed, during his days in Princeton that Wilson began shifting his aspirations away from the pulpit and into the world of statesmanship, which, of course, also meant politics. And for Wilson, much of his focus was on his preferred form of government – the parliamentary system of England.

Wilson continued to be fascinated by the political leaders and institutions that he believed set the British system of government apart from the rest of the world. He was enamored with Cabinet Government, whereby the nation's Prime Minister and Cabinet were selected from the legislature, providing them a platform to truly drive policies into laws that could immediately have an impact. The democratic pressures for performance remained in that mechanisms were in place such that if sustained dissatisfaction were to materialize, the government could simply be changed. However, while the leaders were in power, their built-in majority support in Parliament enabled them to get stuff done. This compared to the inefficient American system whereby the country could select a President in a nationwide vote but then see the administration's platform stymied by an oppositional Congress. While his fellow Americans were celebrating their 100th birthday as a nation, Wilson pointed out to his fellow citizens how much better things would be if his own country "had England's form of government instead of the miserable delusion of a republic. A republic too founded upon the notion of abstract liberty! I venture to say that this country will never celebrate another centennial as a republic. The English form of government is the only true one."[13] To Wilson, the American system was too often an obstacle to implementing the will of the people, something which the British structure was in a better position to overcome.

Wilson also firmly believed in governmental transparency. For this, he was further enamored by the Brits, who debated any and all topics in the open air of the House of Commons. He viewed this approach favorably when compared to the American Congress, which primarily did its work in committees often behind closed doors. These sentiments came through in Wilson's seminal collegiate work, an 8,500-word essay that was published by the prominent *International Review*. According to the college senior, "Congress is a deliberative body in which there is little real deliberation; a legislature which legislates with no real discussion of its business. Our Government is practically carried on by irresponsible committees."[14] Wilson believed the people were best served when politicians participated in public debates where they could be held accountable for their words and deeds. In his widely read article, the 22-

year-old college student boldly advocated for the adoption of the British system by the United States.

While relentlessly pursuing his own intellectual interests throughout his four years at the College of New Jersey, Wilson also found himself immersed in campus life. Things picked up with the opening of Witherspoon Hall. The brand new 80-room dorm, where Wilson would reside for his last two-and-a-half years in college, had all the modern advantages for its residents, including becoming the first college dormitory with indoor plumbing, including a water closet on every floor. It also housed his closest circle of friends (the Witherspoon Gang), many of whom would remain intimates with Wilson for the rest of his life. Wilson also branched out via on-campus activities. In addition to his literary and debate endeavors, he became the President of the Base Ball Association, Secretary of the Football Association, and a frequent spectator at many campus sporting events. He also took the opportunity to share his ideas with students and faculty via opinion pieces in the *Princetonian*, the student newspaper. Wilson rose to be the paper's chief editorial writer, authoring 40 opinion pieces over his last two years on campus.

II-7: Wilson as a senior at The College of New Jersey, 1879 (age 23)

All of these activities and relationships helped form Wilson's worldview as he prepared to leave the rather sheltered confines of the College of New Jersey. While the school would continue to produce many ministers, Tommy Wilson would not be one of them. His father's preferences aside, Wilson saw his path to service to his society in the secular world of statesmanship. "I remember forming with Charlie Talcott (a class-mate and a very intimate friend of mine) a solemn covenant," Wilson later recalled, "that we would school all our powers and passions for the work of establishing the principles we held in common; that we would acquire knowledge that we might have power;

and that we might have facility in leading others into our ways of thinking and enlisting them in our purposes."[15] The young man who finished in the top third of his class with a 90.3 average and was named a "Model Statesman" upon graduating just had to figure out the right path to achieve his newly cemented career ambitions.

Looking at the resumes of America's political leaders, Wilson found the most common theme to be grounded in the law, so that's what he decided to pursue. "The profession I chose was politics; the profession I entered was law," he wrote. "I entered the one because I thought it would lead to the other. It was once the sure road; and Congress is still full of lawyers."[16] By the latter half of the 19th Century, prospective lawyers had their choice on how to qualify for the Bar. Many still "read the law," essentially acting as an apprentice to a practicing attorney. Increasingly, though, others gravitated to established law schools. Wilson would use both methods, and he would rebrand himself along the way. As Wilson settled into the University of Virginia (UVA) Law School, he decided that the name "Tommy" was "'unsuitable' for a grown man."[17] He soon evolved to signing his name as T. Woodrow Wilson before dropping the 'T' altogether, as he formally adopted his mother's maiden name with the professional-sounding Woodrow Wilson, which he believed "sticks to the mind."[18]

Once again, Wilson became deeply enmeshed in campus activities at UVA in addition to his classroom work. He was prominent in the Jefferson Society, the school's leading literary and debating organization. He also became a member of the chapel choir, the glee club, and president of the Phi Kappa Psi fraternity. He continued to advocate for the British system of government, extolling the virtues of British statesmen such as John Bright and William Gladstone in his various speeches. He also revisited his views on his Southern roots and the Confederate cause. "I yield to no one precedence in love for the South," he announced. "But because I love the South, I rejoice in the failure of the Confederacy." He elaborated in this address that "The perpetuation of slavery would, beyond all question, have wrecked our agricultural and commercial interests, at the same time that it supplied a fruitful source of irritation abroad and agitation within. We cannot conceal from ourselves the fact that slavery was enervating our Southern society and exhausting to Southern energies."[19] This speech caught the attention of *Virginia University Magazine*, which reprinted it in full.

Wilson's focus at UVA was not just on the law and academics. For the first time, Wilson was in love. The situation was complicated if for no other reason than the object of his desires, one Harriet ("Hattie") Wilson, was his first cousin. According to Hattie's daughter years later, Wilson "told her how much he loved her, that he could not live without her, and pleaded with her to marry him right away."[20] She cited the close family connection as her initial reason for declining the entreaty, but Wilson tossed that concern aside. Hattie then told him more directly that she just didn't care for him in that way, which he eventually accepted as he sadly withdrew from the relationship. But it didn't stop his yearning for a romantic connection, finding himself "absolutely hungry for a sweetheart."[21]

Wilson's tenure at the UVA Law School ended rather abruptly after just a year and a half. His health was failing again, and his parents urged him to return home to recuperate. Once there, he decided to stay, opting again to continue his educational pursuits on his own. In this regard, he was successful, regaining his strength and readying himself to take the Bar. Wilson's initial license to practice law would come in the state of Georgia. In 1882, he relocated to Atlanta, where he agreed to open up a law practice with a distant relative by the name of Edward Renick. At the age of 25, Wilson found himself with his first full-time job in the largest city in which he had lived, but his newfound career appeared stillborn. He simply had no clients and failed in his efforts to obtain them. He filled his days reading and occasionally writing but was mostly frustrated at his inactivity. "The Law is indeed a hard taskmaster," Wilson confided to his friend Charlie Talcott. "I am struggling, hopefully but with not overmuch courage, through its intricacies, and am swallowing the vast mass of its technicalities with as good a grace and as straight a face as an offended palate will allow."[22] But while his nascent law career was sputtering, his love life was about to take off.

Wilson had some legal work related to an inheritance his mother was going to split with her late sister's husband, James Bones. Wilson decided to make the short trip to Rome, Georgia, to pursue the matter directly in his uncle's hometown. During one of his visits, Wilson attended services at the local Presbyterian Church, where he was introduced to the daughter of the Reverend Samuel Axson. Twenty-three-year-old Ellen Louise Axson was a gifted artist who had received an excellent education at the Rome Female College. Her artwork had been placed on pause due to family commitments related to her mother's recent death, her father's never-ending illnesses, and her commitment to help raise her siblings. But now she had a new entrant in the competition for her attention, and that was the struggling lawyer from Atlanta. Woodrow Wilson was smitten with Ellen from the very beginning. She fit the bill of precisely the kind of mate he had been seeking.

> I had longed to meet some woman of my own age who had acquired a genuine love for intellectual pursuits without becoming bookish, without losing her feminine charm; who had taken to the best literature from a natural, spontaneous taste for it, and not because she needed to make any artificial additions to her attractiveness; whose mind had been cultivated without being stiffened or made masculine ... and I still thought that 'somewhere in the world must be' at least one woman approaching this ideal.[23]

He quickly became convinced that Ellen Axson was the answer to his dreams.

Wilson pursued the match hard, with a regular drumbeat of letters and visits to Rome. It didn't take long before he shared with his "Ellie Lou" that "You were the only woman I had ever met to whom I felt that I could open all my thoughts." He added that he "had begun to realize that you had an irresistible claim upon all that I had to give, of the treasures of my heart as well as of the stores of my mind. I had never dreamed before of meeting any woman who should with no effort on her part make herself mistress of all the forces of my natures."[24] Ellen did not discourage the pursuit, but neither did she jump into her suitor's arms. She had her hands full at home and wasn't prepared to begin a life on her own. Even Wilson knew the timing wasn't quite right, not yet having established himself in a career that

II-8: Ellen Axson, 1883

would support starting a family. For the time being, the pursuit would continue.

The catalyst for finalizing the match appeared to be a chance meeting at the train station in Asheville, North Carolina. Both happened to have a layover at the station on their way in opposite directions. After spotting each other, they spent the time together pouring out their feelings, ultimately leading to a commitment to marry. Any doubts had long left the psyche of Woodrow Wilson, and now Ellen had fallen completely into line. She shared with her brother Stockton after this chance encounter that she was going to marry "the greatest man in the world."[25]

The happy couple wasn't in a rush to take their vows, as Wilson was still searching for stability in his career before settling down. He decided to give up on the law and his life in the deep South. On May 11, 1883, he wrote to his friend R. Heath Dabney, "I can never be happy unless I am enabled to lead an intellectual life; and who can lead an intellectual life in ignorant Georgia?"[26] For Wilson, it was time to go back to school, telling Dabney:

> You know my passion for original work, you know my love for composition, my keen desire to become a master of philosophical discourse, to become capable and apt in instructing as great a number of persons as possible. My plain necessity, then, is some profession which will afford me a moderate support, favorable conditions for study, and considerable leisure; what better can I be, therefore, than a professor, subjects whose study delights me?[27]

Wilson was heading to Baltimore to seek an advanced degree in political science at Johns Hopkins University.

II-9: Hopkins Hall, Johns Hopkins University, Baltimore, MD

Once again, Wilson pursued his own intellectual development in graduate school. He favored the school's adoption of "The German Method," which embraced "individual scientific investigation in pursuit of the truth, [and] original research for its own sake" at the core of the program.[28] He worked himself to the point of exhaustion, continuing to refine his views on the optimal form of government. His seminal work at Johns Hopkins was an extension of his previous leanings toward the British parliamentary system. In January 1885, he released "Congressional Government," which delved deeply into the actual workings of the U.S. Federal government. Wilson portrayed a system dominated by the legislature and its ability to obstruct a presidential administration that had been placed into office by the national electorate. Wilson continued to portray the American system as inferior to the British alternative, whose Cabinet-centric government ensured both authority and clear accountability for effective leadership on behalf of the citizenry. "Power and strict accountability for its use are the essential constituents of good government,"[29] Wilson wrote, something he found in far greater measure on the other side of the Atlantic. Wilson's book caught people's attention. One review in the Minneapolis *Daily Tribune* called it "the best critical writing on the American constitution which has appeared since the 'Federalist' papers."[30] The book's first run of 1000 copies sold quickly, with similar success in academic settings over the next couple of decades, all of which began to elevate Wilson's standing in his profession.

As Wilson was coming into his own professionally, his thoughts were never far from his fiancée. The couple had an extensive correspondence, with daily letters going in each direction, often exceeding 10-12 pages. They shared their experiences, their thoughts, and mostly, their overwhelming love. "If you could know my heart as I know it," Wilson wrote on one of these occasions, "you would have very few doubts and fears as to the future, pet. No love like mine can be a mistaken love, when it is returned by love like yours."[31] In another, he confided, "I am sometimes absolutely frightened by the intensity of my love for you."[32] After her father passed away, Ellen decided to try her hand again at art,

II-10: Wilson at Johns Hopkins University, 1884 (age 27)

ending up at the Art Students League in New York. While she earned praise for her work and enjoyed the experience, her easel was ready to be put aside as she readied to become Mrs. Ellen Wilson. After Wilson's second year at Johns Hopkins, he was offered a full-time teaching position at Bryn Mawr College in Pennsylvania. With a $1,500 salary now secured, the couple could finally tie the knot. The nuptials took place at Ellen's grandfather's house in Savannah, Georgia. After a seven-week honeymoon of pure bliss in Arden, North Carolina, the newlyweds ventured to their new home just outside Philadelphia.

Bryn Mawr had a close relationship with Johns Hopkins, which had been the genesis of the opportunity for Wilson. At first, the new professor was reluctant to take the offer. Bryn Mawr was an all-female college with a total of 14 faculty for the 40 enrolled students. Wilson didn't hide the fact that he thought teaching women was essentially beneath him. As he informed Ellen, "It goes without saying, my darling, I would a great deal rather teach men anywhere, and especially in the South, than girls at Bryn Mawr or anywhere else."[33] Wilson shared the sentiments of many of his era of "the chilled, scandalized feeling that always comes over me when I see and hear women speak in public"[34] – not an optimal perspective for a professor at an all-girls college. His biases showed as he struggled to gain his footing in the classroom. Instead, he focused on

II-11: The first graduating class at Bryn Mawr College (Professor Wilson is in the back row, far right), 1886

his research and his writing. With Ellen at her home in Georgia for the birth of their first child, Wilson poured himself into his latest treatise. He called it "The State" – a comprehensive depiction of governments across the world. It became a classic textbook for college courses on comparative government, adopted nearly immediately by Harvard, Johns Hopkins, and many other institutions. He also hit a milestone by officially earning his Ph.D. from Johns Hopkins. During his tenure at Bryn Mawr, Wilson continued to give occasional lectures at the Hopkins campus in Baltimore. The university made the path to his degree easy when it waived the traditional requirement for mastery of German, which had been a struggle for Wilson, and further allowed him to submit his prior published work rather than a traditional thesis as the foundation for conferring the Ph.D. All of this progress simply made Wilson restless, anxious to advance his career beyond the women's college to which he was currently attached.

After the publication of "The State," other offers started to arrive. Wilson's firm desire was to return to his alma mater, but the College of New Jersey wasn't quite ready to invite him back. The most attractive offer came from Wesleyan University in Middletown, Connecticut, which he accepted. This was his fifth home in his nine years since graduating from college, but this one would be different. This one housed a family of four, as daughters Margaret and Jessie had come into the world during the first couple of years of the Wilsons' marriage. But just as new life came into his world, one notable life was extinguished. Wilson lost his mother in 1888. He never swerved from the affection he held for the woman who brought him into the world and nurtured him during his youth. "I seem to feel still the touch of her hand, and influence of her wonderful character," he

II-12: The Wesleyan Theological College

later noted. "I thank the sweet steadying God to have had such a mother!"[35]

Wilson continued to hone his classroom skills at Wesleyan while also continuing to write. His primary classes were on the history of England and France since the fall of Rome, along with a course in political economy that focused on the U.S. Constitution. Dr. Wilson shared his belief with his students that the Constitution was "not merely a document written down on paper but is a living and organic thing, which, like all living organisms, grows and adapts itself to the circumstances of its environment."[36] When the topic of the regional conflicts between North and South inevitably arose, Wilson shared with his mostly Northern-based students that "in the matter of secession the South was absolutely right from the point of view of a lawyer, though quite wrong from the point of view of a statesman."[37] As Wilson continued to find his voice in the field of political science, he began accepting invitations to speak at other universities to share his perspective on the optimal forms of government. While he expanded his academic network, he also expanded his family, with the Wilsons' third and final daughter entering the world in October 1889. Eleanor (called Nell) would be the closest of the three for Wilson. All in all, these were happy times, both personally and professionally for Wilson and his entire family. "My own thought turns back with the greatest pleasure to the memories of my two years at Wesleyan," he later recalled. "I have always felt that they were among the happiest years of my life, and certainly if I gave anything in those days, I got a great deal in return from the men by whom I was surrounded and with whom I was associated."[38] That said, Wesleyan was never going to be little more than a stopover in the rise of Dr. Woodrow Wilson.

2. Highs and Lows at Princeton

Wilson's academic sights never wavered from the desire to return to his alma mater in Princeton, New Jersey. The opportunity arose when the College of New Jersey decided to start a school of political science. Needing a leader for the institution, they opted to bring back Wilson, whom the trustees elected to become the chair of Jurisprudence and Political Economy in February 1890, with his highest salary to date at $3,000 per year. It was here that Wilson's career really took off. All his academic wanderings had prepared him to shine in his return to Princeton, both in his research and in the classroom. His mastery of his subject matter, coupled with his brilliant oratorical skills, made his classes the most popular on campus. Scholar Bliss Perry was among those who "admitted without question then in Princeton that Wilson was the most brilliant man among the younger faculty. He led us inevitably by his wit, his incisive questioning mind, his courage, and his preeminence in faculty debates."[39] Wilson became thoroughly enmeshed in campus life across a broad spectrum of activities. In addition to his research and teaching, Wilson coached debate, became a member of the Graduate Advisory Committee, as well as an honorary member of the Cap & Gown, one of the newest eating clubs on campus. He made a number of close friends, including Professor John ("Jack") Hibben, who had been the class valedictorian back in 1882. Hibben and Wilson would see each other regularly, often meeting for tea or other opportunities for personal and professional fellowship. The connection brought Wilson satisfaction on many levels. "I have talked with Jack Hibben and I am refreshed," he was known to say.[40] Ellen referred to Hibben as the one friend her husband "took to his bosom,"[41] almost like an extended member of Wilson's close-knit happy family.

II-13: Professor John ("Jack") Hibben

Wilson continued to work as hard as ever, cranking out more and more papers and books. His latest offering was "Division and Reunion," a history of the

United States from 1829 to 1889. On the topic of slavery, Wilson concluded that the practice was economically wasteful and that the South was better off without it. Nevertheless, his sympathy for the Southern cause continued to be woven into many of his works. The book was another hit for Wilson, being embraced in classrooms across the country. It also opened up even more doors for speaking engagements where his expert oratory and subject matter expertise continued his rise as one of the foremost political scientists in the nation.

This rise came with benefits but also serious costs. On the plus side, the remuneration from his books combined with his salary to enable the Wilsons to build their dream home. The family moved into the seven-bedroom abode in February 1896. The joyous times continued in the Wilson household. Ellen's brother, Stockton, who had recently joined the faculty at Princeton, noted:

> I have sometimes wondered how a family composed of varying and very positive elements ever contrived to live in such absolute and undisturbed harmony as did the Wilson family, and I have come to the conclusion that such a result can be attained only in one way, not by any prescription or plan or domestic 'scheme' of action, but only by enthroning love supreme – that where love is always master, every day and every hour, there must be harmony. In the Wilson household love is always law.[42]

Youngest daughter, Nell, described these Princeton years as "deep happy peace [which] permeated the household. So much laughter and teasing and warm friendliness" were the norm.[43] Throughout this period, Ellen continued to be the center of Wilson's universe, with romantic thoughts continuing to permeate their correspondence. "I am madly in love with you," Wilson wrote to his wife in February 1895. "I live upon your love, – would die if I could not win and hold your admiration: the homage of your mind as well as your heart."[44] But despite all this pleasantness, Woodrow Wilson was struggling with his health. Professor Wilson was not a well man.

Wilson had struggled with his health his entire life, but this was different. Wilson had previously complained on occasion of difficulties holding his pen, but in May 1896, this affliction graduated to pain down his entire arm ending with numbness in his fingers. This was likely the result of the first stroke suffered by Woodrow Wilson, which would certainly not be his last. In this instance, his doctors ordered rest. While Ellen stayed home with the children, Wilson ventured back to his roots, a nine-week vacation through England and Scotland. It was a blissful time to explore the homes, landmarks, and academic stomping grounds of the literary greats throughout the region, many of whom were his intellectual heroes. He spent plenty of time leisurely perusing local towns on his bicycle, following his doctor's orders for real rest and relaxation. The getaway did wonders, as Wilson returned home well-rested and ready to jump back into campus life.

For some, Woodrow Wilson's coming out party was the celebration of his school's 150th anniversary. In October 1896, the College of New Jersey was no more, as the institution officially changed its name to Princeton University. Wilson was front and center providing the keynote address, which he entitled "Princeton in the Nation's Service." It was a lofty, visionary portrayal that went to the heart of the university's true mission according to Professor Wilson. Living up to the oratorical standards set by his father, Wilson proclaimed:

> And in days quiet and troubled alike Princeton has stood for the nation's service, to produce men and patriots. Her national tradition began with John Witherspoon, the master, and James Madison, the pupil, and has not been broken until this day. I do not know what the friends of this sound and tested foundation may have in store to build upon it; but whatever they add shall be added in that spirit, and with that conception of duty. There is no better way to build up learning and increase power. A new age is before us, in which, it would seem, we must lead the world.[45]

II-14: Professor Wilson, Princeton University

That leadership needed to be grounded in both moral convictions and practical considerations. He called Princeton "A place where ideals are kept in heart, in an air they can breathe; but no fool's paradise. A place wherein to learn the truth about the past and hold debate about the affairs of the present, with knowledge and without passion; like the world in having all men's life at heart, a place for men and all that concerns them."[46] As he often did in some of his most memorable addresses, Wilson closed with a calling in the form of a question: "Who shall show us the way to this place?" he asked.[47] Wilson was committed to the sons of Princeton being the answer to this noble cause.

Fully rested from his recent vacation and buoyed by his inspirational address, Wilson plowed his energies back into his teaching and his scholarship. "Division and Reunion" turned out to be just the first installment of Wilson's rendering of American history. After quickly producing a biography of George Washington, he was soon working on what would become his five-volume "History of the American People," which Wilson claimed served multiple purposes. "I wrote the history of the United States in order to learn it,"[48] Wilson said, but it was "not to remember what happened, but to find which way we were going."[49] Embedded in these works, along with Wilson's other many public speeches during this time, he continued to emphasize the criticality of effective leadership in shepherding nations to persevere through difficult times and soar to new heights in the best of times. Being constantly attuned to the needs and perspectives of the citizenry was essential for leadership success. According to Dr. Wilson, "the ear of the leader must ring with the voices of the people." Moreover, "the arguments which induce popular action must always be broad and obvious. … Only a very gross substance of concrete conception can make any impression on the minds of the masses."[50] These entreaties were not simply expressed to mold future leaders from the student body at Princeton but also as a means to refine the kind of leader Wilson fashioned for himself. It was obvious to most at Princeton that Woodrow Wilson was destined for positions of leadership, roles for which he had been auditioning since first arriving on campus as an undergraduate a quarter of a century before. The school was about to put this theory to the test, as it was about to elevate Wilson to his first position of executive responsibility.

Professor Wilson was not alone in his dissatisfaction with current university President Francis Patton. Many had become unsettled with Patton's leadership that had been long on promise but short on delivery. Patton had offered a number of assurances over the years, including a recent commitment to adding a law school to the institution that was of particular interest to Wilson. But fundraising was lagging, and there seemed little momentum to fulfilling this and other promises. Moreover, there was discontent among some that Princeton itself had started to wane. The school had developed into a playground for the social elites and wealthy alums who sent their boys to enjoy the last years of their youths rather than dedicate themselves to rigorous study and intellectual pursuits. As Stockton Axson put it, "Gentlemen, whether we like it or not, we shall have to recognize that Princeton is a rich man's college and that rich men frequently do not come to college to study."[51] Such a reality was anathema to Woodrow Wilson and increasingly to other leaders on campus as well. By 1902, the faculty and Board of Trustees had had enough of Patton's tenure, so they offered him a generous package to simply go away. The obvious replacement to most was sitting there amongst the faculty, but it would require a break in tradition to elevate this candidate to the top spot on campus.

Woodrow Wilson had certainly earned the respect and admiration of those entrusted with this decision. He had been enormously productive in his scholarship, cranking out nine books and 35 articles over the past decade, many of which were embraced as new standard offerings on campuses across the country. His famed oratory, which had been similarly welcomed at institutions throughout the nation, had brought distinction to the Princeton brand. To elevate Wilson to the Princeton presidency, though, would require a change. Over the past 150 years, all 12 of Princeton's presidents had been ordained ministers. When the Board of Trustees met to name Patton's successor, none seemed concerned about deviating from this particular tradition. In fact, Wilson was the only candidate considered, receiving the unanimous vote of the Board on the first and only vote. "I never saw so many men of many minds unite to promptly, without debate, without hesitation at the mere mention of a name," recalled S. Bayard Dod.[52] As the delegation arrived at the Wilson home to inform him of the selection, Wilson and Ellen took a moment to share the news with Wilson's nearly 80-year-old father, Joseph, who had recently moved in with the family. The excitement engendered in the former preacher was palpable. "Never forget what I tell you," Joseph Wilson crowed to his granddaughters, "your father is the greatest man I have ever known. … *I* know what I'm talking about. This is only the beginning of a great career."[53]

II-15: Wilson when he became President of Princeton University, 1902 (age 45)

Wilson's elevation to the Princeton presidency was met with cheers by faculty, students, and alums. The four-time most popular professor on campus was now entrusted to lead the university into the 20th Century. His speech at the 150th anniversary had set the table, and now it was time to deliver. He used his inaugural address in October 1902 to lay out his vision, which would require significant reforms to realize the benefits he envisioned. Frankly, in Wilson's eyes, Princeton was failing to live up to its potential, which had implications not just for the university but for the nation as a whole. According to their new president, the university

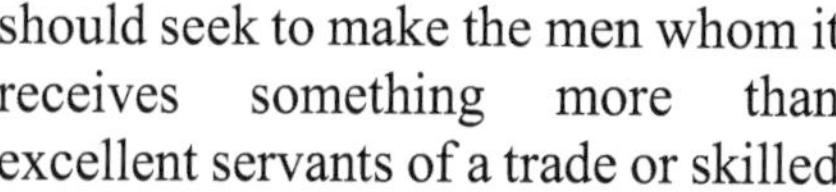

> should seek to make the men whom it receives something more than excellent servants of a trade or skilled practitioners of a profession. It should give them elasticity of faculty and breadth of vision, so that they shall have a surplus of mind to expend, not upon their profession only, for its liberalization and enlargement, but also upon the broader interests which lie about them, in the sphere in which they are to be, not breadwinners merely, but citizens as well, and in their own hearts, where they are to grow to the stature of real nobility.[54]

He forecasted an inclusive environment that was mutually supportive of achieving his vision. Seeing the proposed graduate school, for example, not just as "a body of teachers and students but also a college of residence, where men shall live together in the close and wholesome comradeships of learning." Wilson advocated escaping "the pedantry and narrowness of the old fixed curriculum" and courting "men who care more for principles than for money, for the right adjustments of life than for the gross accumulations of profit." In simple summary, President Wilson proclaimed to his fellow Princetonians, "We must lead the world."[55] And if they would be willing to follow, he would guide them all to the promised land.

The presidency of Princeton came with some immediate perks. The Wilsons sold their home and moved into Prospect, the on-campus estate provided free of charge to the leader of the institution. This benefit, when coupled with his $8,000 salary, put the Wilsons into a truly comfortable economic condition for the first time in their lives. Prospect was large enough for the entire family, which expanded beyond the five Wilsons to include the aging Joseph Wilson as well as Ellen's brother, Stockton – the university professor. Wilson's father did not make life easy for Ellen and her running of the household. The preacher was now an invalid, and a demanding one at that. "He seems to suffer constantly," Ellen shared with her cousin, "and when coming out from his stupors moans and cries – even screams, – for hours. ... It is simply harrowing."[56] The suffering continued for several months before Joseph Wilson finally succumbed to his maladies in January 1903. Wilson mourned the loss for weeks, no longer able to consult with the man who had been his role model in many ways and the greatest influence in his entire existence.

II-16: Prospect, the home for Princeton's Presidents

Woodrow Wilson was ready to begin molding Princeton in his own image from the very outset of his tenure as university president. At his first meeting with the Board of Trustees, he recommended changes to the Princeton curriculum. Wilson believed the student body would be better served by a standard form of study applied to all undergraduates in their first two years on campus, to be followed by a focus on a major course of study and electives in their latter two years. Wilson's approach was not only embraced at Princeton but also adopted as the preferred model at institutions of higher learning throughout the country.

But Wilson believed it wasn't just the content of instruction that needed refinement at Princeton, but also the manner in which these subject matters were delivered. Students were too detached from the purveyors of knowledge in the current classroom setting, so he proposed a variation of the English tutorial system. Wilson called for students to meet in small groups with a preceptor who would engage these gatherings with spirited discussions and debate. It was an opportunity to delve deeply into subjects, far beyond what could be obtained in a large lecture hall with professors who were too busy to provide this attention to detail to the average student. Wilson believed this kind of environment would make for real learning, with applications beyond the words in a textbook. To make this work, Wilson proposed hiring 50 preceptors at a respectable $2,000 per year. He intended to retain them for no more than five years to keep their insights fresh and enthusiasm for the role intact. The Trustees were quick to embrace the concept, which would revolutionize the mode of instruction at college campuses across the nation for the next century and beyond.

Finally, Wilson hit hard the notion that the country club atmosphere that had enveloped Princeton needed to come to an end. He immediately moved to strengthen academic standards, along with the honor code, while frankly putting students on notice. He aimed to "transform thoughtless boys performing tasks into thinking men." For those students who failed to rise to the occasion, he simply stated, "We shall have the pain of parting company with you."[57] He would persist in leading by example, modeling his own standards in the classroom as he continued to teach while pursuing reforms from the seat of the presidency.

Wilson seemed to operate at full speed at all times, embracing every challenge as an opportunity to lead Princeton to its ultimate potential. Such efforts were often more than his frail body could endure. Wilson's ability to overcome his exhaustion with brute force came to a screeching halt in May 1906 when he suddenly lost vision in his left eye. Given his prior history of pain in his arm and numbness in his fingers, the medical specialists to whom he entrusted his care diagnosed another likely stroke.

They warned him of the need to take better care of himself as "50-year-old arteries do not go back to an earlier condition." Dr. Alfred Stengel observed that "You have doubtless done too much in the last few years," with a warning that his current symptoms "simply indicate that excess of work is dangerous."[58] An extended period of complete rest was essential if he expected anything close to a full recovery.

Wilson listened to the professionals. His solution was a family vacation to Europe, the first time the girls were old enough for a meaningful trip. Their primary destination was Rydal in the northern part of England, not far from Scotland. The leisurely pace did Wilson wonders, as the entire family enjoyed lots of walks, bike rides, and quiet family time. The antidote served its patient well, as after three months Wilson informed Cleveland Dodge that "I feel richer for the summer, not only in health but also in thought and in ability to be of service." He was refreshed and ready to get back to work to pursue his newest plans for reform. "A year such as I have planned," he informed Dodge, "ought to set all sorts of processes in order, and that without undue strain on me."[59] Based on the topics he chose to pursue, this would be easier said than done.

Two topics would dominate the last three years of Wilson's tenure as president of Princeton – his quadrangle plan for undergraduate living and engagement, and his approach to the school's long-envisioned graduate school. In terms of the former, over the years Wilson had become increasingly concerned about the caste system which had developed across the student population. The focal point for this inequity lay in the easting clubs on campus. With fraternities and secret societies banned from the Princeton campus, eating clubs popped up as places not only to share meals but also as social gathering spots for those fortunate to be invited to join. That was the rub, according to Wilson. These clubs had evolved into the central point of the entire Princeton experience. However, since family background had become one of the most prominent criteria for admission, the clubs found themselves completely out of reach for at least a third of the campus that didn't hail from the upper crust of society. Moreover, the playful and lackadaisical atmosphere of the eating clubs permeated Princeton, where the enjoyment of the college experience far exceeded student desires to excel in the classroom. "For a great majority of them," Wilson asserted, "residence here meant a happy life of comradeship and sport interrupted by the grind of perfunctory lessons and examinations, to which they attended rather because of the fear of being cut off from the life than because they were seriously engaged in getting the training which would fit their faculties and their spirits for the tasks of the world which they knew they must face after their happy freedom was over."[60] This was not the purpose of a great institution such as Princeton.

While President Wilson acknowledged many of the benefits that students and alums saw emanating from the clubs, he also saw them as undemocratic and serving as both an unhealthy divide and a distraction in the overall campus experience. "My own ideals for the University," Wilson proclaimed, "are those of genuine democracy and serious scholarship. The two, indeed, seem to me to go together. Any organization which introduced elements of social exclusiveness constitutes the worst possible soil for serious intellectual endeavour."[61] For Woodrow Wilson, this was a call to action, and a time for significant change.

Wilson's solution to these insidious challenges was a system of residential quadrangles, where students would not only eat together but also live together, a pure democratic mixture that blended the entire student body into small, egalitarian, and supportive groups. The quads would consist of a dorm, an eating hall, classrooms, and even facilities to offer unmarried faculty the opportunity to live in close proximity to students. These communities would intermix during their leisure hours to expand the educational experience. According to Wilson, "the very best effects of university life are wrought between six and nine o'clock in the evenings, when the professor has gone home, and minds meet minds, and a generating process takes place."[62] His quadrangle plan would at once break down the class divisions that had permeated the institution by way of the eating clubs while also enhancing the opportunity to learn from their colleagues in a mutually supportive environment. While the Board initially balked at the price tag associated with this transformative plan, it generally offered broad support for the concept – at least initially.

As the plan to break down the eating clubs and replace them with Wilson's egalitarian quadrangles became public, resistance mounted quickly. Many students, faculty, and especially alums were deeply invested in the eating clubs, which for many represented their fondest memories of their time on campus. Objections poured into the Board from across the country, including from donors who were threatening to close their checkbooks to Princeton. Woodrow Wilson heard the complaints, but they did nothing to dissuade him from what he saw as a righteous crusade. The fact that social status was front and center of the debate propelled him to fight all the more. To one group, Wilson maintained, "these people are not fighting me out of reason; they are fighting on the basis of their privilege, and privilege never yields."[63] To another, he remarked frankly, "Princeton is exactly what they say of it: a fine country club, where many of the alumni make snobs of their boys."[64] He was determined to put an end to the destructive status quo, but his opposition was equally committed to preserving it.

Some of the most prominent people on campus were antagonistic toward Wilson's vision. This included Andrew West, the gregarious dean of the yet-to-be-constructed graduate school, and his close friend, Grover Cleveland. The nation's 22nd and 24th President had retired to the Princeton community shortly after his second term ended in 1897. He became a regular presence on and around campus and eventually accepted a seat on the Board of Trustees. Cleveland and West joined Moses Pyne, a longtime friend of Wilson's, gearing up to vote against the president's proposal. But the one opponent who really got under Wilson's skin was his closest friend in the world, Professor Jack Hibben.

II-17: Andrew West, Dean of the Princeton Graduate School

II-18: Former President Grover Cleveland, 1904

Try as he might, Wilson was unable to bring Hibben over to his way of thinking on this topic. When Hibben voted against his plan, Wilson saw it as the ultimate act of disloyalty. When the Board formally rejected the quadrangle plan in October 1907, Wilson lost on many levels. His innovation was thwarted, his seeming invincibility as Princeton's sole leader was fractured, and his dearest friendship was shattered. And the battles for control of Princeton University were just beginning.

It should be noted that while Woodrow Wilson sought to democratize the Princeton campus, it was still, in his mind, a place solely for White men. Blacks had been welcomed in small numbers at a handful of U.S. universities by the turn of the 20th Century, including Harvard, Yale, Dartmouth, and Oberlin, but this source of equal access to education would gain no traction in Woodrow Wilson's Princeton. During the debate about the eating clubs and quadrangles, Wilson was asked about incorporating young Black men into this ecosystem. He responded with disfavor. "While there is nothing in the law of the University to prevent a negro's entering," President Wilson stated, "the whole temper and tradition of the place are such that no negro has ever applied for admission, and it seems extremely unlikely that the question will ever assume a practical form."[65] Given the clear message that Blacks were not welcome at Princeton, there was certainly no reason to waste time trying to apply. It would be another four decades before Joseph Moss would become the first Black undergrad admitted to Princeton University.

Knowing his health was fragile, Wilson had gotten better at building periods of relaxation into his otherwise taxing schedule. When he partially lost feeling in his right arm in November 1907, it was clearly time for another break. For this, he ventured to the island of Bermuda, his second visit in as many years. Ellen passed on this trip, but Wilson was hardly alone during his stay. On his previous visit, Wilson had been introduced to Mary Peck, a cultured woman who spent extended stays on the island without her second husband. She often opened her home to the most noteworthy dignitaries to come to Bermuda, and the President of Princeton University fit that bill. When Wilson returned in 1908, he re-engaged with Peck, in what turned into a budding relationship. Wilson found he could tell Peck anything, and she was always there to offer intelligent repartee and unflinching support. Their communications

II-19: Mary Peck and Wilson, Bermuda

continued in the form of lengthy letters that would flow long after Wilson returned home to Princeton.

Wilson shared with Ellen that his newfound friend was "very fine. You must know her for I know that you would like her." But it doesn't appear that Ellen was all that comfortable with her husband's new relationship. While her letter of response is lost to history, Wilson made it a point in his follow-up to emphasize that the situation was "thoroughly wholesome."[66] This debate would come up again as Wilson persisted in corresponding with Peck. While the majority of Peck's letters have been destroyed, many of his were saved and reveal an extremely intimate connection. Many of his more than 200 letters, often delivered at least once a week over the course of several years, began with "Dearest Friend" and closed with "infinite tenderness."[67] A sampling of Wilson's letters to Mrs. Peck included the following references:

> Beauty, charm, companionship, sympathy, quick comprehension and largess of affection will always be the chief and most perfect thing that Bermuda stands for in my thought.
>
> My dear Mary, you are the dearest chum, the most rewarding companion and confidant, the frankest, dearest, most engaging playmate – the smartest woman compact of many charms.
>
> God was very good to me to send me such a friend, so perfectly satisfying and delightful, so delectable.
>
> You are the wonderful lady I knew the moment I looked into your beautiful eyes, and some of the best powers of my life I take from you. I found in my friend … the loving power of a

> great woman, a fearless natural integrity – purity without prudery, rectitude and sincerity without convention, perfect wholesomeness and genuineness, as of a nature without morbidness.[68]

Mrs. Peck shared similar sentiments of attraction to her new pen pal.

> You are an adorable person – and I count it the greatest honor and happiness and privilege of my life that you call me friend. … I miss you horribly – woefully.
>
> You are more wonderful to me every day, so wonderful as to seem not quite human.[69]

After about a year of this back-and-forth, Ellen seems to have grown suspicious. It appears she challenged her husband on the true nature of the relationship with Mary Peck while he was off on another trip, implying he had entered into a bond based on "emotional love" if not a physical connection. Wilson refuted the charge in his attempt to set the record straight.

> You have only to believe in and trust me, darling, and all will come right, what you do not understand included. I know my heart now, if I ever did, and it belongs to you. God give you the gracious strength to be patient with me!
>
> 'Emotional love,'-ah, dearest, that was a cutting and cruel judgment and utterly false; but as natural as false; but I never blamed you for it or wondered at it. I only understood – only saw the thing as you see it and as it is not, and suffered, – am suffering still, ah, how deeply!-but with access of love, constant access of love. My darling! I have never been worthy of you, but I love you with all my poor, mixed, inexplicable nature, with everything fine and tender in me.[70]

Wilson's approach to the situation was to actually bring Peck closer to the family rather than push her further away. Not only would the correspondence continue, but so would visits to each other's homes in the States. These encounters often included Ellen, and even the girls, as Wilson sought to position Peck as the endearing friend of the entire family. Wilson's political enemies would later mount a whisper campaign about Mary Peck, and rumors of an affair became frequent in these circles. But despite many efforts to uncover a physical relationship between the two, no evidence has surfaced to support such a claim. Mary

Peck had become (and would remain for many years) an intimate emotional outlet for Woodrow Wilson, perhaps filling a void in his everyday existence. Ellen seemed to eventually accept this reality, as ongoing objections from her are nowhere to be found. Anything untoward beyond the cozy language which dominates their correspondence is merely speculation.

Perhaps Wilson needed the Mary Peck outlet because things at Princeton were not going his way. Many of the same forces that lined up to defeat his quadrangle plan were now coming forward to oppose his next innovation. Princeton had already committed to building a first-class graduate school. Before ground was even broken, Professor Andrew West was named to spearhead the effort and had spent the past couple of years doing extensive research across the great graduate schools of Europe, as well as conducting broad outreach across Princeton's alumni network. West was determined to locate the graduate school away from the main campus to provide separation for the advanced studies expected to take place, ideally without distraction from the undergraduate cohort. According to West, "Without this much separation … the proper life of the Graduate College cannot be successfully developed."[71] West's ideas were anathema to President Wilson, who wouldn't be moved off his plans to fully integrate all communities from across the institution. As such, Wilson felt the only place to build the graduate school was right in the middle of campus, "not apart, but as nearly as may be at the very heart, the geographical heart, of the university; and its comradeship shall be for young men and old, for the novice as well as for the graduate."[72] Once again, Board members, faculty, and alumni were forced to choose sides in what Wilson believed was a fight for the heart and soul of the institution.

West had powerful allies on his side, including former President Cleveland. He also brought donors to the table, as the university sorely needed hefty donations if it were to realize any of the grand innovations that were being touted by Wilson and the Board. The momentum seemed to shift in 1908 when William Procter, the president of Procter and Gamble who had dropped out of Princeton as a senior in 1883, offered a gift of $500,000 to help build the graduate school, but only in a location approved by Dean West. Wilson refused to be bought, decrying the notion that outside moneyed interests could dictate university policy. Wilson answered the challenge by stating, "I cannot accede to the acceptance of gifts upon terms which take the educational policy of the University out of the hands of the Trustees and Faculty and permit it to be determined by those who give money."[73] Some shared Wilson's view, but many did not. They realized that donations like Procter's didn't come along very often, and the insistence on West's location didn't seem unreasonable for such a generous contribution. At the Board meeting in October 1909, Procter's offer was accepted by a vote of 14-10, despite Wilson's vocal opposition.

Wilson had accepted his earlier defeat over his quadrangle plan, but he was unwilling to let this decision go without further debate. He took his arguments on the road, speaking at numerous alumni events across the country. Moreover, the conflict was no longer limited to the Princetonian world, as the press took the story in a direction that had broader implications for the entire country. The fight had become one of democracy vs. privilege, with Wilson pulling out all the stops to make his case for the principles upon which he believed the university must stand. At a forum in Pittsburgh, Pennsylvania, in April 1910, Wilson asked:

II-20: Wilson, circa 1908 (age ~51)

> Will America tolerate the seclusion of graduate students? Will America tolerate the idea of having graduate students set apart? America will tolerate nothing except unpatronized endeavor. Seclude a man, separate him from the rough and tumble of college life, from all the contacts of every sort and condition of men, and you have done a thing which America will brand with its contemptuous disapproval.[74]

The issue was also becoming a referendum on Wilson's leadership and his standing in the Princeton community. He remarked at a speech in New Hampshire that, "So far as the colleges go, the sideshows have swallowed up the circus, and we don't know what is going on in the main tent and I don't know that I want to continue as ringmaster under those conditions. … Schools like this one and universities like Princeton must pass out of existence unless they adapt themselves to modern life."[75] Wilson's continuation in his current capacity was beginning to hang in the balance of this decision on the location of the graduate school.

In the end, money spoke louder than ideals in this fight between democracy and privilege. On May 18, 1910, Isaac Wyman passed away. The 1848 graduate of Princeton, whose father had fought in the Battle of Princeton in the Revolutionary War, bequeathed nearly $10 million to the university. The executor who would decide how the money would be spent was none other than Dean Andrew West, who had been courting Wyman for months. While the overall donation would ultimately come in at a much smaller number, the gift was enough to swing nearly all the decision makers into West's camp. When he heard the news of the bequest, Wilson knew the game was up. As he told Ellen, "We can beat the living, but we cannot fight the dead."[76] Wilson swallowed his pride, congratulated West on obtaining the gift, and offered his full support. But the ordeal, on top of earlier conflicts, had thrust a wedge into the relationship between the school and its president that was increasingly beyond repair. Fortunately for Wilson, an attractive alternative was presenting itself at just the right time. The professor was finally turning to politics.

3. Rapid Political Rise

A few years earlier, in February 1906, Woodrow Wilson had been the guest of honor at a gathering at the Lotos Club in New York. He was introduced as follows: "There are men whom we admire not because they have accumulated great fortunes, but because they have thought great thoughts."[77] After Wilson's remarks, Colonel George Harvey took the stage. Harvey had made a fortune in the light-rail business and now ran a handful of national publications, including the widely-read *Harper's Weekly*. Harvey closed the festivities with the following prognostication: "As one of a considerable number of Democrats who have become tired of voting Republican tickets, it is with a sense almost of rapture that I contemplate even the remotest possibility of casting a ballot for the president of Princeton University to become President of the United States."[78] Four years later, as Wilson was struggling to maintain his hold on the Princeton campus, Harvey decided to try to fulfill his prior wish. He was ready to lead the Democratic Party to the mantle of Woodrow Wilson, first for governor of New Jersey, and if that went well, then all the way to the White House.

II-21: George Harvey

By January 1910, Harvey was ready to move forward with launching the political career of Woodrow Wilson. He started his play as kingmaker by courting some of the leading political operatives in New Jersey. These were the bosses that essentially ran the political engines that found candidates, offered them full support, and then expected favors in return. This was the seedier side of American politics and something Wilson had historically derided. Nevertheless, he was about to find himself in the crosshairs of the machine with a tantalizing opportunity to leave his misery at Princeton behind and take his rightful place as the leading statesman of his state, and potentially for his entire country. Harvey's

II-22: James Smith, Jr.

prime target was James Smith, Jr., a former U.S. Senator who had become the man behind the curtain for Democrats across the state of New Jersey. Smith was intrigued by Harvey's enthusiasm, seeing Wilson as the kind of serious fresh face that might break through and get his party back into the Governor's seat. He also thought that as a political neophyte, Wilson would be easy to manipulate once in office. He gave Harvey the green light to proceed.

Two months later, on March 17, Harvey and his wife were the Wilsons' guests for dinner at Prospect. After the meal, the men excused themselves to talk politics in Wilson's library. Harvey put his cards on the table: "If I can handle the matter so that the nomination for governor shall be tendered to you on a silver platter, without you turning a hand to obtain it, and without any requirement or suggestion of any pledge whatsoever, what do you think would be your attitude?"[79] After a brief pause to consider the specific request, Wilson gave an encouraging response: "I should regard it as my duty to give the matter very serious consideration."[80] This was, in fact, Wilson's desire all along, to use his legal and academic bona fides as the foundation for his transition to political statesman. That he would be willing to get into bed with Harvey and Smith was an odd combination, but one Wilson believed he could manage as perhaps a necessary evil to get to where he wanted to go.

Harvey and Smith encouraged Wilson to get out on the road and make speeches across the state. Woodrow Wilson was hardly a household name beyond the academic community, and they wanted to gauge his ability to bond with the people via his personality and his policies. All of Wilson's oratorical training was immediately evident as he connected with his audiences with substantive addresses on the topics which he believed would make a difference for the state. Wilson had emerged as a progressive, signing on to the philosophy where government engagement was needed to provide a fair opportunity for all citizens. This meant laws and regulations that would curtail the excesses of management and industry while providing more rights and opportunities for all classes of labor. One of Wilson's most direct appeals came during a speech on the economy to the New York State Bankers Association. With the nation's leading bankers, including the powerful J.P. Morgan, in attendance at the Waldorf Astoria, Wilson essentially lectured these leading financiers with lines such as, "The basis of banking, like the basis of the rest of life, is moral in its character, not financial."[81] There had been an erosion of trust between the people and the bankers, and such a condition was hurting the country and needed to be rectified. After he laid out his policies consistent with this perspective, the audience offered a rousing round of applause. Morgan himself welcomed Wilson back to the head table with a firm handshake – a key sign that was not lost on the budding crop of Wilson supporters.

Wilson's worlds were now going in opposite directions. Princeton was pure misery as he experienced nothing but setbacks in the pursuit of his egalitarian plans for the graduate school, while the magnet of politics was increasingly attractive. The greatest curiosity was how sincere Wilson was in his flirtation with the Democratic bosses. Would he really get in bed with these "politicians" in order to advance his own agenda? The topic continued to come up, and Wilson originally offered conflicting perspectives. On July 12, Wilson addressed a group of New Jersey's political class at the Lawyers' Club in New York. He was asked point blank whether or not he would embrace the input from the leaders of the Democratic Party in the state. "I have always been a believer in party organizations," Wilson said. "If I were elected Governor I should be very glad to consult with the leaders of the Democratic Organization. I should refuse to listen to no man, but I should be especially glad to hear and duly consider the suggestions of my party."[82] But Wilson placed conditions on such a relationship, as articulated in a smaller gathering of party leaders. While he would be open to listening to party input, he would be beholden to no man or organization. According to Wilson, the people:

> … will have confidence in me because they will believe that I am free of the political entanglements which have brought distress to New Jersey, because they are tired of political bargain and sale, because they want their government delivered back into their hands. They want a government pledged to nobody but themselves. Now, don't you see, gentlemen, … I

> must be what the people think I am. I must be free to consider nothing but their interests. There must be no strings tied to your proposal. I cannot consider it an obligation of returned personal favours to any individual.[83]

At this point, all sides were hearing what they wanted to hear. If they could just win the office, then everything would work itself out. Or would it?

The Democrats gathered at the Taylor Opera House in Trenton on September 15, 1910, to choose their nominee for governor. While many in attendance had heard of Wilson or perhaps read some of his speeches, very few had actually met the university president. That hardly mattered. The nomination was in the hands of the bosses – George Harvey, James Smith, and their colleagues – and their adherents were happy to do their bidding. Wilson received 749 votes on the first ballot, more than twice that of the runner-up, and a clear majority to become the Democratic nominee. Wilson did not attend the convention, but he was monitoring the results from his home, which happened to be just a few miles from the Democratic gathering. Once the vote was complete, chairman John Hardin informed his colleagues that "We have just received word that Mr. Wilson, the candidate for the governorship, and the next President of the United States, has received word of his nomination; has left Princeton, and is now on his way to the Convention."[84] The pre-arranged but previously secret move to have Wilson address the crowd was greeted with thunderous applause. And the candidate didn't disappoint. After making a grand entrance, Wilson got down to business. He offered his humble gratitude, and then reinforced the notion that there were no strings attached to his nomination.

> I did not seek this nomination. I have made no pledge and have given no promise. Still more, not only was no promise asked, but as far as I know, none was desired. If elected, as I expect to be, I am left absolutely free to serve you with all singleness of purpose. It is a new era when these things can be said, and in connection with this I feel that the dominant idea of the moment is the responsibility of deserving. I will have to serve the state very well in order to deserve the honor of being at its head.[85]

This was a breath of fresh air for the many in the crowd who could easily have assumed that Wilson had been bought and paid for by the political machines. Wilson appreciated the support of the bosses on the path to the nomination, but he would be obligated to no one, and wanted that clear from the start.

Wilson kept his acceptance speech at a high level but didn't shy away from painting his remarks with broad brushstrokes of progressive-laden patriotism. "When I think of the flag which our ships carry," Wilson concluded while pointing to the flag which hung above the speakers in the hall, "the only touch of colour about them, the only thing that moves as if it had a settled spirit in it in their solid structure, it seems to me I see alternate strips of parchment upon which are written the rights of liberty and justice and strips of blood spilled to vindicate those rights and then – in the corner – a prediction of the blue serene into which every nation may swim which stands for these great things."[86] The crowd was mesmerized. There was something new that this academic was thrusting into the political arena. The way he spoke, the words he used, and the policies he stood for energized and unified the base at once. Among those in the hall that day was Joseph Tumulty, a political operative who had been supporting state senator George Silzer for the gubernatorial nomination. Tumulty was riveted by Wilson. "Attempting none of the cheap 'plays' of the old campaign orator," Tumulty recalled, "he impressively proceeded with his thrilling speech, carrying his audience with him under the spell of his eloquent words. How tense the moment! His words, spoken in tones so soft, so fine, in voice so well modulated, so heart-stirring. Only a few sentences are uttered and our souls are stirred to their very depths. It was not only what he said, but the simple heart-stirring way in which he said it."[87] This was something Tumulty wanted to be a part of.

Wilson, of course, still had his day job to worry about. In fact, the day after receiving the Democratic nomination, Wilson opened the school year for Princeton. But everyone knew the end was near. The move toward divorce had been mounting, and now with the nomination in hand, both sides knew it was time to separate. Wilson initiated the break at his first real opportunity. The next meeting of the Board of Trustees was just a couple of weeks away. When the meeting opened, Wilson asked for regular business to be suspended so he could formally submit his resignation. Within minutes, according to trustee Wilson Farrand, he then "picked up his hat and coat, and while we all stood in silence, passed from the room and from his connection with Princeton."[88] Wilson's tenure leading his alma mater certainly had its high points, but the disappointments overshadowed the successes. Wilson's fervent pursuit on behalf of democracy over privilege primarily failed. He was fortunate that an alternative became available when it did, as it was unclear how much longer Wilson could persist at Princeton. Now, everyone could hold their heads high as the divorce was executed.

In the race for governor, Wilson was up against Republican Vivian Lewis, who had held various political posts for the past dozen years. Wilson dominated the campaign as he continued to advocate for progressive ideals while continuing to distance himself from the political bosses. He gave 50 speeches over the course of six weeks, traveling to all 21 counties across the state. Wilson's major themes were progressive classics, such as regulating corporations, preventing election fraud, controlling public utilities, and protecting workers from on-the-job injuries. He had fought wealth and privilege at Princeton and was now offering his hand to do the same for New Jersey. Wilson also knew that his name was already in the mix for the Democratic nomination for President in 1912, so he didn't shy from broader themes when stumping for governor. "America ... is not a piece of the surface of the earth," he told an audience in Atlantic City. "America is not merely a body of towns. America is an idea, America is an ideal, America is a vision."[89] The people liked what they heard.

II-23: Wilson running for Governor of New Jersey, 1910 (age 53)

This was still a period of transition for Wilson. While he went with his instincts on how to make the pivot from academic to statesman, he also knew he had a lot to learn. Joe Tumulty would become not only his primary support staff but also his political tutor. While Wilson often shunned those who disagreed with him or pointed out his errors, he encouraged just that kind of engagement by Tumulty when deciding to bring him into the campaign. The following early encounter was captured by Tumulty and characterized the essence of their professional relationship.

> 'Doctor, do you really desire an honest opinion of that speech? I really want to serve you but I can do so only by speaking frankly.'
>
> Wilson replied: 'That is what I most desire.'
>
> 'Well,' I said, 'your speech was most disappointing.' I stopped suddenly, feeling that I had done enough damage to the Professor's feelings.
>
> But he urged: 'Please tell me what your criticism is. What I most need is honesty and frankness. You cannot hurt my feelings by truthfully expressing your opinion. Don't forget that I am an amateur at this game and need advice and guidance.'[90]

Such was the beginning of an 11-year relationship where Joe Tumulty was one of the few people Wilson expected to speak his mind, and appreciated it when he did. As for Tumulty, he was a politically-savvy workaholic who was bound to do whatever he could to get Woodrow Wilson elected as the Governor of New Jersey (and beyond).

The only real question about Wilson's candidacy was his relationship with the old guard political bosses, particularly James Smith and one of his closest colleagues James Nugent. The question was formally raised by George Record, a veteran of Republican politics in the state who challenged Wilson with 19 specific questions, mostly related to the influence of the party and the machines on politics in the state in general, and with Wilson in particular. This was the moment of truth for Woodrow Wilson, and he did not disappoint. Record bluntly asked: "Do you admit that the boss system exists as I have described it? … If so, how do you propose to abolish it?" Wilson did not equivocate in his response. "Of course I admit it," wrote Wilson. "Its existence is notorious. I have made it my business for many years to observe and understand that system, and I hate it as thoroughly as I understand it."[91] Wilson went even further, answering beyond Record's specific questions, to leave no doubt about where he stood.

> If elected, I shall not, either in the matter of appointments to office or assent to legislation, or in shaping any part of the policy of my administration, submit to the dictation of any person or persons, special interest or organization. I should deem myself forever disgraced should I in even the slightest degree cooperate in any such system or any such transactions as you describe in your characterization of the 'boss' system.[92]

Record and many of his progressive-leaning Republican colleagues liked what they heard. Surprisingly, Smith, Nugent, and the other bosses didn't seem concerned. Their only comment was that Wilson's response was "a great campaign play."[93] That's because they were career political operatives who often said one thing but meant another. Little did they know how wrongly they were judging the man they were aggressively supporting.

The voters of New Jersey overwhelmingly approved of the first-time politician from the Princeton campus, handing him a landslide victory at the polls. Wilson won by more than 11%, and he had some coattails as the Democrats picked up four seats in each of the two houses of the state legislature. But Wilson had little time to revel in his victory because the machine came calling shortly after the votes were counted and was ready to accept payment for handing Wilson this opportunity in the first place. At the outset of the campaign, James Smith had told Wilson that he had no interest in returning to the U.S. Senate. Now, though, he had changed his mind and expected Wilson's support when the legislature would meet the following month to select the state's next senator. The inevitable clash that had been brewing beneath

II-24: The Wilson Family (circa 1911)
(L to R): Margaret, Ellen, Jessie, Nell, and Gov. Wilson

the surface throughout the campaign immediately came to the fore. Wilson said 'no.' States had recently begun experimenting with new election procedures, following the lead of the progressives to put more power into the hands of the people, specifically through primary elections. In the state of New Jersey, a primary had recently been held in which little-known James Martine had captured the vote of the people for the Democratic nomination for the U.S. Senate. The political bosses, like Smith, felt these primaries were merely advisory, and the state legislature still had the freedom to essentially pick whoever it wanted. Wilson disagreed, and was ready to put his foot down on the topic even before taking his oath of office.

Colonel Harvey joined many who implored Wilson to play the game. If he just let Smith have his way, then that would guarantee support for the governor in the Democratic-controlled legislature. This is how coalitions are formed in order to get things done. But Wilson was unmoved. He told Harvey that Smith's "election would be intolerable to the very people who elected me and gave us a majority in the legislature." If Smith was put forward as a candidate, Wilson would have no choice: "I would have to fight him; and there is nothing I would more sincerely deplore. It would offend every instinct in me, except the instinct as to what was right and necessary from the point of view of the public."[94] As word of the conflict spread, sides were clearly drawn. Some saw Wilson as ungrateful and not a team player, while others saw a principled newcomer trying to do what was right on behalf of the citizenry as a whole. This was going to be an ugly fight that could have significant ramifications for Wilson's ability to lead the state.

Both sides began courting legislators to their side. Smith had the advantage in that most of the Democrats in the statehouse owed him something, and he was not shy about calling in those chits. Wilson took the high road, encouraging the members not to do the expedient thing but the right thing as public servants. "It is clearly the duty of every Democratic legislator who would keep faith with the law of the state with the avowed principles of his party to vote for Mr. Martine," Wilson preached just a couple of weeks before the vote. "It is my duty to advocate his election to urge it by every honourable means at my command," he said.[95] Smith and Nugent countered with name calling, referring to Wilson as "an ingrate and a liar."[96]

Wilson was inaugurated as governor on January 17, 1911. The vote for the next senator from New Jersey occurred in the state legislature one week later. Smith was lobbying members personally from his hotel room until the wee hours of the morning before the vote. Wilson and Tumulty (now his personal secretary/chief of staff) were similarly making calls from the governor's office until around 4:00 am. When the vote began, Martine jumped out to a lead on the first ballot but fell short of a majority. The body adjourned for a short recess, allowing the intense lobbying to resume. When they reconvened, a number of additional members broke from the machine, siding with their new governor. Martine was elected, Smith's power was significantly diminished, and Woodrow Wilson had his first political victory just a week into office. There is little question that Wilson's election as governor in 1910 would not have happened without the support of the Democratic bosses, despite his abhorrence for the concept of political machines. When pressed, though, he wasted no time to set the record straight on where he stood on the issue. It was just a little late for the likes of Smith and Nugent, who would not forget this betrayal, which is how they characterized Wilson's behavior.

II-25: Private Secretary Joe Tumulty and Wilson in the Governor's office, 1911

Wilson had an aggressive agenda to pursue, full of many of the policies common amongst turn-of-the-century progressives. Consistent with his longstanding views on how executives can be most effective in government, Wilson pursued an active engagement with the legislature. He wasn't satisfied simply introducing initiatives, a la the American President. Rather, he intended to follow through with hands-on encounters directly with the legislators themselves, more akin to a British Prime Minister. After one proposal was introduced, Governor Wilson showed up at the Democratic caucus ready to roll up his sleeves to get to work on the bill. The members were taken aback, as governors typically stayed out of the legislative sausage-making. Wilson also didn't just stick with the Democrats. He realized that the progressive ideology had cross-over appeal, so he reached across the aisle for allies. One of his best connections was with George Record, the Republican who had tried to force Wilson to come clean about his relationship with the party bosses during the campaign. Record was more than satisfied with Wilson's responses and found himself aligned with much of the Wilson agenda. Having Record advocating from one end of the political spectrum, and Wilson approaching things from the other, yielded a lot of common ground and a lot of bills being passed. Among the new statutes coming out of Trenton were the state's first official Direct Primary Act, a Corrupt Practices Act, an Employers' Liability Act, and enhanced regulation for utilities which included the railroads. These laws were transformative in nature and popular with the electorate, yielding praise for Wilson from within New Jersey and beyond.

As the governor's supporters were already plotting a run for the White House the following year, Wilson had a couple of connections to make. One key would be party stalwart William Jennings Bryan. "The Commoner" had been the Democratic nominee in three of the previous four presidential campaigns, and while he never won, and was unlikely to get a fourth shot, he was still highly respected in the party and could play a critical role in determining the nominee in 1912. In this case, Ellen Wilson came to her husband's aid. When Ellen heard that Bryan was scheduled to give a talk at Princeton, she took the initiative to invite him to their home for dinner. Bryan gladly accepted, and the evening was a success. Even though they differed on some policy positions, Wilson liked Bryan personally, respected his sincere convictions on a number of key topics, and was pleased to have made a positive connection. "[Bryan] has extraordinary force of personality," Wilson shared with Mary Peck, "and it seems the force of sincerity and conviction. He has himself well

II-26: William Jennings Bryan

in hand at every turn of the thought and talk, too; and his voice is wholly delightful. A truly captivating man, I must admit."[97] It turns out that Wilson had not always felt so warmly to Bryan, however, as a report came out in which Wilson had criticized Bryan a few years before over his position on the currency (one of Bryan's most heartfelt issues). Wilson was quoted as having written in a private letter: "Would that we could do something, at once dignified and effective, to knock Mr. Bryan once for all into a cocked hat!"[98] Many of Bryan's people were taken aback when the quote became public, but Wilson handled the touchy situation perfectly. Without responding to the original charge, Wilson simply took the first opportunity to go out of his way to publicly praise Bryan as a politician and a leader of the Democratic Party. In Bryan's presence, he proclaimed: "When others were faint-hearted, Colonel Bryan carried the Democratic standard. He kept the 'fires burning' which have heartened and encouraged the democracy of the country."[99] Just like that, all was forgiven.

Wilson made another connection in 1911 that would have implications far beyond the upcoming election. "Colonel" Edward House was independently wealthy and had become a bit of a political kingmaker in the state of Texas. He was introduced to Wilson on November 24, and the pair hit it off right away. They first found common cause with their fondness for the British parliamentary system, as well as reminiscing about growing up in the South during the Civil War and Reconstruction, but that was just the beginning. Their belief systems were nearly identical, and their personalities were a perfect match. The key in this case to getting invited into Wilson's inner circle was that House

II-27: Wilson and Colonel Edward House

never seemed to want anything for himself. He didn't want a job, he didn't want money or government contracts, and he didn't want to push his friends into positions of power. He was as selfless as anyone Wilson had ever met, seemingly content to provide assistance in any way Wilson thought House could be helpful but never pushing his own agenda. "What I like about Colonel House," Wilson explained, "is that he holds things at arm's length – objectively. He seems able to penetrate a proposition and get to its very essence quickly. He wants nothing for himself. He will not hold office and is a truly disinterested friend – the most valuable possession a man could have."[100] The attraction was mutual. "The first hour we spent together proved to each of us that there was a sound basis for a fast friendship," House wrote in his diary. "We found ourselves in such complete sympathy, in so many ways that we soon learned to know what each was thinking without either having expressed himself."[101] House was quickly joining Tumulty as Governor Wilson's most intimate political advisers as they geared up for a presidential run.

Wilson lost a bit of momentum in the next round of state elections. The Republicans surged back to the majority in both houses of the New Jersey state legislature, seemingly a rebuke to Wilson and his policies. But the change could be seen more as an act of revenge by the Democratic political bosses, who convinced many of their supporters to stay home and not vote, opening the door for the Republican triumph. It seems they were so angry with Governor Wilson that they'd rather hand the other party a temporary win in order to thwart his agenda. Wilson didn't exactly give up. He still had plenty of progressive ideas to push, and he had some success with topics that had crossover appeal, but every bill was a struggle, and many were dead on arrival as soon as he introduced them. The legislature also tried to push through bills that were counter to his beliefs. In these cases, Wilson was not shy about taking out his veto pen, which he did on 57 occasions. Mostly by now, though, Wilson wasn't focused on his state. Instead, he was getting his message out to the nation to try to secure the Democratic nomination for President of the United States.

Only one Democrat had captured the White House in the last half-century – Wilson's former Princeton colleague, Grover Cleveland. But things looked extremely promising as the Republicans were imploding at the national level. The popular Theodore Roosevelt had left the White

House in the care of William Taft, his hand-picked successor in 1909, but things did not go according to plan. Roosevelt had since grown discouraged by Taft's more conservative policies and felt he had given ill-treatment to many of TR's strongest supporters. By the time the election year rolled around, Roosevelt had had enough and decided to throw his hat back into the ring. In doing so, he broke the Republican Party. The clash came to a head in June 1912 at a divisive convention in which Roosevelt accused the party of stealing the nomination from him and the party faithful. In true Rooseveltian fashion, TR shouted to his supporters, "We fight in honorable fashion for the good of mankind; fearless of the future; unheeding of our individual fates; with unflinching hearts and undimmed eyes; we stand at Armageddon, and we battle for the Lord."[102] Roosevelt lost this fight, as the party regulars rallied around President Taft to hand the incumbent the nomination, but Roosevelt was hardly one to let bygones be bygones. He and his supporters walked out on the Republicans to launch a rival Progressive Party. In a subsequent convention, the Progressives nominated Roosevelt as their standard bearer, creating the perfect opening for whoever could secure the Democratic nomination on the path to the White House. Wilson watched the Republican rupture with a sense of glee. "Good old Teddy," Wilson commented, "—what a help he is."[103]

II-28: Theodore Roosevelt speaking at the first Progressive National Convention in Chicago, August 1912

But Wilson still had his own battle for the Democratic nomination. While he was the fresh face with a lot of momentum, the front-runner heading into the convention in Baltimore was Speaker of the House Champ Clark. Once again, the party's political bosses were taking sides, with the machines all in on Clark and strongly opposed to Wilson after his recent performance in New Jersey. Wilson's team in Baltimore included William McCombs, an attorney who had become an advisor to the governor, and William McAdoo, a railroad man whose claim to fame was building railroad tunnels under the Hudson River to connect New Jersey to Manhattan. They had their work cut out for them, as did the other contenders, knowing they needed 2/3rd of the delegates to vote their way in order to secure the Democratic nomination.

The nominating speeches began late on June 27 and continued into the early morning hours of the 28th. Judge John Wescott placed Wilson's name into nomination around 2:30 in the morning. The process didn't end until close to 7:00 am when the first vote was finally taken. Clark surged to the lead with 440.5 votes, with Wilson in second at 324, followed by former Ohio Governor Judson Harmon with 148, and Oscar Underwood, the Chairman of the House Ways & Means Committee, in fourth place with 84 votes. At that point, the convention recessed so everyone could get a little sleep. They would need their energy as it would take nearly 50 ballots before anyone would top the 2/3rd threshold.

With the New York bosses of Tammany Hall jumping on the Clark bandwagon, the Speaker captured the majority on the ninth ballot with 556 votes. Wilson's man on the ground, McCombs, thought the only way to save the nomination was to make some deals by offering senior positions to key delegates to turn their states in Wilson's direction. But Wilson remained adamantly opposed to anything of this sort. "I am sorry, McCombs, but my statement must stand as I have issued it," Wilson told him on the phone. "There must be no conditions whatever attached to the nomination."[104] At that point, McCombs saw no path to success and recommended Wilson consider releasing his supporters so they could find an alternative. While Wilson started to put pen to paper to do just that, his other advisers encouraged him to wait. Getting to the 2/3rd threshold was still going to be difficult, and there was some grumbling from Baltimore that the Tammany endorsement might actually backfire against Clark. Wilson went to bed thinking he was bound to lose but decided not to concede until a few more ballots revealed something more definitive.

This was a wise move. Clark had hit his high water mark and started to lose some of his traction. Harmon faded completely, Underwood rose a bit, but it was increasingly becoming a two-man race between Clark and Wilson. The governor got a boost when party favorite William Jennings Bryan offered his endorsement during the 14th ballot, but the race remained close, ballot after ballot after ballot. A breakthrough occurred on the 30th ballot when Clark lost his lead for the first time as Iowa put itself into the Wilson column, giving the governor a 460-455 edge. The next break came on the 42nd ballot, as more Midwest states came into the fold, beginning with Indiana and followed by Illinois. The end finally came on the 46th ballot, as Woodrow Wilson surpassed the 2/3rd threshold to become the Democratic nominee for President of the United States. The Wilson household erupted in celebration upon hearing the news, except for the candidate himself. "Governor, you don't seem a bit excited," Joe Tumulty said. Wilson replied, "I can't effervesce in the face of responsibility."[105]

Wilson remained all business when he formally accepted the nomination on August 7, 1912. "We must speak, not to catch votes," he said, "but to satisfy the thought and conscience of a people deeply stirred by the conviction that they have come to a critical turning point in their moral and political development."[106] Interestingly, the statement could just have easily been uttered by one of Wilson's opponents, as Roosevelt also often brought morality into his manner of governing and advocacy. Those two would be the focus of the campaign, as Taft mostly sulked over his disaffection from Roosevelt, and the other two largely ignored the man in the White House as not a legitimate contender in the race. In terms of policies, there was plenty of negative rhetoric that flowed, particularly from Roosevelt to Wilson. "The Democratic platform shows that the Democratic Party now is as stupid, bourbon and reactionary as ever before," Roosevelt declared. "It shows a combination of complete muddleheadedness, with

II-29: Democratic campaign banner for Wilson and VP-candidate Thomas Marshall

great insincerity." In reality, though, there were actually many similarities in what the two candidates were pitching to the electorate when it came to their agendas. Both were staunch progressives with only slightly different focuses. Wilson developed his "New Freedom" agenda, which featured freedom of opportunity for all Americans. Wilson saw the need for a reduced tariff, fundamental changes to monetary policy, even more aggression toward the trusts, and a general curtailment of large businesses from dictating to other Americans directly on the economy and indirectly through the politicians they had in their pockets. Roosevelt wasn't much different with his "New Nationalism" platform. Roosevelt would take progressivism to a new level with robust federal regulation of the economy, new social insurance programs, expanded conservation, and the adoption of an 8-hour workday. William White, a leading progressive throughout this era, offered a colorful comparison of the two programs: "Between the New Nationalism and the New Freedom was that fantastic imaginary gulf that always has existed between tweedled-dum and tweedled-dee."[107] And, in an unguarded moment, even Roosevelt admitted he and Wilson weren't that different when it came to the substance of their domestic agendas. "I suppose," Roosevelt said, "I am a little hard on Wilson. What I object to about him is his mildness of method. I suppose, as a matter of fact, (tapping himself on the chest) Wilson is merely a less virile *me*!"[108] That, of course, was the real difference that was on display throughout the campaign.

The personalities of the two could not have been more different. While both were extremely effective orators, they approached their audiences with a different kind of appeal. Roosevelt was all emotion, punctuating his points by pounding his fists, using inflammatory language that elevated his positions to the highest level while denigrating his opposition in coarse terms. Wilson, on the other hand, played the role of university professor, bringing a calm demeanor to his intellectually laden addresses. Wilson described the difference as follows: Roosevelt was "a real, vivid person, whom they have seen and shouted themselves hoarse over and voted for, millions strong." This compared to himself, who was merely "a vague, conjectural personality, more made up of opinions and academic prepossessions than of human and red corpuscles."[109] But while Wilson had perhaps a less rousing approach, he was nonetheless quite effective on the stump, something for which he had been preparing his entire life. His advocacy came with a force of conviction that was resonating with an electorate that was attracted to his principle-based ideas.

Moreover, Wilson was actually more complex than his own depiction might imply. He had a multi-faceted personality that was strongly influenced by his heritage, as he described to Joe Tumulty shortly after winning the Democratic nomination.

> You know, Tumulty, there are two natures combined in me that every day fight for supremacy and control. On the one side, there is the Irish in me, quick, generous, impulsive, passionate, anxious always to help and to sympathize with those in distress. … And like the Irishman at the Donnybrook Fair, always willin' to raise me shillalah and to hit any head which stands firninst me. Then, on the other side, there is the Scotch – canny, tenacious, cold, and perhaps a little exclusive. I tell you, my dear friend, that when these two fellows get to quarrelling among themselves, it is hard to act as umpire between them.[110]

Only those closest to Wilson, though, really got to know the different sides of his personality.

The presidential general election campaign was a two-month sprint from Labor Day to Election Day. McCombs ran the campaign as Chair of the Democratic Party, with McAdoo as his #2. Henry Morgenthau, the chair of the Finance Committee, was instructed by Wilson not to accept any money from corporations, nor to agree to any deals for donations. Wilson's preference was small donations from as many people as they could get. The results were $1.1 million raised from 90,000 contributors, an average donation of just over $12 apiece. Wilson also had a cadre of policy advisors, none more important than Louis Brandeis, a former valedictorian at Harvard Law School who had become a champion of the progressive cause. Wilson wanted more insight into the latest thinking on combatting trusts, and

II-30: Louis Brandeis

Brandeis favored him with a three-hour lesson. His main point was that regulation had to start long before the trusts ever materialized, enhancing competition to deter the formation of trusts. According to Brandeis, "We must undertake to regulate competition instead of monopoly, for our industrial freedom and our civic freedom go hand in hand."[111] Brandeis's advocacy was soon orthodoxy in the New Freedom agenda.

One voting bloc was anxious to hear where Wilson stood on the topic of civil rights. No Southerner had been elected President since well before the Civil War, and there were concerns in the Black community regarding how Wilson would deal with matters of race. Given his affection for the South that shined through some of his published works, Black leaders were pushing for some kind of indication of how his beliefs would translate into presidential policies. Wilson remained quiet about the topic until finally agreeing to a public statement late in the campaign. In an open letter to Bishop Alexander Walters of the African Methodist Episcopal Zion Church, Wilson offered assurances to "my colored fellow citizens of my earnest wish to see justice done them in every matter, and not mere grudging justice, but justice executed with liberality and cordial good feeling. … They [Blacks] may count upon me for absolute fair dealing and for everything by which I could assist in advancing the interests of their race in the United States."[112] With such a limited political resume, the Black community had little to go on beyond the few utterances such as this from the candidate. When it came time to cast their votes in November, most Blacks were willing to give Wilson the benefit of the doubt. It wouldn't take long, however, to find themselves sorely disappointed in the outcome that followed.

II-31: Wilson during the 1912 presidential election

The campaign came to an abrupt halt about a month

before election day when a man fired a shot into the chest of Theodore Roosevelt from about 30 feet away as the candidate was heading to a campaign event in Milwaukee. The gunman was John Schrank, who was later found not guilty by reason of insanity and spent the rest of his life in a state hospital for the criminally insane. Roosevelt had the good fortune of having his 50-page speech and his glasses case in his coat, both of which slowed down the bullet before it lodged in his chest. Sensing the wound was not fatal, Roosevelt insisted on giving his speech before heading to the hospital. Wilson immediately wired that he was prepared to suspend the campaign until Roosevelt fully recovered, but TR rejected the offer. He insisted the campaign continue, rejoining the fray in just a couple of weeks. Immediately after the incident, Colonel House contacted his friend Bill McDonald, a top marksman who had served valiantly as a captain for the Texas Rangers. While Wilson tried to object to having a bodyguard, his team convinced him otherwise. Bill McDonald remained by Wilson's side until it was time to take his oath of office.

Wilson was on the path to that inaugural after a convincing win in the Electoral College. In the only numbers that mattered, the results were not close. Wilson won 40 out of 48 states, capturing 435 votes in the Electoral College. This compared to 88 votes for Roosevelt (from six states) and only eight votes for President Taft (from just two states). The popular vote, however, told a very different story in terms of 'what might have been' if the Republican Party had remained united. Wilson won only 41.8% of the popular vote, the third lowest in American history. Only John Quincy Adams and Abraham Lincoln (first term) had smaller percentages, as they also were elected from a pool of three or more viable candidates. Roosevelt (27.4%) and Taft (23.2%) combined for 50.6% of the popular vote, approximately 1.3 million votes and nearly nine percentage points better than Wilson. A unified Republican Party may have led to a very different outcome. When all was said and done, this canvass was decided at the conventions. When Roosevelt refused to back down and accept the decision of the Republicans to support Taft for reelection, he destroyed any realistic opportunity to prevent a Democratic victory. Whoever captured the Democratic nomination was almost assuredly going to be the nation's next President, and Woodrow Wilson received that mantle when he outlasted Champ Clark at the Democratic Convention. Wilson's offhand comment at the time ("Good old Teddy,

—what a help he is"[113]) was spot on in identifying what was likely the determining factor in providing him such an easy electoral path to the White House.

4. Putting Plans into Practice

With less than two years of gubernatorial experience under his belt, the former college professor and president had just been elected to the highest office in the land. This was a lifelong dream that had come together quickly, to be able to apply all he had learned in studying, writing, and speaking about politics and government for his entire adult life to the benefit of his country. While confident in his abilities to rise to the occasion, Wilson was pretty even-keeled when the reality began to set in. "I do not feel exuberant or cheerful," he said. "I feel exceedingly solemn. I have no inclination to jump up and crack my heels together. A weight of seriousness and responsibility seems to be pressing down upon me. I feel more like kneeling down and praying for strength to do what is expected of me."[114] More than anything, Wilson was exhausted. His voice was completely gone by election day, and he needed rest. The family left for a month in Bermuda where official business was kept to an absolute minimum. He knew his Cabinet selections needed his attention, but even that could wait a few weeks before he had to start making firm decisions.

Fortunately, Colonel House was on hand to help guide that process. House personally knew many of the people Wilson might consider for Cabinet posts, and Wilson set him loose to start putting together possible lists and vetting candidates. That was true for most Cabinet positions but not the top spot. Wilson believed William Jennings Bryan's lifetime of service to the Democratic Party, along with his strong support in the recent campaign, had earned him a top appointment. Moreover, as Wilson confided with House, their world would be far better with Bryan "in Washington and in harmony with the administration rather than outside and possibly in a critical attitude."[115] Shortly after returning from Bermuda, Wilson welcomed Bryan to his office in Trenton, and they talked about the position of Secretary of State. Bryan was clearly interested and felt they could work well together. He did have a couple of conditions for which he wanted Wilson's support up front. Bryan indicated a desire to pursue reciprocity trade agreements with other countries as a means to prevent war, and, as a teetotaler, he wanted Wilson's approval to refrain from serving alcohol at diplomatic events. Wilson gave his assent to both, and the appointment was announced on December 21.

House continued to vet candidates and funnel recommendations to the President-elect for consideration for the rest of his Cabinet. The most disappointed in the process was William McCombs, who had led the Wilson contingent at both the Democratic Convention and throughout the campaign. The bottom line, though, was that Wilson and his inner circle had lost confidence in McCombs. He had been ill for much of the canvass and behaved erratically when he engaged. Moreover, he was personally considered too ambitious and often appeared suspicious of his colleagues. All of these factors led Wilson to conclude that McCombs would be more trouble than he was worth. McCombs charged Wilson with ingratitude, but no minds were changed in his favor.

II-32: Wilson's First Cabinet
(Clockwise from left): President Wilson, Secretary of the Treasury William McAdoo, Attorney General James McReynolds, Secretary of the Navy Josephus Daniels, Secretary of Agriculture David Houston, Secretary of Labor William Wilson, Secretary of Commerce William Redfield, Secretary of the Interior Franklin Lane, Postmaster General Albert Burleson, Secretary of War Lindley Garrison, and Secretary of State William Bryan

The other leading campaign operative was William McAdoo, whom Wilson wanted to run the Treasury Department. McAdoo had the right balance of business and political experience to be able to help lead the administration's efforts with Congress on topics such as the tariff, trusts, monetary policy, and economic regulation. McAdoo was pleased to accept. Wilson wanted A. Mitchell Palmer, another strong supporter from the campaign, to be the Secretary of War, but, as a Quaker, he did not believe he could serve in that capacity. Instead, Wilson went with Lindley Garrison, the Vice-Chancellor of New Jersey, who Tumulty recommended. Bryan's friend, Josephus Daniels, another ardent progressive, took the portfolio at the Navy Department, with a young Franklin Roosevelt as his top assistant. House continued to work the Cabinet throughout the interregnum, with regular conferences with the President-elect. The two had grown very close very fast, and the mutual trust was at a level Wilson had not experienced previously. "Mr. House is my second personality," Wilson said. "He is my independent self. If I were in his place I would do just as he suggested. If anyone thinks he is reflecting my opinion by whatever action he takes, they are welcome to the conclusion."[116] Wilson offered House a spot in the Cabinet on many occasions, but House declined the entreaty every time it was presented. He had a different role in mind, one that he thought was better suited for both the President and himself. "I very much prefer being a free lance," House wrote in his diary, "and to advise with him regarding matters in general, and to have a roving commission to serve wherever and whenever possible."[117] This unusual arrangement fit perfectly into the President's plans. House was constantly available through the first six years of Wilson's presidency, either in Washington, New York, or Europe as Wilson's eyes and ears throughout the First World War. Wilson trusted House implicitly, in part because he never seemed to want anything for himself. He even refused to draw a salary. When House said he 'just wanted to help,' the offer was genuine, and Wilson placed great stock in that selfless attitude. The two would eventually break over some interactions at the post-war Peace Conference, but for the time being, House was Wilson's unofficial right-hand man, with direct access to the President on almost any topic. The fact that everyone knew the relationship was so tight gave House enormous leverage in his dealings with other politicians and foreign leaders alike.

In early 1913, Woodrow Wilson was still the Governor of New Jersey. He decided to go out with a strong message, advocating the continuance of his progressive agenda, including the ratification of the 16th and 17th Amendments (authorizing a personal income tax and the direct election of senators, respectively). He also signaled he planned to get the work of his presidential administration started as quickly as possible. Unwilling to wait for Congress to open its first session on his watch in December, as was the custom for new Presidents, Wilson indicated he planned to call a Special Session for April to focus on his economic agenda. He was ready to get to work and to apply his long-held views on the role of the national executive, which still favored the function of the Prime Minister under the British parliamentary system. "I can't say in advance what I am going to do," Wilson told a reporter shortly before his inauguration, "but I have a few general ideas. In the first place you may be sure I am going to practice my theory. My views about Executive responsibility will be applied in the Presidency just as much as they were in the Governorship."[118] The professor was more than ready to put his lifetime of study and theories to work on the biggest stage in the world.

Unlike his predecessor's inaugural, which had to be moved indoors because of blizzard-like conditions, the sun broke through to welcome Woodrow Wilson into the American presidency. William Taft was more than ready to vacate the premises, telling Wilson that "I'll be glad to be going, this is the loneliest place in the world."[119] For the time being, Wilson could only speculate on what he meant. After all, it was the first time he'd ever set foot in the White House.

II-33: Wilson meeting outgoing President William Taft at the White House, March 4, 1913

This was indeed a whole new world. At the Capitol that afternoon, Wilson took his oath to "preserve, protect, and defend the Constitution of the United States,"[120] before turning to what many believed was the largest crowd yet to attend a presidential inauguration. To these onlookers, Wilson boldly announced, "There has been a change of government."[121] He painted a vision whereby "Our duty is to cleanse, to reconsider, to restore, to correct the vile without impairing the good, to purify and humanize every process of our common life without weakening or sentimentalizing it.[122] … This is the high enterprise of the new day: To lift everything that concerns our life as a Nation to the light that shines from the hearthfire of every man's conscience and vision of the right. … We shall restore, not destroy."[123] Putting the finishing touches on an oration that would have made his father proud, Wilson reminded his fellow Americans:

> This is not a day of triumph; it is a day of dedication. Here muster, not the forces of party, but the forces of humanity. Men's hearts wait upon us; men's lives hang in the balance; men's hopes call upon us to see what we will do. Who shall live up to the great trust? Who dares fail to try? I summon all honest men, all patriotic, all forward-looking men, to my side.[124]

Many were ready to answer Wilson's inspirational call for a New Freedom for the American people.

II-34: Wilson giving his first Inaugural Address, March 4, 1913

President Wilson brought some of New Jersey with him to the White House. Joe Tumulty would continue as his personal secretary and chief of staff, and Charles Swem tagged along as Wilson's stenographer. Tumulty remained the perfect complement for Wilson, who had little patience for the minute details that needed to be addressed in running the office of the executive. Tumulty worked non-stop behind the scenes, serving as presidential gatekeeper, press liaison, and loyal adviser. He remained one of the few who could speak his mind to the President, including offering counsel when he thought the boss was off track. On top of how much time they spent together, the pair also communicated via memorandum. In fact, that was Wilson's preferred mode of communication. He cared little for the idle chit-chat associated with personal interactions, which he found wasted precious time. Far better was for someone to submit a few focused sentences that went straight to the matter at hand. Those kinds of requests were often the fastest way to get a presidential response, sometimes typed by Wilson himself. Approvals typically came with an "okeh" next to Wilson's signature.[125]

Rounding out the president's inner circle was a Navy Captain by the name of Cary Grayson. Wilson had never had robust health, and he entered the presidency with his customary headaches draining him day after day. Dr. Grayson had previously looked after the health of both Presidents Roosevelt and Taft, and Wilson took to him right off the bat. In one of Grayson's first examinations of the President, he found Wilson had been overmedicating, under-exercising, and failing to set aside sufficient time for rest. He suggested some changes, which immediately generated positive results. Grayson not only served as Wilson's physician throughout his presidency (and beyond), but he also became a close friend and confidant. He was nearly always on hand, and Wilson followed his advice to the letter.

II-35: Dr. Cary Grayson

Wilson had little direct experience in the world of foreign affairs, but the first things that hit his desk came from that realm. During the campaign, Wilson took the high road in his approach to other countries. "We must shape our course of action by the maxims of justice and liberality and good will," Wilson said, "think of the progress of mankind rather than of the progress of this or that investment, of the protection of American honor and the advancement of American ideals rather than always of American contracts, and lift our diplomacy to the levels of what the best minds have planned for mankind."[126] This intent was about to be put to the test. Wilson's first Cabinet meeting focused on a situation with Mexico, which had been dealing with revolution over the last two years of the Taft administration as Francisco Madero had ousted the nation's longtime leader, Porfirio Díaz. Less than a month before Wilson took his oath of office, General Victoriano Huerta initiated a coup. He had Madero executed and named himself President. The British were aligned with Huerta and were pushing other nations to recognize the new government. Wilson thought the whole thing to be a sordid affair that hardly represented the will of the Mexican people. True to his convictions from the campaign, he was not inclined to reward this illegal administration with the imprimatur of American recognition. Moreover, Wilson received reports that the American ambassador, Henry Wilson, may have had a hand in Huerta's rise to power. Before taking any additional action, President Wilson wanted to know the truth. He sent his own emissary, William Hale, to Mexico to investigate. Hale's report was a shock, as he corroborated the rumors, adding the sense among many Mexicans that the entire U.S. government had backed the coup. Wilson took immediate action to replace his rogue ambassador, but he didn't stop there. Taking his own moral counsel, Wilson fired off

II-36: Mexican leader Victoriano Huerta

a letter to President Huerta, suggesting that he step down and call for new elections so the Mexican people could choose their own leader. Huerta defiantly refused. In fact, he published Wilson's letter, decrying the outsider from the north for trying to dictate to the Mexican government. For many Mexicans, Huerta won the day by "exhibiting himself as champion of the national dignity, as defender of the sovereignty of Mexico against the intrusion of a foreign government."[127] Some in Wilson's Cabinet, including War Secretary Garrison, advocated invasion to forcibly remove Huerta and return democracy to Mexico. President Wilson wasn't ready for that step as he looked for other ways to get Huerta to step down. For now, he adopted a policy of "watchful waiting"[128] while he considered all his options.

Woodrow Wilson's view of the national executive was going to be different not only in substance but also in style. Wilson's affinity for the British parliamentary system augured a fresh kind of engagement by the new American President. Just like a British Prime Minister had to be on the hot seat to answer pointed questions in the House of Commons, Wilson decided on his own approach to presidential access and transparency by initiating regular press conferences. Many of Wilson's predecessors had fought hard to control the press to the point where throughout much of American history to date, reporters were not allowed to quote the President directly without his explicit permission. Wilson helped erode those norms with regular sessions with the press, and no questions were deemed off-limits. The scribes had never seen anything like this. "There was something so unaffected and honest about his way of talking," wrote *The New York Times*, "that it won everybody, despite the fact that many of the men there had come prejudiced against him."[129] In his first ten months in office, Wilson held 60 press conferences.

But this was just a start. The last President to speak directly to Congress was the nation's second chief executive, John Adams. Beginning with the administration of Thomas Jefferson, all Presidents had submitted statements, letters, announcements, and even their Annual Messages (now called the State of the Union Address) in writing to be read by a clerk. Oliver Newman, one of the reporters covering the President, suggested in a private meeting with Wilson that he break that tradition and take his wonderful oratory into the well of the House to deliver his messages directly. At first, even Wilson thought this to be a step too far. "I am afraid," Wilson replied, "that it would be too radical.

You know there are certain things which simply can't be done the way you would like to do them. It would be such a shock to the sensibilities of the members of Congress to their orthodox ideas. … The matter of presenting the message might arouse antagonism which would tend to injure my recommendations for legislation."[130] But as he and Tumulty talked it over, they quickly warmed to the idea and decided the benefits outweighed any potential costs. Wilson had already called for Congress to convene in special session just a month into his term to focus on economic legislation that Wilson deemed too sensitive to wait for the normal session to begin in December. Wilson now informed both Houses that he would be opening the session in person. After initially getting over the shock, the Democrat-friendly legislature kindly opened its doors to the representative of their co-equal branch of government. The President got straight to the point – tariff rates had to come down, and protection needed to come to an end. According to Wilson, it was time to "abolish everything that bears even the semblance of privilege or of any kind of artificial advantage, and put our business men and producers under the stimulation of a constant necessity to be efficient, economical, and enterprising, masters of competitive supremacy, better workers and merchants than any in the world."[131] He spoke for only nine minutes and abruptly left the chamber. Riding back to the White House, he couldn't contain his glee over his public address to Congress. "Wouldn't Teddy have been glad to think of that!" he boasted to Ellen, with reference to Roosevelt. "I put one over on Teddy that time and am totally happy!"[132]

Tariff reduction was never easy in the United States as individual members of Congress owed their jobs in many cases to providing protection for their constituents. And since this was typically a regional issue (raw materials producers and farmers in the West and South wanted low tariffs, while finished goods manufacturers in the North and East favored protection), a President typically couldn't count on his party to deliver on this topic. In fact, when President Taft fought for lower tariffs in the first year of his administration, it ended in a disastrous political defeat. But Wilson had this at the top of his agenda for a reason, to set the tone for the progressive agenda he intended to pursue. He also wasn't willing to let Congress debate this to death on its own. He expected to be directly involved, just like a British Premier. So, the day after his speech to Congress, Wilson returned to the Capitol to take part in crafting the final bill in the House and to lobby members to get on board. Oscar

Underwood was the point man in Congress from his perch atop the House Ways and Means Committee. The goal was to dramatically lower rates on all raw materials and necessities, adding as many items to the free list as he could muster from his colleagues. The debate continued for ten weeks, at which point passage of the Underwood Tariff ultimately came easily in the House. That said, a number of tariff reduction bills had found favor in the lower house of Congress only to be stymied in the Senate. Wilson wasn't about to let this happen on his watch, as he continued to directly lobby the members until he got what he wanted. His success came from holding nearly all Democrats in line. Rates came down across the board, on average from 40% down to 25%, with many items added to the free list as well. "I have had the accomplishment of something like this at heart ever since I was a boy,"[133] Wilson said after signing the legislation into law. It was indeed a major triumph for the new President on his first significant legislative effort.

There was one potential problem. Such a dramatic reduction in tariff rates would lead to a direct drop in Federal revenue. While some of that was excess, the totality of the anticipated loss of $50 million per year couldn't simply be absorbed. Wilson and the Democrats had an answer, though, thanks to the recently ratified 16th Amendment to the Constitution, which authorized a personal income tax. As the tariff rates were coming down, the income tax was coming on line. Initially, the law imposed a 1% tax on all personal and corporate income that exceeded $4,000 per year. The lawmakers embraced a progressive system whereby marginal rates would increase at higher income levels. The highest initial bracket was set at 7% for incomes over $100,000 per year. In the first year alone, less than 1% of the population paid $71 million in taxes, generating more than enough revenue to offset the loss from the reduced tariff. This was a turning point in the American economy. In relatively short order, the tariff gave way to the income tax as the primary source of revenue for the Federal government. This would be especially handy in a few years when the country needed to pay for its role in a global war.

The summer months in the nation's capital subjected its inhabitants to stifling heat and humidity. This was one of the reasons why Congress typically left town for an extended period at the start of a new administration. But Wilson was just getting started with this particular special session, with more economic items on his agenda. Dr. Grayson wanted Wilson to slow down, to take at least some time away, but the

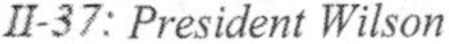

II-37: President Wilson

II-38: First Lady Ellen Wilson

President was unwilling to leave town while there was important work to be done. He sent his family to the shore while he hunkered down in the White House. As busy as ever, Wilson still always had time to correspond with his wife. The letters flowed to and from the White House throughout the long, hot summer, seemingly with as much affection as when the couple first met some 30 years before. "I adore you! No President but myself ever had exactly the right sort of wife!" he wrote. "I am certainly the most fortunate alive!"[134] Ellen responded in kind. "I idolize you," she wrote, "I love you till it hurts."[135] Tumulty and Grayson moved into the White House for the duration of the summer to keep the President company, but it was never quite the same when Ellen was away.

Wilson's next address to a joint session of Congress came on June 23, this time to introduce his plan to fundamentally change the monetary policy of the United States. The nation had a long history of economic panics, where one brokerage house might fall and others would immediately tumble in its wake. These turbulent economic cycles would wreak havoc on the citizenry, calm for a period, but inevitably return, and the Federal government had very few tools at its disposal to do much to prevent these cycles or limit their duration when they occurred. In fact, there was little in the way of Federal oversight or national standards applied to the 7,000 independent banks operating across the country. Moreover, there was no way to efficiently expand or contract the money supply to address the seasonality of key industries, population changes, or other stimuli that impacted the health of the economy. Wilson intended to introduce a new economic structure aimed at overcoming the longstanding deficiencies that contributed to these volatile economic cycles.

Wilson and his advisers had devised a multi-part program to provide the kind of agility the American economy needed to avoid these all-too-frequent panics. The heart of the solution was a decentralized set of a dozen private Federal Reserve Banks that would be overseen by a national Federal Reserve Board. The Board would set national policies, such as the interest rate that banks charge each other and guidance on the money supply, and the regional banks would implement them. These regional banks would not be directly accessible by the public but would provide services to the commercial banks in their areas, including ensuring a proper flow of currency. According to the President, "Our banking laws must mobilize reserves; must not permit the concentration anywhere in a few hands of the monetary resources of the country or their use for speculative purposes in such volume as to hinder or impede or stand in the way of other more legitimate, more fruitful uses."[136] Moreover, by monitoring economic cycles, the Fed could quickly react and insert more money into one region or contract the money supply in another to try to maintain stability before a panic could erupt. As Wilson described, "We must have a currency, not rigid as now, but readily, elastically responsive to sound credit, the expanding and contracting credits of everyday transaction, the normal ebb and flow of personal and corporate dealings."[137] The details of the plan evolved with suggestions coming from both sides of the aisle, but the fundamental structure of the President's plan stayed intact throughout the summer. This included the Federal Reserve Notes that would become the standard currency in the United States, which would be fully backed as government obligations.

The biggest quarrel over the proposal came from the banking industry itself, which was loath to seed so much of its dominion over the economy to the Federal government. To agree to the transformation, the banks wanted their piece of control, which meant seats on the Federal Reserve Board. Secretary of State William Jennings Bryan was among the most vocal opposing such a capitulation to the bankers. Bryan insisted that the Board of Governors be nominated by the President and confirmed by the Senate, enabling them to operate in the best interests of the American people and not the bankers who clearly had a conflict of interest. On this point, the President agreed. "The control of the system of banking and of issue which our new laws are to set up must be public, not private, must be vested in the government itself, so that the banks may be the instruments, not the masters, of business and of individual enterprise and initiative."[138] When a number of the leading bankers came to Washington to lobby the President on this point, Wilson raised a simple question: "Will one of you gentlemen tell me in what civilized country of the earth there are important government boards of control on which private interests are represented?" After a brief pause to let that thought settle in, he added: "Which of you gentlemen thinks the railroads should select members of the Interstate Commerce Commission?"[139] The bankers had no response, and the issue was closed. Wilson's proposal would go to Congress as-is, whether the bankers liked it or not.

Once again, gaining the support of the House of Representatives was relatively straightforward, with all but three Democrats and nearly 50 Republicans voting in favor of the measure. The banking tycoons inundated the Senate Banking Committee to insist on more private sector involvement in the new structure. But this effort was more than countered by the lobbying done by Bryan and Treasury Secretary McAdoo to hold the line in favor of the House-passed bill. They focused on the Democrats in the Senate, who nearly all complied. The Senate bill passed on December 12 with every Democrat and six Republicans voting aye. The conference committee took just three days, and the Federal Reserve System was authorized by President Wilson's signature on December 23. Between the tariff, income tax, and banking restructuring, President Wilson and his Democratic counterparts in Congress had completely remade the structure of the American economy. These reforms were arguably the most lasting effects of the entire Wilson administration and a capper on a highly impactful first year in office.

Through all these legislative triumphs, President Wilson was being attacked for some of his other policies relating to the management of the government itself. Notwithstanding Wilson's statements to the Black community during the campaign, he was true to his Southern roots in formulating policies related to race. For years, Blacks and Whites had worked side-by-side across the Federal government, but that was about

II-39: Secretary of the Treasury William McAdoo

II-40: Postmaster General Albert Burleson

to change. Two Cabinet secretaries, in particular, wanted to re-introduce segregation into their Departments: Treasury Secretary William McAdoo and Postmaster General Albert Burleson, the latter of which had more Federal employees than any other agency. McAdoo was among those who helped drive his personal sentiments into administration policy. "I shall not be a party to the enforced and unwelcome juxtaposition of white and negro employees when it is unnecessary and avoidable without injustice to anybody," the Treasury Secretary wrote, "and when such enforcement would serve only to engender race animosities detrimental to the welfare of both races and injurious to the public service."[140] Particularly offensive to McAdoo was the notion of White women having to report directly to a Black male supervisor, echoing the worst of stereotypes about Black men and their supposed desire to prey on White women. With Wilson's approval, Blacks were transferred to other jobs, with their rights and privileges summarily diminished. Separate restrooms and eating establishments were designated based on race, while photographs were required for job applicants so their race could clearly be assessed upfront. By the end of the summer of Wilson's first year in office, the national headquarters of the postal service, which was home to approximately one thousand employees, had one Black left in the building. Due to the nature of his job, he could not be moved out. But to alleviate the need for Whites to gaze upon this lone Black worker, the department set up screens to encircle his workstation to keep him completely concealed from view. To the Black community, this was the equivalent of placing the man in a cage. Despite these humiliations and the nearly instantaneous collapse of morale among Blacks in the Federal workforce, the Wilson administration continued to believe these moves were actually good for the Black community. This notion of 'separate-but-equal' in Federal employment was deemed a positive as Black workers would now have opportunities for advancement in Black-only units, which would never be available if they had to compete with Whites. The administration posited that segregation would be both culturally and career-enhancing, and President Wilson wholeheartedly agreed. The nation's chief executive regarded the situation "with the idea that the friction, or rather the discontent and uneasiness, which had prevailed in many of the departments would thereby be removed. It is as far as possible from being a movement against the negroes. I sincerely believe it to be in their interest."[141] Of course, the Black community could not disagree more, even though their complaints mostly fell on deaf ears.

W.E.B. Du Bois was serving as the Director of Publicity and Research at the NAACP (National Association for the Advancement of Colored People) at the time of Wilson's elevation to the presidency. In this capacity, he was also the editor of the organization's widely-read monthly magazine, *The Crisis*. Du Bois was one of the leaders of the Black community who had bought into Wilson's rhetoric during the campaign that implied favorable treatment for Black Americans during a Wilson administration. Just a few months into Wilson's first term, however, Du Bois was beyond frustrated, and he decided to make that point in an open letter to the President. According to Du Bois:

> … not a single act and not a single word of yours since the election has given anyone reason to infer that you have the slightest interest in the colored people or desire to alleviate their intolerable position. … The gravest attack on the liberties of our people since emancipation, Public segregation of civil servants in government employ, necessarily involving personal insult and humiliation, has, for the first time in history been made the policy of the United States government. … Here is a plain, flat, disgraceful spitting in the face of people whose

> darkened countenances are already dark with the slime of insult.[142]

Wilson was undeterred by any protests along these lines, continuing to insist that "We are handling the force of colored people who are now in the departments in just the way in which they ought to be handled."[143] This sentiment buttressed Wilson's determination to offer extremely limited political appointments to Blacks. While these were not nonexistent, they were typically for minor positions or ones that could be walled off from the White workers in an agency. His rationale was partly that he needed the support of Southern Democrats to move his New Freedom agenda forward, and he would lose them in protest if he was more generous with Black appointments. The racial policies of the Wilson administration would continue to be implemented with little regard to the forceful protests from the Black community.

Woodrow Wilson had never been a fan of large social gatherings, and that did not change when he became President of the United States. While he continued to adhere to the traditions of certain state dinners, winter receptions, and spring garden parties, he kept them to a bare minimum. While many Presidents not only enjoyed such festivities, they also often found them productive in influencing guests into their way of thinking. This was never Wilson's way. He would just assume to confer by memo, or possibly call a meeting and hammer out the decision at the table. The fact is that Wilson was something of a recluse who cherished his private time with his family. Other than House, Tumulty, and Grayson, very few were welcome for informal gatherings for meals or after-dinner relaxation. And these were never to talk business. In fact, they were just the opposite, the opportunity for Wilson to take his mind off the overwhelming responsibilities that came with his job, even if just for a couple of hours at a time. In many ways, Wilson felt like a captive in his own home, always being watched for every step, word, or action he took. According to reporter David Lawrence, Wilson "was like one under arrest, always guarded, always protected, always awkwardly aware of his own troublesome presence."[144]

Wilson did keep a regular schedule of getting out of the house for at least a little exercise and relaxation. These ventures would typically be an evening performance at the theater, a ride around town, or nine holes of golf (18 on the weekends). Woodrow Wilson played more golf than any President in American history, with well over a thousand rounds to

II-41: Wilson played more golf than any other President

his credit. In fact, Wilson was so determined to pursue this form of distraction that he'd play in almost any weather. When snow was on the ground, the White House staff would color his golf balls so they'd be easier to find. It's not that he was good at the game. In fact, his golf skills were terrible, and they rarely improved despite significant effort. But he enjoyed the distraction and the freedom to be away from the job and the people who always wanted something from him. He chose his golf partners carefully, and those who tried to talk business were almost never invited back. The President rarely missed a day on the links when he was in Washington.

The Wilsons did throw a couple of special parties at the White House, one each in 1913 and 1914. The occasions were the weddings of two of their daughters. Jessie was the first to tie the knot, exchanging vows in the East Room with Francis Sayre in front of 400 guests on November 25, 1913. Sayre was a practicing attorney who had graduated from Williams College and Harvard Law School. Oldest daughter Margaret would never marry, but youngest daughter Nell was just

II-42: Jessie Wilson (center) at her wedding, November 25, 1913

II-43: Eleanor (Nell) Wilson at her wedding, May 7, 1914

a few months away from her nuptials to a powerful player in Washington who was more than twice her age. Nell had started to spend time with Treasury Secretary William McAdoo. He was a 50-year-old widower who had six children from his previous marriage. She was 23 and the apple of her father's eye. Despite the seemingly awkward circumstances, the Wilsons were happy to welcome McAdoo into the family, even though it meant another of the children was leaving the nest. After the ceremony on May 7, 1914, the father of the bride complained in a letter to Mary Peck, "Ah! How desperately my heart aches that she is gone. She was simply part of me, the only delightful part; and I feel the loneliness more than I dare admit even to myself."[145] Nell's wedding was a more modest affair when compared to her sister, in part because Ellen was not well during these many months and had neither the time nor energy to participate in much of the planning. By this point, Wilson had another international crisis on his hand, anyway. Things in Mexico were getting worse.

On April 9, 1914, the USS *Dolphin* docked in the Mexican port city of Tampico on a routine stop to pick up supplies. It turned out the sailors did not have the proper papers, according to some Mexican soldiers, who took a few of the Americans into custody. Once the arrested Americans were seen in town, a more senior official immediately ordered their release, not wanting to bring the wrath of the United States down on his country. The Huerta government quickly issued an apology. But the incident didn't end there, partly because Admiral Henry Mayo, the senior naval official in charge of the region, demanded a different kind of apology. Mayo wanted a 21-gun salute in the vicinity of the *Dolphin* to use military means to demonstrate Mexican remorse. To this, the

Mexicans balked, after which both sides dug in. President Wilson cared little for the military salute, but he was loath to embarrass Admiral Mayo by withdrawing the demand. After eleven days of inaction, Wilson brought the issue to Congress. He expressed a willingness to use the "armed forces of the United States in such ways and to such an extent as may be necessary to obtain from General Huerta and his adherents the fullest recognition of the rights and dignity of the United States."[146] As badly as Wilson wanted to avoid a conflict of arms, he wasn't going to stand for what was now widely understood to be a direct affront to the American military and the people they were charged to protect. This was especially true with President Huerta still clinging to power, something that Wilson abhorred.

The day after this address, the President ordered military action in Mexico. American intelligence uncovered a shipment of 1,000 small arms from Germany bound for the Mexican port of Veracruz. A call was arranged in the middle of the night with the President, Secretary of State Bryan, Navy Secretary Daniels, and Joseph Tumulty on the line. Wilson was told that the shipment had landed and would soon be distributed to the Mexican military to potentially use against Americans. All on the call agreed that they must prevent that outcome, serving as the catalyst for the President to issue the following order: "Daniels, send this message to Admiral Fletcher: 'Take Vera Cruz at Once.'"[147] Secretary Daniels passed the order to Admiral Frank Fletcher: "Seize custom house. Do not permit war supplies to be delivered to Huerta government or to any other party."[148] The Americans landed at Veracruz within hours.

The Mexicans may have been overmatched by the American military, but they did not simply throw down their arms and surrender. The Americans emerged from the fight triumphant, but it was a costly battle on both sides. Nineteen Americans lost their lives and 70 more were wounded in the engagement that also claimed the lives of 126 Mexicans. The city of Veracruz was now firmly in control of the American military, including its custom house and the guns which had recently been received from the Germans. Almost immediately, several South American countries offered to help arbitrate the overarching dispute between their neighbors to the north. Representatives from Argentina, Brazil, and Chile met with American and Mexican diplomats at Niagara Falls, but no agreements were reached as the Wilson administration refused to budge off its longstanding insistence that

President Huerta leave office and the Mexican people be given the opportunity to elect their own leaders in a free and fair election. For the first time, the Americans had real leverage against the Huerta government. Control of Veracruz meant the U.S. could block all shipments that would typically flow through that port on their way across the country. As the nation suffered, the pressure on Huerta mounted to the point where he could no longer resist the call to abdicate. In July 1914, Huerta left Mexico for asylum in Spain. Whether anything would be any better under his replacement would take some time to be seen.

Just south of Mexico was a cause for celebration the following month when the *Ancon*, a U.S. cargo and passenger ship, became the first to traverse the Panama Canal. After decades of wrangling over the optimal path for the connector of the Atlantic and the Pacific, it took only five years of actual construction to bring the canal to life. A last-minute dust-up was facing President Wilson, though, as the first ships readied to sail through the locks. Under the previous administration, the Americans passed a law that exempted U.S. vessels from the fee that would be charged to ships from all other nations for use of the manmade waterway. The rationale was that the Americans had already paid for the construction of the canal, so why should they have to continue to fund the effort on a trip-by-trip basis? The rest of the world, however, cried foul, with the strongest protests coming from the British. After all, it had been the Hay-Pauncefote Treaty signed between the world's leading English-speaking nations that canceled British claims to a Central American canal in return for some key assurances, including that the canal would be built "on terms of entire equality."[149] These new economic rules were a violation of that agreement, and the British led an international contingent of complaints falling at the feet of President Woodrow Wilson.

President Wilson was strongly encouraged to stay the course, to stand up to the British and do what was best for American interests. These people didn't know Woodrow Wilson very well. The President had an overwhelmingly powerful sense of duty, which, in his current role, meant the responsibility to live up to one's commitments. In the case of the Panama Canal tolls, that meant the Americans must pay their fair share because that was a key consideration for the agreement for the British to cast aside their own selfish interests in the first place. "I am the trustee of the people," Wilson shared with his personal secretary, "and I am bound to take cognizance of the fact that by reason of our attitude on

Panama tolls our treaties are discredited in every chancellery of Europe, where we are looked upon as a nation that does not live up to its plighted word. We may have made a very bad bargain with England on Panama tolls, but it will be all the more credit to us if we stand by an agreement even when it entails a sacrifice on our part."[150] Wilson successfully lobbied Congress to rescind the toll exemption, once again restoring the equal terms that had been agreed to at the outset and making a statement to the world in the process. "When everything else about this Administration has been forgotten," Wilson told Tumulty, "its attitude on the Panama Tolls treaty will be remembered as a long forward step in the process of making the conduct between nations the same as that which obtains between honourable individuals dealing with each other, scrupulously respecting their contracts, no matter what the cost."[151] While some protests emanated from within his own country, President Wilson, in this case, was more attuned to the rightful praise coming from Europe for a politician willing to do the right thing, even if not popular amongst his own people. Recently retired British Ambassador James Bryce spoke for many across the Atlantic when he called Wilson's actions on the Panama tolls "the finest, most dignified, most courageous thing done in the United States for many years: perhaps, indeed, since Lincoln's second inaugural."[152]

This sense of a moral duty being integral to proper governance was a dominant theme in the decision-making of Woodrow Wilson, but it was hardly anything new. Wilson had long placed significant weight on fulfilling one's duty regardless of the personal consequences as essential in all human endeavors. He took a moment to try to make his thoughts clear on the topic in another conversation with Joe Tumulty.

> I am cold in a certain sense. Were I a judge and my own son should be convicted of murder, and I was the only judge privileged to pass judgment upon the case, I would do my duty even to the point of sentencing him to death. It would be a hard thing to do but it would be my solemn duty as a judge to do it, but I would do it, because the state cannot be maintained and its sovereignty vindicated or its integrity preserved unless the law is strictly enforced and without favour. It is the business of the judge to uphold it and he must do it to the point of every sacrifice. If he fails, justice fails, the state falls. That looks cold-blooded, doesn't it? But I would do it.[153]

After a brief pause, and to close the thought, Wilson said, "Then, after sentencing my own son to death, I would go out and die of a broken heart, for it would surely kill me." And while this scenario was purely hypothetical, the theme of doing one's duty with lives on the line and personal reputation at risk would be central to the balance of Wilson's tenure as his nation's chief executive.

Since early in the summer, President Wilson knew that Europe was a tinderbox ready to explode. Colonel House had been traveling through the capitals of Europe on behalf of the American President, trying to get a sense of the likelihood of armed conflict on a continent that found itself in a web of secret treaties that mandated military support from partner nations if their allies were ever attacked. As a result, a single dust-up could turn into battles across the continent almost overnight. The encoded telegrams from House were hardly promising. After he finally secured a private meeting with Kaiser Wilhelm of Germany, House informed his President:

> The situation is extraordinary. It is militarism run stark mad. Unless some one acting for you can bring about a different understanding, there is some day to be an awful cataclysm. No one in Europe can do it. There is too much hatred, too many jealousies. … It is an absorbing problem, and one of tremendous consequence.[154]

Just a month after this note, the powder keg exploded.

5. Crises: International and Personal

On June 28, 1914, a Bosnian Serb assassinated Archduke Franz Ferdinand, the heir apparent to the Austro-Hungarian Empire, in Sarajevo. Exactly a month later, Austria declared war on Serbia. Based on existing treaties, Russia was obligated to defend Serbia, so it declared war on Austria. This brought Germany directly into the conflict, committed to defending its ally Austria. Germany declared war on Russia, as well as France, based on a Russo-French alliance. Once France was in the fray, that brought the British in as well. To top things off, Japan declared war on Germany, and World War I was underway. As Europe began to dig in for the long haul of mechanized warfare, the Americans stood firmly on its longstanding tradition of neutrality in foreign conflicts like this one. During one of his press conferences at the time the European conflagration began, President Wilson simply stated, "The United States has never attempted to interfere in European affairs,"[155] dating back to the policies of the nation's first President, George Washington. Wilson saw no reason to change directions at this time. Coincident with the President's affirmation of neutrality, he barred Americans from fighting for either side in the conflict, as well as banned ships from the belligerents from U.S. waters and ports. For now, American companies were free to continue to do business with the warring powers, but they did so at their own risk. Accidents were inevitable on the high seas during war, and American merchantmen were warned by the country's pacifistic Secretary of State William Bryan to be careful as they neared the highly contested waters of Europe.

While the world focused on the crisis in Europe, Woodrow Wilson had more pressing concerns within his Washington, D.C., home. His wife was not well. Ellen Wilson had been suffering from fatigue and other maladies, and things were getting worse. Dr. Grayson had brought in a handful of specialists to see if they could

II-44: First Lady Ellen Wilson

get to the bottom of the situation, and their results were devastating. On the same day that Europe erupted in war, Ellen Wilson was diagnosed with Bright's Disease, a sort-of catch-all title for various ailments of the kidneys, which were almost always fatal. Upon hearing the news, Wilson's daughters saw their father cry for the first time.

Wilson sat with his wife nearly around the clock, following the situation in Europe as best he could, but far more concerned with the woman with whom he had spent more than half his life as his partner and most loyal supporter. By August 6, there was no escaping the outcome. Ellen Wilson was dying, and there was nothing anyone could do to stop it. As the end became near, the First Lady whispered to Dr. Grayson, "Promise me that when I go you will take care of Woodrow."[156] Before the day was out, she was gone.

Wilson was devastated by the loss, not sure which direction to turn. "The days … that followed were heartbreaking," according to Dr. Grayson.[157] Son-in-law Francis Sayre wrote, "It is pathetic to see the President; he hardly knows where to turn."[158] Wilson wrote to Mary Peck (now Mary Hulburt after her recent divorce from Thomas Peck) that "God has stricken me almost beyond what I can bear."[159] Ellen's funeral was held in the East Room of the White House on August 10, after which the family traveled by train to Ellen's hometown of Rome, Georgia for her burial. Wilson stayed glued to her casket the entire journey, and had tears in his eyes throughout the burial at Myrtle Hill Cemetery. All of this personal anguish was occurring while Germany was attacking France (through Belgium) to the west and Russia to the east.

The political calendar in the United States doesn't deviate for personal or national traumas, and there was an election pending that would provide the American people the first opportunity to assess the Wilson administration. Even though his name wasn't on the ballot in these congressional midterms, the President knew that "People . . . know that to vote against a democratic ticket is to vote indirectly against me."[160] The Democrats actually picked up four seats in the Senate but lost 60 in the House, which Wilson took as a public rebuke. His party still maintained majorities in both houses, but the margin for error was greatly decreased. When Wilson spoke to Congress for his Annual Message on December 8, he touted his country's state of peace with the world, and he made it clear he had no plans to institute preparations for armed conflict with anyone. While the war hawks, led by former President Theodore

Roosevelt, lambasted Wilson for his passivity, the current Commander in Chief was convinced the American people were on his side in favor of neutrality.

Wilson was personally on edge, trying to deal with the overwhelming personal loss of his spouse while attempting to navigate his country's stance amidst a war that continued to expand beyond the center of Europe. An eruption was bound to occur, and for Woodrow Wilson, it landed on civil rights advocate William Trotter. Black leaders continued to seethe over Wilson's segregationist policies in the Federal government. Trotter was among those who felt betrayed by Wilson's entreaties to Blacks during the campaign, and he took that message directly to the Oval Office. "Only two years ago you were heralded as perhaps the second Lincoln," Trotter told the President, "and now the Afro-American leaders who supported you are hounded as false leaders and traitors to the race. What a change segregation has wrought!"[161] Trotter was just getting started. "You said that your 'Colored fellow citizens could depend upon you for everything which would assist in advancing the interest of their race in the United States.'" Looking at the results, Trotter asked Wilson whether there was a "new freedom" for White Americans and a "new slavery for your Afro-American fellow citizens."[162] With that, the President had had enough. "Your tone, sir, offends me," Wilson proclaimed. "You are an American citizen, as fully an American citizen as I am, but you are the only American citizen that has ever come into this office who has talked to me with a tone ... of passion that was evident. Now, I want to say that if this association comes again, it must have another spokesman." As Trotter persisted in articulating the complaints of his people, Wilson grew more furious. "You have spoiled the whole cause for which you came,"[163] Wilson declared as he finally brought the meeting to an end.

II-45: William Trotter, circa 1915

Trotter went public with his account of the encounter, which elicited strong reactions from the Black community. According to James Johnson of *The New York Age*, one of the nation's oldest Black newspapers, Wilson "bears the discreditable distinction of being the first President of the United States, since Emancipation, who openly condoned and vindicated prejudice against the Negro."[164] Even many in the White press took Wilson to task, decrying "an Administration so noble in its feeling for the under-dog ... [but] cannot do simple justice when it comes to the color line."[165] None of this had much of an impact on Woodrow Wilson, who still believed in the merits of his racial policies, and, besides, from his perspective, he had a lot more pressing topics to worry about.

Colonel House continued serving as President Wilson's unofficial ambassador at large in Europe. As the calendar switched to 1915, and with Europe in flames, House met with British Monarch George V and Foreign Secretary Sir Edmund Gray before leaving for similar high-level talks in both France and Germany. His messages back to the White House were hardly encouraging. "In each government that I have visited I have found stubbornness, determination, selfishness and cant," House wrote. "My observation is that incompetent statesmanship and selfishness is at the bottom of it all. It is not so much a breaking down of civilization as a lack of wisdom in those that govern; and history, I believe, will bring an awful indictment against those who were short-sighted and selfish enough to let such a tragedy happen."[166] Wilson was adamant that the United States remain neutral, in part because that was the only way for the Americans to deal fairly with all sides if ever permitted to play the role of peacemaker. Wilson had his eyes on the future, trying to envision a peace that would last. He was slowly developing the critical conditions he believed essential for any peace plan. These included the following principles:

> [There] must never again be a foot of ground acquired by conquest
>
> [There] must be recognized in fact that the small nations are on an equality of rights with the great nations
>
> [Ammunition] must be manufactured by governments and not by private individuals
>
> [There] must be some sort of an association of nations wherein all shall guarantee the territorial integrity of each.[167]

Wilson didn't have a peace plan, per se, but he was definitely starting to formulate his thoughts in that direction.

As much as President Wilson wanted to plan for the future, he still had to deal with the immediate implications to his own citizens from the conflict across the Atlantic. Foremost on his mind was the American economy. On the one hand, the war represented an opportunity, as the combatants were anxious to get their hands on American goods that could support the war effort. The problem was that the U.S. lacked sufficient shipping tonnage to transport all these goods. The vast majority of ships that usually carried such cargo were owned by the belligerents and were now banned from doing business with the Americans. Wall Street was nervous during these uncertain times. In a highly unusual move, trade was halted on the jittery U.S. stock exchange, which remained closed for a record four and a half months while the country sought a stabilizing solution. Moreover, tariff revenue fell precipitously, forcing Congress to raise $100 million from an increase in internal taxes to offset those losses to Federal revenue.

Treasury Secretary McAdoo felt the government needed to take action to help American businesses fulfill the demand for U.S. goods. His proposal was for a Ship Purchase Bill that would authorize the government to fund the building of a new fleet of American vessels to carry these goods to the European markets. The administration immediately encountered significant opposition to the plan. Such legislation might jeopardize the true nature of American neutrality, plus it wreaked of socialism with the government getting directly into the shipbuilding business. Republicans in the Senate staged a filibuster toward the end of the congressional session, killing the bill, at least for the time being. Neutrality would remain the watchword of American foreign policy in these early stages of the war.

6. Love Amidst a World at War

Moments of joy were increasingly rare for Woodrow Wilson from the summer of 1914 into the spring of 1915. One bright spot was the birth of his first grandchild, Francis Sayre, Jr., born to Jessie on January 17, 1915. It was a bittersweet moment, to be sure, without Ellen at his side to join in any celebration. But things were about to take a turn for the positive for the nation's President. Just a few months since the passing of his wife, Woodrow Wilson set his sights on another woman. The connection ran through Dr. Grayson, who was about to become engaged to Altrude Gordon. Gordon was friends with a 42-year-old widow by the name of Edith Galt. Galt, who hailed from Wytheville, Virginia, had lost her husband, Norman, about seven years before. She had taken over her husband's jewelry business, residing in a modest home on 20th St. NW. Gordon wanted to bring Galt to the White House to meet both Grayson and the President, but Edith balked, saying such a connection in the world of politics was beyond her comfort level. She did agree, however, to meet Wilson's cousin, Helen Bones, who was living in the White House and helping out since Ellen's passing. Bones was lonely in Washington and looking for companionship, and she and Edith hit it off right away. The first time the President laid eyes on Edith Galt was during a drive with Grayson, who recognized her on the street. After Grayson signaled a greeting in her direction, Wilson asked his physician, "Who is that beautiful woman?"[168]

II-46: President Wilson with his first grandchild, Francis Sayre, Jr.

Helen Bones continued to share stories about Wilson with her new friend, such that Edith's "imagination was fired by the picture Helen gave me of a lonely man, detached from old friends and associations, the fate of official life – uncomplainingly bearing the burden of a great sorrow and keeping his eye single to the responsibilities of a great task."[169] Finally, after one of their walks together, Bones insisted that Edith accompany her to the White House for tea. "Cousin Woodrow asked me the other day why I never brought my friends back there," Bones said. "He really wishes I would have some one in that lonely old house."[170] Besides, the President was playing golf with Dr. Grayson, so Edith had nothing to worry about.

It turns out that all four arrived at the White House at about the same time, creating the first meeting between Wilson and Edith. The President insisted that they all have tea together as soon as he could change his muddy clothes. As Edith later wrote, "This was the accidental meeting which carried out the old adage of 'turn a corner and meet your fate.'"[171] The four spent a lovely evening together, which Edith believed "ended all too soon, for it was the first time I had felt the warm personality of Woodrow Wilson. A boylike simplicity dwelt in the background of an official life which had to be content with the husks of formal contacts when starving for the bread of human companionship. Thereafter I never thought of him as the President of the United States, but as a real friend."[172] Wilson was thinking even more than that.

II-47 Edith Galt

More encounters followed almost immediately, often involving car rides or walks in Rock Creek Park, typically with Bones, Dr. Grayson, or daughter Margaret as chaperone. By the end of April, Wilson and Edith were active in daily correspondence, often with Bones passing the letters between them. The couple was seen in public at a Washington Senators baseball game where the President threw out the first pitch. Edith became a regular at the White House, enjoying dinners and discussions well into the evening with the President. By May 3, just a couple of months since they first met, Woodrow Wilson was alone with Edith at the White House when he expressed his love for her. "Oh, you can't love me," she immediately replied, "for you don't really know me, and it is less than a year since your wife died." But Wilson was determined to make his case. "I know you feel that," he said, "but, little girl, in this place time is not measured by weeks, or months, or years, but by deep human experiences; and since her death I have lived a lifetime of loneliness and heartache. I was afraid, knowing you, I would shock you; but I would be less than a gentleman if I continued to make opportunities to see you without telling you what I have told my daughters and Helen: that I want you to be my wife."[173] Edith almost didn't know what to say, leaving the impression that she was not in favor of the match. The fallout came the next day when Helen Bones was in tears as she told Edith, "Cousin Woodrow looks really ill this morning. … Just as I thought some happiness was coming into his life! And now you are breaking his heart."[174] Wilson, though, was undeterred. His letter writing and gift giving only intensified, convinced that he and Edith were meant to be together.

President Wilson's personal and professional worlds were both heating up at the same time. At one moment, he was wooing Edith Galt, while a minute later he was dealing with German aggression on the high seas. While the land battles in Europe had largely devolved into trench warfare, where thousands were being killed and little ground gained by either side, the conflict at sea had taken on two distinct flavors. The British used their overwhelming superiority with surface ships to blockade German ports, while the Germans used their edge in submarines to put any sailing vessel in the region at risk of being sunk. On May 1, 1915, for example, the American tanker *Gulflight* was torpedoed by a German U-Boat, leaving three U.S. citizens dead. But the big blow came a week later, on May 7, when the Germans sent the British ocean liner RMS *Lusitania* to the bottom of the Irish Sea. Without warning, two torpedoes crashed into the ship bound for England from New York, killing 1,198 people, including 128 Americans. Calls for an armed response echoed throughout the United States. Theodore Roosevelt spoke for many when he told a reporter, "It seems inconceivable that we can refrain from taking action in this matter, for we owe it not only to humanity but to our own self-respect."[175] Some in the Cabinet, like Secretary of War Garrison, agreed, but others, like Secretary of State

II-48: Sinking of the Lusitania, May 7, 1915

Bryan, argued for calm. In this instance, Bryan was sympathetic to the Germans, who claimed the *Lusitania* was carrying ammunition on board bound for the Allies, thereby making it a legitimate military target. The President continued to lean toward neutrality, while his focus was divided. As he was waiting for details on the *Lusitania* disaster, he was writing Edith, "And, oh, how I needed you tonight, my sweet Edith! What a touch of your hand and a look into your eyes would have meant to me of strength and steadfastness as I made the final decision as to what I should say to Germany."[176] The next day, he offered, "You ask why you have been chosen to help me! Ah, dear love, there is a mystery about it ... but there is no mistake and there is no doubt!"[177]

Edith's resistance to the President's charms was quickly breaking down. She traveled with him the next day to Philadelphia where he spoke about world affairs to 15,000 people at Constitution Hall. After expressing his love to Edith, he took the stage to portray why the U.S. would not immediately be taking up arms against anyone. "The example of America must be the example not merely of peace because it will not fight," Wilson proclaimed, "but of peace because it is the healing and elevating influence of the world, and strife is not. There is such a thing as a man being too proud to fight. There is such a thing as a nation being so right that it does not need to convince others by force that it is right."[178]

The President was excoriated for these sentiments by the war hawks in his own country as well as leaders of the nations overseas who felt they had plenty of pride but were nevertheless involved in a righteous undertaking on the field of battle. Nevertheless, Wilson continued to believe the majority of Americans wanted to stay on the sidelines, and he was determined to do so as well.

Wilson did take one step in confronting Germany over the sinking of the *Lusitania* – he wrote them a letter of complaint. The American President demanded a disavowal of the sinking, reparations for the victims, and assurances that neutral ships would not be similarly targeted in the future. Secretary Bryan thought the message was too one-sided and might provoke the Germans to even greater atrocities that would force the Americans into the conflict. He also grumbled over House's role in Europe on behalf of the President, which was undermining his authority in foreign affairs. For the first time, Bryan indicated he might not be able to stay in the Cabinet if things didn't change in these areas. As for the Germans, they rejected the position of the Americans, reiterating that the *Lusitania* was carrying military supplies, which meant it was a legitimate target. While they agreed not to attack truly neutral vessels, they warned ships masquerading as neutral when actually offering aid to the Allies would face the same fate as the *Lusitania*.

The President had begun confiding with Edith Galt across all aspects of his personal and professional life, and she was not shy with her opinions on matters of state. When Wilson informed her that Secretary Bryan was considering resigning, she was more than ready for him to depart. "Good," she answered, "for I hope you can replace him with someone who is able and who would in himself command respect for the office both at home and abroad."[179] Sure enough, as Bryan believed the President's next letter to the Germans continued to portray a one-sided response, Bryan felt he could no longer serve the President and tendered his resignation, which Wilson accepted. Edith was glad to see "that awful Deserter" gone, to which Wilson replied with his own strong feelings about Bryan: "Whew! ... In my secret heart (which is never secret from you) … he is a traitor, though I can say so, as yet, only to you."[180]

Edith remained Wilson's highest priority, determined as ever to convince her to become his bride. In June, Edith joined Wilson, his daughter Margaret, and Helen Bones for a vacation in Cornish, New Hampshire. The setting was perfect for bringing the couple even closer together without the constant distractions of affairs of state. Some were concerned that the President might be shirking his responsibilities at a time of global crisis. Colonel House, for example, noted that "It seems the President is wholly absorbed in this love affair and is neglecting practically everything else."[181] Wilson continued to read dispatches and engage in official correspondence, but most of this six-week period was focused on Edith. And those efforts seemed to be paying off. She later noted, "Those days in Cornish had brought the banishment of any doubt of my love for Woodrow Wilson."[182] Wilson was the first to return to the nation's capital, but even when apart, the couple maintained their connection through lengthy intimate letters. By the time Edith was back in D.C. in late August, she was ready to commit to Wilson. On a drive through Rock Creek Park on September 3, Wilson tried again to seal the deal. "And so, little girl," he said, "I have no right to ask you to help me by sharing this load that is almost breaking my back, for I know your nature and you might do it out of sheer pity." It wasn't a formal proposal, but Edith was ready with her response anyway. As she later recalled, "I put my arms around his neck and said: 'Well, if you won't ask me, I will volunteer, and be ready to be mustered in as soon as can be.'"[183] Wilson's daughters were given the happy news the next day. All three were in favor of the match. Margaret, for one, told Edith, "I'm so glad that he has your love to help him and support him in these terrible times! … I love you dear Edith, and I love to be with you."[184] The world may have been falling apart, but Woodrow Wilson's world was finally coming back together. He could barely contain his joy, often spotted singing aloud, "Oh, you beautiful doll!"[185] which perfectly conveyed his thoughts toward his fiancée. The engagement was made public on October 6.

Edith would be completely devoted to Wilson for the rest of his life, and she would become the center of his universe. The bond between the highly opinionated couple would place strains on some of the President's other relationships, sometimes reflective of Edith's jealousy over who had the greatest influence on her soon-to-be husband. She was particularly cautious about House, whom she described as "not a very strong character . . . a weak vessel."[186] The President didn't pay too much attention to this particular criticism – at least for the time being. However, Wilson did focus briefly on his relationship with Mary Peck. The President nervously confided with Edith some of the details of their intimate correspondence, and that he had recently heard that some of these documents might become public to embarrass him (and her). Edith was unsettled at first by the revelation and spent hours alone thinking about the implications. In the wee hours of the morning, she wrote Wilson a response, making clear she was ready to commit to him, for better or for worse. "This is my pledge, dearest one, I will stand by you – not for duty, not for pity, not for honour – but for love – trusting, protecting, comprehending love. And no matter whether the wine be bitter or sweet we will share it together and find happiness in comradeship."[187] Wilson admitted during their honeymoon that he had been too scared to read her response and only knew things would be right between them when she came to the White House a couple of days later at the request of Dr. Grayson to care for Wilson, who was ill in bed. During their honeymoon, they read the note together, and Wilson "begged that the letter never be destroyed."[188] What would come to an end was Wilson's letter-writing with Mary Peck. While Ellen Wilson had made peace with the relationship, Edith Galt would not, and Wilson would not push the issue. That correspondence was essentially done for good as the President turned the corner to this new phase of his personal life.

II-49: President Wilson with the new First Lady, Edith Wilson

As hundreds of thousands were dying in Europe, President Wilson reaffirmed his stance of remaining "studiously neutral"[189] in his December 7 Annual Message to Congress. Eleven days later, he took his wedding vows in a tiny ceremony at Edith's home. Less than 30 people were invited to cram into the small space, after which the newlyweds hustled off to their honeymoon in Hot Springs, Virginia. Wilson was fundamentally reborn, past the grief of the loss of his first wife, full speed ahead in life and his responsibilities. "We are having a heavenly time here," Wilson wrote. "I shall go back to Washington feeling complete and strong for whatever may betide. I am indeed blessed beyond my (or any other man's) deserts."[190] The return to D.C. would come sooner than planned, as the outside world continued to intrude on Wilson's newest state of bliss.

On December 30, a German submarine torpedoed the British cruiser *Persia* off the coast of Crete. Seventy percent of the ship's 500 passengers perished as the attack came without any warning. Wilson remained adamant about maintaining his nation's neutrality in the conflict but, for the first time, conceded the Americans owed it to themselves to at least begin preparations in the event that war could no longer be avoided. In early 1916, he launched the "President's Preparedness Campaign" with a series of speeches in cities such as Pittsburgh, Cleveland, Chicago, and Des Moines. He emphasized that any effort to join the war must be preceded by clear support from a strong majority of the American people.

> I hate war; I loathe it as either a means or an end, but when I do wage it, believe me it is going to be to the limit. But it must be with a united national sentiment. Nothing short of that must be back of the boys who go. The instant I see we have this united national sentiment, I'll light the spark. But until I am convinced of that, I am willing to be misunderstood. Better misunderstood in peace than underarmed in war.[191]

For the time being, Wilson refused to pick sides in the war and tried to deflect any suggestions that the Americans were close to joining the fight.

While Secretary Bryan had resigned from the Cabinet over what he believed to be the President's overly belligerent stance against the Germans, Secretary of War Garrison resigned in February 1916 for exactly the opposite reason. Garrison had always been one of the leading hawks in the Cabinet, and he felt he could no longer sit inside an administration that refused to engage in a fight for the future of mankind. Garrison had actually offered to resign previously, but Wilson had refused to accept. Not anymore. He wanted unity lined up behind his leadership, so Garrison was out, and Newton Baker was in. Baker had no background in military affairs, but he had known Wilson since their days together at Johns Hopkins, had supported him during the campaign, and could be counted on as a reliable subordinate. He had his hands full in the post, beginning with his first day on the job.

That day was March 9, which saw a new spark in the American conflict with Mexico. After President Huerta left the previous year, the country split into two camps – one behind Venustiano Carranza and the other behind Pancho Villa. Just within the past few months, the United States had joined most of the nations of the world in formally recognizing the Carranza government, which Villa saw as a national betrayal. He and his armed followers were champing at the bit to fight for their rights, with the Americans perceived as an enemy preventing their legitimate rise to power. On Baker's first day in office, Villa crossed the border with 1,500 men, initiating an attack on Americans in Columbus, New Mexico, three miles inside U.S. territory. Villa's band of marauders burned buildings and shot up the town, killing 17 Americans before U.S. soldiers responded and forced the attackers back across the Mexican border. All eyes focused on President Wilson to see how he might react to this unprovoked attack on his fellow citizens on American soil.

II-50: Pancho Villa

Wilson did not seek a declaration of war against Mexico, as he believed Villa's band did not represent the official government of the American neighbor to the south. Nevertheless, he did agree that a military response was needed. The President selected Brigadier General John Pershing to lead a force of approximately 5,000 men into Mexico to capture Villa and bring him to justice. Wilson had hoped the Carranza government would assist the Americans, but the Mexicans refused. Instead, they decried the American response as simply an invasion of their country. These protestations aside, Pershing's men aggressively pursued Villa's trail, leading to a direct confrontation on June 21 at the Battle of Carrizal. Both sides were bloodied, with nine Americans killed, a dozen wounded, and 25 captured, while 30 Mexicans lost their lives. But the bottom line was that Villa and most of his men escaped, leaving the U.S. Commander-in-Chief despondent over his army's inability to complete its mission. "The break seems to have come in Mexico," Wilson wrote Colonel House, "and all my patience seems to have gone for nothing. I am infinitely sad about it."[192] While Pershing wanted to continue the pursuit, Wilson decided to cut his losses and bring the effort to an end. As the situation in Europe increasingly demanded the administration's focus, Wilson quietly withdrew the U.S. troops from Mexico and, within a few more months, formalized full diplomatic relations with the Carranza government. Trouble would continue to persist south of the U.S.-Mexican border, including the assassination of Carranza in 1920, but the Wilson administration would mostly be observers and not participants in these subsequent activities.

The latest atrocity on the high seas occurred in March 1916 when the Germans sunk the SS *Sussex*, resulting in the loss of 50 lives, including several Americans. As before, the cries for war heated up, but President Wilson continued to resist the call. Once again, he picked up his pen to complain. This time he threatened "that unless the Imperial German Government should now immediately declare and effect an abandonment of its present methods of warfare against passenger and freight-carrying vessels this government can have no choice but to sever diplomatic relations with the government of the German Empire altogether."[193] The Germans were trying to balance their need to deny shipments to the Allies while highly desirous of keeping the Americans on the sidelines. Their diplomatic response to Wilson's outreach indicated that Germany was "prepared to do its utmost to confine the operations of war for the rest of its duration to the fighting forces of the belligerents, thereby also insuring the freedom of the seas."[194] But was there any substance behind that statement? In this case, the answer appeared to be yes – at least for several months before conditions would change yet again.

Woodrow Wilson was fully aware that he had entered the year in which the American people would decide whether he would continue as the nation's chief executive. It was a busy year on the domestic front, which often took a back seat to the historic happenings in foreign affairs. But Wilson kept his progressive agenda going, seeing not only righteous causes which merited enabling legislation but also good politics. Working with Congress, Wilson brought to life the National Park Service Act, which authorized the regulation of existing parks as well as opened the door for the addition of new parks into the national program. Also

II-51: President Wilson in the White House

coming on line was new legislation in the areas of child labor protections, worker's compensation for Federal employees, and a Revenue Act that increased tax rates and added an estate tax on assets worth over $5 million. The administration's boldest move came amid a pending national railroad strike that would have crippled the country's transportation network at a time when bringing goods to export markets was critical to the health of the American economy and the war effort of the Allies. The President brought labor and management to Washington, and putting aside his sense of neutrality, he told the parties that "The Allies are fighting our battle, the battle of civilization, across the way. They cannot carry on without supplies and means of sustenance which the railroads of America bring to them. I am probably asking you to make a sacrifice at this time, but is not the sacrifice worth while because of the things involved?"[195] But neither side was willing to budge despite the urging of the President. So, Wilson decided to take matters into his own hands and proposed a legislative solution to the most important topic in the dispute. He advocated for what would be called the Adamson Act, which imposed an eight-hour workday on the railroad industry. This provision had long been sought by progressives and would quickly be adopted across most American industries. The strike was averted, and the progressive agenda had another win.

The President also made some noise in the spring of 1916 after the death of Supreme Court Associate Justice Joseph Lamar. Wilson's choice to fill the vacancy was Louis Brandeis, the man who had been so helpful in discussing economic issues during Wilson's first campaign for the presidency. Brandeis was a leading progressive and was sure to bring a new perspective to a fairly conservative Court. Many thought the appointment to be too radical and were not shy about voicing their opposition. Among the most vocal was former President William Taft, who cherished the judiciary and thought this appointment was destructive to that branch of government and the Constitution. The usually mild-mannered Taft called the move by Wilson "one of the deepest wounds that I have suffered as an American and as a lover of the Constitution … that such a man as Brandeis could be put on the court. … He is a muckraker, an emotionalist for his own purposes, a socialist ... a man who has certain ideals ... of great tenacity of purpose, and in my judgment of much power for evil."[196] At the time, Supreme Court nominations were typically a one day affair. Not so the appointment of Louis Brandeis. For the first time, a Supreme Court nominee faced difficult questions in the form of a confirmation hearing, after which the debate continued for close to four months. Woodrow Wilson, for one, was not backing down, offering a strong public statement of support for his nominee.

> I cannot speak too highly of his impartial, impersonal, orderly, and constructive mind, his rare analytical powers, his deep human sympathy, his profound acquaintance with the historical roots of our institutions and insight into their spirit, or of the many evidences he has given of being imbued to the very heart with our American ideals of economic conditions and of the way they bear upon the masses of the people.[197]

Wilson's persistence paid off, as Brandeis was eventually confirmed, becoming the first Jew to sit on the U.S. Supreme Court.

Despite all this activity, in a very consequential first term, Wilson's reelection prospects really came down to six words: "He kept us out of war."[198] That was the campaign theme upon which the American people would render their verdict on the Wilson administration when they went to the polls on November 7, 1916. Wilson knew that the easiest way to secure re-election was by taking his country to war, but he refused to consider such a proposition. "Tumulty," he said to his personal secretary, "you may as well understand my position right now. If my re-election as President depends upon my getting into war, I don't want to be President. … I have made up my mind that I am more interested in the opinion that the country will have of me ten years from now than the opinion it may be willing to express today. Of course, I understand that the country wants action ... but I will not be rushed into war, no matter if every damned congressman and senator stands up on his hind legs and proclaims me a coward."[199] Instead, Wilson appealed to the American people that his neutral stand was in the best interest of the United States, and the only way to preserve American independence when it came time to assist in the negotiations of a meaningful peace that would stand the test of time. The Democratic Convention was a short affair, as Wilson and Vice President Marshall were both renominated without dissent, with the platform entirely conforming to the President's worldview. The Republicans were eager to offer an alternative that would take the country in a different direction.

The opposition party continued to be fractured, not yet recovering from the Roosevelt/Taft split from the previous canvass. Roosevelt would have welcomed the Republican nomination in 1916, but the party was hardly ready to welcome him back into the fold after the destruction he had caused four years before. This time, however, Roosevelt spurned another nomination from his Progressive Party, knowing that such a move would simply guarantee four more years of Woodrow Wilson. Instead, he agreed to support the nomination of Associate Justice Charles Evans Hughes, who had been on the Supreme Court for the last six years after serving as Governor of New York. Hughes was pro-business and pro-war, the latter perspective likely to be the determining factor in the election.

II-52: Campaign pin for Republican Charles Evans Hughes, 1916

Wilson mostly shied away from public campaigning, although he did offer a weekly campaign-style address throughout the summer months. Hughes, on the other hand, barnstormed the country after tendering his resignation from the Court. Hughes's attack lines focused his criticism on Wilson's policies over the war in Europe, the conflict with Mexico, and what he labeled as socialist tendencies in domestic affairs. Wilson could count on the Solid South, while Hughes and the Republicans found their strength in the North and East. The election would likely be decided in the Midwest and

West in what was expected to be a very close race. In fact, Wilson went to bed on election night assuming that he had lost. As the results began to be tallied, the path to victory appeared exceptionally small. After losing his home state of New Jersey by 12 points, along with a number of the other large states in the East, he told his wife, "Well, little girl, you were right in expecting we should lose the election. Frankly I did not, but we can now do some of the things we want to do."[200] But Tumulty was among those unwilling to give up until all the votes were counted. He was getting some reports that the Republicans weren't ready to claim victory, as some of the races in the West were still too close to call. While Woodrow Wilson slept, the political teams spent the night looking for a conclusive sign, particularly from California, which was going to go down to the wire.

It would take another three days before the results in California could be called, with its decisive 13 electoral votes hanging in the balance. In the end, Wilson edged Hughes in California by just over 3,000 votes out of more than one million cast (.003%). That gave Wilson 277 electoral votes compared to 254 for Hughes. Hughes didn't concede right away, waiting for the official tally to be tabulated on November 22, at which time he acknowledged the race was over. Things were close in Congress as well. Wilson's Democrats lost two seats in the Senate but still held a 54-42 advantage. Things were not so positive in the House, where the Republicans gained enough seats such that the Democrats needed to partner with a few Progressives to maintain their majority. While the country was clearly divided, Wilson had his four more years locked up, and he was determined to stay the course on the policies which he believed had been validated by the electorate.

To this end, the President decided to take out his pen and draft an open letter to the belligerents. Wilson's so-called "peace note" was intended to force both sides to make clear their specific goals from the conflict as a possible starting point on the path to peace. Colonel House and Robert Lansing, who had taken over for Bryan at the State Department, were both opposed to the effort as appearing too pro-German when most Americans had chosen sides with the Allies. After Wilson sent the note, House confided in his diary that it "nearly destroyed all the work I have done in Europe"[201] as the Allies were not inclined to become party to any peace effort that would not validate their claims against the German aggressors. Secretary Lansing went even further, taking public his concerns about the pro-German perception of the President's note. On his own accord, Lansing sought to clarify "that we are drawing nearer to the verge of war ourselves, and therefore we are entitled to know exactly what each belligerent seeks in order that we may regulate our conduct in the future."[202] The President was outraged, as he (and many others) interpreted Lansing's public missive as forecasting war for the Americans rather than Wilson's desire to achieve peace without entering the conflict. After nearly terminating Lansing over this insubordination, the President settled for a clarifying statement from his Secretary of State, who immediately complied.

II-53: President Wilson, 1917 (age 60)

Wilson kept up the pressure with another major address to Congress on January 22, 1917. This speech introduced new rhetoric for the quickest path to peace – "peace without victory."[203] With the two sides so evenly matched, and the casualties continuing to mount to levels never before seen in the history of the world, Wilson emphasized that:

> It must be a peace without victory … Victory would mean peace forced upon the loser, a victor's terms imposed upon the vanquished. It would be accepted in humiliation, under duress, at an intolerable sacrifice, and would leave a sting, a resentment, a bitter memory upon which terms of peace would rest, not permanently, but only as upon quicksand. Only a peace between equals can last.[204]

The President's lofty vision aside, there were no takers abroad and plenty of dissent domestically as well. While he was focused on ensuring a lasting peace such that this kind of war would never take place again, victory remained the sole objective of the belligerents – one of which was about to change the course of the war while convincing even Woodrow Wilson to finally bring his country into the conflict.

7. World War

Throughout the past several months of Wilson's first term as President, the damage to American shipping in the war zone had been curtailed by the Germans who were working hard to keep the United States out of the war. But there were leaders in Germany who had come to believe the country's only path to victory was via an all-out blitz against the enemy, including maximum destruction by its fleet of submarines, the greatest military advantage the Germans had at their disposal. The militants prevailed in their argument to launch unrestricted submarine warfare against any vessel – military or commercial – found in the war zone. American ships would no longer be bypassed. All ships were now in danger of being sunk without warning. "When the most ruthless methods are considered the best calculated to lead us to victory and to a swift victory," the German Chancellor announced, "they must be employed."[205] The Germans were well aware that this policy change would likely bring the Americans into the war on the side of the Allies, but they believed if executed properly, they could force the enemy to capitulate before the Americans could effectively mobilize and bring their forces to battle. Knowing how little the Americans had invested in growing and preparing their small standing army to participate in the global conflict, the Germans determined they might have a year or so to drive to victory before the Americans could be ready to mobilize against them. This would be a race to the finish, but only if Wilson would finally release the reins and permit the Americans to take part in the fight. When the President was informed of the new German policy, he was realistic in his assessment. "This means war," he told Tumulty. "The break that we have tried so hard to prevent now seems inevitable."[206]

Nevertheless, President Wilson was *still* unwilling to pull the trigger and request a declaration of war. He did sever diplomatic relations with Germany but was not ready to initiate war, something which his political enemies considered nearly treasonous. "These professional pacifists, through President Wilson, have forced the country into a path of shame and dishonor during the past eighteen months," bellowed Theodore Roosevelt. "Thanks to President Wilson, the most powerful of Democratic nations has refused to recognize the binding moral force of international public law. Our country has shirked its clear duty."[207] Wilson did agree the military change in tactics by the Germans necessitated greater protection for American shipping, so he went to Congress to propose legislation that would allow the government to begin arming commercial vessels so they could protect themselves. He called it "armed neutrality."[208] Despite strong support in Congress, the bill died at the end of the session due to a filibuster maintained for the last couple of days by a cadre of 11 senators who were strongly opposed to anything that might imply military action on behalf of the Americans. Wilson was in a foul mood over the Congressional inaction as he prepared to take his oath of office for the second time. "In the immediate presence of a crisis fraught with more subtle and far-reaching possibilities of national danger than any other the Government has known within the whole history of its international relations," the President fumed, "the Congress has been unable to act either to safeguard the country or to vindicate the elementary rights of its citizens."[209] The President concluded, "A little group of willful men … have rendered the great Government of the United States helpless and contemptible."[210]

It turns out the Germans had another angle to try to distract the Americans from coming to the aid of the Allies. Just prior to announcing their adoption of unrestricted submarine warfare, the Germans reached out to Mexico to seek a mutually beneficial alliance. The British intercepted the coded message from German Foreign Minister Arthur Zimmerman to Heinrich von Eckhardt, the German Minister to Mexico, with instructions to "propose an alliance with Mexico on the following basis: That we shall make war together and together make peace. We shall give general financial support and it is understood that Mexico is to reconquer the lost territory in New Mexico, Texas and Arizona."[211] The Mexicans were not persuaded by the chance to reclaim this territory that had been lost to the Americans nearly seventy years before. They had enough problems to deal with without taking up arms against the Americans. When *The New York Times* broke the story, it prompted yet another chorus of calls for President Wilson to bring the fight to Germany, which was clearly taking action to make the United States its enemy. But Wilson went into his inaugural a few days later still trying to find a way to avoid bringing his country into the war.

With March 4, 1917, falling on a Sunday, Wilson's public inaugural was switched to the following day, when he once again took his oath from Chief Justice Edward White. Wilson opened with a few self-congratulatory remarks for his domestic accomplishments, but most of his address was focused on the global war, the position his country continued to take, and his vision for the future to make these kinds of conflicts a thing for the history books alone. "We stand firm in armed neutrality," the President declared, "since it seems that in no other way we can demonstrate what it is we insist upon and cannot forget." But Wilson also acknowledged that the time might be coming when neutrality would no longer be viable. "We may even be drawn on, by circumstances, not by our own purpose or desire, to a more active assertion of our rights as we see them and a more immediate association with the great struggle itself."[212] If the Americans were forced to enter the war, Wilson wanted to be clear about the goals he had for such an undertaking, including introducing mechanisms for the world that would prevent such a cataclysm from ever happening again. "The community of interest and of power upon which peace must henceforth depend," he declared, "imposes upon each nation the duty of seeing to it that all influences proceeding from its own citizens meant to encourage or assist revolution in other states should be sternly and effectually suppressed and prevented."[213] He concluded his second Inaugural Address with the notion that whatever course the Americans take, it will be a righteous cause. "The shadows that now lie dark upon our path will soon be dispelled," he said, "and we shall walk with the light all about us if we be but true to ourselves – to ourselves as we have wished to be known in the counsels of the world and in the thought of all those who love liberty and justice and the right exalted."[214]

While the President had tried to portray continuing to remain neutral as a viable proposition, he was one of the few left in his country to think so. For Wilson, it all came to a head in a Cabinet meeting just two weeks into his second term. At this session, for the first time, he found complete agreement on the need to enter the war in order to thwart Germany's newfound aggression. With a couple of American ships already being sunk by the German U-Boats in the last few weeks, time was of the essence to Wilson's senior advisers. Secretary of State Lansing was not shy about his advocacy to engage, proclaiming the "duty of this and every other democratic nation to suppress an autocratic government like the German … because it was a menace to the national safety of this country and of all other countries with liberal systems of government."[215] Treasury Secretary McAdoo was right behind him. If the President didn't seek a declaration of war on his own, "the American people would compel action and we would be in the position of being pushed forward instead of leading, which would be humiliating and unwise," McAdoo said.[216] As the President went around the room, the sentiments remained consistent with this view that the Americans had no choice but to join the conflict on behalf of the Allies. Perhaps the nail in the coffin came from Navy Secretary Daniels, a close ally of former Secretary of State Bryan and among the last holdouts against war. But even Daniels threw his lot in with the others. "Having tried patience," Daniels said, there was "no course open to us except to protect our rights on the seas."[217] And armed neutrality would no longer be adequate now that the Germans were intent on sinking every vessel that came within its reach. As Colonel House had recently noted, based on the German plans, "we are already in the war" and might as well "throw all our resources against Germany."[218] Wilson's advisers had spoken as one, and the President finally allowed himself to join the call for war. The man who had been elected just a few months before as the man who "kept us out of war," was about to turn in the exact opposite direction just a couple of weeks into his second term.

For the last few days of March, Wilson isolated himself in his White House study to craft his request for a declaration of war. Edith was the only one privy to the President's thoughts regarding the specifics, but the intent was clear when Wilson requested time to speak to a joint session of Congress on April 2. With the House chamber full, Wilson placed the blame entirely on the Germans. He called the "present German submarine warfare against commerce, … a war against all nations [and a] challenge to all mankind."[219] The time had come for American engagement in the conflict. "There is one choice we cannot make, we are incapable of making," the President declared; "we will not choose the path of submission and suffer the most sacred rights of our nation and our people to be ignored, or violated. The wrongs against which we now array ourselves are no common wrongs; they cut to the very roots of human life."[220] As a result, the time had come "to fight thus for the ultimate peace of the world and for the liberation of its people, the German people included; for the rights of nations great and small and the privilege of men everywhere to choose their way of life and of obedience. The world must be made safe for democracy."[221] With that, the chamber erupted in applause. Similar reactions were heard across the country and throughout many parts of the world. To Wilson, it was actually an odd response, given the ominous nature of what was being cheered. "Think what it was

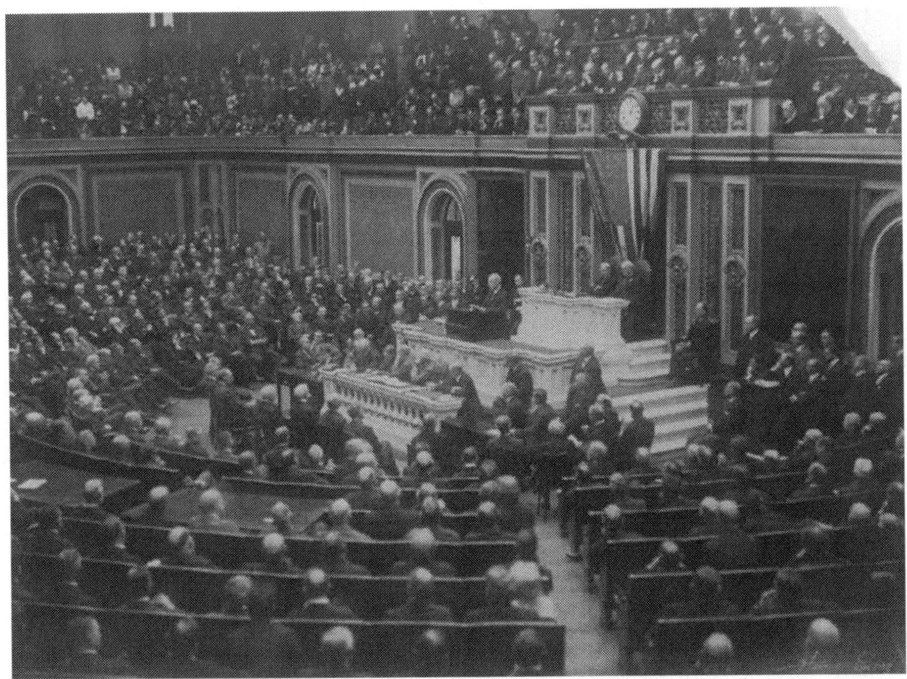

II-54: Wilson speaking to a joint session of Congress to seek a declaration of war against Germany, April 2, 1917

they were applauding," the President told Tumulty later that night. "My message to-day was a message of death for our young men. How strange it seems to applaud that."[222] Congress took only a few days before voting overwhelmingly in favor of Wilson's request for war. The President signed the statute into law at 1:19 pm on April 6. The United States had finally entered the World War.

Wilson knew it had been a circuitous path to war, as he further explained in a private conversation with his personal secretary.

> Tumulty, from the very beginning I saw the end of this horrible thing; but I could not move faster than the great mass of our people would permit. Very few understood the difficult and trying position I have been placed in during the years through which we have just passed. In the policy of patience and forbearance I pursued I tried to make every part of America and the varied elements of our population understand that we were willing to go any length rather than resort to war with Germany. As I told you months ago, it would have been foolish for us to have been rushed off our feet and to have gone to war

> over an isolated affair like the *Lusitania*. But now we are certain that there will be no regrets or looking back on the part of our people. There is but one course now left open to us. Our consciences are clear, and we must prepare for the inevitable – a fight to the end.[223]

Now that he had taken his country into the conflict, the man who "kept us out of war" immediately shifted to bringing the full power of the United States to bear against the Germans. As determined as he had been to remain neutral for as long as possible, he was now even more focused on ensuring a swift and complete victory.

Despite some limited preparations made over the course of the past year, the war effort was very much a start-up effort. The country faced immediate challenges in ramping up and transporting millions of soldiers directly into the fight while shifting the nation's giant economic engine to providing the tools needed to defeat the enemy. Among the very first military decisions the Commander-in-Chief needed to make involved a volunteer who showed up at the White House just three days after the President's address to seek permission to raise a regiment and head to France immediately, to jump-start the American effort while waiting for full training and mobilization to kick in. This visitor wasn't just an ordinary American, however. This was Wilson's chief political rival – Theodore Roosevelt. Roosevelt's greatest experience in life was what he called his "crowded hour," the time he led his fellow Rough Riders into the line of fire up the hills of San Juan Heights in the critical land battle of the Spanish-American War. Roosevelt had always wanted to test his bravery in combat and cherished his success under the greatest of pressures. Now, he wanted to do it again. Sure, he was 58 years old and not in great health, but he saw the value of a former President leading Americans on the battlefield as a boost to morale for troops on both sides of the Atlantic. He was the perfect person to raise a regiment and get the Americans into the fight right away, if only President Wilson would accept his offer.

It was surely an odd get-together at the White House given how aggressively Roosevelt had been excoriating Wilson for the past several years. In a single utterance, TR dismissed all those prior disagreements as no longer relevant given the new circumstances. "Mr. President," Roosevelt said to Wilson, "what I have said and thought, and what others have said and thought, is all dust in a windy street."[224] Roosevelt went on to make his case on why his proposal was good for everyone involved. Wilson heard him out over what turned out to be a pleasant conversation. He told the former President he would think about it. After Roosevelt left, Wilson turned to Tumulty and said, "Yes, he is a great big boy. I was, as formerly, charmed by his personality. There is a sweetness about him that is very compelling. You can't resist the man. I can easily understand why his followers are so fond of him."[225] But would he let him go to war?

The answer to that question came quickly – no. Wilson determined such a stunt would be a distraction at a time when full mobilization required everyone's attention. Wilson planned to recruit his army and navy through a draft and told Roosevelt that approving his request would disrupt that effort. While Roosevelt shouldn't have been surprised by Wilson's refusal to go along with his proposal, he was angry nonetheless. "I cannot overstate how bitterly I regret that the President refused my offer to raise troops,"[226] Roosevelt wrote the French Prime Minister Georges Clemenceau. But while Roosevelt hung on to his resentment, President Wilson moved on quickly. He had a war to fight, his nation had a long way to go to get ready, and not much time to do it. The Germans were doing everything they could to destroy their enemies before the Americans could engage with all their might. An additional complication was the revolution in Russia which brought the Communists to power under Vladimir Lenin. The new Russian government was now seeking its own peace with Germany, which would free up hundreds of thousands of German troops to shift to the western front. Without the influx of Americans, it was doubtful the Allies could hold off the Germans for long.

At President Wilson's request, Congress authorized conscription to provide the number of soldiers and sailors needed to put a stop to this German aggression. All males between the ages of 21 to 30 were required to register for the draft. Ten million entered their names into the lottery system in time for the first numbers to be randomly selected on June 5, 1917. Of the more than four million Americans who served in the war, some 2.7 million came into the service via the draft, which was later expanded to 18 to 45-year-olds when more men were needed. Encampments were built across the country to stage units, provide initial training, and prepare these raw recruits for the fights to come.

President Wilson also had to quickly put his military leadership into place to organize and strategize for this massive undertaking. The previous year, many believed General Frederick Funston would lead the American war effort if the U.S. ever entered the conflict. But Funston, a medal of honor winner, was no longer an option after recently dying from a heart attack. Some considered General Leonard Wood, who very much wanted the job, as the next logical choice given his experience on the battlefields of Cuba in the Spanish-American War. But Wood was extremely close to Roosevelt, and Wilson was uncomfortable with how that connection might interfere with the chain of command. So, the President selected General John Pershing to lead the American army into battle. Even though Pershing had failed to capture Pancho Villa in the recent raids into Mexico, Wilson had a lot of confidence in the West Point graduate who had led troops in Cuba and the Philippines and had served on the General Staff for the past three years. "Black Jack" Pershing would be joined in command by Admiral William Sims, who would lead the American navy in the conflict.

II-55: General John Pershing arriving in France, June 13, 1917

President Wilson was not a military man, and he knew it. He viewed his job as Commander-in-Chief was to provide the overarching strategy and all the means to successfully prosecute the war while leaving the detailed military tactics to the professionals. He did have one requirement, though, and that was that Americans would fight in American units and not be rushed to the battlefield as replacements to fill out French or British divisions that had been depleted. "Nothing except sudden and manifest emergency," Wilson instructed Secretary of War Baker, should "be suffered to interfere with the building up of a great distinct American force at the front, acting under its own flag and its own officers."[227] The President insisted on maintaining American unity and morale with this approach, but that wasn't his only reason for keeping American fighting units separate from the Allies. The President was "determined that it shall be known to the world that this country is acting independently of our allies" to better position the Americans for a separate voice when it came time to negotiate peace. "England and France have not the same views with regard to peace that we have by any means,"[228] Wilson wrote to Colonel House, indicating that he was already thinking of the end game, and how he believed he would need independence and leverage if he was going to be able to mold the peace in his image, something which he knew could be very different from the desires of the Allies.

While Wilson left his military leaders to build the detailed plans for the fight to come, he and his administration focused on bringing the rest of the nation's power to bear for the overall campaign. This meant funding, materiel, food, transportation, and every other detail that could make a difference in winning or losing this fight for democracy over autocracy. Treasury Secretary McAdoo was placed in charge of figuring out how to pay for the war in his role as the Chair of the War Finance Board. The President wanted the current generation to pay for as much of the expense as possible in the form of tax increases, but there were limits to this approach. While taxes paid for about a third of the war effort, the rest was resourced through borrowing, particularly through the sale of Liberty Bonds. At McAdoo's request, Congress approved the largest bond issuance in American history – $7 billion just to start. The administration solicited the help of celebrities such as Charlie Chaplin, Mary Pickford, and Douglas Fairbanks, along with former politicians, including Republicans like Theodore Roosevelt and William Taft, to appeal to the nation's patriotism and invest in these bonds. The bonds were priced at $50 each, making them attractive to the broadest number of citizens. The first campaign looked to sell $2 billion in bonds at 3.5% interest. The offering was oversubscribed in just one month on the market. Four million Americans opened their wallets on behalf of the war effort, a prideful moment even for those who could only afford a single bond. The war would not be cheap, as President Wilson was committed to not letting inadequate resourcing become an excuse when the future of civilization was at stake. The numbers help tell the story.

For a country that had approximately $1 billion in debt in 1916 and $2 billion in 1917, those figures leaped to $14 billion in 1918 and $19 billion in 1919. Most Americans had finally concluded that this was a reasonable price to pay to save the world.

Wilson took it upon himself to prepare his fellow citizens for the sacrifices needed during these perilous times. The country needed to become "more prolific and more efficient than ever," to set loose "a great international ... army ... engaged in the service of the nation and the world, the efficient friends and saviors of free men everywhere," the President declared.[229] To that end, Americans needed to look beyond themselves, to the greater good. This required a movement to "expedite shipments of supplies of every kind." His message to American businessmen was simple: "Small profits and quick services." According to the President, "The supreme test of the nation has come. We must all speak, act, and serve together!"[230] The patriotic overtones of the President's messages were evident from the very beginning of the mobilization effort. On Flag Day, June 14, 1917, Wilson proclaimed:

> For us there is but one choice. We have made it. Woe be to the man or group of men that seeks to stand in our way in this day of high resolution, when every principle we hold dearest is to be vindicated and made secure for the salvation of the nations. We are ready to plead at the bar of history, and our flag shall wear a new luster. Once more we shall make good with our lives and fortunes the great faith to which we were born, and a new glory shall shine in the face of our people.[231]

To fulfill these goals, Wilson needed a team around him of highly competent businessmen who knew how to get stuff done.

Several European nations had created War Cabinets, bringing in members of all political parties to unite around the singular goal of victory. President Wilson rejected the notion, seeking to maintain complete conformity to his leadership during the crisis. That said, Wilson did seek the highest skilled advisors in a number of key areas beyond the formal Cabinet regardless of political affiliation. The President established a Council of National Defense to serve as advisory bodies as well as execution authorities across all manner of war-related industries. In most cases, the purpose was acceleration, to cut through the traditional bureaucratic red tape in Washington that all too often introduced barriers to real progress. Wilson had no patience for such administrative obstacles, and he charged his leadership team with an aggressive push to prevent any impediments to getting the Americans fully into the war as quickly as possible.

Bernard Baruch was a self-made financial whiz whom Wilson brought in from Wall Street to oversee preparation efforts across the American economy in his role as the Chair of the War Industries Board. Baruch tried to see the big picture to help guide his prioritization efforts in the production and transportation of war-related goods, making decisions in the best interest of the nation as a whole. If there were conflicts or delays in the supply chain, Baruch and his team rolled up their sleeves to figure it out and solve the problem. While Democratic Party Chair Vance McCormick was put in charge of the War Trade Board, as mentioned, a number of the key wartime leaders hailed from the opposition party. One of the first priorities to aid the war effort was food. Some areas of Europe were dangerously close to all-out starvation as the army and navy blockades continued to disrupt food production and transportation. Republican Herbert Hoover, an engineer by trade, had volunteered early in the conflict to lead the effort to get food to the Belgians, who were caught in the middle of the warring factions. President Wilson was so impressed with Hoover's accomplishments that he placed him in charge of the new Food Administration. Hoover agreed to take on the role as long as he could continue supporting the people of Belgium as well. Hoover was relentless, seeking to maximize every morsel of food available for the war effort. This meant increased production and decreased consumption across the American landscape. Hoover introduced Meatless Tuesdays and Wheatless Wednesdays, leveraging the rise in national spirit to achieve widespread adoption of his policies. The Wilsons not only participated in these efforts to preserve scarce food for the actions in Europe, but they also planted a vegetable garden at the White House to grow some of their own.

II-56: Herbert Hoover, Chair of the Food Administration

The First Family also brought in a flock of sheep to save money in cutting the White House grass, as well as to generate more than 100 pounds of wool that was auctioned off to raise more funds. Every little bit helped. The results of Hoover's food campaign proved to be nothing short of a miracle, as nearly the entire American citizenry embraced the opportunity to make a real difference in feeding the troops and the Allies.

II-57: Sheep grazing on the White House grounds during World War I

Other Republicans signed on to help, including former President William Taft, who took a one-year leave of absence from his teaching position at Yale to lead the National War Labor Board. His job was to prevent strikes that could disrupt the war effort. By one count, Taft's board helped avert some 138 potential work stoppages. Dr. Harry Garfield, the son of another former President and currently the President of Williams College, had similar success as the Chair of the Fuel Administration. Even Charles Evans Hughes, the man Wilson recently edged for the presidency, answered the President's call for assistance. The former Supreme Court Justice was asked to lead an investigation into corruption charges against the Aircraft Board. The World War required unity of effort regardless of political affiliation, and these leaders (along with many others) answered that call in the service of their country. Such bipartisan cooperation was a critical success factor in winning the conflict. The fact that it disappeared almost as quickly as it materialized as soon as the fighting overseas ended could not have been a surprise either.

II-58: George Creel, Chair of the Committee of Public Information (CPI)

The administration knew it needed to win the hearts and minds of the citizenry to complete this all-of-nation approach. While the President led the messaging, he couldn't do it alone. For this effort, he established the Committee of Public Information (CPI), with Denver journalist George Creel in charge. Creel called it "the world's greatest adventure in advertising."[232] The CPI utilized speakers, articles, posters, motion pictures, and anything else they could think of to get out its patriotic messages. This was no longer an even-sided affair. The Americans were now all-in with the Allies, who were portrayed as the heroic saviors of mankind, while the Central Powers were the evil-doing instigators who must be stopped at all costs. "The trial of strength was not only between massed bodies of armed men," according to Creel, "but between opposed ideals, and moral verdicts took on all the value of military decision."[233] The core messages that were repeated over and over revolved around the themes of unity, sacrifice, and service. By all accounts, the CPI delivered exactly what the President was looking for to rally the people at home to do whatever they could to enable their fathers, brothers, and sons to win abroad.

While the CPI was delivering pro-American propaganda, there were still those opposed to the war who wanted the right to speak their minds. Woodrow Wilson was among those who sought to curtail this dissent. In some of the nation's past wars, the U.S. government had clamped down on those who spoke out against the war effort. Just a few years after the ratification of the First Amendment, which protected freedom of speech, President John Adams signed into law the Sedition Act of 1798 to put a stop to negative press during the Quasi-War with France. Abraham Lincoln took similar steps through executive order to silence opposition in the North during the Civil War. As an academic, Woodrow Wilson had criticized these infringements on the rights of citizens, even in times of war. Wilson wrote that the actions of the Adams administration, for example, "cut perilously near the root of freedom of speech and of the press. There was no telling where such exercises of power would stop. Their only limitations and safeguards lay in the temper and good sense of the President and the Attorney General."[234] That very responsibility was now in his hands, along with those of his AG Thomas Gregory, after Congress passed the Espionage Act of 1917 – a move that Wilson now fully supported. "I honestly think that it would be impossible for me to conduct the war with success if I am to be placed under daily espionage," the President wrote to Senator Robert Owen.[235] The most controversial part of the original bill gave the government the ability to censor the press, which elicited strenuous opposition when initially introduced. In order to secure passage of the overall measure, the censorship provision was dropped – but only temporarily. A standalone sedition bill came along the following year, which was put to great use by the administration. Gregory greatly expanded the power of the Bureau of Investigation (later, the FBI), while Postmaster General Burleson was aggressive in shuttering publications that were critical of the government's prosecution of the war. One of those who continued to speak in harsh terms toward the government was former President Roosevelt, but Wilson had a different approach than prosecution to deal with TR. "I really think the best way to treat Mr. Roosevelt is to take no notice of him," Wilson said. "That breaks his heart and is the best punishment that can be administered."[236] Many of Roosevelt's fellow citizens were not so fortunate if they decided to voice their displeasure while the global conflict played itself out.

8. Fourteen Points and Victory

While all national power was being brought to bear to get the Americans into the present fight, President Wilson was already thinking about the future. He didn't just bring the United States into the war to beat back the Germans and force their capitulation. Such an outcome, to Wilson, was only the means to an end. His higher purpose was to make real the phrase author H.G. Wells used to describe the current conflict as "the war that will end war."[237] Among the many responsibilities Colonel House had undertaken on behalf of the President during the war was to initiate a group called "The Inquiry," which began working on defining the kind of structural solution that would prevent these kinds of horrific armed conflicts from ever happening again. Walter Lippman, the future Pulitzer Prize-winning journalist, was part of the brain trust that produced a series of memos that informed Wilson's thinking. Out of this came Wilson's famous Fourteen Points.

Wilson announced the conditions upon which the current war would end and future wars would be avoided when he spoke to a joint session of Congress on January 8, 1918. His Points fell into three categories. The first five Points were general principles that he believed were imperative to be adopted to prevent future armed conflicts.

14 CONDITIONS FOR PEACE ARE PROPOSED BY WILSON

WILSON'S PEACE SPEECH IN FULL

The Evening World. FINAL EDITION

NEW YORK, TUESDAY, JANUARY 8, 1918

WIDE SPLIT IN GERMANY CAUSED BY LLOYD GEORGE AND RUSSIAN NEGOTIATIONS

Socialists Stand Firmly for Bolsheviki Terms—Harden Warns Against

EQUAL PLACE IN THE WORLD OFFERED TO GERMANY

RUSSIAN PLANS, GERMAN OFFERS AND ALLIED AIMS ALL CONSIDERED

SUMMARY OF WILSON'S PROGRAM TO CONGRESS FOR WORLD PEACE

II-59: Headline in the New York Evening World announcing Wilson's Fourteen Points

Points six through 13 were specific to how the national boundaries of the primarily affected nations should be addressed in a final peace agreement. Finally, the Fourteenth Point envisioned an international body charged with preventing war in the future. The National World War I Museum and Memorial summarized Wilson's Points as follows:

1. Open diplomacy without secret treaties

2. Economic free trade on the seas during war and peace
3. Equal trade conditions
4. Decrease armaments among all nations
5. Adjust colonial claims
6. Evacuation of all Central Powers from Russia and allow it to define its own independence
7. Belgium to be evacuated and restored
8. Return of the Alsace-Lorraine region and all French territories
9. Readjust Italian borders
10. Austria-Hungary to be provided an opportunity for self-determination
11. Redraw the borders of the Balkan region creating Romania, Serbia, and Montenegro
12. Creation of a Turkish state with guaranteed free trade with the Dardanelles
13. Creation of an independent Polish state
14. Creation of a League of Nations[238]

If all of the Fourteen Points were adopted by all the warring parties, then, and only then, could a *lasting* peace be accomplished. "What is at stake now is the peace of the world," Wilson told Congress. "What we are striving for is a new international order based upon broad and universal principles of right and justice, no mere peace of shreds and patches." Wilson emphasized that unless each of the problems cited in the Fourteen Points "are dealt with in a spirit of unselfish and unbiased justice, with a view to the wishes, the natural connections, the racial aspirations, the security, and the peace of mind of the peoples involved, no permanent peace will have been attained."[239] The Fourteen Points were hardly a sop to the Allies. Wilson realized that in going to war against Germany that the goal was a military victory against the common foe of all the Allies. But peace should not be one-sided, according to Wilson. Those peace agreements never last. Real peace must be based on universal principles that are implemented fairly to all the nations of the world. As he would add later in the year while pitching the adoption of the Fourteen Points, "The impartial justice meted out must involve no discrimination between those to whom we wish to be just and those to whom we do not wish to be just. It must be a justice that plays no favorites and knows no standard but the equal rights of the several peoples concerned."[240] Woodrow Wilson was making it clear that he didn't take his country into World

War I just to beat the Germans; he did it under the lofty notion of saving the world from such a conflict every happening again.

For Wilson, his Fourteenth Point was the key to making all of this work – the establishment of a League of Nations. The Fourteenth Point stated: "A general association of nations must be formed under specific covenants for the purpose of affording mutual guarantees of political independence and territorial integrity to great and small states alike."[241] This organization would be structured to address future disagreements based on well-defined authorities and mechanisms that would find a resolution before a call to arms. If any rogue state decided to take matters into its own hands, Wilson's League would immediately respond, isolating the aggressor from the rest of the world with crippling economic sanctions, to be followed by a global military intervention if all other measures failed to deliver the desired results. How this would all come together would be ironed out at the Peace Conference, with Wilson's blueprint envisioned as the starting point for negotiations.

Woodrow Wilson was not the first to embrace the concept of a global association designed to help avoid wars. In many ways, its predecessor concept was called the League to Enforce Peace, which had been embraced by a handful of Democrats and Republicans alike over the last three years, but without a lot of momentum behind it. Among the staunchest supporters of this League were two prominent Republicans: former President William Taft and former Senator Elihu Root, with Taft serving as the fledgling organization's president. Another Republican supporter in 1917 was Henry Cabot Lodge of Massachusetts, the chair of the Senate Foreign Relations Committee. Speaking at an event sponsored by Taft, Lodge declared:

II-60: Senator Henry Lodge

> It may seem Utopian at this moment to suggest a union of civilized nations in order to put a controlling force behind the maintenance of peace and international order; but it is through the aspiration for perfection, through the search for Utopias,

> that the real advances have been made. At all events, it is along this path that we must travel if we are to attain in any measure to the end we all desire of peace upon earth.[242]

In less than a year, however, Henry Lodge would become the strongest foe of the version of the League that Wilson would negotiate with the other countries of the world at the postwar Peace Conference. The fact that the American system of government required the consent of 2/3rd of the U.S. Senate to ratify a treaty meant Lodge's opinions could carry significant weight. President Wilson's pursuit of peace without engaging Republicans in the Senate would be done at his own peril.

None of this would matter if the Allies didn't win the fight on the battlefield in the first place. And things weren't going very well for the Allied cause. The Americans did manage to slow down the terrifying German U-boat attacks by using American warships to escort commercial and transportation vessels, making it much more difficult for the submarines to get close enough to launch their torpedoes. The U.S. navy also placed thousands of mines outside the waters through which many of the German subs needed to transit. But, in terms of the land war, the earliest that American soldiers would be ready to engage was either May or June 1918, and the Germans weren't about to wait to go on a full-scale attack. On March 21, the Germans launched their spring offensive with a four-pronged attack against the Allied lines. Initially, they made significant progress, taking town after town while advancing deeper into Allied territory before the defensive line finally held about 60 miles outside of Paris. Massive casualties resulted from the campaign, with 1.5 million being killed, wounded, or missing in action for the two sides combined. If that wasn't distressing enough, an outbreak of the Spanish Flu had reached pandemic status. Ultimately a billion people across the globe would be infected, with more than 100 million fatalities. In fact, approximately half the deaths of U.S. soldiers during the war came from the influenza pandemic. Amidst all this chaos and catastrophe, the U.S. mobilization effort continued full speed ahead.

Meanwhile, President Wilson had two groups fighting for their rights at home while their fellow Americans were heading overseas to fight for the rights of the people of the world. The Black community had already become severely disenchanted with the Wilson administration, but the outbreak of war had made things worse in many parts of the country. Many Blacks wanted to fight and felt Wilson's global challenge was the perfect vehicle to integrate the armed services. That was a non-starter with the President. The door was open to Black servicemen, but Wilson wouldn't force Whites to fight alongside Blacks in any army under his command. Four-hundred-thousand Blacks became American soldiers during World War I. They all served in segregated units, mostly in support roles and not on the front lines. But this selfless service to the country was hardly celebrated at home, particularly in the South. While fighting units were segregated, training bases housed both Black and White units, including on bases in the South where Whites were offended even by the notion of training near Black soldiers. Many Whites in the North and South were also angered by the sight of Blacks filling the jobs of White Americans who had been sent overseas. Throughout this period of mobilization, racial tensions boiled out of control. Race riots and lynchings were on the rise across the South. Many pleaded with the President to, at a minimum, speak out and condemn such actions, but for weeks Wilson resisted. His rationale was these were local issues not under his direct purview. By late summer, however, as the violence continued unabated, the President relented. He gave a speech on July 26, 1918, in which he said:

> There have been many lynchings, and every one of them has been a blow at the heart of ordered law and humane justice. … Every American who takes part in the action of a mob or gives it any sort of countenance is no true son of this great Democracy, but its betrayer, and does more to discredit her by that single disloyalty to her standards of law and of right than the words of her statesmen or the sacrifices of her heroic boys in the trenches can do to make suffering peoples believe her to be their savior.[243]

It was the most forceful civil rights address Wilson had ever given. Unfortunately, his remarks didn't do much good, and he did little to follow his rhetoric with any meaningful action.

The other group that finally wanted its just due was women. The object of their desire was the Constitutional right to vote. Women were critical to the war effort, leaving their homes in droves to backfill the men who had vacated all manner of jobs so they could head overseas. The manufacturing behemoth that the Americans would bring to the fight would not have been possible without women joining the workforce. Women had gained access to the franchise in several states but had yet to fulfill the breakthrough many had long sought at the national level. In this regard, they did not have an ally in the White House, at least not initially. Woodrow Wilson felt the cons outweighed the pros when it came to women and the vote. "Suffrage for women," Wilson said earlier in his presidency, "will make absolutely no change in politics – it is the home that will be disastrously affected. Somebody has to make the home and who is going to do it if the women don't?"[244] Moreover, the President believed this was not a matter to be adjudicated at the national level. "I ... am tied to a conviction, which I have had all my life," Wilson said in 1915, "that changes of this sort ought to be brought about state by state."[245] The leading suffragists were bound and determined to change the President's mind, so they started showing up at his home every day to state their case. Wilson didn't seem bothered by the protests in front of the White House. "Let them alone," the President said. "They don't worry me a particle. If they derive any satisfaction out of parading about the White House or standing with their banners, for goodness' sake let them do it. Let them picket to their heart's content."[246] Wilson wasn't offering his support to the cause, but neither did he see any advantage in making martyrs out of the protesters. In fact, he was annoyed when several were taken into custody, urging security officials, "Don't arrest them, that is exactly what they want."[247] When one of the leading suffragists, Alice Paul, found herself incarcerated in November 1917, she went on a hunger strike. When she was force-fed through a tube down her throat, it made national news. The entire movement was winning converts, including a couple very close to the President.

The saying that "all politics is local" may have had a hand in getting Wilson to change course and support a constitutional amendment that would guarantee women the right to vote in every state in the Union. His daughters were strongly in favor, and that seemed to be one of the final catalysts to get the President to weigh in on the topic. When the House of Representatives took up the amendment for women's suffrage, it passed by a single vote (274 to 136), just beyond the 2/3rd threshold needed for constitutional amendments. The Senate, however, was going to be a tougher hill to climb. Most senators had already staked out their positions, and the body appeared to be two votes short. Treasury Secretary McAdoo took the opportunity to encourage the President to take his case directly to the legislature, just as he had on so many topics thus far in his presidency. If anyone could shake loose a couple more votes, it was President Woodrow Wilson. So, he agreed to give it a try. During his 15-minute address, the President asserted, "I regard the concurrence of the Senate in the constitutional amendment proposing the extension of the suffrage to women as vitally essential to the successful prosecution of the great war of humanity in which we are engaged." He reminded the senators that the world was looking "to the great, powerful, famous Democracy of the West to lead them to the new day ... and they think, in their logical simplicity, that democracy means that women shall play their part in affairs alongside men and upon an equal footing with them."[248] In this instance, Wilson couldn't move a single vote. When the tally was taken in the Senate, the total remained two votes short of the necessary supermajority. The amendment would eventually be sent to the states by both Houses of Congress on Wilson's watch, but it would take another two years for that vote to come in.

The President had additional domestic challenges, including those related to the Sedition Act that passed on May 16, 1918. As a follow-up to the Espionage Act from the year before, the government now had the authority to go after speech (written or spoken) that was critical of that government or the war effort. Postmaster General Burleson was on point to scour the mails looking for seditious content and refer the perpetrators to the Attorney General when he found it. The Justice Department had its own investigations as well, with a particular focus on the labor movement. Workers uniting against management at a time of war could impact the military effort abroad, so labor leaders were on notice that what they said may very well be used against them. Advocates for socialism were also deemed dangerous, and their speech was closely monitored as well. The fact that Eugene Debs was one of the leaders of the powerful Industrial Workers of the World (IWW) Union, and had

II-61: Eugene Debs speaking in Canton, OH, after which he was arrested for violating the Sedition Act

been the Socialist Party candidate for President on three previous occasions, certainly put him in the cross hairs. The speech that got him arrested was given on June 16, 1918, in Canton, Ohio. In his remarks, Debs openly opposed the war and, in particular, the military draft. Two weeks later, he was taken into custody and charged with ten counts of sedition. In his defense at trial, Debs spoke for two hours on the legitimacy of his claims and the constitutional basis that protected him for articulating them. His arguments made no difference. Debs was convicted and sentenced to ten years in prison. At his sentencing, Debs took one more opportunity to make the point about the righteous nature of his position. "Your Honor, years ago I recognized my kinship with all living beings, and I made up my mind that I was not one bit better than the meanest on earth," Debs declared in open court. "I said then, and I say now, that while there is a lower class, I am in it, and while there is a criminal element I am of it, and while there is a soul in prison, I am not free."[249] With that, he was taken to his new home behind bars.

One person who had absolutely no sympathy for Debs was the man in the White House. Wilson was offended that anyone would speak out with the stakes being so high for the country and the world. "While the flower of American youth was pouring out its blood to vindicate the cause of civilization, this man, Debs, stood behind the lines, sniping, attacking, and denouncing them,"[250] Wilson said after the conviction was announced. According to the President, Debs got what he deserved. Debs appealed his case to the Supreme Court, which continued to rule that the government's actions under the Espionage Act and the Sedition Act during this time of war were authorized under the Constitution. Eugene Debs would remain in prison for stating his controversial opinions, at least as long as Woodrow Wilson was the President of the United States.

The first real combat for American soldiers in World War I occurred on May 28, 1918, a little more than a year after Congress had approved President Wilson's request for a declaration of war. Nearly 3,500 Americans from the 28th Infantry engaged the enemy at Cantigny, a town just north of Paris. Working closely with the more experienced French fighters, the Allies took the town in about a half hour. The victory yielded a huge boost to morale, not only for the Americans but also for the Allies, who finally saw first-hand the determination and skill the Americans could bring to the fight. While General Pershing coordinated closely with

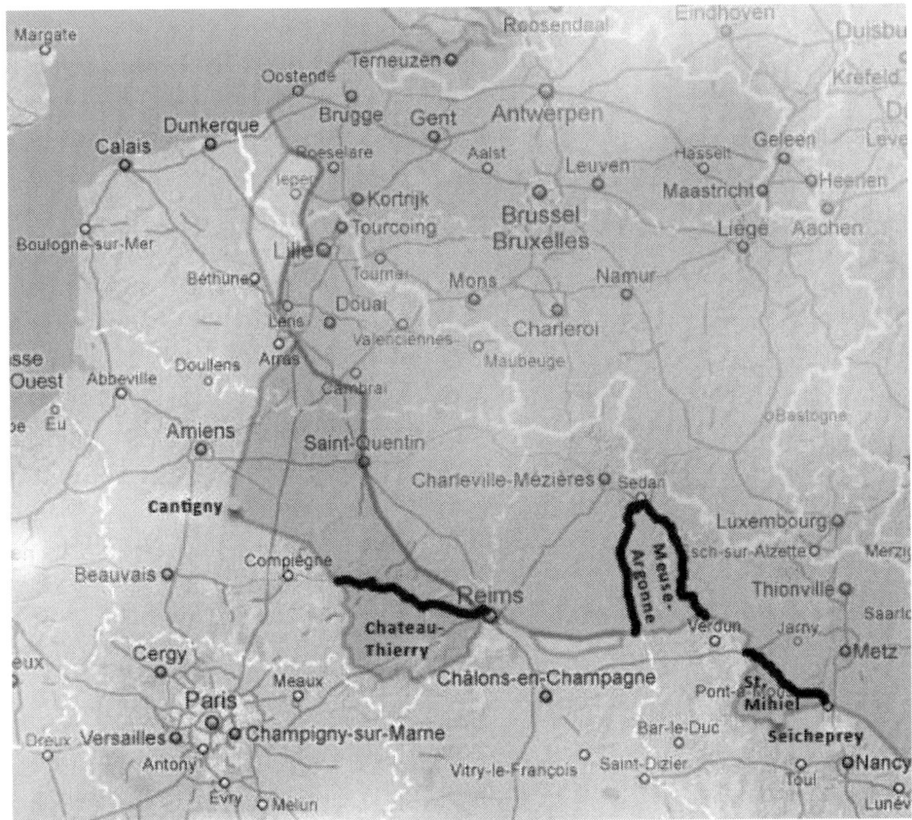

II-62: Map of the location of the American Expeditionary Forces during World War I, including major engagements

the Supreme Allied Commander, Marshal Ferdinand Foch, he remained under orders to keep his units intact, fighting under American leaders and the American flag. The U.S. was assigned duty on the front lines in the sector between Verdun and Belfort. Over the course of the next five months, approximately half of the two million American soldiers stationed in France would face the enemy in combat on the front lines, recording one triumph after another on the way to total victory before the year was out.

After the Battle of Belleau Wood, the tide shifted for good in favor of the Allies on July 18, as the Americans and French broke through the German lines in fighting along the Marne. Step by step, the Germans were pushed back as the Allies retook ground that had been lost at great cost. The Battle of Amiens was followed by the Battle of the Somme, the

II-63: American soldiers fighting in Séchault, France, during the Meuse-Argonne Offensive, September 29, 1918

Battle of the Argonne Forest, and eventually the Battle of St. Michiel. Every fight was costly. Over the course of 150 days of bloody fighting, 116,000 Americans lay dead, half from battle and half from disease. Another 204,000 lay wounded. But the German losses were much worse, and while the Americans were bringing another 10,000 boys into the fight every day, the Germans had no way to replace the men and materiel that were lost on the battlefield. The tide had clearly turned.

The first of the Central Powers to fall was Bulgaria, which surrendered to the Allies in late September. Turkey was next in October, with Austria-Hungary next to lay down its arms. A clear rupture had opened in the German government as well. Kaiser Wilhelm wanted to continue the fight, but he was losing control of his country with one defeat after another. On October 6, the Germans first signaled their willingness to accept a truce based on Woodrow Wilson's Fourteen Points – likely the best terms they could possibly get from the Allies. The German Chancellor, Prince Max, sent the following note to the Americans:

> The German Government accepts, as a basis for the peace negotiations, the programme laid down by the President of the United States in his Message to Congress of January 8, 1918, and in his subsequent pronouncements particularly in his address of September 27, 1918. In order to avoid further bloodshed, the German Government requests the President of the United States of America to bring about the immediate conclusion of a general armistice on land, on water, and in the air.[251]

The U.S. President was certainly intrigued but also skeptical that those reaching out were really speaking for the German government, which was clearly falling apart. Besides, the request was a non-starter until the Germans offered guarantees that they would evacuate all conquered territory that was still under their control. The end seemed near, but for now, the fight would continue.

All of this was occurring as Americans were about to go to the polls in the 1918 midterm elections. Wilson's name wasn't on any ballot, but the Republicans were making this election a referendum on the President's administration of the war and his Fourteen Points. Theodore Roosevelt was back on the stump trashing the President, calling the Fourteen Points "thoroughly mischievous" and saying that any peace based on Wilson's proposal "would represent not the unconditional surrender of Germany but the conditional surrender of the United States."[252] The election was critical to Wilson's plans, particularly in the Senate, which would have to vote on any peace treaty negotiated by the executive branch. Wilson decided to weigh in late in the campaign. He not only put forward a strong defense of his actions during the war, but he also made a highly partisan plea to send Democrats to Washington so he could complete the effort.

> My Fellow Countrymen: The Congressional elections are at hand. They occur in the most critical period our country has ever faced or is likely to face in our time. If you have approved of my leadership and wish me to continue to be your unembarrassed spokesman in affairs at home and abroad, I earnestly beg that you will express yourself unmistakably to that effect by returning a Democratic majority to both the Senate and the House of Representatives. …[253]

> The leaders of the minority have unquestionably been pro-war, but they have been anti-administration. At almost every turn, since we entered the war, they have sought to take the choice of policy and the conduct of the war out of my hands and put it under the control of instrumentalities of their own choosing. … The return of a Republican majority to either house of the Congress would, moreover, certainly be interpreted on the other side of the water as a repudiation of my leadership.[254]

Wilson's entreaty dramatically backfired, as he was castigated for using the war as a political prop. His defenders were quick to point out that Woodrow Wilson was hardly the first President to play politics with war. Just two decades earlier, William McKinley called for the people to send Republicans to Congress in the midterm elections while the final negotiations over the conclusion of the Spanish-American War were still hanging in the balance. "This is no time for divided councils," McKinley urged at the time. "If I would have you remember anything I have said in these desultory remarks, it would be to remember at this critical hour in the nation's history we must not be divided. The triumphs of the war are yet to be written in the articles of peace."[255] There were no negative ramifications to McKinley's partisan remarks just prior to the election in 1898, but that was not the case for Woodrow Wilson, who was slammed far and wide for his partisan advocacy in the days leading up to the vote.

The final say in the matter was in the hands of the electorate, which issued a strong rebuke to President Wilson and the Democrats. The Republicans took control of both Houses of Congress, picking up 25 seats in the House and five in the Senate. With the war winding to a close, partisan politics were back in full swing in the United States, and that political tension was only going to increase as the international effort shifted from winning the war to winning the peace.

The end of the fighting came just a few days after the Americans went to the polls. Prince Max resigned as the German Chancellor on October 30. At the same time, Colonel House received confirmation that the British and French would support a negotiated peace based on Wilson's Fourteen Points. An agreement was reached for the combatants to meet on November 8 to secure a formal armistice. The venue was the train that was serving as the mobile headquarters of Marshal Foch. It was currently parked off the beaten path outside Rethondes in the forest of Compiegne. The Supreme Allied Commander was prepared to welcome

II-64: Supreme Allied Commander Marshal Ferdinand Foch (standing) and colleagues great German representatives Matthias Erzberger and his colleagues in Foch's mobile headquarters, November 1918

the Germans' Matthias Erzberger and his small team, but it was hardly a friendly encounter. The initial discussion was tense, with little toleration for sympathy on the part of the Allies. Their demands were unilateral and nonnegotiable, including complete and immediate demilitarization by the Germans. Without that, the Allies would ramp up the fighting again. The Germans were given 72 hours to accept or face the consequences of the resumption of military devastation.

Part of the challenge for the Germans was figuring out who was in charge to make the decision to sign the armistice. The day after the terms were offered, Kaiser Wilhelm abdicated, moving to Holland, where he would reside in exile for the rest of his life. Knowing the clock was ticking, a new German government was quickly assembled in the form of a republic. Friedrich Ebert was selected as the Chancellor. Without any other realistic options, Ebert gave the approval to agree to the Allies' terms. That decision came at 5:00 am on the 11th of November. Both sides agreed the fighting would cease later that morning – at the 11th hour on the 11th day of the 11th month of the year. Woodrow Wilson had been anxiously waiting with Edith in the White House to get the official word from Colonel House, who sent the following encoded message: "Autocracy is dead. [Long live] democracy and its immortal leader. In this great hour my heart goes out to you in pride, admiration and love."[256] Edith Wilson later wrote, "Many persons have asked me what we did, and all I can answer is, we stood mute – unable to grasp the full significance of the words."[257] Emotions flowed around the country and across the globe as the most horrific conflict in the history of the world had finally come to an end.

II-65: American soldiers of the 64th Regiment, 7th Infantry Division, celebrating the news of the armistice, November 11, 1918

President Wilson spoke to a joint session of Congress the next day where he unveiled the 35 terms contained in the armistice agreement. The harsher the terms, the louder the applause from the congressmen. The Americans certainly had a lot to be proud of. There was no doubt that the U.S. entry played the critical role in bringing about the final result, ensuring a timely conclusion with the Allies prevailing in the end. It is easy to imagine an opposite outcome if the U.S. had remained on the sidelines. Woodrow Wilson planned to use that fact as leverage when the formal Peace Conference would convene to negotiate the final terms of surrender along with the many other decisions that still hung in the balance concerning territorial alignment, reparations, and, of course, Wilson's League of Nations.

The Americans were only in the fight in Europe for about six months. Their contributions were instrumental in the outcome, but also extremely costly. Just over 116,000 members of the U.S. military died in World War I, with nearly twice that many wounded. As devastating as these numbers were, they paled in comparison to some of the nations who were in the fight for four long years. The Allies suffered approximately six million dead and another 12 million wounded. The biggest casualty figures came from Russia (more than 1.7 million killed and another four million wounded), France (more than 1.4 million killed and another 4.2 million wounded), and the United Kingdom and its colonies (nearly 900,000 killed and another 1.6 million wounded). The Central Powers were similarly devastated, with the human toll accounting for more than four million killed and another 8.5 million wounded. Germany took the greatest hit, losing just over two million killed and 4.2 million wounded. The grim numbers go on and on and on. Empires were devastated, cities and towns were obliterated, and families were left to mourn the loss of lives and livelihoods. These results continued to motivate Woodrow Wilson to fight for his Fourteen Points, which he believed offered the only recipe to ensure such a cataclysmic event would never happen again.

9. Peace Conference: Round One

One question on minds on both sides of the Atlantic was whether President Wilson would personally lead the American delegation to the upcoming Peace Conference in Paris. No American President had ever taken on such a diplomatic role before, and, frankly, the leaders of the Allies didn't want Wilson at the table. In the United States, the President is both the Head of State and the Head of Government. That's different from the parliamentary systems in Europe, where a monarch is typically the Head of State and a Prime Minster is the Head of Government. The Prime Ministers of France and Britain were not shy about their feelings that having an American President directly involved in the talks would be out of balance with the rest of the negotiators. French Premier Georges Clemenceau sent word to President Wilson that "he hoped you will not sit in the Congress because no head of a State should sit there. The same feeling prevails in England."[258] The opinion overseas was that the Secretary of State would be the logical choice to lead the American delegation. President Wilson, however, would have none of this. First of all, it was obvious that such a move would place the Americans at an immediate disadvantage in the negotiations when going up against the Prime Ministers of Europe, which he was hardly inclined to do. Second, Wilson felt it was his duty to go and fight for his Fourteen Points, even if the move was unprecedented in American history. "I owe it to [the American soldiers] to see to it, so far as in me lies, that no false or mistaken interpretation is put upon them, and no possible effort omitted to realize them," Wilson explained. He was determined to "play my full part in making good what they offered their life's blood to obtain."[259] Finally, Wilson didn't trust the Allies to adhere to his vision for the postwar settlement. He was convinced his European counterparts were more focused on vengeance against Germany and the other Central Powers than the future safety of mankind. Co-mingled with this concern was the selfish nature of the most prominent victors, who could use the Conference to further their own aims at the expense of others, including many who had joined them in the trenches against their enemy. "I infer the French and British leaders desire to exclude me from the Conference for fear I might there lead the weaker nations against them," Wilson cabled Colonel House.[260] For all these reasons, Wilson made it clear he would lead the American delegation and do so in person.

If his own participation was an easy decision for the President, determining who would join him at the Conference was a little more challenging. Secretary of State Lansing was an obvious selection as one of the four commissioners joining the President, but beyond that, things were a little tricky. Given all the work that the Secretaries of War and the Navy had to do with respect to demobilization, Wilson opted for a military man to represent the military's interest. Army Chief of Staff, General Tasker Bliss, would have a seat at the table. Next, the President appointed Colonel House to an official position for the first time. The man who had operated for six years as a free agent, supporting the President in any area he needed assistance but without a specific portfolio of his own, was formally added to the team. While the President could have used House's relationships with the European leaders in an informal capacity, as he had done before, in this instance, he decided to make it official. The real question concerned the last spot on the delegation, and whether Wilson would invite a Republican to join the team.

II-66: The American Delegation to the Paris Peace Conference (L to R): Edward House, Robert Lansing, President Wilson, Henry White, and General Tasker Bliss

With the recent election handing the majority in the Senate to the Republicans, many encouraged Wilson to invite a member of that body to be alongside for the negotiations. However, this was a political game Wilson refused to play, perhaps at his own peril. The role and power of government executives had been a focus for Woodrow Wilson most of his adult life. His preference had always been for the British parliamentary system which entrusted power in the hands of a Prime Minister who represented the majority in Parliament and therefore had complete confidence that his negotiations in foreign affairs would be supported by the legislature. That was not the case in the United States, where the executive has the authority to negotiate treaties, but those agreements couldn't go into effect without the concurrence of 2/3rd of the Senate – a body that was now in the hands of Wilson's political opposition. In one of his earliest pieces of scholarship from his days as a college senior in 1879, Wilson decried the American system where "The President can seldom make himself recognized as a leader. He is merely the executor of the sovereign legislative will; his Cabinet officers are little more than chief clerks, or superintendents, in the Executive departments, who advise the President on matters in most of which he has no power of action independently of the concurrence of the Senate."[261] Wilson didn't stop over the years from advocating for greater power and independence for the President. As Princeton's president in 1908, Wilson said:

> Our President must always, henceforth, be one of the great powers of the world, whether he act greatly and wisely or not. … We can never hide our President again as a mere domestic officer. … He must stand always at the front of our affairs, and the office will be as big and as influential as the man who occupies it.[262]

Sounding eerily like Theodore Roosevelt, Wilson then opined that "The personal force of the President is perfectly Constitutional to any extent to which he chooses to exercise it."[263] This power was especially true when it came to international affairs. He continued in this address from 1908:

> One of the greatest of the President's powers I have not yet spoken of at all: his control, which is very absolute, of the foreign relations of the nation. The initiative in foreign affairs, which the President possesses without any restriction whatever, is virtually the power to control them absolutely. … He (the President) need disclose no step of negotiation until it

> is complete, and when in any critical matter it is completed the Government is virtually committed. Whatever its disinclination, the Senate may feel itself committed also.[264]

Now a decade later, Woodrow Wilson still held these very same views – a belief that would lead to the biggest failure of his life.

Confident that even a Republican-controlled Senate wouldn't rebuke the American President on the international stage, Wilson declined all suggestions to include a Republican member of that body as the final member of his delegation. In public, he cited the Constitution as the basis for his decision. According to Article I, Section 6:

> No Senator or Representative shall, during the time for which he was elected, be appointed to any civil office under the authority of the United States, which shall have been created, or the emoluments whereof shall have been increased during such time; and no person holding any office under the United States, shall be a member of either House during his continuance in office.[265]

According to the President, this clause disqualified any sitting member of Congress from participating in the upcoming mission. Wilson saw the delegation as a purely executive function, and the inclusion of a member of Congress would violate the separation of powers. It would also be inappropriate, in Wilson's mind, for anyone to participate in negotiating a treaty for which he would then have to turn around and vote to provide legislative consent. Wilson cared little for precedents where previous administrations had no trouble placing current congressmen on identical missions. In fact, just a couple of decades before, President William McKinley placed senators from both political parties on the team to negotiate the end of the Spanish-American War. Wilson viewed that decision as a mistake, and one he vowed not to repeat.

Of course, the primary reason that Wilson refused to include a Republican senator on his team was that he wanted complete unity of purpose, with a group that would follow his lead no matter what. A Republican senator would put that at risk and inhibit Wilson's ability to forcefully insist that the Allies adopt his vision for the future security of the world. This meant most other Republicans were out of consideration as well. The two names that were most prominently raised were those of former President William Taft and former Senator and Secretary of State Elihu Root. Not only did both have the stature in the party that could be

II-67: William Taft with Elihu Root, during the Roosevelt administration, circa 1904

useful to lobby for ratification, but they had also been strong proponents for Wilson's prized League of Nations. While they may have differing views on other points in the negotiation, Wilson could likely count on their support on the topic that he cared the most about. Moreover, both had also served in a Cabinet, understood the chain of command, and were interested in the assignment. But Wilson was unmoved. He was down on Taft because of recent critical comments he had made during the midterm elections, and he didn't trust Root, who was still close to Theodore Roosevelt. Joe Tumulty acknowledged that Taft and Root were both considered by Wilson, but rejected. The President did select a Republican for the final spot, Henry White, who had served as the U.S. ambassador to Italy and France. However, White was not a strong player in the party and would be unlikely to have much influence when it came time for the Senate to consider the treaty. Wilson remained unconcerned.

The President went to Congress on December 2 for his Annual Message. He recounted the successes of his administration before pivoting to his plans to secure the peace based on the Fourteen Points he had announced the year before. Frankly, the reception in the House chamber was cold. The Senate Republicans felt shut out and mostly sat quietly as the President delivered his address. It was an ominous sign that didn't seem to concern Wilson much at all. The President was entirely focused on winning over the Allies in Europe, with little attention paid to winning over his political opposition at home, despite the constitutional risk that came with that perspective.

The American entourage was feted to a grand send-off in New York on December 4, 1918. After nine days of travel, the USS *George*

Washington docked in Brest before the President's party traveled by train to Paris. The reception was unlike anything Wilson had ever seen before, and by some accounts, was on a scale never experienced by anyone in the history of mankind. An estimated two million people lined the streets of Paris to welcome the man who had sent them the army that saved the world as they knew it. Edith Wilson captured the scene as follows:

> Every inch was covered with cheering, shouting humanity. The sidewalks, the buildings, even the stately horse-chestnut trees were peopled with men and boys perched like sparrows in their very tops. Roofs were filled, windows overflowed until one grew giddy trying to greet the bursts of welcome that came like the surging of untamed waters. Flowers rained upon us until we were nearly buried.[266]

II-68: Millions lined the streets of Paris to welcome President Wilson

The reporter for the *New York World*, William Bolitho, made it clear who was the center of all this attention. "No one has ever had such cheers," according to Bolitho. "I, who heard them in the streets of Paris, can never forget them in my life. I saw Foch pass, Clemenceau pass, Lloyd George, generals, returning troops, banners, but Wilson heard from his carriage, something different, inhuman – or superhuman."[267] French President Raymond Poincaré said the reception for the American President "stood

II-69: President Wilson riding with French President Raymond Poincaré during the welcome in Paris

alone among the welcome given any previous visitor to Paris."[268] And the Europeans were just getting started.

It would be a few weeks before all the dignitaries would arrive, so Wilson had a little time on his hands, with plenty of invitations to fill his calendar. After reviewing the American troops in Chaumont on Christmas Eve, it was off to London to meet a grateful King George V and Prime Minister David Lloyd George. Knowing the latter might have different priorities heading into the negotiations, there was some tension as the two leaders got to know each other. There was little reason to be concerned, as Wilson and Lloyd George hit it off right away, carrying a wave of optimism as the Americans returned to France. The other major player at the Peace Conference was going to be Italian Prime Minister Vittorio Orlando, so when the Italians extended an invitation, Wilson agreed to accept as a start to another key relationship. The welcome Wilson received in Italy reportedly topped all the others in Europe. "The reception in Rome," according to Secret Service agent Edmund Starling, "exceeded anything I have ever seen in all my years of witnessing public demonstrations. The people literally hailed the President as a god – 'The God of Peace.'"[269] Herbert Hoover, who was traveling with the American delegation to focus on the immediate needs of the starving people across Europe, simply observed that "Woodrow Wilson had reached the zenith of intellectual and spiritual leadership of the whole world, never hitherto known in history."[270] It was here that references to Wilson being the Lord's representative started to enter the conversation, such were the expectations of global peace that the American President had been preaching. Many of Wilson's critics started decrying his "Messiah Complex" around this time as dangerous to the work ahead, sensing he might be so entrenched in his divinely inspired ideas that he would be difficult to work with. The perception of Wilson's sanctimonious attitude was one that played well in public but may be harmful to the negotiations ahead. Even Wilson knew the current enthusiasm would likely fade once they got down to the task at hand. "There is bound to be a reaction to this sort of thing," Wilson said to Dr. Grayson, who had recently been promoted to the rank of Admiral. "I am now at the apex of my glory in the hearts of these people, but they are thinking of me only as one who has come to save Italy, and I have got to pool the interests of Italy with the interests of all the world, and when I do that I am afraid they are going to be disappointed and turn about and hiss me."[271] How right he was.

The world took notice in early January 1918 when another American headlined the news for the final time – Theodore Roosevelt died in his sleep. Roosevelt was true to his nature right to the end, continuing to criticize Wilson and his Fourteen Points. Even with Roosevelt's voice silenced, there would be plenty of condemnation from the Republicans back home. Senator Lodge, a close friend of Roosevelt's for years, was ready to take up that mantle. And it was clearly personal for Lodge, just as it had been for TR. "I never expected to hate anyone in politics with the hatred I feel toward Wilson," Lodge shared with Roosevelt shortly before the latter's death.[272] All of these personal sentiments would eventually come into play, despite the grand receptions Wilson enjoyed in his first month in Europe.

Wilson had one more public appearance before the start of the Peace Conference. The setting was Sorbonne University in Paris where Wilson became the first person in seven centuries to receive an honorary degree from the institution. The President used the opportunity to again elevate the possibilities uniquely available to these delegates at this point in world history. "There is a great wind of moral force moving through the world," Wilson said while warning his audience that "every man who opposes himself to that wind will go down in disgrace."[273] He committed to reminding the conference attendees that "they are the servants of mankind, and if we do not heed the mandates of mankind we shall make ourselves the most conspicuous and deserved failures in the history of the world."[274] The stakes could not be higher, with Europe still smoldering, large swaths of people facing imminent starvation, whole industries decimated with no funds to rebuild, and political chaos manifesting as governments were trying once again to find their footing after years of subjugation by the enemy. On top of all this was the specter of communism that had mostly taken control in Russia in the form of Lenin's Bolsheviks. The Russians were the lone major country missing in action from the Allies at the Peace Conference as they were still sorting out the winners and losers of their recent revolution. But the prospect of communism as the answer to the political and economic woes across Europe terrified many of the leaders across the Continent. These were very real problems that weighed heavily on nearly every delegate in attendance, but less so on Woodrow Wilson. Besides the concern about the rise of communism, Wilson's own country was primarily immune from these immediate fears. This enabled him to focus much more on the long-term future than the terrors of the present, which would make for some interesting negotiations in the days and weeks ahead.

The Quaid d'Orsay, the headquarters of the French Ministry of Foreign Affairs, was the site of the Peace Conference. There were approximately 70 official delegates on hand representing 30 countries. Only the Allies were present. The Central Powers would be invited to Paris only when their fate had already been determined. Woodrow Wilson woke up with a cold on January 18, 1819, the day of the first plenary session, but he rallied to full strength by the time of the opening remarks that afternoon. Wilson took the opportunity to nominate Clemenceau to be the permanent chairman of the Conference, a fitting position for the lead representative from the host nation. That was the only decision made that day, with the next session scheduled for the following week.

Four leaders would stand out in the negotiations to follow. France, Britain, and Italy were the most powerful European nations amongst the Allies, had led the war effort, and suffered the highest numbers of casualties (not including the absent Russians). Their Prime Ministers (Clemenceau, Lloyd George, and Orlando) were charged by their governments to negotiate the specific terms on reparations, new geographical boundaries, the resolution of governance for prior colonies in a new world order, as well as the fate of President Wilson's League of Nations. The United States was the outsider but with enormous leverage for its role in bringing the war to a successful conclusion. President Wilson would be the fourth prominent member of the lead negotiators, intent on pushing for each of his Fourteen Points. Wilson perceived Clemenceau to likely be his greatest obstacle. John Maynard Keynes,

II-70: The "Big Four" at the Paris Peace Conference
(L to R): Italian Prime Minister Vittorio Orlando, British Prime Minister David Lloyd George, French Prime Minister Georges Clemenceau, and American President Woodrow Wilson

who was early in what would become a renowned career as an economist, was supporting the British delegation in Paris. Keynes described Clemenceau as "a foremost believer in the view of German psychology which thinks that the German understands and can understand nothing but intimidation, that he is without generosity or remorse in negotiation."[275] Keynes saw Clemenceau as seeking revenge against Germany and security for his home country as the primary objectives of the Conference. With this mindset, he was bound to clash with President Wilson, who would make the point repeatedly that vindictive terms imposed on the Central Powers would only mean another war down the road. Balancing these interests was going to be the focal point and primary challenge of the negotiations.

As the Conference got underway, there was a nagging tension in the air over the fact that, unlike all the European leaders, the American President had never laid eyes on the massive destruction inflicted during the war. Wilson had been urged since arriving on the Continent to visit some of the battlefields to try to get a true sense of what the Allies had been through over the past four years. At this stage, Wilson refused to make such a trip. He thought he needed to maintain his objectivity concerning the overarching objectives of the Conference and was afraid such a visit would trigger an emotional response that might affect his judgment. "I don't want to get mad over here because I think there ought to be one person at that peace table who isn't mad," Wilson explained as the rationale for his resistance. "I'm afraid if I visited the devastated areas I would get mad, too, and I'm not going to permit myself to do so."[276] The Europeans were taken aback at this stance, but it was just another signal that Wilson's perspective on the Conference was on a different plane from his colleagues.

Wilson knew that the Peace Conference could only do so much and that concessions may need to be made that individual parties would later regret. This was another point in favor of Wilson's League of Nations. He saw the League as a never-ending Peace Conference, the kind of formal body that could continue to address the challenges between nations in a structured, rules-based manner that was anchored by a moral foundation based on an overriding mutual desire for peace. "I now realize, more than ever before," he told Edith, "that once established the League can arbitrate and correct mistakes which are inevitable in the Treaty we are trying to make at this time. The resentments and injustices caused by the War are still too poignant, and the wounds too fresh. They must have time to heal, and when they have done so, one by one the mistakes can be brought to the League for readjustment, and the League will act as a permanent clearinghouse where every nation can come, the small as well as the great."[277] This view was one of the reasons that Wilson wanted the League to be the first topic discussed amongst the delegates. On January 25, Wilson was center stage at the second plenary session to introduce what he believed the League to be all about. "We have assembled for two purposes," Wilson shared with his colleagues, "to make the present settlements which have been rendered necessary by this war, and also to secure the peace of the world." The League of Nations, according to Wilson, "seems to me to be necessary for both of these purposes." Without the League, "no arrangement that you can make would either set up or steady the peace of the world."[278] He shared with his fellow delegates how the League had the potential for mutual guarantees of political and territorial integrity, processes to arbitrate disputes, and, if necessary, the kind of consequences that nations would face if they violated the rules to which the members agreed to adhere. After Wilson concluded his remarks, a commission was established to work out the details and report back to the Conference as a whole the proposed framework for the League of Nations. All would progress forward despite an undercurrent among many of the delegations that lacked interest in Wilson's League and would rather just focus on the immediate punishment of the Central Powers and recovery of their own countries (including territorial adjustments). But there was no way to try to formally deny the American leader his primary objective given the critical role the United States played in winning the war.

Over the course of the following week, before the League Commission would start its formal discussions, delegations started meeting to advocate for how to allocate the remnants of the German and Ottoman Empires. Questions needed to be addressed, including where new geographical boundaries would be drawn, what former colonies would be recognized as independent nations, and what to do with former colonies which weren't ready or able to establish themselves as sovereign countries at this time. Woodrow Wilson's first Thirteen Points were intended to guide these discussions, but disagreements quickly materialized as selfish motives typically outweighed Wilson's principles-based rubric. While some clear-cut issues were resolved early on, many more controversial topics simply revealed the disconnects that would make an ultimate agreement difficult to achieve. To try to tamp down the noise, the Big Four (Clemenceau, Lloyd George, Orlando, and Wilson) made it clear that they would be the ones figuring out these complex decisions, and would do so mostly in small, private sessions behind closed doors. Wilson's first "point" ("open covenants of peace, openly arrived at") was at risk of being violated right out of the gate.

During this week, President Wilson finally relented and agreed to visit some of the devastation caused by the war. He was the primary guest on a tour of Belleau Wood, Chateau-Thierry, and Reims, the sites of tens of thousands of American casualties. Wilson found utter destruction at every turn. "No one can put into words the impressions received amid such scenes of desolation from the Federation of Protestant and ruin," Wilson said upon his return to Paris. Nevertheless, Wilson remained committed to compartmentalizing these observations and the associated emotions. He still intended to be the one man at the table who wasn't acting out of revenge for past sins but would remain focused on how to prevent these catastrophic events in the future.

The League of Nations Commission met nearly every day from February 3 to 13 to hammer out a Covenant to define the purpose, structure, major responsibilities, and commitments associated with the new global body. Fourteen nations were represented, but this was primarily a Woodrow Wilson show. He had already sketched out the concept and was mostly seeking concurrence with his ideas. Historian Harold Black offered the following summary:

> Its terms were general rather than specific. Its aim was disarmament and the promotion of harmony and cooperation among the nations. … The members of the League were not to make war on each other without first arbitrating the questions in dispute. Effective means, such as an economic boycott, or, if necessary, the use of military force, were provided, – means which might be employed against any nation refusing to abide by the decision thus reached.[279]

The League would consist of a Council which would be comprised of the nine most powerful nations in the world. The Council would be the decision-making body for all major moves by the League, and its decisions would need to be unanimous to be placed into effect. All country members would comprise the Assembly which would basically serve as advisors to the Council. A permanent Secretariat would be hired to manage the day-to-day operations of the organization.

The League Covenant was captured in 26 Articles, but the one that was truly the heart of the construct, as well as the most controversial, was Article 10, which read as follows:

> The Members of the League undertake to respect and preserve as against external aggression the territorial integrity and existing political independence of all Members of the League. In case of any such aggression or in case of any threat or danger of such aggression the Council shall advise upon the means by which this obligation shall be fulfilled.[280]

Those means were intended to be economic in nature to start but could be elevated to joint military action based on a unanimous vote of the Council. The League was not authorized to manage a standing military operation of its own but would form coalitions of military capabilities from across the membership on a case-by-case basis. This was the stick that was intended to keep the members in line by making the prospect of war so unattractive that countries would do everything they could to avoid it. But Article 10 immediately raised concerns in the United States, particularly with members of Congress, who saw their exclusive constitutional power to declare war potentially being outsourced to an independent body. Woodrow Wilson continued to make no effort to consult those members, including the senators who would ultimately decide whether anything Wilson negotiated in Paris would actually be approved by his own country.

For now, Wilson was focused on getting the approval of the delegates at the Peace Conference, and for that, things came together quickly. The members of the League Commission voted unanimously to approve the Covenant. The next day, February 14, Wilson presented the results at the third plenary session. Knowing the importance of this presentation, Edith and Dr. Grayson asked permission to be in the room. Prime Minister Clemenceau agreed to this exception to the protocol established for the Conference, but with discretion. The pair would have to sit in an alcove in the back concealed by some heavy curtains. They would have to arrive early and leave after everyone else, but they could attend and peek through the curtains to observe Wilson's big moment.

After reading through all 25 Articles, Wilson then offered some perspective. He provided a brief description of what they were tasked to do. "This conference had entrusted to us the expression of one of its highest and most important purposes," Wilson shared, "to see to it that the concord of the world in the future with regard to the objects of justice should not be subject to doubt or uncertainty; that the cooperation of the great body of nations should be assured from the first in the maintenance of peace upon the terms of honor and of the strict regard for international obligation."[281] A key to the success of the League, according to Wilson, was the foundational empowerment that went beyond the body being created.

> Throughout this instrument we are depending primarily and chiefly upon one great force, and that is the moral force of the public opinion of the world—the cleansing and clarifying and compelling influences of publicity—so that intrigues can no longer have their coverts, so that designs that are sinister can at

> any time be drawn into the open, so that those things that are destroyed by the light may be properly destroyed by the overwhelming light of the universal expression of the condemnation of the world.[282]

And, in case moral suasion didn't work, there was the military option that would be the final insurance policy against violent aggression. "Armed force is in the background in this program," Wilson said, "but it is in the background, and if the moral force of the world will not suffice, the physical force of the world shall. But that is the last resort, because this is intended as a constitution of peace, not as a league of war."[283] As he closed his address, Wilson once again returned to the vision upon which the League would be based: "We are brothers and have a common purpose. We did not realize it before, but now we do realize it, and this is our covenant of fraternity and of friendship."[284]

Wilson was pleased with the Covenant and his presentation and was confident that the delegates would adopt it. It was his highest priority, and everyone knew it. More than anything else, he saw this as his gift to the world and the most important item that would emanate from the entire Conference. He was also insistent that the League Covenant be adopted as part of the final Peace Treaty. He was adamantly opposed to making it a separate agreement, which was being advocated by some of the other prominent delegates who weren't as enamored with the entire concept. That was a non-starter for Wilson, who was concerned that if the Covenant wasn't part and parcel of the final product, it might be left behind. He was determined not to let that happen.

II-71: Wilson at the Paris Peace Conference, 1919

But Wilson would do no lobbying for the League with the delegates right away because he had a boat to catch. As President of the United States, he needed to return to Washington, DC, for a brief period to be available to sign (or veto) legislation that was being approved before the current congressional session would close on March 4. It would also be an opportunity to begin advocating for the League Covenant with the senators who would have to approve it before the United States could ever become a member. This latter point was more on the mind of Colonel House than it was for President Wilson. House made two recommendations to the President as he prepared to depart. First, he suggested arriving in Boston, rather than New York or Virginia, in order to increase the likelihood of a grand reception, which House thought would also be impactful on the minds of the Europeans who would continue at the Conference. Wilson agreed, Boston it would be, which also happened to be the home of Republican Senator Lodge. House's second suggestion also concerned Senator Lodge and his colleagues on the Foreign Relations Committee. He believed the President should schedule a dinner and interactive discussion with committee members from both parties to explain the League Covenant and answer whatever questions they might have. On this, Wilson initially balked. He thought one of his typical addresses to all of Congress would make more sense, but House convinced him that a more informal setting at the White House would be more conducive to getting the senators who mattered most on board. Ultimately, the President agreed. While Secretary Lansing, as the senior government official, would technically be the leader of the American delegation while Wilson was away, everyone knew that the President placed House in charge. Wilson's primary advice to his alter-ego was to hold the line and not make any major decisions without him. "I beg that you will hold things steady with regard to everything but the strictly naval and military terms until I return," Wilson told House. After years of reliable service, the President had no reason for concern – at least for now.

Wilson's party left from Brest on the *George Washington* late on February 14, arriving in Boston ten days later. Anxious to get back to Washington, he made only a few brief addresses to the large throngs who welcomed him back to the United States. "And now these ideals have wrought this new magic that all the peoples of Europe are buoyed up and confident in the spirit of hope," the President proclaimed, "because they believe that we are at the eve of a new age in the world, when nations will understand one another; when nations will support one another in every just cause; when nations will unite every moral and every physical strength to see that right shall prevail. If America were at this juncture to fail the world, what would come of it?"[285] Wilson was starting his two-pronged approach to advocate for the League in his home country. At the same time, he would both accentuate the benefits of the League while also painting a picture of doom if the Senate failed to approve the product emanating from the Peace Conference. This was fine in Boston, where the reception was as desired, but it would not play well in the upcoming meeting with the senators.

After Wilson's train arrived in Washington, the President went straight to the White House, where Joe Tumulty was waiting for him with mounds of papers ready for his review and signature. Wilson then met with his Cabinet before preparing to welcome the invited senators to the White House. Senator Lodge and his colleagues had not been sitting idly by while the President was serving as the leader of the American delegation abroad. They had been building their opposition to Wilson's League, which had only ramped up since they had received the details from Paris. Article 10 was squarely in their sights, but there were other concerns as well, mostly related to items that were perceived to infringe on the sovereignty of the United States and/or the constitutional prerogatives of the U.S. Congress. The meeting at the White House did not go well. The Republican senators basically sat on their hands, asked very few questions, and gave little indication they were going to support the most important initiative of Wilson's entire life. Annoyed by the gathering, the President blamed House for the idea of the dinner in the first place, which was just the start of the Republican effort to thwart Wilson's grand idea.

With the passing of Theodore Roosevelt earlier in the year, his close friend Henry Lodge had taken center stage in opposition to Wilson's League. Again, the issue of American independent thought and action was at the heart of his concern. "One of the reasons why I object to the provisions of this treaty," Lodge said, "is that it endangers the sovereignty and the independence of the United States. I think now, as I always have thought and believed, that the United States is the best hope of mankind and will remain so as long as we do not destroy it by mingling in every broil and quarrel that may desolate the earth."[286] In this case, the senator was hardly alone in his views. On March 4, as the congressional session was gaveled to a close, Lodge issued a letter signed by 37 senators opposed to the League as currently proposed. The number was significant, as it represented 39% of the total number of senators, more than enough to kill the proposal. The letter urged the President to renegotiate several of the articles, which, if he did, could pave the way for their support. The letter received an icy reception at the other end of Pennsylvania Avenue. As Wilson prepared to return to Europe, he responded to Lodge and his fellow naysayers by writing, "When that treaty comes back, gentlemen on this side will find the Covenant not only in it, but so many threads of the treaty tied to the Covenant that you cannot dissect the Covenant from the treaty without destroying the whole vital structure."[287] The President continued to evade any meaningful negotiations with his senatorial opposition. Rather, his words and tone implied a man who was locked in and ready to stand firm in the face of this opposition. How he intended to get the constitutional sanction from the Senate to put the agreement into effect was anybody's guess.

10. Peace Conference: Round Two

The day after the congressional session came to an end, the Wilsons left on the *George Washington* for the return journey to France. The President was anxious to get back to the negotiating table. Arriving in Brest on March 13, he was met by Colonel House, and the news was not good. According to House, the League of Nations had been under attack throughout Wilson's absence. Specifically, the French were seeking to separate the League from the Peace Treaty, and they had been succeeding in recruiting other nations to join their push. The European sentiment was fixated on the need to solve today's problems today, and focus on tomorrow's problems down the road. Unlike the United States, whose territory had escaped the devastation of the war, Europe was crumbling and needed a final peace. Widespread starvation, economic and political chaos, and the looming threat of Bolshevism were foremost on their minds, with far less interest in Wilson's League. The French were also pushing a proposal to establish a so-called Rhinish Republic as a buffer state (under French control) on the west bank of the Rhine. It was already clear that the Alsace-Lorraine region would be returned to France as part of the Peace Treaty, but the French were adamant that this was insufficient to protect them from a future German attack. The challenge was the large German-speaking population throughout that region, placing the proposal squarely at odds with Wilson's Fifth Point ("a strict observance of the principle that in determining all such questions of sovereignty the interests of the population concerned must have equal weight with the equitable government whose title is to be determined"[288]). Wilson's bedrock principle of self-determination was under assault.

The President was furious after receiving House's report, and he placed the blame squarely on the shoulders of the man he had once called "my second personality … my independent self."[289] The President turned to Edith to convey his disgust over the situation. "House has given away everything I had won before we left Paris," he said. "He has compromised on every side, and so I have to start all over again and this time it will be harder, as he has given the impression that my delegates are not in sympathy with me."[290] Secretary Lansing was seemingly the most out of sync with the President, something Wilson had previously suspected but was becoming increasingly clear. This incident was the first crack in the previously impenetrable relationship between Wilson and Colonel House.

By the time Wilson's train arrived in Paris, he was primed and ready to stop these desertions from his Fourteen Points. After doing the rounds with the American delegation, he sought out the other 'Big Three,' telling Clemenceau, Lloyd George, and Orlando that a treaty without the League was a non-starter for the United States. As he forcefully reminded them that they wouldn't be sitting there on the victorious side of the conflict without the commitment and sacrifice of the American people, he also re-stated his case on why the League was not only essential but also needed to be joined at the hip with all the other elements of any Peace Treaty. On this point, he seemed to make headway, based on the public statement released on March 15: "The President said to day that the decision made at the Peace Conference at its plenary session, January 25, 1919, to the effect that the establishment of a League of Nations should be made an integral part of the Treaty of Peace is of final force and that there is no basis whatever for the reports that a change in this decision was contemplated."[291] What Wilson didn't know at the time was how costly this stand was going to be, both at the Conference and at home. The other Allies finally understood that threatening to withdraw support from the League was the quickest way to get Wilson to cave on some of the other controversial decisions that were still pending. Interestingly, Wilson seemed willing to trade away some of his other precious Fourteen Points to preserve the League with the Allies, but he gave no sign of any concessions toward the Republican senators back home.

As the negotiations resumed, they increasingly became a four-person affair. The leaders from Britain, France, Italy, and the United States were now frequently meeting in private to try to break through the numerous roadblocks that had materialized. But even these smaller sessions were not going well, with Wilson often the odd man out. On the topic of reparations, for example, Clemenceau was leading the charge to inflict maximum punishment on the Germans. The Sub-Committee of the Commission on Reparations of Damage had been compiling the numbers for weeks, trying to quantify the suffering the Germans and the Central Powers had inflicted on the Allied Nations. Still a work in progress, the numbers were nonetheless staggering. When all factors were accounted for, the sub-committee identified nearly $40 billion in damages (more than $725 billion in inflation-adjusted numbers[292]). They all knew that Germany had no capacity to pay this astronomical sum, even if the terms were spread over many years, but Clemenceau (and others) were determined that the Germans must be held to fully account for their atrocities. Wilson pleaded with his colleagues that imposing such damages would put the Germans in an impossible situation, likely leading to years of discontent that would eventually explode into an inevitable military clash. "Our greatest error," Wilson said, "would be to give [Germany] powerful reasons for one day wishing to take revenge. Excessive demands would most certainly sow the seeds of war."[293] The tension was mounting and finally came to a head in a meeting of the Big Four on March 27. Continuing to argue over both territorial claims and the magnitude of the reparations, Clemenceau grew exasperated, charging that Wilson had become "the friend of Germany." Wilson was shocked at the statement, given all his country had done to save France from complete subjugation by Germany. After charging the French Premier with stating untruths, Wilson asked with a bitter tone, "In that event, do you wish me to return home?"[294] Clemenceau told Wilson not to bother; he would take leave himself. With that, he walked out the door. The agreement the entire world was waiting for appeared to be falling apart amongst the bickering "allies."

As much as Wilson had intended the negotiations to stay clear of emotionally charged motivations, the strong sentiments of the Allied leaders had clearly come to the fore. The Europeans were tired of being dictated to by the sanctimonious man from across the Atlantic. Wilson's single-minded stubbornness was increasingly seen as a manifestation of his "Messiah Complex," projecting a sense of Divine purpose in his Fourteen Points, and particularly the League of Nations. That Wilson's religiosity was deeply embedded in his soul was not a revelation given his upbringing, as well as his many statements over the years that tied religious-based morality to public policy. Wilson, who engaged in morning prayers, evening prayers, and Bible-reading every day throughout his life, had once said during his tenure as President of Princeton that "I believe in Divine Providence. If I did not I would go crazy."[295] Biographer Ray Baker noted that Wilson's religious ideals tended to be even more prominent in his speeches during periods of crisis, such as the acrimonious relationship Wilson encountered in the second half of his presidency at Princeton. "As in all previous crises of his life," noted Baker, "it also seemed to have a religious side. We find him speaking again and again that winter and spring [in 1906-1907] on religious subjects or to religious gatherings. Many of his other addresses breathe a religious aspiration."[296] Facing the greatest crisis of his life, it is not surprising that many began to sense Wilson pitching ideas in a Christ-like manner of a man on a mission to save the world.

Several of those closest to Wilson during the negotiations in Paris brought up the comparison. Clemenceau commented that Wilson "thought himself another Jesus Christ come upon the earth to reform men."[297] Colonel House, who knew Wilson as well as anyone, observed that "There is a bon mot going around in Paris and London, 'Wilson talks like Jesus Christ and acts like Lloyd George.'"[298] One of those who developed the theory of Wilson's "Messiah Complex" was none other than famed psychologist Sigmund Freud. Freud teamed with William Bullitt to perform "A Psychological Study" of Wilson in a book by that title. Neither man cared for Wilson, nor were they shy about those feelings. As will soon be seen, Bullitt was part of the American delegation in France, but he resigned via a public letter citing his disillusionment over Wilson's backtracking from the vision of the Fourteen Points. Freud talked openly in the book's introduction about his "antipathy" for Wilson, and, in particular, how his performance at the Peace Conference made him "unsympathetic to me, and that this aversion increased in the course of years the more I learned about him."[299] Despite this obvious bias, it is hard to simply ignore the views of someone like Freud who has such renown in the field. Weaving through all the commentary about Wilson's Ego and Super-Ego, and the unsurprising discussion about the relationships Wilson had with his mother and father

II-72: Sigmund Freud

(classic Freudian material), is the theme that Wilson had embraced the notion that he was God's messenger to deliver this new world order that would preserve peace for all time. "Wilson's unconscious identification of himself with the Saviour had become so obvious that it compelled even those who had never studied the deeper psychic strata to recognize its existence," the authors wrote.[300] They further noted that these beliefs allowed Wilson to stay the course with "a great wind of moral force" that he believed was so strong that "every man who opposes himself to that wind will go down in disgrace."[301] Wilson undoubtedly believed that the outcome he was determined to achieve was, at a minimum, Divinely-inspired. In some ways, it was his source of strength amidst powerful opposition. However, his preaching often rubbed others the wrong way, not to mention his unwillingness to embrace any alternatives from his own Divinely-inspired ideas regarding the formation of the League. This obstinance created deep fissures with critical stakeholders on both sides of the Atlantic. Acting like a man on a "mission from God," Wilson's stubbornness would help establish the League, but he sacrificed a lot of his other "Points" in getting there, as well as his own country's participation.

If God was indeed watching over Woodrow Wilson during these negotiations in Paris, he might have been sending some sort of a warning when the American President came down with a violent illness. Dr. Grayson had been worried for weeks that Wilson was once again working himself too hard, avoiding exercise and rest, and that his body may not withstand the pace and pressure. On April 3, Wilson's body gave out, as Grayson shared in a letter to Tumulty:

II-73: Wilson with Rear Admiral Cary Grayson, 1919

> The President was taken violently sick last Thursday. The attack was very sudden. At three o'clock he was

> apparently all right; at six he was seized with violent paroxysms of coughing, which were so severe and frequent that it interfered with his breathing. He had a fever of 103 and a profuse diarrhea. That night was one of the worst through which I have ever passed.[302]

After a brief doctor-mandated rest, Wilson slowly started to regain his strength and was anxious to get back to the negotiating table. Nevertheless, some observers noticed changes in the President beginning with this attack. White House Chief Usher Ike Hoover, who ran the household during the Wilsons' stay in Europe, remarked, "We could but surmise that something queer was happening in his mind [and that] he was never the same after this little spell of sickness."[303] In fact, the President's symptoms lingered for weeks, during which he had a short fuse with everyone, from world leaders to his personal staff. He was more likely to express his anger than anyone could remember. The intensity of the negotiations certainly played a significant role in these mood swings, but those around him sensed something different after the onset of this illness. It didn't help that Wilson refused to stand down and take an extended rest, as recommended by Dr. Grayson – not with the future of mankind hanging in the balance.

So, the Big Four continued to meet. Many of the sessions took place in the Wilson residence, with some even occurring in the President's bedroom. The biggest remaining issues were concerned with drawing the new geographic boundaries of Europe. What new nations would be created? What colonies would persist, and under whose authorities? One of the most heated arguments was between Clemenceau and Wilson over the Saar Valley, a critical coal-producing region that had historically been part of Germany, but France Premier was insisting on making its own. Wilson extensively argued that this was completely counter to the theory of self-determination, but the French remained adamant. Wilson's frustration, fueled partly by his illness, started to bubble over. "The whole course of the conference has been made up of a series of attempts, especially by France, to break down this agreement, to get territory, and to impose crushing indemnities," Wilson asserted.[304] He stunned the participants by ordering his team to get the *George Washington* back into port, paving the way for a quick departure if he decided to exit the Conference. Everyone around Wilson was taken aback. Clemenceau posed the question to Dr. Grayson, "It is a bluff, isn't it?" The President's physician responded, "He hasn't a bluffing corpuscle in his body."[305] In this instance, however, no one was ready to give up, so the long days of tense negotiations continued.

That week was actually a turning point in the talks, and not in the direction that Wilson desired. Despite his threat to walk away, the American President was the one who started to give in. The key to everything was the League of Nations. Whether consciously or not, Wilson was willing to sacrifice many of his other Points in order to get his League established. Since the Allies had figured this out, they pressed their demands, and Wilson began to relent. The Saar Valley, for example, would eventually enjoy self-determination, but not for another 15 years. In the meantime, the French would control the mines and reap the benefits of their vast production generated by the mostly German-speaking workers. A similar solution was proposed for the west bank of the Rhine. The French would control the territory for 15 years, with a plebiscite then taking place to determine its long-term future, once again giving no say to the predominately German-speaking population throughout the region for the next decade and a half. And when the French insisted on even greater security guarantees for the area, Wilson agreed to a side deal whereby the United States and Britain would immediately come to the aid of the French if Germany ever invaded again – precisely the kind of agreement he sought to banish with the first of his Fourteen Points. Other regions with large German populations were similarly affected. Italy would receive Tyrol, south of the Bremer Pass, and Poland would become an independent nation. In both cases, large German communities were being separated from their Mother Country. Wilson maintained that "The only real interest of France in Poland is in weakening Germany by giving Poland territory to which she has no right."[306] Nevertheless, Wilson agreed to each of these items, despite the fact they ran counter to many of his Fourteen Points.

As for the previous colonial holdings of both the German and Austro-Hungarian empires that were deemed unfit for self-rule at that time, colonialism would persist, just under a different name and new territorial masters. They called it the "Mandate System." Instead of their previous colonial powers, these states or regions would be overseen by "Mandatory Powers," which, not surprisingly, ended up being Britain and France in many instances. Impacted states were to be found in the Middle East, Africa, and Asia Pacific. In the Middle East, for example, France was handed responsibility for Lebanon and Syria, while Britain took on the new states of Palestine, Jordan, and Iraq – the latter including the combination of the traditional enemies of the Shiites, Sunnis, and Kurds. A number of smaller constructs were established as well, including isolated Mandate responsibilities for Belgium, Australia, Japan, and New Zealand for landholdings in the other regions covered by the system. Wilson was convinced this structure was not colonialism by another name. He thought this would be different. He had asserted when the Covenant for the League of Nations was announced:

> We recognize in the most solemn manner that the helpless and undeveloped peoples of the world, being in that condition, put an obligation upon us to look after their interests primarily before we use them for our interest; and that in all cases of this sort hereafter it shall be the duty of the league to see that the nations who are assigned as the tutors and advisers and directors of those peoples shall look to their interest and to their development before they look to the interests and material desires of the mandatory nation itself. There has been no greater advance than this, gentlemen.[307]

But these thoughts were more in Wilson's visionary mind than in the plans of the Mandatory Powers. They were happy to agree to Wilson's rhetoric, knowing that once the Conference was over, they would be able to lead these areas in any manner they saw fit. Similar to the American holdings over the Philippines during this era, most of these lands would eventually receive their independence. But, also like the Philippines, that would often take several decades to come to fruition.

There were some other areas where President Wilson also gave in to the demands of the Allies so he could protect the League from any adjustments. He relented on the Allies' insistence that the Peace Treaty include a specific reference

II-74: President Wilson

that German aggression was the sole cause of the war in the first place. In addition, against his previous stand, Wilson concurred with the provision that would permit Kaiser Wilhelm to be tried for war crimes. And, most significantly, he caved on the magnitude of the reparations, which leaned toward the astronomically high numbers that had been put forward by the French. The down payment would be £1 billion to be paid over two years, with another £6 billion to follow. Wilson knew the risks associated with many of these concessions. He fully acknowledged the possibility of motivating future armed conflict on the part of the Central Powers based on the crushing nature of the terms, as well as the erosion of many of his Fourteen Points, but he believed if he could just get the League of Nations up and running, it would be worth it. Wilson concluded this was the only path to a treaty that included the League, and the League would be the mechanism whereby any injustices incorporated into the treaty could be addressed at some future time.

The last couple of territorial decisions were perhaps the most controversial and difficult to resolve. The first determination involved Italy and its claim for Fiume, the growing port city that sat at the convergence of Italy and Croatia. This was Prime Minister Orlando's top priority in the talks. In this instance, Wilson held his ground. Despite the fervent plea from Orlando, Wilson thought the move would be such a blatant violation of the concept of self-determination that he simply could not concede. He also saw Fiume as critical to the economic future of the Slavic nations and, if taken by Italy, could devastate the well-being of the entire region. Orlando threatened to leave the Conference if Wilson wouldn't change his mind, but the President, on this decision, remained obstinate. When Orlando realized he would not get Wilson's support, he reportedly went to the window, burst into tears, and left the meeting. The next day, he took his delegation and returned to Italy. Just a few months before, Wilson had been hailed as the Second Coming during his reception in Italy prior to the start of the Conference. Now, as he had predicted, he was vilified throughout that land.

The last topic of debate was between Japan and China. The Japanese had been relatively quiet during the Conference. They had made one intriguing proposal which would have included a clause in the Treaty that committed the signatories to "racial equality." While a majority of the delegates voted to approve the measure, Woodrow Wilson was adamantly opposed and effectively killed the proposition. Wilson cited the need to receive unanimous approval for adoption, as opposed to a majority vote, despite the fact that no such rule had been formally adopted by the delegates and a number of other proposals had been embraced without unanimous support. Wilson's motivation may have been from his own personal sentiments, for which there had been a long record demonstrating an aversion to dealing with the different races on equal terms. It is also likely that he was concerned that the measure would be a poison pill in a U.S. Senate that the President knew would never embrace the concept. The result, though, was that the Japanese were on edge and particularly insistent on their one other major proposal. This one involved the Shantung Province.

Shantung is a region of approximately sixty-thousand square miles smack in the middle of the eastern seaboard of China. It is located on the Yellow Sea, directly across from what is now known as South Korea. Shantung's port city of Qingdao is approximately one-thousand miles from the western Japanese city of Fukuoka. Yet the Japanese were insistent that it be awarded Shantung as part of the post-war settlement. This was based on one of those secret side deals that President Wilson was so anxious to eliminate from international agreements. Germany had captured Shantung from the Chinese during the war, and the British enticed the Japanese with the offer of Shantung if they would enter the war on behalf of the Allies. The Japanese agreed, and now it was time to collect its reward. This was despite the fact that it violated several of Wilson's Fourteen Points, most particularly the right of self-determination. Shantung happened to be the birthplace of Confucius, and the Chinese wanted it back. The British supported the position of the Japanese, who, after the earlier setback on racial equality, were now threatening to quit the Conference if they didn't get what had been promised to them. Woodrow Wilson found himself in yet another bind. He knew handing Shantung to the Japanese violated his tenets, but he was also concerned that the Conference might fall apart if he didn't relent. With the Italians having already departed, if the Japanese also left, it would be difficult to make the case that any treaty coming out of the Conference truly had the support of the world. The League of Nations was, therefore, once again at risk. So, Wilson reluctantly gave in … again.

This time, several members of the American delegation voiced opposition to their chief. Secretary Lansing was perhaps the most vocal in his protests, calling the decision a "surrender of the principle of self-determination, a transfer of millions of Chinese from one foreign master to another." General Bliss wrote the President on behalf of Henry White and Herbert Hoover, citing the impossible-to-explain inconsistency in this abdication of principle when compared to other decisions about which the President had been so insistent. "If it be right for Japan to annex the territory of an Ally [China], then it cannot be wrong for Italy to retain Fiume taken from the enemy," Bliss wrote.[308] Wilson found himself in the grip of *realpolitik,* compelled to sacrifice principle for the greater good, but hardly consistent with the utopian rhetoric he often espoused. His lone fallback remained that perhaps the League would be able to fix this situation down the road. "I would never have done that if I had not been sure that the League of Nations would revise that decision," Wilson remarked.[309]

There were immediate ramifications to this decision. While the Japanese were appeased, the Chinese were outraged, both in Paris and in Peking. China would no longer sign onto the treaty, would initiate a boycott with Japan, and a new set of revolutionary leaders would begin to rise. For Woodrow Wilson, he now had a fractured team, loud protests in Washington, and a diplomat who couldn't take these concessions anymore from the President. That diplomat was William Bullitt, the man who would go on to co-author the psychological study of Wilson with Sigmund Freud. Bullitt was an assistant in the State Department, serving as an attaché to the American delegation. His principal mission had been to go to Russia to see if there were opportunities to forge a positive relationship with Vladimir Lenin and his new government. Bullitt returned to Pairs with optimism based on his interactions with Lenin, but the Allies, led by the British, rejected the entreaty. Now, President Wilson's decision on Shantung Province was the last straw in a series of concessions that Bullitt concluded represented such a degree of abdication of the original Fourteen Points that they were no longer

II-75: William Bullitt

recognizable. Bullitt decided he could no longer support his President, and submitted his resignation with a lengthy note directly to Wilson.

> I was one of the millions who trusted confidently and implicitly in your leadership and believed that you would take nothing less than 'a permanent peace' based upon 'unselfish and unbiased justice.' But our Government has consented now to deliver the suffering peoples of the world to new oppressions, subjections, and dismemberments - a new century of war. And I can convince myself no longer that effective labor for 'a new world order' is possible as a servant of this Government. … Unjust decisions of the Conference in regard to Shantung, the Tyrol, Thrace, Hungary, East Prussia, Danzig, the Saar Valley, and the abandonment of the principle of the freedom of the seas, make new international conflicts certain.[310]

Despite these protests, Wilson agreed to the assignment of Shantung to Japan, which would now sign the Treaty and support Wilson's League in return. For Woodrow Wilson, that result trumped all other considerations, including those directly stated in his original Fourteen Points.

The one member of Wilson's entourage who was mostly supportive of the President's concessions was Colonel House, who was generally willing to compromise to get to closure on an issue. But while House continued to be part of Wilson's working team, he was no longer as intimate as he had been over the past six years. Ever since House had let Wilson down during the President's interlude in Washington, things had not been the same. According to Ray Baker, "From this time onward there began to grow up a coldness between the two men."[311] And things got chillier still in April 1919, shortly after Wilson had come down with his serious illness. One day when House showed up at the Wilson house to check on his boss, he was met at the door by Edith Wilson, who had a newspaper in her hand. It was the latest issue of the Paris *Daily Mail*, and contained a very flattering article about House by reporter Wickham Steed. It was entitled *Colonel House's Services*.

> Insofar as there is a real improvement in the prospects of the Conference, it is believed to be attributable chiefly to its practical statesmanship of Colonel House, who, in view of President Wilson's indisposition, has once again placed his savoir faire and conciliatory temperament at the disposal of the

> chief peacemakers. … If there is now a chance that the Conference may be hauled back from the brink of failure on to relatively safe ground, it is mainly due to the efforts of Colonel House.[312]

Before House could comment, and with Edith glaring at him, he was whisked away to see the President, but he realized this would be trouble. House knew as well as anyone that Wilson did not like being upstaged. In fact, a key part of his success had been his ability to remain the man in the background, offering counsel and support but never detracting from the man in charge. This article represented another wedge in the relationship, one which was undoubtedly encouraged by Mrs. Wilson who never cared for House and was extremely protective of her husband.

By early May, the final pieces of the treaty were settling into place. Then, out of the blue, Vittorio Orlando suddenly reappeared. The Italian Premier decided Italy still needed its seat at the table, with him as the leading member of the delegation once more. He was just in time for the Allies to summon the Germans to hear their fate (separate treaties would be presented later to the other members of the Central Powers). The session was scheduled for May 7 and took place at King Louis XIV's palatial estate at Versailles, located about 12 miles outside of Paris. The German delegation was led by Foreign Minister Ulrich von Brocldorff-Rantza, who acknowledged up front, even before reading the treaty, that while Germany had been defeated, the Allies should be cautious about imposing excessively harsh terms. And then he read the document and wondered how any nation could be expected to absorb such punishment. Back in Germany, the President of the National Assembly at Weimar responded by directing his ire at Woodrow Wilson, stating, "It is incomprehensible that a man who had promised the world a peace of justice, upon which a society of nations would be founded has been able to assist in framing this project dictated by hate." The Germans, who were given no opportunity to negotiate and only 15 days to place their signature on the document, declared that the treaty revealed that "on essential points the basis of the Peace of Right, agreed upon between the belligerents, has been abandoned," that some of the demands were such as "no nation could endure," and that "many of them could not possibly be carried out."[313] The Allies maintained their 'take it or leave it stance,' with the threat of military decimation as the only alternative.

While the Germans tried to figure out what to do, President Wilson made one more trip to honor the American boys who had died fighting for peace in the world. The occasion was the dedication of an American military cemetery outside of Paris. It was held on Decoration Day, which had become an annual commemoration of American military sacrifice since the Civil War. This was another emotional experience for a President who still felt responsible for sending so many soldiers to their deaths, even if for the most righteous of causes. The President offered these words to open the dedication ceremony:

> No one with a heart in his breast, no American, no lover of humanity, can stand in the presence of these graves without the most profound emotion. These men who lie here are men of unique breed. Their like has not been seen since the far days of the Crusades. Never before have men crossed the seas to a foreign land to fight for a cause which they did not pretend was peculiarly their own, but knew was the cause of humanity and of mankind.[314]

Wilson's purpose in life remained to create a mechanism that would alleviate future American Presidents from presiding over similar ceremonies in the future.

As the allotted duration for the Germans began to wind down, there was real concern that they would refuse to sign. In fact, German Chancellor Philipp Scheidermann found the terms so unreasonable that he opposed accepting them regardless of the consequences. The Germans formally responded with a 119-page counterproposal, with strong disagreements with just about every clause as originally presented. They expected the decrees they were issued for demilitarization, including the dramatic reduction in the size of the German army and navy, as well as the ban on submarines from their military, but many of the other clauses were difficult to fathom. The magnitude of the reparations was beyond anything they felt they could repay while also trying to rebuild their own nation, which had mostly been destroyed. They also objected to many of the territorial outcomes, a number of which clearly violated one or more of Wilson's Fourteen Points. And then there was the so-called "war guilt clause" which required the Germans to admit that they were solely responsible for instigating the war. They disputed the validity of the statement and worried that it would wound the soul of their nation if they signed off on it. These protestations fell on deaf ears amongst the Allies.

The choice remained, to accept the treaty as presented or be prepared to be invaded. While most Germans were appalled at the terms, they feared a resumption of arms even more. Scheidermann's government fell, and just a few hours before the deadline, the new Chancellor, Gustav Bauer, authorized the German representatives to accept the Treaty as presented.

II-76: The signing of the Treaty of Versailles, June 28, 1919
Seated (L to R): General Tasker Bliss (U.S.), Edward House (U.S.), Henry White (U.S.), Robert Lansing (U.S.), President Wilson (U.S.), Georges Clemenceau (France), David Lloyd George (Britain), A. Bonar Law (Britain), Arthur Balfour (Britain), Viscount Milner (Britain), G.N. Barnes (Britain), and The Marquis Sainozi (Japan)

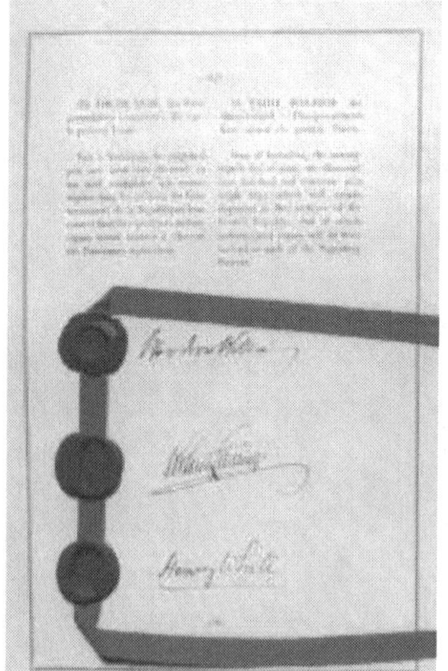

II-77: The signatures of President Wilson, Robert Lansing, and Henry White from the American delegation on the Treaty of Versailles

The signing ceremony took place in the Hall of Mirrors at Versailles on June 28, 1919 – five years to the day since the assassination of Archduke Ferdinand. All five members of the American delegation placed their signatures on the document, with the President going first. After Wilson returned to his seat, he leaned over to Secretary Lansing and said, "I did not know I was excited until I found my hand trembling when I wrote my name."[315] As far as Wilson was concerned, his mission was accomplished. He had made what he called "many minor compromises,"[316] but the League was intact, and the rest, in his mind, was more than acceptable.

In his own words, "many of the results arrived at are far from ideal," but he insisted that "on the whole we have been able to keep tolerably close to the lines laid down at the outset."[317] At least that was what he told himself. In fact, the final treaty was a far cry from the Fourteen Points he had initially unveiled and had been the basis for the German capitulation. Historian Louis Auchincloss aptly summarized how far the Treaty of Versailles had deviated from Wilson's Fourteen Points.

> Covenants were not openly arrived at; the freedom of the seas was not even mentioned; free trade and disarmament (except in the case of the enemy) were ignored; the German colonies were divided up among the victors. More specifically, the Saar Valley was ceded to France for fifteen years; the province of Shandong in China went to Japan; … and despite the affirmation of self-determination of peoples, a Polish Corridor was stretched across Teutonic territory to the Baltic. Worst of all, Germany was crippled with reparations impossible to pay, including pensions for Allied servicemen, and made to sign a humiliating and pointless war-guilt clause.[318]

Central to all of these concessions to his ideals was the fact that Wilson agreed to most of them to keep his beloved League of Nations intact. Despite yielding on so many points, Wilson remained comforted that the League could still right some of these wrongs. Lost in all the intensity of the past two months was that Wilson still had no clear path to gaining the consent of the U.S. Senate for the Treaty, without which

II-78: President Wilson (center) leaves the signing of the Treaty of Versailles alongside French Prime Minister Georges Clemenceau and British Prime Minister David Lloyd George

the United States would be shut out of the League on which Wilson had staked so much. That battle was waiting to resume, with Senator Lodge and his colleagues more than ready to take on the President.

As soon as the Treaty was signed, Wilson was ready to get on the *George Washington* and sail home. The principals departed on a high note, with a sense of mutual appreciation for what they had accomplished, despite the difficulties along the way. "You have done more than any one man to bring about further cordial and friendly relations between England and the United States," Lloyd George told Wilson as they said goodbye. "You have brought the two countries closer together than any other individual in history." Clemenceau told Wilson that he felt like he was "saying good-bye to my best friend."[319] As for Wilson's former closest friend – Colonel Edward House – that relationship had come to an end. At the time of Wilson's departure, House suggested that the President return in a conciliatory spirit in order to enhance the likelihood of securing the support of the Senate. The President rejected the counsel. "House," the President said, "I have found one can never get anything in this life that is worthwhile without fighting for it." House disagreed, suggesting "that a fight was the last thing to be brought about, and then only when it could not be avoided."[320] These were the last words the two ever said to each other. After this, the President cut Colonel Edward House out of his life. The man who had been his most intimate advisor, and occasional alter ego, had been cast aside in the same manner in which Professor Jack Hibben had been exiled at Princeton when Wilson believed he had been disloyal. No explanation was ever given to House for the reason behind the rupture. "My separation from Woodrow Wilson was and is to me a tragic mystery, a mystery that now can never be dispelled, for its explanation lies buried with him," House later wrote.[321] Wilson's inner circle was always very small, usually just family and a few key advisors or friends. House would not be the last of these special few to eventually be completely cast aside.

11. Fighting for the League, and His Life

Huge crowds greeted the President when he arrived in New Jersey on July 8. He was then whisked away to New York for a speech at Carnegie Hall before taking the train to Union Station for another large public reception in Washington. Two days later, Wilson presented the Treaty of Versailles to the Senate, placing before that body the magnitude of the responsibility that was now entrusted to their care. The League of Nations, Wilson announced, was "the hope of the world. ... Shall we or any other free people hesitate to accept this great duty? Dare we reject it and break the heart of the world?" Clearly, in the eyes of the President, failure to consent to the treaty was not an option. "The stage is set, the destiny disclosed. It has come about by no plan of our conceiving, but by the hand of God who led us into this way. We cannot turn back. We can only go forward, with lifted eyes and freshened spirit, to follow the vision. It was of this that we dreamed at our birth. America shall in truth show the way. The light streams upon the path ahead, and nowhere else."[322] Woodrow Wilson had spent a lifetime convincing people to follow his lead with his well-crafted speeches and powerful oratory. But there had also been times when his powers of persuasion failed to move his opposition, most notably in the fights for his quadrangle and graduate school plans at Princeton. All indications were that the U.S. Senate was lining up to be the reincarnation of Princeton's Board of Trustees. In the most significant political battle of his life, Woodrow Wilson may have once again met his match.

Senator Henry Lodge had spent weeks gearing up to take on the President's League of Nations. While there was plenty of consternation about the overall Treaty of Versailles, particularly the capitulation to the Japanese over the Shantung Province, the primary source of discontent for Lodge and his followers was the Covenant for the League that had been included in the agreement. And while concerns with the Covenant also included such topics as implications for domestic policies of the United States as well as the principles adopted in the Monroe Doctrine, the primary angst was centered on Article 10. Lodge couldn't get past what he perceived as a potential demand for action this treaty could place upon his country, which was seemingly dismissive of the constitutional authorities explicitly granted to the US. Congress when it comes to deciding to send American troops into a conflict. "These constitutional rights of Congress must not be impaired by any agreements such as are presented in this treaty," Lodge maintained, "nor can any opportunity of charging the United States with bad faith be permitted. No American soldiers or sailors must be sent to fight in other lands at the bidding of a league of nations. American lives must not be sacrificed except by the will and command of the American people acting through their constitutional representatives in Congress."[323] Lodge made it clear that he didn't oppose the entire treaty or even the notion of the League of Nations, but he and many of his fellow senators did have a number of strong objections. They insisted on introducing amendments that, if approved, could get them to vote aye. While President Wilson gave no indication that he was open to any such amendments, Lodge and the Senate moved forward anyway.

After Lodge put on a bit of a show by reading aloud all 440 articles of the Treaty of Versailles to his Foreign Relations Committee, he then initiated six weeks of hearings. Sixty witnesses were brought in to share their views and perspectives. While a handful were supporters from the administration, the vast majority were coming to voice objections to various parts of the agreement. President Wilson thought about adding his own name to the witness list, but he was talked out of it as inappropriate for the national executive. Instead, he invited the committee to essentially convene an informal session on his turf in the East Room of the White House. Wilson performed well under the three hours of questioning, particularly the eloquence with which he continued to advocate for the lofty ideals the League was uniquely positioned to deliver. But there was no evidence he changed any of the minds of the senators. Many also resented the manner in which Wilson was essentially dictating to them a take-it-or-leave-it solution. That wasn't the way legislators thought. They expected to have input, and at this stage, the so-called "reservationists" had enough of the numbers to prevent passage in the current form.

They were called "reservationists" because that's how they referred to their suggested changes. When the President made it clear that "amendments" could not be considered, former Senator Elihu Root came up with the idea of listing "reservations," which represented specific concerns that would need to be addressed before the U.S. would ratify the treaty and, therefore, be eligible to join the League. With about a third of the senators in this camp, the fate of the treaty was in their hands, but only if President Wilson would agree to support any of these "reservations." At this point at least, the answer was a definitive 'no.' Wilson reiterated this stance with a message to Tumulty on June 25:

> My clear conviction is that the adoption of the treaty by the Senate with reservations will put the United States as clearly out of the concert of nations as a rejection. We ought either to go in or stay out. To stay out would be fatal to the influence and even to the commercial prospects of the United States, and to go in would give her a leading place in the affairs of the world. Reservations would either mean nothing or postpone the conclusion of peace, so far as America is concerned, until every other principal nation concerned in the treaty had found out by negotiation what the reservations practically meant and whether they could associate themselves with the United States on the terms of the reservations or not.[324]

Wilson viewed the situation as comparable to the ratification of the U.S. Constitution in 1787-1788. Several states had pushed for amendments to the Constitution before willing to sign onto the new structure, but the framers made it clear that amendments would only be considered after adoption. Wilson may have been channeling James Madison, who left no doubt at the Virginia Ratifying Convention when he declared that "previous amendments are but another name [for] rejection."[325] If the Senate had concerns, the League would have procedures to address them. However, like the Constitution, the President saw no practical way to insist on changes up front without re-opening the negotiations with all the signatories to the Treaty. In Wilson's mind, if the Senate continued to insist on consent with reservations, then that would mean rejection. And if that came to pass, it would not only be the greatest disappointment in Woodrow Wilson's life but, he believed, would create a backlash of discontent around the world.

Neither Wilson nor Lodge was inclined to compromise as the clash became increasingly personal. As Lodge had come to detest Wilson, that animosity was clearly mutual. Wilson's calm, stoic public demeanor aside, there was an underlying passion that was always just below the surface. Sometimes those emotions were joyful and productive, while on other occasions they were angry and even vengeful. In a review of statements made by people who knew Wilson well, there was a remarkable consistency concerning the revulsion for others the President could bring to bear. Here's a sample of Wilson's ability to hate:

> Ray Baker: Wilson was "a good hater – & does hate those obstructive Senators."[326]
>
> Secretary of State Robert Lansing (at the Paris Peace Conference): "The President is a wonderful hater."[327]
>
> Secretary of the Treasury William McAdoo: "Like Andrew Jackson, he was a good hater."[328]
>
> Even Dr. Cary Grayson added: "He has to hate somebody."[329]

These were not exactly the kinds of statements one would expect concerning someone associated with a "Messiah Complex," but such was the complicated psyche of one Woodrow Wilson. It was also a mindset that was getting in the way of finding common ground with his rivals in the Senate about whom he said, "Anyone who opposes me in [the treaty], I'll crush!"[330] But a frontal assault wasn't the only way for Wilson to try to get his way with the Senate. In fact, the President decided he had a different card to play, and one suited to his strengths. His idea was to get public opinion to be so strongly on his side that the senators would have no choice but to accept the Treaty as-is. So, Woodrow Wilson decided to take his case to the American people with a campaign-style tour to advocate for the agreement.

Those closest to Wilson tried to talk him out of the trip. Mrs. Wilson, Tumulty, and Dr. Grayson had complete confidence in the President's ability to swing the people to his side, but they all believed that the President simply wasn't healthy enough to take on what would undoubtedly be a grueling experience. Wilson was still suffering from the lingering side effects from his illness in Paris, and, with his history of physical breakdowns and strokes, there was a very real fear that this trip could do him in. Wilson was not oblivious to the risks, but he was beyond the point of thinking about himself. The Treaty and the League were bigger than anyone, including him. This was the message he conveyed to Tumulty:

> I know that I am at the end of my tether, but my friends on the Hill say that the trip is necessary to save the treaty and I am willing to make whatever personal sacrifice is required, for if the treaty should be defeated, God only knows what would

> happen to the world as a result of it. In the presence of the great tragedy which now faces the world, no decent man can count his own personal fortunes in the reckoning. Even though, in my condition, it might mean the giving up of my life, I will gladly make the sacrifice to save the treaty.[331]

Tumulty had been side-by-side with Woodrow Wilson for nearly a decade. In that time, he had watched his boss age considerably under the stress and strain of his executive positions. "In those days [in New Jersey], he was a vigorous, agile, slender man, active and alert, his hair but slightly streaked with gray," Tumulty noted. "Now, as he stood before me discussing the necessity for the Western trip, he was an old man, grown grayer and grayer, but grimmer and grimmer in his determination, like an old warrior, to fight to the end."[332] And that fight would definitely take its toll on the 62-year-old President of the United States.

The presidential train left the nation's capital on September 3, 1919, for what was expected to be approximately a one-month tour of the country. The plan was to make speeches from the back of the train at local stops, as well as major addresses in large halls in the biggest cities across the several states. He would summon the energy for up to four speeches per day, with an average of one major address and a few minor ones every day of the trip. Wilson continued to craft his own remarks, usually making a few notes in advance but then letting his natural oratorical skills take over. Typically, Wilson would rise to the occasion with powerful, moving remarks when it came time to address the people, but each speech would take its toll, leaving the President increasingly exhausted and Dr. Grayson more and more worried about his patient and friend.

Wilson's speeches were indeed compelling. This was the cause for which Woodrow Wilson had been preparing his entire life. He got the Allies to accept his League as the means to ensure the peace of the world, and he made it clear to each and every audience the criticality for the United States to sign on as well. "I have come out to fight for a cause," Wilson proclaimed to the crowd at Richmond, Indiana – one of the first stops on the trip. "That cause is greater than the Senate. It is greater than the government. It is as great as the cause of mankind, and I intend, in office or out, to fight that battle as long as I live."[333] After stops in St. Louis and Kansas City, he placed the importance of the League in context in remarks in Des Moines, Iowa. "I want to say that [the Treaty of

II-79: President Wilson on his tour to promote the League of Nations, September 1919

Versailles] is an unparalleled achievement of thoughtful civilization," Wilson said. "To my dying day I shall esteem it the crowning privilege of my life to have been permitted to put my name to a document like that."[334] Then, at the Armory in Sioux Falls, South Dakota, he added a personal touch. "Sometimes people call me an idealist," Wilson noted. "Well, that is the way I know I am an American."[335] By the time he got to the west coast, Wilson was selling hard, focusing on his belief in the once-in-a-lifetime benefits uniquely offered by the Treaty and the League. In Spokane, Washington, he asserted, "this is a ninety-nine percent insurance against war."[336] And then, at the Auditorium in Portland, Oregon, he added, "Peace can only be maintained by putting behind it the force of united nations determined to uphold it and prevent war."[337] By nearly all accounts, Wilson's message was resonating, particularly out West. The crowds were enthusiastic, cheering his advocacy at just about every stop, elevating the President's spirits as he sensed the people were with him more and more each day. Nevertheless, there seemed to be little movement with the senators in Washington, D.C.

While Wilson was on the road with the people, Senator Lodge continued to hold his hearings. One witness, in particular, offered some bombshell testimony. The featured witness was William Bullitt, the man who had resigned after becoming disillusioned with all the concessions the President had made during the negotiations in Paris. In his remarks to the Senate Foreign Relations Committee, Bullitt made it clear that he wasn't the only one who voiced concerns about the President's agreements at the Peace Conference. He brought Secretary Lansing directly into the debate. Bullitt read from his notes, which quoted Lansing as having told him, "I consider that the league of nations at present is entirely useless. The great powers have simply gone ahead and arranged the world to suit themselves. England and France in particular have gotten out of the treaty everything that they wanted, and the league of nations can do nothing to alter any of the unjust clauses of the treaty."[338] This was the kind of fissure Lodge was looking to exploit. It also caused an uproar on the President's train. "Were I in Washington," Wilson told Tumulty, "I would at once demand [Lansing's] resignation! That kind of disloyalty must not be permitted to go unchallenged for a single minute." The President saw Bullitt's testimony as a validation of his own suspicions about Lansing. "Here in his own statement is a verification at last of everything I have suspected," he said. "Think of it! This from a man whom I raised from the level of a subordinate to the great office of Secretary of State of the United States. My God! I did not think it was possible for Lansing to act in this way."[339] Not for a moment did Wilson stop to consider the legitimacy of Lansing's assessment, which was objectively sound. But the President had completely tuned out such objections in France and continued to dismiss them in the midst of his battle back home. All of this contributed to the fragile state of the President's health, which continued to weigh on Edith and Dr. Grayson in particular. At this stage of the trip, Mrs. Wilson observed:

> With each revolution of the wheels my anxieties for my husband's health increased. He grew thinner and the headaches increased in duration and in intensity until he was almost blind during the attacks. Coming in from a reception or dinner I have seen him sit with his head bowed on the back of a chair in front of him while trying to dictate and keep abreast of his mountainous correspondence.[340]

Wilson knew he was breaking down, but he still refused any delay in further taking his message to the people.

Part of that message was focused on Senator Lodge himself. The President took every opportunity to remind his audiences that Lodge had previously voiced strong support for the League in 1916. But Lodge made no effort to hide from his prior statements. Rather, as he got more information and studied the implications of the subject as fully developed at the Peace Conference, he had simply rethought his conclusions. "The mere fact that a man happens to have changed his mind, if he has changed it, does not bear on the merits of any question," Lodge wrote, "and even if a man happens to be a convert, some good work has been done by converts from the days of St. Paul to the present time."[341] In fact, Lodge had a ready-made example of someone else who had changed his mind for the better, and that was Woodrow Wilson himself. After all, Wilson was the man who had been re-elected after spending two years as the person who "kept us out of war," only to pivot to a call for war a mere month into his second term. "When we entered the war, on the 6th of April, 1917," Lodge wrote, "evidently the President had seen reason to change his mind – very fortunately, as I think, and greatly to his credit. But if we are looking for inconsistencies they can be found even in the greatest men."[342] In this case, Lodge had a pretty good point, although it didn't deter the President from continuing to call out the Senator from Massachusetts for hypocrisy.

The President's train took him to California for major speeches in San Francisco, Oakland, and Berkeley, where he continued to deliver strong addresses but then suffer from debilitating headaches as soon as he left the stage. The largest reception of the entire tour then came in Los Angeles, where some two-hundred-thousand people lined the streets to greet the President's entourage. As the train continued to work its way through Nevada, Utah, and Wyoming, Senator Lodge was wrapping up the work of the Foreign Relations Committee, preparing to issue a report condemning the League if reservations were not adopted. From that report:

> The Committee believe that the league as it stands will breed wars instead of securing peace. They also believe that the covenant of the league demands sacrifices of American independence and sovereignty which would in no way promote the world's peace but which are fraught with the gravest dangers to the future safety and well being of the United States. The amendments and reservations alike are governed by a single purpose and that is to guard American rights and American sovereignty, the invasion of which would stimulate of faith, encourage conflicts, and generate wars.[343]

Dozens of reservations were highlighted in the report, but the concern about Article 10 continued to overshadow all the others. As the Lodge report stated, "This reservation is intended to meet the most vital objection to the league covenant as it stands. Under no circumstances must there be any legal or moral obligation upon the United States to enter into war or to send its Army and Navy abroad, or without the unfettered action of Congress to impose economic boycotts on other countries. Under the Constitution of the United States the Congress alone has the power to declare war."[344] Wilson continued to insist that this was more about partisan politics than any legitimate concerns since Article 10 didn't require any action on behalf of the League membership unless there was a *unanimous* vote in the Council, to which the United States would be a member. In other words, the Americans couldn't be forced into any military action without their consent. The senators continued to point out the constitutional flaw in that argument. The *executive branch* would represent the United States in the League Council, whose vote could mandate American entry into a war. Since that power was exclusively given to the *legislative branch* in the U.S. Constitution, the arrangement, as described, would deny the people's representatives the opportunity to fulfill one of their most precious duties. None of this swayed Wilson from his firm belief that no signatory to the Treaty could insist on amendments until after the League was established, so all this talk about prior reservations was a waste of time. On September 23, the President responded to Senator Lodge's report by saying, "That is a rejection of the covenant. That is an absolute refusal to carry any part of the same responsibility that the other members of the League carry. This [Article 10] is the heart of the covenant."[345] The battle lines remained drawn.

As the President's train crossed into Colorado, the concerns for the President's health were reaching new heights. Wilson continued to suffer not only from debilitating headaches but also serious bouts of asthma and coughing spells to go along with overwhelming fatigue. In Denver, on the 25th of September, Edith tried to convince her husband to take a few days to rest up. The President was unmoved. "No, I have caught the imagination of the people," he told Edith. "They are eager to hear what the League stands for; and I should fail in my duty if I disappointed them."[346] After his remarks in Denver, the President's train continued to Pueblo, Colorado, for another address that evening. With 3,000 citizens jammed into Memorial Hall, Wilson gave one of the longest and most emotional speeches of the trip. He referred to the dedication of the American cemetery outside of Paris. "I wish some of the men who are now opposing the settlement for which those men died could visit such a spot as that. I wish they could feel the moral obligation that rests upon us not to go back on those boys, but to see this thing through to the end and make good their redemption of the world."[347] Wilson, for one, wouldn't turn his back on those who gave their lives for the cause of world peace. "They believe, and they rightly believe, that their sons saved the liberty of the world. They believe that wrapped up with the liberty of the world is the continuous protection of that liberty by the concerted powers of all the civilized world. These men were crusaders. They were going forth to prove the might of justice and right."[348] In summary, "For nothing less depends upon this decision, nothing less than the liberation and salvation of the world."[349] Tumulty would later describe the reaction by the crowd to this address in Pueblo as "a great wave of emotion, such as I have never witnessed at a public meeting, swept through the whole amphitheatre."[350]

Wilson may have been making inroads with his audiences, but his body was simply about to give out. The night after the speech in Pueblo, while the train was making its way to Wichita, Kansas, Wilson was exhausted but unable to sleep. At 11:30 pm, he went into Edith's cabin with complaints of headache, nausea, his worst asthma attack of the trip, and even a bit of a twitch in his face. Edith was frightened, and immediately called for Dr. Grayson. The President's symptoms were worse than before, as his entire left side had gone numb. Edith became forceful for shutting down the tour. For the first time, Wilson admitted she might be right. "I don't seem to realize it, but I seem to have gone to pieces," the President said. "The doctor is right. I am not in condition to go on. I have never been in a condition like this, and I just feel as if I am going to pieces."[351] Later that night, which Edith called "the longest and most heartbreaking of my life,"[352] Wilson argued once again to stay the course. He returned to his position that he must continue for all that was at stake, which was more important than the health of any one man, even if that man was the President of the United States. "Don't you see," Wilson told Tumulty, "that if you cancel this trip, Senator Lodge and his friends will say that I am a quitter and that the Western trip was a failure, and the Treaty will be lost."[353] But this time, Wilson could not prevail against the evidence that he had fallen apart to the point where continuing was impossible. Tumulty made the official announcement the next morning in Wichita, reporting that Wilson had "so spent himself without reserve on this trip that it brought on a nervous reaction in his digestive organs."[354] No other details were given, other than the presidential party

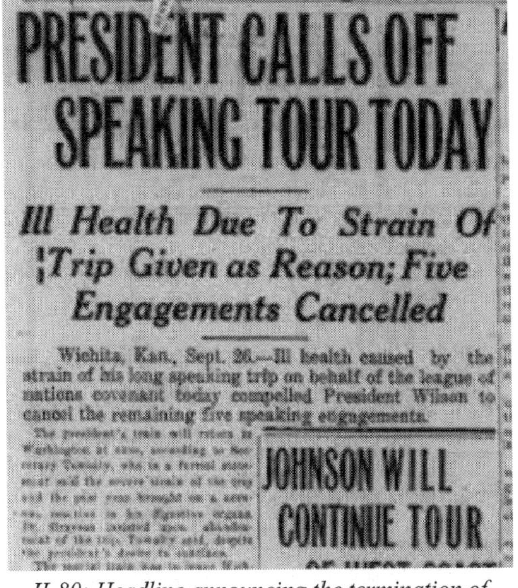

PRESIDENT CALLS OFF SPEAKING TOUR TODAY

Ill Health Due To Strain Of Trip Given as Reason; Five Engagements Cancelled

Wichita, Kan., Sept. 26.—Ill health caused by the strain of his long speaking trip on behalf of the league of nations covenant today compelled President Wilson to cancel the remaining five speaking engagements.

JOHNSON WILL CONTINUE TOUR

II-80: Headline announcing the termination of President Wilson's tour, September 26, 1919

would return to Washington immediately, at which point Wilson would be subject to "a complete rest, not partial rest." Dr. Grayson added that "nothing was to be allowed to interfere with the President's restoration to health if possible."[355]

Unfortunately, Wilson's broken-down body had been pushed too far, and despite reaching the comforts of the White House, his next setback would be the worst, creating a presidential crisis the likes of which the nation had never previously experienced. Four days after returning to Washington, Edith Wilson went to check on her husband.

> At five or six in the morning I found him still sleeping normally, as it appeared. Relieved, I dozed off again until after eight. This time I found him sitting on the side of the bed trying to reach a water bottle. As I handed it to him I noticed that his left hand hung loosely. 'I have no feeling in that hand,' he said. 'Will you rub it? But first help me to the bathroom.' He moved with great difficulty, and every move brought spasms of pain; but with my help he gained the bathroom. This so alarmed me that I asked if I could leave him long enough to telephone the Doctor. He said yes, and hurrying into my room I reached Dr. Grayson at his house. While at the phone I heard a slight noise, and rushing into my husband's apartment found him on the bathroom floor unconscious.[356]

When Dr. Grayson arrived, he found the President completely unable to move his left side. "My God, the President is paralyzed!" the doctor said to Ike Hoover.[357] Hoover later recalled that the man he saw stretched out in the Lincoln Bedroom "looked as if he were dead."[358]

12. Who's Running the Country?

Dr. Grayson called in several specialists to examine the President, and the news was difficult to hear. The doctors diagnosed a serious ischemic stroke. It appeared Wilson's powers to think and speak were unaffected, but he still had no movement in his left arm or leg ("a condition of complete flaccid paralysis,"[359] according to Dr. Francis Dercum, the highly accomplished professor of nervous and mental disorders at Philadelphia's Jefferson Medical College who was brought in to evaluate the President's condition). In addition, the left side of his face was drooping, his vision was impaired, he had difficulty swallowing, and he was exceptionally fatigued. Edith pressed the doctors on what to do with a President in such a state of physical collapse. Years later, Mrs. Wilson described at length in her memoirs what the specialist told her next:

> Dr. Dercum leaned towards me and said: 'Madam, it is a grave situation, but I think you can solve it. Have everything come to you; weigh the importance of each matter, and see if it is possible by consultations with the respective heads of the Departments to solve them without the guidance of your husband. In this way you can save him a great deal. But always keep in mind that every time you take him a new anxiety or problem to excite him, you are turning a knife in an open wound. His nerves are crying out for rest, and any excitement is torture to him.'[360]

II-81: Dr. Francis Dercum

Based on this information, Edith wrote that she suggested that her husband should consider resigning and pass the strains of the presidency to Vice President Thomas Marshall. According to Mrs. Wilson, Dr. Dercum strongly discouraged such a move.

> For Mr. Wilson to resign would have a bad effect on the country, and a serious effect on our patient. He has staked his life and made his promise to the world to do all in his power to get the Treaty ratified and make the League of Nations complete. If he resigns, the greatest incentive to recovery is gone; and as his mind is clear as crystal he can still do more with even a maimed body than any one else. [361]

Again, according to Edith's memoirs, Dr. Dercum continued to advocate for her to take on this role for which he believed she was well suited to perform. "Dr. Grayson tells me [the President] has always discussed public affairs with you; so you will not come to them uninformed,"[362] Dr. Dercum told Mrs. Wilson, leaving her with the most important decision a First Lady had ever been asked to make.

Edith Wilson agreed to follow the doctor's advice. "So began my stewardship," she later wrote. "I studied every paper, sent from the different Secretaries or Senators, and tried to digest and present in tabloid form the things that, despite my vigilance, had to go to the President. I, myself, never made a single decision regarding the disposition of public affairs. The only decision that was mine was what was important and what was not, and the very important decision of when to present matters to my husband."[363] In what turned out to be not only a short-term approach to national governance but also one that persisted for the balance of Wilson's second term, First Lady Edith Wilson took over almost complete control of the information provided to the President of the United States and the dissemination of his decisions.

II-82: First Lady Edith Wilson guiding her husband, President Wilson, to sign documents, June 1920

Some perspective is needed on these maneuverings that were made entirely behind the scenes without input by anyone who had been elected by the American people other than the seriously ill President. First, we only have Edith's words regarding the medical justification for taking on the role of presidential gatekeeper. Others have questioned the veracity of her story, speculating that the decision was simply made by Edith Wilson herself, or perhaps in consultation with Dr. Grayson. While Dr. Dercum left detailed notes about his four examinations of President Wilson during these first couple of weeks of October, there is no written evidence of his supposed guidance to Mrs. Wilson other than what she offered in her memoirs nearly two decades later. The doctor's official documentation is, as one might expect, entirely about the medical condition of his patient, with no commentary on the impact to the country regarding the League of Nations or any other aspect of public affairs. Further, the language cited by Mrs. Wilson is also suspect. Colloquial phrases such as "turning a knife in an open wound," or "excitement is torture," or "mind is clear as crystal," are very different from the fact-based, medically-focused terminology used throughout Dr. Dercum's documentation and letters as contained in the exhaustive papers of Dr. Grayson. In one memo, for example, after being pressed to counter some rumors in the press about the President's mental state, Dr. Dercum would only assert that President Wilson's "mentality is today keen."[364] That's very different from, "as his mind is clear as crystal he can still do more with even a maimed body than any one else." The latter comment is also odd as it does not appear Dr. Dercum had ever met Woodrow Wilson prior to this medical event, calling into question any basis for such a conclusion, or whether it came from the doctor at all. There is simply nothing in Dr. Dercum's official records, in tone or substance, to corroborate Mrs. Wilson's version of events leading to her decision to begin her "stewardship." That doesn't necessarily mean he didn't provide the explicit guidance quoted by Mrs. Wilson, but it does call it into question.

Dr. Grayson's own summary of the President's stroke from October 1919 also makes numerous references to Dr. Dercum's memorandum but without any mention of a suggestion to Mrs. Wilson to take on the role of presidential gatekeeper. In terms of transparency, Grayson's summary did highlight Mrs. Wilson being "adamantly opposed" to providing the public with any information other than "general statements" about the

President's condition, but he referenced nothing but detailed medical commentary from Dr. Dercum.[365] Edith Wilson has also been portrayed as the consistent leading voice against the President ever resigning his office, calling into question her suggestion to Dr. Dercum that he do just that. Finally, the timing of Edith Wilson's memoirs is also intriguing, coming nearly a decade and a half after her husband's passing. Dr. Dercum died in 1931, followed by Dr. Grayson in 1938, the latter occurring just a few months before Mrs. Wilson finally published her book. By the time she decided to release her memoirs, there was no one left to refute her account.

Edith's claim that she "never made a single decision regarding the disposition of public affairs" also must be viewed as disingenuous at best since she, and she alone, decided what matters ever reached the President for a decision over the final year and a half of his presidency. That fact alone had a direct impact on the public affairs of the country. Even Joe Tumulty was given only limited access to the President, as he mostly submitted his comments and suggestions in the form of memos that Edith would then decide which to present and the large volume which she opted to lay off to the side. The Cabinet and the Vice President were given zero access to the President, to either assess his condition or discuss pressing matters of the public's business. The sole decision on what to bring to the President was in the hands of the First Lady, along with delivering for action what she claimed were the decisions of the President. Since no one else was ever in the room, there is no way to validate if Mrs. Wilson's assertions were true. Some have claimed that after the President's collapse on October 2, 1919, Edith Wilson became the first female President of the United States. This overstates the case. If anything, she nudged Tumulty aside and took over as Chief of Staff. There is no evidence that Mrs. Wilson developed public policy or put any into motion on her own, like a President does on a daily basis. Her primary influence (which was significant) was in deciding what subjects to bring to the President and when. This certainly made her the most influential First Lady to date in American history. It was also consistent with a wife who was committed to protecting and caring for her husband. In her memoirs, Edith admitted that during her "stewardship," "Woodrow Wilson was first my beloved husband whose life I was trying to save, fighting with my back to the wall – after that he was the President of the United States."[366] That statement, perhaps, sheds more light on the steps she followed in the wake of this medical crisis than any guidance she supposedly received from Dr. Dercum. It also raises grave constitutional concerns that directly impacted the functioning governance of the United States. So, was Edith Wilson just following doctor's orders in assuming these unprecedented responsibilities for a First Lady, or did she use her book to provide a cover story for her spousal coup that could no longer be refuted due to the deaths of the only people who might know differently? Posterity will likely never know for sure. In the end, the most apt description of the entire situation was that the United States was mostly without a President for the last year-and-a-half of Woodrow Wilson's second term, as opposed to her taking over the presidency. Affairs of state essentially came to a halt throughout this period, which was completely shrouded in mystery.

In the meantime, Secretary Lansing, who was still in his job leading the State Department despite the vitriol the President displayed about him during the recent trip, was the most aggressive in trying to figure out what was really going on. He went to Tumulty with his Constitution in hand. Lansing pointed to Article II, Section I, which stated:

> In case of the removal of the President from office, or of his death, resignation, or inability to discharge the powers and duties of the said office, the same shall devolve on the Vice-President, and the Congress may by law provide for the case of removal, death, resignation, or inability, both of the President and Vice President, declaring what officer shall then act as President, and such officer shall act accordingly until the disability be removed or a President shall be elected.[367]

But what was meant by "inability to discharge the powers and duties of the said office," and who had the authority to make that determination? Lansing suggested either Tumulty or Dr. Grayson could come forward with a public statement that would put the constitutional provision into motion. To this, both men adamantly refused. "Doctor Grayson left no doubt in Mr. Lansing's mind that he would not do as Mr. Lansing suggested," Tumulty later wrote. "I then notified Mr. Lansing that if anybody outside of the White House circle attempted to certify to the President's disability, that Grayson and I would stand together and repudiate it. I added that if the President were in a condition to know of this episode he would, in my opinion, take decisive measures. That ended the interview."[368] The President's innermost circle had closed ranks, and there didn't seem to be any mechanism to force the issue as long as Wilson himself insisted on continuing his term of office.

Lansing decided to call the Cabinet together, if for no other reason than to present some sign to the American people that the government was still functioning. But the Cabinet had no direct line to the President, so very little got done in this or any other subsequent gatherings. Tumulty did his best to keep the office of the President performing the people's business, but it was a losing battle as Edith continued to prevent most official work from reaching her husband's bedroom. Occasionally, the President would put his name on bills, but he was slow to respond to almost all other requests. Executive branch vacancies mounted as few new appointments were made. The President did issue one veto during this period. He had never been a fan of the 18th Amendment, which banned the sale and consumption of alcohol throughout the United States. When Congress passed the Volstead Act to provide the statutory details needed to enforce the Amendment, Wilson balked. At a minimum, he wanted exceptions for light wine and beer. His veto was quickly overridden by a Congress that was full of prohibitionists.

II-83: Secretary of State Robert Lansing

Throughout the course of October, Wilson slowly saw some modest physical improvements, but his general symptoms remained. And then he took a turn for the worse. He developed a urinary obstruction that was threatening multiple systems of his weakened body. Some called for surgery, but Dr. Grayson urged caution, concerned that the surgery itself might be too much for the President's body to handle. The decision whether to operate was yet another made by Edith Wilson. Based on the potential complications, Edith told Dr. Grayson, "Then we will not operate. You know more than anyone else of the real chances of recovery. So go down and tell them I feel that Nature will finally take care of things, and we will wait."[369] The emergency did pass without surgery, but the President's remaining symptoms continued to keep him an invalid who was confined to his bedroom with virtually no access beyond his doctors, nurses, and immediate family.

There has been much speculation as to the impact the stroke had on Wilson's mental capacity. According to Ike Hoover, "There was never a moment during all that time when he was more than a shadow of his former self. He had changed from a giant to a pygmy in every wise. He was physically almost incapacitated; he could articulate but indistinctly and think but feebly."[370] Those last words ("think but feebly") certainly give one pause considering the patient was the most powerful man in the country. Others admitted to the sick room shared observations of increased emotional outbursts, overall testiness, frustration over all things (big and small), a quickness to tearing up, as well as lapses in memory. The degree to which these symptoms affected the performance of his presidential duties remains the subject of speculation since so few first-hand interactions were permitted, let alone preserved for history.

In the meantime, the battle over the League of Nations continued in the U.S. Senate. Senator Lodge remained unrelenting in forging his alliance to stand up against Article 10 and some of the other objectionable measures embedded in the Covenant. He insisted that support for the League would only occur with the adoption of a number of reservations. This continued to be a non-starter for President Wilson. With the vote in the Senate scheduled for November 19, the President agreed to meet with Senator Gilbert Hitchcock of Nebraska, who had been the administration's point person in advocating for the League in the Foreign Relations Committee. Hitchcock emerged from the meeting with a clear message. "I am merely told 'the President will not budge an inch,'" Hitchcock informed his colleagues. "His honor is at stake. He feels he would be dishonored if he failed to live up to the pledges made to his fellow delegates in Paris."[371] When the President was advised such an obstinate approach might mean the death of the League, Wilson refused to budge. "Let Lodge compromise," he told Hitchcock.[372] As Edith saw her husband's health continue to sag, and with the greatest dream of his professional life hanging in the balance, even she urged some concessions. "For my sake, won't you accept these reservations and get this awful thing settled?" she pleaded with her husband. But Wilson simply took her hand and said: "Little girl, don't you desert me. That I cannot stand."[373] Wilson's obstinance was complete heading into the crucial vote.

With both sides unwilling to budge, the Treaty of Versailles, including U.S. participation in the League of Nations, went down to defeat in the United States Senate. There were a number of votes on the matter, with two being the most critical. In one tally, the Senate voted against the Treaty *with* the Lodge Reservations (39 in favor to 55 opposed). Another vote was then taken for the Treaty *without* the Lodge Reservations, and that went down by a similar count (38 ayes to 53 nays). The bitterness was profound with both antagonists, and plenty of blame to go around. Wilson believed the Republicans would pay the price at the polls the following year. "They will have to answer to the country in the future for their acts," Wilson said. "They must answer to the people." He was also determined to continue to fight for the League. "I am going to debate this issue with these gentlemen in their respective states whenever they come up for re-election. ... I shall do this even if I have to give my life to it."[374] On the other hand, Senator Lodge made it clear in his mind who was to blame for the defeat. "He [Wilson] was so set upon having his own way that he was ready to destroy the treaty of Versailles, which was framed to replace a victorious war with a victorious peace," Lodge wrote, "rather than permit any modification in the terms of the League of Nations which he had identified with himself."[375] He concluded that Wilson "would have had the world at his feet, but he could think only of himself, and his own idea was and had been for a long time that the part for him to play was that of the great peacemaker."[376] There was plenty of blame to go around. The most obvious source of failure was the unwillingness of the principal political combatants (President Wilson and Senator Lodge) to make any reasonable effort to find common ground. Both started locked in with their opposition, and neither showed any inclination to compromise. Despite all the concessions Wilson was willing to make in his negotiations on so many of his Fourteen Points with the Allies, he was unwilling to concede anything with the U.S. Senate. But the fault here wasn't purely ideological on the substance of the League Covenant, it was also political and even personal. The fact that Wilson refused to invite Senate Republicans into the peace negotiations in the first place was the first nail in the coffin of the League in the United States. His refusal to recognize the limitations of an American President when it came to foreign affairs and treaties when compared to his preferred parliamentary system in nations such as Britain and France was a fatal flaw in this entire process. While the outcome may not have changed, it is reasonable to surmise that if Wilson had been more open and engaging with the decision-makers in the Senate from the beginning of the peace process, he may have at least had a chance to forge an agreement that could get 2/3rd support in that body. His alienation of those whose votes ultimately had the final say on whatever Wilson negotiated overseas was a political strategy that completely failed. The result was a catastrophic setback in the most important initiative in Woodrow Wilson's life.

13. Invalid … and Failure

Wilson still had a little more than a year left in his presidency, yet there was no indication that he was physically up to doing the job. Nevertheless, with Tumulty, Dr. Grayson, and Mrs. Wilson closing ranks around the President, there didn't seem to be any constitutional mechanism to change the leadership in the executive branch. Edith continued to be the presidential gatekeeper. "Many leases or transfers came to the President's desk for signature," she later wrote. "It was my habit to acquaint myself with the context of each matter and put the papers in convenient stacks before carrying them to him for his signature. We would prop him up in bed, and he would sign as many as he could before growing exhausted."[377] The wheels of government continued to turn, but slowly. Many memos went unanswered as many were never delivered to the President. Countless positions remained vacant, including ambassadorships and key domestic posts. Policy decisions that were deemed by Edith to be either too trivial or too taxing for her husband often sat in a growing pile of paperwork that would never be seen by the President.

In some cases, such as Cabinet openings, it was the First Lady who put into motion the requests of the President. When Carter Glass, who had taken over for William McAdoo as Secretary of the Treasury shortly after the armistice, resigned to take a seat in the U.S. Senate, it was Edith who took steps to arrange for the backfill on behalf of her husband. Mrs. Wilson was the one who contacted Agriculture Secretary David Houston, met with him at the White House, and offered Houston the switch to Treasury. Similarly, when Interior Secretary Franklin Lane submitted his resignation later in the year, Edith took the action to contact Judge John Payne, interview him for the position, and ultimately provide him the offer on behalf of the President. Neither met directly with the President in receiving these new positions. These were clearly unchartered territories for a First Lady of the United States. As Ray Baker noted, "Everything must come through one overstrained woman!"[378] Yet, there was no indication of any change in sight.

There was one more Cabinet change around which Woodrow and Edith Wilson were completely aligned – the ultimate departure of Secretary of State Robert Lansing. Lansing had continued to call Cabinet meetings while also questioning whether Wilson was healthy enough to fulfill his constitutional responsibilities. In terms of those Cabinet sessions, President Wilson eventually was sufficiently annoyed to bring them to an end. He sent Grayson with the query as to "what authority [the Cabinet] was meeting while he was in Washington without a call from him."[379] He may have been an invalid but he was still the President, and the Cabinet should only be meeting with him present or at his discretion. "The disloyalty is a personal act; the calling of meetings of the Cabinet is official insubordination; it is my duty to put a stop to that," President Wilson said according to Edith.[380] He did, and Lansing's days in the Cabinet were clearly numbered.

As for the Secretary of State, he too was beside himself, trying to figure out how to fulfill his responsibilities with a President who was either unwilling or unable to perform his duties. "It is not Woodrow Wilson but the President of the United States who is ill," Lansing wrote in a memo to himself. "His family and his physicians have no right to shroud the whole affair in mystery as they have done."[381] Yet there was nothing Lansing could do to change this dynamic, as he grew increasingly bitter and distraught over the entire affair. In February 1920, Lansing wrote, "I must continue … though the irrascibility [sic] and tyranny of the President, whose worst qualities have come to the surface during his sickness, cannot be borne much longer. … His violent passions and exaggerated ego have free rein."[382] Lansing acknowledged his tenure could not continue much longer under these circumstances. "Woodrow Wilson is a tyrant," he wrote, "who even goes so far as to demand that all men shall think as he does else be branded as traitors or ingrates. ... Thank God I shall soon be a free man!"[383] Lansing submitted his resignation two days later, which the President was happy to accept. Wilson handed the job to Bainbridge Colby, one of the founders of the Progressive Party who had no experience whatsoever in foreign affairs. But he did have a more important qualification – he was completely loyal to Woodrow Wilson.

The congressional session had a couple more months to go before the nation's politicians would turn their attention to the upcoming election season. This meant one more opportunity to reconsider the Treaty of Versailles and the League Covenant. Outside forces continued to try to bridge the Wilson/Lodge divide with some sort of compromise. Among those pushing were former Secretary of State William Jennings Bryan and former President William Taft, the latter of whom had been the foremost champion of the League before Wilson had made the concept his own. Taft came to Washington to lobby his fellow Republicans to put personal differences aside and not let this unique opportunity to enhance peace in the world pass them by. "I don't like Wilson any better than you do," Taft told his colleagues, "but I think I can rise above my personal attitude in order to help along the world and the country. I don't care who gets credit for the League of Nations, if it goes through."[384] He added, "I beg you, consider the consequences if you defeat the treaty. ... We are in sight of the promised land. Don't prevent our reaching there."[385] Despite these entreaties, there was no sign of any thawing in the stubbornly held positions on either side of the divide.

For this go-around, Senator Lodge introduced 14 reservations that he considered essential to protect the interests of the United States. President Wilson wouldn't agree to a single concession. "We cannot rewrite this Treaty," Wilson wrote in January 1920. "We must take it without changes which alter its meaning, or leave it and then, after the rest of be the world have signed it, we must face the unthinkable task of making another and separate kind of treaty with Germany."[386] Any vote in the Senate to add *any* reservations as conditions for approval of the Treaty would signal defeat, according to the President. "I hear of reservationists and mild reservationists," Wilson wrote to Senator Hitchcock just before the final vote, "but I cannot understand the difference between a nullifier and a mild nullifier."[387] Senator Lodge countered by reiterating where he placed blame for the failure to make progress. "Since the man who really seeks the establishment of an ideal will never sacrifice it because he cannot secure everything he wants at once," Lodge railed, "and always estimates the principle as more important than its details and qualifications,"[388] the upcoming vote was bound to fall short. Senator Frank Brandegee of Connecticut concurred, saying, "The President has strangled his own child."[389] Overseas, there was similar criticism of the American President and his unflinching obstinance. Harold Nicholson, who had been part of the British delegation to the Peace Conference, chided Wilson:

> He possessed no gift for differentiation, no capacity for adjustment to circumstances. It was his spiritual and mental rigidity which proved his undoing. It rendered him as incapable of withstanding criticism as of absorbing advice. It rendered him blind to all realities which did not accord with his

> preconceived theory, even to the realities of his own decisions.[390]

Wilson's "Messiah Complex" continued to be espoused, preventing the President from any deviation from his Divinely-inspired handiwork.

With no sign of movement on either side of the debate, the results of the vote in the Senate on March 15 were completely predictable. While the vote *with* reservations received more than a majority of support, it fell seven votes short of the 2/3rd needed for senatorial consent. But since Wilson would have vetoed any resolution that had reservations attached, in reality, the outcome was not as close as it seemed. When the President heard the results of the vote, he bitterly told Tumulty, "They have shamed us in the eyes of the world."[391] Dr. Grayson further described the President's reaction, noting that Wilson "showed every evidence of being very blue and depressed." He told Grayson directly, "I feel like going to bed and staying there."[392]

The question that must be addressed is whether any form of compromise could have satisfied both Wilson and Lodge and rendered a different result. Such a solution would have to have met the President's insistence that the Treaty be accepted as-is, as well as Lodge's primary requirement that the U.S. could not be committed to war without infringing on its national sovereignty or without the proper sanction by the American Congress. While reservations were raised on other topics as well, this was the heart of the debate, all of which centered on Article 10. First, any objection by the Senate that the League Covenant dealt a fatal blow to the sovereignty of the United States was simply nonsense. Lodge interpreted the first sentence in Article 10 to be instantly binding on all members, such that any "external aggression" against the "territorial integrity and existing political independence" of any member of the League would automatically *require* the United States to go to war against the violator without any say in the matter. But that view completely ignored the second sentence of the Article, which stated: "In case of any such aggression or in case of any threat or danger of such aggression *the Council shall advise upon the means by which this obligation shall be fulfilled* (emphasis added)."[393] Nothing was automatic. Decisions to generate a military response by the League had to be approved by the Council. Article 16 further emphasized the role of the Council in determining any military action by the membership ("It shall be the duty of the Council in such case [of an act of war by one member against another] to recommend to the several Governments concerned what effective military, naval or air force the Members of the League shall severally contribute to the armed forces to be used to protect the covenants of the League.")[394] Moreover, Article 5 of the Covenant stated that "decisions at any meeting of the Assembly or of the Council shall require the agreement of *all* the Members of the League represented at the meeting (emphasis added)."[395] Given that the United States was a permanent member of the decision-making Council, and since all decisions needed to be unanimous, there was no way for the League to commit to any action without the concurrence of the United States. National sovereignty was simply not at risk.

That said, Senator Lodge did have a legitimate concern regarding the potential usurpation of Congress's sole constitutional power to declare war. As previously stated, since the executive branch would have the seat in the League Council, an American President could potentially instruct the country's representative to vote in favor of armed conflict without congressional sanction. Under this scenario, such a move would appear to be a violation of the war powers clause in Article I, Section 8, which places that decision entirely in the hands of the national legislature. But this did not need to be the deal-breaker that it appeared to be. In fact, a simple constitutional amendment could have overcome this impasse. Such an amendment could have required the President to submit any questions about going to war to the American Congress whenever the topic is under consideration by the League Council (or any similar international forum in which the United States agreed to participate). If Congress concurred, then the American representative at the League could vote yes. If Congress failed to provide its assent, then the U.S. would have to vote 'no' at the Council. The only objection to this approach would potentially be timing where such consultation with Congress could not happen in time to influence the vote. But this theoretical concern is unconvincing given that these are not the kinds of decisions that are made in a matter of hours or even days. Just as an American President can't commit the country to wars without the approval of Congress, this amendment would ensure that no such decision is made by the American representative in the League Council without similar authorization. The amendment would satisfy Senator Lodge's concern about outsourcing war decisions to other parties (including the American executive) without running afoul of President

Wilson's stipulation that nothing done during the ratification process would require re-opening negotiations with the other signatories to the Treaty of Versailles. This change to the U.S. Constitution would simply address the internal processes of the United States in determining how to vote in certain matters, which would have had no bearing on any of the commitments made by the signatories to the Treaty. The American Founders included Article V in the Constitution anticipating amendments would be needed throughout the life of the country. While amendments have generally been rare, that had not been the case in the early 20th Century. In fact, in the most recent decade, four amendments had been added to the Constitution, including the authorization of the income tax (#16 in 1913), the direct election of senators (#17 in 1913), the adoption of prohibition (#18 in 1919), and the approval of women's right to vote (#19 in 1920). Adding one more, as described above, could have overcome the primary objections of the antagonists regarding the League and the Treaty of Versailles. However, such a move does not appear to have even been considered. Both sides were locked in, and, as a result, the U.S. would never join the League of Nations.

It was around this time that Woodrow Wilson went outside for the first time since his stroke. He went for a drive, appearing in public wearing a cape instead of an overcoat as it was easier to put on over his immobile left arm. He used a cane whenever he tried to walk without assistance. In the meantime, Wilson's presidential routine was devoid of almost any real business. Edith was always at his side, whether it was when Wilson occasionally spent time in the White House garden, or on their afternoon drives, or their movies which they watched just about every day in the East Room. Difficulty with Wilson's vision led Edith to read to him since he struggled to do so on his own. A limited amount of official paperwork was squeezed into the routine, but when it came to running the government and politics, Wilson mostly just stewed over the loss of the Treaty in the Senate.

The most prevalent sign that the President had lost touch with reality was his insistence that he should not rule out running for a third term as the only way to resurrect the Treaty and the League. "Everyone seems to be opposed to my running," the President acknowledged shortly before the conventions were to gather to select the party nominees, but he maintained a belief that "there may be practically a universal demand for the selection of someone to lead them out of the wilderness."[396] While

Dr. Grayson had been unflinching in his loyal support to the President throughout his illness and attempted recovery, he was adamant that another term was out of the question. "No matter what others may tell you," Grayson said to party official Robert Woolley, "no matter what you may read about the President being on the road to recovery, I tell you that he is permanently ill physically, is gradually weakening mentally and can't recover. He couldn't possibly survive the campaign."[397] The Democrats meeting in San Francisco needed little convincing. While a couple of dozen candidates received votes in the contest, it was really a three-person race through most of the 44 ballots it took to pick a nominee. Wilson's son-in-law, William McAdoo, led the pack on the first ballot, with a slight edge over Wilson's third and final Attorney General, A. Mitchell Palmer, and Ohio Governor James Cox. As the balloting progressed, Cox rose while Palmer fell, creating a two-person race at the top of the balloting. Cox took the lead from the 12th to the 29th ballots, McAdoo recaptured the top spot from the 30th to the 38th, but as Palmer continued to fade, his supporters primarily gravitated to Cox, who finally went over the top. Woodrow Wilson's name was called just once during the count when he recorded two votes on the 22nd ballot. Wilson supported the choice of the convention as Cox and his vice presidential nominee, Franklin Roosevelt, were both committed to the President's League of Nations. Wilson welcomed the ticket to the White House to try to provide some momentum for the general election race. It would be a clear choice for the electorate, with Senator Warren Harding of Ohio as the standard bearer for the Republicans.

II-84: 1920 Democratic Campaign Banner: James Cox and Franklin Roosevelt

Harding had been side-by-side with Senator Lodge in opposition to the League unless reservations were adopted. His campaign was premised on a "return to normalcy," where the Americans would go back to focusing on their own country, with practical solutions to address their immediate needs, rather than the idealism by which Wilson had steered the nation in what was portrayed as lofty, yet unproductive ways. Once again, Wilson was not on the ballot, but his name was everywhere throughout the campaign. Former President Taft, for example, campaigned at an event in Port Huron, Michigan, just a couple of weeks before voters were to cast their ballots. Greatly disappointed over Wilson's mismanagement of the ratification process for the League that he had long supported, Taft told the electorate that Wilson was to blame and it was time to move in a different direction.

> When the war came on, both Republicans and Democrats, had to extend to the Executive much arbitrary authority. No czar or king ever had greater power than Woodrow Wilson during the war, and no potentate ever exercised it with less willingness to consult those interested. He established a seclusion from conference with members of the Senate and members of the House unheard of before in this country. … Mr. Wilson should have opened arms and invited to his assistance all Republicans capable of rendering service, but this he did not do. … Mr. Wilson's failure to secure his League was due in great part to his desire always to exercise one-man power.[398]

For many, this was the epitaph of a presidency that had generated so much promise but ended with such profound disappointment. And there would be no immediate second chances for the ideals of the Wilson administration, as Harding defeated Cox in a rout, 404 to 137 in the Electoral College. While the Democrats held the Solid South, Harding ran the table across the rest of the nation, winning 37 states to 11 for Cox. The popular vote difference accentuated the landslide, with Harding capturing 60.4% of the vote compared to

II-85: Senator Warren Harding during the 1920 presidential campaign

34.1% for Cox. The difference among the electorate was seven million votes, the largest margin of victory to date in American history – by far.

The results of the election were generally seen as a repudiation of Wilson and his policies. Not surprisingly, Senator Lodge led the way in this regard. "The League of Nations was the one question above all others which the people wished to hear discussed," Lodge declared. "Mr. Wilson desired and had demanded an appeal to the people. That appeal was duly made and fully met and the result is history."[399] As for the incumbent President, Wilson acknowledged the setback but still believed he and his policies would be vindicated in the end. "Of course, I am disappointed by the results of the election for I felt sure that a great programme that sought to bring peace to the world would arouse American idealism, and that the Nation's support would be given to it," he told Tumulty. "The enemies of this enterprise cleverly aroused every racial passion and prejudice, and by poisonous propaganda made it appear that the League of Nations was a great Juggernaut which was intended to crush and destroy instead of saving and bringing peace to the world. The people will have to learn now by bitter experience just what they have lost." The President remained convinced that "the people will soon witness the tragedy of disappointment and then they will turn upon those who made that disappointment possible."[400] Wilson was clinging to his convictions, despite an unambiguous verdict by the American people to take the country on a path that was very different from what he had advocated for so long.

The United States may have rejected the League of Nations, but just over a week after the 1920 U.S. elections, the League opened for business in Geneva, Switzerland. The world was still optimistic as to the benefits of the League, even without the United States. That included the committee which awarded Woodrow Wilson the Nobel Peace Prize for his leadership in bringing the League of Nations to life. Forty-two countries comprised the founding members of the League, with more to follow over time. Germany was finally granted admission in 1926 and the Soviet Union entered the body in 1934. The bottom line on Wilson's utopian vision, however, was that the League failed in its most important mission – to keep the world safe and prevent future wars. Despite the protocols for mutual support against aggression, and a few modest successes, the League did nothing to stop Italy from doing battle with Ethiopia in 1936, Germany from re-militarizing the Rhineland in 1936,

Japan from invading China in 1937, and the Soviet Union from attacking Finland in 1939. Kicking these perpetrators out of the League was the only real form of punishment for these countries, which hardly deterred them from their aggressive actions. World War II followed in 1939. The League remained intact throughout that war, but without much effect, and then faded entirely in 1946 after being superseded by the post-war establishment of the United Nations. Wilson's efforts to prevent war didn't even last one generation.

Many of the other aspects of the Treaty of Versailles would also collapse over the next decade and a half. For example, many of the territorial decisions made at the Peace Conference also fell apart, either by force (such as Italy taking Fiume in 1922) or by the vote of the locals (such as the return of the Saar Valley and much of the area on the west bank of the Rhine to eventually reunite with Germany). More significantly, Germany turned inward and grew angry over being forced to take all the blame for World War I and for the massive reparations that prevented the German economy from recovering. German governments fell, as none could provide the relief the people were looking for. This dynamic helped give rise to Adolph Hitler, who fueled the anger of the German people, directing that discontent and rage against the Allies by railing against the Treaty throughout the following decade. In 1923, just a few months before leading an armed uprising in Munich on behalf of his newly established Nazi Party, Hitler proclaimed, "With the armistice begins the humiliation of Germany. … So long as this Treaty stands there can be no resurrection of the German people; no social reform of any kind is possible! The Treaty was made in order to bring 20 million Germans to their deaths and to ruin the German nation."[401] A decade later, shortly after Hitler became the Chancellor of Germany, he said to the members of the Reichstag:

> All the problems which are causing such unrest today lie in the deficiencies of the Treaty of Peace which did not succeed in solving in a clear and reasonable way the questions of the most decisive importance for the future. Neither national nor economic—to say nothing of legal—problems and demands of the nations were settled by this treaty in such a way as to stand the criticism of reason in the future. … The idea that the economic extermination of a nation of sixty-five millions would be of service to other nations is absurd. … The Treaty

> of Versailles is to blame for having inaugurated a period in which financial calculations appear to destroy economic reason.[402]

II-86: German Chancellor Adolph Hitler, circa 1937

Within a few months of this address, Hitler withdrew Germany from the League of Nations and ordered a dramatic increase in the size of the German military – in direct violation of the Treaty of Versailles. Another decade later, as captured by historian Harold Black, Hitler was still blaming the Treaty (and specifically Woodrow Wilson) as the cause of the Second World War. According to Hitler, "The fact that in 1918 the German nation, led astray by the lying words of the United States President, believed it could hasten the end by a voluntary armistice not only drove Germany into the present disaster but was responsible for the present war."[403] Of course, this was almost exactly what Wilson predicted when he warned the other Big Three at the Paris Peace Conference against imposing on the German nation "excessive demands [that] would most certainly sow the seeds of war."[404] But Wilson was so concerned about the League of Nations that he conceded point after point during the negotiations in Paris to yield a vengeful collection of stipulations for the Germans that did precisely what he predicted – sow the seeds of war. Rather than put together an agreement that would truly make World War I the "war to end all wars," an even more terrifying and destructive global conflict sprung from the center of Europe, much of it as a direct backlash to those terms imposed by the Allies in the Treaty of Versailles. Woodrow Wilson and his colleagues created an agreement that could only be described as one of the biggest diplomatic failures in the history of the world.

Wilson spent his last few weeks in the White House wallowing in bitterness over the way everything had fallen apart over the past year and a half. His list of enemies had grown, and he was not in any mood to offer compassion to anyone on that docket. That included Eugene Debs, who remained in prison for his conviction under the Sedition Act. Despite calls for mercy, the President wouldn't even consider a pardon or commutation. "I will never consent to the pardon of this man," he told Tumulty.

> I know that in certain quarters of the country there is a popular demand for the pardon of Debs, but it shall never be accomplished with my consent. … They will say I am cold-blooded and indifferent, but it will make no impression on me. This man was a traitor to his country and he will never be pardoned during my administration.[405]

Wilson's enemies would receive no sympathy as his presidency wound its way to an end.

President Wilson welcomed President-elect Harding to the White House for a traditional gathering of tea on the day before the transfer of power. The pair then rode together to the Capitol on the morning of March 4, 1921. Wilson still had a few final responsibilities as President, with Congress presenting him with a handful of bills for his signature to round out the session. A number of congressmen stopped by to pay their respects, as did General Pershing, but these final minutes leading to the noon transition were mostly a sad sight for the beleaguered outgoing executive. There was also one moment of tension. Of all people, Senator Henry Lodge appeared to communicate the formal end of the congressional session. This was typically a perfunctory moment but was tinged with bitterness this go around. "This committee begs to inform you," said Senator Lodge, "that the two Houses have completed their work and are prepared to receive any further communications from you." The outgoing President gazed hard into the eyes of his adversary, while coldly responding, "I have no further communication. I would be glad if you would inform both Houses and thank them for their courtesy – good morning, sir."[406] Harding then asked Wilson if he thought he could make it to the outside ceremony, which was about to begin. But Wilson wasn't physically up to it. The steps were too daunting, so he wisely decided, "I guess I had better not try it."[407] As the participants for the Harding inaugural headed to the east front of the Capitol, Wilson, Edith, Dr.

Grayson, and Tumulty quietly got into their car to take the Wilsons to their new home and their post-presidential lives.

Unlike most Presidents, the Wilsons didn't have a real home base to which they were likely to return. They discussed several possible cities but eventually decided to stay in the nation's capital, which had been Edith Wilson's home for most of the past two decades. After deciding they didn't have enough funds to build their dream home overlooking the Potomac River, Edith settled on a four-story house on S St., just off Embassy Row, that she described as "an unpretentious, comfortable, dignified house, fitted to the needs of a gentleman's home."[408] After installing the one major addition they needed – an elevator – Edith went about fixing up the place to mirror their White House residence in an effort to ease the transition for her husband.

There would be some familiar faces at the S St. home. Edith was never far from her husband's side, and Grayson was a regular as well. President Harding generously assigned the navy admiral to stay in Washington and be available full-time to continue to take care of his friend and patient. Ray Baker was also often around, having been selected by Wilson to manage his papers and eventually write his official biography. Isaac and Mary Scott were hired by Mrs. Wilson as the principal servants in the home, which was mostly a quiet, slow-moving existence for the former First Couple. In many ways, it was a somber home, with little joy, as Wilson continued to struggle from the fatigue and weakness that still plagued him from his massive stroke. Just a couple of weeks into Wilson's retirement, Baker observed the former President as "looking inconceivably old,

II-87: The Wilsons' post-presidential home on S St. in Washington, D.C.

gray, worn, tired. … He has been lost. . . He seems lonelier, more cut-off than ever before. His mind still works with power, but with nothing to work upon! Only memories & regrets. He feels himself bitterly misunderstood & unjustly attacked; and being broken in health, cannot rally under it."[409] The one man surprisingly no longer on the inside was Joe Tumulty. The man who had been Wilson's most intimate aide and political adviser for the past decade, was not offered a position in the Wilson household. Instead, Edith's brother, John Bolling, took over Wilson's secretarial duties. There were some grumblings that Tumulty had been on the outs with Wilson since the days of the Peace Conference when the President was reportedly "highly displeased at some of the policies of the White House during his absence," with Tumulty the center of that discontent.[410] Tumulty continued his duties during the President's illness, but engagement with Wilson was almost entirely through memos and discussions with the First Lady. The level of intimacy they had once enjoyed appeared to be on the wane, and now in Wilson's post-presidential world, Tumulty seemed to be on the outs.

Wilson spent most of his time in his bedroom, the upstairs sunroom, or in his wood-paneled library which housed his collection of more than 8,000 books and his White House mementos. His exercise primarily consisted of small walks around the house, along with his afternoon drives, which he took nearly every day around 3:00 pm. As the Wilsons' car became easily recognized, members of the public would often cheer as Wilson drove by, something which often brought a smile and a wave from the former President. The Wilsons' special outing each week was a visit on Saturday nights to nearby Keith's Theater. The owner would save a couple of seats in the back row for Mr. and Mrs. Wilson, who were happy to attend whatever was playing that night. In the evenings, after Wilson ate his dinner, Edith would often read to him before he retired. Only then would Edith take a break and have a meal for herself. Wilson's left arm and leg remained primarily immobile, his digestive system was always a problem, and even shaving – one of the few activities he continued to insist on performing by himself – was often difficult to complete.

Despite his lengthy list of maladies, Woodrow Wilson wasn't ready to just give up on life. In fact, in a strange turn of events, he decided to open a law partnership with his last Secretary of State, Bainbridge Colby. The firm was based in New York, but the pair opened an office for Wilson in Washington, D.C. However, this venture was doomed from the start. First, Wilson refused to let Colby take on any business that related to his presidency. Client after client were rejected by Wilson, who was unwilling to trade on his prior position. Wilson was also physically never up to the task of returning to the practice of law and almost never stepped foot in the D.C. office. After a few months, Edith stepped in and pointed out to her husband that Colby was being hurt by the partnership and he should be released from the commitment. Wilson agreed, and the partnership of Wilson & Colby was dissolved after just a few months.

Wilson watched with regret as President Harding took the United States in very different directions from what he had tried to pursue. A number of Wilson's domestic accomplishments were withdrawn or curtailed, and the Americans also signed separate peace treaties with Germany, Austria, and Hungary, which included some of the reservations requested by Senator Lodge. Harding also commuted the sentence of Eugene Debs and named William Taft as the new Chief Justice of the Supreme Court after the death of Edward White. But Harding did graciously reach out to Wilson when it came time to commemorate the third anniversary of the armistice on November 11, 1921. The event would include a long procession from downtown Washington to Arlington National Cemetery, where a tribute would take place for the Tomb of the Unknown Soldier. It was a somber affair, but when spectators on the route recognized Wilson in his open carriage, many broke the silence with rounds of applause. Afterward, some twenty-thousand made their way to the Wilsons' home on S St. to pay their respects. Wilson was visibly moved by the outpouring of support, bringing both him and his wife to tears. "I wish

II-88: Former President Wilson and Edith Wilson in the procession for the dedication of the Tomb of the Unknown Solider, November 11, 1921

that I had the voice to reply and to thank you for the wonderful tribute that you have paid me," Wilson told the crowd. "I can only say God bless you."[411] Even after he went back inside, thousands remained in a mostly silent vigil outside the Wilson home.

There was one final event in the life of Woodrow Wilson that can only be described as sad. Joe Tumulty was still trying to get back into Wilson's world. Writing a book without the boss's knowledge was definitely not a step in the right direction. Tumulty's book, "Woodrow Wilson: As I Know Him," came out within a year of the end of Wilson's presidency. It was largely a favorable portrayal, with extensive first-person conversations captured in detail. But the book reportedly caught Wilson by surprise, with no advance notice that Tumulty was even working on a book, let alone providing him any opportunity to review the content before publication. Wilson reportedly was "enraged" when the book hit the shelves and he finally had a chance to read it.[412] The formal break between the two came the following April when Tumulty encouraged his former chief to send a note to the National Democratic Club of New York City to be read at its annual Jefferson Day Dinner. Many of Wilson's old guard would be on hand, and Tumulty thought it would be a gesture that would be well-received and perhaps generate some positive press. To Tumulty's disappointment, Wilson declined, concluding he didn't really have anything meaningful to say. Tumulty appealed to Edith to advocate with Wilson on the subject, but she shot him down as well. "No, Mr. Tumulty," said [Edith], "you know him well enough to know that when he has thought a thing out and decided it there is no use to continue argument; and besides, I thoroughly agree with him."[413] Nevertheless, in this case, Tumulty decided not to take "no" for an answer. On his own authority, he penned what appeared to be a fairly benign greeting from Wilson to the Club. "Say to the Democrats of New York that I am ready to support any man who stands for the salvation of America, and the salvation of America is justice to all classes," read the note.[414] Tumulty's indiscretion took a difficult turn when the press interpreted Wilson's note as an endorsement for James Cox to repeat as the Democratic nominee in 1924, a notion Wilson did not support. Tumulty's note never mentioned Cox, but since Cox, who was the featured speaker at the event, took the stage directly after the Wilson/Tumulty note had been read to the gathering, the press drew its own conclusions and made the link in the next day's newspapers. All of this took Wilson by surprise when he read about his supposed endorsement in the press.

Wilson wrote to *The New York Times* demanding a retraction. He then contacted Tumulty to inquire "what [was] the real source of the alleged message"[415] that prompted the press to draw such conclusions. Tumulty was now trapped, and he knew it. He was terrified of having to admit that he had sent the message without Wilson's permission. Such a transgression could be professionally fatal, in his mind, in terms of how Wilson, the public, the press, and the political class would view him. He offered an immediate apology to Wilson and practically begged him to agree to a statement to the effect that while Wilson had not written the note himself, it reflected his general feelings that had been communicated verbally to Tumulty to pass along. Wilson would agree to no such thing. According to Edith Wilson's memoirs, Wilson directed that Tumulty be told "that without stultifying myself I could not do what he asks; that he is entirely mistaken about its 'ruining' him, or disgracing his wife and children; that it is too small a matter to attract the attention of the public unless he himself dramatizes it, which he seems to be trying to do."[416] In this instance, Tumulty was hung out to dry. Moreover, the main people to which this was hardly a "small matter" were Woodrow and Edith Wilson. Joe Tumulty was cut off from his former boss for good. Despite efforts to get back into Wilson's good graces, Edith helped make sure that Tumulty would never see Wilson in person again. There are certainly multiple sides to the story of the break between Woodrow Wilson and Joe Tumulty, with both participants likely sharing some responsibility for a split that seemingly had been growing for months. Nevertheless, the general consensus is that Tumulty had served as the quintessential loyal aide to Wilson for more than a decade and likely deserved a better fate. But the pattern of Woodrow Wilson and his disaffection with his closest intimates persisted to the end. From Jack Hibben to Edward House to Joe Tumulty, years of unflinching loyalty and comradery were once again permanently cast aside by the man at the center of all these relationships – one Woodrow Wilson.

Wilson did begin to receive a handful of special guests at the S St. home. This included separate visits from Georges Clemenceau and David Lloyd George, mostly to reminisce. Other members from his administration might be granted an appearance here and there, but not many. Colonel House stopped by to drop off his card, hoping to get a return call and invitation to meet. His outreach, however, never received a response. There would be no reunions for those Wilson had previously cast aside.

While Wilson's body remained broken, his mind continued to churn out ideas, including those related to politics. He worked on a project that he called "The Document," which he intended to offer his fellow Democrats as a blueprint for the 1924 party platform. He also crafted one article called "The Road Away from Revolution," which ran in the *Atlantic Monthly*. His message was a warning about both Bolshevism and an overly selfish implementation of capitalism. Wilson's final outreach to the American people came in a radio address on the eve of the 1923 anniversary of the armistice that ended the fighting overseas. He called his speech "The Significance of Armistice Day," which he delivered from his home. Engineers arrived on the morning of the broadcast to wire Wilson's library for his remarks. Wilson was in bed all day with a pounding headache, but as he usually did, he rose to the occasion when it came time to speak that evening. Some three million people tuned in across the country to hear the voice of their former leader on a matter for which he was uniquely qualified to speak. Wilson continued to regret the Senate's failure to ratify the Treaty that he originally negotiated, but he remained confident that the country would "retrieve that fatal error and assume once more the role of courage, self-respect and helpfulness which every true American must wish to regard as our natural part in the affairs of the world."[417] The next day, another large gathering appeared outside the Wilson home to commemorate the solemn anniversary. In his brief remarks to the crowd, Wilson reiterated his confidence that his views would ultimately prevail. "I am not one of those that have the least

II-89: Former President Wilson, 1923 (age 66)

anxiety about the triumph of the principles I have stood for," Wilson said. "I have seen fools resist Providence before, and I have seen their destruction, as will come upon these again, utter destruction and contempt. That we shall prevail is as sure as that God reigns."[418] The crowd responded with loud applause as Wilson returned to the quiet of his home.

Wilson had some generous friends who wanted to help him during the final period of his life. A previous collection of $100,000 had gone a long way to paying for the home on S St., and now a few wealthy compatriots surprised him on his 67th birthday with a $12,000 Rolls Royce Silver Ghost, a beautiful six-passenger limousine that the former President greatly appreciated. Knowing that presidential pensions still did not exist, those same friends also arranged for a $10,000/year annuity that would help care for Edith after Wilson had passed. As the end drew near, at least he had comfort in the fact that Edith would not want for much after he was gone.

The end came just a month later. On January 26, 1924, Dr. Grayson finally agreed to take a vacation, even though his patient was not doing well. After just a couple of days, Edith grew more and more concerned. She reached Grayson and asked him to come back. The admiral returned on the 31st and agreed to stay overnight to ease Edith's worry. The next morning, Wilson's systems started to shut down. Word got out, and the press and public gathered for what amounted to a death watch outside the S St. home. Tumulty was among those who arrived, and tried several times to see his former boss, but he was denied access at every turn. Many other dignitaries stopped by to pay their respects, dropping off their cards as a sign of their affection. Besides the doctors, nurses, and house servants, Edith and daughter Margaret kept everyone else out. In a moment when Wilson appeared alert, Dr. Grayson told him the end was near. "I am ready," Wilson responded. "I am a broken piece of machinery. When the machinery is broken …" After failing to complete that thought, he reiterated in a whisper, "I am ready."[419] On February 3, the former President spent most of the day unconscious, with Edith on one side holding his right hand and Margaret on the other holding the left. For a brief moment, Wilson suddenly opened his eyes, but then they closed almost as quickly. Shortly thereafter, with tears streaming down his face, Dr. Grayson informed those gathered around the Wilsons' home that the former President had taken his last breath at 11:15 am.

The Wilsons had selected the recently completed Washington National Cathedral as his final resting place. After a brief ceremony at the home on S St., the invited mourners traveled the short two miles for the final service and burial at the Bethlehem Chapel within the grand Cathedral. A few years later, Wilson's body was reinterred to his own bay on the south side of the nave. Edith would join him there when she finally passed nearly four decades later, on December 28, 1961, at the age of 89.

Woodrow Wilson was born to lead. He inherited the gift of oratory from his father, used the skill to educate and inspire, and ultimately led others to join the pursuit of his lofty goals throughout his career. Spending the last two decades of his life in executive positions, Wilson reached the heights of academia as the President of Princeton University, led his state as the Governor of New Jersey, was twice elected President of the United States, and led an international effort to devise a system that was intended to prevent future wars. But for every major accomplishment stemming from these leadership roles, there were also significant defeats. As an academic innovator, Wilson successfully changed the way the country educated students at the collegiate level. At the same time, when he challenged the elitist and undemocratic status quo on campus, he fell to crushing defeats at the hands of the Board of Trustees. As his nation's President, Wilson personally pursued a bold, progressive agenda that led to a number of legislative triumphs, including the establishment of the Federal Reserve System that revised and stabilized the foundation of the American economy. At the same time, his southern roots came to the fore with his racist policies that segregated Federal agencies, crushing the morale and career prospects across the Black community. He began his administration as the most transparent President in history with his public addresses to Congress and numerous on-the-record press conferences, but he spent the last year of his presidency shrouded in mystery as an invalid who was almost completely hidden from view and barely able to do any work. He kept his country out of war until circumstances demanded engagement and then turned the full power of the United States into a war machine that changed the trajectory of the contest and brought victory to the Allies. But when his greatest mission in life was at hand, Woodrow Wilson dramatically failed in his effort to win the peace.

Wilson's most obvious failure in the aftermath of World War I was his inability to get the U.S. Senate to ratify the Treaty of Versailles, including its Covenant for the League of Nations. While Wilson was willing to make numerous concessions in his negotiations with the Prime Ministers of Europe in formulating the treaty, he was unwilling to negotiate anything with the Senate Republicans, without whom he had no way to get his own country to agree to his handiwork. Yes, Wilson always admired the British parliamentary system, with its powerful executive who could count on his legislature to back him up, particularly on the international scene. Wilson spent his academic career extolling the virtues of such a system and why he preferred it to the American democratic construct. But Wilson was not a prime minister, and did not operate in a parliamentary system. He was the President of the United States, who was bound by the separation of powers and oppositional government. Among the most dramatic failures of the nation's only Ph.D. President was to behave like a prime minister while serving in a presidential system. And while his goals may have been righteous, his execution was amateurish that fell prey to professional opposition that seemed to understand the American system far better than the political science expert. In the end, with the citizens of his nation and around the world watching his every move, Professor Woodrow Wilson flunked this final exam in the most important cause of his entire life.

But the greater failure for Wilson, and the world, actually occurred before Wilson ever presented the Treaty to the Senate – it was encapsulated in the Treaty itself. Woodrow Wilson went to the Paris Peace Conference fully expecting to guide the Allies to embrace his League of Nations while also adhering to his Fourteen Points. He was mistaken. The Allies didn't care much for either, focusing more on their own selfish aims and the need to punish the Central Powers. To preserve the League, Wilson conceded point after point, sacrificing his principles in the areas of self-determination and reasonable reparations to yield a treaty that was far afield from what he originally intended. Even with his League of Nations in place, it could do nothing to prevent the backlash that predictably developed in Germany over the vindictive terms of the Treaty of Versailles, ultimately serving as one of the major catalysts for an even more horrific war less than a generation away. The treaty to which Wilson put his name proved to be a disaster, as was his League, which spectacularly failed in its effort to prevent future armed conflicts.

The greatest failure in the life of Woodrow Wilson wasn't that he couldn't get the Treaty of Versailles ratified by the U.S. Senate. Wilson's greatest failure was the sacrifice of his principles, forfeiting so many of his Fourteen Points upon which he had staked the future peace of the world. As Wilson had rightly predicted, those concessions resulted in a one-sided agreement that gave rise to the ultra-nationalist Nazis who craved revenge on their neighbors. The American President's inability to hold the line against his European counterparts was itself a catalyst for the subsequent global conflagration, thereby representing one of the greatest collective failures in the history of the world.

20 Quotations from Woodrow Wilson

Date	Context and Source	Quote
1908	On the role of the American President in foreign affairs; From his book *Constitutional Government in the United States* (Lawrence. p. 316)	"One of the greatest of the President's powers I have not yet spoken of at all: his control, which is very absolute, of the foreign relations of the nation. The initiative in foreign affairs, which the President possesses without any restriction whatever, is virtually the power to control them absolutely. … He (the President) need disclose no step of negotiation until it is complete, and when in any critical matter it is completed the Government is virtually committed. Whatever its disinclination, the Senate may feel itself committed also."
October 1910	Thoughts on America during his New Jersey gubernatorial campaign; From a speech to an audience in Atlantic City (Berg. p. 201)	"America ... is not a piece of the surface of the earth. … America is not merely a body of towns. America is an idea, America is an ideal, America is a vision."
October 24, 1910	On what his approach would be to the "boss system" in New Jersey if elected governor; From his response to a query from Republican George Record (Clements. p. 58)	"If elected, I shall not, either in the matter of appointments to office or assent to legislation, or in shaping any part of the policy of my administration, submit to the dictation of any person or persons, special interest or organization. I should deem myself forever disgraced should I in even the slightest degree cooperate in any such system or any such transactions as you describe in your characterization of the 'boss' system."
~ 1912	On Colonel Edward House (Auchincloss. p. 35)	"Mr. House is my second personality. He is my independent self. If I were in his place I would do just as he suggested. If anyone thinks he is reflecting my opinion by whatever action he takes, they are welcome to the conclusion."
January 1915	On his initial opposition to a constitutional amendment for women's suffrage; From remarks to Nancy Toy	"Suffrage for women, will make absolutely no change in politics – it is the home that will be disastrously affected. Somebody has to make the home and who is going to do it if the women don't?"

	(Berg. p. 488)	
May 10, 1915	Continues to resist bringing the United States into World War I; From a speech at Constitution Hall in Philadelphia (Auchincloss. p. 72)	"The example of America must be the example not merely of peace because it will not fight, but of peace because it is the healing and elevating influence of the world, and strife is not. There is such a thing as a man being too proud to fight. There is such a thing as a nation being so right that it does not need to convince others by force that it is right."
Early 1916	Expressing his views on war and what it would take for him to bring the U.S. into World War I; From comments to a newspaper reporter on his Preparedness Tour (Black. p. 161)	"I hate war; I loathe it as either a means or an end, but when I do wage it, believe me it is going to be to the limit. But it must be with a united national sentiment. Nothing short of that must be back of the boys who go. The instant I see we have this united national sentiment, I'll light the spark. But until I am convinced of that, I am willing to be misunderstood. Better misunderstood in peace than underarmed in war."
January 22, 1917	Advocates for a "peace without victory" in World War I; From a speech to Congress (Thompson. p. 133)	"It must be a peace without victory … Victory would mean peace forced upon the loser, a victor's terms imposed upon the vanquished. It would be accepted in humiliation, under duress, at an intolerable sacrifice, and would leave a sting, a resentment, a bitter memory upon which terms of peace would rest, not permanently, but only as upon quicksand. Only a peace between equals can last."
April 2, 1917	On why the U.S. must now enter World War I; From a speech to Congress (Black. p. 168)	The time had come "to fight thus for the ultimate peace of the world and for the liberation of its people, the German people included; for the rights of nations great and small and the privilege of men everywhere to choose their way of life and of obedience. The world must be made safe for democracy."
April 2, 1917	On why he decided the time had finally come to enter World War I; From remarks to Joe Tumulty (immediately after his speech to Congress) (Tumulty, p. 257)	"Tumulty, from the very beginning I saw the end of this horrible thing; but I could not move faster than the great mass of our people would permit. Very few understood the difficult and trying position I have been placed in during the years through which we have just passed. In the policy of patience and forbearance I pursued I tried to make every part of America and the varied elements of our population understand that we were willing to go any length rather than resort to war with

		Germany. As I told you months ago, it would have been foolish for us to have been rushed off our feet and to have gone to war over an isolated affair like the *Lusitania*. But now we are certain that there will be no regrets or looking back on the part of our people. There is but one course now left open to us. Our consciences are clear, and we must prepare for the inevitable – a fight to the end."
January 8, 1918	On his goals at the conclusion of World War I; From his address to Congress introducing his Fourteen Points (Berg. p. 472)	"What is at stake now is the peace of the world. … What we are striving for is a new international order based upon broad and universal principles of right and justice, no mere peace of shreds and patches. … [Unless these problems] are dealt with in a spirit of unselfish and unbiased justice, with a view to the wishes, the natural connections, the racial aspirations, the security, and the peace of mind of the peoples involved, no permanent peace will have been attained."
January 8, 1918	On the League of Nations; From his address to Congress introducing his Fourteen Points (Berg. p. 471)	"A general association of nations must be formed under specific covenants for the purpose of affording mutual guarantees of political independence and territorial integrity to great and small states alike."
October 25, 1918	Advocating for Democratic votes in the 1918 midterm elections; From a press release (Lawrence. p. 238)	"The leaders of the minority have unquestionably been pro-war, but they have been anti-administration. At almost every turn, since we entered the war, they have sought to take the choice of policy and the conduct of the war out of my hands and put it under the control of instrumentalities of their own choosing. … The return of a Republican majority to either house of the Congress would, moreover, certainly be interpreted on the other side of the water as a repudiation of my leadership."
February 14, 1919	On the elements needed for the League of Nations to be successful; From remarks to the delegates at the Paris Peace Conference introducing the League Covenant	"Throughout this instrument we are depending primarily and chiefly upon one great force, and that is the moral force of the public opinion of the world—the cleansing and clarifying and compelling influences of publicity—so that intrigues can no longer have their coverts, so that designs that are sinister can at any time be drawn into the open, so that those things

	(Retrieved from "The American Presidency Project." U.C. Santa Barbara)	that are destroyed by the light may be properly destroyed by the overwhelming light of the universal expression of the condemnation of the world."
February 14, 1919	On the imperative of the League of Nations; From comments to Edith Wilson (Berg. p. 545)	"Once established the League can arbitrate and correct mistakes which are inevitable in the Treaty we are trying to make at this time. The resentments and injustices caused by the War are still too poignant, and the wounds too fresh. They must have time to heal, and when they have done so, one by one the mistakes can be brought to the League for readjustment, and the League will act as a permanent clearinghouse where every nation can come, the small as well as the great."
June 25, 1919	On his refusal to accept reservations to the Treaty; From a memo to Joe Tumulty (Tumulty. p. 452)	"My clear conviction is that the adoption of the treaty by the Senate with reservations will put the United States as clearly out of the concert of nations as a rejection. We ought either to go in or stay out. To stay out would be fatal to the influence and even to the commercial prospects of the United States, and to go in would give her a leading place in the affairs of the world. Reservations would either mean nothing or postpone the conclusion of peace, so far as America is concerned, until every other principal nation concerned in the treaty had found out by negotiation what the reservations practically meant and whether they could associate themselves with the United States on the terms of the reservations or not."
July 10, 1919	Urging Congress to support the Treaty of Versailles; From his remarks to Congress (Clements. p. 212)	"The stage is set, the destiny disclosed. It has come about by no plan of our conceiving, but by the hand of God who led us into this way. We cannot turn back. We can only go forward, with lifted eyes and freshened spirit, to follow the vision. It was of this that we dreamed at our birth. America shall in truth show the way. The light streams upon the path ahead, and nowhere else."
August 1919	On the need to go on his tour across the country to advocate for the League of Nations; From remarks to Joe Tumulty	"I know that I am at the end of my tether, but my friends on the Hill say that the trip is necessary to save the treaty and I am willing to make whatever personal sacrifice is required, for if the treaty should be defeated, God only knows what

	(Freud and Bullitt. p. 284)	would happen to the world as a result of it. In the presence of the great tragedy which now faces the world, no decent man can count his own personal fortunes in the reckoning. Even though, in my condition, it might mean the giving up of my life, I will gladly make the sacrifice to save the treaty."
January 8, 1920	Continues to refuse to consider the Senate's reservations over the Treaty and the League Covenant; From a letter to the Jackson Day Banquet of the Democratic Party of Washington (Lawrence. p. 292)	"We cannot rewrite this Treaty. … We must take it without changes of it which alter its meaning, or leave it and then, after the rest of be the world have signed it, we must face the unthinkable task of making another and separate kind of treaty with Germany."
November 1920	On his reaction to the results of the election of 1920; From remarks to Joe Tumulty (Tumulty. p. 501)	"The enemies of this enterprise cleverly aroused every racial passion and prejudice, and by poisonous propaganda made it appear that the League of Nations was a great Juggernaut which was intended to crush and destroy instead of saving and bringing peace to the world. The people will have to learn now by bitter experience just what they have lost."

Primary Sources

Berg, A. Scott.

Wilson. G.P. Putnam's Sons. New York, NY. 2013.

Black, Harold.

The True Woodrow Wilson: Crusader for Democracy. Fleming H. Revell Company. New York, NY. 1946.

Clements, Kendrick.

Woodrow Wilson: World Statesman. Twayne Publishers. Boston, MA. 1987.

Freud, Sigmund and William Bullitt.

Thomas Woodrow Wilson: A Psychological Study. Houghton Mifflin Company. Boston, MA. 1966.

Lodge, Henry.

The Senate and the League of Nations. Charles Scribner's Sons. New York, NY. 1925.

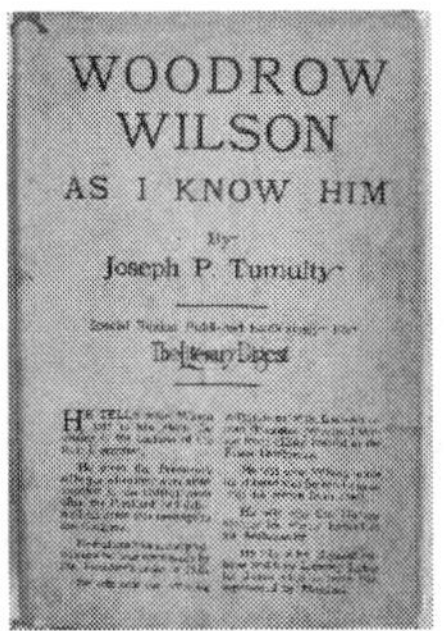

Tumulty, Joseph.

Woodrow Wilson: As I Know Him. The Literary Digest. Doubleday, Page & Co. Garden City, NY. 1921.

Wilson, Edith.

My Memoir. The Bobbs-Merrill Company. New York, NY. 1938.

Primary Sources Specifically for Illustrations

Annin, Robert.

Woodrow Wilson: A Character Study. Dodd, Mead and Company. New York, NY. 1925.

Baker, Ray.

Woodrow Wilson: Life and Letters – Volume I: Youth (1856-1890). Doubleday, Page & Co. Garden City, NY. 1927. [Baker (1)]

Baker, Ray.

Woodrow Wilson: Life and Letters – Volume II: Princeton (1890-1910). Doubleday, Page & Co. Garden City, NY. 1927. [Baker (2)]

Daniels, Josephus.

The Life of Woodrow Wilson (1856-1924). Will H. Johnston. 1924.

Eaton, William.
Woodrow Wilson: His Life and Work. C.E. Thomas. 1919.

Hale, William.

Woodrow Wilson: The Story of His Life. Doubleday, Page & Company. Garden City, NY. 1912.

Hosford, Hester.

Woodrow Wilson and New Jersey Made Over. The Knickerbocker Press. G.P. Putnam's Sons. New York, NY. 1912.

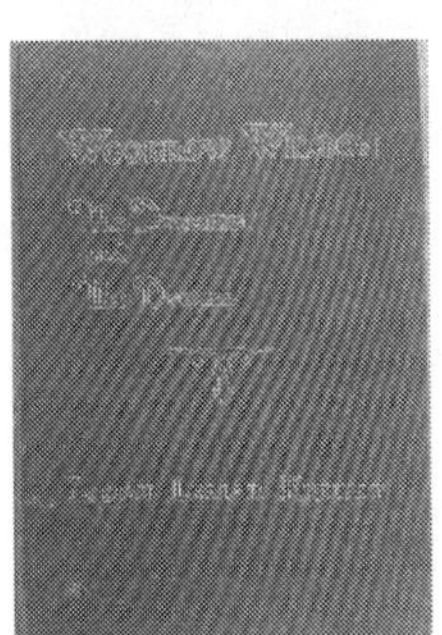

Knight, Lucian.

Woodrow Wilson: The Dreamer and The Dream. The Johnson-Dallis Company. Atlanta, GA. 1924.

Illustrations and Their Sources

II-19: **Mary Peck and Wilson, Bermuda** (Artist: Unknown. Retrieved from *The Washington Post. A President's secret letters to another woman that he never wanted public* by Molly McCartney. Posted on September 16, 2018. https://www.washingtonpost.com/news/retropolis/wp/2018/09/16/the-secret-letters-to-another-woman-that-a-president-never-wanted-public/)

II-20: **Wilson, circa 1908 (age ~51)** (Artist: McManus. New York, NY. circa 1908. Retrieved from the Library of Congress. www.loc.gov/item/94508334/)

II-21: **George Harvey** (Artist: Unknown. Blog: The Importance of the Obvious. *On George Harvey*. Posted November 26, 2013. https://crackerpilgrim.com/2013/11/26/on-george-harvey/)

II-22: **James Smith, Jr.** (Artist: Brown Bros. Hosford. p. 42)

II-23: **Wilson running for Governor of New Jersey, 1910 (age 53)** (Artist: Unknown. 1910. National Portrait Gallery, Smithsonian Institution. https://www.si.edu/object/woodrow-wilson:npg_NPG.77.110)

II-24: **The Wilson Family (circa 1911): (L to R): Margaret, Ellen, Jessie, Nell, and Gov. Wilson** (Artist: Pach Brothers Studio. circa 1911. Retrieved from the National Portrait Gallery, Smithsonian Institution. https://www.si.edu/object/wilson-family:npg_NPG.93.388.41)

II-25: **Private Secretary Joe Tumulty and Wilson in the Governor's office, 1911** (Artist: Brown Bros. Hosford. p. 120)

II-26: **William Jennings Bryan** (Artist: Harris & Ewing. Retrieved from the Library of Congress. https://www.loc.gov/pictures/item/2016856655/)

II-27: **Wilson and Colonel Edward House** (Artist: Unknown. Retrieved from the Texas State Historical Society. Posted in 1952. Updated February 16, 2017. https://www.tshaonline.org/handbook/entries/house-edward-mandell)

II-28: **Theodore Roosevelt speaking at the first Progressive National Convention in Chicago, August 1912** (Artist: Bain News Service. August 1912. Retrieved from the Library of Congress. https://www.loc.gov/pictures/item/2014691372/)

II-29: **Democratic campaign banner for Wilson and VP-candidate Thomas Marshall** (Artist: Manhattan Slide Company, Inc. 1912. Retrieved from the Library of Congress. www.loc.gov/item/2007680381/)

II-30: **Louis Brandeis** (Artist: Unknown. 1915. Brandeis University. Retrieved from Wikipedia. https://en.wikipedia.org/wiki/Louis_Brandeis#/media/File:Louis_Brandeis_portrait,_1915.jpg)

II-31: **Wilson during the 1912 presidential election** (Artist: Udo Keppler. Published by Keppler & Schwarzmann, Puck Building. New York, NY. 1912. Retrieved from the Library of Congress. www.loc.gov/item/2011649367/)

II-32: **Wilson's First Cabinet: (Clockwise from left): President Wilson, Secretary of the Treasury William McAdoo, Attorney General James McReynolds, Secretary of the Navy Josephus Daniels, Secretary of Agriculture David Houston, Secretary of Labor William Wilson, Secretary of Commerce William Redfield, Secretary of the Interior Franklin Lane, Postmaster General Albert Burleson, Secretary of War Lindley Garrison, and Secretary of State William Bryan** (Artist: Harris & Ewing. 1913. National Portrait Gallery, Smithsonian Institution. https://www.si.edu/object/woodrow-wilson-and-his-cabinet:npg_S_NPG.84.299)

II-33: **Wilson meeting outgoing President William Taft at the White House, March 4, 1913** (Artist: Unknown. March 4, 1913. Retrieved from the National Park Service. https://www.nps.gov/parkhistory/online_books/presidents/introa.htm)

II-34: **Wilson giving his first Inaugural Address, March 4, 1913** (Artist: Unknown. March 4, 1913. Eaton. p. 92)

II-35: **Dr. Cary Grayson** (Artist: Harris & Ewing. Retrieved from the Library of Congress. https://www.loc.gov/pictures/resource/hec.21511/)

II-36: **Mexican leader Victoriano Huerta** (Artist: Unknown. 1913-1914. Retrieved from Wikipedia. https://en.wikipedia.org/wiki/Victoriano_Huerta#/media/File:V_Huerta.jpg)

II-37: **President Wilson** (Artist: Rose. Hosford. Frontispiece)

II-38: **First Lady Ellen Wilson** (Artist: Unknown. Eaton. p. 165)

II-39: **Secretary of the Treasury William McAdoo** (Artist: Unknown. Eaton. p. 390)

II-40: **Postmaster General Albert Burleson** (Artist: Unknown. National Postal Museum, Smithsonian Institution. https://www.si.edu/object/photograph-postmaster-general-albert-s-burleson:npm_1982.0157.687)

II-41: **Wilson played more golf than any other President** (Artist: Unknown. Eaton. p. 221)

II-42: **Jessie Wilson (center) at her wedding, November 25, 1913** (Artist: Harris & Ewing. November 25, 1913. Retrieved from *Town & Country* Magazine. https://www.townandcountrymag.com/society/politics/g40604858/white-house-wedding-history-photos/)

II-43: **Eleanor (Nell) Wilson at her wedding, May 7, 1914** (Artist: Unknown. May 7, 1914. Retrieved from *Town & Country* Magazine. https://www.townandcountrymag.com/society/politics/g40604858/white-house-wedding-history-photos/)

II-44: **First Lady Ellen Wilson** (Artist: Bain News Service. Retrieved from the Library of Congress. https://www.loc.gov/resource/ggbain.11469/)

II-45: **William Trotter, circa 1915** (Artist: Unknown. "William Monroe Trotter, circa 1915," House Divided: The Civil War Research Engine at Dickinson College. https://hd.housedivided.dickinson.edu/node/35232)

II-46: **President Wilson with his first grandchild, Francis Sayre, Jr.** (Artist: Harris & Ewing. 1915. Retrieved from the Library of Congress. https://www.loc.gov/resource/hec.17927/)

II-47: **Edith Galt** (Artist: Unknown. Edith Wilson Juvenile/Educational Biography. Retrieved from the National First Ladies' Library. http://www.firstladies.org/curriculum/educational-biography.aspx?biography=29)

II-48: **Sinking of the Lusitania, May 7, 1915** (Artist: Charles Topin. Picture from the National Defence, courtesy of the Canadian Navy. Retrieved from ThoughtCo. *Sinking of the Lusitania* by Jennifer Rosenberg. Updated on March 9, 2020. https://www.thoughtco.com/sinking-of-the-lusitania-1778317)

II-49: **President Wilson with the new First Lady, Edith Wilson** (Artist: Harris & Ewing. Knight. p. 98)

II-50: **Pancho Villa** (Artist: Unknown. Part of the George Bain Collection. circa 1910-1915. Retrieved from the Library of Congress. https://www.loc.gov/item/2014689241/)

II-51: **President Wilson in the White House** (Artist: Underwood & Underwood. Daniels. p. 194)

II-52: **Campaign pin for Republican Charles Evans Hughes, 1916** (Artist: Unknown. Retrieved from Heritage Auctions. https://historical.ha.com/itm/political/pinback-buttons-1896-present-/charles-evans-hughes-republican-candidate-button/a/6221-43204.s)

II-53: **President Wilson, 1917 (age 60)** (Artist: Unknown. 1917. Retrieved from the National Portrait Gallery, Smithsonian Institution. Gift of Oswald D. Reich. https://www.si.edu/object/woodrow-wilson:npg_S_NPG.67.86)

II-54: **Wilson speaking to a joint session of Congress to seek a declaration of war against Germany, April 2, 1917** (Artist: Harris & Ewing. April 2, 1917. Retrieved from the National Portrait Gallery, Smithsonian Institution. https://www.si.edu/object/woodrow-wilson:npg_S_NPG.84.297)

II-55: **General John Pershing arriving in France, June 13, 1917** (Artist: Bettman/CORBIS. June 13, 1917. Retrieved from "Almost Chosen People." https://almostchosenpeople.wordpress.com/2017/06/16/june-14-1917-pershing-arrives-in-france/general-john-j-pershing-arriving-in-france/)

II-56: **Herbert Hoover, Chair of the Food Administration** (Artist: Underwood & Underwood. Eaton. p. 277)

II-57: **Sheep grazing on the White House grounds during World War I** (Artist: Martin Gruber. 1919. Smithsonian Institution Archives, Record Unit 7355, Martin A. Gruber Photograph Collection, Image No. SIA2010-1986. https://www.si.edu/object/president-wilsons-sheep-white-house:siris_arc_291781)

II-58: **George Creel, Chair of the Committee of Public Information (CPI)** (Artist: Unknown. 1919. Original stored at the National Archives: File:111-SC-36878 - NARA - 55232937-cropped.jpg. Retrieved from Wikipedia. https://en.wikipedia.org/wiki/George_Creel#/media/File:111-SC-36878_-_NARA_-_55232937-cropped.jpg)

II-59: **Headline in the New York *Evening World* announcing Wilson's Fourteen Points** (New York *Evening World*. Originally appeared on January 8, 1918)

II-60: **Senator Henry Lodge** (Artist: James Purdy. circa 1901. Retrieved from the Library of Congress. https://www.loc.gov/pictures/item/2005685687/)

II-61: **Eugene Debs speaking in Canton, OH, after which he was arrested for violating the Sedition Act** (Artist: Unknown. 1918. Originally appeared in CantonRep.com: The Repository. Retrieved from Wikipedia. https://en.wikipedia.org/wiki/Eugene_V._Debs#/media/File:Debs_Canton_1918_large.jpg)

II-62: **Map of the location of the American Expeditionary Forces during World War I, including major engagements** (Artist: Unknown. 1918. Retrieved from American Expeditionary Force: Doughboys in WWI. https://www.usaww1.com/American-Expeditionary-Force/American-Expeditionary-Force-Maps.php5)

II-63: **American soldiers fighting in Séchault, France, during the Meuse-Argonne Offensive, September 29, 1918** (Artist: Unknown. Source: H. Charles McBarron,

Jr. Retrieved from Wikipedia. https://en.wikipedia.org/wiki/United_States_campaigns_in_World_War_I#/media/File:Harlem_Hell_Fighters_in_S%C3%A9chault,_France_on_September_29_1918_during_the_Meuse-Argonne_Offensive.jpg)

II-64: **Supreme Allied Commander Marshal Ferdinand Foch (standing) and colleagues great German representatives Matthias Erzberger and his colleagues in Foch's mobile headquarters, November 1918** (Artist: Maurice Pillard Verneuil. Retrieved from Wikipedia. https://en.wikipedia.org/wiki/Armistice_of_11_November_1918#/media/File:Waffenstillstand_gr.jpg)

II-65: **American soldiers of the 64th Regiment, 7th Infantry Division, celebrating the news of the armistice, November 11, 1918** (Artist: Unknown. November 11, 1918. U.S. Army – U.S. National Archive. Retrieved from Wikipedia. https://en.wikipedia.org/wiki/Armistice_of_11_November_1918#/media/File:US_64th_regiment_celebrate_the_Armistice.jpg)

II-66: **The American Delegation to the Paris Peace Conference: (L to R): Edward House, Robert Lansing, President Wilson, Henry White, and General Tasker Bliss** (Artist: Unknown. Eaton. p. 556)

II-67: **William Taft with Elihu Root, during the Roosevelt administration, circa 1904** (Artist: B.M. Clinedinst. circa 1904. Retrieved from the Library of Congress. www.loc.gov/item/2003688477/)

II-68: **Millions lined the streets of Paris to welcome President Wilson** (Artist: Unknown. Eaton. p. 631)

II-69: **President Wilson riding with French President Raymond Poincaré during the welcome in Paris** (Artist: Unknown. Eaton. p. 611)

II-70: **The "Big Four" at the Paris Peace Conference: (L to R): Italian Prime Minister Vittorio Orlando, British Prime Minister David Lloyd George, French Prime Minister Georges Clemenceau, and American President Woodrow Wilson** (Artist: Bettman/Getty. Retrieved from the *New Yorker*. https://www.newyorker.com/news/daily-comment/woodrow-wilsons-case-of-the-flu-and-how-pandemics-change-history)

II-71: **Wilson at the Paris Peace Conference, 1919** (Artist: John Johansen. circa 1919. Retrieved from the National Portrait Gallery, Smithsonian Institution; transfer from the Smithsonian American Art Museum; gift of an anonymous donor, 1926. https://www.si.edu/object/woodrow-wilson:npg_NPG.65.84)

II-72: **Sigmund Freud** (Artist: Max Halberstadt. circa 1921. Retrieved from christies.com. https://www.christies.com/lot/lot-6116407/?intObjectID=6116407)

II-73: **Wilson with Rear Admiral Cary Grayson, 1919** (Artist: Underwood & Underwood. Daniels. p. 282)

II-74: **President Wilson** (Artist: Jacques Reich. Copy after Pach Brothers Studio. 1914. Retrieved from the National Portrait Gallery, Smithsonian Institution; gift of Oswald D. Reich. https://www.si.edu/object/woodrow-wilson:npg_S_NPG.67.88)

II-75: **William Bullitt** (Artist: Unknown. Courtesy of the U.S. Department of State. Retrieved from Wikipedia. https://en.wikipedia.org/wiki/William_Christian_Bullitt_Jr.#/media/File:William_C_Bullitt.jpg)

II-76: **The signing of the Treaty of Versailles, June 28, 1919 – Seated (L to R): General Tasker Bliss, Edward House, Henry White, Robert Lansing, Wilson, Georges Clemenceau (France), David Lloyd George (Britain), A. Bonar Law (Britain), Arthur Balfour (Britain), Viscount Milner (Britain), G.N. Barnes (Britain), and The Marquis Sainozi (Japan)** (Artist: Sir William Orpen. Retrieved from Wikimedia Commons. https://commons.wikimedia.org/wiki/File:William_Orpen_%E2%80%93_The_Signing_of_Peace_in_the_Hall_of_Mirrors,_Versailles_1919,_Ausschnitt.jpg)

II-77: **The signatures of President Wilson, Robert Lansing, and Henry White from the American delegation on the Treaty of Versailles** (Universal History Archive/UIG/Getty Images. "The Treaty of Versailles Punished Defeated Germany With These Provisions." Retrieved from history.com. https://www.history.com/news/treaty-of-versailles-provisions)

II-78: **President Wilson (center) leaves the signing of the Treaty of Versailles alongside French Prime Minister Georges Clemenceau and British Prime Minister David Lloyd George** (Artist: Keystone View Company. Meadville, PA. 1919. circa 1918. Retrieved from the Library of Congress. www.loc.gov/item/2016646069/)

II-79: **President Wilson on his tour to promote the League of Nations, September 1919** (Artist: Unknown. "President Wilson Surveying Crowd during Trip West," 1919, WWPL2504, Woodrow Wilson Presidential Library Photo Collection, *Woodrow Wilson Presidential Library & Museum, Staunton, Virginia*. http://presidentwilson.org/items/show/27457)

II-80: **Headline announcing the termination of President Wilson's tour, September 26, 1919** (September 26, 1919. Retrieved from "Salem Breakfast on Bikes." http://breakfastonbikes.blogspot.com/2019/10/president-wilsons-strokes-and-persistent-race-riots-made-1919-tense-year.html)

II-81: **Dr. Francis Dercum** (Artist: Bain News Service. circa 1920. Source: Flickr Commons project, 2017. Retrieved from the Library of Congress. https://www.loc.gov/item/2014709684/)

II-82: **First Lady Edith Wilson guiding her husband, President Wilson, to sign documents, June 1920** (Artist: Harris & Ewing. June 1920. Retrieved from the Library of Congress. https://www.loc.gov/item/2005684886/)

II-83: **Secretary of State Robert Lansing** (Artist: Unknown. Eaton. p. 277)

II-84: **1920 Democratic Campaign Banner: James Cox and Franklin Roosevelt** (Artist: Unknown. 1920. Heritage Auctions. Retrieved from Retro Campaigns. https://retrocampaigns.tumblr.com/post/17955541149/james-m-cox-franklin-d-roosevelt-1920/amp)

II-85: **Senator Warren Harding during the 1920 presidential campaign** (Artist: Unknown. June 17, 1920. National Photo Company Collection (Library of Congress). Gift of Herbert French (1947). https://www.loc.gov/resource/npcc.01846/)

II-86: **German Chancellor Adolph Hitler, circa 1937** (Artist: Unknown. Associated Press. Retrieved from *The New York Times*. "How Hitler Took the World Into War." August 5, 1920. https://www.nytimes.com/2020/08/05/books/review/the-nazi-menace-benjamin-carter-hett.html)

II-87: **The Wilsons' post-presidential home on S St. in Washington, D.C.** (Author photo)

II-88: **Former President Wilson and Edith Wilson in the procession for the dedication of the Tomb of the Unknown Solider, November 11, 1921** (Artist: Underwood & Underwood. Daniels. p. 314)

II-89: **Former President Wilson, 1923 (age 66)** (Artist: Harris & Ewing. Annin. p. 370)

Notes

[1] Black. 16.
[2] Berg. 31.
[3] Berg. 32.
[4] Berg. 58.
[5] Berg. 38.
[6] Black. 24.
[7] Lawrence. 18.
[8] Berg. 47.
[9] Berg. 66.
[10] Freud and Bullitt. 58.
[11] Berg. 64.
[12] Black. 35.
[13] Berg. 62.
[14] Berg. 71.
[15] Freud and Bullitt. 20.
[16] Freud and Bullitt. 22.
[17] Berg. 81.
[18] Black. 39.
[19] Berg. 78.
[20] Berg. 83.
[21] Berg. 87.
[22] Black .37.
[23] Berg. 89.
[24] Berg. 90.
[25] Berg. 92.
[26] Berg. 87.
[27] Black. 42.
[28] Berg. 92.
[29] Thompson. 28.
[30] Berg. 100.
[31] Clements. 12.
[32] Auchincloss. 11.
[33] Clements. 17.
[34] Auchincloss. 16.
[35] Black. 19.
[36] Berg. 110.
[37] Berg. 110.
[38] Black. 53.
[39] Berg. 118.
[40] Berg. 119.
[41] Berg. 120.
[42] Black. 66.
[43] Berg. 120.
[44] Berg. 120.
[45] Lawrence. 22.
[46] Lawrence. 21.
[47] Lawrence. 21.
[48] Berg. 134.
[49] Clements. 23.
[50] Thompson. 37.

[51] Berg. 135.
[52] Berg. 135.
[53] Berg. 135.
[54] Clements. 29.
[55] Berg. 138.
[56] Clements. 31.
[57] Berg. 141.
[58] Berg. 151.
[59] Berg. 153.
[60] Black. 71.
[61] Berg. 154.
[62] Clements. 31.
[63] Clements. 40.
[64] Auchincloss. 22.
[65] Berg. 155.
[66] Berg. 43-44.
[67] Saunders, Frances. *Love and Guilt: Woodrow Wilson and Mary Hulbert*. American Heritage. Volume 30, Issue 3. April/May 1979. https://www.americanheritage.com/love-and-guilt-woodrow-wilson-and-mary-hulbert
[68] Saunders, Frances. *Love and Guilt: Woodrow Wilson and Mary Hulbert*. American Heritage. Volume 30, Issue 3. April/May 1979. https://www.americanheritage.com/love-and-guilt-woodrow-wilson-and-mary-hulbert
[69] Saunders, Frances. *Love and Guilt: Woodrow Wilson and Mary Hulbert*. American Heritage. Volume 30, Issue 3. April/May 1979. https://www.americanheritage.com/love-and-guilt-woodrow-wilson-and-mary-hulbert
[70] Clements. 44.
[71] Clements. 43.
[72] Berg. 158.
[73] Clements. 47.
[74] Black. 80.
[75] Berg. 175.
[76] Auchincloss. 25.
[77] Berg. 146.
[78] Berg. 146.
[79] Berg. 182.
[80] Berg. 182.
[81] Berg. 182.
[82] Clements. 55.
[83] Tumulty. 470.
[84] Tumulty. 19.
[85] Black .97.
[86] Tumulty. 21.
[87] Tumulty. 20.
[88] Berg. 197.
[89] Berg. 201.
[90] Tumulty. 28.
[91] Tumulty. 41.
[92] Clements. 58.
[93] Berg. 203.
[94] Berg. 206.
[95] Tumulty. 60.

---

[96] Auchincloss. 32.
[97] Berg. 215.
[98] Black. 108.
[99] Tumulty. 97.
[100] Lawrence. 68.
[101] Berg. 227.
[102] Manners, William. *TR and Will: A Friendship that Split the Republican Party*. Harcourt, Brace & World, Inc. New York, NY. 1969. p. 238.
[103] Berg. 236.
[104] Tumulty. 117.
[105] Berg. 234.
[106] Berg. 236.
[107] Cooper, Jr., John. *The Warrior and the Priest: Woodrow Wilson and Theodore Roosevelt*. The Belknap Press of Harvard University Press. Cambridge, MA. 1983. p. 208.
[108] Lawrence. 84.
[109] Clements. 80.
[110] Tumulty. 457.
[111] Berg. 240.
[112] Berg. 269.
[113] Berg. 236.
[114] Lawrence. 63.
[115] Clements. 90.
[116] Auchincloss. 35.
[117] Clements. 91.
[118] Lawrence. 82.
[119] Anderson, Judith. *William Howard Taft: An Intimate History*. W.W. Norton & Company. New York, NY. 1981. p. 250.
[120] Constitution of the United States: A Transcription. Article II, Section 1. America's Founding Documents. National Archives. https://www.archives.gov/founding-docs/constitution-transcript
[121] Berg. 275.
[122] Berg. 276.
[123] Auchincloss. 46.
[124] Lawrence. 85.
[125] Lawrence. 232.
[126] Clements. 124.
[127] Berg. 288.
[128] Tumulty. 147.
[129] Berg. 291.
[130] Lawrence. 83.
[131] Berg. 294.
[132] Black. 118.
[133] Berg. 315.
[134] Berg. 313.
[135] Berg. 313.
[136] Black. 119.
[137] Black. 119.
[138] Black. 119.
[139] Berg. 300.
[140] Berg. 312.
[141] Berg. 309.

[142] Du Bois, W.E.B. "Another Open Letter to Woodrow Wilson." September 1913. *Teaching American History*. Retrieved no October 19, 2022. https://teachingamericanhistory.org/document/another-open-letter-to-woodrow-wilson/
[143] Berg. 308.
[144] Lawrence. 109.
[145] Berg. 329.
[146] Black. 125.
[147] Tumulty. 152.
[148] Black. 125.
[149] Tumulty. 163.
[150] Black. 121.
[151] Tumulty. 162.
[152] Berg. 325.
[153] Tumulty. 473.
[154] Black. 144.
[155] Berg. 344.
[156] Black. 138.
[157] Berg. 336.
[158] Berg. 335.
[159] Berg. 336.
[160] Berg. 344.
[161] Berg. 346.
[162] Berg. 346.
[163] Berg. 346.
[164] Berg. 347.
[165] Berg. 347.
[166] Auchincloss. 71.
[167] Berg. 351.
[168] Berg. 355.
[169] E. Wilson. 54.
[170] E. Wilson. 56.
[171] E. Wilson. 56.
[172] E. Wilson. 58.
[173] E. Wilson. 60.
[174] E. Wilson. 61.
[175] Manners, William. *TR and Will: A Friendship that Split the Republican Party*. Harcourt, Brace & World, Inc. New York, NY. 1969. p. 296.
[176] Auchincloss. 61.
[177] Berg. 364.
[178] Auchincloss. 72.
[179] E. Wilson. 63.
[180] Berg. 368.
[181] Auchincloss. 62.
[182] Berg. 372.
[183] E. Wilson. 75.
[184] Berg. 374.
[185] Berg. 377.
[186] Clements. 198.
[187] E. Wilson. 77.
[188] E. Wilson. 78.
[189] Berg. 377.

[190] Berg. 383.
[191] Black. 161.
[192] Berg. 392.
[193] Berg. 396.
[194] Berg. 396.
[195] Tumulty. 200.
[196] Burton, David. *William Howard Taft: In the Public Service*. Robert E. Krieger Publishing Company. Malabar, FL. 1986. p. 132.
[197] Berg. 401.
[198] Clements. 163.
[199] Berg. 384.
[200] E. Wilson. 116.
[201] Clements. 164.
[202] Clements. 165.
[203] Clements. 165.
[204] Thompson. 133.
[205] Black. 165.
[206] Tumulty. 255.
[207] Thayer, William. *Theodore Roosevelt: An Intimate Biography*. Houghton Mifflin Company. Boston, MA. 1919. p. 419.
[208] Lawrence. 203.
[209] Berg. 426.
[210] Clements. 167.
[211] Tumulty. 160.
[212] Wilson, Woodrow. Second Inaugural Address. March 5, 1917. Retrieved from: *Presidential Inaugural Addresses*. Word Cloud Classics. San Diego, CA. 2019. p. 251.
[213] Wilson, Woodrow. Second Inaugural Address. March 5, 1917. Retrieved from: *Presidential Inaugural Addresses*. Word Cloud Classics. San Diego, CA. 2019. p. 252.
[214] Wilson, Woodrow. Second Inaugural Address. March 5, 1917. Retrieved from: *Presidential Inaugural Addresses*. Word Cloud Classics. San Diego, CA. 2019. p. 253.
[215] Berg. 431.
[216] Berg. 431.
[217] Berg. 432.
[218] Clements. 168.
[219] Berg. 435.
[220] Lawrence. 208.
[221] Black. 168.
[222] Tumulty. 256.
[223] Tumulty. 257.
[224] Brands, H.W. *T.R.: The Last Romantic*. BasicBooks. New York, NY. 1997. p. 781.
[225] Tumulty. 288.
[226] Brands, H.W. *T.R.: The Last Romantic*. BasicBooks. New York, NY. 1997. p. 784.
[227] Clements. 188.
[228] Clements. 188.
[229] Berg. 441.
[230] Berg. 442.
[231] Black. 178.
[232] Clements. 173.
[233] Berg. 450.
[234] Berg. 494.
[235] Clements. 183.

[236] Brands, H.W. *T.R.: The Last Romantic*. BasicBooks. New York, NY. 1997. p. 788.
[237] Wells, H.G. *The War that Will End War*. Frank & Cecil Palmer. Red Lion Court, E.C. London. 1914.
[238] Wilson, Woodrow. *The Fourteen Points*. January 1918. *The Points, Summarized.* The National WWI Museum and Memorial. Kansas City, MO. Retrieved November 7, 2022. https://www.theworldwar.org/learn/peace/fourteen-points
[239] Berg. 472.
[240] Freud and Bullitt. 270.
[241] Berg. 471.
[242] Lodge. 130.
[243] Berg. 485.
[244] Berg. 488.
[245] Berg. 487.
[246] Lawrence. 137.
[247] Lawrence. 138.
[248] Berg. 493.
[249] Berg. 496.
[250] Berg. 497.
[251] Tumulty, 307.
[252] Lawrence. 236.
[253] Tumulty. 330.
[254] Lawrence. 238.
[255] Tumulty. 328.
[256] Berg. 513.
[257] E. Wilson. 170.
[258] Berg. 515.
[259] Berg. 519.
[260] Freud and Bullitt. 251.
[261] Lawrence. 313.
[262] Lawrence. 313.
[263] Lawrence. 314.
[264] Lawrence. 316.
[265] Constitution of the United States: A Transcription. Article I, Section 6. America's Founding Documents. National Archives. https://www.archives.gov/founding-docs/constitution-transcript
[266] Berg. 18.
[267] Black. 190.
[268] Berg. 18.
[269] Berg. 521.
[270] Berg. 523.
[271] Berg. 521.
[272] Berg. 612.
[273] Berg. 20.
[274] Clements. 198.
[275] Berg. 524.
[276] Lawrence. 259.
[277] Berg. 545.
[278] Berg. 533.
[279] Black. 203.
[280] Lodge. 82.

[281] Wilson, Woodrow. "Address at the Third Plenary Session of the Peace Conference, Paris, France." February 14, 1919. Retrieved from "The American Presidency Project." U.C. Santa Barbara. https://www.presidency.ucsb.edu/documents/address-the-third-plenary-session-the-peace-conference-paris-france

[282] Wilson, Woodrow. "Address at the Third Plenary Session of the Peace Conference, Paris, France." February 14, 1919. Retrieved from "The American Presidency Project." U.C. Santa Barbara. https://www.presidency.ucsb.edu/documents/address-the-third-plenary-session-the-peace-conference-paris-france

[283] Wilson, Woodrow. "Address at the Third Plenary Session of the Peace Conference, Paris, France." February 14, 1919. Retrieved from "The American Presidency Project." U.C. Santa Barbara. https://www.presidency.ucsb.edu/documents/address-the-third-plenary-session-the-peace-conference-paris-france

[284] Wilson, Woodrow. "Address at the Third Plenary Session of the Peace Conference, Paris, France." February 14, 1919. Retrieved from "The American Presidency Project." U.C. Santa Barbara. https://www.presidency.ucsb.edu/documents/address-the-third-plenary-session-the-peace-conference-paris-france

[285] Freud and Bullitt. 228.

[286] Lodge. 145.

[287] Freud & Bullitt. 229.

[288] Knight, Lucian. *Woodrow Wilson: The Dreamer and The Dream*. The Johnson-Dallis Company. Atlanta, GA. 1924. p. 130.

[289] Auchincloss. 35.

[290] Berg. 556.

[291] Freud and Bullitt. 238.

[292] CPI Inflation Calculator. U.S. Bureau of Labor Statistics. Date Range: March 1919 to October 2022. https://www.bls.gov/data/inflation_calculator.htm

[293] Berg. 566.

[294] Berg. 567.

[295] Freud and Bullitt. 66.

[296] Freud and Bullitt. 115.

[297] Berg. 566.

[298] Freud and Bullitt. 274.

[299] Freud and Bullitt. xi.

[300] Freud and Bullitt. 243.

[301] Clements. 204.

[302] Tumulty. 350.

[303] Berg. 570.

[304] Freud and Bullitt. 254.

[305] Freud and Bullitt. 253.

[306] Freud and Bullitt. 254.

[307] Wilson, Woodrow. "Address at the Third Plenary Session of the Peace Conference, Paris, France." February 14, 1919. Retrieved from "The American Presidency Project." U.C. Santa Barbara. https://www.presidency.ucsb.edu/documents/address-the-third-plenary-session-the-peace-conference-paris-france

[308] Berg. 580.

[309] Freud and Bullitt. 261.

[310] Freud and Bullitt. 271.

[311] Freud and Bullitt. 233.

[312] Freud and Bullitt. 256.

[313] Freud and Bullitt. 268.

[314] Berg. 593.

[315] Berg. 600.
[316] Berg. 606.
[317] Clements. 211.
[318] Auchincloss. 95.
[319] Berg. 601.
[320] Berg. 601.
[321] Auchincloss. 124.
[322] Clements. 212.
[323] Lodge. 174.
[324] Tumulty. 452.
[325] Gutzman, Kevin. *James Madison and the Making of America*. St. Martin's Press. New York, NY. 2012. p. 89.
[326] Berg. 552.
[327] Berg. 567.
[328] Black. 252.
[329] Berg. 721.
[330] Auchincloss. 112.
[331] Freud and Bullitt. 284.
[332] Tumulty. 435.
[333] Berg. 623.
[334] Freud and Bullitt. 286.
[335] Berg. 624.
[336] Freud and Bullitt. 287.
[337] Berg. 628.
[338] Berg. 627.
[339] Tumulty. 442.
[340] E. Wilson. 280.
[341] Lodge. 136.
[342] Lodge. 138.
[343] Lodge. 175.
[344] Lodge. 173.
[345] Lodge. 184.
[346] E. Wilson. 282.
[347] E. Wilson. 263.
[348] Black. 220.
[349] Freud and Bullitt. 290.
[350] Berg. 634.
[351] Clements. 215.
[352] E. Wilson. 284.
[353] Tumulty. 447.
[354] Lawrence. 279.
[355] Berg. 639.
[356] E. Wilson. 287.
[357] Berg. 641.
[358] Berg. 642.
[359] Dercum, Francis. "Dr. Dercum's Memoranda." October 20, 1919. Cary T. Grayson Papers. Woodrow Wilson Presidential Library, Staunton, Virginia. http://presidentwilson.org/items/show/21527.
[360] E. Wilson. 289.
[361] E. Wilson. 289.
[362] E. Wilson. 289.

[363] E. Wilson. 289.
[364] Dercum, Francis X. (Francis Xavier), 1856-1931 and Philadelphia Press, "President Will Never Recover, Is View of Dr. Bevan," 1920 February 16, WWP16188, Cary T. Grayson Papers, *Woodrow Wilson Presidential Library & Museum, Staunton, Virginia.*
[365] Grayson, Cary T. (Cary Travers), 1878-1938, "Woodrow Wilson Stroke," 1919 October, WWP16061, Cary T. Grayson Papers, *Woodrow Wilson Presidential Library & Museum, Staunton, Virginia.*
[366] E. Wilson. 290.
[367] Lawrence. 283.
[368] Tumulty. 444.
[369] E. Wilson. 291.
[370] Berg. 648.
[371] Berg. 655.
[372] Clements. 218.
[373] Auchincloss. 118.
[374] Berg. 656.
[375] Lodge. 216.
[376] Lodge. 213.
[377] E. Wilson. 301.
[378] Berg. 674.
[379] Berg. 647.
[380] E. Wilson. 301.
[381] Berg. 661.
[382] Berg. 666.
[383] Berg. 667.
[384] Severn, Bill. *William Howard Taft: The President Who Became Chief Justice*. David McKay Company, Inc. New York, NY. 1970. p. 148.
[385] Severn, Bill. *William Howard Taft: The President Who Became Chief Justice*. David McKay Company, Inc. New York, NY. 1970. p. 152.
[386] Lawrence. 292.
[387] Clements. 220.
[388] Lodge. 225.
[389] Berg. 677.
[390] Berg. 592
[391] Berg. 677.
[392] Grayson, Cary T. (Cary Travers), 1878-1938, "Cary T. Grayson Diary," 1920 March 20, WWP16224, Cary T. Grayson Papers, *Woodrow Wilson Presidential Library & Museum, Staunton, Virginia.*
[393] Lodge. 82.
[394] "The Covenant of the League of Nations." (Article 1-26) Retrieved from the Department of State, Office of the Historian. https://history.state.gov/historicaldocuments/frus1919Parisv13/ch10subch1
[395] "The Covenant of the League of Nations." (Article 1-26) Retrieved from the Department of State, Office of the Historian. https://history.state.gov/historicaldocuments/frus1919Parisv13/ch10subch1
[396] Berg. 684.
[397] Berg. 689.
[398] Lawrence. 301.
[399] Lodge. 210
[400] Tumulty. 501.

[401] Hitler, Adolph. Speech on the Treaty of Versailles. April 17, 1923. Retrieved from Bartleby. https://www.bartleby.com/questions-and-answers/speech-on-the-treaty-of-versailles-april-17-1923-adolf-hitler/e1637696-c88a-4fc8-9027-0fab923d3453

[402] Hitler, Adolph. Speech to the German Reichstag. May 17, 1933. Originally from "The Speeches of Adolph Hitler." Edited by Norman Baynes. April 1922-August 1939. Vol. 2. New York, NY. 1969. Retrieved from "American Foreign Relations" – Encyclopedia of American Foriegn Policy. Viewed on November 30, 2022. https://www.americanforeignrelations.com/E-N/Loans-and-Debt-Resolution-Hitler-repudiates-the-versailles-treaty-and-reparations.html

[403] Black. 233.

[404] Berg. 566.

[405] Berg. 686.

[406] Lawrence. 309.

[407] Lawrence. 308.

[408] E. Wilson. 312.

[409] Berg. 708.

[410] Holmes, George. *Wilson-Tumulty Breach Widened by Repudiation of 'Message.' The Pittsburgh-Post Gazette.* April 14, 1922. https://news.google.com/newspapers?nid=1144&dat=19220414&id=drgaAAAAIBAJ&sjid=xkkEAAAAIBAJ&pg=1143,5360412

[411] Berg. 716.

[412] Holmes, George. *Wilson-Tumulty Breach Widened by Repudiation of 'Message.' The Pittsburgh-Post Gazette.* April 14, 1922. https://news.google.com/newspapers?nid=1144&dat=19220414&id=drgaAAAAIBAJ&sjid=xkkEAAAAIBAJ&pg=1143,5360412

[413] E. Wilson. 333.

[414] Berg. 719.

[415] E. Wilson. 335.

[416] E. Wilson. 337.

[417] Cooper, John. *Woodrow Wilson: A Biography*. Alfred A Knopf. New York, NY. 2009. p. 591.

[418] E. Wilson. 356.

[419] Berg. 736.

Index

PRESIDENTIAL CHRONICLES
VOLUME VI: PROGRESSIVISM AND PROSPERITY
III: THE LIFE OF WARREN HARDING
DAVID FISHER

III: The Life of Warren Harding

Preface

Teapot Dome. Those two words seem to represent the lasting legacy of the nation's 29th President, Warren Harding, and they connote a legacy of scandal. And while there was some malfeasance in and around the Harding administration, there was so much more to this man's life and political career. Warren Harding won a landslide victory to become his nation's leader in 1920. The American people widely embraced his "Return to Normalcy" campaign as an antidote to the visionary efforts yet ultimate failures of his predecessor, Woodrow Wilson. Harding remained popular throughout his two-and-a-half years in office, persevering through challenging economic times before the American economy began to soar shortly before his untimely death. His international disarmament conference yielded landmark agreements among the major powers of the earth, earning high praise for the American executive, once again in sharp contrast to his predecessor's inability to ratify his global diplomatic endeavors. Harding died unexpectedly while on a goodwill tour of the American West, including the first visit by an American President to the territory of Alaska. As the nation mourned, many assumed that Harding would be fondly remembered by posterity. That would not be the case.

There was an undercurrent of corruption that ran through Washington, D.C. during Harding's tenure in office. Those rumors became front-page news in the immediate aftermath of Harding's death with a series of highly publicized congressional hearings and court cases. Flamboyant characters took the witness stand offering wild tales of pervasive graft that reached into the President's Cabinet. For the first time in American history, a Cabinet Secretary was convicted of a crime and sent to prison. Additional charges were levied against members of the so-called "Ohio Gang," which primarily consisted of Harding cronies who weren't government officials but were portrayed as coming to Washington to peddle influence to anyone with sufficient cash. While some truth could be found in these troubling tales, much of the damning testimony was exaggerated, some was outright fabricated, and none directly implicated Harding in any corrupt act. Nevertheless, the sensational accounts found the headlines and into the psyche of the American people, while any retractions were typically ignored.

And then there were the affairs. Harding had two long-term extramarital dalliances that also became very public after his death. One was the subject of a highly detailed tell-all memoir from the young woman who claimed to be the father of Harding's only child. While Harding's friends and family sought to discredit Nan Britton's story, the public gobbled up her book and kept the salacious nature of the Harding presidency in the minds of the American people. Over the ensuing decades, more details would emerge, including the often lurid letters Harding had written to the other object of his affections, one Carrie Phillips. Those letters were finally released to the public in 2015, around the same time that DNA evidence pointed directly to Harding as the father of Nan Britton's child. Warren Harding has been dead for 100 years, but had rarely rested in peace.

Harding was hardly the only President to have affairs. Nor was he the only one to have associates charged with crimes, even though little if any of the wrongdoing was directly traced to Harding himself. Yet the sensational nature of the charges against his administration, the drip-drip-drip of new tales of misconduct, and the never-ending revelations of his affairs, have propelled Harding's reputation into the cellar of presidential estimation. This was not the Harding as viewed by his contemporaries. What the people around the dawn of the 20th Century experienced was a generous, hard-working man who personally shepherded a defunct small-town newspaper into a thriving business. They saw someone promoting the best in people, serving as a harmonizer in his community and in politics. They cherished a kind man who enjoyed life and relished his interactions with people of all sorts. They enjoyed someone aptly described as "just plain folks." Unfortunately, "just plain folks" didn't translate well to the spotlight of the presidency and the nation's capital. For "just plain folks" also often have skeletons in their closet and friends who deceive, characteristics that are rarely forgiven in the highest world of American politics. The goodwill that Warren Harding generated through a lifetime of good works, including some noteworthy accomplishments as his nation's President, quickly got washed out of his story in favor of the scandals. The full story is certainly more nuanced than that, and deserves to be told.

1. A Young Man Buys a Newspaper

A few years after William Bradford and his Pilgrims landed the *Mayflower* at Plymouth Rock in 1620, the first of the Harding clan followed. It was just three years later when Richard Harding, of English Puritan ancestry, settled just to the north of that initial landing in a town called Braintree. Over the course of the next century and a half, the Harding family grew, only to be decimated during an Indian massacre during the Revolutionary War. As the survivors got on with their lives after the Americans won their independence, some of the Hardings sought opportunities elsewhere, particularly in northern Pennsylvania. By 1820, some were ready to move again, with Amos Harding in the lead, loading up his family members and their belongings into covered wagons for the trek into neighboring Ohio. These folks finally settled in the tiny hamlet of Blooming Grove, in the central portion of the relatively new state. These pioneers essentially built their town from scratch, primarily working the land to feed themselves and make ends meet.

As the generations evolved, along came George Harding, who was mostly referred to by his middle name, Tryon. Tryon was raised as a farmer but didn't feel restricted to that profession. After graduating from the college in nearby Iberia, he volunteered to serve in the Union Army during the Civil War, even meeting President Abraham Lincoln on an occasion that brought him to the nation's capital. While home recuperating from an illness, Tryon married Phoebe Dickerson, a woman of Dutch heritage who was a devout Methodist. Phoebe became a leader in religious activities that often served as key social events in the small community.

III-1: Harding's father, Dr. George (Tryon) Harding

After the war, Tryon supplemented his farming duties with work as a teacher and eventually decided to become a homeopathic physician, which was in high demand on the rural

III-2: Harding's mother, Phoebe Harding

plains. Phoebe would also make her way into the medical field, serving as a midwife. But her primary responsibilities were in the home, raising the couple's eight children, the first of whom was born on November 2, 1865. In their two-story farmhouse, built of walnut with an oak frame and surrounded by cherry trees, Warren Harding came into the world, the first President to be born after the Civil War.

Harding was raised in farm country, spending his first eight years in Blooming Grove. It was a tiny town featuring a store, hotel, post office, and a couple of taverns, but mostly surrounded by farms. Harding's most intimate relationship in his youth was with his mother, who was considered quiet but firm, deeply religious, and protective of her children. She loved flowers, which had an effect on her Winnie (the name she always used for her eldest child), who, in his adult years, always arranged to send her a fresh bouquet every Sunday morning even when he was out of town. While Tryon and Phoebe were constantly pulled away from the farm to perform medical house calls, there was little money generated from these duties.

III-3: The home of Harding's birth in Blooming Grove, OH

By 1873, the Hardings decided to make a move, heading to Caledonia, a slightly larger community about 15 miles to the west. They settled into a white frame house with green trimmings a few doors down from the town square. Here they found more opportunities for paying customers for their medical services, but the farm continued to be the principal source of their existence. Warren Harding performed all the typical jobs one would expect on a family farm in the latter half of the 19th Century. He milked the cows, watered and fed the horses, cleared the land, and tilled the soil. He attended the local school and learned to play a variety of brass instruments after his father bought him a cornet at the age of ten. He even served as drum major for a time for the Caledonia Brass Band. Harding was happy to take on odd jobs around town, and he and a buddy became particularly adept at painting neighborhood barns. Mostly, Harding was known for his warm, genial personality. As he was throughout his life, he liked people and they liked him.

At the age of 12, Harding got his first taste of the career which would occupy most of his adult life. "Caledonia is the town where I first got printer's ink on my fingers," Harding later recalled. "I was a 'devil,' as print-shop apprentices are known, in the office of the *Caledonia Argus*, and learned to stick type, feed press, make up forms and wash rollers there."[1] Tryon had bought a half-interest in the paper, and Harding was anxious to help out. Little did he know at the time that he would spend nearly four decades in the newspaper business.

It was a difficult time for the Hardings. Money was tight for the growing family, so they picked up stakes again and settled onto a 42-acre farm, needing to rely more on agriculture than medicine to pay the bills. And then tragedy struck when two of Harding's siblings, five-year-old Charley and seven-year-old Persilla, both died of jaundice in 1878. Persevering through these challenges, the family remained committed to education, and Harding led the way by following in his father's footsteps. Ohio Central College in Iberia offered a secondary education for

III-4: Ohio Central College in Iberia, OH

farm boys like him throughout the region. Using some of the same textbooks his father had stored away after his tenure in Iberia, Harding joined some 60 students and three faculty for the four-year program, which he found to be a good fit. "I am still persuaded that the smaller college, with the personal contact between the members of the faculty and student body, was the best educational institution of which we have ever been able to boast," Harding later recalled.[2] Harding was active in and out of the classroom. He became president of the Philomathic Literary Society, played alto horn in the Iberia Brass Band, and became editor of the college newspaper. The Iberia *Spectator* was his primary focus in his final term at Ohio Central, getting a four-page issue out the door every two weeks – a total of six issues before graduating. "The *Spectator*," Harding said, "is taken by every family in our city excepting a few stingy old grumblers who take no more interest in home enterprise than a mule in a hive of bees."[3] Harding clearly had a knack and a fondness for the newspaper business from a very early age.

When Harding left Iberia in 1882, he didn't return to Caledonia, as the family was on the move again. The next settlement took them another ten miles to the west, to the growing town of Marion – the place Harding would call home for the rest of his life. For Harding, Marion represented a significant change from his earlier surroundings. "My first impression [of Marion] was that of very much a city, in which I feared I should be hopelessly lost," he later recalled. "I came from the farm and village, and the county seat of 4,000 loomed big in my vision, because I had seen nothing greater."[4] Marion was indeed an up-and-coming community, already boasting three rail lines passing through, with direct connections to Chicago, Indianapolis, and the state capital at Columbus. With a new courthouse being built, and some manufacturing companies settling in, Marion had moved beyond a collection of farms. As a recent college graduate, Warren Harding was ready to

III-5: Marion, Ohio (1887)

find his place in the world.

He started with some teaching, signing on at the Little White Schoolhouse, making about $30/month. While he looked back fondly on the profession, later saying, "The school teacher is now and will ever remain one of the most important factors in building up the citizenship of America,"[5] the experiment was short-lived. Harding spent just one year in the classroom. He tried to study law, but Blackstone's *Commentaries* bored him, and he gave up the pursuit partly because he needed money. Harding did have some accomplishments selling insurance for a brief period, but none of these activities caught his fancy. Where he did have success was making friends. Harding quickly emerged as "one of the boys," enjoying playing pool and poker, spending time at the Merry-Roll-Round roller skating rink, serving as the back-up first baseman on the local baseball team, and finding a real home with the Marion People's Band. Harding not only played in the street concerts every Saturday night, he also became the band manager. In May 1883, he entered the band into a state tournament in Findlay, about 50 miles away. He convinced everyone to borrow money to pay for the uniforms required for the competition. Harding was proud that the Marion entry earned first place in its division and also relieved that the result came with a $150 prize that more than paid for the uniforms.

III-6: Harding as a teacher, circa 1882 (age ~17)

But none of these ventures was establishing Harding in any form of a career. Fortunately, his father was often dabbling in various businesses beyond the farm and his medical opportunities, and once again, Tryon decided to invest in a newspaper. Tryon partnered with Ben Demster to purchase the *Marion Daily Star* out of bankruptcy in May 1884. Given his prior experience in Caledonia and Iberia, the 18-year-old Harding was tasked to be the editor of the enterprise. Almost immediately, he took advantage of one of the perks of a local paper, which was free passes to ride most trains. Just a month after his entry into the newspaper business,

Harding found himself at the Republican National Convention in Chicago. He was there as a reporter, but also as an advocate. Harding had followed his father into the Republican political camp, and he was particularly enamored with the former Speaker of the House and Senator from Maine, James Blaine, who finally earned his party's nomination that year after several previous attempts had failed. Harding was thrilled at the result and couldn't wait to return to Marion to share the stories of the convention with the readers of the *Star*. Unfortunately, as soon as he returned home, he found a padlock on the door to the *Star's* office. While he was gone, a judgment had been placed against the property his father had put up to secure his loan to buy his portion of the paper, upon which the sheriff once again took possession of the property. Just like that, Warren Harding was out of the newspaper business just over a month after getting into it.

The *Daily Star* was the smallest of the three newspapers serving the town of Marion. Local papers were typically aligned with one of the major political parties, partly because this assured them of getting the printing business and announcements emanating from the local government. The revenue from these government contracts was often essential to keeping a local paper afloat. Also in town was the *Mirror*, which was run by James Vaughn. It was a Democratic paper, like much of the county. Then there was the *Independent*, which, despite its name, was staunchly Republican in its editorial views, and under the longtime care of George Crawford. When the *Star* was shuttered, Harding sought to stay in the business by seeking employment at one of the other papers in town. Vaughn found Harding likable (as did everyone) and decided to give him a chance. Despite his Republican leanings, Harding signed on as a reporter for the *Mirror* for $7/week. This ended up as another short-term venture. Late in the presidential campaign, Harding showed up to work sporting a James Blaine hat. When Crawford told him to take it off and never wear it to work again, Harding decided to keep the hat on his head and leave the *Mirror* behind him. He then watched Blaine go down to defeat in an extremely close election at the hands of Grover Cleveland, leaving Harding disappointed in politics and once again out of a job. But that election night in 1884 served as a turning point in the career and the life of Warren Harding, as he ventured to get back into the newspaper business, and this time for good.

Sulking over the loss of Blaine, Harding went to grab a bite on election night at Meily's Restaurant on N. Main Street with a couple of buddies and an idea he wanted to pitch. Over a round of oysters, Harding asked his friends Jack Warwick and John Sickel to become his partners, purchase the *Daily Star*, and bring it back to life. Harding estimated $300 should do it. Mind you, Warren Harding was only 19 years old, while Sickel was 20, and Warwick was the senior of the bunch at 23. None of this mattered to the young entrepreneurs who agreed to make the run as newspapermen. Sickel had recently inherited around $1,600, so coming up with his portion was no problem. He then loaned Warwick his $100 contribution, and it is believed that Harding got his stake from his father. With the payment, the sheriff took the lock off the door, and the three young men went to work in the tiny two rooms that housed the entire operation of the *Star*. It was a bit of a sorry sight according to Warwick, who claimed, "There never was a place more generally and particularly unfitted, in all its appointments, for a newspaper office than this second floor front and back which we occupied immediately following the adoption of the sick kitten."[6] Harding's goal wasn't just to resuscitate the "sick kitten," but to turn it into a thriving concern.

This was not going to be easy. The *Star's* rivals weren't about to cede any of their business to these upstarts. This was particularly true of Crawford, who used his editorial page to scoff at the new owners of the *Star*, implying almost immediately after their purchase that the new ownership wouldn't last. Harding took up his pen to respond immediately to these charges, doing so in no uncertain terms. "Some man is a willful liar," Harding wrote. "We refer to the man who is telling around that there will be another change in the *Star*. The only change anticipated is that of making the paper better. Persons expecting to damage the *Star* by their silly lies are wasting their breath."[7] If he was going to go down, it certainly wasn't going to be

III-7: Harding, shortly after he purchased the Star, circa 1885 (age ~20)

quietly. And Harding was serious, fully intending to make the *Star* a success. He decided to make those intentions clear to all of Marion.

> Many times we have been interrogated as to our intentions. 'Are you going to sell soon?' 'When will the next change occur?' and like questions reach us daily. To answer these questions emphatically, we say, 'Look for no more changes.' Our egotism tells us that if we can't make the *Star* a success, no one can. … We believe that we will gain your confidence, at least we hope to merit it, and then we shall certainly obtain your patronage. Try the *Star* and if it doesn't suit you, stop it. We are pleasantly located on the second floor of the Miller block, where we invite you to call and see us. Pardon us for these remarks concerning ourselves and hereafter we will not parade the columns of the *Star* with the publishers' intentions.[8]

And with that, they continued to dive headfirst into making the *Star* a success.

Neither the *Mirror* nor the *Independent* was a daily paper, and Harding was committed to getting his product out every evening. At the start, each issue carried four pages. The front page typically featured national and international news, most often taken from other papers via a cooperative agreement. Every day dozens of papers would arrive at the Marion post office and train station. Harding would scan these for topics he felt would be interesting to Marionites, and the front page would be constructed accordingly. The local features typically began on Page 2, and this was where Harding shined ahead of his peers. Harding was everywhere looking for stories. He introduced himself to folks at the coffee shop, local stores, the hotel, bank, roller rink, courthouse, and street corner. He got to know the people of Marion and was happy to share their stories. He wasn't looking for dirt but rather seeking

MARION DAILY STAR.

500 OVERCOATS
MEN, BOYS
CHILDREN!!
VERY LOWEST!!
SAM. OPPENHEIMER

III-8: Marion Daily Star, December 1, 1885

positive stories that would make people feel good about themselves and their community.

The *Star* was initially a tiny operation where Harding performed just about every job. He edited the national page, served as a local reporter, wrote editorials (which reflected his Republican leanings), and regularly set the type, made up the forms, applied the ink, and ran the press. His writing was plain – as straightforward as the man himself. He worked non-stop, living at home with his parents while walking to and from the office several times a day. "[Harding's desk] looked like a jumble of things," according to Warwick, "but he knew the location of the papers and clippings stowed away. His early habits as a printer looking after matters about the shop caused him to use a desk but seldom. He acquired the habit of writing with his copy paper perched on his knee, or on the arm of a chair."[9] It may have been a bit messy, but Harding was crafting his own style and starting to have an impact.

III-9: Harding's desk at the Daily Star

After only a few weeks, Sickel decided this wasn't the life for him and sold his share to Harding. Warwick stuck with the effort for several years, contributing anywhere he was needed. In the early years, the paper always seemed a day or two away from insolvency. The *Star* had about 500 subscribers from the previous owners. They paid ten cents a week for the paper, while single issues were available for three cents apiece. Initially, there was no delivery service. People just stopped by the office, had a brief chat, and left with their paper in hand. But none of this was going to keep the paper afloat without advertisers, and the *Star* was in short supply at the beginning of the venture. Harding made it his mission to visit local shop owners and businessmen every day, trying to convince them that advertising in the *Star* was the best investment they could make. "Run an ad in the *Star*," he would tell them, "and you'll boost your sales."

Putting his money where his mouth was, at times he would go further. "If your business doesn't show an increase you needn't pay for the ad" he might offer[10] – anything to get folks to give him a chance. It didn't take long for people to start paying attention to the product Harding was producing. Less than six months after they re-started the paper, the Delaware (OH) *Chronicle* noted that "The little twinkling Star at Marion has at last fallen into good hands, and shows its effect by getting out a daily that contains much more news and with each succeeding issue is improving. Marionites could do no better thing than by giving it a most liberal support."[11] Yes, it was a good start, but taking on the entrenched competition was hardly going to be easy.

In order to grow the *Star* into a thriving concern, Harding had to deal with an aggressive competitor in the form of George Crawford. Crawford had been running the *Independent* for more than two decades by the time Harding purchased the *Star*. The former attorney resented the young upstart, including the potential competition for Republican government advertising and notices. When Harding started to push for competitive bidding for some of these contracts, Crawford ratcheted up the noxious rhetoric in his own publication. While Harding sought to stay above the fray, there were some occasions when he couldn't hold back. One of the most acerbic responses from Harding came after the *Independent* attacked Harding's father in February 1886, calling him a fake Republican and a quack doctor. Harding refused to take the insult lying down. Speaking of Crawford, Harding wrote:

> His sordid soul is gangrened with jealousy. This sour, disgruntled and disappointed old ass gets frenzied at the prospects of a successful rival, and must vent the feelings of his miserable soul by lying about those he cannot browbeat or cajole. He belittles men whose shoes he is unfit to lace, and his mind has become a heterogeneous mass of jealous ideas and dissatisfaction. But his colossal self-adulation is tumbled mightily, for no one trembles when he barks. His acquaintance is tottering him; he only remains an imbecile whose fits will make him a paralytic, then his way of spitting venom will end.[12]

The attacks, however, did not abate.

The ultimate confrontation between Harding and Crawford took place in May 1887. There had long been rumors going back several

III-10: Harding, circa 1887 (age ~22)

generations at Blooming Grove that the Hardings came from a mixed-race background. The details often changed with whoever was telling the story, and there was never any evidence to justify the claim, but the rumor still persisted, and would continue to do so when Harding eventually got into politics. An exasperated George Crawford, whose *Independent* was consistently losing ground to Harding's *Star*, decided to put a reference to the rumor into print. Crawford wrote: "We have no desire to draw the color line on the kink-haired youth that sees fit to use his smut machine only as a receptacle for a low order or adjectives – as nature did it for him."[13] The reference was clear, and this time Harding didn't wait for his next edition to respond. With his father (who was reportedly even more upset at Crawford's unsubstantiated insinuation) in tow, the Hardings headed over to the offices of the *Independent* to demand an immediate retraction. Some versions of the story have Tryon Harding appearing with a shotgun under his arm to make his point perfectly clear. Crawford apparently realized he had gone too far and agreed to write the retraction. For the foreseeable future, the *Star* stopped being the foil for the *Independent's* editorial pages. The antagonism had reached its apex and began to subside. And so did the *Independent*, which continued to fade as the *Star* continued to rise.

For the most part, these disparaging editorials were the exception and not the norm for Warren Harding's *Daily Star*. He responded when attacked, particularly in the early years, but such aggression was never his innate style, which always leaned toward the positive. Harding's approach was eventually captured in the creed of the *Star*, which was imprinted on the walls of the office.

> Remember there are two sides to every question. Get them both.
>
> Be truthful. Get the facts.

> Mistakes are inevitable, but strive for accuracy. I would rather have one story exactly right than a hundred half wrong.
>
> Be decent, be fair, be generous.
>
> Boost-don't knock.
>
> There's good in everybody. Bring out the good and never needlessly hurt the feelings of anybody.
>
> In reporting a political gathering give the facts, tell the story as it is, not as you would like to have it. Treat all parties alike. If there's any politics to be played we will play it in our editorial columns.
>
> Treat all religious matter reverently.
>
> If it can possibly be avoided never bring ignominy to an innocent man or child in telling of the misdeed or misfortune of a relative.
>
> Don't wait to be asked, but do it without asking and, above all, be clean and never let a dirty word or suggestive story get into type.
>
> I want this paper to be so conducted that it can go into any home without destroying the innocence of children.[14]

Notwithstanding the early battles with Crawford, these principles largely held true as Harding turned his paper into a profitable enterprise and a staple in the community. According to Jack Warwick, "Gathering his daily harvest of small stories, he rejoiced in type with the parents of new babies, said pretty things of the newly-weds, jubilated with the jubilant and commiserated with the afflicted."[15] A typical story might be how Harding recounted a civic modernization in Marion in 1888:

> The era of electric street lighting has come, the inauguration of the improvement occurring Wednesday night. At 7:30 p.m., Miss Della Barnhart, daughter of President Barnhart of the Electric Light Company, made the connection at the station, with the street circuit, and instantly fifteen arcs shed their brightening rays on the street. The effect was charming. The smoky gas lights were doing poor service, and the blazing forth of the electric lights was like a marvelous transformation and the streets presented a truly novel appearance for Marion.[16]

As noted in his creed, Harding's goal was to "boost – don't knock." Harding was a "booster" and the people of Marion appreciated it. They liked seeing these positive stories in the paper, learning about their neighbors in a form of social media that long pre-dated the World Wide Web. Harding's *Star* gave the people of Marion an outlet to share the stories of their lives, and the more he told, the more papers he sold. By 1890, circulation was up to 1,100. By 1895, it was 2,500 for the expanded 8-page paper.

That circulation grew in part because Marion was growing, increasing in population by about 50% every decade during this era. With no electronic media yet available, the local newspaper was the principal source of news for most of small-town America. Part of the attraction was political, which provided fodder for conversations across these communities. Harding's county leaned Democratic while the state leaned Republican, but even that wasn't so simple. Ohio's Republicans were divided into factions during this period, with Mark Hanna leading out of Cleveland and Joseph Foraker from Cincinnati. Hanna emerged nationally by helping Ohio's William McKinley reach the presidency in 1896, while Foraker led his organization based on his long-term service as the state's Governor and one of its two senators. Harding was aligned with Foraker, but his gregarious personality made him acceptable to most factions. In fact, most Democrats liked him as well. James Blaine continued to be his national hero, and the *Star* celebrated when Benjamin Harrison won the presidency in 1888 and named Blaine as his Secretary of State. It was around this time Harding made his first sojourn to the nation's capital. Using his free rail passes, he began what became an annual trip to Washington where he got to know not only the members of the Ohio delegation but also other key leaders in the Republican Party, including up-and-comers like Theodore Roosevelt and Henry Cabot Lodge. There was little thought at the time of having Harding run for office himself, but as the editor of the leading local paper, he had a prominent political voice, and earned his reputation from these early days as a staunch loyalist of the Republican Party.

Warren Harding was a tall, handsome man who was coming into his own as the publisher and editor of the *Daily Star*. There did not appear to be any serious romantic relationships, though, in his life prior to 1890 when he started dating Florence Kling. Kling was the daughter of Amos Kling, who happened to be the wealthiest man in town. Amos started out in the hardware business and then made big money in real estate, a local hotel, and banking. Florence was his only daughter, and she inherited his headstrong personality. The two rarely saw eye-to-eye. Florence was well-read, loved the outdoors and animals (especially dogs and horses), and had a knack for music. These latter skills were honed at the Cincinnati Conservatory of Music. At the age of 19, Florence got married, despite strong objections from her father. Her beau was Henry De Wolfe (also known as "Pete"), and since their lone child was born less than nine months after the wedding, there may have been extenuating circumstances that led to the nuptials. The marriage did not go well, nor did it last. The divorce wasn't finalized until 1886, but separation had occurred long before. Life was hardly settled, though, just because De Wolfe was out of the picture. Florence never took to motherhood, and it was decided that her parents would raise her son, Marshall. In fact, Florence was unwelcome at the Kling home throughout this period, forcing her to find a room to rent and teach piano lessons to pay her own way in life. She looked back at these days with disdain. "That short, unhappy period in my life is dead and buried," she later recalled. "It was a great mistake. It was my own private affair and my mistake. I did all that was possible to correct it and obliterate it."[17] She had very little relationship with her only child, and Marshall struggled dearly, primarily with alcohol, before succumbing to tuberculosis at the age of 35.

Florence was 30 years old when she started dating Warren Harding, who was five years her junior. As far as Amos Kling was concerned, the young newspaperman was even a worse match than De Wolfe. Amos did everything he could to keep the couple apart, including resurfacing the rumors about Harding having "Black blood" running through his veins. As it increasingly appeared that wedding bells were on the horizon, Amos flat-out threatened to disown his daughter if she went ahead with the match. As soon as the couple

III-11: Florence Harding

exchanged their vows on July 8, 1891, that is exactly what he did. Amos didn't speak to his daughter for the next seven years and wouldn't step foot into her new home for another eight years after that. Only late in life did he finally soften and eventually re-establish relations with his daughter and became friendly with Harding.

For once, Harding was a subject on which his own paper could report.

> It isn't often that the Star records marriages of its own force, and there might be pardon for unusual notice to the nuptials of the editor, but it is quite sufficient to say that Warren G. Harding and Florence M. Kling were happily married. … Reverend R. Wallace officiated. Quite a pleasant company of friends were present to witness the ceremony and extend congratulations.[18]

After the ceremony, the couple left for a honeymoon tour of the Midwest, undoubtedly taking advantage of the editor's free rail passes. Upon their return, the newlyweds moved into the home they had recently built on a vacant lot on Marion's Mount Vernon Avenue. When Warren Harding returned to work at the *Star*, he had a new member to add to the staff.

Florence Harding had no experience in the newspaper business, but she had a good head on her shoulders and a natural sense of discipline and efficiency, qualities the *Star* workforce lacked. Harding had recently started delivery service for his subscribers, but it was a regular struggle to get the boys to do the job at the level Harding expected. This was a perfect call for Florence, who set out to recruit a team of youngsters who took their duties seriously and agreed to adhere to her directives. One of those was timely collections. As she was wont to say, "if the subscribers cannot pay ten cents for one week, they cannot pay twenty cents for two weeks."[19] In a business where pennies were material to the bottom line, this kind of discipline paid off handsomely for the business side of the paper. So, Florence became a part of the team. "I went down there," she later recalled, "intending to help out for a few days and remained fourteen years."[20] Eventually, she earned the title of Circulation Manager. But it was still her husband's newspaper, and by all accounts, the *Star* was beginning to thrive.

Warren Harding was known for his loyalties, which were on full display with the workforce at the *Star*. In his more than three decades running the paper, he never fired anybody or cut their wages. Over time, he started a profit-sharing program and even offered some stock in the company to the members of his team. When a push for newspapers to unionize reached Marion, Harding did nothing to stand in the way of his staff signing up. In fact, he joined them, carrying a union card for the rest of his life. The paper was surely a business, but it was also a family, and it served a purpose about which the workforce could be proud. The *Marion Daily Star* told the stories of the people of that community, and Warren Harding was increasingly hailed as the friendly neighbor who made it all happen.

While Harding and his wife watched their pennies, they were also willing to invest in their operation. Harding twice moved his offices, eventually taking over the majority of a three-story building on East Center Street. One of the other tenants was Harding's father, who opened up his medical office on the second floor, directly across from his son's office. Harding was also constantly modernizing his equipment, willing to go into short-term debt to generate greater long-term efficiencies for the business. In 1895, he installed a state-of-the-art Cox Duplex Perfecting Press, and a decade after that, he became one of the first country dailies to employ a linotype type-setting machine. Harding made sure his staff was fully trained on the machinery, including himself. There wasn't any job associated with the *Star* that Harding couldn't do himself, if need be. It also turned out that Harding's success at the *Star* wasn't an end in and of itself. It was also his entrée on the path to politics.

III-12: The longtime home of the Daily Star on East Center Street in Marion, OH

2. From the Paper to Politics

Newspapers and politics very much went hand-in-hand throughout the history of the United States. From the earliest days of the Republic, newspapers served as the mouthpiece of political administrations, as well as the voice of their opposition. High-profile editors had great influence in political parties, often using their platforms to advocate for individual candidates and party positions. Thurlow Weed and his *Albany Evening Journal*, for example, helped turn career soldier Zachary Taylor into a legitimate presidential contender. Once in a while, some of these newsmen even found themselves on national tickets. Horace Greeley, founder and editor of the *New York Tribune*, led the Democratic and Liberal Republican tickets in a losing effort against Ulysses Grant in 1872. In the most recent election, Whitelaw Reid, who had taken over the *Tribune* after Greeley's death, was the choice of Harding's Republicans as the Vice Presidential candidate in a losing effort alongside President Benjamin Harrison. The next election would feature newsman William Jennings Bryan as the standard bearer of the Democrats. Warren Harding's affinity for politics was well known, but his initial transition from the news business to a political candidate was hardly a well-planned, long-sought initiative. In fact, Harding's first run for office was basically a spur-of-the-moment decision made out of loyalty to his party.

By 1895, Harding was not only a prominent citizen of Marion but also a leading member of the local Republican Party. He was one of the founding members of Marion's Young Men's Republican Club and was a consistent voice on behalf of the party on the editorial pages of the *Star*. So, he was taken aback when the Republican County Convention met that year without a single candidate to make a run for county auditor. Democrats continued to dominate county elections and most considered the effort futile. Some even suggested not wasting any time on the race and just accept another loss. This defeatist attitude lit a fire under Harding. Unwilling to concede without a fight, he told the gathering, "I'll accept [the nomination] and make the run"[21] if the delegates would support him. They did, he ran, and, as predicted, he lost badly. But at least he made the effort and learned from the experience. "Real success is often built upon preliminary failures spurring on to greater achievements,"[22] Harding said at the time of his defeat. This was typical for Harding who was always looking on the bright side of things.

Harding began to spread his wings, reaching beyond the confines of Marion. He had an excellent voice for public speaking and was popular on the stump. He was happy to advocate for Ohio's William McKinley in the 1896 campaign, both in the *Star* and in his community. He started to take positions on issues, aligning with McKinley on a high protective tariff and the commitment to a sound currency backed by gold, both sentiments in direct opposition to the Democrats of the day. Harding also started to accept invitations to join the Chautauqua Speaking Circuit, an annual journey of political and other leaders sharing their views with local communities throughout Ohio. In addition to Republican political doctrine, Harding spoke in patriotic tones with hearty pro-American sentiments. He captivated his audiences with tales of the Founding Fathers, with special emphasis on his personal hero, Alexander Hamilton. "Lofty statesmanship and unselfish patriotism were demanded," he told his fellow Ohioans. "When it was most needed, there arose the greatest genius of the Republic, Alexander Hamilton. Without Hamilton there would be no American Republic today, to astonish the world with its resources and its progress."[23] These addresses were typically received with great applause as Harding's name (and voice) began gaining attention across the state.

If Harding was ever going to win an election, he needed to branch out beyond his home county, which remained decidedly Democratic. In 1899, he decided to toss his name into the ring for an opening in the state senate. These positions typically rotated between the four counties that comprised the 13th Ohio District. That year was Marion's turn, and Harding expressed his interest. He was by no means a shoo-in, with others also seeking the post, but he prevailed by a narrow margin at the Republican nominating convention. Harding hit the campaign trail on his own behalf, preaching core Republican ideas with a patriotic American flare. Along the campaign trail, Harding met Harry Daugherty for the first time. Daugherty was originally from the small town of Washington Court House. He graduated from the University of Michigan, became a lawyer, and served in the state legislature from 1889-1894. Daugherty was politically savvy and well-connected but came with a reputation for dishonesty and dirty dealings. While no charges ever seemed to stick to Daugherty, he suffered in the opinion of many who mattered, which may have been why he lost every election he ran after his stint in the state legislature. This included runs for Congress (both House and Senate), state Attorney General, and Governor of Ohio. Daugherty had settled in as a lobbyist, making it his business to get to know anyone who might have a position of power in the state capital. Harding first crossed paths with Daugherty during his current campaign at a party rally in Union County. The two became friends almost immediately. They became political bedfellows only over time.

When the votes were tallied, Warren Harding emerged as the victor for the first time in a political campaign. Among the proudest was (not surprisingly) his mother Phoebe, who told her son, "Warren Harding, this settles it. You are going to be President some day."[24] Harding took the comment for what it was – an endearing sentiment from his adoring mother. Beyond that, he didn't give it another thought. He had much bigger things to worry about, including how the *Daily Star* would operate without him while he was on duty in Columbus. Fortunately, he had two qualified leaders to take over in his absence. George Van Fleet had signed on at the *Star* in 1895 as telegraph editor and city editor. He had earned his stripes and had already taken on additional responsibilities when Harding put him in charge of the editorial side of the paper when he had to be out of town. And then there was Florence, who was entrusted to run the business operations, which had become her domain in many ways already. The *Star* had matured to the point where it would be OK without its founder in place every day as Harding officially veered into the world of politics.

III-13: State Senator Harding, 1908 (age 33)

Being the outgoing people-person that he was, Harding easily made the transition to being a state legislator, where relationships were essential to getting things done. Just as he had so successfully charmed the people of Marion with his genial personality, he had similar good fortune with his new political colleagues. And, unlike many other politicians, those connections were not just limited to the members of his own party. Harding was a loyal Republican and a reliable party-line vote, but his friendliness did not stop at the line of partisanship. This natural gift for fellowship put Harding in position to serve as a harmonizer on divisive issues, rarely straying from Republican doctrine but reaching across the aisle to get opposing sides closer together to move legislation forward. Some of this facilitation occurred during the course of the business day, but Harding was equally effective after hours. As one reporter covering the statehouse wrote at the time, "It was not long before Harding was the most popular man in the legislature. He had the inestimable gift of never forgetting a man's face or name. He was a regular he-man in the sign-manual of those days, a great poker-player, and not at all averse to putting a foot on the brass rail."[25] Harding loved to play cards, which was a perfect fit in Columbus. He rarely turned down the opportunity to play poker with some of his colleagues or other prominent people in town. These weren't high-stakes games, but they were certainly competitive – Harding always played to win – but the real joy came from the comradery of men around the table, smoking cigars, swapping stories, taking a drink or two (rarely more than that for Harding), and occasionally talking shop. He also became a popular after-dinner speaker, adjusting his typically "Marion-First" and "America-First" messaging to "Ohio-First" for these new audiences.

Legislation was not Harding's strong suit. He was rarely out front on the issues. He preferred to work behind the scenes as others proposed new bills, perhaps help to get people on the same page, and then cast his vote in conjunction with his Republican colleagues. The record shows Harding introduced only 15 bills during his time in Columbus, 14 of which were specific to his home community at Marion. Many of these were non-controversial "vanity bills" that helped build reputations back home. But this limited input in leading new legislation should not be taken as an indicator of poor performance. Harding's contributions were valued across the capital, even though they were more behind the scenes than from the floor of the statehouse. Governor George Nash perhaps best summed up Harding's stint as an Ohio legislator when he said, "There may be an abler man in the Senate than Harding, but when I want things done I go to him"[26] – certainly high praise in the world of politics.

The general understanding in Ohio politics, and certainly in his district, was a belief in the concept of rotation in office. In other words, leading members of communities would be elected, serve their constituents for a single term, and then pass the baton to someone else. In fact, it had been more than half a century since anyone from Ohio's 13th District had served consecutive terms. But that was about to change.

Harding's popularity, both in the district and the state capital, was such that he was approached about serving a second two-year term. With the *Star* continuing to perform well while he was away, he was happy to consent and was easily re-elected. Harding's second term differed from his first in that he was now a senior member of the legislative body. Two-thirds of the senators were new, many of whom now looked to Harding for leadership and guidance. He became the Floor Leader and frequent spokesman for the state Republican Party. His primary contributions remained as a harmonizer, where he continued to be extremely effective, but he was more out front on issues than he had been in his first term in office.

The turn of the century brought forward a new element in the Republican Party, and much of it started at the top. After the assassination of William McKinley in September 1901, Theodore Roosevelt became the nation's youngest President. Roosevelt's arrival provided the progressive era with a champion to lead the country in new directions, particularly with respect to the role of government. Roosevelt and the progressives believed that an active government could play a key role in improving the lives of the citizenry. New laws were passed governing labor, trade, the environment, and many social issues for which the government in the past had mostly stayed on the sidelines. These sentiments were beginning to find a voice at the state level as well, but not with Warren Harding. Harding was conservative by nature, a "stand-patter" to use the term of art of the day. Harding would eventually go along with many progressive initiatives as they began to permeate Republican ideology, but this was neither his style nor his preference. Harding typically felt more at ease alongside the conservative Old Guard of the Republican Party, which would find itself fighting with the progressive wing for prominence over the next couple of decades.

While Harding had been granted an exception to the rotation in office norms to let him serve a second term in the state legislature, a third term was never going to be an option. Nevertheless, his popularity within the party put him in contention for a higher position within the state, and Harding was definitely interested. What he really wanted was the top spot (Governor), but the fractious nature of Ohio Republican politics made such a proposition difficult to maneuver. The major power brokers in the party remained Mark Hanna and Joseph Foraker, who were currently occupying both of Ohio's seats in the U.S. Senate. Hanna backed Myron Herrick for Governor in 1903, while Foraker was in Harding's corner. This time, Hanna had the majority of the party lined up behind him, and Herrick got the top spot on the ticket. As a consolation prize for Foraker, and to promote party unity, Harding was offered the nomination for Lieutenant Governor, an opportunity he was pleased to accept. With Ohio (and the country) still leaning Republican, the Herrick-Harding ticket carried the day, elevating the 38-year-old newspaper publisher from Marion to the number two spot in the state.

The position of Lieutenant Governor was an even better fit for Harding than as a state legislator. While the position assigned him the role of presiding officer of the state senate, that role was mostly as a facilitator and not an active participant in any legislative debates. In fact, the Lieutenant Governor of Ohio had relatively few responsibilities. Nevertheless, someone in that seat could be immensely valuable as a conciliator, keeping the party aligned, which was often a challenging task but one for which Harding was perfectly suited. He was considered at the top of his game when he played the harmonizing role at the raucous Republican state convention of 1904 that was responsible for selecting delegates to the national convention. As the forces behind Hanna and Foraker were jockeying for position, Harding used his floor time to preach unity and collaboration. According to the Cleveland *Plain Dealer*:

> The man who stepped into the breach today was Lieutenant Governor Harding. ... By the use of a rare flow of words the lieutenant governor for the moment made the delegates believe that the word 'harmony' had been written with indelible ink. Roused from a condition of lethargy produced by the previous monotony of the convention, the delegates vociferously cheered the name of each one of the men who will constitute the Republican 'Big Four,' and at the end poured forth approval on Harding himself. If the enthusiasm this afternoon is any criterion, Lieutenant Governor Harding is destined to figure in an increasing extent in the future counsels of the party.[27]

Senator Hanna, who would pass from the scene later in the year, recognized the glow around Harding at the event. In fact, he used the opportunity to nudge him in a direction less aligned with Foraker. "Harding, you know every Ohio boy has his hope of the Presidency,"

Hanna said, "and it looks to me that you are heading that way. Just keep closer in touch with us fellows up at Cleveland and not so damned exclusively intimate with the trouble-makers down in Cincinnati."[28] Hanna knew a lot about making Ohioans into Presidents, having been instrumental in William McKinley's rise to the national executive, but it was still far too early to be considering such a possibility. In fact, Harding was a lot more concerned about what political post he would hold after his current term expired at the beginning of 1906. To his great disappointment, the answer would be "none."

Governor Herrick was not inclined to simply step aside after one term and hand the reigns of the state over to his Lieutenant Governor. By this point, after six years of service in Columbus, Harding really only wanted a shot at the top spot. If that path was blocked, perhaps it was time to return to Marion and the *Star* and reassess his political fortunes. While he could have run for re-election for his current post, he declined to be considered. Perhaps it was for the best. Herrick found himself on the wrong side of the progressives and prohibitionists in the state and lost his seat to Democrat John Pattison.

Harding's political career was not over, but it was definitely at a crossroads. He had emerged as a leader in the Republican Party in Ohio and was well-liked across the political spectrum. He had greatly expanded his network over the past six years, including some men who would become among his closest friends. This included Malcolm Jennings, the assistant clerk of the Assembly, and Frank Scobey, the clerk of the Senate, who became Harding intimates for the rest of his life. He also got closer to Harry Daugherty, the Republican operative/lobbyist who would play such a pivotal role in Harding's political future. But, for now, it was time for a break from politics and a return to his life as one of the leading men of Marion.

Harding had never been far from the *Star* even when he was in Columbus, maintaining regular communications with his team in Marion. George Van Fleet had done well leading the editorial side of the paper, which continued to increase its penetration across the community. Upon Harding's return, he jumped back into the *Star's* operations, but more in the role of publisher than editor, leaving much of the detailed day-to-day grind to Van Fleet. Harding could still be found on the street corner, hanging out with neighbors and friends, swapping stories that would inevitably make their way into the paper, but the pressure to perform was now spread across many other qualified leaders and staff who continued to take great pride in producing a product that adhered to Harding's creed and provided the community with something they looked forward to receiving each and every day.

Harding relished his newfound stature in the community and welcomed the opportunity to join just about every civic organization Marion had to offer. He proudly wore the hats and participated in the rituals of the Elks, Red Men, Hoo Hoos, Oddfellows, Moose, and many other similar associations. Each afforded him opportunities to hang out with the fellows, smoke cigars, play cards, and enjoy the comradery of the men of Marion. He even bought his first automobile, a real status symbol that was still only for those who had really begun to prosper. He also spent quality time on the road, using those free rail passes to visit various parts of the country, almost always with Florence along for the ride.

There has been considerable speculation about the true nature of the relationship between Warren and Florence Harding. Given that there is no surviving correspondence from the couple, third-party perspectives have fueled this narrative in the context of Harding's extramarital activity. Many have concluded that Florence was cold, prone to nagging, and not interested in physical intimacy, all of which led Harding to stray. There was certainly some truth to these assessments. But, while Harding's affairs filled gaps that existed in his marriage, it would also be a mistake to assume that there weren't positives in the relationship that Harding truly valued. After all, Harding stayed with Florence despite aggressive efforts by at least one of his mistresses to get him to move on. Yes, it may have been politically ruinous for Harding to divorce Florence in the early

III-14: Warren and Florence Harding, later in life, as seen during the 1920 presidential campaign

days of the 20th Century, but there seems to be more to Harding's decision than just protecting his political prospects. Florence was his foundation, the stable center of his life that he could rely on. She believed in him, supported him, looked out for him, and at times protected him. As First Lady, for example, she told a group of girl scouts that "My hobby is my husband, girls, just my husband."[29] This focus and stability were characteristics that were valuable to the more free-wheeling Harding and not something he was ever willing to toss aside, despite alternate temptations.

The most favorable descriptions of Florence, and the couple's relationship, come from the memoirs of Harry Daugherty, who was close to both of them. "I found in Mrs. Harding always a strong champion and an inspiring friend," Daugherty wrote. "She was natural – always herself. In an age of jazz she was simple and old-fashioned and made no attempt either to change the world or her own outlook on it. She took life as it came, always finding her happiness in the success of her husband."[30] In terms of the relationship between the two, Daugherty wrote:

> They were of more help to each other than any other man and woman I have ever known. She was interested in his work and watched carefully to see that he made no mistakes. If he did she was keen to 'pick him up,' though she did it in a way that never nagged. Their discussions were heated at times, but never quarrelsome or bitter.[31]

There were clearly things missing from the relationship that Harding sought elsewhere, but Florence was his partner in many ways for the better part of 32 years, with plenty of companionship and friendship, if not the kind of physical intimacy Harding also craved.

It was around this time that Harding found himself in the arms of another woman for the first time since his marriage to Florence. And he didn't have to look far to find it. The Hardings were close friends with James (Jim) and Carrie Phillips. Jim was the co-owner of the Uhler-Phillips Company, one of Marion's leading dry goods establishments. Unlike Florence, Carrie was emotional, sensual, and among the most attractive women in Marion. She could carry on a conversation on just about any topic, as well as ignite Harding's libido in a manner that Florence seemingly could not. The couples often socialized together and collectively enjoyed each other's company. Then, both couples went through a rough period around 1905. As Harding's stint as Lieutenant

III-15: Carrie Phillips

Governor was coming to an end, Florence became quite ill. She was suffering from a serious ailment, necessitating the removal of one of her kidneys. It took her months to recover, and she suffered through kidney issues for the rest of her life. At the same time, the Phillipses lost their youngest child, James, Jr., succumbing to jaundice at the age of two. The parents were devastated to the point where Jim needed some time in a sanitarium to recover. Amidst these tragedies, the nature of the relationship between Warren Harding and Carrie Phillips began to change. It would be another couple of years before it is believed that the connection became physical, which will become vividly clear in the ten years of letters that survive beginning from 1910. But the affair got underway a few years before, during these challenging days as Harding transitioned back to his full-time life in Marion.

Another person entered Harding's life around this time, one he had known for years but had previously avoided him like the plague – his father-in-law Amos Kling. Kling has softened a bit over the years, having begun to re-establish a relationship with his daughter after effectively disowning her upon her marriage to Harding. After losing his own wife, Kling began to open up to Florence, particularly around the time of her kidney surgery in 1905. Kling was vacationing in Florida when he heard about his daughter's operation and sent her a telegram that read, "Be calm cheerful and full of hope for you will surely be well again."[32] What was even more dramatic was that Kling also started to correspond with Harding. Harding got the ball rolling after coming back from a recent trip. He sent Kling several issues of the *Star* to help him stay close to the activities in Marion. Upon receipt, Kling responded. "This is a duty as well as a pleasure on which I ought to have realized long ago," Kling wrote, "answering your nice letter upon your return home. You seemed to have had a rip-roaring time."[33] More letters followed, and the tone softened the more he wrote. Kling went from opening with "Dear Sir" to "Dear Warren" and eventually started signing his letters "Daddy."[34] After a decade and a half of ostracizing his son-in-law, Kling apparently started to see what most people saw in Harding, a warm, gregarious, earnest person who was fun to be around. Kling only had a few years left before he would pass, but at least he would end his relationship with the Hardings on a positive note.

The Harding family suffered some losses of their own in this period, most profoundly being the death of Warren's blessed mother in 1910. Phoebe Harding suffered a fall and was bedridden for months before she passed. Harding adored his mother and drew much strength from the person who saw so much good in him. As she was laid to rest, Harding wrote to his sister Carolyn, "Surely, yea, surely, there are for her all the rewards in eternity that God bestows on his very own. I could not speak for myself, but dear, dear Mother will wear a crown if ever a Christian woman does – and I can believe in eternal compensations for such as her."[35] It was a difficult loss for Harding to absorb, which was coupled with the death of his sister, Mary, not long after.

In the meantime, the Republican Party was on the verge of coming apart at the seams, both in Ohio and on the national scene. It didn't take long after Theodore Roosevelt turned over the White House to his handpicked successor William Taft that the former's legion of followers began to cry foul. Taft wasn't progressive enough, he was soft on conservation, he had no spark of personality. In other words, he simply couldn't measure up to TR. The party started to fracture along the TR/Taft fault lines, with Warren Harding very much in the camp of the more conservative Taft. In Ohio, it was also a changing of the guard, with new leaders jockeying for position. Hanna had died and Foraker had fallen out of favor over reports in the Hearst newspapers that he was in the pocket of John Rockefeller and Standard Oil. The progressives in the party were battling with the conservatives for control of the party, and a unifying presence was needed if the Republicans were going to have a chance to regain the statehouse. All eyes turned to Warren Harding.

Harding had wanted to run for Governor in 1905 but was denied the opportunity when Myron Herrick insisted on running for a second term. Herrick lost that race, and the rival Democrats had been in the seat ever since. The incumbent was Judson Harmon, who was going to be tough to beat, especially with the lack of alignment in the Republican ranks.

III-16: Harding as a gubernatorial candidate, 1910 (age 44)

Harry Daugherty was among those pushing Harding to make the race, eventually running his campaign once Harding agreed to toss his hat into the ring. Daugherty remained controversial. While many begrudgingly admired him for his success as a party operative, he was also held in contempt for his unscrupulous tactics as a means to an end. Harding was aware of these concerns, but he had grown close to Daugherty over the years, saw him as a friend and an effective political organizer, and welcomed his support. For the first six months of 1910 Harding criss-crossed the state, giving some 300 speeches, preaching the Republican gospel. "I believe that the Republican party has the conscience and the purpose to solve every problem attending our marvelous development," Harding declared on the eve of the state convention.[36] In a competitive contest, he secured the nomination of his party, setting up a showdown with Harmon for the top political spot in the state.

As a politician, Harding was rarely out front on controversial issues. He was more inclined to follow his party's leadership than be a first-mover on a topic. But certain issues were finally unavoidable in the showdown for Governor. People insisted on knowing, for example, where Harding stood on the movement to ban alcohol in the United States. Harding was a social drinker himself and did his best to avoid taking a stand. The best he would offer the electorate was the following statement just a couple of weeks before Ohioans went to the polls:

> The temperance question is legislative rather than executive, and is not to transcend all other important issues in this campaign. My legislative record is written in the journals of two general assemblies. I couldn't change that record if I would. I stand for enforcement of the law and would not be worthy of your suffrages if I did not.[37]

Harding was still trying to straddle the fence as best he could.

In the end, the result was not close. Harmon won a second term by a convincing margin of just over 100,000 votes, a whopping 11-point margin of victory. The bottom line was that most progressive Republicans stayed home rather than vote for the conservative Harding, who ultimately never had a chance against a unified Democratic opposition. While disappointed in the outcome, Harding also felt some relief. He put things in perspective in a letter to one of his supporters:

> I am serene and happy, if not quite so confident as I have been in the good faith of all people. I have the germ eradicated from my system, and can go ahead and do other things which please me more than hunting men of 'abiding honesty' to appoint to places, and listening to the appeal for the pardon of dishonest ones in the penitentiary. I will not in the future have to be either 'wet' or 'dry' or to shape my course within the lines of any faction.[38]

To his wife, he shared, "Now, Duchess (his long-term nickname for Florence), we still have our wagon hitched to a Star and we will keep right on running the newspaper and make a trip on the salt seas to bury our sorrow."[39] The couple set off on a couple of trips around this time, visiting the Mediterranean and then the Bahamas. In both cases, their traveling companions were Jim and Carrie Phillips.

Harding certainly tried to keep his affairs a secret and had an agreement with Carrie that they would destroy their love letters. Harding complied with this understanding, but Carrie did not, which provides us deep insight into some very personal communications. The letters are a story in and of themselves. They were found in a box in a closet after Carrie's death in 1960. A multi-year tussle ensued between historians and the Harding family, which fought to keep them sealed. Harding's reputation had already suffered over the years, and the release of these 240 time bombs was simply expected to make things even worse. So they went to court, and a ruling was handed down. The letters would become public, but not for another 50 years. The Harding Memorial Association would maintain them under lock and key until 2014, when they would be made available to the public. When they were finally released by the Library of Congress, the initial attention was on the overtly sexual nature of many of these lengthy hand-written notes, but these must be viewed in the context of a couple that appeared to be very much in love. "I love you more than all the world," Harding wrote to Carrie in December 1914, "and have no hope of reward on earth or hereafter, so precious as that in your dear arms, in your thrilling lips, in your matchless breasts, in your incomparable embrace."[40] Sometimes Harding wrote in verse, such as this creation from January 1912.

> I love your poise
> Of perfect thighs
> When they hold me
> in paradise. …
>
> I love to suck
> Your breath away
> I love to cling —
> There long to stay
>
> I love you garb'd
> But naked more
> Love your beauty
> To thus adore. …[41]

But there was much more to this correspondence, in letters that would sometimes go on for 40 or 50 handwritten pages. Harding shared all aspects of his life with Carrie, including the *Star*, politics, the happenings in Marion, and his frequent travels. Sometimes these trips afforded opportunities to share a couple of days (and nights) away from Jim and Florence. When Harding traveled alone, it was an opportunity to pour out his heart in a way that he never could with his wife, using stationary from whatever hotel in which he happened to find himself on any particular night. Both relationships mattered to Harding, but in different ways. Carrie offered Harding a level of intimacy, both emotional and physical, that appeared to most as foreign to Florence. He not only embraced the opportunity to fill this gap in his life – he relished it.

Only one side of these conversations has been preserved, but one can infer much from Harding's responses to Carrie's letters. And the correspondence was not always harmonious. Over time, Carrie pushed Harding to leave his wife and to drop politics, ostensibly so he could spend more time with her. She was needy and was not averse to attempting to bully Harding to try to get her way. She occasionally threatened to expose his letters if he didn't give her what she wanted. Sometimes she would engage in emotional blackmail, highlighting new male friends she had met on her own travels, to get him to comply.

These tensions became more pronounced when Carrie up and left to live in Europe in 1911. On a trip with her family, she fell in love with all

III-17: A small sampling of the correspondence over the years from Harding to Carrie Phillips

things German and decided to relocate. Her husband returned to Marion, but Carrie enrolled her daughter (Isabelle) at a boarding school in Switzerland and thrust herself into the cultural and social aspects of Berlin and the neighboring communities. For Harding, absence appeared to make the heart grow fonder as the passion in his letters continued unabated.

> Honestly, I hurt with the insatiate longing, until I feel that there will never be any relief until I take a long, deep, wild draught on your lips and then bury my face on your pillowing breasts. Oh, Carrie! I want the solace you only can give. It is awful to hunger so and be so wholly denied. … Oh, Carrie mine! You can see I have yielded and written myself into wild desire. I could beg. And Jerry came and will not go, says he loves you, that you are the only, only love worthwhile in all this world, and I must tell you so and a score or more of other fond things he suggests, but I spare you.[42]

"Jerry" was a reference to Harding's genitalia. He and Carrie developed an elaborate set of code words, primarily related to how to continue to correspond and meet without anyone catching on. But some of these terms were sexual. Carrie's private parts were referred to as Mrs. Pouterson. So, many yearnings and emotions flowed across the pond, a nice distraction from Harding's day-to-day existence in Marion, Ohio, at a time when politics was about to re-enter his life.

3. Senator Harding

Harding was, in fact, perfectly content with his life. The *Star* was doing extremely well, and the demands on his time were far less intense than in the early days when he was building his baby into a thriving concern. He had plenty of time for his civic organizations, playing golf during the day and poker at night, and spending time with his newest dog, Hub, a Boston terrier who joined him at the *Star* just about every day. He had Florence at home and Carrie in his thoughts and letters to satisfy his private needs. Politics, however, always seemed to come knocking at the door just when Harding was ready to put it all behind him. The opening in 1912 was mostly an honorific, the opportunity to formally place President William Taft's name into nomination at the Republican National Convention. By now, the Republican Party had completely fractured, with the progressives urging Theodore Roosevelt to make another run for the White House while the Old Guard conservatives rallied around Taft. Harding had been with Taft throughout the party's rupture, and his fellow Ohioan in the White House reached out to request Harding's support at the Chicago Convention. "It is a good deal of a task to do this," Taft wrote, "but I know your earnest support of me, and I hope that you will feel like assuming the burden. I know you can do it well, and I shall be delighted to be able to have it done by a man who represents the state so worthily as you do."[43] This was a no-brainer for Harding. "I think I was more honored by that request," he wrote a decade later "than I was by my own nomination, in my own appraisal."[44]

III-18: Former President Theodore Roosevelt

The 1912 Republican Convention was a complete and utter mess. Before the first session was even gaveled to order, there were intense battles over which delegates would be seated. Since the Old Guard essentially ran the convention for the party, virtually all of these disputes were decided in Taft's favor, leading Roosevelt to erupt in furor. TR traveled to Chicago and accused the party leaders of outright fraud. "We fight in honorable fashion for the good of mankind," Roosevelt bellowed to a large gathering of his supporters, "fearless of the future;

unheeding of our individual fates; with unflinching hearts and undimmed eyes; we stand at Armageddon, and we battle for the Lord!"[45] But Roosevelt didn't have the numbers, and eventually instructed his followers to refrain from voting for anyone out of protest.

Amid all this turmoil stood Warren Harding waiting to offer his heartfelt advocacy for four more years of Taft. He went the route of alliteration to try to convince his fellow delegates that Taft represented the entire party, including the progressive wing.

> Progress is not proclamation nor palaver. It is not pretence nor play on prejudice. It is not the perturbation of a people passion-wrought, nor a promise proposed. Progression is everlastingly lifting the standards that marked the end of the world's march yesterday and planting them on new and advanced heights today. Tested by such a standard, President Taft is the greatest Progressive of the age.[46]

That last statement was certainly a stretch, but the speech was well-received. While Taft won the nomination, the party was completely broken. The progressives bolted, stood up their own convention, and rallied around Roosevelt as their standard-bearer. Throughout the volatile campaign, Harding maintained his loyalty to Taft. He hit the campaign trail, not just in Ohio but also offering enthusiastic addresses in Indiana, Missouri, Iowa, and Michigan. He further took Roosevelt to task on the editorial pages of the *Star*, at one point calling him "the greatest fakir of all times."[47] But these efforts were entirely futile. Roosevelt's third-party run siphoned off millions of votes from the Republican ranks, providing Democrat Woodrow Wilson a landslide victory in the Electoral College despite capturing slightly less than 42% of the nationwide popular vote. For only the second time since the Civil War a Democrat was heading to the White House. It was a disappointing (but not surprising) outcome to Warren Harding.

Harding's loyalty to Taft placed him in an excellent position with the Old Guard Republicans, such that his name surfaced when the next election cycle started to heat up. This latest opportunity surrounded the upcoming election for the open Senate seat from Ohio. The rise of the progressives had upended the political process in a number of important ways. The 17th Amendment, which was ratified in April 1913, mandated the popular election of senators, taking that power away from state legislatures. Also now in vogue were formal primaries in most states, eschewing political conventions that had traditionally made nominations on behalf of the party. These changes created a new set of challenges, causing some politicians to opt out. This included incumbent Senator Theodore Burton, creating an open seat for the 1914 election. Harry Daugherty was back in Marion pushing Harding to make the race.

At first, Harding demurred. After all, he had been trounced in his most recent campaign for Governor and had no interest in repeating that experience. He also believed his former patron, Joseph Foraker, was interested in his old seat, creating a potential conflict that Harding preferred to avoid. Moreover, he was happy and saw no reason to disrupt his current existence. And then there was Carrie Phillips, who was steadfast against Harding's re-entry into politics. Harding confided with her on his thoughts in November 1913, about a half year before the primary and a full year before the general election.

> I find among the political buzzing I still have some supporters, who are generous with their suggestions. … It tickles one's vanity a bit to hear from them, here and there, but there is no lure to mislead me. I shall not aspire again. There are more attractive things in life. I believe I should like to live a life of contented love, with you, in preference to all else.[48]

Nevertheless, the entreaties persisted. While still conflicted over whether to make the run, Harding ventured out on a hunting expedition for a couple of months to think it over. When he returned, he was inclined to toss his hat into the ring, as long as Foraker was OK with it. Harding visited Foraker at his home, and as Harding indicated he planned to run, Foraker raised no objection to him pursuing the seat. With that, the race for the U.S. Senate was on.

Harding had plenty of supporters, including former President Taft, who continued to have a strong influence with many Republicans in the state of Ohio. Taft officially endorsed Harding as the best choice for the people of their state, calling him "a man of marked ability, of sanity, of much legislative experience, and he is a regular Republican of principle, and not a 'trimmer.'"[49] That didn't mean the nomination was going to be handed to Harding on a silver platter. Others coveted the spot, and their supporters were equally passionate about their candidates. Particularly aggressive were the progressives who were still seeking a dominant spot in the Republican ranks. At one event, Harding was being heckled to the point that brought the proceedings to a halt. In this instance, the typically mild-mannered Harding firmly stood his ground. "I came here to do one thing," he told the raucous crowd, "and that is to speak. And I am going to speak if I have to stand here all night and whip one or two of your best men on the stage, or wait for you to get tired and go to sleep."[50] This did the trick, and he moved out on his two-hour address. Most of Harding's speeches were filled with his typical "America First" kind of rhetoric, carefully avoiding the most controversial domestic topics, such as prohibition and women's suffrage. His approach worked. When Ohioans went to cast their ballots for the Republican primary, Harding outpolled Foraker by a 6% margin, putting him against the Attorney General, Democrat Timothy Hogan, for the coveted Senate seat.

The backdrop of this race was the onset of global war. On June 28, Archduke Franz Ferdinand, the heir apparent to the Austro-Hungarian empire, was gunned down by a Bosnian Serb. Based on a complex web of bilateral defense treaties across Europe, when Austria declared war on Serbia, the entire continent jumped into the fray. World War I was on. President Wilson committed the United States to a firm position of neutrality, aligning with neither the Central Powers (led by Germany and Austria-Hungary) nor the Allies (led by Britain, France, and Italy). Along with most Americans at this stage in the conflict, Harding supported the President, seeing no upside to an American entry. American politicians would watch the situation closely, eventually dividing on whether to join the fray.

In the meantime, there was one direct impact on Harding as a result of the onset of war in Europe – Carrie Phillips reluctantly agreed to leave her beloved Germany behind and return to the safety of the United States. Despite some of the tension that had developed between Carrie and Harding during her three years abroad, they seemed glad to be reunited as the physical nature of their relationship quickly resumed. It turned out to be a banner year for Harding, as not only did he have Carrie back in his arms, he also had himself a seat in the United States Senate. Ohio's Republican party had unified behind Harding and other candidates in 1914, sending Frank Willis to the Governor's chair and Warren Harding to the Senate. Harding had completely reversed the outcome from his gubernatorial race from four years before. He had lost that race by 100,000 votes and now won the current contest by 102,000. The outcome meant a great deal to Harding, the man who started a newspaper with next to nothing but his own grit and determination at the age of 19 and was now heading to his nation's capital as one of the two men to represent his state in the United States Senate. "This is the zenith of my political ambition," Harding remarked. "I am going to try to be a good Senator."[51]

While Harding would be sworn in on March 4, 1915, the first session of Congress would not begin until December of that year, giving him a full year before his duties would commence. He took the opportunity for some travel with Florence. The Phillipses did not accompany them. Something had come between the couples over the previous year. Whether Florence found out about the affair is unknown, but some sort of conflict led to the cessation of joint activities. The Hardings enjoyed some time in Texas with Frank Scobey and then ventured to Hawaii. It was here the couple made the acquaintance of Charles Forbes, a charming man who helped show them around the island. Forbes was a man of Harding's ilk. He enjoyed cigars and poker, making a perfect companion for the Senator-elect and an ally for the future. One member of the family that would not be traveling to Washington was the Hardings' dog Hub who had recently died. Harding's sentimentality showed through the announcement of Hub's passing in the *Star*:

> Perhaps you wouldn't devote these lines to a dog. But Hub was a *Star* office visitor nearly every day of the six years in which he deepened attachment. He was a grateful and devoted dog, with a dozen lovable attributes, and it somehow voices the yearning of broken companionship to pay his memory deserved tribute. It isn't orthodox to ascribe a soul to a dog – if soul means immortality. But Hub was loving and loyal, with the jealousy that tests its quality. He was reverent, patient, faithful. ... He couldn't speak our language, though he somehow understood, but he could be and was eloquent with uttering eye and wagging tail and the other expressions of knowing dogs. No, perhaps he had no soul, but in these things are the essence of soul and the spirit of lovable life.[52]

Becoming a U.S. Senator provided Harding with his first job outside his home state, and the change in circumstances was going to take some getting used to. Fortunately, he didn't have to worry much about money. Harding was still taking in around $20,000 a year from the highly profitable *Daily Star*, and with his Senate salary of $7,500, he would be quite comfortable. He and Florence moved into a duplex on Wyoming Avenue in Washington before settling into his seat on the Senate floor. Harding's strength as a legislator in the state of Ohio always played out behind the scenes, making friends with everyone and serving as a harmonizer on difficult issues. He brought the same approach to Capitol Hill. He was rarely out front on any issue, certainly anything controversial, making very few noteworthy speeches throughout his six years in office. He was always a reliable Republican vote, just as he had been in Ohio. "Believing as I do in political parties and government through political parties," he noted, "I had much rather that the party to which I belong should, in its conferences, make a declaration, than to assume a leadership or take an individual position on the question."[53] Harding was seen as generally pro-business and against excessive regulations and high taxes, mostly because those were the positions of the Republican Party. He did introduce 134 bills during his tenure, but over 90% of those were to satisfy purely local interests in his home state. Harding always maintained his close ties to Marion, about which he was fully informed thanks to the regular arrival of copies of the *Daily Star* which he dutifully read cover-to-cover. He was also in regular communication with George Van Fleet, who continued to run the paper on a day-to-day basis. Harding may have become a senator, but that didn't mean he stopped being a newspaperman. The *Star* was never far from his mind, and Van Fleet deferred to the boss on almost all major decisions regarding the paper.

III-19: Harding had always been a hands-on newspaper owner at the Marion Daily Star

III-20: Senator Harding, circa 1918 (age ~53)

The U.S. Senate often felt like an exclusive club, and Harding was happy to be a member. As with most clubs, there was the business for which they had been formed that needed to be addressed, but there was also a social aspect, which is where Warren Harding shined. As he had in Ohio, Harding made friends across the aisle and saw many of his fellow senators as much outside the office as within. One of his new companions was James Wadsworth of New York, who was seated near Harding from the beginning and became so close that whenever one moved his seat, the other followed along. "I was his neighbor during those six years," Wadsworth wrote of Harding. "I was very fond of him. He was essentially an honest man. He disliked sham and was deeply concerned over the influence of demagogues in American public life."[54] Rarely would Harding pass on an opportunity to play golf (during the day) or poker (at night) with his colleagues. The Chevy Chase Club became his preferred golf course, and the home of Nicholas and Alice Longworth was a frequent location for evening poker games. Alice was the oldest (and wildest) child of Theodore Roosevelt, and all of Washington seemed to want to join her social circle. "From the time he came to Washington as Senator in 1915, he and Mrs. Harding came to our house a great deal, chiefly to play poker, a game to which he was devoted," Alice later wrote. "Though Mrs. Harding did not play, she always came, too, and the job of the 'Duchess,' as she was called, was to 'tend bar.'"[55] Florence looked forward to being included in the world of the Roosevelts, although it appears that Alice never returned the favor, never stepping foot in the Harding home on Wyoming Avenue.

Not long after Harding took his seat in the Senate, a presidential election was once again in play. Woodrow Wilson was the unanimous pick to run for a second term by the Democrats and was pitched as the "man who kept us out of war." Many Republicans, egged on by Roosevelt, believed the time had come for the United States to enter the contest on the side of the Allies. American commercial ships had come under fire by German submarines, despite commitments to avoid conflict with neutral vessels. When the British ocean liner *Lusitania* was sent to the bottom of the Irish Sea via an unprovoked German torpedo assault, killing 1,198 people (including 128 Americans), popular opinion began to surge away from the administration's hardline stance of neutrality. But President Wilson remained convinced that engaging in the fight was not in the best interest of the United States. This created a clear divide across the country that would sit at the center of the upcoming presidential race.

The topic of the war was a personal one for Harding, not particularly for himself but rather through the eyes of Carrie Phillips. Even though Carrie had returned to the United States, she continued to espouse her pro-German sentiments. With the Central Powers increasingly out of favor in the U.S., this was creating a challenge for Senator Harding, who was caught between Carrie and his own conscience. "I have never approved of your war attitude," Harding wrote to Carrie in March 1915, "but I have loved you no less. I have deplored it for your sake and my own because I have been conscious of the embarrassments which might attend. I am sure you understand. But I know as well as I live that you would not respect me, were my attitude different. I couldn't be other than for my country, in the best way that I know to show my devotion."[56] If there was political tension in the correspondence during this period, it didn't detract from the sexual messaging conveyed in this very same letter.

> Jerry — you recall Jerry — ... came in while I was pondering your notes in glad reflection. ... He told me to say that you are the best and darlingest in the world, and if he could have but one wish, it would be to be held in your darling embrace and be thrilled by your pink lips that convey the surpassing rapture of human touch and the unspeakable joy of love's surpassing embrace. I cordially agree with all he said.[57]

Harding had many motivations guiding his thoughts as the country prepared to choose its next President, with participation in the World War very much the central issue of the election.

Roosevelt desperately wanted the Republican nomination in 1916 and was attacking President Wilson with a vengeance over the administration's passivity, but the bad blood from the previous canvass left many Republicans with a sour taste in their mouth when it came to TR. He had broken the party four years before, and many were not inclined to welcome him back into the fold, let alone place him at the top of the ticket. Warren Harding was among those who saw value in Roosevelt as a strong voice in the party but was not inclined to support his bid for the nomination. And Harding would not simply be an innocent bystander at the upcoming convention in Chicago. With the party still divided between the conservative and progressive wings, the Republican leadership sought someone who could help unify the gathering as the convention chair. Harry Daugherty was among those advocating for "Harding the Harmonizer" as the best man for the job, and the party elites agreed. Harding would preside, which also gave him the honor of offering the convention's keynote address. For two hours he tried to rouse the spirits of the attendees, but by nearly all accounts, his effort fell short. Harding's oratory, always long on platitudes and limited with specifics, might have been expected to spur some enthusiasm, but for the most part, his remarks fell flat. "We proclaim justice and we love peace, and we mean to have them – and we are not too proud to fight for them!" Harding bellowed in a direct attack on a recent Wilson proclamation. It was time for "the mistaken policy of watchful waiting and wabbling warfare" of the Wilson administration to come to an end, he emphasized. He took Wilson to task for domestic policies as well, claiming, "The strength of the business heart shows in every countenance in all the land, and the weakness of that heart holds a nation ill."[58] When he was finally done, Harding left the stage, receiving a smattering of polite applause. "When he got through there was no demonstration," according to the report in *The New York Times*, "only the same courteous and necessary noise that had been made to do duty for a cheer wherever in his speech he had paused for one."[59] Harding was sorely disappointed by these muted reactions.

Harding had always been confident in his ability to connect with a crowd and to move them with his words. Here on the national scene,

Harding's high-level patriotic phrases that tended to be short on substance were picked apart by the press and the opposition. Treasury Secretary William McAdoo, a future Democratic candidate for President, once said that Harding's "speeches leave the impression of an army of pompous phrases moving over the landscape in search of an idea; sometimes these meandering words would actually capture a straggling thought and bear it triumphantly, a prisoner in their midst, until it died of servitude and overwork."[60] Harding was taken aback by his performance in the wake of the criticism. "Since the roasting I received at Chicago," he confided to his friend Malcolm Jennings, "I no longer harbor any too great self-confidence in the matter of speechmaking."[61] Harding persevered through the convention, trying to maintain party unity, but lamented his wasted opportunity to lead and inspire in a way that could also enhance his own standing in the process.

As for the main purpose of the convention, a loose alignment came together for the sake of trying to defeat Woodrow Wilson in the fall. The party rallied around Supreme Court Associate Justice Charles Evans Hughes, sufficiently appealing to the various party factions to come together on just the second ballot. Twenty-one people received at least one vote, including Warren Harding, who picked up a single tally in the second ballot thanks to a delegate from New Jersey. Roosevelt never inched higher than sixth before Hughes went over the top. The progressives ran their own convention across town for the second cycle in a row and once again nominated TR to try to regain the White House. But, this time Roosevelt turned them down. He knew as well as anyone that his third-party run in 1912 had handed the presidency to Wilson, and his hatred for the incumbent and what he was doing to the country was sufficient to get him to put his large ego aside and commit to fully support the Republican Hughes. The electorate would have a clear choice when going to the polls in November 1916.

Harding did his best to rally the citizenry to return the Republicans to power, both on the stump and with his influence in the *Daily Star*. The election turned out to be extremely close, with the outcome undetermined for three days after the polls had closed. The decision fell to California, a state that was too close to call for those three long days, before Wilson's lead of about 3,000 votes (out of a million cast) was solid enough to declare the winner, resulting in four more years for the incumbent. Harding's own Ohio was a disappointment, with Wilson beating Hughes by a convincing 70,000 votes. It was the only state in the Midwest not to go for Hughes, helping Wilson eke out his victory.

Before Wilson would even take his oath of office for his second term, the entire calculus for American involvement in World War I was upended. The man who had clung to neutrality finally changed his tune when the Germans announced a policy of unrestricted submarine warfare, placing American vessels directly at peril just by appearing in waters near the belligerents. This policy shift turned even the most pacifistic members of Wilson's Cabinet toward a war posture, and the President finally was inclined to go along. With many Republicans long clamoring for war, it was not a surprise to find Harding ready to cast his vote in favor of entering the conflict. He had only one source of minor hesitation – the steadfast objections of Carrie Phillips. It can be inferred from his letters that Carrie began pressuring Harding to vote against U.S. involvement in the war if such a vote materialized. "Frankly, I have all along recognized your intense partisanship and sympathy for and devotion to Germany," Harding wrote to Carrie in February 1917, "and have respected it because you are you, and most of the cutting things said I have been able to pass by. … But I can and will do my duty accordingly to my best conscience and understanding and then take the consequences. I do not know now whether I shall vote for war. I may not be called upon to so vote. When I do vote for it, I shall do so with such conviction that I shall enlist to fight as I vote."[62] Things got dicier in April when Wilson formally asked Congress for a declaration of war. Carrie overtly threatened Harding to get him to vote against the measure. "My mind reverts momentarily to the shock I received at Baltimore," Harding wrote in April, "when out of the very halo of blissful existence, when sweet and holy reflections made an air of paradise, you suddenly threatened me with exposure to the Germans."[63] Harding would go to great lengths to keep his affair secret, but he was not about to deviate from his true convictions on a topic of such great importance. The vote for war quickly passed the Senate by a count of 82-6, with Harding solidly in favor of the measure. He provided the following explanation for his vote as in the best interest of the American people:

> I want it known to the people of my State, and to the Nation that I am voting for war to-night for the maintenance of just American rights, which is the first essential to the preservation of the soul of this Republic. … A war not for

> the cause of the allies of Europe; a war not for France, beautiful as the sentiment may be in reviving at least our gratitude to the French people; not precisely a war for civilization, worthy and inspiring as that would be; but a war that speaks for the majesty of a people popularly governed, who finally are brought to the crucial test where they are resolved to get together and wage a conflict for the maintenance of their rights.[64]

Most Ohioans were fully supportive of the war posture and Harding's vote. Carrie Phillips was surely disappointed but made no move to expose their affair.

At least at the outset of the conflict, most Americans rallied around their Commander-in-Chief. Harding was among those who voted in favor of a number of war measures that provided the government with significant new authorities to aggressively prosecute the war. This included a national draft, an Espionage Act, food control measures, and many other acts related to war mobilization and execution. This was no time for partisanship or even short-sighted constitutional nitpicking, according to Senator Harding. "I must say that he is not my choice," Harding remarked about Wilson, "but the people of the country have chosen him. ... He is already by the inevitable force of events our partial dictator. Why not make him complete and supreme dictator? He will have to answer to the people and to history eventually for his stewardship. Why not give him a full and free hand, not for his sake, but for our sake?"[65] Harding's personal antipathy for Wilson and many of his policies was not going to prevent him from providing the national executive with everything he needed to defeat the enemy now that his country had opted into the global fight.

As usual, Harding was not a driver for most of the consequential war-related decisions being made in the Senate. However, there was one measure for which he did engage directly, and not without controversy. Theodore Roosevelt had been one of President Wilson's harshest critics for not being more proactive in preparing for potential war and for delaying his decision to enter the conflict. But now he found himself at Wilson's doorstep seeking a favor. Roosevelt's greatest memory was in leading his fellow Rough Riders in battle in Cuba during the Spanish-American War, and he wanted to return to those glory days by leading an all-American volunteer regiment into France. Roosevelt knew it would take many months before the U.S. Army was ready to deploy men to the front lines, and he thought it would be a great morale boost to the Allies to have a former American President bring an initial set of troops into the fight right away. One of Roosevelt's strongest supporters in this initiative was none other than Senator Warren Harding. Harding had completely broken with Roosevelt over the latter's defection from the Republican Party in the 1912 election, but during the recent canvass they had found common cause once again in the Republican ranks. As Roosevelt went to see Wilson in the White House to make his pitch about leading American volunteers into battle, Harding was offering the legal authority to sanction such a move. "An immediate force of American volunteers," Harding told his colleagues, "would put new life in every Allied trench and a new glow in every Allied campfire on every battlefront in Europe."[66] Harding's measure authorized the President to raise three such volunteer regiments to accelerate American involvement on the front lines, a move greatly valued by the former President. "I deeply appreciate your patriotic work," Roosevelt wrote to Harding. "Opposition is of course merely political."[67] But that opposition was formidable. President Wilson had no intention of providing one of his greatest political rivals a platform to re-establish himself as the Great American Hero. Wilson signed the broader legislation to which Harding had attached his amendment but took no steps to raise any of these regiments. The bulk of the American fighting force would come through the draft and take about a year before appearing on the field of battle. Roosevelt returned to his posture as Wilson's #1 critic, with heartfelt gratitude to Harding for his personal efforts to try to get him back into uniform leading American troops in battle.

Senator Harding joined his fellow Americans in doing what he could to support the war effort. This was going to be a period of sacrifice, not only for the citizen soldiers who were about to be deployed to the trenches of Europe but also for the men and women staying home to enable the fight abroad. The entire American economy shifted to a war footing as the massive training and mobilization effort touched every aspect of American lives. One of the most direct impacts was in the area of food. President Wilson and his Food Administrator, Herbert Hoover, preached maximum production and conservation in order to feed the people and soldiers in Europe. Hoover was an engineer by training but had emerged in the early stages of the war as a management and logistics guru, helping to feed the starving people of Belgium. President Wilson now tapped him to take over similar responsibilities for a wider audience. Plenty of people tried to squeeze a few minutes into Hoover's packed schedule to offer advice, as well as make a seemingly endless run of requests and even complaints. Senator Harding was among those who showed up at Hoover's Washington office, but, as Hoover later recalled, Harding's visit was different. The Senator had no agenda to pursue, just a genuine offer to help. "I haven't come to get anything," Harding said. "I just want you to know that if you wish the help of a friend, telephone me what you want. I am here to serve and to help."[68] And then he left. It was an act of selfless generosity that was typical of Harding's persona, and one that Herbert Hoover never forgot.

While the nation sought to channel its anxiety into the sole purpose of defeating a global enemy, Warren Harding also had some other things on his mind. This included his extramarital relationship with Carrie Phillips, which was in a particularly tenuous state over the pair's divergent views on all things German. But while that connection may have been at a crossroads, along came Nan Britton. Britton had been "in love with Warren Harding"[69] since she was a 14-year-old high school freshman. That year was 1910, when the newspaperman was making his run for Governor of Ohio. Nan's primary connection to the Harding family was through Abigail ("Daisy") Harding, Warren's sister, who happened to be her teacher. Nan was smitten with the handsome, gregarious Harding, adorning her walls with pictures from his campaign posters, as well as watching him from a distance as he walked to and from the offices of the *Star*. One of the few times she had actually spoken to Harding was when he won his seat in the Senate, as Nan and a friend joined the myriad of Marionites who made their way to the Harding home to offer congratulations. As the Hardings shifted to Washington, D.C., the Brittons left Marion for Cleveland, but Nan never lost her crush on the senator. Harding was, of course, oblivious to all of this when he received a letter from Nan on May 8, 1917. Now living in New York, she wanted help getting a job.

> HON. WARREN G. HARDING
> UNITED STATES SENATE
> WASHINGTON, D. C.
>
> MY DEAR MR. HARDING:

> I wonder if you will remember me; my father was Dr. Britton, of Marion, Ohio. I have been away from Marion for about two years, and, up until last November, have been working. But it was work which promised no future. Through the kindness of one of my father's Kenyon classmates, Mr. Grover Carter, of this city, I have been enabled to take up a secretarial course, which course I shall finish in less than three weeks. I have been reading of the imperative demand for stenographers and typists throughout the country, and the apparent scarcity, and it has occurred to me that you are in a position to help me along this line if there is an opening. … Now that I am about to look for an all-day position I do so want to get into something which will afford me prospects of advancement. Any suggestions or help you might give me would be greatly appreciated, I assure you, and it would please me so to hear from you.
>
> Sincerely,
> NAN BRITTON[70]

According to Nan, Harding responded immediately, telling her he remembered her well: "… you may be sure of that, and I remember you most agreeably, too."[71] In fact, he would be happy to meet with her in New York in just a few days.[1] They set a date, and he sent word that he would look for her in the lobby of the Mayflower Hotel. When their eyes

---

[1] The source for nearly all the information on the relationship between Warren Harding and Nan Britton comes from her book, *The President's Daughter*, published in 1927, four years after his death. For decades, Britton's memoirs were a source of conflict, with many friends and supporters of President Harding denying her assertions and ridiculing her in the process. It was only when DNA evidence substantiated her claims of maternity of Harding's only child that her credibility was given a second look. Britton's book is extremely detailed with a strong sense of authenticity. The DNA results not only confirm her primary allegation that she and Harding had a baby together, but enhances the reliability of many of her other claims. That said, given that the entire historical record of letters between the couple was intentionally destroyed in order to maintain secrecy, many of Britton's assertions cannot be verified. Historians are often confronted with aspects of history which cannot be validated, and Nan Britton's tale certainly fits that bill. In light of the DNA results, Britton deserves a general benefit of the doubt for much of her story. Areas which are potentially questionable, will be noted, including any direct quotes from Harding. Britton's book is filled with such quotes, but given that no records were kept, the accuracy of these quotations are questionable. For this rendering, most of those direct quotes have been avoided, although some paraphrasing has been incorporated, when deemed appropriate.

met, he certainly liked what he saw. Nan was a 20-year-old beauty who seemed to relish just being in his presence. It wasn't long before the pair made their way to Harding's room. "He asked me to come up there with him so that we might continue our conversation without interruptions or annoyances. … We had scarcely closed the door behind us when we shared our first kiss."[72] And Warren Harding's latest fling was on. The physical nature of the relationship didn't go beyond kissing at this first encounter, but that was only a matter of time. The 50-year-old senator was infatuated with this young darling who seemed completely smitten with him. She came with none of the pestering or baggage that had become common in his association with Carrie Phillips. This seemed like pure fun, filling yet another gap in Harding's personal life. He was happy to help Nan get a secretarial job at U.S. Steel and provided her with some spending money as they said their goodbyes in New York. Harding's travel schedule immediately increased as the passionate side of the relationship accelerated quickly.

III-21: Nan Britton at the time she began her affair with Harding, 1917 (age 20)

In addition to the hotel liaisons in New York, Harding invited Nan to accompany him on a trip to Chicago in June 1917. "What a maze of emotions!" Nan thought after that trip. "I knew I loved Warren Harding more than anything in all the world."[73] And through the many twists and turns of their relationship, she never seemed to waver in her attraction to Harding. Her memoirs carry with them a naïve quality, reflecting a young lady who had become overtaken by a school-girl crush, and couldn't believe her good fortune when the object of her desires seemed all too happy to reciprocate in the attachment. Unlike the demanding Carrie Phillips, Nan Britton was easy, just waiting for Harding to guide her for when to meet and what to do, always with a handful of cash on the way out the door to keep Nan well until their next get-together. "There was an element of naivete about my suggestions of which I was blissfully unaware," Nan later admitted.[74] She represented a complete escape for Harding, from any of the dreary aspects of his personal and professional life. "Our conversation was not principally political but warmly personal,"[75] Nan remarked – again, very different from Florence or Carrie. All that was pending was the consummation of the relationship, which occurred on July 30 at a hotel on Broadway in New York. "I became Mr. Harding's bride – as he called me – on that day,"[76] Nan later wrote to commemorate the loss of her virginity. As long as Harding could keep this latest affair a secret, another gap in his life would be fulfilled. Unlike Carrie, who covertly kept all his revealing letters, Nan was compliant in destroying any such evidence. "Through mutual recognition of the trouble we might cause each other and the ensuing happiness that might befall," she later wrote, "we early decided to destroy all love-letters."[77] Harding had a new source of joy, which was only exceeded by Nan's sense of revelry. Oblivious to the world around her, Nan felt that "The two years the United States was in the war were the two years I shall ever look back upon as the happiest of my life, as one cherishes the memory of precious hours with one's sweetheart."[78] There were indeed plenty of those hours together during this period for the Senator and his young fling, with little concern about the propriety of an affair with someone who was less than half his age.

As Harding's new relationship advanced with joy, his other illicit liaison was proving to be nothing but trouble. Carrie Phillips had a mind of her own, which continued to portray her pro-German sympathies at a time when the vast majority of Americans had deemed the Germans to be their mortal enemies. Harding was sufficiently concerned about Carrie's rhetoric that he wrote her a series of warnings to watch her mouth.

> It is quite all right for you to express yourself freely on war matters to me. This does not say you are right, but there is no harm in free expression to me. I can understand. But do, please, I beg you, be prudent in talking to others. If things go as you have foreseen, in the serene aftermath you can have your consolation. Remember, your country is in war, and things are not normal, and toleration is not universal, and justice is not always discriminating. You know I am only for your good. If you are right, your triumph will be complete; if you are wrong, you will have no words to eat, and meanwhile you will be secure from misrepresentation.[79]

Harding's mistresses represented plenty of risks, from the physical to the political. Nevertheless, he made no moves to sever either relationship. Just a couple of months after warning Carrie about her pro-German sentiments, Harding sent another note focused entirely on the more pleasurable aspects of their connection. "Wish I could take you to Mount Jerry," he wrote. "Wonderful spot. Not in the geographies but a heavenly place, and I have seen some passing views there and reveled in them. Gee! How I wish you might be along."[80]

Meanwhile, the country's business progressed forward, with a unified effort to secure victory over Germany and the Central Powers. It took almost a year before the American servicemen were ready to fully deploy, and when they did, they didn't disappoint. The Americans helped secure the defensive line protecting Paris and other parts of France and were then at the pointy end of the spear in the fight to push the Germans back to their homeland. Victories at the Battles of Amiens, the Somme, the Argonne Forest, and St. Michiel were costly but decisive. Casualties accrued on both sides of the lines, but while the Americans were bringing in 10,000 fresh troops per day, the Germans had no way to replenish their losses in men and materiel. By the fall, it was only a matter of time for the Central Powers to admit defeat. The armistice was eventually signed on November 11, 1918, bringing the fighting to a close, and readying a pitched battle to win the peace.

Harding had been proud to support President Wilson in the prosecution of the war, but now that the guns had been silenced, a reversion to partisan politics was quick to re-emerge. Wilson fueled some of this animosity as he insisted on personally leading the American delegation to the Peace Conference in France that would settle the terms to be imposed on the Central Powers. When Wilson named his delegation, it was devoid of any outreach to the other side of the aisle, despite the fact that any treaty negotiated abroad would require the support of 2/3rd of the members of the U.S. Senate. Wilson claimed he needed complete unity in the American delegation if he was going to be able to forge an agreement with the Allies to support his Fourteen Points, including the establishment of a League of Nations as a mechanism to avoid future wars. There were plenty of prominent Republicans who supported the core elements of Wilson's plan, and could have been useful when it came time to ratify any agreements, but Wilson refused to engage the opposition, simply expecting compliance when he would return with a treaty. The Ph.D. President, who was one of the nation's leading political scientists, completely misjudged his political reality. Senator Warren Harding was among those who found themselves in direct opposition to the national executive.

Henry Cabot Lodge was a former political scientist himself, now representing the people of Massachusetts in the United States Senate. Lodge was the chairman of the Foreign Relations Committee, placing him on the front lines in consideration of any peace treaty negotiated by the delegation in Paris. Harding had recently been elevated to a spot on Foreign Relations as well, and he found himself in complete alliance with Lodge against the Treaty of Versailles as negotiated by Wilson. The crux of the concern was the Covenant for Wilson's beloved League of Nations, with the strongest objections emanating from Article Ten, which stated:

> The Members of the League undertake to respect and preserve as against external aggression the territorial integrity and existing political independence of all Members of the League. In case of any such aggression or in case of any threat or danger of such aggression the Council shall advise upon the means by which this obligation shall be fulfilled.[81]

This part of the pact was taken by many Republicans in the Senate as an attack on American sovereignty, potentially requiring the United States to come to the aid of another member of the League even if the conflict had nothing to do with the U.S. As the debates began in the Senate, numerous objections were raised. They were termed "reservations" and their proponents were tagged as "reservationists," of which Warren Harding was proud to be a member. The reservationists weren't opposed to *any* League, just the one negotiated by Wilson. They were insisting that the President return to the bargaining table with changes to accommodate their concerns. To this, Wilson absolutely refused. He had made a deal in good faith and had no inclination to modify that agreement to deal with concerns that he believed were unfounded in the first place.

Lodge led the opposition to the President, with Senator Harding among his chief allies. When Lodge floated a "round-robin" letter advocating opposition to the Peace Treaty without acceptance of reservations, Harding was among the 37 senators to sign the missive. Harding's "America First" perspective was at the heart of his concerns:

> These reservations must be strong and unmistakable. I could no more support mild reservations than I could support mild Americanism. These reservations come of a purpose to protect America first and still save a framework on which to build intelligent co-operation. ... I do not believe, Senators, that it is going 'to break the heart of the world' to make this covenant right, or at least free from perils which would endanger our own independence. But it were better to witness this rhetorical tragedy than destroy the soul of this great Republic.[82]

The debate over the Treaty became personal and heated. Lodge led hearings in the Senate, inviting a majority of witnesses to share their objections. Meanwhile, President Wilson took his message on the road, beginning a grueling campaign-style tour to generate support for his efforts. The always frail Wilson was not up to the task, suffering a physical breakdown after giving a lengthy address to a packed crowd in Pueblo, Colorado. Wilson's wife and physician shut down the tour, ordering an immediate return to Washington, but the damage had already been done. Just a couple of days after settling back into the White House, Wilson suffered a massive stroke that would leave him an invalid for the last four-and-a-half years of his life.

Wilson's failing health did not bring the debate over the League of Nations to an end, as a vote on the proposed Treaty was still pending in the Senate. Harding took the floor of the Senate for a major speech on the League, reiterating his insistence on passage only with the adoption of the stated reservations. "To accept it unaltered would be a betrayal of America," Harding maintained.[83] The majority of senators agreed, refusing to vote for Wilson's Treaty without modifications when the vote was called on November 19. As far as Harding was concerned, the blame for the defeat fell squarely on the stubborn executive who refused to find common ground with the political opposition, something that was required to put most treaties into effect under the American system of government. "That is not the fault of the Senate," Harding maintained, "that is the fault of him who negotiated without recognizing that there is a Senate."[84] As far as Harding was concerned, "There was but one man in the United States of America, who did not know that this treaty could never be ratified without reservations." Thus, Wilson was responsible for "the colossal blunder of all time," and those who supported him participated in "a knowing betrayal of the Republic."[85]

Harding wasn't completely opposed to the idea of an international body whose purpose was to reduce the likelihood of future wars. He would have supported an alternative structure that was less binding on the member states to deploy arms where it might not be in their best interest to do so. Harding thought the right construct would be less of a League and more of a Court. Harding gave a speech in which he advocated for "An international arbitration and a world court for justiciable disputes." He claimed such an institution would:

> … appeal to all who think justice is sustained in reason rather than in armed disputes. The establishment of an agency for the revelation of the moral judgment of the world can never be amiss. These things might well have come out of the combined consciences of the nations awakened to new ideas amid the sufferings of war, and they will yet come. But it does not require a supergovernment to effect them, nor the surrender of nationality and independence of action to sanction them.[86]

A commitment to arbitration was a principle for which Harding was pleased to advocate as far preferable to the interests of the United States than the agreement put forward by Wilson and the Allies in France. But Wilson was no longer listening to any outside suggestions. While his work was significantly curtailed due to his ill health, Wilson found the strength to continuously reject any modifications to the original Treaty of Versailles. As a result, when another vote was taken in the Senate in March 1919, it suffered the same fate as before. The League of Nations would shortly go into effect, but without the United States as a member. Wilson was convinced that all of this would be reversed after the upcoming election when the American people would demand the adoption of his treaty. The electorate would indeed weigh in on this topic in the subsequent canvass, but hardly in the way anticipated by the incumbent President.

4. The Dark Horse from Ohio

Most Republicans anticipated the return of Theodore Roosevelt to the presidential canvass in 1920. The party had once again rallied around Roosevelt as among the most outspoken and dogged in the criticism of President Wilson, both during the war and in the subsequent negotiations for peace. Harding was now in good stead with Roosevelt and was ready to once again support the former President to re-unify the party and return Republican ideology to the White House. But Roosevelt suddenly died on January 6, 1919. Harding was given the honor to eulogize TR in front of the Ohio General Assembly:

> In any appraisal Colonel Roosevelt's name will be inseparably linked with the finding of the American soul, with the great awakening and consecration. Now and hereafter let it be said: 'Here was a great and courageous American, who called to the slumbering spirit of the republic and made it American in fact as well as in name.'[87]

Once the tears subsided, the political reality set in. With Roosevelt's passing, the Republicans were now facing a wide-open field in the race for the 1920 nomination. Harry Daugherty re-entered the Harding orbit to once again push his longtime friend to go for higher office – in this case, the presidency itself. Harding had a number of things going for him, not the least of which was the simple fact that he hailed from Ohio. The midwestern state had become a breeding ground for American Presidents, with six of the past ten national executives hailing from Harding's home state. Harding was also likable thanks to a career of getting along with just about everyone. And he had been on the right side of the debate over the League as far as most Republicans were concerned. But Harding also had very little in the way of a national following and had hardly been a leader in the Senate. He was always a reliable Republican vote but was rarely out front on issues or made his mark with any major legislation. Daugherty wasn't worried. These details would work themselves out. For now, all Daugherty wanted was Harding's commitment to make the race, and he would take care of the rest.

Harding was seriously conflicted by the entire proposition. Harding had a great life. He had few worries, had all the time he wanted to carouse with the boys on the golf course or at the poker table, and could still rely on a steady stream of income from the hometown paper that he continued to own. George Christian had come to Washington with Harding, serving as his personal secretary. He knew Harding as well as anyone and had an interesting take on Harding the politician. "He had no taste for politics," Christian once claimed. "Never had." When queried about whether he liked being a Senator, Christian replied: "No: he didn't like being a Senator. He liked being in the Senate."[88] Harding was a member in good standing of the greatest club in the world, with his most significant worries tied to keeping his extramarital affairs under wraps. He was perfectly content with his station in life, with re-election to the Senate on the horizon. Why would he risk all that for one of the toughest jobs on the planet? He said as much in a letter to his friend, Samuel McClure. "I am very happy in the Senate and much prefer to remain there," Harding wrote. "I do not believe I could be happy as President. I don't want it."[89] When Daugherty approached Florence Harding on the subject, he received a similar reply. "We are happy in our home in Washington," she told Daugherty. "He likes the Senate. I like being a Senator's wife. There is no strain. No pressure. No nerve-racking anxieties. We have charming friends. Warren is making a fine record. He can stay here as long as he likes."[90]

Harding expanded on his reluctance in a letter to another friend back home.

> Honestly, I would not have [the presidency] if I could reach out and grasp it, and I really do not want any of my friends to promote it in any way. … I find it difficult to make a good many people believe that one can feel this way. … Of course, I am human enough to enjoy having friends who think well enough of me to suggest me for the position, and I confess some pleasure in knowing that events have so broken thus far that I should attract some favorable mention, but when it comes down to serious consideration I am wholly truthful when I say that I had rather no mention were made whatever.[91]

Harding also humbly expressed reluctance to enter the contest out of concern for his ability to meet the demands of the position. This included the following note to his friend E. Mont Reily:

> Truly, my dear Reily, … I do not want to be considered in that connection. … I must assert the conviction that I do not

> possess the elements of leadership or the widespread acquaintances which are essential to the ideal leadership of our Party in 1920. I think I owe it to the Party to say these things, because I know better than some who over-estimate both my ability and availability.[92]

These weren't the only reasons for Harding's hesitation. He had two other concerns, one named Carrie and the other named Nan.

Carrie Phillips continued to badger Harding about getting out of politics. She wanted the Senator to divorce his wife and return to Marion to be with her full time. Her threats also became more overt, not only wanting him but demanding money as well. Harding responded: "Your proposal to destroy me, and yourself in doing so, will only add to the ill we have already done. It doesn't seem like you to think of such a fatal course. I can't believe your purpose is to destroy me for paying the tribute so freely uttered and so often shown." That led to the discussion of payment.

> I'll pay this price to save my own disgrace and your own self-destruction to destroy me. That is one proposal, complete, final, and covers all. Here is another. If you think I can be more helpful by having a public position and influence, probably a situation to do some things worthwhile for myself and you and yours, I will pay you $5,000 per year, in March each year, so long as I am in that public service. It is not big, but it will add to your comfort and make you independent to a reasonable degree. It is most within my capacity. I wish it might be more, but we can only do that which is in his power. Destroy me, and I have no capacity, while the object of your dislike is capable of going on in her own account.[93]

Needless to say, Carrie continued to keep the affair quiet.

Harding received no threats from Nan Britton, but he had a very different kind of challenge with mistress #2. Early in 1919 Nan became pregnant. Harding tried to counsel her to have an abortion or to give the child up for adoption, but the expectant mother wanted nothing more in the world than to bear Warren Harding's child, and she had no plans to do otherwise now that the miracle of life was growing inside her. Harding continued to pay Nan's bills, getting her a room in Asbury Park, New Jersey, for which she registered under the name Nan Christian. It was in this private setting that she could obtain medical attention while waiting for the big day to arrive. It was around 2:00 pm on October 22 when Nan Britton gave birth to Warren Harding's only child. Seeking to keep their secret quiet, she named her precious little girl Elizabeth Ann Christian. Shortly after the birth, Nan returned to Chicago where she and the baby moved in with her sister, Elizabeth Willits, and her husband Scott. Harding kept track of these events from afar, continuing to write letters and sending a few hundred dollars here and there. He had every intention of continuing the affair while desperately trying to keep the whole thing quiet.

So, Warren Harding had a lot on his mind as the calendar flipped to 1920 and he mulled over the possibility of running for President of the United States. Harry Daugherty continued to push Harding to commit to making the race. This included a trip to Washington to convince the Ohio congressional delegation to stand up for Harding as the state's favorite son candidate. He then went for the big guns, homing in on Florence, who was reluctant at first but eventually offered her support. Despite this growing list of advocates, Daugherty was still struggling to get Harding himself on board, in part because he wasn't sure he could trust his primary suitor. Many people had warned Harding about Daugherty. As Harding's close friend Charles Hard put it, "[Harry] always 'busts up' anything he is in because he plays it too hard and is too combative"[94] – very much the opposite of Warren Harding. Daugherty tried to spin the difference as a positive. "I am far more comfortable as to your ability to cope with great public questions and public appearances, positions and utterances, than I am for you to deal with those who are engaged in intrigue," Daugherty said to Harding. "I will take care of the latter and together we will make a fair combination in this great enterprise."[95] Harding wasn't so sure. After some of his own disagreements with Daugherty, he decided to put his cards on the table. "The trouble with you, my dear Daugherty, in your political relations with me," Harding wrote, "is that you appraise my political sense so far below par that you have no confidence in me or my judgement. Pray do not think because I can and do listen in politeness to much that is said to me, that I am always being 'strung.' I cannot and will not suspect everyone of wanting to use me. I must and will believe in professed political friendship until I find myself imposed upon. It is the only way that I know of to political happiness."[96] By now, it was mid-December 1919, and decisions had to be made. Harding and Daugherty had a final heart-to-heart, and the latter finally prevailed. Despite the myriad concerns infecting his thought process, on December 17, Harding consented to become a candidate for the Republican nomination for President. This was still a long shot at best, with Daugherty one of the few who really thought Harding had much of a chance at securing the nomination. But now the work could begin.

Two major themes would develop for Harding's 1920 campaign. The first had been Harding's calling card for years – a nationalistic view predicated on an "America First" mindset and related policies. These perspectives were on full display from the beginning of the campaign, which included a speech in New York City to the Ohio Club of New York on January 10.

> I have a confidence in our America that requires no council of foreign powers to point the way of American duty. We wish to counsel, coöperate and contribute, but we arrogate to ourselves the keeping of the American conscience and every concept of our moral obligations. It is fine to idealize, but it is very practical to make sure our own house is in perfect order before we attempt the miracle of the Old-World stabilization.
>
> Call it the selfishness of nationality if you will, I think it an inspiration to patriotic devotion:
>
> To safeguard America first.
> To stabilize America first.
> To prosper America first.
> To think of America first.
> To exalt America first.
> To live for and revere America first.[97]

III-22: Poster from Harding's "America First" presidential campaign, 1920

Harding's nationalistic sentiments were popular when held in contrast to the worldview espoused by President Wilson which had failed to catch on with the U.S. Senate and much of the American citizenry. Harding's second theme was also a direct contrast to the incumbent President. According to Harding, it was time to slow things down, to stop trying to change the world, to limit the radical notions of the progressives, and return to the good ol' days. In Harding's words, he was advocating for a "Return to Normalcy." Harding told the Home Market Club in Boston in May that "America's present need is not heroics, but healing; not nostrums but normalcy; not revolution but restoration ... not surgery but serenity."[98] Harding further defined the concept as follows: "By 'normalcy' I don't mean the old order, but a regular steady order of things. I mean normal procedure, the natural way, without excess. I don't believe the old order can or should come back, but we must have normal order or, as I have said, 'normalcy.'"[99] The rhetoric sounded appealing, but it was still coming from a one-term senator with very little in the way of a national following. The nomination still felt to most as a bridge too far.

In recent political cycles, states were increasingly adopting primaries to choose delegates for the national conventions for the major political parties. Harding expected to sweep the primary in his home state of Ohio, but even that turned out not to be an easy task. The Republican front-runner emerging in the race was Roosevelt's close friend, General Leonard Wood. Wood was a career army officer, a physician by trade, who had won the medal of honor in the 1886 Geronimo Campaign before serving as TR's commanding officer in the Rough Riders' appearance in Cuba. After the Spanish-American War, Wood served as the Governor General in Cuba before becoming Chief of Staff of the Army. Also in the mix was Illinois Governor Frank Lowden, who was more popular with the Old Guard members of the party compared to

III-23: General Leonard Wood, 1920

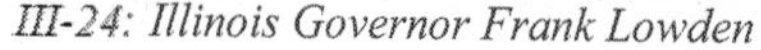

III-24: Illinois Governor Frank Lowden

III-25: Hiram Johnson, 1920

Wood. Lowden had previously served five years in the House of Representatives and had been a member of the Republican National Committee. The last of the front-runners was Hiram Johnson, the former Governor of California and the leading progressive back in the Republican ranks. Johnson was popular with a key segment of the electorate but had burned his bridges with the party leadership by joining Roosevelt for the party fracture in 1912 and then refusing to support Charles Evans Hughes in 1916. Three strong candidates, but with very different appeals, made for a wide-open contest. This was what Harry Daugherty was counting on. Daugherty knew Harding wouldn't be the favorite heading into the convention, but he did have confidence that he could be the second, third, or fourth choice of just about every delegate, perhaps serving as the classic "available man" if a deadlock occurred among the favorites. In fact, Daugherty predicted as much in an interview with *The New York Times* early in the campaign:

> I don't expect Senator Harding to be nominated on the first, second, or third ballots, but I think we can afford to take chances that, about eleven minutes after two, Friday morning of the convention, when ten or twenty weary men are sitting around a table, someone will say, 'Who will we

> nominate?' At that decisive time the friends of Harding will suggest him and can well afford to abide by the result.[100]

Daugherty's prophecy would pretty nearly come true. But none of that could materialize if Harding didn't at least demonstrate his prowess in the primary in his home state of Ohio, which Leonard Wood was actively trying to disrupt.

Wood had never served in elective office. He had received just one vote at the Republican Convention in 1916 (the same as Harding). But he had attracted significant support for this go-around, in part because he was seen as the man to carry forward in the tradition of his friend, Theodore Roosevelt. Wood's team was being aggressive, entering primary races across the country, including Ohio, where Harding was feeling the pressure. "We have a pretty stiff fight on in Ohio," Harding bemoaned to Charles Forbes on April 1, "and it gives me a great deal of annoyance that I am obliged to give the slightest attention to my home State."[101] Harding went on to win the Ohio primary, but, in many ways, the result was disappointing. Wood captured nine of the 48 delegates – a mixed bag, at best, for Harding who had hoped to head to Chicago with all of Ohio in his pocket. But the bad news for Harding was actually just beginning. Daugherty had convinced Harding to enter two other primaries to try to pick up a few more delegates heading into the convention. Daugherty identified Indiana and Montana as attractive primaries to enter. These were disastrous for Harding, who showed little ability to garner virtually any support outside of his home state. He not only captured zero delegates in these two primaries, but he also received only 723 votes out of more than 40,000 cast in Montana. Once these results were in, Harding thought this was the end of the line. "Well," he sighed, "it looks like we're done for."[102] *The New York Times* seemed to agree. "Harding is eliminated," the *Times* reported. "Even if his name is presented to the convention … everyone will know that he is an impossible candidate."[103] Harding talked about giving up. Florence wasn't giving in to this defeatist attitude, however, at least not at this stage of the campaign. "Wurr'n Harding," she declared in her typical pronunciation of her husband's name, "what are you doing? Give up? Not until the convention is over. Think of your friends in Ohio!"[104] Harding *was* thinking about Ohio, about how he could continue to support the people of his state in the Senate and forget about this presidential stuff. He still wanted to register for the Senate race, despite the pushback from

Daugherty, who thought it would send a terrible signal to his presidential supporters. "You don't want me to give up the senatorship, do you?" he said to Daugherty in a fit of exasperation. "I haven't got a ghost of a chance at the Presidency."[105] He wasn't dropping out of anything at this stage but wanted to keep his options open with no real cause for any optimism emanating from the presidential contest.

Fortunately for Harding, the leading contenders all had baggage that was hurting their candidacies. Wood, for example, was being pounded as the rich man's candidate thanks to the overwhelming advantage he had accumulated with campaign donors. According to reporting by Louis Seibold in the New York *World*, Wood's political war chest had been filled by a handful of millionaires. The list included "oil-man E. L. Doheny, metal-man Ambrose Monel, utilities-man H.M. Byllesby, copper-man William Boyce Thompson, steel-man and banker Dan Hann, sports promoter E.E. Smathers, and grocer A.A. Sprague."[106] And then there was William Procter, the head of Procter & Gamble with seemingly unlimited funds, who was emerging as the top contributor to the Wood campaign. These reports caused a backlash from voters and politicians. Senator William Borah, a supporter of the progressive candidate Hiram Johnson, formed a committee under Senator William Kenyon to investigate the matter. The Kenyon Committee issued a report just two weeks before the Republican Convention, and the numbers didn't look good for Wood, who had already spent nearly $1.8M in the campaign. This compared to $414,000 by Lowden (most of which was his own money), $194,000 by Johnson, $173,000 by Herbert Hoover, and $113,000 by Harding.[107] Wood was blasted as caring only for the rich and out of control with his exorbitant spending. Lowden's personal wealth, which was significantly enhanced when he married into the family that owned the Pullman Company and its famous rail cars, was also an issue, along with some rumors that his campaign was trying to buy off a couple of delegates with cash. None of these issues was decisive, but it ensured that every candidate had areas of concern heading into the national convention in June.

The Republican Convention of 1920 was united in at least one thing – its complete rebuke of all things Woodrow Wilson. Wilson's failures over the Treaty of Versailles and the League of Nations were just the starting point. He was also taken to task for his intrusive domestic policies, as well as his elitist and dictatorial personality. The fact that he

III-26: 1920 Republican National Convention, Chicago Coliseum, June 1920

had been bedridden for months had the Republicans champing at the bit to paint the Democrats as incapable of governing, opening the door for wholesale change. With this in mind, Senator Henry Cabot Lodge, Wilson's chief opponent in the fight over the League, was selected to chair the Republican Convention. Lodge set the tone for the entire event with his anti-Wilson keynote address:

> Mr. Wilson and his dynasty, his heirs and assigns, or anybody that is his, anybody who with bent knee has served his purposes, must be driven from all control, from all influence upon the government of the United States. They must be driven from office and power not because they are Democrats but because Mr. Wilson stands for a theory of administration and government which is not American.[108]

While the 940 delegates were undoubtedly in complete agreement with these sentiments, that didn't mean they were ready to rally around a single candidate to win back the White House. In fact, Harry Daugherty was counting on that. Daugherty consolidated the Harding forces at Chicago's Congress Hotel, but he had supporters fan out to all the hotels, buttonholing delegates to keep Harding in mind as a second or third option in case a deadlock materialized during the upcoming balloting.

Harding arrived in the Windy City uncharacteristically depressed. He was still smarting from his poor showing in the primaries and was basically thinking this was all a waste of time. He had his friend George Harris standing by in Columbus to enter his Declaration of Candidacy for re-election to the Senate, fully expecting that to be his only political option in the very near future. He also visited a "friend" in Chicago as the proceedings were getting underway. Nan Britton was living in the city with her sister and their daughter. Nan desperately wanted Harding to meet his little girl – to hold her, play with her, and love her – but he always had a reason why such a meeting couldn't take place. Harding saw Nan a couple of times during the convention and secured her a seat in the gallery so she could witness the festivities, but he never laid eyes on little Elizabeth Ann.

Before the balloting for the Republican nomination for President and Vice President could begin, speeches were delivered to nominate the various candidates for consideration. For Harding, that honor went to former Ohio Governor Frank Willis. Willis addressed his comments to the "boys-and-girls" in the audience,[109] acknowledging the 27 women serving as delegates to a national convention for the first time. He then got down to the business at hand, selling Warren Harding to this Republican gathering as a winning contrast to the other people in the race.

> The record of Ohio's candidate is the record of the Republican party for the last decade. … He is one of the common folks, best loved by those who know him best. With no working capital, other than his own ability and his capacity for toil, he has built up a prosperous business, employing many men, and in his shop, where he works side by side with his men, there has never been an hour of labor trouble in twenty-five years of friendly co-operation. He is a stalwart fighting Republican, who believes in the efficacy of representative government under party sponsorship. His face is toward the future.[110]

That same day, Friday, June 11, the roll call of states commenced amid sweltering conditions in the packed Coliseum, with 471 votes needed to capture the nomination.

More than a dozen candidates received votes on the first ballot, but Wood was clearly in command at the outset with 287 ½ votes, followed by Lowden with 211 ½ and Johnson with 133 ½. Harding was sixth on the first ballot with 65 ½. Three more ballots were held that day with very little movement. When a recess was called, Wood had risen to 314 ½ votes followed by Lowden at 289. Harding was up one spot to fifth place but had actually lost some votes, checking in at 61 ½. Harding wanted to throw in the towel and get out of town. He was moping around his hotel, showing "great mental distress," according to Jacob Meckstroth of the *Ohio State Journal*. "Discouragement hung about him like a cloud. He was not interested in anything."[111] Harding was focused on the only sure task ahead of him, and that was to ensure that George Harris filed those papers to officially get him into the race for his senate seat. Those papers were filed at 11:58 pm that night, two minutes before the deadline. But political conventions were known to be highly unpredictable, and a lot would transpire over the next 24 hours on the path to the Republican nomination.

The convention was essentially stuck, with neither Wood nor Lowden interested in making a deal or compromising to get the nomination. When Wood was offered the support of the large delegation from Pennsylvania in return for some patronage guarantees in the Cabinet and other postings, he rejected it out of hand. "Shady business, gentlemen," Wood replied, "and I'll have nothing to do with it."[112] Wood and Lowden were both approached about a unity ticket between the two of them, but neither was interested in being the VP to the other. Another push was for Johnson to be the VP, but Wood, Lowden, and even Johnson rejected that overture. There did not seem to be any path that would get one of the front runners over the top. Given all the problems the party had had at its most recent conventions, a number of leaders were concerned about the negative perceptions that might result from a protracted fight for the nomination. Meetings took place across Chicago that night, trying to figure out a way to resolve the impasse.

The most famous of these smoke-filled room gatherings took place at the Blackstone Hotel in the suite of Party Chairman Will Hays. For several hours, Republican senators filed in and out of the room to listen in and make their case on how to get to an acceptable nominee. Among those present for much of the night included Senators Henry Lodge (MA), Charles Curtis (KS), Reed Smoot (UT), and Frank Brandegee (CT), along with newspaperman George Harvey. Harvey was a former Democrat and early supporter of Woodrow Wilson but had defected to the Republican cause during Wilson's presidency. As the senators each made the case for his favorite, others quickly weighed in with their opposition. This included the front-runners and the next tier as well. The only person for which there were seemingly no negatives was everyone's friend, Warren Harding. Harding seemed to check all the right boxes. He had been loyal to the Old Guard in 1912, he was for the League of Nations but *only* by adopting the Senate's reservations, he had always been a loyal Republican vote in the Senate, he was completely opposite to the pompous and elitist Wilson in personality, and he was someone with whom these leading senators felt they could work. Plus, he hailed from Ohio, which continued to resonate among the delegates as a tried and true resume item that had worked so many times before.

Senator Harding did not step foot into Chairman Hays's suite during these discussions. He agreed with Daugherty to take one meeting that night, and that was to keep the Ohio delegation firmly in his camp even after news spread that Harding had registered for his re-election to the Senate. This mission accomplished, it was around 2:00 am when Harding was summoned to the smoke-filled room where he met with Brandegee and Harvey after the others had departed. According to Harvey, Harding was told that if the stalemate persisted at the top of the balloting, these senators were prepared to swing votes in Harding's direction to make him the nominee. But first, he put Harding on the spot. "We think, you may be nominated tomorrow," Harvey reportedly told Harding, but "before acting finally, we think you should tell us, on your conscience and before God, whether there is anything that might be brought up against you that would embarrass the party, any impediment that might disqualify you or make you inexpedient, either as candidate or as President."[113] Harding was surprised at the question and asked for a few minutes to think, undoubtedly with visions of Carrie Phillips, Nan Britton, and his daughter Elizabeth rolling around in his head. When he returned, Harding told Harvey he had no concerns about anything in his past.

Rumors of a pro-Harding movement began filtering through the various camps, as well as with the reporters covering the convention. The Associated Press put it this way: "Harding of Ohio emerged this morning from all-night conferences of Republican chieftains as the man with whom they hoped to break the imminent deadlock. Delicate relationships were involved ... but most of the leaders appeared agreeable to trying Harding first among the large field of dark horses."[114] Harding appeared reborn the next morning, emerging from the gloom of the previous days with all smiles and handshakes once again. Harry Daugherty, who always downplayed the importance of the meeting of the senators, remained indefatigable in placing Harding as everyone's second choice, waiting for the deadlock and the switch to the "most available man."

Balloting resumed on the morning of Saturday, June 12, and things picked up pretty much where they left off the night before. There was no immediate surge for Harding, and most of the senators involved in the previous night's debates remained initially unmoved in their own votes from the previous day. It appeared that Wood, Lowden, and Johnson would still be given the chance to break through, with Harding waiting in the wings in case the deadlock persisted. By the sixth ballot, Wood and Lowden were tied at 311 ½ votes each, followed by Johnson at 110 and Harding up to 89. Harding passed Johnson on the next ballot, and while he was inching closer to the leaders, he remained in third place after the eighth ballot. At this point, a recess was called by the Wood and Lowden supporters to try to salvage their candidacies and halt the momentum that Harding was experiencing. There was a move to shut down for the day, take Sunday off, and come back and start again on Monday. Such a delay could have been disastrous for Harding, but it did not come to pass. Chairman Lodge gaveled the convention back to order a little before 5:00 pm, and the balloting resumed.

Lowden saw the writing on the wall and began to release his delegates, almost all of whom jumped on the Harding bandwagon. Connecticut was the first to switch, followed by Florida, Kansas, and Kentucky. When New York cast its ballots for Harding, it gave the Senator from Ohio a strong lead at 374 ½ (compared to 249 for Wood and 121 ½ for Lowden). Daugherty saw his strategy paying off, with Harding sitting there as the attractive alternative to the initial frontrunners who now appeared to have no path to a majority. After that ninth ballot, a confident Daugherty proclaimed, "It was all over but the shouting and it began in short order. Our men leaped to their feet and yelled themselves hoarse. They marched down the aisles with banners and streamers, and exhorted sinners to repent before it was too late."[115] New Harding postcards were dropped from the rafters, anticipating one more ballot should put him over the top.

That tenth ballot was more of the same, with Pennsylvania casting the decisive votes that made Warren Harding the 1920 Republican nominee for President of the United States. What a remarkable turnaround in less than a day's time! "A cheer rose that shook the earth,"

Daugherty later recalled. "The vast spaces of the Coliseum echoed with demoniac screams. Ambitions crumbled! And a new figure in history emerged from the din."[116] Harding may have only been the first choice of a handful of delegates from Ohio, but American political conventions were full of dark horses emerging when the front runners failed to get to a majority, and this time Harding was in the right place at the right time to get the nomination. Leave it to Harding to come up with an apt analogy tied to his favorite game – poker. "I feel like a man who goes in on a pair of eights and comes out with aces full," Harding said.[117]

There were many takes on why Harding emerged from the Chicago Convention with his party's nomination. Senator Brandegee spoke for many when he said, "There ain't any first-raters this year. This ain't 1880 or any 1904; we haven't any John Shermans or Theodore Roosevelts; we got a lot of second-raters and Warren Harding is the best of the second-raters."[118] Moreover, since Harding was known as much more of a loyal party follower than a leader, many assumed that the senators picked Harding as their dark horse primarily because they were convinced they could control him. The New York *Evening Journal* echoed this sentiment when it declared that the Republicans "did not nominate a man; they nominated a group, an oligarchy."[119] As for Harding, he described in simple, natural terms why the nomination came to him:

> With Wood, Johnson and Lowden out of the way, I knew I could count on friends in every one of their delegations, because I had followed in my pre-convention campaigning the rule that has guided me throughout my political career, which is not to hurt any one's feelings or to step on anybody's toes if I could find foot room elsewhere. I figured that if politeness and an honest desire not to humiliate any rival just for the sake of winning a few votes were ever going to produce anything, this was the time. Other fellows, just as competent as I, or more so, had made enemies, and it looked to me that there was no one in sight that the convention could unite on except myself.[120]

Perhaps nice guys don't always finish last, as the saying goes. Warren Harding was out to prove quite the opposite.

There was still a little business to wrap up before everyone left town. A vice presidential candidate needed to be named as well. A number of leading senators were out front pushing for their colleague Irvine Lenroot of Wisconsin. But the delegates almost immediately balked at the suggestion, not interested in a Senate-dominated ticket. A quick surge developed for Massachusetts Governor Calvin Coolidge, whose greatest claim to fame had been standing firm in a face-off with striking Boston policemen the year before. Governor Coolidge's assertion that "There is no right to strike against the public safety by anybody, anytime, anywhere"[121] elevated his standing in the party across the country. Coolidge had tapped out at 34 votes in the presidential balloting but captured the VP nomination on the first ballot with 674 votes. As the delegates left the Coliseum on their way out of town, Harding had one more stop to make. He once again called upon Nan Britton. Things were going to be different going forward if for no other reason than his every movement was going to be tracked by both the secret service and the press. Harding assured Nan that their relationship would continue, but they were going to need to be even more discreet. Nan wanted to help the cause and eventually took a position in Chicago working on the campaign from afar. Harding still did not agree to meet his daughter, claiming the logistics were impossible now that he was under the microscope.

III-27: 1920 Republican campaign banner featuring the ticket of Warren Harding and Calvin Coolidge

The 1920 election was an all-Ohio affair, as the Democrats selected the sitting Governor, James Cox, to oppose Harding. An up-and-comer from New York by the name of Franklin Roosevelt was selected as the VP candidate. It was a clear choice for the electorate, both in terms of policies and personalities. The hot topic for national debate continued to be the League of Nations. Cox headed to the White House to celebrate his nomination and confer with President Wilson. He emerged with a full-throated support for the League as negotiated by Wilson. On the flip side, Harding had become even more steadfast in his opposition to Wilson's League unless significant changes were made. Cox became the aggressor on the campaign trail, barnstorming the country to reach nearly two million voters with his message. Harding had no interest in that kind of campaign, opting to follow the lead of another Ohioan from a couple of decades before. When William McKinley ran for the presidency, he did so from his front porch, playing the kind host to anyone who wanted to show up and hear him speak. Harding was one of those who visited Canton, Ohio, during that campaign and liked what he saw. Upon leaving Chicago, Harding made his intentions clear. "I must first go to Washington and clean up my work," he declared, "then to Marion for a porch campaign."[122]

III-28: 1920 Democratic campaign banner featuring the ticket of James Cox and Franklin Roosevelt

Fortunately, the front porch at the Harding home had undergone a major renovation and expansion, creating a near-perfect setting for the Republican nominee to make his case to the American people. Yes, there were prepared speeches each day, with the assistance of party leaders such as George Harvey and Richard Child, but the main attraction to the 600,000 or so people who showed up during the general election campaign was Harding himself. People got a chance to see the man up close and started to understand why those who knew him liked him so much. His messaging was simple and straightforward, extending his themes of "America First" and "Return to Normalcy." He was humble and sincere in every appearance and made virtually no gaffes. He was the genuine article, as portrayed by an editorial in the *Morrow County Sentinel*.

> The proudest moment in Morrow County's history has come. A native son has been selected as the candidate of a

III-29: A modern look at the Harding home on Mount Vernon Avenue

> great party for the highest office within the gift of the people. … Warren G. Harding's boyhood was not materially different from that of other boys of the community. He simply made the most of his limited opportunities. He worked, obtained an education, and his life has demonstrated his superior industry, capacity, intelligence and leadership. Harding is worthy. He is just plain folks.[123]

Indeed he was.

The official launch of the fall campaign took place on July 22 when representatives from all 48 states and the leadership of the Republican Party converged on Marion to formally offer Harding the nomination. This was one of the most substantive addresses for Harding throughout the entire campaign, touching on a number of the important issues facing the country. He spoke about the challenges of labor, the railroads, the economy (in particular as it related to farmers), the needs of war veterans, and women's suffrage. In terms of foreign affairs, Harding committed to officially ending the war with Germany and Austria-Hungary, but

III-30: Harding speaking to one of the large crowds gathered for the Front Porch Campaign of 1920

without signing on to the Treaty of Versailles or its League of Nations. He acknowledged some of his own limitations while committing to doing his best. "I will gladly give all that is in me, all of heart, soul and mind and abiding love of country, to service in our common cause," he remarked. "I can only pray to the omnipotent God that I may be worthy in service as I know myself to be faithful in thought and purpose. One can not give more."[124] He concluded by stating that he moved forward with complete confidence in his faith in the American people, the American system of government, and his Republican Party.

All of Marion came alive to put its best foot forward for the visitors who arrived daily at the local train station. The Marion Civic Association helped to organize the festivities, which included bands to greet the guests, glee clubs to serenade them, and members of the local fraternal organizations to show them around and pitch their friend, Warren Harding, as the right man to lead the country. Harding had long been a member of most of these organizations, and now he could add one more. After barring his admission for years, even the Masons now opened their doors to Harding. One of the most popular songs heard in Marion was a new Al Jolson tune written especially for the campaign, "Harding, You're the Man for Us." It featured lines such as:

> We think the country's ready
> For another man like Teddy
> We need another Lincoln
> To do the country's thinkin'[125]

Two people who were not around to partake in the festivities were Jim and Carrie Phillips. Shortly after Harding received the Republican nomination, the couple hit the road for Asia. It appears that Harding may have confided with party officials about his affair with Carrie, and donors were lined up to raise funds to keep the Phillipses out-of-sight and out-of-mind for the duration of the campaign. The couple got a free extended trip abroad, while Harding (and his fellow Republicans) got some peace of mind. The letter writing between Harding and Carrie Phillips also came to an end, with the last letter saved by Carrie passing between them during the 1920 campaign.

The press arrived in droves to share stories of Harding with the rest of the country. Being a newspaperman himself, Harding tried his best to take care of the reporters. He had a three-room bungalow built behind his home and stocked it with telegraph lines, telephones, typewriters, and plenty of cigars. Harding made himself available to the press, was sensitive to their deadlines, and was in his element whether he was swapping stories or pitching horseshoes. The press coverage was consistently favorable, a reflection not only of the candidate but also of his treatment of the reporters. In general, there was very little mudslinging in the campaign, as it neither fit the style of Harding nor Cox. But there was one exception that drew the ire of both campaigns which refused to take part in dredging up the unproven smear that Harding came from a mixed-race background.

William Chandler was a professor at Ohio's Wooster College. He had become almost obsessed with proving that Harding's lineage included "Black blood." He spent weeks roaming Blooming Grove, giving life to every rumor dating back several generations. During the campaign, Chandler's research became embedded in a book that was quickly condemned by leading Republicans and Democrats alike. Efforts were made to halt the publication and destroy copies that had made it into print. Chandler was called on the carpet by the college's leadership, demanding proof of his assertions. Given that he had no proof, the school's president, the Reverend Doctor Charles Wishart, demanded (and received) Chandler's resignation. The New York *Herald* reported on the rumormongering as: "In all our political history there is nothing comparable to this foul, eleventh-hour attack on a Presidential Candidate made without conscience or moral sense, solely for the purpose of defrauding the Republican Party of its impending victory. This is desperation carried to the verge of criminality."[126] Harding wanted to respond, but everyone talked him out of it. He was counseled that it was better to let the story die off without dignifying it with any statement whatsoever. Harding relented, although he burned inside over a story that never seemed to go away.

Harding did agree to hit the road for much of the last month of the campaign. He brought his folksy charm and "Return to Normalcy" messaging to 13 states. As the economy continued to sour as the campaign wore on, Harding offered more specifics on his plans for reducing taxes and raising the protective tariff, but Harding the human being continued to be the main attraction. Harding thoroughly enjoyed himself throughout the campaign. After all, he was spending time doing the things he liked the most – meeting people, getting to know them, and sharing a connection or story to bring a smile to their faces. Florence Harding also reveled during the months-long campaign, watching her husband thrive as the center of attention. "No matter what comes into my life," she wrote to her friend Evalyn McLean, "I shall always regard this summer as one of the greatest epochs."[127]

That epoch concluded with a resounding victory at the polls. Harding celebrated his 55th birthday with a landslide win over James Cox. The Democrat didn't even keep the Solid South, with Tennessee and Oklahoma both going for Harding. In total, Harding captured 37 states to 11 for Cox, resulting in an Electoral College rout to the tune of 404-127. The popular vote was similarly one-sided. Harding captured 60.4% of the vote, compared to 34.1% for Cox. In raw numbers, Harding outpolled Cox by more than seven million votes, the largest margin of victory (by far) in American history to date. When the crowds gathered around the Harding home to celebrate the triumph, he emerged to offer a few words to his neighbors and friends. "You and I have been associated together for many years," he told them. "I know you and you know me. I

THE MARION DAILY STAR.

Harding Wins

HARDING BREAKS SOUTH IN A STUPENDOUS VICTORY SCORED BY REPUBLICANS

A MIGHTY LANDSLIDE SWEEPS REPUBLICANS TO UNPRECEDENTED VICTORY

III-31: Banner headline in the Daily Star announcing Harding's election as President of the United States, November 3, 1920

am about to be called to a position of great responsibility. I have been on the square with you and I want to be on the square with all the world."[128] Harding would be going to Washington with Republican majorities in both houses of Congress. In fact, the House would provide a supermajority with more than 2/3rd of the members from the Grand Old Party.

It should not be forgotten that there was one man who wasn't on the ballot who had an outsized impact on the election – President Woodrow Wilson. The results of the 1920 election were seen as a complete repudiation of Wilson and his policies by the American people. Wilson had bungled the peace treaty, had initiated unpopular measures during the war that had yet to be repealed, and his lack of transparency since his debilitating stroke had turned a strong majority of Americans into looking for an alternative. Cox offered "more of the same," while Harding was promising a "Return to Normalcy." After eight years of Wilson, "normalcy" sounded pretty good.

5. Return to Normalcy

Presidents-elect typically focused on two things during their interregnums – selecting a Cabinet and crafting an Inaugural Address. Harding would focus on both, but not before a three-week vacation through Central America to unwind from the campaign and prepare for the arduous task ahead. In addition to Florence, Harry Daugherty, and his close associate Jess Smith, several friendly senators joined the excursion as well. This included Theodore Frelinghuysen from New Jersey, Davis Elkins from West Virginia, Frederick Hale from Maine, and Albert Fall from New Mexico. These were Harding's golfing buddies and poker companions, with both activities prominent throughout the journey. There was also plenty of alcohol aboard the ship, despite the recent passage of the 18th Amendment banning the production and sale of alcohol in the United States. After passing through Oklahoma and Texas, Harding spoke at a reception in New Orleans before heading toward the Panama Canal. Prior to leaving the confines of the United States, Harding proudly espoused his patriotic sentimentalities:

III-32: Harding disembarking the SS Pastores during his trip through the Panama Canal in December 1920

> Our great assurance at home lies in a virile, intelligent, resolute people, in a land unravaged by war, at enmity with no people, envying none, coveting nothing, seeking no territory, striving for no glories, which do not become a righteous nation. This republic cannot, will not fail, if each of us does his part.[129]

Harding's party received generous welcomes and receptions in Panama and the island of Jamaica before sailing back to Hampton Roads on December 4. That date was key, as the lame-duck session of the U.S. Senate was due to begin on the 5th. Harding was technically still a member of that body, and he wanted to take his seat for the last time. Amid much handshaking and best wishes, Harding offered a few departing remarks to his senatorial colleagues, telling them that he looked forward "to find a common ground in the spirit of service."[130]

While there was joy in celebrating his election, this was also a sober period for Harding, who was coming to grips with the reality of the task before him. He was no longer going to be a backbencher in the Senate but rather the leader of more than 100 million people. He also felt isolated in a way that he had never previously experienced. He spoke to a group of Masons in Columbus, telling them:

> There is an aloofness of one's friends [to the President-elect], and that is one of the sad things; and in me there is a deepening sense of responsibility. I have found already there is intrigue and untruth that must be guarded against. One must ever be on his guard. This everlasting standing on one's guard spoils a man.[131]

It's not that he lacked people who wanted to spend time with him. But this was different. Everyone seemed to want something from him. The naturally gregarious Harding was already growing a bit cautious about whom to engage and whom to trust.

This sense made getting Harding's Cabinet selections right all the more important. The President-elect received advice from just about every direction on whom to appoint. This included a visit to Marion by former President Taft, who continued to be close to Harding. After offering a number of suggestions at their private breakfast, Taft was surprised when Harding remarked, "By the way, I want to ask you, would you accept a position on the Supreme Bench because if you would, I'll put you on the court."[132] This was music to Taft's ears. He had never wanted to be President but had always longed for a seat on the Court. Perhaps his ambition might finally be realized. Many others were welcomed for private conferences, assessments of candidates, and direct interviews. Harding was heading into unchartered territory for him as the nation's executive, and he wanted what he called the "best minds"[133] to advise him on how to meet the challenges of the American people. One of the leading contenders for the top spot at the State Department certainly fit that description. Charles Evans Hughes had been the Governor of New York, an Associate Justice on the Supreme Court, and the Republican nominee for President just four years before. Hughes would bring instant credibility to the administration, both at home and abroad. Harding met with Hughes and quietly offered him the position on December 10. Hughes immediately accepted, even though none of Harding's Cabinet appointments would be made public until February.

Another of the "best minds" was Herbert Hoover, the man who helped feed the western world during the darkest days of World War I. Hoover was well-known and generally well-respected, but there was early pushback when rumors of his candidacy for Commerce Secretary were raised. The progressives in the Senate were particularly concerned about Hoover. Harding didn't seem to care. He wanted Hoover and was determined to nominate him regardless of these stated objections. For the Treasury Department, Harding was intrigued by a suggestion from the senators from Pennsylvania to consider the banker from Pittsburgh, Andrew Mellon, who happened to be the second richest man in the world (behind John Rockefeller). Mellon had no experience in government and didn't think he would be a good fit, but Harding saw him as among the country's most successful businessmen and wanted his expertise in banking and finance. He referred to Mellon as "the ubiquitous financier of the universe"[134] and a man who "knows how to turn red ink conditions into profits."[135] To Harding's delight, Mellon agreed to serve.

Not surprisingly, Harding sought to achieve party harmony by bringing his primary rivals for the Republican nomination into his inner circle. General Wood was offered a spot as Secretary of War, and Governor Lowden was approached to be the Secretary of the Navy. Neither was interested, although Wood eventually did agree to serve as the Governor-General of the Philippines. John Weeks, who had previously represented his state of Massachusetts in both the U.S. House and Senate, accepted the portfolio at the War Department, while Edwin Denby, a former congressman from Michigan who had served as Chairman of the Committee on Naval Affairs, became the Secretary of the Navy.

There were other appointments that were more personal to Harding, men who he liked or felt he owed for their support. The most controversial was Harry Daugherty, Harding's longtime friend who had been instrumental in helping to secure the Republican nomination and win the presidential election. Daugherty claimed in his memoirs that he didn't want the job of Attorney General or any position in the Cabinet, but like many things in Daugherty's book, statements such as these are hard to take at face value. Daugherty had finally won the brass ring as Harding's campaign manager, and he undoubtedly expected a reward. Harding was determined to give him one, despite some furious opposition. Former Ohio Governor Myron Herrick simply told Harding, "Harry Daugherty will wreck your administration."[136] Daugherty was competent to perform the role, but his methods and ethics remained highly suspect. His reputation for running over and through people to get what he wanted was well known. While never caught violating the law, he was generally seen as operating very close to the edge, which was a dicey proposition for the top law enforcement official in the country. But Harding stood firm. He pushed back on Senator James Wadsworth with respect to a Daugherty appointment, telling him that "Harry Daugherty has been my best friend from the beginning of this whole thing. I have told him that he can have any place in my Cabinet he wants, outside of Secretary of State. He tells me that he wants to be Attorney General and by God he will be Attorney General!"[137]

III-33: President Harding and his initial Cabinet, 1921

(Clockwise, beginning at the left): President Harding, Treasury Secretary Andrew Mellon, Attorney General Harry Daugherty, Navy Secretary Edwin Denby, Agriculture Secretary Henry Wallace, Labor Secretary James Davis, Vice President Calvin Coolidge (who sat in on Cabinet meetings), Commerce Secretary Herbert Hoover, Interior Secretary Albert Fall, Postmaster General Will Hays, War Secretary John Weeks, and Secretary of State Charles Evans Hughes

Harding rounded out his Cabinet with a friend from the Senate, New Mexico's Albert Fall. Harding told some folks that he initially considered Fall for Secretary of State, but the best fit for the westerner was at the Interior Department. Fall was an expert on natural resources having been a farmer, rancher, and miner before becoming a judge and eventually a United States Senator. Fall and Harding grew close during their years in the Senate, which extended to the poker table as well. Harding had complete confidence in the man and was happy when he agreed to join his Cabinet.

The Hardings had a few last-minute to-dos before officially beginning their new adventure. Harding said his goodbyes to the employees at the *Daily Star* on March 2. He would still own the paper, but Van Fleet would run the show. Another round of goodbyes occurred on March 3 from the Harding porch on Mount Vernon Avenue, which had just been rented out for the duration of his presidency. The following day, the couple was at the White House, ready for the transfer of power. President-elect Harding traveled side-by-side with outgoing President Wilson to the Capitol for the ceremonies. It was quite a contrast between the invalid incumbent and his vigorous successor. Wilson completed his duties in the Senate chamber by signing the last remaining bills from the 66th Congress but was too ill to walk the stairs for the outdoor swearing-in ceremony. The Wilsons quietly slipped away to their retirement home in Washington while the Hardings made their way to the East Front of the Capitol. Florence was by her husband's side, along with his sister, Daisy, and his father, Tryon. Harding undoubtedly would have agreed with his father when he said, "Oh, how I wish Warren's mother could have been here. He had a wonderful mother, a Christian and a saint."[138] After Chief Justice Edward White administered the oath of office, Harding stepped forward to give his Inaugural Address. For the first time, amplifiers were installed, so none of the 100,000 spectators should have had any trouble hearing from the new President.

Not surprisingly, Harding emphasized his "America First" bona fides in his remarks. "Liberty – liberty within the law – and civilization are inseparable," he said, "and though both were threatened, we find them now secure, and there comes to Americans the profound assurance that our representative government is the highest expression and surest guaranty of both."[139] He then brought forward his campaign theme of "Return to Normalcy" with a new administration and no more war.

III-34: Harding giving his Inaugural Address, March 4, 1921

> Our supreme task is the resumption of our onward, normal way. Reconstruction, readjustment, restoration – all these must follow. I would like to hasten them. If it will lighten the spirit and add to the resolution with which we take up the task, let me repeat for our nation, we shall give no people just cause to make war.[140]

Normalcy would be the goal in both foreign and domestic operations. On the home front, Harding touched on many of the issues facing the country related to demobilization, unemployment, agriculture, tariffs, taxes, and what Harding called "more efficient business in government administration."[141] Each of these topics would be prominently featured in the new President's agenda. Finally, Harding reiterated his stance against the League of Nations as proposed by his predecessor.

> We crave friendship and harbor no hate. But America, our America, the America builded on the foundation laid by the inspired fathers, can be a party to no permanent military alliance. It can enter into no political commitments, nor assume any economic obligations which will subject our decisions to any other than our own authority. … A world supergovernment is contrary to everything we cherish and can have no sanction by our Republic. This is not selfishness; it is sanctity. It is not aloofness; it is security. It is not suspicion of others; it is patriotic adherence to the things which made us what we are.[142]

Harding was still interested in international engagements that could prevent future wars, but not on the model negotiated by Woodrow Wilson.

When the ceremonies were complete, Harding did something no President had done before. He accompanied Vice President Coolidge onto the dais on the floor of the Senate. He decided to present his Cabinet appointments in person. "I have chosen my Cabinet in accordance with my best judgment and my personal wishes," he told his former colleagues. "I trust it will meet with your speedy approval."[143] It did. The Senate provided the new President with the fastest confirmations of an initial Cabinet in history.

The tone of Washington seemed to change instantly when Harding settled into the White House. Gone were the doldrums and mysteries of the sick house that the executive mansion had become. The standoffish Wilson had been replaced by the convivial Harding. Harding ordered the gates to his new home, which had been closed since the start of the war, opened. He announced that every day would be a "reception day,"[144] where Harding would welcome all-comers around noon to shake hands and take pictures with their President for about a half hour. When his secretary George Christian advised him this would take up too much of his time and energy, Harding rejected the notion. "I love to meet people," he told Christian. "It is the most pleasant thing I do; it is really the only fun I have. It does not tax me, and it seems to be a very great pleasure to them."[145] Even Florence got into the spirit of the new openness at 1600 Pennsylvania Avenue. She ordered the staff to open the blinds, which had also been closed by the Wilsons to keep people from peering in. "It's their White House," Florence said, "let them look in if they want to."[146]

III-35: The Harding White House

Another sense of openness arrived when Harding reintroduced the twice-weekly press conferences that had been started but eventually abandoned by Wilson. Harding still considered himself a newspaperman, and he was perfectly comfortable with those charged with covering him and his administration. There were rules against quoting him directly, but since Harding trusted his former colleagues, he was happy to take them into his confidence on a regular basis. Harding enjoyed the give-and-take with the reporters, who appreciated his candidness. The approach seemed to pay off. Harding enjoyed very favorable press coverage during his presidency. This changed dramatically after he died, but for the duration of his time in office, the stories were generally positive.

Harding may have been all smiles on the outside, but his gut must have been churning on the inside with the huge challenges that had just been dumped in his lap. The nation was struggling. After all, the Wilson administration had essentially gone dark for the last year-and-a-half since his stroke, leaving a slew of unresolved issues for his successor. The economy was in a funk, with prices falling as supply far exceeded demand in many industries as the artificial uptick in production during the war had suddenly become obsolete. The agriculture sector was hit the hardest, but the manufacturing sphere was starting to feel the effects as well. Workers were suffering as the period of near full-time employment during the war had come to an end, and unemployment was on the rise with more than five million Americans out of work. Racial tensions were also running hot, with race riots and lynchings occurring not only in the South but in many other regions across the country. And there were still outstanding issues in foreign affairs in the wake of the Senate's rejection of the Treaty of Versailles. The U.S. needed to negotiate a separate peace with the Central Powers, and needed a final resolution in terms of participation in the League of Nations, which was up and running in Geneva without any engagement by the United States. Typically, new Presidents would enjoy a bit of a honeymoon with Congress in recess until December of their first year in office, but Harding was not inclined to wait. There were too many pressing issues, so he decided to use his Constitutional authority to call Congress in for a Special Session beginning just a month into his term. Congress would stay in session for nearly all of the first two years Harding was in office.

Harding followed Wilson's precedent to deliver speeches in person to Congress. This included the opening remarks for this Special Session that reflected his "America First" mentality. He continued to make clear his position on the possibility of the Americans joining Wilson's League.

III-36: President Harding delivering remarks to Congress

"In the existing League of Nations, world-governing with its super-powers, this republic will have no part," Harding said to mostly cheers from the floor and the galleries.[147] But the most robust part of the discussion was on domestic issues. Higher tariffs and lower taxes were foremost on his mind, but he did not stop there. The new President wanted Congress to focus on immigration reform, the creation of a Veterans Bureau to unify the nation's management of veteran services, offering new programs to aid farmers, the establishment of a national budget system, and a reduction in government expenditures. The most immediate needs were an emergency tariff to protect struggling American industries and to officially end World War I. Since the Treaty of Versailles failed to pass the Senate, the U.S. was technically still at war with Germany and Austria. Wars typically end with treaties, but Harding believed that while the administration continued to pursue bilateral negotiations with the former combatants, Congress had the immediate authority to essentially declare peace, just as it had the power to declare war. To this end, Harding sent a note the next day to Congress. "To establish the state of technical peace without further delay," he declared, "I should approve a declaratory resolution by Congress to that effect, with the qualifications essential to protect all our rights."[148] This brought both houses of Congress into the mix, which was no problem, as the passage of the act immediately followed, and Harding's signature completed the transaction that had been left open by the previous administration. Separate peace treaties were subsequently negotiated with Germany, Austria, and Hungary in August, and ratifications were secured on these separate agreements in November. The negotiations were all straightforward, as the treaties embraced the vast majority of the terms in the Treaty of Versailles. The exceptions mirrored those brought forth by the likes of Lodge and Harding during the previous administration, including no mention of American involvement in the League of Nations. The fighting had ended three years before under President Wilson, but only now, under Harding, was peace formally established between the U.S. and each of the Central Powers.

The "America First" agenda moved forward apace with emergency tariff legislation and new immigration restrictions. Congress increased import duties on wheat, sugar, meat, wool, and dozens of agricultural products to keep Europe from dumping cheap goods onto the American people. European countries immediately retaliated with protective tariffs of their own, slowing American exports, but prices in the U.S. slowly began to stabilize. The measure was temporary, with more permanent tariff reforms still to be negotiated. Just like inexpensive imports had been hurting the American economy, labor organizations felt similar angst over the large numbers of immigrants who were pouring into the U.S., many of whom were willing to work for incredibly low wages. Congress responded with the Emergency Quota Act, which established a formula based on the 1910 census on how many immigrants from each country would be allowed going forward. The formula greatly favored Northern and Western Europe, while significantly restricting access for Eastern and Southern Europeans and people from non-European countries. The impact was immediate. In the fiscal year ending June 30, 1921, the United States welcomed 805,000 immigrants to its shores. The following year, that number fell by more than 60% to 309,000, with only a slightly larger influx the following year. The targeting also worked as designed, keeping most of the low-paid manual laborers from Southern and Eastern Europe out of the U.S. during Harding's term in office.

Then there was the issue of taxes. Not surprisingly, the wealthy businessman running the Treasury Department sought dramatic reductions to help spur investments in the postwar economy. Secretary Andrew Mellon wanted rates brought down for personal and corporate income taxes, as well as sizeable cuts to the excess profits tax that had been put into place during the war. In a number of these technical issues, Harding knew his limitations. He shared with one of his aides, Judson Welliver, "I can't make a damn thing out of this tax problem. I listen to one side and they seem right, and then-God! I talk to the other side, and they seem just as right."[149] Harding is often taken to task by historians for his lack of knowledge and experience in many political issues, but that's not why the American people hired Harding to be their President. They wanted his leadership, his sense of direction, and his personality, and they were confident in his "best minds" Cabinet to help guide him along the way. They also knew him to be a "harmonizer," someone who would work behind the scenes to get the best deal that was primarily consistent with his Republican ideals. When it came to taxes, Congress was only partially helpful in this regard. For example, while Mellon wanted to drop the excess profits tax from 65% to 33%, Harding proposed 40% to the legislature. Congress passed the bill at 50%, disappointing the administration. At least it was moving in the right direction, so Harding signed the measure into law, but it was also clear that even with strong Republican majorities in Congress, there were no guarantees that the administration would always get what it wanted.

Next up was the budget. And for Harding, this wasn't just about the amount of federal spending but also the manner in which the budget was constructed. President Taft had been the first to unify annual budget requests from the executive branch for Congressional consideration, but he did so by executive order, and Congress barely paid attention, still negotiating budgets on an agency-by-agency basis. Harding knew this was leading to wasteful spending, and he was determined to change course. At Harding's instigation, Congress passed the Budget and Accounting Act of 1921, requiring the President to submit a consolidated budget request to Congress. It created a Bureau of the Budget to facilitate the process, which included pushing back on duplicative spending requests from the various agencies. Administrations would now also be responsible for producing statements of revenues and expenditures on an annual basis, and the act established the General Accounting Office to audit the executive branch going forward. These kinds of administrative reforms do little for the popularity of Presidents, but this measure fundamentally transformed a significant function of the Federal government for the next hundred years (and beyond). Harding turned to Charles Dawes as the first Director of the Budget Bureau. Dawes was another wealthy banker, but one with significant public sector experience. He had served as the Comptroller in the Treasury Department under President McKinley and most recently returned from volunteer duty in World War I, where he served as an invaluable aide to Commanding General John Pershing. Dawes had been commissioned a major but was promoted three times, leaving the service as a brigadier general.

On June 29, 1921, Harding and Dawes convened the Conference on Business Organization of the Government. President Harding provided the opening remarks, telling the 1,200 assembled leaders from across the executive branch, "The present administration is committed to a period of economy in government. There is not a menace in the world today like that of growing public indebtedness and mounting public expenditures. … We want to reverse things."[150] Dawes appropriately gets a lot of credit for the critical first year of operation of the new system, taking a $6.8 billion post-war federal budget from 1920 to $5.5 billion in 1921 and down to $3.7 billion in 1922, a reduction of 46% over just two budget cycles. But none of this would have happened without the support and advocacy of President Harding. It would have been easy for Cabinet Secretaries to try to go around Dawes, cozy up to Harding, and get him to approve individual budget increases. But while some may have tried this technique, very few succeeded. "America First" required a lean Federal government that needed less revenue from taxes to cover expenditures, keeping more money in the pockets of American citizens. This seemingly mundane administrative change had significant impacts, both in the short and long terms.

III-37: President Harding with Chief Justice William Taft, circa 1921

Another impactful decision took place when Harding fulfilled his pledge to William Taft to name him to the Supreme Court if the opportunity presented itself. In fact, just a few months into Harding's term, Chief Justice Edward White died. Harding took a few weeks before making his appointment, but when he did, Taft's name was emboldened on the nomination sent to the Senate. During his tenure in office, Harding added three additional members to the Court, all of whom maintained a conservative view of the law. Taft was an expert in all three branches of government and decided to use his opportunity atop the Court to fight for some overdue reforms. He worked closely with Attorney General Daugherty to suggest language that would be signed into law by Harding as the Judges Act of 1922. This law embodied mostly administrative changes but ones that enhanced the organization and reliability of the entire Federal judiciary to resolve longstanding backlogs in cases and bring more timely justice to the American people.

In just a few months, Harding had worked with Congress to raise the tariff, cut some taxes, curtail immigration, select a new Chief Justice, and lower the Federal budget – all consistent with his campaign pledges and his "America First" mentality. While many problems persisted across the country, things seemed to be moving again and in the right direction. But there was one constituency that was unimpressed. The agriculture sector continued to be awash in debt, foreclosures, and prices so low that it was not economical for some even to produce their crops. The emergency tariff helped a bit, but it was only a band-aid and not a cure. What the farmers wanted were price controls to truly stabilize prices in a way that would guarantee some degree of profitability. In this instance, Warren Harding said "no." The President thought this kind of intrusion into the economy was a bridge too far in keeping with long-standing American traditions. "Government paternalism," Harding declared, "whether applied to agriculture or to any other of our great national industries, would stifle ambition, impair efficiency, lessen production and make us a nation of dependent incompetents. The farmer requires no special favors at the hands of the government. All he needs is a fair chance."[151] With Communism on the rise in Russia and trying to spread to other parts of the world, Harding balked at too much deviation from the free flow of goods in a capitalistic structure. The farmers would continue to suffer and be the last industry to emerge from the doldrums as the post-war economy began to pick up in the latter half of Harding's term.

Harding had certainly hit the ground running, and by most accounts, he was exceeding expectations for his direct engagement in driving legislative solutions to the country's problems. Harding was not one to sit around. He worked hard and he played hard, and as President he did plenty of both. He was up at 7:00 am each day, went straight to the office, and worked well into the afternoon (including the midday welcome receptions to meet the public). But, just as he did in the Senate, Harding had plenty of other activities to fill his schedule. Always a big baseball fan, Harding loved to catch a ballgame at Griffith Stadium, where he always kept score in his own hand. Harding became friendly with New York Yankees star Babe Ruth, who visited with Harding at the White House on several occasions. Golf remained a mainstay for Harding, continuing his regular appearances at the Chevy Chase Club. Senators Frelinghuysen and Hale, along with Agriculture Secretary Henry Wallace, buddy Ned McLean (the wealthy publisher of the *Washington Post*), and personal secretary

III-38: President Harding befriended New York Yankees star Babe Ruth

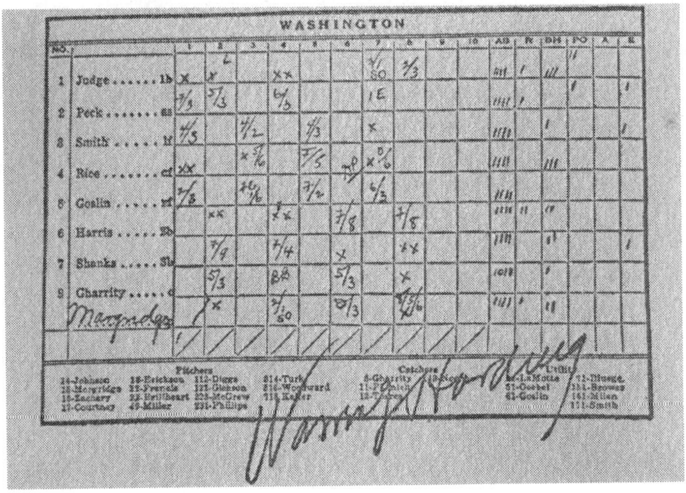

III-39: President Harding liked to keep score in his own hand at Major League Baseball games

III-40: President Harding on the golf course

George Christian were among his regular playing partners. Harding was highly competitive by nature and expected everyone to bring their best to see if they could top his 22-handicap. According to Edmund Starling, the lead secret service agent on Harding's detail, "The President insisted on being treated without respect for his office. No matter how bad his lie, he played it, even when his opponents begged him to pick it up. 'Forget that I am President of the United States,' he would say. 'I'm Warren Harding, playing with some friends, and I'm going to beat hell out of them.'"[152] The gambler in Harding was ever-present on the golf course as well, with side bets galore. "He made so many bets that sometimes he was betting against himself," Starling recalled. "I had to keep accounts, and it was a job for a Philadelphia lawyer."[153]

Harding's gambling instinct typically kicked in at night, with regular poker games at the White House. In addition to his golfing pals, other Cabinet members often joined in, including Daugherty and Fall. Hughes and Hoover were invited once but didn't play and never came back. It wasn't their scene, which was very much an old boys club where swapping stories, smoking cigars, and a round of drinks almost always accompanied the gaiety. Now that he was President, Alice and Nicholas Longworth finally came to his house to play cards. Alice described a typical evening in her memoirs. "No rumor could have exceeded the reality," she wrote. "The study was filled with cronies, Daugherty, Jess Smith [Daugherty's aide], Alec Moore, and others, the air heavy with tobacco smoke, trays with bottles containing every imaginable brand of whisky stood about, cards and poker chips ready to hand – a general atmosphere of waistcoat unbuttoned, feet on the desk, and the spittoon alongside."[154] This was heaven for Harding, letting loose at night to prepare for another day of the presidency in the morning. Florence was not left out. While the First Lady didn't play with the boys, she often attended these sessions and supported her husband while playing hostess to the men around the table.

Tobacco and alcohol were certainly part of the Harding routine. While Florence forbade him from chewing tobacco in the public areas of the White House, he occasionally took a dip in the residence upstairs. This would go along with his two cigars per day habit and an occasional cigarette as well. And while the consumption of alcohol was a direct violation of the U.S. Constitution, thanks to the recently passed 18th Amendment, Harding's White House looked the other way. Harding was never a heavy drinker, but he did enjoy 1-2 drinks on many occasions and felt it was his duty to provide alcoholic beverages to his guests. It did not escape him when people pointed out the hypocrisy of advocating for the enforcement of Prohibition from the bully pulpit of the White House while directly violating the mandate (and his oath of office) behind the curtains of the executive mansion. In public, he made statements such as, "Prohibition is a constitutional mandate and I hold it to be absolutely necessary to give it a fair and thorough trial."[155] But things were very different behind the scenes. In one instance, while discussing the situation with reporter Mark Sullivan, Harding grew exasperated and invited Sullivan upstairs *for a drink* to further the conversation. "We both think that we ought not to drink in the White House," Harding said, "but we feel that our own bedrooms are our house and we can do as we like here."[156] So, alcohol would continue to flow in the Harding White House – one of the most willful and blatant constitutional violations in the history of the presidency.

Alcohol also flowed at 1625 K Street, a building that became known simply as the "Little Green House." Some of the accounts of scandal related to the Harding presidency focused on this house where many of his Ohio friends would gather, play poker, drink, and peddle influence. Harding had given a number of jobs to his pals, including Ed Scobey as the Director of the Mint, the Reverend Heber Votaw (his brother-in-law) as the Superintendent of Federal Prisons, Daniel Crissinger as the Comptroller of the Currency, Charles Forbes as the head of the Bureau of War Risk Insurance and eventually the Director of the new Veterans Bureau, and Charles Sawyer as the White House Physician. Sawyer had been Florence's doctor through her kidney ailments, and she wanted him close by. Harding enjoyed his company and his poker playing, so he made Sawyer a Brigadier General in the Army Medical Corps Reserve, and he was a constant presence wherever the Hardings went. Some of these folks were not necessarily qualified for these appointed positions, but they were happy to be included in the spoils of victory by their buddy, who now happened to be the President of the United States. Many of the Harding cronies, an apt title by which they were commonly referred, often gathered to carouse at the Little Green House. What else happened there has been the subject of many wild tales, but the degree to which it ventured into the realm of illegal activity (beyond the consumption of alcohol) remains a bit of a mystery.

III-41: The so-called "Little Green House" on K Street

The Little Green House was rented in May 1921 by Howard Mannington, a friend of Harding's from Marion who had helped run the front porch campaign. Attorney General Daugherty's friend, Jess Smith, was also one of the leaders of the so-called "Ohio Gang" that frequented the house. Smith did not have a job in the Federal government, but he acted like he did. He had an office near Daugherty inside the Department of Justice and often ran errands for him. Daugherty's wife remained very ill, and Smith often helped care for her. Smith and Daugherty shared a home in Washington, and Smith kept track of Daugherty's books and some of his correspondence. Everybody liked Jess Smith. He was a happy-go-lucky soul who wanted everyone to have a good time. Harding enjoyed his company and liked having him around. Smith was among those who were accused of taking advantage of his situation, purportedly accepting cash in return for introductions to senior officials, influencing prosecutorial and pardon decisions emanating from the Justice Department, and for securing sought-after liquor permits (individual exceptions to the 18th Amendment granted by the Federal government for medicinal purposes) for bootleggers. According to these accusations, all of this graft was for sale, and the place to get them was the Little Green House. As will be seen, there was corruption in the Harding administration, and some of it stemmed from the Ohio Gang. In many instances, the degree and the particulars remain unproven, including any direct connections to Harding. But some of his cronies did take advantage of their access and the trust of the President, were caught, and paid the price – along with the hit to Harding's reputation.

Many members of the Ohio Gang were frequent visitors to Harding at the White House, where Florence and Warren lived alone, at least as far as human occupants were concerned. The Hardings did have a dog in the White House – one of the most famous presidential pets in part because he was the only other member of the First Family in residence. His name was Laddie Boy, an Airedale Terrier that caught the public's imagination. Harding trained him to bring him his newspaper in the morning and was a constant presence at the White House, often wandering in and out of meetings. Press coverage of Laddie Boy was extensive, and always positive. When children wrote letters to Laddie Boy on behalf of their own pets, Harding occasionally responded, speaking for his beloved pet – all part of the charming personality of the Harding presidency.

III-42: Presidential pet, Laddie Boy

Of course, Warren Harding did have a child, just not with Florence. When he took his oath of office, Elizabeth Ann Christian was nearly a year-and-a-half old. Harding had continued his correspondence with Nan Britton, and, according to her, he had every intention of continuing the affair. But first, he wanted some stable parentage for his daughter that would also deflect any potential connection to himself. Harding met directly with Nan's sister, Elizabeth, and encouraged her to formally adopt the little girl. Nan was initially opposed when she was brought into the discussion, but eventually she consented as long as she could remain in Elizabeth Ann's life. On March 15, 1921, less than two weeks after being sworn in as President, Harding's daughter officially became Elizabeth Ann Willits.

Nan's memoirs make it clear that the physical nature of her relationship with Harding continued almost from the beginning of his presidency. She described in detail an encounter in June 1921 when she was escorted by a secret service agent to a private room so she could be alone with the President.

> Then I preceded him into a very small adjoining room, a room with one window. He explained to me that this was the ante-room, and crossed over to another door which led into his own private office. … This was a small closet in the ante-room, evidently a place for hats and coats, but entirely empty most of the times we used it, for we repaired there many times in the course of my visits to the White House, and in the darkness of a space not more than five feet square the President of the United States and his adoring sweetheart made love.[157]

Additional encounters would continue, always aided by the agent that Nan referred to as 'Tim Slade' in her memoirs. These accounts have also been disputed. Agent Starling, who was constantly by the President's side, acknowledged Nan's account in her book, including the alleged assistance from another member of the secret service. Nevertheless, he denied that relations between the President and Nan occurred in the White House. According to Agent Starling:

> The Nan Britton affair, if it happened (and I would be foolish to say that I am certain it did, for I am not), began while Harding was in the Senate and ended before he entered the White House. From the moment of his election until the hour of his death he was never free from our surveillance. His acts are things to which I can swear. He never did anything more reprehensible than cuss mildly at a golf ball and play poker with his friends. He was the kindest man I ever knew. But he was weak, and he trusted everyone.[158]

Ike Hoover served ten Presidents in his more than 40 years in the White House, most of which were in the role of Chief Usher. He also denied that Harding had an affair in the White House. "There was never a gadabout by that name or any other name in the White House. Nan Britton is a liar."[159] People called Nan a liar for years before DNA evidence substantiated her claim of Harding's paternity of Elizabeth Ann. Whether the affair persisted inside the executive mansion remains, however, in dispute. Nan's extremely detailed descriptions of the inner sanctum of the White House and the veracity of her claims of paternity certainly weigh in favor of her credibility. At the same time, there is simply no independent physical evidence to substantiate Nan's claim of sexual relations with the President inside the executive mansion.

Harding loved meeting people and didn't want to be confined to the nation's capital. While it was harder to get away with Congress in session, he did like to take the presidency directly to the people. As his first summer in office wore on, the President accepted an invitation to speak at an event honoring the 300th anniversary of the initial landing of the Pilgrims at Plymouth Rock in Massachusetts. They were actually about a year too late, but the initial plans for a presidential-led celebration had been postponed because of Woodrow Wilson's illness. Vice President Coolidge, who hailed from Massachusetts, received a warm welcome, but the featured attraction was the President, who was happy to address the crowd at the festive occasion.

III-43: Florence and President Harding at the 300th anniversary of the landing at Plymouth Rock, August 1921

> The pageant which we have just seen, shows in vivid spectacular form how much we of today owe to that sturdy Pilgrim spirit which the first founders of our nation brought

> with them from across the seas. I believe most firmly that this stern, indomitable spirit with which the Pilgrims faced the perils of an unknown land for the sake of conscience, represented that which is truest and best in the America of today.[160]

While some Presidents grew to loathe these time-consuming press-the-flesh events, Harding never tired of them. Plus, they offered a nice respite from the business of the country, which continued full steam ahead throughout his first year in office.

As the Harding administration sought to tackle the myriad challenges facing the country in 1921, it held a number of conferences to bring together leaders from across the country with both expertise and equities in specific areas. Just a couple of months after the conference on the Business Organization of the Government, the administration hosted a Conference on Unemployment. Commerce Secretary Herbert Hoover, who had emerged as a key adviser to President Harding in several areas, including those traditionally outside the scope of the Commerce Department, was in charge of the gathering (as opposed to Labor Secretary James Davis, who participated in more of a support role). Unemployment had fallen to practically zero during the war but had risen rapidly since demobilization kicked in, running at about 12% at the time of the conference. Harding and Hoover welcomed some 300 delegates to Washington to discuss options to improve the situation, but all were put on notice at the outset not to look for handouts from the Federal government as part of any solution. Just like with the plight of the farmers, Harding saw only a limited role for the Federal government to become directly involved. "I would have little enthusiasm for any proposed relief which seeks either palliation or tonic from the

III-44: Harding's Secretary of Commerce, Herbert Hoover

Public Treasury," Harding said in his opening remarks.[161] Harding did his typical "boosting," encouraging state and local governments to look for every opportunity to accelerate work opportunities such as pending construction projects, and further suggested that other Cabinet secretaries be on the lookout for Federal building opportunities as well to possibly put people to work, but cash handouts to those out of work were not going to be on the table. Harding believed the collective moves by the administration to stimulate the domestic economy, along with local stimulus, would augment the natural economic cycle and start to turn the tide. While the short-term pain was very real, the Harding approach generated positive results in relatively short order. By the Spring of 1922, national unemployment had fallen under 8%. By 1923, it was back under 4%. It was a dramatic turnaround in just two years in office, setting the stage for additional economic prosperity for the next several years.

6. Disarmament

All of the major conferences of the Harding administration were focused on domestic challenges except for one. That one would turn out to be the apex of Harding's presidency, an event in which he became a true international statesman who delivered a major diplomatic feat. The idea for a global disarmament conference preceded Harding's term in office. Senator William Borah had twice introduced in Congress during the waning days of the Wilson administration a motion to pause American naval shipbuilding for six months as a signal to all the major powers of the world that another arms race was not the obligatory response to the end of the recent global conflict. Borah further proposed a gathering of leaders from the United States, Britain, and Japan to negotiate arms limitations that would be binding on each of the leading naval powers of the world. Borah's motivation was two-fold. First was to lessen the likelihood of future military conflicts, and second, to preserve capital for productive purposes other than a model of never-ending military expenditures that would suck the public treasury dry. Borah's motions did not pass in the previous Congress, but they received a new look and fresh promotion from the incoming administration.

Secretary of State Charles Hughes led the push, one in which he found common cause with his President. Both were aligned on the notion of U.S. leadership in pursuing global disarmament as a path to avoid future wars. They also embraced the opportunity to cut government spending, which was another priority for the administration. Harding decided to build on Borah's proposal to not only invite Britain and Japan to participate in the discussions but also include major powers France and Italy, as well as the next tier of global leaders from China, Belgium, the Netherlands, and Portugal. Invitations were sent by the Americans in August 1921 for an event planned for November in Washington, D.C. The focus would be disarmament, as well as the opportunity to resolve some ongoing disputes in the Asia-Pacific region. Based on some preliminary back-channel discussions, these invites were warmly embraced by all parties. An optimistic tone permeated the upcoming venture. *The New York Times* labeled the invites as "inspiring news." "The President is truly responding to the desire of all nations," the *Times* wrote. "He has given to [this country] the high distinction of leading in a noble work for civilization."[162]

Before the delegates gathered in the U.S. capital, President Harding took a moment to focus on race relations in his own country at a time when racial tensions (and violence) remained at a boiling point. Many White laborers harbored bitter resentment toward Blacks who were competing for jobs, with significant anxiety attached to returning soldiers who were looking to resume their pre-war careers. Harding had virtually no record on the topic of civil rights. His only action to date as President was to allow President Wilson's move to segregate the Postal Service and Treasury Department to persist in his administration. He had offered support for anti-lynching legislation at the outset of the Special Session in April when he proposed that "Congress ought to rid the stain of barbaric lynching from the banner of a free and orderly representative democracy,"[163] but he had done little beyond this mention to pursue the cause. On October 26, 1921, Harding ventured into the heart of this debate. He became the first President to travel into the South to speak about race relations since the Civil War. The location was Capitol Park in Birmingham, Alabama, where Harding addressed a crowd of 20,000 Whites and 10,000 Blacks in a completely segregated audience. It was a bold speech that generated strong reactions that spanned the spectrum of high praise to outright condemnation.

Harding saw the races as fundamentally different when it came to social and cultural aspects but did not believe these differences justified unequal opportunities in the political and economic realms of American society. "Politically and economically there need be no occasion for great and permanent differentiation, for limitations of the individual's opportunity," Harding asserted, "provided that on both sides there shall be recognition of the absolute divergence in things social and racial.[164] … Natural segregations" should be

III-45: President Harding addressing race relations and civil rights in Birmingham, AL, October 26, 1921

accepted, "satisfying natural inclinations and adding notably to happiness and contentment. ... Racial amalgamation there cannot be."[165] This sounded eerily similar to something Woodrow Wilson (and many of his other predecessors) may have asserted. That said, while segregation of the races made sense to Harding, that didn't mean Blacks should be denied equal access to the vote or robust economic opportunities in the labor force. Harding promoted an expanded push for vocational training for Blacks in the South as a means to prepare them for participation in the modern American workforce. He advocated for the elimination of discriminatory laws that were preventing Blacks from participating in the political process at the ballot box. "I want to see the time come when black men will regard themselves as full participants in the benefits and duties of American citizenship," Harding asserted.[166] The notion of "separate but equal" was filtered throughout Harding's remarks in Birmingham.

The reaction to the President's speech ran the gamut. Senator Pat Harrison from the neighboring state of Mississippi condemned it as "a blow to the white civilization."[167] Blacks were split. Many in the Black section of the crowd enthusiastically applauded the speech in real time. Educator J. Wilson Pettus wrote the President, calling the speech "The most notable and courageous expression on the race question made by any President of the United States since Lincoln."[168] Civil rights advocate W.E.B. Du Bois took a very different view, calling Harding's concession of social inequality for the races "inconceivably dangerous and undemocratic."[169] Harding was generally praised for placing the topic front and center and for being brave enough to take his message into the heart of the South. But the nuanced distinctions on where the equality line should be drawn left many feeling cold. More significantly, Congress did little in the aftermath of the speech to take up the mantle with any meaningful legislation. Harding once again pushed an anti-lynching bill in early 1922, but after a filibuster in the Senate from members from the Solid South, the notion was eventually dropped from consideration. The Birmingham speech aside, President Harding did little to advance the cause of civil rights during his tenure in the White House.

The Disarmament Conference was originally timed to start on the third anniversary of the armistice, which ended the fighting in World War I. But the opening session was delayed by one day so all of Washington, including the foreign representatives, could pay their respects at the dedication of the Tomb of the Unknown Soldier at Arlington National Cemetery. The unknown soldier's remains had been exhumed from the Romagne Military Cemetery in France. The body was shipped to Washington, where it lay in state in the Capitol Rotunda on the same catafalque that had supported the caskets of slain Presidents Lincoln, Garfield, and McKinley. President Harding and General Pershing marched side-by-side as the fallen soldier's body was first led to the White House before the somber procession continued on to Arlington. Harding had made a special effort to include the ailing former President Wilson in the event. Harding had already offered help to his predecessor by assigning Admiral Cary Grayson, who had served as Wilson's physician throughout his presidency, to continue his duty in the nation's capital with ongoing responsibilities to look after Wilson's health. Wilson appreciated the move and now readily accepted the opportunity to participate in the military honors being bestowed on soldiers he had sent into harm's way.

Thousands gathered for the somber ceremony where President Harding presided over the dedication. Millions more could listen in to the President's remarks thanks to innovations in radio broadcasting which were just starting to be realized. "As we return this poor clay to its mother soil," Harding said, "garlanded by love and covered with the decorations that only nations can bestow, I can sense the prayers of our people, of all peoples, that this Armistice Day shall mark the beginning of a new and lasting era of peace on earth, good will among men."[170] This statement was a

III-46: President Harding presides over the dedication for the Tomb of the Unknown Soldier, Arlington National Cemetery, November 11, 1921

perfect lead-in to the Conference for the Limitation of Armament that would gavel to order the following day.

The Americans had held their cards close to their chests in the days leading up to the Conference. No specific proposals had been circulated prior to the arrival of the delegates, so everyone was anxious to listen to the opening remarks to see what the hosts truly had in mind. Unlike President Wilson, who had named himself as the leading delegate to the Paris Peace Conference three years prior, President Harding would not serve as an active member of the gathering. However, he did take center stage to welcome the diplomats to Washington and to set the tone for an aggressive push on the topic at hand.

> I can speak officially only for the United States. Our hundred millions frankly want less of armament and none of war. Wholly free from guile, sure in our own minds that we harbor no unworthy designs, we accredit the world with the same good intent. So I welcome you, not alone in good-will and high purpose, but with high faith.[171]

Harding earned the respect of the august delegates in attendance with his remarks, which were greeted with cheers and hearty handshakes as Harding circled the room before taking his leave. Secretary of State Charles Evans Hughes took over from there with a bold proposal that caught many off-guard. Hughes started out by advocating a complete halt to military shipbuilding across the globe. "It would seem to be a vital part of a plan for the limitation of naval armament that there should be a naval holiday," Hughes proclaimed. "It is proposed that for a period of not less than ten years there should be no further construction of capital ships."[172] And Hughes was just getting started. He also proposed that the leading navies of the world scrap parts of their existing fleets to achieve strict national limits at a ratio of 5:5:3 for the U.S., Britain, and Japan, respectively, with France and Italy capped at about half the level of the Japanese. Many in the audience weren't sure how to react. Colonel Charles Repington, who was a member of the British

III-47: Harding's Secretary of State, Charles Evans Hughes

III-48: The opening session of the Conference on the Limitation of Armament, Memorial Continental Hall, Washington, D.C., November 12, 1921

delegation, made the following observation: "Secretary Hughes sunk in thirty-five minutes more ships than all the admirals of the world have sunk in a cycle of centuries."[173] The plenary session ended and the conference went into recess for the weekend so the delegates could absorb the daring American proposal, which journalist William Allen White still maintained a quarter-of-a-century later as "the most intensely dramatic moment I have ever witnessed."[174]

When the delegates returned, they voiced strong support for the direction the Americans wanted to pursue. Premier Aristide Briand led the delegation from France. He announced, "The United States has had a powerful share, together with our other Allies, in saving the independence and life of my country. Therefore, having won the war together, we for ourselves cannot remain deaf to the eloquent appeal that was addressed to us, in order to win peace together. … If the necessary precautions are taken, in order to insure her life and safety, France, like you, gentlemen, is ready to say 'Down arms!'"[175] Japan had emerged as a force to be reckoned with throughout the Pacific, with fears by others of imperialistic inclinations by the Empire. The Japanese had recently brought online the *Mutsu*, believed to be the most formidable battleship yet deployed by any nation. Yet, the lead representative from Japan joined the chorus of support for Hughes's proposition. "The world needs peace," proclaimed first Prince Iyesato Tokugawa, the president of the

House of Peers. "It calls for political and economic stability. And to co-operate with the powers here so worthily represented for the accomplishment of such a lofty end, under the guidance of the distinguished presiding officer, it will be for Japan a source of greatest pleasure."[176] Representatives from the other nations present followed with a similar willingness to follow the Americans' lead.

Negotiations over the next 12 weeks were challenging but productive. The French, in particular, remained loath to reduce armaments too far, fearful of perhaps lethal exposure if Germany ever decided to re-arm in violation of the Treaty of Versailles. As such, agreements were light when it came to land armaments and even submarines. But the bulk of the Americans' original proposal about naval vessels eventually made it into the Five-Power Naval Treaty that was signed at the end of the conference by the primary naval powers of the world. But this wasn't all the conference accomplished. All nine participants agreed to a separate pact that re-committed the parties to the Open Door policy related to equal access to Chinese markets. Moreover, Japan agreed to return the Shantung Province to China after aggressively fighting to acquire the Chinese region during the recent peace talks in Paris. The previous decision had been among the most unpopular pieces of the Treaty of Versailles in the United States, partly because it represented a complete abrogation of one of President Wilson's Fourteen Points related to self-determination. That wrong had now been righted at Harding's Disarmament Conference. Finally, a Four-Power Treaty was signed between Britain, France, Japan, and the United States to respect the rights of the other signatories with respect to territories in the Pacific. This ten-year agreement also called for a joint conference to settle any disputes.

President Harding stayed away from the meetings until the end, although he was in constant communication with Secretary Hughes throughout the course of the negotiations. In the end, he was confident the agreements reached would make a positive difference across the globe. In closing remarks on February 6, 1922, he told the delegates:

> This conference has wrought a truly great achievement. It is hazardous sometimes to speak in superlatives [but the result is] so fine, so gratifying, so reassuring, so full of promise, that above the murmurings of a world sorrow not yet silenced; above the groans which come of excessive burdens

> not yet lifted but soon to be lightened; above the discouragements of a world struggling to find itself after surpassing upheaval, there is the note of rejoicing which is not alone ours or yours, or all of us, but comes from the hearts of men of all the world.[177]

The delegates left Washington on a high. After all, in their parliamentary systems of government, these foreign dignitaries had every reason to believe their national legislatures would sign on to these agreements. As recent history had showed, however, such an outcome was hardly guaranteed in the United States.

President Wilson learned the hard way that while American executive branch officials could freely negotiate any treaty they wanted, none would go into effect without positive concurrence from 2/3rd of the members of the U.S. Senate. To his own detriment, Wilson had completely ignored the Senate and its Republican majority when he refused to include any of the leaders of the opposition party in the delegation that joined him in Paris. Warren Harding was a first-hand witness to this impolitic choice, aligning with Henry Cabot Lodge to thwart the passage of Wilson's Treaty, including participation in the League of Nations, at every turn. Woodrow Wilson's greatest mission in life ended in defeat – a failure that lay very much at his own two feet. The nation's leading political scientist had failed U.S. Government 101, the basic premise of divided government and separation of powers which required some degree of collaboration to secure the passage of international treaties. Warren Harding would not make the same mistake. In fact, when compared to the nation's only Ph.D. President, the much more lightly educated Harding proved to be very much the master politician.

First of all, unlike Wilson, Harding did not make this all about himself. He opened and closed the conference and gave it his full support, but he did not take over the proceedings in a way that might alienate the opposition. More significantly were the people he chose to represent his country's interests. In addition to Hughes, who was masterful in shepherding the entire event, Harding not only selected leading Republican Senators Henry Lodge and Elihu Root, but he also appointed Oscar Underwood, the *Minority* Leader in the Senate and the ranking Democrat on the Foreign Relations Committee to represent America's interests. All four men were highly respected, but they were brought in not only for their expertise but also because they would be critical to securing passage of any agreement in the Senate. In a true bipartisan spirit, Lodge and Underwood equally embraced the pacts emanating from the talks and enthusiastically brought that endorsement to their colleagues on Capitol Hill – a complete reversal from the period following Wilson's negotiations in Paris. This didn't mean passage was assured, as ratification of treaties is rarely simple in the U.S. Senator Borah, who was personally bitter over not being selected as a delegate after his proposals had sparked many of the ideas pursued at the conference in the first place, was among those opposed to the treaties as presented. Harding was anxious about the results as Lodge and Underwood led the negotiations with their colleagues. The President told H.H. Kohlsaat just before the votes:

> The success or failure of this administration depends on the ratification of these treaties. Every administration's name rests on one or two acts. If these treaties are ratified by the Senate, then this administration's name is secure in history. If the treaties are defeated, nothing I can do in the balance of my term will be of more than passing interest.[178]

Fortunately for Harding, every proposal received the sanction of the supermajority needed in the U.S. Senate.

As Harding noted, the treaties stemming from the Disarmament Conference represented the apex of his presidency. They were not permanent, and eventually were overcome by other events as Japan gave in to its imperialist faction and Germany began to re-arm in the early 1930s. But, for a decade, the arms race was slowed to an agreed-upon formula, helping to sustain several years of global peace and save billions of dollars in the process. Just about a year into his presidency, on top of his domestic advances, this success at international diplomacy led to a string of compliments directed toward the President. Secretary Hughes was thrilled at the recent results and consistently praised Harding as a key catalyst to achieving a successful outcome. "The tranquilizing spirit of President Harding permeated the endeavors of the Conference," Hughes noted.[179] He wrote to Harding to thank him for "the opportunity you have given to work for worth-while results under your leadership. Such an experience makes one feel younger despite the flight of time."[180] Fellow delegate Elihu Root, who during the election campaign "did not believe that Harding was of big enough calibre for the Presidency," had changed his mind. "I knew him very slightly at the time he was elected and I was afraid he was going to be too anxious to please everybody," Root wrote, "but he has shown himself to have a decision of character and cheerful courage that are most gratifying."[181] Vice President Coolidge shared his admiration with Harding after the conference, telling the President that "I am very proud of your accomplishments, and feel certain that no one can examine the record, either now or hereafter, without being thankful for what you have done for the welfare of America."[182] Reporters heaped on the praise as well. *The New York Times* commented that "President Harding is gradually assuming undisputed leadership and without offending his former associates in the Senate."[183] Many had anticipated that the actions of the Senate cabal in the smoke-filled room at the Republican Convention would make Harding a tool of the Senate. A year into his term, reporter Mark Sullivan painted a very different picture.

> On this point – of his capacity to stand on his own bottom – Harding was not merely underestimated. He was totally misapprehended. It was only a year ago that the phrase 'creature of a Senatorial oligarchy' was the epithet of the opposition party, supposed to be potent to deprive Harding of votes. [Now,] if that phrase is recalled at all, it is to point a joke on those who once believed it.[184]

Harding had enjoyed a packed first year in office. He had taken the lead on critical issues that were both foreign and domestic in nature. He had set the agenda and worked with Congress to fulfill it. The economy was moving in the right direction, and he had accomplished a major diplomatic triumph that was in marked contrast to the failure of his predecessor. For the most part, the Harding presidency was looking pretty good. And Harding had one more piece of welcome news to pass along, continuing to return the country to normalcy by putting some additional painful leftovers of the war behind them.

When Warren Harding took over the presidency in March 1921, the U.S. still had about 200 people in prison related to wartime convictions under the Espionage and Sedition Acts. While Britain and most other members of the Allies had established general amnesty programs for similar wartime crimes, the U.S. had not followed suit. While many of these so-called "political prisoners" had been released, President Harding directed a case-by-case review before opening the cell doors to freedom. The most famous of the prisoners still behind bars was Eugene Debs, the

III-49: Eugene Debs, outside the office of Attorney General Harry Daugherty, December 1921

former union leader and perennial candidate for President for the Socialist Party of America. Debs had been convicted of sedition in June 1918 while speaking out against the war and the draft. He was serving a ten-year sentence, with no mercy from either President Wilson or the Supreme Court. Despite cries for leniency toward the end of the prior administration, Wilson was unrelenting on the punishment for Debs. "This man was a traitor to his country and he will never be pardoned during my administration," Wilson said bluntly at the time.[185] Harding wasn't so sure. Perhaps the Return to Normalcy meant putting such divisiveness behind them. The President directed his Attorney General to meet with Debs and make a recommendation. Daugherty sent for Debs to come to Washington in December 1921 so he could make his own assessment. By all accounts, Debs had been a model prisoner, so Daugherty saw no reason for him to be guarded on his journey. Debs traveled in civilian clothes by himself on the train to the nation's capital before heading to the meeting at the Justice Department, where the two spoke for several hours. The discussion was pleasant and respectful, according to Daugherty, who was impressed by the man who stood by his convictions. "I found him a charming personality, with a deep love for his fellow man," Daugherty later wrote. "To my mind, of course, absolutely wrong in his ideas on government and society, yet always sincere, truthful and honest."[186] The Attorney General was convinced that justice would be best served by sending Debs home after having spent the past three years behind bars. He recommended that the President issue the commutation effective at the end of the year. Harding offered his concurrence, except for the timing. "I want him to eat his Christmas dinner with his wife," the President said, accelerating the release to December 24. "I was persuaded in my own mind that it was the right thing to do," Harding added. "I thought the spirit of clemency was quite in harmony with the things we were trying to do here in Washington."[187] Those efforts were not just restricted to Eugene Debs. On the same day Debs was released, Harding commuted the sentences of 23 other prisoners held under similar charges. By the end of the following year, only 62 of these inmates remained behind bars. By the time Harding left on his trip to Alaska in 1923, that number was down to 21 as the President continued to move the country forward, erasing painful elements of the recent past.

7. Second Year Challenges

The President and First Lady opened the new year in grand style with a six-hour public reception at the White House. They each shook hands with approximately 6,500 of their fellow citizens and other dignitaries. Harding thoroughly enjoyed the smiles, back-slapping, and pleasant chit-chat of these kinds of festivities, but it didn't mean that the strain of being President of the United States wasn't beginning to show. Despite a productive first year in office that delivered on a number of elements of the Republican platform and his Return to Normalcy agenda, Harding couldn't escape the daily grind of political challenges that never seemed to go away. There were never enough patronage jobs to go around, and those who failed to win these posts were often left embittered toward the man in charge. And despite the solid Republican majorities in both Houses of Congress, there were party fractures that were making almost every effort painful. The Senate, in particular, was increasingly divided, with the progressives still seeking their place in the power structure and sectional conflicts also maintaining prominence in key areas. Some of the more reliable Republican leaders had passed (such as Boies Penrose, who died on New Year's Eve), and others, such as Henry Lodge and Philander Knox, were aging and beginning to lose some of their clout. During his tenure in the Senate, Harding had typically been in the background, enjoying the experience with little pressure to lead. That dynamic was no longer in play, and with the schisms growing on Capitol

III-50: President Harding and First Lady Florence Harding, circa 1921

Hill, Harding's second year in office seemed destined to be even more demanding than the first.

A couple of prime examples of these challenges were a permanent fix for the tariff and Harding's plans for the country's merchant marine. Congress had approved an emergency set of tariff increases at the beginning of its Special Session the prior April, but Harding was opening the new year with a continued push for more permanent fixes as part of his America First agenda. His proposal included some statutory flexibility for the national executive that he believed essential to providing both agility and stability to the nation's economy going forward. He continued this push in his Annual Message in December 1921, which opened the first regular session of the 64th Congress. "I hope a way will be found to make for flexibility and elasticity so that rates may be adjusted to meet unusual and changing conditions which cannot be accurately anticipated," the President declared.[188] But making changes to the tariff had never been easy for presidential administrations due to the cross-party conflicts the topic typically generated. Plus, Congress was loath to entrust the President with flexibilities that had traditionally been exclusive to the realm of the legislature. Harding and his team pushed for months before eventually achieving their legislative victory. When Harding finally signed the Fordney-McCumber Tariff in September 1922, he got most of what he was seeking. Rates were among the highest in history, and the President was given the authority to make adjustments by up to 50% in either direction on a go-forward basis. These were to be informed by recommendations of the Tariff Commission, but this counsel was not binding on the President. Harding was relieved to finally realize the outcome he had been seeking. "This law has been long in the making," he told those assembled at the signing ceremony. "I don't know how many are in accord with me, but if we succeed in making effective the elastic provisions of the measure it will make the greatest contribution to tariff making in the nation's history."[189]

While the long-fought tariff battle eventually yielded productive results, the same could not be said for Harding's push to aid the country's merchant marine. The Federal government had taken over much of the nation's commercial shipbuilding as critical to the rapid mobilization needed for the recent war effort. But now that same government was straddled with a massive fleet that it didn't need, losing more than $16 million a month in the cost of operations. Harding appointed his friend

Albert Lasker, a wealthy ad executive known for his aggressive business tactics but no experience in the shipping industry, to be the head of the United States Shipping Board. Harding and Lasker both believed that the government needed to sell off much of this fleet of commercial ships to private industry and further subsidize that industry to build modern ships of their own. Unfortunately, the market wasn't responding. When Lasker went to sell the first batch of 205 all-wooden ships, only one buyer was interested, yielding only a tiny return on their initial investment. Congress was split over the matter, with farmers and labor crying foul over any economic incentives for this specific industry while so many others were still struggling. While Harding continued to fight for the ship subsidy bill "above everything else,"[190] Congress lacked the same level of conviction. The tariff fight drowned out most other issues in Congress in 1922, including this one, and when labor strife struck the nation in the middle of that year, even the administration realized that it had too many fights on its hands. By August, Harding agreed it would be a bridge too far to get congressional approval, and the ship subsidy effort was eventually dropped.

The President was also at odds with Congress over a proposed bonus bill for veterans from World War I. Similar bonuses had become popular parts of the Republican agenda over the course of several administrations in the aftermath of the Civil War, and many in Congress were anxious to further the tradition of these popular handouts. But President Harding was firmly opposed unless there was a way to pay for the bonuses without incurring additional debt that would be paid for by future generations. Harding was fighting to stabilize the post-war economy, and encumbering the Federal budget with this large new expenditure was irresponsible in his view. He told Congress that "This menacing effort to expend billions in gratuities" could crush the entire economic revival that was underway but remained tenuous. "We may rely on the sacrifices of patriotism in war," Harding said, "but to-day we face markets, and the effects of supply and demand, and the inexorable law of credits in time of peace. ... A modest offering to the millions of service men is a poor palliative to more millions who may be out of employment."[191] When Congress passed the measure anyway, Harding stuck to his guns and wrote out one of the six vetoes issued during his presidency. Given the popularity of the bill, a congressional override was certainly possible. In fact, the House had the votes to overturn the veto, but the Senate fell four votes short. Harding's firmness carried the day but continued to show how difficult things had become even with strong Republican majorities in both houses of Congress.

The constituency most aggrieved heading into Harding's second year remained the farmers. While other parts of the economy had started to see positive momentum, agriculture continued to lag. While the migration from farm to factories had been moving apace since before the turn of the century, approximately 30% of the nation's workforce was still engaged on the farm.[192] Despite the adjustments to the tariff, farm prices continued to sag, creating economic peril throughout the agriculture sector. The Farm Bloc in Congress, led by Iowans William Kenyon in the Senate and Lester Dickinson in the House, was pushing for action, but President Harding remained reluctant to put the power of the Federal government too heavily into any particular sector of the economy. Harding's Agriculture Secretary Henry Wallace was pushing the President to hold another of his national conferences to focus on possible solutions everyone could support. Wallace was close to Harding, having become one of his golf and poker buddies. Harding also trusted Wallace's relationships with the farm community. Wallace had been a farmer himself, had studied and taught agriculture at Iowa State University, and had been a popular journalist as editor of *Wallace's Farmer*. When Wallace continued to push for the national gathering, Harding finally relented, and the National Agriculture Conference was held over the course of five days toward the end of January 1922. More than 300 delegates from 37 states convened to discuss possible solutions to the ongoing plight of this community. And while some measures were embraced, including a Farm Loan Act that made it easier for farmers to get loans and for higher amounts, as well as improvements to facilitate cooperative marketing for farm products, President Harding remained reticent to bring the full power of the Federal government to bear, particularly when it came to controlling prices. "While I believe in every possible help which is consistent with sane government," Harding said just before this conference, "I do fear that in our modern agricultural life we have become too prone to expect the government to cure every ill which is encountered."[193] Despite some modest actions emanating from the conference, the agricultural sector continued to lag behind the rebound being experienced by much of the rest of the economy.

The highlight of 1922 for Harding was likely his summer vacation when he returned home to Marion for the 4th of July celebration. Being hailed as the returning hero in the context of some of his notable accomplishments made for a personal highlight for Harding. According to secret service agent Edmund Starling:

> Those brief days in his home town were the happiest of President Harding's career, I think. He was at the peak of his national popularity, and the enthusiasm of his fellow townspeople was a reflection of the way the whole country felt about him. A man who loved all people, and who wanted all people to love him, could have asked for no more. His cup was filled.[194]

Unfortunately for Harding, the celebration was short-lived. While still fighting for major tariff reform, struggling with his Ship Subsidy plan, and getting called out for lack of progress by the farmers, Harding was about to face a severe test as hundreds of thousands of coal miners and railroad shopmen had just gone on strike.

Circumstances for labor had been generally positive during the war as employment was at capacity and wages were strong. However, demobilization had challenged a number of industries that were still adjusting to post-war economics. Wages had fallen and changes were being made to the work week that were unfavorable to the labor force. Textile workers in New England were the first to strike in 1922, with one hundred thousand walking off their jobs for six months before settling with management. The coal miners were next, with 650,000 going on strike in April. This was merely problematic over the spring and summer but could become catastrophic if the walkout persisted into the cold winter months. At first, the administration stayed on the sidelines, following the traditional hands-off approach by the Federal government regarding work stoppages. But things intensified when 20 strikebreakers were killed in a violent attack by striking workers in late June in Herrin, Illinois. Nevertheless, Harding was still reluctant to engage directly. "I suppose nobody felt worse than I did about the Herrin matter," Harding shared with his friend Malcolm Jennings, "but there is not anything that the federal administration could do except talk about it, and I have a very strong aversion to a government official indulging in excessive talk and inadequate action."[195] The President did try to take on his customary role as a harmonizer, inviting both sides to Washington to try to settle the dispute. However, neither party was interested in backing down from its demands. As winter approached, the administration started to feel the weight of the issue and opened to the possibility of using Federal troops to seize the mines and protect the strikebreakers. While no plans were ever finalized, the talk alone gave the operators the leverage they needed to force a settlement with the union. The agreement stipulated that the wage rules in place prior to the strike would remain in effect until at least April 1923 (i.e., after the dangers of a frigid winter had passed) and that another presidential commission would be established to study the situation and make recommendations. Feeling backed into a corner, the union agreed to these terms, but with tremendous enmity for a presidential administration that influenced an outcome that gave them little to show for their months-long strike.

That same summer, some 400,000 railroad shopmen walked off their jobs on July 1, fighting back against postwar wage reductions and unfair working conditions. Harding looked to the National Railroad Labor Board to help settle the matter, but the workers weren't inclined to bargain with a Federal entity that had sanctioned their recent cuts in pay. It was this work stoppage that drew the ire of Attorney General Harry Daugherty. Daugherty was already inclined to blame all of the labor disputes his country was facing on the Russian Communists, whom he fervently believed were seeking to rally workers across the globe to overthrow management and create a new structure with themselves at the center. In August, Daugherty started pushing the President to consider going for a legal injunction against the striking railway workers. With Federal equities at stake, ranging from interstate commerce to the delivery of the U.S. mail, Harding signaled to Congress that the administration was poised to take action. "There are

III-51: Harding's Attorney General, Harry Daugherty

statutes forbidding conspiracy to hinder interstate commerce," Harding declared. "There are laws to assure the highest possible safety in railway service. It is my purpose to invoke these laws, civil and criminal, against all offenders alike."[196] This sentiment may have been channeling former President Grover Cleveland, who brought in Federal troops to ensure that the nation's trains would once again be up and running amid the nationwide Pulman strike in 1894 – an act which almost instantaneously broke the strike and handed management a major victory. In Harding's administration, Daugherty was on point, personally heading to Chicago and the courtroom of James Wilkerson to seek the injunction. "Unions should not be destroyed," Daugherty told Judge Wilkerson, "but they should be corrected and restrained. If the acts of violence and murder are inspired by the unions then it is time for the government to call a halt. … No union or combination of unions can under our laws dictate to the American Union."[197] Wilkerson, who had recently sentenced Al Capone to prison, had been recommended for his post by Daugherty and appointed by Harding. He was more than happy to issue the injunction, which was one of the most sweeping orders ever imposed on organized labor. Not only were the workers prohibited from continuing their strike, but according to Harding biographer Robert Murray, the order also

> enjoined rail workers from tampering in any manner with the operation of the railroads. ... The strikers, their associates, attorneys, and leaders were forbidden to encourage continuance of the strike by letters, telegrams, telephones, or word of mouth; they could not picket, issue strike directions, or use union funds to continue the conflict.[198]

The injunction did the trick, as the strike cratered almost as soon as the ink dried on the judge's order. But what was generally perceived as a positive outcome for the American people faced a serious backlash inside the Harding Cabinet and on Capitol Hill. Commerce Secretary Hoover was the most outspoken against the administration's move that he believed imperiled basic rights granted under the Constitution. "I was outraged by its obvious transgression of the most rudimentary rights of the men," Hoover later wrote.[199] Secretaries Hughes and Fall joined the chorus denouncing the breadth of the injunction Daugherty had pursued. President Harding saw the merits of some of this pushback and instructed Daugherty to pull back on some of the elements of the injunction when he went to argue for Wilkerson's order to become permanent. Daugherty complied, but by this point, it didn't make much difference. The strikers couldn't stand up to the power of the Federal executive and judicial branches, and the strike completely evaporated.

The ire against Harry Daugherty extended beyond the Cabinet Room in the White House. Organized labor made him their public enemy number one, and several members of Congress took up their fight. Daugherty was never well-liked by the establishment in Washington. His reputation for unscrupulous behavior preceded his arrival, and the rough elbows he brought to bear in fulfilling his responsibilities as Attorney General rubbed many in Washington the wrong way. Congressman Oscar Keller, a Republican from Minnesota, took advantage of the flap over the injunction to pursue articles of impeachment against Harding's AG. The charges themselves were light on specifics, and both the Judiciary Committee and the full House voted down the measure by a large margin. But this would not be the last time Daugherty would find himself in the crosshairs of the U.S. Congress.

Harding tried to take each of these issues as he saw them, seeking to balance the competing interests in an America First Return to Normalcy. While labor often saw itself on the losing side of the administration's positions, there was one area in which Harding persisted for more than a year to get a positive result for the working man. The steel industry was one of the few left in the U.S. that still employed a mandatory 12-hour workday. Harding thought this was wrong and put the power of his office behind bringing it to an end. He called industry leaders to Washington in May 1922 to discuss the issue, and Elbert Gary, the head of U.S. Steel, agreed to study the matter. That study lagged for months before a report was issued in November. The industry leaders concluded that while some limited changes to the policy could be adopted, the essence of the 12-hour workday needed to remain in place. In this instance, President Harding refused to take "no" for the answer. He continued to badger industry leaders to reconsider their conclusion. Egged on by Commerce Secretary Hoover, Harding proclaimed, "It has seemed to me for a long time that the twelve-hour day and the type of worker it produces have outlived their usefulness and their part in American life in the interests of good citizenship, of good business, and of economic stability. The old order of the twelve-hour day must give way."[200] It took another eight months for U.S. Steel to come to this same conclusion, but it did, announcing the end of the 12-hour day in early August 1923. Harding was hardly beloved by the labor movement, but he did come through with this notable accomplishment, which went into effect just before his death.

The fall of 1922 was particularly challenging for President Harding. First, his wife was sick again. Florence's kidney ailment often flared, but had mostly been manageable with Doc Sawyer always at her side. But on September 8, things took a turn for the worse. Sawyer reported that the First Lady "developed complications Thursday and Thursday night which make her condition critical. These complications are so serious that recovery is not yet assured."[201] Harding spent the next ten days mostly by his wife's side, never sure if she was going to make it. To everyone's relief, Florence turned the corner on the 19th, even though it would take months before she was once again near full strength. Harding suffered through his own illness during this period as well, something he personally described as the grippe. It was a combination of flu-like symptoms and an intestinal disorder, which took weeks to clear. Daugherty, whose wife continued to suffer from her medical ailments, also succumbed to illness, keeping him in bed for about six weeks.

III-52: First Lady Florence Harding

Through this physical suffering came the anguish associated with a serious setback for Harding's Republican Party in the midterm elections. Farmers, other workers, and war veterans were expressing their dissatisfaction with the folks in Washington who they believed weren't doing enough to help them get their share of benefits as part of the post-war recovery. Progressives were also making another push to lead the political agenda for the country. In total, Republicans lost 69 seats in the

House and seven in the Senate. Harding's party maintained majorities in both houses of Congress, but their margins were greatly diminished. Moreover, given that a number of progressive Republicans were more aligned on policy with the Democrats, passing legislation was going to be much more difficult in the second half of Harding's term. "For such blame as the administration must assume I am willing to bear my share," Harding admitted after the results were known. "It is a very difficult thing to recover from the aftermath of war and get ourselves firmly on our feet. … However, I hope we shall do better in the two years before us."[202] A potential reason for optimism was that there was a sense that Harding wasn't nearly as unpopular as Congress had become. According to *The New York Times*, "Mr. Harding retains his popularity in a large degree. Congress has utterly lost whatever it had."[203] The dynamics would surely weigh on the second half of Harding's term in office.

Other than the flap about Daugherty's push for the injunction against the striking railway workers, the Harding administration to date had been relatively scandal free. That was about to change in a couple of specific instances. The first round of disloyalty to the President came from Charles Forbes, the former war hero who had earned a congressional medal for his service in World War I and had befriended the Hardings on their trip to Hawaii several years before. Forbes had become a close friend (and poker partner) and Harding first rewarded him with the leadership position at the War Risk Bureau and then as the first director of the Veterans Bureau. Before establishing this new organization, veterans had to navigate numerous Federal agencies to get the services they sought. The new Bureau was intended to consolidate those services, ranging from caring for wounded vets, establishing and maintaining veterans' hospitals, providing vocational training, and managing the large number of supplies needed to address veterans' needs. Forbes was

III-53: Harding's friend and head of the Veterans Bureau, Charles Forbes

popular and his nomination was well-received by organizations such as the American Legion.

The Veterans Bureau under Forbes was entrusted with more than a half billion dollars in Federal funding, which proved too tempting for him to let pass by without some sticking to his hands. The corruption started with the $17 million he was given for new hospital sites and construction. Forbes awarded those contracts based on guaranteed kickbacks that he baked into the overall cost. He then turned to the supplies, with millions of dollars in products sitting in warehouses such as the depot at Perryville, Maryland. Forbes deemed many of these perfectly good items to be obsolete and started selling them for pennies on the dollar to the Boston-based firm Thompson & Kelley, again with kickbacks built in. One of those who smelled a rat and sought to expose Forbes was the White House physician, Charles Sawyer. Sawyer didn't care for Forbes and personally investigated the situation at Perryville. He shared his concerns with the President, who proved obstinate with his support for his good friend, Forbes. While Harding refused to believe Sawyer's accusations, he did agree to an investigation by the Justice Department, which substantiated the charges against Forbes. Harding was saddened and angered by the betrayal, reportedly shouting at Forbes when he confronted him at the White House. Harding sent Forbes off to Europe where he was allowed to quietly submit his resignation. The President was deeply wounded by the man he had welcomed into his inner circle. While rumors of corruption linked to Daugherty and the Ohio Gang at the Little Green House were ever-present during the Harding administration, this was the first time that malfeasance was confirmed, and Harding took

III-54: Harding's friend and White House Physician, Dr. Charles Sawyer

it hard. The First Lady told E. Mont Reily that her husband "never recovered from Forbes's betrayal of himself and the Administration. It was his first experience of treachery; probably his bitterest."[204] Daugherty confirmed the sentiment. "I think nothing in Harding's life ever cut him so deeply as this man's betrayal of the trust he had placed in him,"[205] Daugherty later wrote. An exasperated Harding bemoaned to journalist William White, "My God, this is a hell of a job! I have no trouble with my enemies. I can take care of my enemies all right. But my damn friends, my God-damn friends, White, they're the ones that keep me walking the floor nights!"[206] Harding never saw Forbes again, but that was hardly the end of the saga. A congressional investigation led to formal charges against Forbes, who was convicted of conspiracy to defraud the Federal government. He was sentenced to two years in prison and fined $10,000. Forbes's general counsel, Charles Cramer, resigned and committed suicide over the affair. No one ever charged Harding with being personally complicit in any of these acts of corruption at the Veterans Bureau, but any such treachery inevitably puts a stain on the President in office. This would not be the last time such a blemish would be smeared across the Harding administration.

The major scandal that has become synonymous with the Harding Administration goes by the term "Teapot Dome." Teapot Dome was the name of a rock formation in Natrona County, Wyoming. It was the landmark for an oil reserve that had been set aside in the previous administration to secure precious oil for the U.S. Navy. Similar reserves were established at Elk Hills and Buena Vista Oil Fields in Kern County, California. These reserves were placed under the auspices of the Department of the Navy. In February 1920, President Wilson signed into law the General Leasing Act, which authorized the Secretary of the Navy to grant private leases within these reserves when deemed appropriate. One such reason was to prevent private oil interests from drilling at the border of these reserves and essentially siphoning off drainage that may have spilled into their neighboring lands. The Act authorized the granting of these leases without competition at the discretion of the Navy Secretary.

While the Navy had never managed such a leasing endeavor, this was the bread and butter of the Interior Department, so Navy Secretary Denby had little concern when Interior Secretary Fall offered to take over the responsibility on the Navy's behalf. Some in the Navy chain of

III-55: Harding's Secretary of the Navy, Edwin Denby

III-56: Harding's Secretary of the Interior, Albert Fall

command, such as Admirals Robert Griffin and John Robison, objected to the switch as potentially putting Navy equities at risk, but Denby seemed unconcerned. To him, this was simply putting the experts in charge, and the Navy would still retain the right of refusal on any actions the folks at Interior wanted to pursue. Secretary Fall sought to assuage any concerns on behalf of the Navy by ensuring the service would benefit directly from the sale of these leases. Ordinarily, the profits from such transactions would go directly into the Treasury, but Fall moved to generate a direct return to the Navy. Fall proposed that some of the royalties from the leases would include the trade of goods. Specifically, the producers would deliver some of the oil pumped from these reserves to the Navy, and they would also build tanks to hold that oil, particularly at the growing naval presence at Pearl Harbor in Hawaii. This was a win-win that protected the naval reserves from theft while producing tangible benefits for the Navy.

Fall moved forward with granting leases for commercial drilling at Teapot Dome and Elk Hills. The lease to the former went to Harry Sinclair and his Mammoth Oil Company which was created specifically

III-57: Oilman Harry Sinclair

III-58: Oilman Edward Doheny

for this venture. The Elk Hills lease went to Edward Doheny, who had known Fall for decades, and his Pan-American Petroleum Company. Both were no-bid contracts, so no other vendors were considered. The initial constituency that objected to the deals were the conservationists who felt the entire program was a step backward for their cause. They complained to Congress, where some members were open to investigating, particularly because of the use of no-bid contracts, even though they were specifically authorized in the General Leasing statute. Progressive-leaning senators led the questioning, including Robert La Follette (R-WI), Thomas Walsh (D-MT), and John Kendrick (D-WY). President Harding pushed back against any objections, making it clear he fully supported the policy. "I think it is only fair to say in this connection," Harding maintained, "that the policy which has been adopted by the Secretary of the Interior, in dealing with these matters, was submitted to me prior to the adoption thereof and the policy decided upon and the subsequent acts have at all times had my entire approval."[207] When others questioned Fall's actions, the ever-trusting Harding offered his Secretary his full support. "I have both a very high regard for your ability," Harding wrote to Fall on July 14, 1922, "and an unfaltering belief in your integrity. I had these impressions when I asked you to come into the Cabinet, and I have had no reason of any kind to modify my earlier impressions concerning you as either friend or public servant."[208] Harding had seen no evidence that anything untoward had been going on with respect to the leases to Doheny and Sinclair, even after Fall resigned from the Cabinet and took a lucrative position in Sinclair's oil business in January 1923. But what Harding didn't see at the time was the money Fall had taken under the table to grease the skids for making both of these awards. Those discoveries, which would come to light after Harding's death, would paint the darkest cloud over the entire Harding presidency.

As Harding neared the halfway point of his four-year term, he continued to focus primarily on domestic issues but never put the international scene out of his sight. He trusted Secretary Hughes to lead the way in discussions about recognizing the new government in Mexico (he supported), to not recognize the Communist government in Russia (with Daugherty as a strong ally), to work out a treaty with Colombia that offered compensation for the role of the U.S. under President Roosevelt in the Panamanian Revolution, and to prepare to remove American troops from Santo Domingo. Moreover, when Harding was in the Senate, he had been the chair of the Philippine Committee at a time when he believed the archipelago was not yet ready to receive its independence. Locals in the islands were once again pushing for their freedom from American control, so Harding asked for an updated review of the matter from former Governor-General Cameron Forbes and his replacement Leonard Wood. Both felt that the Filipinos would be lost without American oversight, and the President agreed. "I must say to you that the time is not yet for independence," Harding announced to the people of the Philippines. "Meanwhile, I can only renew the proven assurances of our good intentions ... no backward step is contemplated. … Our relation to your domestic affairs is that of an unselfish devotion which is born of our fate in opening to you the way of liberty of which you dreamed."[209] The Filipinos would have to continue to wait, though, for that dream to be realized.

While Harding remained adamant against the U.S. joining the current form of the League of Nations, he did continue to look for ways for his country to engage in international affairs. This included agreeing to send American observers to be on hand for some League activities. For example, when the League invited the Americans to participate in one of its conferences on international health, the President gave Secretary Hughes the go-ahead. "I can see no consistency in studied effort on our part to ignore the work of the League because we do not find it consistent to accept membership therein," Harding said. "I think we ought to maintain a position in which we may be able to commend the good which it accomplishes."[210] And while such participation was not a signal that the Americans were changing their minds about entry into the League, it did indicate the President's openness to other kinds of organized international engagement. The one initiative in which he continued to push for American involvement was the World Court, which had been established by the League but operated completely independently. The goal of the Court was to use peaceful arbitration as a means to avoid war. Republicans had long championed the idea of expanding the use of binding arbitration to settle international disputes, and with Hughes and Hoover, the true internationalists in the Cabinet, encouraging him, Harding formally recommended participation to Congress on February 24, 1923. It was not well received. In fact, Congress buried the proposal without consideration. Harding was frustrated, as he shared in a letter to Malcolm Jennings.

> The great hubbub over the World Court was largely bunk. Most of it emanates from members of the Senate who have very little concern about the favor with which the administration is regarded, and the remainder of it come [sic] from those who are nuts either for or against the League. The League advocates have somewhat embarrassed the situation, but I do not fear the outcome. A good many people have urged me to drop the matter, but I do not find myself ready to accept that sort of a sneaking program.[211]

Harding was in on this matter for the long run. He felt he had planted the seed with Congress and would not be discouraged. There would be plenty of additional opportunities to push for inclusion in the Court in the second half of his term, or perhaps a second term.

8. Alaska and Untimely Death

The President had remained silent as to whether he would run for another four years as his nation's executive. The job was exhausting. Even for a man who found plenty of time to relax, there was always another pile of work waiting for him when he returned. "I never find myself done," he told a gathering at the National Press Club in early 1923. "I never find myself with my work completed. I don't believe there is a human being who can do all the work there is to be done in the President's office. It seems as though I have been President for twenty years."[212] Harding also chafed at the lack of freedom imposed on a President, where his every step was watched (and often criticized). Nevertheless, Harding had also warmed to the role and believed his administration was, in fact, making progress on behalf of the American people. While he was still contemplating his future, Harry Daugherty beat him to the punch. In what appeared to be a surprise to the President, Daugherty decided to make a public announcement that Harding would be on the ballot again in 1924. When the Hardings were on a brief golfing holiday in Florida with the McLeans, Daugherty issued the following announcement, which appeared in *The New York Times* on March 18, 1923: "The President will be a candidate for renomination. ... The President will be renominated and re-elected because the country will demand it."[213] Harding was caught a bit unawares when the announcement hit the papers, but he did nothing to repudiate the statement. With unemployment down, government expenditures and the national debt reduced, railroad traffic up, wages solid, prices mostly stabilized, and the positive sentiments that still held true from the Disarmament Conference, Harding had every reason to believe he would be in good shape to win another four-year term.

With this backdrop, Harding chose to make some changes that would impact his retirement, whenever that came to pass. First, he decided to solidify his roots going back to his youth at Blooming Grove. Harding decided to buy his childhood home, with plans to spend at least some portion of his retirement in what he hoped to be a peaceful setting for which he retained a strong emotional attachment. "My one dream is to restore the old houses of your father and Great-grandfather Harding," the President wrote to his aunt Ella Dickerson. "I think they can be restored as they were on the exterior and made modern on the interior, and be combined into a very attractive group of farmhouses. … The addition of the Finney Farm was made in the hope of acquiring ... ground along the road for a sufficient distance to provide a nine-hole golf course."[214] Harding would have 266 acres to play with as he visualized his retirement homestead. Harding wouldn't need to live in Marion partly because he finally decided to sell the *Daily Star*. Harding had received many offers over the years for his newspaper but could never part with something that was part and parcel of the man himself. For nearly four decades, Harding and the *Star* went hand-in-hand, growing up together on the path to success. The daily routine of the paper still penetrated his psyche even while serving as President of the United States. Harding had recently confided with reporter William White that:

III-59: President Harding, 1922 (age 56)

> Every day at three-thirty, here in the midst of affairs of state, I go to press on the *Marion Star*. I wonder what kind of layout the boys have got on the first page. I wonder how much advertising there is; whether they are keeping up with this week last year. I would like to walk out in the composing room and look over the forms before they go to the stereotyper. There never was a day in all the years I ran the paper that I didn't get some thrill out of it.[215]

It must have come as a bit of a shock when Harding agreed to sell. Louis Brush and Roy Moore had put an offer of nearly $550,000 on the table ($423,000 of which would go into Harding's pockets). Some thought it was an exorbitant offer, perhaps a cover for something nefarious, but the fact was it was a reasonable price. The *Star*'s circulation was now more than 11,000, and the paper had made a profit of $60,000 in the past year. Plus, Harding agreed to write a column for the paper in his post-presidential years, adding to the value even further. Harding never fully explained why he decided to sell, but he did take one additional action as a result of the transaction – he updated his will. Just before leaving on an extensive tour to the West, he pulled Harry Daugherty aside and asked him to prepare the new document, which reflected both the sale of the *Star* and the purchase at Blooming Grove. The paperwork was fairly routine, with little additional thought given once the signatures affirmed the President's wishes.

The trip Harding was planning was supposed to be just what the doctor ordered – a chance to get away, make a few speeches, but get in a lot of relaxation as the President geared up for the next congressional term. Congress had been in session for all but two of the first 24 months of the Harding administration, but it was finally entering a lengthy recess that would span from March to December 1923. Harding wanted to get away from Washington, meet his fellow citizens, see the sights of his country, and re-energize after a taxing two years in office. His primary destination was Alaska, the vast but lightly populated territory the U.S. had purchased from Russia in 1867. The region was overseen by a variety of Federal agencies, and Harding thought improvements could be made in some of those arrangements. He wanted to bring some Cabinet secretaries with him to evaluate the situation first-hand and make policy adjustments as circumstances warranted. The plan was to travel by train through the western part of the country, then board a ship for Alaska and tour the far reaches of the territory before returning through California, take a ship through the Panama Canal, and visit the American territory of Puerto Rico before returning to Washington. Harding had Walter Brown serving as his advance man to plan the itinerary, but he was growing concerned that Brown was packing the schedule to make the trip all work and no play. "Brown is making a circus out of the trip," the President complained to Agent Starling. "He has booked me for from eight to ten hours of constant activity every place we are to stop. I won't get a minute's rest. … I want to do as little work as possible on this trip and I am depending on you to help me out."[216] Things didn't work out as Harding had initially envisioned for the expedition.

Jess Smith, AG Daugherty's aide and everyone's pal, was looking forward to being part of the traveling party on Harding's upcoming "Voyage of Discovery." He was on the original list, but his spot was canceled, apparently at the direction of the President. According to Daugherty, the President told him, "I am informed he [Smith] is running

III-60: Jess Smith

with a gay crowd, attending all sorts of parties. And you should know too that he is using the Attorney-General's car until all hours of the night." Harding added, "for the good of all concerned it would be well to advise him to go home."[217] Shortly thereafter, Jess Smith was dead. Daugherty wrote at great length in his memoirs about Smith in his final days. He documented Smith's depression over not being able to go on the trip to Alaska. He was further down because of health issues, struggling to recover from an appendectomy that did not heal well and required hospitalization for the better part of a month. Daugherty and Smith traveled to Ohio, where the latter was expected to stay. But Smith asked to return to DC one more time to wrap up his affairs and say goodbye to some of his friends. Daugherty agreed.

On May 29, 1923, Smith played a round of golf, met with a handful of folks, cleared out some of his files at the Justice Department, and then had a brief meeting with President Harding at the White House. According to Daugherty, the AG had previously committed to spending a few days at the White House, but he didn't want Smith to be alone, so he asked his special assistant, Wayne Martin, to spend the night with Smith at their suite at the Wardman Hotel. In the middle of the night, after destroying not only his own papers but also Daugherty's personal papers that he typically managed, Smith committed suicide. He used a gun he had purchased on the recent trip to Ohio.

The death of Jess Smith affected a lot of people, including the President and Mrs. Harding, who were both fond of the man. Daugherty was shocked and saddened, as were the hundreds of people who had befriended Smith during his two years in Washington. Reporter Mark Sullivan, for example, wrote to Daugherty when he heard the news. "He was such a wholesome, optimistic fellow," Sullivan wrote. "I always thought of him as a man who enjoyed life fully, and as one who got immense pleasure out of devotion to his friends. I had come to like him with unusual feelings, and to think of myself as a friend of his."[218] But there were also questions about Smith, around whom rumors had already been swirling about his influence peddling and potentially dirty deals. Folks behind these rumors saw Smith as the center of the Ohio Gang, which was described in many circles as a criminal enterprise operating out of the Little Green House. This line of thinking often included the Attorney General as one of the leaders of these corrupt schemes. There were calls for an investigation, including the possibility that Smith had actually been murdered to cover up his crimes and the crimes of others. Smith's death left more questions than answers, in part because so many of the people who opined on the sad event had powerful reasons to lie. Undoubtedly many did, which complicated so many of the stories about scandals during the Harding administration that surfaced after the President's death. But there is one source who had no reason to lie, and his account may be the most credible. That source is Herbert Hoover.

The future President served the entire Harding administration as Secretary of Commerce. Hoover later captured in his memoirs a conversation he had with Harding during the trip to Alaska. Several Harding biographers have focused on Hoover's recollection of this discussion, which began with Harding asking, "If you knew of a great scandal in our administration, would you for the good of the country and the party expose it publicly or would you bury it?" According to Hoover:

> My natural reply was, 'Publish it, and at least get credit for integrity on your side.' He [Harding] remarked that this method might be politically dangerous. I asked for more particulars. He said that he had received some rumors of irregularities, centering around [Jess] Smith, in connection with cases in the Department of Justice. … I asked what Daugherty's relations to the affair were. He abruptly dried up and never raised the question again.[219]

The interesting thing is that this extensive quotation in these Harding biographies used the ellipsis to omit four critically important sentences. From Hoover's original text, the following lines are also present:

> He [Harding] had followed the matter up and finally sent for Smith. After a painful session he told Smith that he would be arrested in the morning. Smith went home, burned all his

> papers, and committed suicide. Harding gave me no information about what Smith had been up to.[220]

Harry Daugherty made no mention in his memoirs of the pending arrest which the President had conveyed to Smith and about which he must have been aware. According to a lengthy section in Daugherty's book, Smith was simply depressed over his health and for being sent away for "running with a gay crowd." The specific dirty deal in which Smith was rumored to be involved and was potentially going to send him to prison was never clarified. Any connections to Daugherty were also clouded in mystery and lies. We do know from Hoover's statement from the President that something nefarious was going on. We also know that the Attorney General tried to distract from any such charges with a much more innocent rationale for Smith's suicide. The truth lies buried with Jess Smith, with no shortage of speculation on what was really going on. Once again, there were no substantiated charges that President Harding was in on any of the activities at the Little Green House or going on behind the scenes at the Justice Department. His only guilt was by association, for placing his trust in friends who, at times, trampled on that faith and goodwill. But when you're the President of the United States, all scandals seem to find their way to your doorstep. And the death of Jess Smith contributed to the growing list of untoward activities being perpetrated by the friends of Warren Harding that raised questions about the ethics of this administration.

III-61: President Harding advocates for membership in the World Court in a radio address from St. Louis, MO, June 21, 1923 (age 57)

Less than a month after Smith's suicide, President Harding and his entourage left Union Station to begin their lengthy journey to the West. The schedule was indeed grueling, as Harding gave 85 speeches over the course of the next six weeks. Many were delivered in the heat of the day from the back of the presidential train, while others were in larger auditoriums in some of the major cities. St. Louis was one of the first stops, where Harding focused on his advocacy for the U.S. to join the World Court. With many listeners tuning into the remarks on the radio, Harding proclaimed:

> I shall not restrict my appeal to your reason, I shall call upon your patriotism. I shall beseech your humanity. … I shall reach to the very depths of love for your fellow countrymen of whatever race or creed throughout the world. … My soul yearns for peace. My heart is anguished by the sufferings of war. My spirit is eager to serve. My passion is for justice over force. My hope is in the great court. My mind is made up. My resolution is fixed.[221]

In Kansas, the President felt at home on a farm where he rode a tractor in the fields. In Jackson Hole, Wyoming, Harding made a rare venture into the world of conservation, advocating for setting aside 400,000 acres for the public domain. It was "not desirable that the West should fall into the hands of bonanza corporations seeking to exploit it for the profit of stockholders,"[222] Harding told an approving audience. Things were a little trickier for the President when he talked about the imperative of law and order to the 12,000 in attendance. Specifically, he was talking about Prohibition. "I am convinced," he proclaimed, "that they are a small and a greatly mistaken minority who believe that the Eighteenth Amendment will ever be repealed." Harding did not believe that would be the case, and, as such, "The country and the nation will not permit the law of the land to be made a byword."[223] That remained the official position of the government, regardless of how many drinks were served behind the scenes at the White House or even for the current traveling party. More speeches followed in Salt Lake City, Zion National Park, and Yellowstone Park, where the President had the opportunity to go on hikes, feed the bears, and see Old Faithful blow its top. The Fourth of July found the President in Portland, Oregon, where he celebrated American independence with local schoolchildren who kindly brought him flowers. The final stop before boarding the USS *Henderson* for Alaska was Tacoma, Washington. The President put in another plug for gutting the 12-hour workday in the steel industry, with agreement from the leadership at U.S. Steel finally only a few days away.

By this point, Harding was completely exhausted. Dr. Sawyer had tried for days to restrict the President's activities (not unlike when physician Cary Grayson had tried to limit Woodrow Wilson's speeches in his ill-fated tour to promote the League of Nations in 1920, which abruptly ended when his body completely broke down just before a massive stroke), but he had little impact on Harding's schedule. Plus, the President would resort to card games until the wee hours of the morning rather than get his rest. Commerce Secretary Hoover and his wife joined the traveling party just prior to the journey to Alaska. "As soon as we were aboard ship," Hoover later recalled, "he insisted on playing bridge, beginning every day immediately after breakfast and continuing except for mealtime often until after midnight. There were only four other bridge players in the party, and we soon set up shifts so that one at a time had some relief. For some reason I developed a distaste for bridge on this journey and never played it again."[224] Pure rest and relaxation remained elusive for President Harding.

The *Henderson* left Tacoma with a 21-gun salute and an escort of two Navy destroyers to begin the 1,000-mile journey to Alaska. The population of the entire territory was only around 55,000 people, half of whom were native Indians and Eskimos. The massive 300 million acres had been paved thus far with only 400 miles of motor roads. The most recent modernization was the completion of the 497-mile Alaskan Central Railway, which was built by the Federal government to open travel to the Yukon. As a U.S. territory, it was led by a governor (Scott Bone), along with one Federal Judge, a U.S. Marshal, and a U.S. Attorney. Alaska had huge deposits of natural resources, including oil, gold, silver, copper, zinc, coal, and wood pulp. The soil was fertile, with crops ranging from potatoes to alfalfa to blueberries, along with flowers galore. But most of this was completely unknown to the vast majority of Americans. President Harding wanted to see this beautiful part of his country for himself, to assess this land of opportunity, and determine how best the Federal government could assist in helping Alaska live up to its full potential. In addition to Commerce Secretary Hoover, he brought Agriculture Secretary Wallace and Interior Secretary Hubert Work (who had taken over for Albert Fall just a few months before) to help with the fact-finding and to develop policy recommendations that would not only help the Alaskans but also potentially the rest of the American people. "What we want, boys, is to understand the actual situation in Alaska now," Harding told the members of his entourage. "Keep your eyes and ears open, get acquainted with the people, and tell the folks back home what the real Alaska of today is like."[225]

III-62: President Harding raising an American flag in Matlakatla, Alaska Territory, July 1923

The *Henderson's* first stop was Metlakatla, where the President was met by Governor Bone and entertained by 500 native-born Alaskans. Harding raised an American flag and was presented with a fresh four-foot salmon. The first port on the mainland of Alaska was Ketchikan, where the Hardings celebrated their 32nd wedding anniversary. Next up was a visit to Wrangell, where the President paused to reflect on his view of the people of Alaska. "You know, I do enjoy meeting these people," he said. "They help me more than I can tell them. They have preserved the sturdy spirit

III-63: President Harding admiring the mammoth salmon in Matlakatla, Alaska Territory, July 1923

of the pioneer, and without our pioneers and frontiers we are likely to lose the self-reliance and upstanding courage which have made our nation grow."[226] Harding next had a busy round of meetings with politicians and leading citizens in Juneau, the capital of the territory, on the only day the entire trip when it rained, followed by a visit to Skagway, the site of the previous gold rush. Harding was truly forming a bond with the people of Alaska. "Here the people have achieved, in this great out-of-doors, a freedom from the restraints of conventionality that help in the making of strong characters and strong friendships," Harding said. "The longer I live the more firm is my belief that the greatest possession in the world is dependable friendships."[227] *Dependable* friendships, Harding noted, at a time when he was struggling with betrayal from some of those back home to whom he had given his trust.

The presidential party next headed out on a three-day journey across the Gulf of Alaska to Seward and Resurrection Bay, the terminus of the new Central Railway. Next was a visit to Anchorage, a city that was only nine years old. The travelers arrived at 11:00 pm with the sun still shining as brightly as ever. From here, the President got his first glimpse of Mt. McKinley with its peak of 20,464 feet representing the highest point of land in the Western Hemisphere. It was surrounded by the Mt. McKinley National Park and its 3,000 square miles of untouched wild-game preserve – the largest national park in the United States. In the Yukon District, Harding hammered home the Golden Spike to complete the transition of the Alaska Railroad from the narrow gauge to standard gauge, enhancing the connection from the Pacific to the Artic Oceans. In Fairbanks, Harding visited with the first

III-64: President Harding in the engine of the Alaska Railway, July 1923

graduating class of the Agricultural and Mining College. Harding felt at home when he stopped by the local newspaper, happy to set type and help make up the forms like the professional that he was. At each of these stops, Harding gave speeches, but he also listened to the locals, gaining a true appreciation for their lives, their goals, and their challenges. Doctor Sawyer was often badgering Harding to take breaks and get more rest, but he was constantly losing that battle with a President who continued to go at full speed from early morning until late at night.

The final part of the Alaskan journey went through Sitka, the ancient Russian capital of the territory. From there, it was off to Vancouver, where Harding became the first American President to speak on Canadian soil. He brought his folksy charm to the occasion, telling the locals, "I like that word – neighbors. I like the sort of neighbors who borrow eggs over the back fence."[228] American battleships were waiting when the *Henderson* found its way back to American soil, docking in Seattle. The President was clearly weary from his travels, but he insisted on keeping his commitments. "I cannot disappoint them," he said. "I must go on."[229] And he did, speaking to more than 60,000 people gathered in Seattle Stadium under a scorching sun. "He managed to get through the speech," Secretary Hoover later wrote. "As soon as he finished, Speaker [Frederick] Gillett, Secretary [Hubert] Work, the White House physician, Dr. Sawyer, and I hustled him to the special train, put him to bed, and canceled the engagements for the evening."[230] Dr. Joel Boone, a cardiac specialist, was called in as well. He diagnosed an enlarged heart. The planned visit to Portland was canceled, and the presidential train made its way directly to San Francisco, where it was believed the President could recover at the

III-65: President Harding arriving in San Francisco, July 1923

Palace Hotel while getting the best medical attention available on the West Coast. On July 29, two experts were brought in, including another heart specialist, Dr. Charles Cooper, and Dr. Ray Wilbur, the president of nearby Stanford University and a future President of the American Medical Association. After a couple of days, the patient showed real signs of improvement. X-rays indicated that Harding's lungs were clear, and on August 1, Dr. Sawyer pronounced the crisis had passed. He spoke too soon.

The very next day, at 7:35 pm, Florence was reading to her husband an article in the *Saturday Evening Post* entitled *A Calm View of a Calm Man*, when the end came. "He seemed so well and so cheerful this evening that I began to read it again to him," Florence later told Daugherty. "I stopped for a moment, thinking that he had fallen asleep, when he looked at me and said: 'That's good, read some more.' I turned to the page again and as I did he threw his right arm over his head. I saw his face twitch. I leaped to my feet, bent over him. He was dead. It all happened in a second."[231] According to a statement released by his doctors, "Death was apparently due to some brain evolvement, probably an apoplexy."[232] The cause was later changed to a heart attack, although no autopsy was performed at the direction of Mrs. Harding.

Part One

THE MARION DAILY STAR.

Pages 1-14

TWENTY-TWO PAGES

PRESIDENT HARDING SUCCUMBS TO DEATH; CALVIN COOLIDGE SUCCEEDS HIM AS PRESIDENT

NEWS OF DEATH SHOCKS NATION

DEEP MOURNING MARKS CAPITAL

COOLIDGE NOW THE PRESIDENT

WILSON LEARNS NEWS OF DEATH

MRS. HARDING HEROIC FIGURE

FRANCE DEEPLY MOVED BY NEWS

COLUMBUS ASKS TO GIVE HONORS

FIND PRESIDENT TRUE AMERICAN

III-66: Coverage of President Harding's death in the Marion Daily Star, August 3, 1923

The nation poured out its emotions for the 57-year-old self-made newspaperman who had led the country for 882 days before his sudden passing, the fourth shortest tenure in American history. Harding had been a breath of fresh air after the war years, making good on his Return to Normalcy pledge, helping turn the American economy into positive territory, and orchestrating the most significant arms limitation agreement in the history of the world. But mostly Harding was beloved because of his personality. He was folksy and charming, patiently shaking hands and engaging in chit-chat with his fellow citizens without airs or any sense of superiority. And just like that, he was gone, a shock to the entire country.

The eulogies poured in from all directions. Among the first was the one personally written by George Van Fleet that appeared the day after Harding's death in the *Marion Daily Star*.

> President Harding is dead. This brief message, flashed around the globe, brought sorrow to the nation and touched the tenderest sympathies of the liberty-loving people of every land. But here in Marion, where we knew and loved him as Harding, the man; Harding, the fellow-citizen; Harding, the neighbor; and Harding, the friend rather than Harding, the president the blackest grief obtains.[233]

Secretary of State Charles Evans Hughes, the leading intellectual in Harding's Cabinet, noted that:

> He was a man of the people, indulging no consciousness of superiority, incapable of arrogance. Nothing human was alien to him and he had the divine gift of sympathy. He wrought mightily for the prosperity of the Nation and for the peace of the world, but he clothed the exercise of power with the beautiful garments of gentleness. He gave his life for his country. No one can do more than that. He exhausted himself in service, a martyr in fidelity to the interests of the people for whom he labored with a passionate devotion.[234]

The new President, Calvin Coolidge, honored his predecessor by proclaiming, "It would be difficult to find two years of peacetime history in all the record of our republic that were marked with more important and far-reaching accomplishments."[235] Coolidge committed himself to continue to pursue the Harding agenda through the balance of the term.

The Mourning of Warren Harding

III-67: Harding's body being removed from the Palace Hotel in San Francisco, CA, August 3, 1923

III-68: Thousands gather to mourn President Harding as the funeral train passes through Chicago, IL

The Mourning of Warren Harding

III-69: Harding's body lying in state in the East Room of the White House, August 8, 1923

III-70: Harding's funeral procession on Pennsylvania Avenue in Washington, D.C., August 8, 1923

President Coolidge welcomed the deceased President's train when it returned to Washington after millions had turned out in silence to line the tracks on the coast-to-coast journey. Formal services were held on the morning of August 8 at the White House, with former Presidents Taft and Wilson joining the mourners. General John Pershing then led a procession to the Capitol where Harding's body lay in state on the same catafalque that had been used for the Unknown Soldier less than two years before. At noon there was a national moment of silence, after which thousands of American citizens paid their last respects during the five-hour period where final views were permitted. A military escort then brought Harding's body to Union Station for the final train trip to Marion. Arriving on August 9, Marion's most famous citizen lay in state in his father's home. Thousands were on hand the next day as Harding was laid to rest at the Marion Cemetery, buried amidst a rendering of Taps and a 21-gun salute.

III-71: Harding's burial at the Marion Cemetery, August 10, 1923

This was not the final resting place for Harding. The Warren Harding Memorial Association was established and raised $700,000 for a proper presidential memorial, which was constructed not far from the Harding home. Florence died just over a year after her husband, and both would lay for eternity side-by-side in this grand tomb in their precious hometown of Marion, Ohio. However, it would take a few years before the cornerstone was laid, and several additional years before the formal dedication took place. The reason for the delay? Scandals.

9. Scandals

Warren Harding had been in his grave for only a handful of weeks before the tales of corruption about his administration began to come to the fore. Accusations, congressional hearings, press investigations, court cases, tell-all books, secret letters, and eventually even DNA testing all contributed to developing a picture that sent Harding's reputation into the toilet. The biggest challenge in relating this portion of the Harding story is that so much of it is based on self-serving lies – lies from those making the charges as well as those defending the actions of the President and the administration. If all "evidence" is simply taken at face value, then it is easy to conclude (as many have done) that Harding's administration was one of the most corrupt in the nation's history. But doing so would also be inaccurate. Liars abound in the scandal portion of the Harding story, making definitive conclusions extremely difficult.

During Harding's tenure in office, the most public form of wrongdoing that had come to light was the corruption employed by Charles Forbes while running the Veterans Bureau. A congressional investigation uncovered many of Forbes's illegal actions and referred those findings to the Justice Department for prosecution. The subsequent trial ended in conviction, grabbing headlines along the way. President Harding was not directly linked to the malfeasance, but it happened on his watch and was executed by one of his friends, so the taint to Harding was not surprising. Forbes served 20 months of his two-year sentence at the Leavenworth Federal Penitentiary beginning in May 1926.

Next up was the oil scandal, beginning with a congressional investigation just a couple of months after Harding's death and carrying forward for years. The catchy name "Teapot Dome" became part of the American vernacular, seemingly equivalent to "massive corruption." A pair of zealous senators were at the forefront of the investigation. Thomas Walsh of Montana and John Kendrick of Wyoming pursued charges against the Harding administration and oil industry executives for more than two years, with a non-stop drumbeat of hearings and accusations, many of which were the kind of headline-grabbing fare that sells a lot of newspapers. As related earlier, "Teapot Dome" referred to a series of leases sold to two oil companies that paid the government for the right to drill on fields that had been set aside for the U.S. Navy. The policy, which President Harding supported, was fully consistent with the law. The accusation, however, was that those leases resulted from some form of malfeasance on behalf of the oil executives and their dealings with Interior Secretary Albert Fall. The Walsh/Kendrick investigations were determined to uncover the corruption and expose all involved. President Harding was less a direct subject of the inquiry, but Fall, Navy Secretary Denby, Attorney General Daugherty, and oil executives Edward Doheny and Harry Sinclair were very much in their crosshairs.

Fall was one of the early witnesses, and he vigorously defended his actions. Fall claimed the leases represented good policy, were consistent with the law, and generated positive results for the Federal government. He highlighted the revenue arranged from the deals, as well as the national security benefits that had accrued in Hawaii with the construction of tanks and placement of oil in that strategic location. One senator asked him why he didn't use competitive bids, which were not legally required in this instance, but represented the typical government practice. Fall's response was: "Business purely. I knew I could get a better price without calling for bids." When pressed on whether other bids might have been received if solicited, Fall replied, "Oh, I might have gotten bids. There was only one bid I could have gotten that I could have considered, however, in my judgment, and that is the bid that was finally accepted."[236] Doheny and Sinclair were both called to testify, and they fully backed Fall, claiming nothing untoward in their financial relationship with him when he was Secretary of the Interior.

After the committee went into recess, some stories began to emerge about lavish spending by Fall at his ranch in New Mexico. The *State Tribune* reported extravagant upgrades in and around the ranch, the payment of back taxes which had been stuck in limbo for years, and a general rise in his standard of living. Further digging led to the discovery of a $100,000 payment to Fall prior to the awarding of the leases. That payment was made in cash and believed to have been personally delivered in a black satchel by Doheny's son. More payments were then uncovered, this time from Sinclair's company to Fall in the form of Liberty Bonds. Within a month of the no-bid contract being awarded to Sinclair to drill at Teapot Dome, $198,000 of those bonds were transferred from Sinclair's Continental Trading Company to Fall's son-in-law. Another $35,000 payment followed shortly thereafter. Fall, Doheny, and Sinclair clearly had some explaining to do, and were called to Washington to do just that. Sinclair claimed, then and forever more, that his payments had nothing to do with the contract award. Rather, they were an investment on his part, believing the funds would be used to upgrade Fall's ranch so it could become an income-generating tourist destination. When Senator Irvine Lenroot asked whether Fall had received "any benefits or profits, directly or indirectly, in any manner whatsoever" by awarding the leases to Sinclair, the oilman replied, "No, sir, none."[237] While skeptics abounded, there was no hard evidence to prove otherwise.

As for that $100,000 in cash from Doheny, that saga took a bizarre twist when Fall tried to get someone else to admit on the record to providing the payment, to throw the investigators off track. After initially striking out with Price McKinney, Fall found someone else to say he was the source of the funds. Fall wrote the committee on Christmas Day:

> The gentleman from whom I obtained it and who furnished me the cash was the Hon. Edward B. McLean of Washington, D.C. ... I have never approached E. L. Doheny or anyone connected with him or any of his corporations, or Mr. H. F. Sinclair or anyone connected with him or any of his corporations; nor have I ever received from either of said parties one cent on account of any oil lease or upon any other account whatsoever.[238]

McLean even wrote out a check for the $100K for Fall to show as evidence, even though Fall had agreed never to cash the check. Senator Walsh frankly didn't believe the story and hit the road to visit with McLean at his vacation home in Palm Beach, Florida. McLean realized the morass he had stepped into and came clean with Walsh, blowing Fall's credibility out of the water. It was also one of the catalysts that led Fall to the bottle, which coincided with numerous ailments cropping up. Evalyn McLean commented on her friend that "For the first time in my life, I saw a man crumble right before my eyes. ... Drinking had changed [Fall] from a virile, sharp-witted man into a trembling wreck."[239] Fall claimed he was too ill to testify again, so Walsh focused on Doheny, who reappeared before the Senate committee on January 21, 1924. Doheny admitted to giving the money to Fall, but he claimed it was a personal loan that had nothing to do with granting the oil leases. "This sum was loaned to Mr. Fall by me personally. It was my own money and did not belong in whole or in part to any oil company with which I am or have been connected. This loan had no relation to any of the subsequent transactions."[240] Such statements were met with pure skepticism, although it was still unclear if any of the accusations could be proven if taken to the courts. Sinclair also appeared in front of the Senate investigators and remained defiant. After refusing to answer some questions, he was referred to the Justice Department for charges of contempt of Congress.

To sensationalize things even further, additional hearings made the names Gaston Means and Roxie Stinson household names. Means was a professional con man who had been ripping people off for years with a variety of elaborate schemes. One of his trademark techniques was to swear to public officials that he had documents to substantiate his claims, but rarely ever did he actually produce the evidence. Means would often begin his accusations with a sliver of truth to try to sway his skeptics, but then go off the reservation with wild stories that could never be confirmed. Despite his checkered past, William Burns, the aggressive head of Harry Daugherty's FBI, hired Means as a government detective. This supposedly gave him inside access to illegal activity. Always looking to be in the spotlight, Means approached the senators with tales of corruption that led directly to President Harding and Attorney General Daugherty. For example, he claimed they were fully aware that the government was turning a blind eye to failures to enforce the Prohibition Amendment as a result of payoffs from bootleggers. When called to produce the documents that he claimed would substantiate his testimony, Means failed to deliver. It turned out that the investigation actually revealed that Means was directly involved in Prohibition-related bribes. He was charged with perjury, convicted in Federal court, and sent to prison for two years.

III-72: Gaston Means

But Means wasn't done. He had more stories to tell and convinced a journalist by the name of Mae Thacker to ghostwrite a book that went

III-73: "The Strange Death of President Harding" by Gaston Means

beyond the accusations Means had delivered to Congress. The title of the book was the clue to where the story was heading – *The Strange Death of President Harding*. According to Means, he had been employed by Florence Harding to track her husband's infidelities. Through his access, he claimed to have uncovered the real cause of the President's death – poison. Means identified the perpetrator as none other than the First Lady herself, who was supposedly in cahoots with Doctor Sawyer, both of whom had already died before the book came out. According to Means, Harding's sudden demise was due to Florence's attempt to distract from his crimes and affairs before they blew up in his face. This took the Harding corruption stories well into the 1930s, with the book becoming a best-seller, despite the fact that nearly all of the sensational tales were pure fiction. Once again, Means was challenged to produce the documentary evidence to support his claims, but once again, he was unable to do so. This eventually caused his ghostwriter to repudiate the entire effort. Thacker told *Liberty Magazine* in November 1931 that the Means book was a "colossal hoax – a tissue of falsehood from beginning to end."[241] But that didn't mean the public simply forgot his allegations. According to Agent Starling, Means was "a man who would not have been caught dead telling the truth … smeared the President and the administration with vicious and scandalous lies which are still quoted as truth by most of the public."[242] That was part of the problem for Harding. Once these fictitious stories started to fill the nation's newspapers, they began to cloud people's recollections of Harding in a way that was not easily undone.

A similar story revolves around the testimony of Roxie Stinson who was the ex-wife of Jess Smith, the happy-go-lucky unofficial aide to Daugherty who had committed suicide in 1923. Ms. Stinson was the one who broke open the story about the Little Green House and its wild, alcohol-infused parties that took place while bribes were paid and influence peddled. Senator Burton Wheeler of Montana led the crusade

III-74: Roxie Stinson

against Daugherty's Justice Department and used his hearings to elicit sensational claims from both Means and Stinson. But just as the Means testimony would eventually be repudiated, there were serious questions about Stinson's as well. She had come across as rehearsed and coached and, of course, had no first-hand knowledge of any of her assertions as she had never even been to the Little Green House. All of her testimony came from stories supposedly told to her by Smith, who could no longer corroborate anything. The more outrageous the claims, the more the public gobbled them up, despite the likelihood of fabrication.

The Attorney General refused to testify to Wheeler's Committee or even provide access to Department of Justice records. For several months, President Coolidge stood by Daugherty despite calls for his dismissal, including by some from within the administration. At one point Coolidge told Senator William Borah, who was demanding the Attorney General's ouster, "Daugherty was Harding's friend. He stands high with the Republican organization. I do not see how I can do it."[243] But, eventually, the rumors and accusations heading in Daugherty's direction proved too much, and in March 1924, the President decided to make a change. The AG agreed to step down, but the story was hardly over. It was time for the courts to take over and try to sort out all of this mess.

Albert Fall, Edward Doheny, Harry Sinclair, and eventually Harry Daugherty were the star attractions in a series of trials in the latter half of the 1920s. The primary charges related to conspiracy to defraud the Federal government. In the first round, the jury came back with acquittals for both Fall and Doheny in December 1926. After the Supreme Court subsequently invalidated the drilling leases associated with Teapot Dome and Elk Hills in December 1927 on the grounds of collusion and conspiracy, Fall and Sinclair went to trial and were also acquitted of bribery conspiracy. New evidence continued to crop up, and more charges ensued. In one of the most bizarre twists to the story, the first conviction associated with Teapot Dome was handed down in October 1929 when a broken and wheelchair-bound Albert Fall was found guilty of accepting a bribe from Doheny. The twist came less than six months later when, in the same courtroom and in front of the same judge, Doheny was found *not* guilty of offering that very bribe. This meant Fall was going to prison for accepting a bribe that the legal system determined Doheny never offered in the first place. After years of investigations, someone was finally going to jail – the first time a Cabinet official was sentenced to time behind bars for crimes committed during his service. Fall spent a year in the state penitentiary at Santa Fe beginning in July 1931. He was also fined $100,000, equivalent to the amount of the bribe he was found guilty of accepting.

Harry Sinclair was never found guilty of bribing a Federal official, but he was sentenced to jail terms on two occasions throughout this ordeal. The first was a conviction over the contempt of Congress charges that emanated from his testimony during his congressional hearing. Sinclair was later found guilty of jury tampering, which cost him another six months behind bars. Doheny was never sanctioned for any of his actions. To add insult to injury, Doheny foreclosed on Fall's home for not paying back the $100,000 cash "loan" he had provided to start the entire sordid affair, merely adding to the misery of Albert Fall.

Through the course of all these investigations, headline-grabbing charges, court cases, and eventually a conviction of a Cabinet official, Warren Harding's name was dragged through the mud. Yet, when the Teapot Dome scandal is fully unpacked, none of the corruption actually involved the President of the United States. The entire set of actions, including the transfer of authority from the Navy to the Interior, the issuing of leases to drill on these naval reserve lands, the use of no-bid contracts to make the awards, and the subsequent drilling activities were all permissible policies within the confines of existing law. Harding knew about each of these steps, and he approved of them, which should bear no connotation of corruption. The malfeasance was limited to Albert Fall, a man Harding believed he had every reason to trust. This was poor judgment and a common theme for Harding in Washington, as Fall wasn't the only one who let him down. But, it was hardly criminal or even truly "scandalous" on the part of Warren Harding. The bribes Fall accepted from Doheny and Sinclair were unknown to anyone until after Harding was dead. There have been some accounts that link the oil conspiracy back to the Republican Convention, claiming Harding had been bought and paid for by the industry from the very beginning. The evidence to support this claim is weak, relying on self-serving testimonies that have largely been discredited. Trustworthy accounts of the era simply do not support the conclusion that Harding had anything to do with the illegal portion of the Teapot Dome scandal. But the story sure has had legs, as Teapot Dome remains the primary bumper sticker for Harding's presidency in most historical accounts.

There was one other Cabinet official who was also charged with crimes but was never convicted, and that's former Attorney General Harry Daugherty. Senator Wheeler's investigation led to criminal charges against Daugherty in 1926. While accepting bribes for favors from his perch atop the Justice Department was the frequent allegation against Daugherty, that was not the actual charge that he faced in court. Daugherty was charged with negligence in the performance of his duty for refusing to prosecute allegedly fraudulent transactions in a case related to the American Metal Company. In Daugherty's own words, "The American Metals case involved the return of alien property which had been unlawfully taken during the war and subsequently returned to its rightful owners."[244] His accusers believed the property did not meet the standard and should not have been returned. At trial, there were allegations that Jess Smith had influenced this decision in Daugherty's Justice Department and had received tens of thousands of dollars in return for helping determine the outcome and expedite the decision. While Daugherty's supposed accomplice, Thomas Miller, was convicted and sentenced to 13 months for arranging the illegal transfer of American Metals, a hung jury was the result in not one but two attempts to convict Daugherty. While the jury vote in the second trial was 11-1 to convict, Daugherty can correctly claim that he was never found guilty in any court of law. There was nothing in any of these charges against Daugherty which directly implicated Warren Harding in any wrongdoing.

Was there corruption in the Harding presidency? Yes. Albert Fall betrayed the trust of his President and the American people by taking a pair of bribes that illegally influenced his decision to award lucrative leasing contracts to two oil companies. After years of investigations, Fall was finally caught in his lies, convicted in a court of law, fined, and sent to prison for a year. A similar case of corruption materialized in the

Veterans Bureau under Charles Forbes, who also ended up in prison for his efforts to make a quick buck at the expense of returning war heroes and American taxpayers. The Ohio Gang that met at the Little Green House undoubtedly engaged in some forms of influence peddling as well, although Jess Smith appears to be the only one of the group who was going to be charged with a crime. These activities appropriately left a stain on the legacy of Warren Harding, but the size of that stain seems out of proportion to the actual malfeasance that took place, particularly since there is little to no credible evidence that Harding was personally involved in any of these corrupt acts. For some perspective, none of this compares to the corruption that permeated the Cabinet of Ulysses Grant a half-century before. *Four* of Grant's Cabinet secretaries resigned in disgrace associated with bribes or kickbacks. Moreover, his appointees a step below the Cabinet were caught in the tax-cheating Whiskey Rings, which also led to the resignation of Grant's personal secretary in the White House. The corruption under Warren Harding pales in comparison, yet Teapot Dome has stuck in the American psyche as the epitome of degenerate service, bringing Harding's reputation down with it, with virtually no mention of the positive contributions he made in his two-and-a-half years in office. When looking at the entirety of the Harding presidency, the overwhelmingly negative reaction seems disproportionate to the actual performance of his administration.

That reaction, however, was the principal reason that the dedication of Harding's final resting place took so long to occur as the country's leaders were skittish about commemorating the former President while the nation's capital was swirling with all these terrible tales. President Coolidge demurred every time the topic came up throughout his full term in office. When Herbert Hoover took over the White House in 1929, he initially balked as well. But, by 1931, Harding's former Commerce Secretary agreed it was time for closure on this piece of history, and a date was set for the official ceremony. It was an awkward affair in that while Hoover sought to praise his former boss (and he did), he also was not silent concerning all the stories of wrongdoing that had circulated since Harding's death.

> Here was a man whose soul was seared by a great disillusionment. We saw him gradually weaken not only from physical exhaustion but also from mental anxiety. Warren Harding had a dim realization that he had been

III-75: A modern day view of the Harding Memorial in Marion, OH

> betrayed by a few of the men whom he had trusted, by men whom he had believed were his devoted friends. It was later proved in the courts of the land that these men had betrayed not only the friendship and trust of their staunch and loyal friend but they had betrayed their country. That was the tragedy of the life of Warren Harding.[245]

Hoover tried to be diplomatic in his remarks, offering further perspective on Harding and his administration.

> These acts never touched Warren Harding. ... He was a man of delicate sense of honor, of sympathetic heart, of transcendent gentleness of soul ... who reached out for friendship ... who gave of it loyally and generously. ... a man of passionate patriotism. … But any objective weighing of Mr. Harding's Presidential contribution in the balances of time must show that his playmates tipped the scales from his very considerable accomplishments in national progress toward national degeneration.[246]

That taint was already setting in for the historical perspective on the presidency of Warren Harding.

Of course, these political scandals were also only part of the story on the seedier side of Warren Harding. He was hardly the only President to have extramarital affairs, either before or during their presidencies. But the public rendering of these affairs certainly contributed to the blot on Harding's reputation. The Carrie Phillips affair was more of an open secret to the people of Marion but took on a whole new flavor when Harding's steamy letters to Phillips were unsealed. The overtly sexual nature of the letters certainly caught the imagination of the public, adding to the tawdry reputation that had already been attached to Harding after the publication of Nan Britton's book, *The President's Daughter,* in

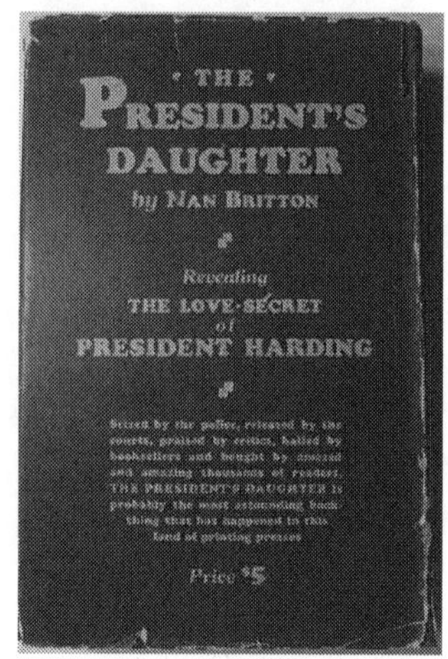

III-76: "The President's Daughter" by Nan Britton

1927. The story behind that book deserves some exploration. According to Nan, her affair with Harding continued throughout his presidency. They had only limited opportunities to be together physically, but according to her accounts, they did find time to connect, including in that closet in the White House. Correspondence flowed regularly as well, with Nan including sealed notes inside the main envelope, passing these through Harding's valet Arthur Brooks. Harding regularly dispatched cash to Nan to pay for her expenses and those of their daughter, although he always avoided being in the same room as Elizabeth Ann. He never laid eyes on his only child. According to Nan, the last time she saw Harding was in January 1923. When the Hardings left for Alaska later in the year, Nan was off to Europe with a friend on a trip paid for by the President. She was in France when news of Harding's illness became public. She was crushed when she heard of his passing and quickly returned to the United States. Amid her personal grief, which was profound, she was also confused. Harding's will generously provided hefty sums for both Florence and Tryon Harding. He also made bequests to his brothers and sisters, the Marion Park Commission, the Baptist Church of Marion, along with some small amounts to various nieces, nephews, Florence's grandchildren, and some longtime employees of the *Star*. Nan Britton and her daughter Elizabeth Ann were not mentioned. "I could not understand this," Nan later wrote. "He had always been so generous. … And now for me to think that Warren Harding had not made ample provision for his child, and her mother as well, would be for me to impute cowardice and injustice to one who, I knew always bravely met life-issues."[247] This had to be a mistake. She was convinced that Harding had accounted for his only child, if not in his will, then in some other arrangement. She understood his desire to maintain their secret, but she could not conceive that the man she loved would simply abandon her and their offspring.

As the months passed, there was no secret outreach to Nan with a bucket of Harding money. She eventually contacted the secret service agent who had helped her during Harding's presidency – the man she referred to as Tim Slade. Slade helped her out with small amounts of cash from his own pocket while agreeing to quietly inquire from Harding's friends if any arrangements had been made for "anyone else" who might have been deserving of some of Harding's estate. No one Slade approached knew anything about what he was talking about. In the meantime, Nan was trying to make do on a $35-a-week secretarial position in the little work she was qualified to obtain.

A bit out of desperation, Nan agreed to marry in January 1924 to a man she called "Captain Angus Neilson" in her memoirs, a seafaring man from Europe who had been kind to her in her grief. Neilson claimed he had lots of money back in his home country, or at least he could sell some assets and bring the cash back to the U.S. to provide for both Nan and her daughter. Nan agreed to Neilson's proposal but couldn't get her mind off of Warren Harding. When Neilson failed to deliver on his economic promises, an unhappy Nan sued for divorce after only a couple of years together.

Nan did have an encounter with one of the Hardings in 1924. It was her old teacher, Harding's sister, Daisy, who was in New York for a visit, and Nan reached out to her. They had always been friendly, and Nan looked forward to having Elizabeth Ann, now almost five years old, meet her "Aunt Daisy." Nan kept her secret but was pleased to make the connection. A year later, a bewildered and frustrated Nan felt she had to do something to obtain the funds Elizabeth Ann deserved. Her little girl had been back and forth from Chicago to New York several times based on Nan's financial situation, with the Willitses generously taking care of their officially adopted daughter whenever Nan needed help. By the summer of 1925, she had grown desperate and decided to share her full story with Daisy Harding. She wasn't seeking any grand public disclosure but wanted the Harding family to know about the

III-77: Nan Britton, 1926 (age 29)

President's daughter and, frankly, to get them to help out. Nan went to Marion and called upon Daisy (now Daisy Lewis after her recent marriage).

Nan and Daisy spent hours together as the former pupil poured out the details of her affair and all about Elizabeth Ann. She also made clear she was destitute and needed help. Daisy appeared sympathetic, and even offered small amounts of cash, but made no commitments. This kind of relationship continued over the course of the next several months. Daisy agreed to provide some support for Elizabeth Ann, particularly for schooling and clothing, and while these payments were appreciated, they were insufficient to provide the kind of stability Nan was looking for for her child. In July 1925, she pushed for more funds, making it clear to Daisy in a letter that her recent outreach "had been for the express purpose of bringing the Harding family to a realization that there existed an obligation on their part to Elizabeth Ann, and not merely to solicit sympathy and discuss the intimate details of my relationship with her brother."[248]

Over time, Nan's secret was shared with two more Harding siblings. First was Carrie Votaw, who was not inclined to offer any support. Votaw's husband, Heber, who had served in Harding's administration, did not believe Nan's story and tried to keep her at bay. Eventually, Daisy and Carrie decided to share Nan's story with their brother, Dr. George Harding (known as "Deac"). Deac Harding was also very skeptical of the entire account. After all, Nan had no evidence to substantiate her story. Unlike Carrie Phillips, who had retained all of Harding's correspondence, Nan had dutifully destroyed all the letters she received. Without any concrete proof, the judgment by the men in the Harding family led to a collective conclusion that Nan's story was simply a shakedown for cash. There was no way to prove paternity at the time, and the family was not inclined to take Nan's word for a story that could not be verified through any other source.

The showdown between Nan and Deac took place in Marion on April 1, 1926. The two-hour meeting was confrontational as Deac sought proof of Nan's claims. She shared what she had, but knew it was likely to be unconvincing. She cited dates and locations for her liaisons with Harding but could not substantiate any of these details with any documentation. Toward the end of the session, Deac bluntly asked Nan what she wanted.

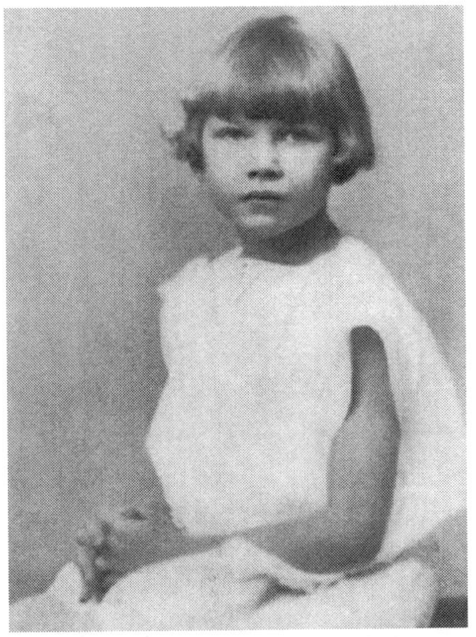
III-78: Harding's daughter, Elizabeth Ann Willits

He wanted numbers, and Nan responded as follows: "I mean that she [Elizabeth Ann] should get a fair amount, say $50,000, to be put into a trust fund so that she would have a monthly income to live upon." Deac responded, "And is that *all*?" Nan continued: "No, I think also that I should have enough to settle my indebtedness which were incurred directly as a result of my attempt to keep my daughter with me during my marriage, and $2500 would allow me to settle these debts and have a balance upon which to 'turn around' as it were."[249] Deac took careful notes of the entire conversation and then said he would look into the matter. No commitments were made.

Eventually, the Harding siblings decided to cut Nan off. She had come across as a gold digger with no proof of her claims, and they had no intention of parting with tens of thousands of dollars based on this flimsy story. The rejection by Daisy hurt Nan most of all. "It seemed to me that I had been cruelly dismissed from further loving consideration by her who had once termed herself one 'who never fails a friend,'"[250] Nan wrote. She felt betrayed, and she was desperate. This was what led to her going public with the story in the form of her book.

Nan opened her memoir with a statement about a mission broader than herself. "The author has had but one motive in writing for publication the story of her love-life with Mr. Harding," she wrote on page one. "This motive is grounded in what seems to her to be the need for legal and social recognition and protection of all children in these United States born out of wedlock."[251] There may have been some truth in this sentiment, but by this point, the book was really about money. For more than three years Nan had tried everything she could to penetrate Harding's inner circle, to find someone who would believe her story and be willing to do the right thing. She had been denied at every turn and had no prospects of finding the kind of resources she felt were rightfully hers. Thus was born *The President's Daughter*.

The first "tell-all" memoir of its kind in American presidential history was a sensation. While none of the established publishing houses would agree to publish the book, Nan went out on her own, creating the Elizabeth Ann Guild to bring her story to the public. If money was her object, she might have even exceeded her expectations. Ninety-thousand copies were sold at $5 a book, generating a nice windfall for the mother of Warren Harding's child. She also suffered terribly for her efforts. Critics abounded, calling her a money-grubbing fraud. She had earned some financial security for her family, but she paid a steep price in public opinion – as did the reputation of her lover, Warren Harding. Nan's book came to market at the same time as the various trials over Teapot Dome and the alleged misconduct of Harry Daugherty, creating a stench over the Harding presidency that persisted long after all the characters passed from the scene. Nan Britton lived until the ripe old age of 94, dying at her final home in Sandy, Oregon, in 1991. She had spent the bulk of her adult life living quietly in obscurity but never lost her infatuation with Warren Harding that jumped off the pages of her book. One of Nan's grandchildren, James Blaesing, described Nan's relationship with Harding as a true love story. "She loved him until the day she died," Blaesing said. "When she talked about him, she would get the biggest smile on her face. She just loved this guy. He was everything."[252] As for Elizabeth Ann, she married Henry Blaesing in 1938. The couple had three children (including James). She was aware of her mother's claims about her paternity, but had no interest in pursuing the matter or even talking about it, denying requests over the years from Harding biographers to discuss the situation. Elizabeth Ann Blaesing died 14 years after her mother, in 2005, at the age of 86. At the time of their deaths, few believed Nan Britton's story.

But along came DNA testing, spurred on by curiosity. One of Harding's grand nephews, Dr. Peter Harding, and his cousin Abigail Harding, thought it was time to solve the mystery of Elizabeth Ann's paternity. They contacted James Blaesing to see if he would be interested in submitting his DNA for testing. Ancestry.com did the analysis, and in August 2015, the match was confirmed – Elizabeth Ann shared roots with both the Harding and Blaesing families. "We're looking at the genetic scene to see if Warren Harding and Nan Britton had a baby together and all these signs are pointing to yes," said Stephen Baloglu, an executive at Ancestry. "The technology that we're using is at a level of specificity that there's no need to do more DNA testing. This is the definitive answer."[253] The DNA testing cleared up one of the other Harding mysteries as well, those rumors that he came from a mixed-race background. The DNA testing confirmed the answer was "no" – Harding "had no ancestors from sub-Saharan Africa."[254] If only DNA testing had existed a hundred years before, reputations might have turned out very different than they did.

One question clearly remains, though: Why did Warren Harding not take any steps to make provisions for his only child in the event of his death? Those who argue that his death was sudden and he just hadn't gotten around to it need to remember that Harding updated his will just a couple of weeks before he died. Harry Daugherty helped Harding pull together his new will and made clear that "It would have been the work of but a few minutes for me to draft in my own handwriting a deed of trust that would have made ample provision for Nan Britton and her child, outside the terms of his regular will."[255] Yet, Harding took no such steps. Perhaps Harding didn't believe that Elizabeth Ann was his, and therefore not his responsibility. Many believed Harding was sterile, perhaps due to a childhood case of the mumps, given that no children resulted from his marriage to Florence, who had had a child of her own in a prior marriage. Maybe Harding just wanted to keep his secret for all eternity to protect his reputation. Daugherty's perspective on the situation is telling, in part because he knew Harding as well as anyone ever did. Daugherty did not believe a word of Nan's tale, writing in his memoirs that "Fake" should be written "over every page of the book that bears the name of Nan Britton."[256] The opposite was unfathomable to Daugherty. First, Harding's longtime friend said it was inconceivable that Harding would refuse to see his own child, as Nan claimed in her book. "It is unthinkable that a man of Harding's temperament," Daugherty wrote, "if he had taken all the risks of hotel registers in New York, of Pullman rides across half a dozen states, could not create an opportunity to see his baby! If he had ever been the father of one, no power on earth could have kept him from it. The thing is preposterous on the author's own showing."[257] And second, according to Daugherty, if there was anything true in Nan's account, nothing would have prevented Harding from taking care of his own daughter after his death.

> It is easy to say that a man neglects to do such things often until it is too late. Many men do. But Harding could not have done such a thing. He was too gentle, too kind, too sentimental. He never had any such relations with Nan Britton as she claims in the book in which she boasts of her own shame. If he had, he would have provided for the child on this memorable day of his life. He was that kind of a man. For in these friendly hours [when they updated Harding's will] we talked of the deep things of life and death and eternity.[258]

But now we know through DNA testing that all the doubters were wrong.

Warren's Harding's presidency is remembered primarily for scandals, which is both too simplistic a summary and, to a great degree, unfair. Harding was a decent President who had some notable accomplishments during his time in office. He helped the country "Return to Normalcy" with an "America First" agenda that helped spur the nation onto a path of prosperity while notching a major triumph in the world of international diplomacy. President Harding also stumbled by associating with some people who sought to take advantage of their situation, with a few committing criminal acts that betrayed his trust and that of the American people. Harding's presidency was hardly the most scandalous in American history, and no charge of corruption against him personally has ever been sustained. Nevertheless, it also wasn't scandal-free, with implications for some members of his administration as well as in his personal life. And we now also have proof with letters in his own hand and DNA testing that confirm two affairs, including one that spawned his only child. Cutting through all the sensationalistic allegations, including many that don't stand up to scrutiny, this is the essence of the legacy of Warren Harding. Except for Elizabeth Ann. As Harry Daugherty stated so emphatically, it is simply hard to imagine that the kind, generous, gregarious people-person who had befriended so many over the years with his affable and caring personality could simply abandon his only child upon his death. That decision – not Teapot Dome, or the Ohio Gang, or his two extramarital affairs – represents the greatest mystery of Warren G. Harding, and also his primary source of shame.

20 Quotations from Warren Harding

Date	Context and Source	Quote
1895	Remark after losing his first political race, for county auditor; One of his favorite sayings (Chapple (1). p. 70)	"Real success is often built upon preliminary failures spurring on to greater achievements."
December 24, 1910	Expressing his feelings to Carrie Phillips; From a letter to Carrie Phillips (As reported in *The New York Times Magazine*)	"I love you more than all the world, and have no hope of reward on earth or hereafter, so precious as that in your dear arms, in your thrilling lips, in your matchless breasts, in your incomparable embrace."
June 24, 1915	Expresses his view on the appropriateness of following the Republican leadership in the Senate; From a speech to a delegation from the Ohio Convention of the Congressional Union (Sinclair. p. 63)	"Believing as I do in political parties and government through political parties, I had much rather that the party to which I belong should, in its conferences, make a declaration, than to assume a leadership or take an individual position on the question."
June 7, 1916	Critical of Woodrow Wilson's policies regarding World War I; From his Keynote Address at the 1916 Republican National Convention (As reported in *The New York Times*)	"We proclaim justice and we love peace, and we mean to have them – and we are not too proud to fight for them! … [It was time for] the mistaken policy of watchful waiting and wabbling warfare" of the Wilson administration to come to an end, he emphasized.
April 4, 1917	Provides rationale for his vote to go to war against Germany and the Central Powers; From a speech to the Senate (Sinclair. p. 87)	"I want it known to the people of my State, and to the Nation that I am voting for war to-night for the maintenance of just American rights, which is the first essential to the preservation of the soul of this Republic. … A war that speaks for the majesty of a people popularly governed, who finally are brought to the crucial test where they are resolved to get together and wage a conflict for the maintenance of their rights."
March 1919	Explaining his position on signing Senator Henry Lodge's "Round Robin" letter opposing the	"These reservations come of a purpose to protect America first and still save a framework on which to build intelligent co-operation. ... I do not believe, Senators, that it

	League of Nations as negotiated by President Woodrow Wilson; From a speech to the Senate (Adams. p. 94)	is going 'to break the heart of the world' to make this covenant right, or at least free from perils which would endanger our own independence. But it were better to witness this rhetorical tragedy than destroy the soul of this great Republic."
1919	Expresses why he doesn't want to run for President; From a letter to a friend in Marion (Mee. p. 79)	"Honestly, I would not have [the presidency] if I could reach out and grasp it, and I really do not want any of my friends to promote it in any way. … I find it difficult to make a good many people believe that one can feel this way. … Of course, I am human enough to enjoy having friends who think well enough of me to suggest me for the position, and I confess some pleasure in knowing that events have so broken thus far that I should attract some favorable mention, but when it comes down to serious consideration I am wholly truthful when I say that I had rather no mention were made whatever."
January 10, 1920	Expressing his "America First" perspective at the outset of the 1920 campaign; From a speech to the Ohio Club of New York in New York City (Johnson. p. 144)	"I have a confidence in our America that requires no council of foreign powers to point the way of American duty. We wish to counsel, coöperate and contribute, but we arrogate to ourselves the keeping of the American conscience and every concept of our moral obligations. It is fine to idealize, but it is very practical to make sure our own house is in perfect order before we attempt the miracle of the Old-World stabilization. Call it the selfishness of nationalist if you will, I think it an inspiration to patriotic devotion: To safeguard America first. To stabilize America first. To prosper America first. To think of America first. To exalt America first. To live for and revere America first."
March 4, 1921	Expressing his "Return to Normalcy" theme; From his Inaugural Address (Chapple (1). p. 296)	"Our supreme task is the resumption of our onward, normal way. Reconstruction, readjustment, restoration – all these must follow. I would like to hasten them. If it will lighten the spirit and add to the resolution with which we take up the task, let me repeat for our nation, we shall give no people just cause to make war."
March 4, 1921	Maintains his objection to joining the League of Nations as currently	"We crave friendship and harbor no hate. But America, our America, the America builded on the foundation laid by the inspired fathers, can be a party to no permanent military

	structured; From his Inaugural Address (Chapple (1). p. 294)	alliance. It can enter into no political commitments, nor assume any economic obligations which will subject our decisions to any other than our own authority. … A world supergovernment is contrary to everything we cherish and can have no sanction by our Republic. This is not selfishness; it is sanctity. It is not aloofness; it is security. It is not suspicion of others; it is patriotic adherence to the things which made us what we are."
1921	On enjoying meeting people and shaking hands as President; From remarks to George Christian (Russell. p. 438)	"I love to meet people. It is the most pleasant thing I do; it is really the only fun I have. It does not tax me, and it seems to be a very great pleasure to them."
1921	Opposes implementing price controls for farmers; In response to an appeal from farmers for relief (Sinclair. p. 203)	"Government paternalism, whether applied to agriculture or to any other of our great national industries, would stifle ambition, impair efficiency, lessen production and make us a nation of dependent incompetents. The farmer requires no special favors at the hands of the government. All he needs is a fair chance."
October 26, 1921	Views on race relations and civil rights; From a speech in Birmingham, AL (Sinclair. p. 231)	"Politically and economically there need be no occasion for great and permanent differentiation, for limitations of the individual's opportunity, provided that on both sides there shall be recognition of the absolute divergence in things social and racial. … Natural segregations [should be accepted] satisfying natural inclinations and adding notably to happiness and contentment. … Racial amalgamation there cannot be."
November 12, 1921	Views on disarmament and war; From his welcoming remarks at the Conference for the Limitation of Armament (Johnson. p. 162)	"I can speak officially only for the United States. Our hundred millions frankly want less of armament and none of war. Wholly free from guile, sure in our own minds that we harbor no unworthy designs, we accredit the world with the same good intent. So I welcome you, not alone in good-will and high purpose, but with high faith."
February 6, 1922	On the results of the Disarmament Conference; From his closing remarks at the Conference for the Limitation of Armament	"This conference has wrought a truly great achievement. It is hazardous sometimes to speak in superlatives [but the result is] so fine, so gratifying, so reassuring, so full of promise, that above the murmurings of a world sorrow not yet silenced; above the

	(Murray. p. 157)	groans which come of excessive burdens not yet lifted but soon to be lightened; above the discouragements of a world struggling to find itself after surpassing upheaval, there is the note of rejoicing which is not alone ours or yours, or all of us, but comes from the hearts of men of all the world."
1922	On the importance of the Senate votes on the treaties coming out of the Conference for the Limitation of Armament; From remarks to H.H. Kohlsaat (Russell. p. 485)	"The success or failure of this administration depends on the ratification of these treaties. Every administration's name rests on one or two acts. If these treaties are ratified by the Senate, then this administration's name is secure in history. If the treaties are defeated, nothing I can do in the balance of my term will be of more than passing interest."
1922	Makes clear his support of the policies of Interior Secretary Albert Fall re: granting leases to drill on Naval Reserves; From a letter to a congressional committee investigating the leases (Daugherty. p. 195)	"I think it is only fair to say in this connection, that the policy which has been adopted by the Secretary of the Interior, in dealing with these matters, was submitted to me prior to the adoption thereof and the policy decided upon and the subsequent acts have at all times had my entire approval."
1923	On the challenges his friends were creating for him; From remarks to journalist William Allen White (Murray. p. 436)	"My God, this is a hell of a job! I have no trouble with my enemies. I can take care of my enemies all right. But my damn friends, my God-damn friends, White, they're the ones that keep me walking the floor nights!"
June 21, 1923	Advocates for the U.S. joining the World Court; From a speech/radio address in St. Louis, MO (Mee. p. 217)	"I shall not restrict my appeal to your reason, I shall call upon your patriotism. I shall beseech your humanity. … I shall reach to the very depths of love for your fellow countrymen of whatever race or creed throughout the world. … My soul yearns for peace. My heart is anguished by the sufferings of war. My spirit is eager to serve. My passion is for justice over force. My hope is in the great court. My mind is made up. My resolution is fixed."
July 1923	On how much he enjoyed meeting the people of Alaska; From remarks to Joe Chapple (Chapple (1). p. 238)	"You know, I do enjoy meeting these people. They help me more than I can tell them. They have preserved the sturdy spirit of the pioneer, and without our pioneers and frontiers we are likely to lose the self-reliance and upstanding courage which have made our nation grow."

Primary Sources

Adams, Samuel.

Incredible Era: The Life and Times of Warren Gamaliel Harding. The Riverside Press. Houghton Mifflin Company. Boston, MA. 1939.

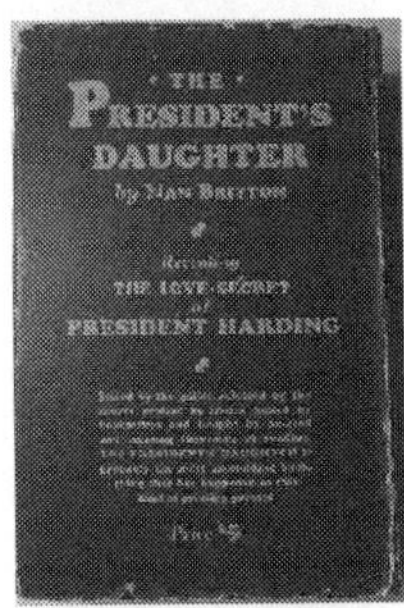

Britton, Nan.

The President's Daughter. Elizabeth Ann Guild, Inc. New York, NY. 1927.

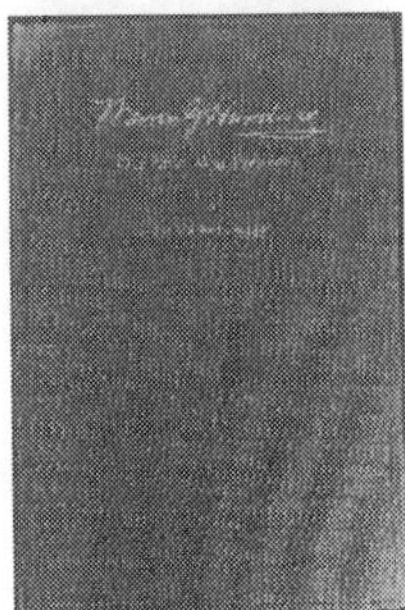

Chapple, Joe.

Life and Times of Warren G. Harding: Our After-War President. Chapple Publishing Company, Limited. Boston, MA. 1924. [Chapple (1)]

Daugherty, Harry.

The Inside Story of the Harding Tragedy. The Churchill Company. New York, NY. 1932.

Hall, Sheryl.

Warren G. Harding & the Marion Daily Star. The History Press. Charleston, SC. 2014.

Johnson, Willis.

The Life of Warren G. Harding. William H. Johnston. 1923.

Murray, Robert.

The Harding Era: Warren G. Harding and His Administration. University of Minnesota Press. Minneapolis, MN. 1969.

Russell, Francis.

The Shadow of Blooming Grove: Warren G. Harding in His Times. McGraw-Hill Book Company. New York, NY. 1968.

Sinclair, Andrew.

The Available Man: Warren Gamaliel Harding. The MacMillan Company. New York, NY. 1965.

Primary Sources Specifically for Illustrations

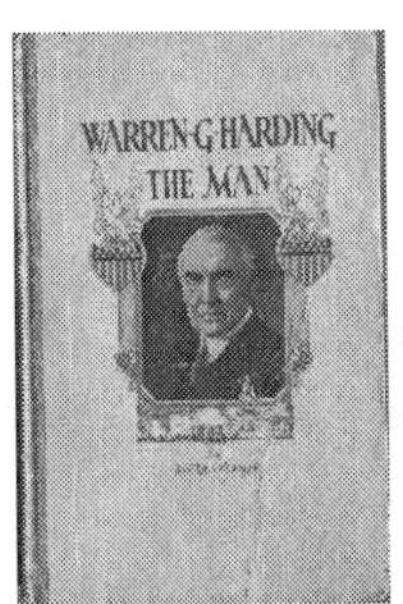

Chapple, Joe.

Warren G. Harding – The Man. Chapple Publishing Company, Limited. Boston, MA. 1920. [Chapple (2)]

Cuneo, Sherman.

From Printer to President: The Story of Warren G. Harding. Dorrance & Co., Inc. Philadelphia, PA. 1922.

Russell, Thomas.

From Farm to White House: The Illustrious Life and Work of Warren G. Harding. Thomas Russell. 1923.

Illustrations and Their Sources

Cover: **President Warren Harding** (Artist: Margaret Williams. 1923. Retrieved from the National Portrait Gallery, Smithsonian Institution. https://npg.si.edu/object/npg_NPG.66.21?destination=edan-search/default_search%3Fedan_local%3D1%26edan_q%3Dwarren%252Bharding)

III-1: **Harding's father, Dr. George (Tryon) Harding** (Artist: Unknown. Chapple (2). p. 32)

III-2: **Harding's mother, Phoebe Harding** (Artist: Unknown. Johnson. p. 21)

III-3: **The home of Harding's birth in Blooming Grove, OH** (Artist: Unknown. Chapple (2). p. 112)

III-4: **Ohio Central College in Iberia, OH** (Artist: Unknown. Russell, T. p. 64)

III-5: **Marion, Ohio (1887)** (Artist: Wm. H. Moore. Marion, OH. 1887. Retrieved from: https://freepages.rootsweb.com/~henryhowesbook/genealogy/marion.html)

III-6: **Harding as a teacher, circa 1882 (age ~17)** (Artist: Unknown. Chapple (1). p. 9)

III-7: **Harding, shortly after he purchased the *Star*, circa 1885 (age ~20)** (Artist: Unknown. Chapple (1). p. 20)

III-8: ***Marion Daily Star*, December 1, 1885** (*Marion Daily* Star, December 1, 1885. Retrieved from newsapaperarchive.com. https://newspaperarchive.com/marion-daily-star-nov-12-1885-p-1/)

III-9: **Harding's desk at the *Daily Star*** (Artist: Unknown. Chapple (2). p. 96)

III-10: **Harding, circa 1887 (age ~22)** (Artist: Unknown. Chapple (1). 148)

III-11: **Florence Harding** (Artist: Unknown. Retrieved from the National First Ladies' Library. http://www.firstladies.org/biographies/firstladies.aspx?biography=30)

III-12: **The longtime home of the *Daily Star* on East Center Street in Marion, OH** (Artist: Unknown. Johnson. p. 29)

III-13: **State Senator Harding, 1908** (age 33) (Artist: Unknown. 1908. Chapple (1). p. 165)

III-14: **Warren and Florence Harding, later in life, seen during the 1920 presidential campaign** (Artist: The International Film Service Co., Inc. Chicago, IL. 1920. Retrieved from the National First Ladies' Library.)

III-15: **Carrie Phillips** (Artist: Unknown. Believed to be from 1913. Retrieved from the Library of Congress. From the Phillips/Mathee collection. https://www.loc.gov/resource/mss85928.0105?sp=10&r=-0.736,-0.139,2.473,1.414,0)

III-16: **Harding as a gubernatorial candidate, 1910 (age 44)** (Artist: Unknown. circa 1910. Retrieved from the Library of Congress. https://www.loc.gov/item/mss485950101/)

III-17: **A small sampling of the correspondence over the years from Harding to Carrie Phillips** (Author: Warren Harding. Retrieved from the Library of Congress. "Warren G. Harding – Carrie Fulton Phillips Correspondence."

https://www.loc.gov/collections/warren-harding-carrie-fulton-phillips-correspondence/about-this-collection/)

III-18: **Former President Theodore Roosevelt** (Artist: Harris & Ewing. Retrieved from *The Marvelous Career of Theodore Roosevelt* by Charles Morris. W. E. Scull. 1910. Frontispiece)

III-19: **Harding had always been a hands-on newspaper owner at the *Marion Daily Star*** (Artist: Unknown. Cuneo. p. 42)

III-20: **Senator Harding, circa 1918 (age ~53)** (Artist: National Photo Company. circa 1919. Retrieved from the Library of Congress. Gift from Herbert French. https://www.loc.gov/pictures/item/2016819939/)

III-21: **Nan Britton at the time she began her affair with Harding, 1917 (age 20)** (Artist: Unknown. Britton. p. 26)

III-22: **Poster from Harding's "America First" presidential campaign, 1920** (Artist: Christy. Ritchey Litho. Corp. Amalgamated Lithographers of America. 1920. Retrieved from Cowan's Auctions. https://www.cowanauctions.com/lot/warren-g-harding-campaign-poster-by-howard-chandler-christy-previously-unrecorded-116006)

III-23: **General Leonard Wood, 1920** (Artists: William Hobbs and Henry Wood. G.P. Putnam's Sons. New York, NY. 1920. Retrieved from Wikipedia. https://en.wikipedia.org/wiki/Leonard_Wood#/media/File:Leonard_Wood,_administrator,_soldier,_and_citizen_(1920)_(14579077497).jpg)

III-24: **Illinois Governor Frank Lowden** (Artist: Unknown. Originally appeared in "Illinois in the World War: An Illustrated History of the Thirty-third Division" by Donald Biggs. Chicago, IL. 1921. Frontispiece. Retrieved from Wikipedia. https://en.wikipedia.org/wiki/Frank_Orren_Lowden#/media/File:Frank_O_Lowden_portrait.jpg)

III-25: **Hiram Johnson, 1920** (Artist: National Photo Company. December 1920. Retrieved from the Library of Congress. Gift of Herbert French. https://www.loc.gov/resource/npcc.03123/)

III-26: **1920 Republican National Convention, Chicago Coliseum, June 1920** (Artists: Moffett Studio and Kaufmann & Fabry Co. Retrieved from the Library of Congress. https://www.loc.gov/pictures/item/2007663528/)

III-27: **1920 Republican campaign banner featuring the ticket of Warren Harding and Calvin Coolidge** (Artist: Unknown. 1920. Retrieved from Anderson Americana. http://www.anderson-auction.com/harding-coolidge-poster-lot61326.aspx)

III-28: **1920 Democratic campaign banner featuring the ticket of James Cox and Franklin Roosevelt** (Artist: Unknown. 1920. Retrieved from Pixels. https://pixels.com/featured/1920-cox-roosevelt-presidential-campaign-advertisement-redemption-road.html)

III-29: **A modern look at the Harding home on Mount Vernon Avenue** (Author photo, 2022)

III-30: **Harding speaking to one of the large crowds gathered for the Front Porch Campaign of 1920** (Artist: Unknown. Retrieved from *The Washington Post*. "Biden campaigns from his basement. Harding ran for president from his porch."

By Ronald Shafer. Posted May 3, 2020. https://www.washingtonpost.com/history/2020/05/03/harding-porch-biden-basement/)

III-31: **Banner headline in the *Daily Star* announcing Harding's election as President of the United States, November 3, 1920** (*Marion Daily Star*, November 3, 1920. Retrieved from newsapaperarchive.com. https://newspaperarchive.com/marion-daily-star-nov-03-1920-p-6/)

III-32: **Harding disembarking the SS *Pastores* during his trip through the Panama Canal in December 1920** (Artist: Unknown. Chapple (1). p. 245)

III-33: **President Harding and his initial Cabinet, 1921 (Clockwise, beginning at the left): President Harding, Treasury Secretary Andrew Mellon, Attorney General Harry Daugherty, Navy Secretary Edwin Denby, Agriculture Secretary Henry Wallace, Labor Secretary James Davis, Vice President Calvin Coolidge (who sat in on Cabinet meetings), Commerce Secretary Herbert Hoover, Interior Secretary Albert Fall, Postmaster General Will Hays, War Secretary John Weeks, and Secretary of State Charles Evans Hughes)** (Artist: Harris & Ewing. 1921. Retrieved from the National Portrait Gallery, Smithsonian Institution. https://www.si.edu/object/warren-harding-and-his-cabinet:npg_S_NPG.84.301)

III-34: **Harding giving his Inaugural Address, March 4, 1921** (Artist: Unknown. Chapple (1). p. 180)

III-35: **The Harding White House** (Artist: Unknown. Johnson. p. 140)

III-36: **President Harding delivering remarks to Congress** (Artist: Unknown. Johnson. p. 149)

III-37: **President Warren Harding with Chief Justice William Taft, circa 1921** (Artist: Harris & Ewing. circa 1921. Retrieved from the Library of Congress. www.loc.gov/item/2016885827/)

III-38: **President Harding befriended New York Yankees star Babe Ruth** (Artist: Unknown. Chapple (1). p. 212)

III-39: **President Harding liked to keep score in his own hand at Major League Baseball games** (Artist: Warren Harding. Opening Day, 1923. Johnson. p. 120)

III-40: **President Harding on the golf course** (Artist: Unknown. Johnson. p. 124)

III-41: **The so-called "Little Green House" on K Street** (Artist: National Photo Company. Retrieved from Wikipedia. https://en.wikipedia.org/wiki/Little_Green_House_on_K_Street#/media/File:LittleGreenHouseKStreetLOC.jpg)

III-42: **Presidential pet, Laddie Boy** (Artist: Unknown. Johnson. p. 229)

III-43: **Florence and President Harding at the 300th anniversary of the landing at Plymouth Rock, August 1921** (Artist: Unknown. Chapple (1). p. 196)

III-44: **Harding's Secretary of Commerce, Herbert Hoover** (Artist: Unknown. Retrieved from the Commerce Research Library, U.S. Department of Commerce. https://library.doc.gov/digital-exhibits/hoover-digital-exhibit)

III-45: **President Harding addressing race relations and civil rights in Birmingham, AL, October 26, 1921** (Artist: Keystone View Company. Originally appeared in

"The Literary Digest," New York, NY. November 19, 1921. https://archive.org/details/literarydigest71newy/page/n471/mode/2up)

III-46: **President Harding presides over the dedication for the Tomb of the Unknown Soldier, Arlington National Cemetery, November 11, 1921** (Artist: Unknown. November 11, 1921. Retrieved from the Library of Congress. https://www.loc.gov/resource/cph.3b38302/)

III-47: **Harding's Secretary of State, Charles Evans Hughes** (Artist: National Photo Company. 1924. Retrieved from the Library of Congress. https://www.loc.gov/resource/cph.3c11374/)

III-48: **The opening session of the Conference on the Limitation of Armament, Memorial Continental Hall, Washington, D.C., November 12, 1921** (Artist: Underwood & Underwood. November 12, 1921. Retrieved from the Daughters of the American Revolution. https://blog.dar.org/new-era-international-policy-centennial-washington-naval-conference)

III-49: **Eugene Debs, outside the office of Attorney General Harry Daugherty, December 1921** (Artist: Unknown. Retrieved from Washington Area Spark. 1921. https://washingtonareaspark.com/2016/01/10/unbowed-unbroken-debs-comes-to-washington-1921/)

III-50: **President Harding and First Lady Florence Harding, circa 1921** (Artist: Harris & Ewing. Retrieved from the Library of Congress. www.loc.gov/item/2016885037/)

III-51: **Harding's Attorney General, Harry Daugherty** (Artist: National Photo Company. circa 1921-22. Retrieved from the Library of Congress. Gift from Herbert French. https://www.loc.gov/resource/npcc.21120/)

III-52: **First Lady Florence Harding** (Artist: Unknown. Retrieved from the National First Ladies' Library)

III-53: **Harding's friend and head of the Veterans Bureau, Charles Forbes** (Artist: Unknown. Adams. p. 234)

III-54: **Harding's friend and White House Physician, Dr. Charles Sawyer** (Artist: Harris & Ewing. 1923. Retrieved from the Library of Congress. https://www.loc.gov/pictures/item/2016892576/)

III-55: **Harding's Secretary of the Navy, Edwin Denby** (Artist: Unknown. Adams. p. 354)

III-56: **Harding's Secretary of the Interior, Albert Fall** (Artist: Unknown. Adams. p. 354)

III-57: **Oilman Harry Sinclair** (Artist: Unknown. Adams. p. 354)

III-58: **Oilman Edward Doheny** (Artist: Unknown. Retrieved from Wikipedia. https://en.wikipedia.org/wiki/Edward_L._Doheny#/media/File:Edward_L._Doheny.jpg)

III-59: **President Harding, 1922 (age 56)** (Artist: Jacques Reich. 1922. Retrieved from the National Portrait Gallery, Smithsonian Institution. https://www.si.edu/object/warren-g-harding:npg_NPG.67.71)

III-60: **Jess Smith** (Artist: National Photo Company. December 1920. Retrieved from the Library of Congress. https://www.loc.gov/pictures/item/2016829357/)

III-61: **President Harding advocates for membership in the World Court in a radio address from St. Louis, MO, June 21, 1923 (age 57)** (Artist: Unknown. Chapple (1). 356)

III-62: **President Harding raising an American flag in Matlakatla, Alaska Territory, July 1923** (Artist: unknown. Chapple (1). p. 309)

III-63: **President Harding admiring the mammoth salmon in Matlakatla, Alaska Territory, July 1923** (Artist: Unknown. Chapple (1). p. 73)

III-64: **President Harding in the engine of the Alaska Railway, July 1923** (Artist: Unknown. Johnson. p. 228)

III-65: **President Harding arriving in San Francisco, July 1923** (Artist: Unknown. Chapple (1). p. 340)

III-66: **Coverage of President Harding's death in the *Marion Daily Star*, August 3, 1923** (*Marion Daily* Star, August. 3, 1923. Retrieved from newsapapers.com. https://www.facebook.com/newspaperscom/photos/a.312842978821852/2863893090383482/?type=3)

III-67: **Harding's body being removed from the Palace Hotel in San Francisco, CA, August 3, 1923** (Artist: Unknown. August 3, 1923. Russell, T. p. 257)

III-68: **Thousands gather to mourn President Harding as the funeral train passes through Chicago, IL** (Artist: Unknown. Russell, T. p. 288)

III-69: **Harding's body lying in state in the East Room of the White House, August 8, 1923** (Artist: Unknown. Russell, T. p. 257)

III-70: **Harding's funeral procession on Pennsylvania Avenue in Washington, D.C., August 8, 1923** (Artist: Unknown. August 8, 1923. Russell, T. p. 257)

III-71: **Harding's burial at the Marion Cemetery, August 10, 1923** (Artist: Unknown. August 10, 1923. Russell, T. p. 289)

III-72: **Gaston Means** (Artist: Unknown. Adams. p. 354)

III-73: **"The Strange Death of President Harding" by Gaston Means** (Means, Gaston, as told to May Thacker. "The Strange Death of President Harding." Guild Publishing Company. New York, NY. 1930. Cover. Image retrieved from AbeBooks. https://www.abebooks.com/STRANGE-DEATH-PRESIDENT-HARDING-MEANS-GASTON/12219058989/bd)

III-74: **Roxie Stinson** (Artist: Harris & Ewing. 1924. Retrieved from the Library of Congress. https://www.loc.gov/resource/hec.44044/)

III-75: **A modern day view of the Harding Memorial in Marion, OH** (Author photo, 2022)

III-76: **"The President's Daughter" by Nan Britton** (Britton, Nan. "The President's Daughter." Elizabeth Ann Guild, Inc. New York, NY. 1927. Cover)

III-77: **Nan Britton, 1926 (age 29)** (Artist: Unknown. Britton. p. 436)

III-78: **Harding's daughter, Elizabeth Ann Willits** (Artist: Unknown. Britton. Frontispiece)

Notes

[1] Johnson. 36.
[2] Sinclair. 14.
[3] Russell, F. 46.
[4] Sinclair. 11.
[5] Chapple (1). 37.
[6] Hall. 20.
[7] Hall. 35.
[8] Hall. 24.
[9] Hall. 21.
[10] Adams. 16.
[11] Russell, F. 64.
[12] Russell, F. 72.
[13] Hall. 38.
[14] Johnson. 51.
[15] Hall. 64.
[16] Hall. 47.
[17] Hall. 70.
[18] Hall. 54.
[19] Chapple (1). 59.
[20] Adams. 25.
[21] Chapple (1). 69.
[22] Chapple (1). 70.
[23] Russell, F. 161.
[24] Chapple (1). 74.
[25] Adams. 51.
[26] Mee. 59.
[27] Adams. 58.
[28] Chapple (1). 81.
[29] Chapple (1). 60.
[30] Daugherty. 170.
[31] Daugherty. 170.
[32] Russell, F. 165.
[33] Russell, F. 179.
[34] Russell, F. 201.
[35] Russell, F. 202.
[36] Russell, F. 206.
[37] Adams. 72.
[38] Russell, F. 213.
[39] Chapple (1). 84.
[40] Harding, Warren to Carrie Phillips. December 24, 1910. Retrieved from *The New York Times Magazine*. "The Letters that Warren G. Harding's Family Didn't Want You to See" by Jordan Michael Smith. July 7, 2014. https://www.nytimes.com/2014/07/13/magazine/letters-warren-g-harding.html
[41] Harding, Warren to Carrie Phillips. January 28, 1912. Retrieved from *The New York Times Magazine*. "The Letters that Warren G. Harding's Family Didn't Want You to See" by Jordan Michael Smith. July 7, 2014. https://www.nytimes.com/2014/07/13/magazine/letters-warren-g-harding.html

[42] Harding, Warren to Carrie Phillips. September 15, 1913. Retrieved from *The New York Times Magazine*. "The Letters that Warren G. Harding's Family Didn't Want You to See" by Jordan Michael Smith. July 7, 2014. https://www.nytimes.com/2014/07/13/magazine/letters-warren-g-harding.html
[43] Russell, F. 224.
[44] Russell, F. 224.
[45] Manners, William. *TR and Will: A Friendship that Split the Republican Party*. Harcourt, Brace & World, Inc. New York, NY. 1969. p. 238.
[46] Russell, F. 230.
[47] Sinclair. 50.
[48] Harding, Warren to Carrie Phillips. November 11-15, 1913. Retrieved from *The New York Times Magazine*. "The Letters that Warren G. Harding's Family Didn't Want You to See" by Jordan Michael Smith. July 7, 2014. https://www.nytimes.com/2014/07/13/magazine/letters-warren-g-harding.html
[49] Sinclair. 56.
[50] Chapple (1). 89.
[51] Chapple (1). 92.
[52] Johnson. 33.
[53] Sinclair. 63.
[54] Russell, F. 264.
[55] Adams. 99.
[56] Harding, Warren to Carrie Phillips. March 12, 1915. Retrieved from *The New York Times Magazine*. "The Letters that Warren G. Harding's Family Didn't Want You to See" by Jordan Michael Smith. July 7, 2014. https://www.nytimes.com/2014/07/13/magazine/letters-warren-g-harding.html
[57] Harding, Warren to Carrie Phillips. March 12, 1915. Retrieved from *The New York Times Magazine*. "The Letters that Warren G. Harding's Family Didn't Want You to See" by Jordan Michael Smith. July 7, 2014. https://www.nytimes.com/2014/07/13/magazine/letters-warren-g-harding.html
[58] Harding, Warren. Keynote Address to the Republican National Convention, June 7, 1916. Retrieved from *The New York Times*. "Republicans to Discuss Harmony With Progressive Committee Today; Conventions Hold First Sessions." Originally written June 8, 1916. https://archive.nytimes.com/www.nytimes.com/library/politics/camp/160608convention-gop-ra.html
[59] Harding, Warren. Keynote Address to the Republican National Convention, June 7, 1916. Retrieved from *The New York Times*. "Republicans to Discuss Harmony With Progressive Committee Today; Conventions Hold First Sessions." Originally written June 8, 1916. https://archive.nytimes.com/www.nytimes.com/library/politics/camp/160608convention-gop-ra.html
[60] Adams. 115.
[61] Russell, F. 275.
[62] Harding, Warren to Carrie Phillips. February 16 ,1917. Retrieved from *The New York Times Magazine*. "The Letters that Warren G. Harding's Family Didn't Want You to See" by Jordan Michael Smith. July 7, 2014. https://www.nytimes.com/2014/07/13/magazine/letters-warren-g-harding.html
[63] Harding, Warren to Carrie Phillips. February 16 ,1917. Retrieved from *The New York Times Magazine*. "The Letters that Warren G. Harding's Family Didn't Want You to See" by Jordan

Michael Smith. July 7, 2014. https://www.nytimes.com/2014/07/13/magazine/letters-warren-g-harding.html
[64] Sinclair. 87.
[65] Russell, F. 295.
[66] Russell, F. 268.
[67] Russell, F. 268.
[68] Adams. 93.
[69] Britton. 5.
[70] Britton. 25.
[71] Britton. 27.
[72] Britton. 32.
[73] Britton. 43.
[74] Britton. 63.
[75] Britton. 62.
[76] Britton. 49.
[77] Britton. 77.
[78] Britton. 100.
[79] Harding, Warren to Carrie Phillips. February 17, 1918. Retrieved from *The New York Times Magazine*. "The Letters that Warren G. Harding's Family Didn't Want You to See" by Jordan Michael Smith. July 7, 2014. https://www.nytimes.com/2014/07/13/magazine/letters-warren-g-harding.html
[80] Harding, Warren to Carrie Phillips. August 20, 1918. Retrieved from *The New York Times Magazine*. "The Letters that Warren G. Harding's Family Didn't Want You to See" by Jordan Michael Smith. July 7, 2014. https://www.nytimes.com/2014/07/13/magazine/letters-warren-g-harding.html
[81] Lodge. 82.
[82] Adams. 94.
[83] Sinclair. 95.
[84] Sinclair. 100.
[85] Sinclair. 99.
[86] Johnson. 74.
[87] Johnson. 151.
[88] Adams. 84.
[89] Adams, 192.
[90] Daugherty. 15.
[91] Mee. 79.
[92] Russell, F. 313.
[93] Harding, Warren to Carrie Phillips. February 2, 1920. Retrieved from *The New York Times Magazine*. "The Letters that Warren G. Harding's Family Didn't Want You to See" by Jordan Michael Smith. July 7, 2014. https://www.nytimes.com/2014/07/13/magazine/letters-warren-g-harding.html
[94] Murray. 26.
[95] Sinclair. 121.
[96] Sinclair. 110.
[97] Johnson. 144.
[98] Murray. 70.
[99] Murray. 70.
[100] Adams. 130.

---

[101] Sinclair. 132.
[102] Daugherty. 31.
[103] Murray. 30.
[104] Russell, F. 347.
[105] Adams. 131.
[106] Adams. 128.
[107] Adams. 129.
[108] Russell, F. 366.
[109] Sinclair. 140.
[110] Chapple (1). 109.
[111] Adams. 151.
[112] Russell, F. 385.
[113] Mee. 92.
[114] Russell, F. 386.
[115] Daugherty. 52.
[116] Daugherty. 54.
[117] Adams. 163.
[118] Mee. 92.
[119] Sinclair. 156.
[120] Sinclair. 136.
[121] Sinclair. 150.
[122] Chapple (1). 112.
[123] Chapple (1). 126.
[124] Chapple (1). 120.
[125] Russell, F. 407.
[126] Daugherty. 59.
[127] Murray. 49.
[128] Hall. 109.
[129] Chapple (1). 147.
[130] Russell, F. 424.
[131] Sinclair. 182.
[132] Burton, David. *William Howard Taft: In the Public Service*. Robert E. Krieger Publishing Company. Malabar, FL. 1986. p. 122.
[133] Johnson. 95.
[134] Sinclair. 185.
[135] Chapple (1). 133.
[136] Adams. 196.
[137] Russell, F. 427.
[138] Chapple (1). 163.
[139] Chapple (1). 293.
[140] Chapple (1). 296.
[141] Chapple (1). 297.
[142] Chapple (1). 294.
[143] Daugherty. 82.
[144] Chapple (1). 169.
[145] Russell, F. 438.
[146] Murray. 113.

[147] Russell, F. 456.
[148] Sinclair. 206.
[149] Murray. 185.
[150] Murray. 175.
[151] Sinclair. 203.
[152] Starling, Edmund and Thomas Sugrue. *Starling of the White House*. Peoples Book Club. Simon & Schuster. Chicago, IL. 1946. p. 169.
[153] Starling, Edmund and Thomas Sugrue. *Starling of the White House*. Peoples Book Club. Simon & Schuster. Chicago, IL. 1946. p. 168.
[154] Sinclair. 262.
[155] Murray. 403.
[156] Adams. 271.
[157] Britton. 172.
[158] Starling, Edmund and Thomas Sugrue. *Starling of the White House*. Peoples Book Club. Simon & Schuster. Chicago, IL. 1946. p. 171.
[159] Murray. 489.
[160] Chapple (1). 178.
[161] Murray. 232.
[162] Murray. 148.
[163] Murray. 398.
[164] Sinclair. 231.
[165] Sinclair. 232.
[166] Russell, F. 471.
[167] Murray. 400.
[168] Russell, F. 472.
[169] Sinclair. 235.
[170] Murray. 149.
[171] Johnson. 162.
[172] Chapple (1). 194.
[173] Adams. 249.
[174] Murray. 152.
[175] Chapple (1). 196.
[176] Chapple (1). 197.
[177] Murray. 157.
[178] Russell, F. 485.
[179] Murray. 157.
[180] Russell, F. 536.
[181] Adams. 299
[182] Russell, F. 539.
[183] Russell, F. 470.
[184] Sinclair. 211.
[185] Berg, A. Scott. *Wilson*. G.P. Putnam's Sons. New York, NY. 2013. p. 686.
[186] Daugherty. 118.
[187] Hall. 115.
[188] Murray. 274.
[189] Murray. 277.
[190] Murray. 290.
[191] Sinclair. 212.

[192] Dmitri, Carolyn, Anne Effland, and Neilson Conklin. *The 20th Century Transformation of U.S. Agriculture and Farm Policy*. United States Department of Agriculture. June 2005.
[193] Sinclair. 250.
[194] Starling, Edmund and Thomas Sugrue. *Starling of the White House*. Peoples Book Club. Simon & Schuster. Chicago, IL. 1946. p. 185.
[195] Sinclair. 256.
[196] Sinclair. 258.
[197] Daugherty. 145.
[198] Murray. 255.
[199] Hoover, Herbert. *The Memoirs of Herbert Hoover (Volume II): The Cabinet and the Presidency (1920-1933).* The Macmillan Company. New York, NY. 1952. p.47.
[200] Murray. 236.
[201] Russell, F. 549.
[202] Murray. 320.
[203] Murray. 316.
[204] Adams. 297.
[205] Daugherty. 185.
[206] Murray. 436.
[207] Daugherty. 195.
[208] Sinclair. 266.
[209] Murray. 347.
[210] Murray. 367.
[211] Russell, F. 561.
[212] Murray. 417.
[213] Adams. 303.
[214] Russell, F. 554.
[215] Russell, F. 541.
[216] Starling, Edmund and Thomas Sugrue. *Starling of the White House*. Peoples Book Club. Simon & Schuster. Chicago, IL. 1946. p. 195.
[217] Daugherty. 248.
[218] Daugherty. 244.
[219] Hoover, Herbert. *The Memoirs of Herbert Hoover (Volume II): The Cabinet and the Presidency (1920-1933).* The Macmillan Company. New York, NY. 1952. p. 49.
[220] Hoover, Herbert. *The Memoirs of Herbert Hoover (Volume II): The Cabinet and the Presidency (1920-1933).* The Macmillan Company. New York, NY. 1952. p. 49.
[221] Mee. 217.
[222] Russell, F. 580.
[223] Adams. 369.
[224] Hoover, Herbert. *The Memoirs of Herbert Hoover (Volume II): The Cabinet and the Presidency (1920-1933).* The Macmillan Company. New York, NY. 1952. p. 49.
[225] Chapple (1).231.
[226] Chapple (1). 238.
[227] Chapple (1). 241.
[228] Russell, F. 588.
[229] Chapple (1). 283.
[230] Hoover, Herbert. *The Memoirs of Herbert Hoover (Volume II): The Cabinet and the Presidency (1920-1933).* The Macmillan Company. New York, NY. 1952. p. 50.

[231] Daugherty. 272.
[232] Johnson. 236.
[233] Hall. 121.
[234] Daugherty. 298.
[235] Murray. 533.
[236] Adams. 353.
[237] Murray. 467.
[238] Adams. 397.
[239] Russell, F. 612.
[240] Adams. 402.
[241] Daugherty. 238.
[242] Starling. 182.
[243] Russell, F. 620.
[244] Daugherty. 253.
[245] Russell, F. 640.
[246] Hoover, Herbert. *The Memoirs of Herbert Hoover (Volume II): The Cabinet and the Presidency (1920-1933).* The Macmillan Company. New York, NY. 1952. p. 53.
[247] Britton. 286.
[248] Britton. 342.
[249] Britton. 400.
[250] Britton. 408.
[251] Britton. 1.
[252] Baker, Peter. *DNA is Said to Solve a Mystery of Warren Harding's Love Life. The New York Times*. August 12, 1915. https://www.nytimes.com/2015/08/13/us/dna-is-said-to-solve-a-mystery-of-warren-hardings-love-life.html
[253] Baker, Peter. *DNA is Said to Solve a Mystery of Warren Harding's Love Life. The New York Times*. August 12, 1915. https://www.nytimes.com/2015/08/13/us/dna-is-said-to-solve-a-mystery-of-warren-hardings-love-life.html
[254] Baker, Peter. *DNA is Said to Solve a Mystery of Warren Harding's Love Life. The New York Times*. August 12, 1915. https://www.nytimes.com/2015/08/13/us/dna-is-said-to-solve-a-mystery-of-warren-hardings-love-life.html
[255] Daugherty. 263.
[256] Daugherty. 263.
[257] Daugherty. 265.
[258] Daugherty. 263.

Index

PRESIDENTIAL CHRONICLES
VOLUME VI: PROGRESSIVISM AND PROSPERITY
IV: THE LIFE OF CALVIN COOLIDGE
DAVID FISHER

IV: The Life of Calvin Coolidge

Preface

Calvin Coolidge was very much a product of his environment. The boy reared on the farm at the Notch in Plymouth, Vermont, was weaned on the Puritan ethic of selfless hard work. The man known as "Silent Cal" let his work speak for him, keeping conversation at a minimum. He was an unremarkable youth who stayed true to the righteous elements of his upbringing and education to appeal to his fellow citizens in a way that ultimately elevated him from the bottom of the political ladder to its very pinnacle. Coolidge was hardly a natural politician, but he offered a no-nonsense, trustworthy persona during an era when the American electorate was looking for someone on whom it could rely.

In some ways, Coolidge was often in the right place at the right time – circumstances which some have simply called the "Coolidge Luck." But Calvin Coolidge made his own luck by proactively seeking one political opportunity after another, learning intently at each step of the way, and creating his own opportunities from these pursuits. And at crucial moments, he acted, whether that meant locking up the position of President of the State Senate in Massachusetts before anyone else could jump into the race in 1913 or taking charge of the Boston Police Strike as the state's Governor in 1919. In the latter case, Coolidge captured the nation's attention when he stood for principle, stood for community, and stood for law and order when he boldly declared, "There is no right to strike against the public safety by anybody, anywhere, any time."[1] That statement propelled Coolidge to the Republican nomination for Vice President of the United States and eventually the presidency itself.

In his five and a half years in the Oval Office, Coolidge was laser focused on putting his own stamp on the agenda he inherited from Warren Harding, which was built to improve the nation's post-war economy. By every conceivable measure, he was successful. Coolidge's combination of tax cuts, protective tariffs, and dramatic curtailment of government expenditures, paired with a leap in technological innovation, raised the American economy to heights it had never seen before. The Roaring Twenties brought prosperity and joy throughout the land, overseen by the quiet, steadfast leadership of the nation's 30th President. Of course, the rise was unsustainable and came crashing down just a few months after Coolidge left the White House in the form of the worst economic depression the nation had ever seen. How much credit and blame Coolidge gets for these phenomena can still be debated, as informed by the story of his remarkable rise to the highest office his nation has to bestow.

1. From Plymouth to Amherst

Calvin Coolidge's Puritan roots date back to the beginning of European immigration to North America. His early relatives sailed from Cottenham, England, in 1630, around the same time John Winthrop made the trek to the spot in North America that eventually became known as the Massachusetts Bay Colony. Many Coolidges stayed in the Boston area, settling just west in the community of Watertown. Coolidge's Great-Great Grandfather, Captain John Coolidge, joined in the fight at Lexington that sparked a revolution. After independence, the Coolidges remained in New England, but spread out a bit, including an offshoot of the clan settling in the tiny hamlet of Saltash in Vermont – later renamed Plymouth after the original settlement in Massachusetts.

While many New England communities grew into villages, towns, and cities, Plymouth remained stuck in time as an isolated assemblage of local farmers trying to persevere on the rocky soil of the Green Mountain State, which had many of the same characteristics as its neighbor, the Granite State of New Hampshire. Vermont was dominated by hills such that many farms would be nestled into their slopes, anything to find ground on which to try to grow crops. While the railroad was transforming communities throughout the nation, enabling the efficient transportation of people and goods, Plymouth was mostly bypassed by this form of modernization. The nearest depot was Ludlow, which was a dozen miles away. The people of Plymouth didn't know what they were missing, and didn't seem to care, perfectly content to raise their families generation after generation as prideful, thrifty, self-sustaining, and honest descendants carrying on the Puritan tradition.

IV-1: Coolidge's Father, John Coolidge

John Coolidge represented the ninth generation of his family lineage in North America, operating the village store next to his own farm in Plymouth Notch, an unincorporated section of Plymouth in Windsor County. The primitive village had a church, a small schoolhouse, a store, a cemetery, and a handful of outbuildings surrounded by a number of farmhouses, which were the primary source of subsistence. John was a jack-of-all-trades, a master with his hands, able to perform just about any task the rough farm life thrust in his direction. He was also a prominent member of this small community, serving in a variety of roles that ranged from constable, deputy sheriff, superintendent of schools, notary public, postmaster, and eventually state legislator. He was a gruff, no-nonsense man who took great pride in doing things the right way, which meant acting mostly independently and without airs or any sense of fanfare.

John Coolidge married Victoria Moor on May 6, 1868. Both were in their early twenties. They brought two children into the world. The first was a boy who arrived on the nation's birthday, July 4, 1872, in the backroom of a 1½ story cottage that was attached to the family's store. Amid the maple trees, lilac bushes, and picket fence surrounding their home, the tenth generation of Coolidges arrived with the birth of John Calvin Coolidge, who was known as Calvin from the earliest days of his life. It was a foundation that Coolidge never forgot. He later noted:

IV-2: Coolidge's Mother, Victoria Coolidge

> Vermont is my birthright. Here, one gets close to nature, in the mountains, in the brooks, the waters of which hurry to the sea; in the lakes, shining like silver in their green setting; fields tilled, not by machinery but by the brain and hand of man. My folks are happy and contented. They belong to themselves, live within their income, and fear no man.[2]

Typical of Vermont families of this era, everyone contributed to the family's well-being, although there was a little twist for the Coolidges. Just a couple of months after Coolidge's birth, his father was elected to the state legislature. When he was away on state business, Victoria was in charge of both the farm and the store, as well as raising their young family, which added a girl by the name of Abigail (Abbie) in 1875.

IV-3: The Coolidge's store and attached home where Coolidge was born, Plymouth Notch, VT,

Victoria was on point to raise the children, including using the Bible to teach them to read, and while Coolidge adored his mother, it was his father that the young boy always wanted to impress.

The family store was a successful enterprise, netting a profit of about $100 a month. This enabled the Coolidges to expand their holdings, moving across the road to a new setting that came with several barns and a blacksmith shop. Around the age of three, young Calvin was taken to visit his father at the state capital of Montpelier and given a chance to sit for a few moments in the Governor's chair. By his own recollection, he was more impressed by the stuffed catamount in the capital museum. Times were not easy, especially after Victoria became ill, struggling as an invalid, likely suffering from tuberculosis. She did the best she could around the house, as her sister described her as "quiet, refined, orderly, conscientious, even in her disposition, and a model housekeeper."[3] She instilled in her children an upbringing premised on religious faith that was ever-present in the long days on the farm. Coolidge took his chores seriously, always seeking to demonstrate his own prowess for one new skill after another such that his father might acknowledge his contributions. "My father had qualities that were greater than any I possess," Coolidge later recalled. "He was a man of untiring industry and great tenacity of purpose. … It always seemed possible for him to form an unerring judgment of men and things. I cannot recall that I ever knew of his doing a wrong thing. He would be classed as decidedly a man of character."[4] These were all qualities Coolidge spent a lifetime trying to emulate.

While Coolidge always looked back fondly on these days of his youth, he also acknowledged the difficulty of his early surroundings. "They were English Puritan stock, and their choice of a habitation stamps them with a courageous pioneering spirit," he wrote in his post-presidential *Autobiography*. "It was a hard but wholesome life, under which the people suffered many privations and enjoyed many advantages, without any clear realization of the existence of either one of them."[5] As he grew older, Coolidge's contributions to the family farm increased as well. Over time, he learned how to mend fences, participate in the spring planting, feed the animals, milk the cows, use reapers in the hay fields, sheer the sheep, pick the apples, and extract sap from the numerous maple trees. Maple sugar season was one of Coolidge's favorites, as each April the family focused on generating anywhere from 800 to 2000 pounds of syrup for sale. According to his father, young Calvin could get "more sap out of a maple tree than the other boys around here."[6] He and Abbie attended Sunday School each week, and there were annual trips to the circus and county fair, but mostly life for young Calvin Coolidge was spent helping the family make ends meet on the farm.

IV-4: Coolidge's sister, Abigail ("Abbie") Coolidge

There was also time for education. Some of this came within the home but also in the local schoolhouse. At just five years old, Coolidge was the youngest of the 23 pupils who attended the local school beginning in 1877. One of his teachers was C. Ellen Dunbar. "I remember Calvin at school," she later wrote. "He studied. It was the job. It was to be done, so do it. Cal wasn't brilliant. If I were asked to describe him at that time I would say 'Good little boy, good in school.'" As for Coolidge's character, Mrs. Dunbar noted, "He wouldn't lie to save himself from the gallows."[7] The other characteristic commonly recalled about Coolidge was his taciturnity, even at a very young age. Toward the end of his career, the man who became known as "Silent Cal" linked this trait back to his early youth.

IV-5: Coolidge, 1879 (age 7)

> Do you know, I've never really grown up? It's a hard thing for me to play this game. In politics, one must meet people, and that's not easy for me. … It's been hard for me all my life. When I was a little fellow, as long ago as I can remember, I would go into a panic if I heard strange voices in the kitchen. I felt I just couldn't meet the people and shake hands with them. Most of the visitors would sit with Father and Mother in the kitchen, and the hardest thing in the world was to have to go through the kitchen door and give them a greeting. I was almost ten before I realized I couldn't go on that way. And by fighting hard I used to manage to get through that door. I'm all right with old friends, but every time I meet a stranger, I've got to go through the old kitchen door, back home, and it's not easy.[8]

It is remarkable that such a description would come from a career politician who eventually made it all the way to the White House.

The most difficult moment in Calvin Coolidge's youth came when his mother's health finally gave way. Victoria Coolidge died on her 39th birthday in 1885 when Coolidge was only 12 years old. "In an hour she was gone," Coolidge later recalled. "We laid her away in the blustering snows of March. The greatest grief that can come to a boy came to me. Life was never to seem the same again."[9] Coolidge's grandmother, Sarah

IV-6: Coolidge's mother, Victoria Coolidge

(sometimes known as Aunt Mede), stepped in to help raise the children after Victoria's passing. Coolidge would often visit his mother's grave in the nearby cemetery. He would also keep his mother near him, both in his heart and his eyes, by placing her picture on his desk at each stop throughout his political rise.

The phrase "all politics is local" could easily have been written with Plymouth Notch in mind. Cut off from the day-to-day happenings in the rest of the world, the 250 or so residents of the Notch brought democracy to life through the form of the local town meeting. The red-haired Coolidge stood out among the attendees, selling apples and popcorn at the local gathering, as his father and grandfather had done before him. Decisions about local policies (including taxation) were made by the popular vote of the citizenry, making a strong impression on the young man. "By reason of what I saw and heard in my early life," Coolidge later wrote, "I came to have a good working knowledge of the practical side of government. I understood that it consisted of restraints which the people had imposed upon themselves in order to promote the common welfare."[10] Some of these impressions were further cemented when Coolidge had a first-hand opportunity to hear from a sitting President. Benjamin Harrison was his nation's chief executive when he came to Vermont in 1891 to dedicate a memorial to the men who fought and died in the Civil War. Coolidge was among the 15,000 citizens on hand to hear the President declare:

> The courage of those who fought at Bennington was born of high trust in God. … That devotion to local self-government which originated and for so long maintained the town meeting, establishing and perpetuating a true democracy, an equal, full participation and responsibility in all public affairs on the part of every citizen, was the cause of the development

> of the love of social order and respect for laws which has characterized your communities, has made them safe and commemorable abodes for young people.[11]

One of those young people in attendance, Calvin Coolidge, would certainly agree.

Coolidge ventured out on his own for the first time about a year after his mother's death. Both of his parents had taken classes years before at the Black River Academy in nearby Ludlow, and now it was Calvin's turn. The institution with a Baptist foundation was celebrating its 50th anniversary when Coolidge enrolled in 1886. He was one of approximately 125 students who came to the three-story red brick building to gain an education. The school had no dormitories, so Coolidge boarded with local families throughout his tenure. It was a rough transition. Coolidge was often ill, both physically and homesick, and struggled to fit in – yet he persevered. "Going away to school was my first great adventure in life," he later wrote. "I shall never forget the impression it made on me. It was so deep and remains so vivid that whenever I have started out on a new enterprise a like feeling always returns to me."[12] Some of those feelings likely made him queasy, given his challenge of being a bit of a quiet outcast. He was also a prankster – a tease, whose humor sometimes only appealed to himself. Whether at home or at school, Coolidge was often on his own. "Cal always was a student," his childhood friend Herbert Moore later recalled. "Unlike most of us who had to work hard on the farm and could not get away for any long periods, he always went to school. He didn't play ball or skate, nor did he hunt,

IV-7: Coolidge as a student at the Black River Academy, circa 1890 (age ~18)

swim, fish, or go in for any sports, except that he walked a great deal. When he was in the academy, he went to the public library every day, and I think he read every book in it."[13] Home was also never too far away. Coolidge's father made the 12-mile journey each way nearly every weekend to bring his son home to the family and the farm, and, like most of his fellow students, he spent the summer months doing all manner of farm work. But his education was always front and center.

Coolidge's father did not discriminate against his daughter when it came to getting an education, enrolling Abbie at Black River a year and a half after Calvin. But when the teenagers returned home for a break, Abbie became sick. The pains in her stomach worsened quickly, and the doctors had no cure. She died suddenly in March 1890, just shy of her 15th birthday. The cause of death was subsequently identified as appendicitis. It was another tough loss for young Calvin. "I went home when her condition became critical," he later wrote, "and staid beside her until she passed to join our mother. The memory of the charm of her presence and her dignified devotion to the right will always abide with me."[14] The following month, after returning to Black River, Coolidge wrote his father in his typically understated way, "It is lonesome here without Abbie."[15]

A little more than a year later, Coolidge graduated from the Black River Academy along with four other boys and four girls. He was selected to make an address during the commencement ceremonies, which he titled "Oratory in History" – an intriguing topic for someone notorious for his reticence for speaking in public. The *Vermont Tribune* had a reporter at the ceremonies who called Coolidge's speech "masterly in its conception and arrangement."[16] Graduating from Black River was an inflection point for Coolidge as he determined his next steps in life. When he proposed going on to college, his father wasn't quite sure it was the right move. Colonel Coolidge, as his father was commonly known after working on the staff of Governor William Stickney, later shared with George Olds that "he was not sure his son was the right type, and that he finally decided he had better apprentice him to a pharmacist in a neighboring drugstore. At that time all drugstores had liquor in stock, and after the Colonel told Calvin of his decision, his son thought for a minute or two, and then said: 'Father! Sell rum?' That ended it."[17] Coolidge received encouragement from George Sherman, the man who had recently become the principal at Black River Academy. Sherman was pushing Coolidge to attend his alma mater at Amherst, about a hundred miles due south in the state of Massachusetts. But when Coolidge attempted the Amherst entrance exams, he was under the weather and ultimately fell short. After discussions with his father and principal Sherman, Coolidge spent the next several months on a crash course at St. Johnsbury Academy, focusing primarily on Latin, Greek, algebra, and elocution. When the term came to an end, a certificate came with it, providing automatic entry into Amherst without further examinations. In September 1891, Calvin Coolidge was off to college.

Once again, the shy and quiet Coolidge found himself like a fish out of water. Life on the Amherst Campus was centered on the nine fraternities to which nearly everyone sought entry. "The societies are a great factor of Amherst and of course I want to join one if I can," Coolidge wrote his father. "It means something to get into a good society at Amherst; they don't take in everybody."[18] They actually took in approximately 80% of the student body, but not Calvin Coolidge, who was left on the outside looking in. He was off to a rough start. "I am in a pleasant place and like very much," Coolidge wrote home in his freshman year, "but suppose I shall like better as [I] become better acquainted, I don't seem to get acquainted very fast however."[19] In fact, Coolidge struggled to make any impression at all at the time. Once of his classmates noted, "A drabber, more colorless boy I never knew than

IV-8: View from the Library at Amherst College, 1891

Calvin Coolidge when he came to Amherst. He was a perfect enigma to us all. He attended class regularly, but did not show any very great interest."[20] Coolidge had no hobbies, did not play sports, and mostly stuck to himself. When he wasn't in class, he was typically in the library or by himself at his boarding house on Pleasant Street. His initial grades were below par.

Around this time, Coolidge acquired a new pen pal. Six years after his mother died, Coolidge's father remarried. Her name was Carrie Brown, a local schoolteacher who was 13 years younger than Coolidge's father. She immediately established a loving rapport with her stepson, writing to him regularly with phrases of affection and support. "After being without a mother nearly seven years I was greatly pleased to find in her all the motherly devotion that she could have given me if I had been her own son," Coolidge wrote in his post-presidential years. "Loving books and music she was not only a mother to me but a teacher. For thirty years she watched over me and loved me, welcoming me when I went home, writing me often when I was away, and encouraging me in all my efforts."[21] Coolidge wrote many letters home, often including a request for cash. His father not only paid for Coolidge's education but also parceled out additional funds on an as-needed basis. Coolidge thought nothing of highlighting those moments of need. One such request came at the beginning of his junior year at Amherst.

> In view of the fact that yesterday I put a debate said to be the best heard on the floor of the chapel this term, in view of the fact that my name was read as one of the first ten in French, in view of the fact that I passed in Natural philosophy with a fair mark whereas many failed, and lastly in view of the fact that the purchase clause of Sherman Bill has been repealed thus relieved the cause of financial panic, can you send me $25 the forepart of next week?[22]

Colonel Coolidge knew his son to be as frugal as he, so when he asked for money, he knew the need was legitimate and invariably sent the cash.

The contemporary reflections of Coolidge from his Amherst days were unremarkable. "Coolidge was a very retiring, silent individual, with few friends, and not at all an outstanding figure, even in his class," recalled Frederick Fales, who was one year behind Coolidge at Amherst. Another friend offered, "He remained through his college course the same quiet, faithful, unpretentious figure that he was as President."[23] A Mr. Hardy offered the following characterization:

> He was just the same kind of a boy that I have known him as a man, quiet, faithful, studious, dependable, doing the day's work and doing it well, staying on the job until it was done. Probably no one thought that he would be President of the United States, but we who knew him best knew that he was the stuff out of which great men are made.[24]

Some of those more positive perspectives started to reveal themselves in Coolidge's junior year. He began speaking out a bit more, performing well in formal debates. Classmate Charles Andrews noted that "when we got into the debating, he began to emerge and become one of the best debaters in his class, distinguished for the directness and brevity of his style, the soundness of his logic, the aptness of his humor. By the time we got to be juniors we all knew that Calvin was a real fellow and that the quality of his college course was excellent."[25] Coolidge later recalled sensing his own maturity around this time. "If we keep our faith in ourselves," he later wrote, "and what is even more important, keep our faith in regular and persistent application to hard work, we need not worry about the outcome."[26] Some of this confidence emanated from the two classes that left the greatest impression on him from his entire Amherst experience.

IV-9: Coolidge as a student at Amherst, circa 1894 (age ~22)

Professor Anson Morse inspired Coolidge with his course on history and politics. Morse brought his subject to life, beginning with a journey through European history before focusing attention on the political history of the United States. "The whole course was a thesis on good citizenship and good government," Coolidge later recalled. "Those who took it came to a clearer comprehension not only of their rights and liberties but of their duties and responsibilities."[27] But it was Charles Garman's course that embodied philosophy, psychology, politics, and ethics that left the greatest impression on Coolidge and most of his fellow students. Garman had graduated from Amherst in 1872, returning to teach eight years later. He engaged more in seminars than lectures, challenging his students to question everything. He spurred intellectual curiosity, using logic and reason to find the truth, typically in the context of religious teachings. Garman encouraged individual discovery but clearly guided his subjects to similar conclusions that celebrated the necessity and dignity of work, the importance of the individual over groups, and the power of the independent thinker. Mostly, he taught service to humanity as the ultimate righteous cause, whether in religious or sectarian settings. In his *Autobiography*, Coolidge described Garman's teachings and the impact they had on the students at Amherst:

IV-10: Professor Charles Garman

> Above all we were taught to follow the truth whithersoever it might lead. We were warned that this would oftentimes be very difficult and result in much opposition, for there would be many who were not going that way, but if we pressed on steadfastly it was sure to yield the peaceable fruits of the mind. It does. Our investigation revealed that man is endowed with reason, that the human mind has the power to weigh evidence, to distinguish between right and wrong and to know the truth. I should call this the central theme of his philosophy. …[28]
>
> In ethics he taught us that there is a standard of righteousness, that might does not make right, that the end does not justify the means and that expediency as a working principle is bound to fail. The only hope of perfecting human

> relationship is in accordance with the law of service under which men are not so solicitous about what they shall get as they are about what they shall give.[29]

As for the collective esteem for which he and his classmates held for Professor Garman, Coolidge wrote simply, "We looked upon Garman as a man who walked with God."[30] Throughout his life, Coolidge typically kept two books on the night table next to his bed. The first was the Bible, while the second was *The Life and Letters of Charles E. Garman.*[1]

Garman's class was spread over the last year and a half Coolidge spent at Amherst. While he remained generally shy and aloof, Coolidge did begin to make a name for himself on campus, particularly in his senior year. His confidence grew, especially in the area of speech and debate. "There is nothing in the world gives me so much pleasure as to feel I have made a good speech and nothing gives me more pain than to feel I have made a poor one," he wrote at the time. "I think I must stand very well in college now."[31] He was indeed recognized for coming out of his shell, earning a share of the J. Wesley Ledd prize for public debate. Coolidge won another award during his senior year as well. He entered a national essay contest sponsored by the Sons of the American Revolution. The topic was "The Principles Fought For in the American Revolution." "The real principle was not one of the right of the state or the duty of citizens,"

---

[1] Coolidge wrote another lengthy piece in which he sought to explain some of Garman's teachings. Coolidge referenced one of Garman's lectures in which he stated: "Critics have noticed three stages in the development of human civilization. First: the let-alone policy; every man to look out for number one. This is the age of selfishness. Second: the opposite pole of thinking; every man to do somebody else's work for him. This is the dry rot of sentimentality that feeds tramps and elect laws that excite the indignation of Herbert Spencer. But the third stage is represented by our formula: every man must render and receive the best possible service, except in the case of inequality, and there the strong must help the weak to help themselves; only on this condition is help given. This is the true interpretation of the life of Christ. On the first basis He would have remained in heaven and let the earth take care of itself. On the second basis He would have come to earth with His hands full of gold and silver treasures satisfying every want that unfortunate humanity could have devised. But on the third basis He comes to earth in the form of a servant who is at the same time a master commanding His disciples to take up their cross and follow Him; it is sovereignty through service as opposed to slavery through service. He refuses to make the world wealthy, but He offers to help them make themselves wealthy with the true riches which shall be a hundred-fold more, even in this life, than that which was offered them by any former system." (Sobel. p. 37)

Coolidge wrote, "it was a question of government, a question of form and method. … It was not so much a revolution, a propagation of new ideas, as the maintenance of the old forms of representative government, of chartered rights and constitutional liberty."[32] He concluded: "If the leading principle was the preservation of the English constitutional government from the encroachments of King and Parliament, there is another principle, as far-reaching as the development of the state in government. Sovereignty is always finally vested in the people."[33] Coolidge not only won top honors amongst his fellow Amherst students, but he also won the national gold medal and $150 in prize money that came with the award. Typical for Coolidge, he failed to inform anyone about his accomplishment, at one point telling a colleague after the result was featured in the local newspaper that he "didn't know you would be interested."[34] Calvin Coolidge could never be charged with tooting his own horn.

IV-11: Coolidge as a student at Amherst, 1895 (age 22)

Coolidge could rejoice in another element of his senior year – he was finally admitted into an Amherst fraternity. It was actually a new house for the Amherst campus, and Coolidge's friend John Deering convinced him to try to gain acceptance with their fellow students who were aligning themselves with Phi Gamma Delta. Little changed for Coolidge upon joining the fraternity. He continued to live elsewhere and was not one to participate in the consumption of alcohol or other acts of late-night revelry. Nevertheless, it was a new source of friendship and belonging which stayed with Coolidge long after he left the Amherst campus. The quietest member of Phi Gamma Delta later volunteered to periodically provide legal counsel to the fraternity, for which he never charged a cent in fees.

Coolidge graduated from Amherst in 1895, just shy of his 23rd birthday. He finished with an average score of 78.71 for his four years in the classroom, good enough to earn *cum laude* honors but short of Phi Betta Kappa. Future Attorney General and Supreme Court Justice Harlan

Stone, who was a year behind Coolidge at Amherst, offered the following reflection: "I doubt if many of his fellow students were intimate with him. His extreme reticence made that difficult. To those who knew him casually he seemed odd or queer, but it only required a slight acquaintance to appreciate his quiet dignity and the self-respect which commanded the respect of others."[35] The standout pupil in Coolidge's class was Dwight Morrow, who was selected by his peers as the Most Likely to Succeed. Coolidge did get one vote in that tally, and it came from Dwight Morrow himself.

Coolidge had impressed enough of his fellow students with his oratory and debate skills to be selected to give the Grove Oration on Class Day shortly before commencement. The Grove Oration was set aside for witty putdowns and inside jokes to make light of certain experiences by both students and faculty. It was an odd assignment for Coolidge, who admitted it wasn't really his style. "While my effort was not without some success," he later wrote, "I very soon learned that making fun of people in a public way was not a good method to secure friends, or likely to lead to much advancement, and I have scrupulously avoided it."[36] It was another practical life lesson that Coolidge would embrace throughout his political career. He did end his oration on a strong, pro-Amherst note. "Wherever we go, whatever we are, scientific or classical, conditioned or unconditioned, degreed or disagreed, we are going to be Amherst men," Coolidge proclaimed. "And whoever sees a purple and white button marked with '95 shall see the emblem of a class spirit that will say, 'Old Amherst, doubtless always right, but right or wrong, Old Amherst!'"[37] Coolidge's ties to his alma mater would run deep, as he remained connected to the school and many of its vast network of successful graduates throughout the rest of his life.

2. Law and Politics

Calvin Coolidge found himself at a crossroads as he left the friendly confines of Amherst to find his way in the professional world. He had options, including heading back home to Plymouth and the small-town life he had known since birth. He sought the advice of his father as he leaned toward a career in the law, perhaps a profession in which he could make a difference in his community. "I should like to live where I can be of some use to the world and not simply where I should get a few dollars together," he noted in a letter to his father.[38] After some back and forth, Coolidge made up his mind to pursue the law, but he still had a significant decision to make. By the turn of the century, more and more law pupils were getting their education from law schools at some of the country's top universities, as opposed to "reading the law" with an established attorney, which had been the norm for the first century of the American republic. Money was a factor for the Coolidges who collectively decided a law school education was simply beyond their means. Coolidge initially sought an apprenticeship in the law practice of former Vermont Governor William Dillingham – a former colleague of his father's – but when Dillingham was slow to respond, Coolidge pursued an option in Northampton, Massachusetts, a city just across the Connecticut River from Amherst. Two of the leading attorneys in the city were partners John Hammond and Henry Field, both of whom had strong ties to Amherst. In fact, Hammond had been on-hand for Coolidge's Grove Oration at the recent graduation and liked what he heard. When offered the position, Coolidge accepted on the spot.

IV-12: Coolidge after graduating from Amherst, 1895 (age 23)

Northampton was a city of some 18,000 residents as the 19th Century was coming to an end. The community was greatly influenced by the number of colleges and universities in the surrounding area. In addition to Amherst, Smith College for Women had opened in Northampton two decades before. Also nearby were Mount Holyoke College, the Massachusetts Agricultural College, and the Clarke Institute for the Deaf. The offices of Hammond and Field were located in the bank building on the corner of Main and King Streets, which is where Coolidge spent much of his time when he wasn't at the courthouse or studying in the Forbes Library. Coolidge received very little instruction from the firm's partners, mostly left to his own devices to master his new profession. His closest companions were books – James Kent's *Commentaries on American Law* and William Blackstone's *Commentaries on the Law of England.* There is little record of Coolidge pursuing any outside activities during this period of his life, focusing his energies on learning the law. In Northampton, there were three civil and two criminal terms for the courts each year, and during these sessions, Coolidge would spend full days in the courtroom, watching and learning. In between, he would assist the partners by helping to prepare writs, deeds, wills, and other similar documents. And he did all of this in nearly complete silence. Henry Field once noted that, "I guess we've added the Sphinx to our staff."[39] Despite being quiet, Coolidge still made a positive impression. "That young fellow isn't much when it comes to gab," Hammond once

IV-13: Coolidge (center) with the law partners under whom he served his apprenticeship, Henry Field (left) and John Hammond (right), shown later in life

remarked, "but he's a hog for work. … He's only been in this office a few months, but I've found out that when he says a thing is so, it is."[40] Coolidge's diligence paid off. He was admitted to the Bar on June 29, 1897, about a year earlier than originally projected. Just shy of his 25th birthday, he was ready to hang out his shingle and would do so while casting aside earlier versions of his name. Even in formal settings, he would no longer be John Calvin Coolidge or even J. Calvin Coolidge. It would just be "Calvin Coolidge" from now on.

Coolidge and his father weighed several options before he decided to remain in Northampton to start his legal practice. He rented two rooms in the new Masonic Building on lower Main Street, not far from Hammond and Field, opening his doors on February 1, 1898. He always ensured to be at his desk, where people could find him. While Coolidge was able to piece together some work for writs, deeds, and rent collection issues, there were plenty of more experienced lawyers in town, so his legal career got off to a slow start. While he earned about $500 in his first year, he struggled to meet even his meager expenses, which included $200 in rent for his office. He still received financial support from home. "I shall make my expenses as reasonable as possibilities permit," he wrote his father. "You will have to peace [sic] out my income until I can make it meet my expenses as you do now."[41] Things improved in his second year, with revenues topping $1400. He started to get some corporate accounts, including becoming counsel to the Nonotuck Savings Bank. He still had a small practice but was getting closer to financial independence for the first time in his life.

Coolidge also got his first taste of politics in the last few years of the 19th Century. He supported both of his former bosses, who each ran for local office. Coolidge helped Field's victorious campaign for mayor of Northampton, as well as Hammond's successful run for District Attorney. With Republican blood fervently coursing through his veins, he then supported William McKinley in the 1896 presidential canvass. Coolidge strongly opposed the "free silver" campaign of Democrat William Jennings Bryan, participating in a local debate at Plymouth Union, where he argued in favor of the gold standard. Coolidge's first entry into politics followed McKinley's victory at the polls, being named to the Republican City Committee for Northampton's Ward Two. This unpaid position provided an entry point into the local Republican ranks, becoming an active attendee at various events for which he was rewarded by being named ward leader. The following year, he ran for one of the three seats from Ward Two on the city council. Again, there was no pay, but his name recognition was increasing, opening the door to move on to other steps up the political ladder.

The position Coolidge coveted in these early days of his legal and political careers was City Solicitor. While the $600 salary was attractive, on top of what he could continue to earn in private practice, money was never his primary motivator. "I wanted to be City Solicitor," he later wrote, "because I believed it would make me a better lawyer. … It gave me a start in the law which I was ever after able to hold."[42] Coolidge won the race in 1899 and was re-elected the following year but he lost out in 1901 to his Democratic counterpart. It was one of only two elections Coolidge would lose in his entire career.

IV-14: Coolidge, circa 1900 (age ~28)

For Coolidge, there was always another rung to climb on the legal or political ladder. The next was one for which he was extremely proud, calling it "the greatest compliment ever paid to my professional ability."[43] William Clapp had been the longtime Clerk of the Courts in Northampton, responsible for maintaining the records of the Superior Court and the Supreme Judicial Court of the county. When Clapp died in 1903, the sitting justices offered the position to Coolidge. He accepted, but only for the balance of the year. While he was honored by the recognition, and welcomed the $2,300 annual salary, he thought the role could take him only so far, so he declined to run for the seat when the election came around in the fall. He wanted the freedom to continue to grow his private practice, as well as run for other political offices, and the Clerk position would have made that impossible.

By this point, Coolidge was eight years removed from college and five years since he passed the Bar. His career was progressing, albeit slowly. His greatest frustration, however, was personal. Calvin Coolidge longed for a wife and family. Unfortunately, his overwhelming shyness

IV-15: Grace Goodhue around the time she met Coolidge (circa 1904)

and limited social interactions were keeping him a lonely young man. But then he got a break. Coolidge was staying in a room in the home of Robert Weir, who happened to be the steward for the Clarke School for the Deaf. Living next door was a pupil at the Clarke School by the name of Grace Goodhue. Like Coolidge, Grace originally hailed from Vermont. After graduating from the University of Vermont, she made her way to Northampton specifically to attend the Clarke School. The first encounter between Coolidge and Grace, who were six and a half years apart in age, took place over the fence line between their places of residence. Grace took the initiative, following up by sending Coolidge a potted plant as a gift. He reciprocated by sending her his card, requesting to see her socially.

In most respects, Calvin Coolidge and Grace Goodhue were complete opposites. Grace's biographer, Ishbel Ross, put it this way:

> No two people could have been more unlike. In all respects Grace Coolidge was the opposite of Calvin Coolidge, except for their basic sincerity and high principles. She was gregarious where he was solitary. She was joyous where he was glum. She was responsive where he was aloof. She loved a good time. He took a dim view of social pleasures. She was impulsive. He was cautious.[44]

Regardless of these clear differences, the relationship prospered. After one of their dates, Coolidge wrote, "You made Tuesday evening so pleasant for me that I am wondering when I may come back."[45] A couple of months later, he shared with her, "Sometimes I think the best part of having you with me is after you are gone. For it is only when I am alone again that I realize how much pleasure you really made for me and remember that I express so little of it to you at parting. ... if *you* gave me much practice I *might* learn to do a *little* better."[46] Not everyone was in favor of the match, however. Grace's mother, Lemira, was the most outspoken in her opposition, finding it impossible to warm up to Coolidge's rather cool personality.

Grace also learned the hard way not to expect Coolidge to be anyone but himself. While they were courting, she arranged for Coolidge to meet one of her friends. Grace knew Coolidge was less than enthusiastic about the gathering, but she was still taken aback by his behavior. While sitting on the edge of her friend's sofa, Grace noted that "Not one word did he utter and when, at last, he could bear it no longer, he arose and said simply, with one of his best smiles, 'We'll be going now.'" While preparing to leave, her friend whispered, "My land, Grace, I'd be afraid of him!" Grace was annoyed. "Now, why did you act like that?" she asked. "She thinks that you are a perfect stick and said she'd be afraid of you." Coolidge's response: "She'll find I'm human."[47] And a peculiar kind of human (particularly for a politician) who refused to perform for others. Grace Goodhue would not try to pressure him into being something he was not. She understood his Puritan roots, which impacted his work ethic and his personality. In total, she liked what she saw, so when he proposed, she said yes (against her mother's wishes). The nuptials took place in a small ceremony in the Goodhue home in Burlington, Vermont, on October 4, 1905. The couple whisked away to Montreal for their honeymoon, but they cut the trip short, returning after just one of the two planned weeks away. Coolidge reasoned they had already seen all the sights, and it wasn't worth the expense to stay any longer. Plus, he was about to run for office again. Grace shared Coolidge's innate frugality and did not object to returning earlier than planned.

Coolidge was still making his way through relatively minor political postings at this stage of his career. After being named the Chairman of the Republican City Committee in 1904, he was now put up to run for membership on the school committee. The votes were cast just three months after his wedding, and for the second time in his career, he came up just short. This circumstance involved poor campaign management on the part of the local Republicans. Coolidge found himself not only facing a Democrat in the canvass but he was also opposed by a fellow Republican. The result was a split vote within the Grand Old Party, paving the way for a 100-vote victory for Democrat John Kennedy. This was the last race Calvin Coolidge would lose in his 30 years in politics.

Coolidge spent the next year continuing to build his law practice while settling down with his new bride before entering another political contest. The couple initially rented a room at the Norwood Hotel, but their stay was short as the establishment closed down. The closure had one distinct advantage as the Coolidges bought up sheets, pillowcases, and table linens on the cheap during the hotel's going-out-of-business sale. For years, the Coolidges enjoyed these household goods, ignoring the large stamp "Norwood Hotel" which adorned each of these items. The next stop would be their home for the next 20 years. Coolidge was not only frugal, but he was also extremely leery of any kind of debt, so buying a home at this stage of his career was out of the question. "I know very well what it means to awake in the night and realize that the rent is coming due," he commented, "wondering where the money is coming from with which to pay it. The only way I know of to escape from that constant tragedy is to keep running expenses low enough so that something may be saved to meet the day when earnings may be small."[48] So, the Coolidges were content to rent half of a duplex at 21 Massasoit Street for $27 a month. The home came with three upstairs bedrooms and a bath, along with a parlor, dining room, kitchen, and pantry on the first level. It also had a cellar and attic for storage. While Coolidge had plenty of chances to improve on this simple abode, he saw no reason to make the change. "So long as I lived there," he later wrote, "I could be

IV-16: The Coolidge's home at 21 Massasoit Street in Northampton, MA (they rented one side of the duplex)

independent and serve the public without ever thinking that I could not maintain my position if I lost my office. … This left me free to make my own decisions in accordance with what I thought was the public good. We lived where we did that I might better serve the people."[49] Material items rarely registered as important to Calvin Coolidge, which Grace learned to understand and accept as well.

Coolidge could be gruff and direct with his wife at times. In terms of money, there was the time when a pregnant Grace said yes to a salesman who came to their door pitching a book entitled "Our Family Physician." Grace made the $8 purchase, knowing her husband might question the extravagance. She placed the book on a table in the home, which Coolidge saw but refrained from any comment. He chose a different route to express his disapproval. Several weeks later, Grace picked up the book to see a handwritten note on the flyleaf that read, "Don't see any receipt here for curing suckers!"[50] Until they moved to Washington, D.C. after the 1920 election, Grace's place was almost entirely in the home. She no longer pursued teaching and was also not involved in Coolidge's career in any way. He did not share his work with her, did not ask her advice, and at times didn't even want her around. In one instance early in the marriage, when Coolidge was heading out for a speech, Grace started to put on her coat when her husband asked where she was going. "Oh, I thought I'd go out and hear you talk," she replied. Coolidge looked at her and simply stated, "Better not."[51] Grace Coolidge stayed home. While these encounters appear harsh, there is no evidence that Grace pushed back against any of these dynamics. She was raised in a similar household in Vermont and understood the traditional division of responsibilities for couples from the state who were raised on Puritan values. In his *Autobiography*, Coolidge would write, "We thought we were made for each other. For almost a quarter of a century she has borne with my infirmities, and I have rejoiced in her graces."[52] He wasn't an easy man to live with and was certainly not the warmest husband, but they remained committed to each other throughout their adult lives, with no indication of any serious dissatisfaction from either party. Differences notwithstanding, they knew their roles, accepted them, and for the most part, were very content throughout their life together.

Less than a year into their marriage, the Coolidges experienced both a loss and an addition to their family. Gone was Coolidge's grandmother, Sarah, the woman who had helped raise him after his mother had passed when he was just 12 years old. Grace joined him for the trip to Plymouth for the funeral. Shortly thereafter, the couple welcomed their first child into the world. John Coolidge was born on September 7, 1906. "Little John is as strong and smart as can be," Coolidge wrote to his stepmother, Carrie. "He has blue eyes and red eyebrows. Grace calls his hair red. … They say he looks just like me."[53] The proud papa was hardly content to sit at home and take care of the baby, though. He was already in the midst of another political campaign.

The state legislature in Massachusetts is known as the General Court, dating to colonial days when the state assembly not only made laws but also served as a judicial court of appeals. Coolidge set his sights on the lower house of the bicameral body. Coolidge was hardly a typical campaigner. He rarely riled up a crowd. His customary outreach in his door-to-door canvassing went something like, "I want your vote. I need it. I shall appreciate it."[54] But Coolidge had already served in several local positions, and his Republican-leaning district gave him a majority over Democrat Moses Bassett by a margin of 264 votes. The General Court met in the state capital of Boston for roughly six months out of the year, taking Coolidge away from Grace and baby John. He minimized the time away by taking the three-hour train ride every Monday morning and returning to Northampton every Friday evening. The one-year term was hardly lucrative, earning him only $750 per year in salary plus per diem. He likely made money on the expenses as he joined many of his fellow legislators in staying at the Adams House hotel. The cost of his single room (and shared bathroom) was $1 per day.

IV-17: Coolidge as a State Legislator, 1908 (age 36)

Coolidge was hardly an impressive figure as he arrived in Boston to take his seat in the state's House of Representatives. One colleague, Democrat Martin Lomasney, described him as "either a schoolteacher or an undertaker."[55] Coolidge's friend, Dick Irwin, tried to help by sending House Speaker John Cole a letter of introduction, which concluded, "He's better than he looks, like a singed cat."[56] That was yet to be seen. Coolidge was ever-present when the House was in session, but he was as quiet as ever, rarely socializing with his colleagues. He took most of his meals by himself and spent most evenings alone in his room. Over the course of the term, Coolidge did begin to establish some working relationships with his fellow politicians from across the state, including those across the aisle. They appreciated the fact that he studied each bill and was well-prepared for every vote, but at times he was so quiet that he was barely noticed. His bland personality also materialized in a variety of settings. During this period, for example, Coolidge was invited to an elaborate dinner given by state senator Allen Treadway, someone with whom Coolidge had collaborated on some legislation. While each course of fancy dishes was being served, Coolidge could be seen just sitting there, not touching his food. Treadway recognized that Coolidge wasn't eating, and asked if he could get the chef to prepare something more to his liking. After successive prodding, Coolidge finally responded, "Well, if you insist, I'd like some dry toast and a cup of weak tea."[57] To many of his colleagues, that was Calvin Coolidge in a nutshell – a piece of dry toast and a cup of weak tea.

That said, Coolidge performed well enough in the eyes of his constituents to be sent back to the statehouse for a second term, just barely edging Democrat Alfred Preece by 63 votes. Coolidge's two years in the House coincided with the rise of the progressive movement under President Theodore Roosevelt. Roosevelt used the "bully pulpit" of the White House to push for reforms that sought to utilize government for the direct benefit of the common man. Coolidge was always conservative by nature, but his party had turned progressive, and at this stage, he was on board. During the 1908 term, Coolidge supported an anti-monopoly bill along with pro-labor legislation that made obligatory one day's rest in seven and special low railway rates for workingmen and their children. Coolidge also benefited by finding his first political patron in the form of U.S. Senator Murray Crane. Crane had served

IV-18: Coolidge's political mentor, Murray Crane

three terms as the state's Lieutenant Governor followed by three terms as Governor before landing in the U.S. Senate. He was one of the leading Republicans in the state, along with fellow Senator Henry Lodge, who had become his political rival. Crane liked Coolidge and took him under his wing, a real boon to someone who was still trying to figure out his place in Massachusetts politics. "In all political affairs he [Crane] had a wonderful wisdom," Coolidge once remarked, "and in everything he was preeminently a man of judgment, who was the most disinterested public servant I ever saw and the greatest influence for good government with which I ever came in contact."[58] Coolidge didn't have many intimate political mentors or even allies, but Murray Crane was one who really mattered, now and later, when Coolidge returned to state government after a brief hiatus.

The people of Massachusetts appreciated the notion of rotation in office, not wanting any individual to stay in the same seat of power for more than 2-3 years. After his second year in the House, Coolidge adhered to this tradition by declining to run for a third term. Besides, he had another mouth to feed, so he needed to focus on generating a little more income from his law practice. The couple's second child was born on April 13, 1908. They named him after his father, Calvin Coolidge, Jr. Coolidge settled back into his Northampton law office fulltime, adding some corporate clients, including the Knickerbocker Trust Company and the Springfield Brewing Company. The latter was a bit of a dicey proposition for a lawyer who was also a politician at a time when many folks across the country were advocating a national ban on alcohol. Coolidge was not a fan of the movement, believing the prospect of state-ordered temperance to be an intrusion on individual liberty. He had no issue providing legal advice to the brewery, which also contributed a welcome source of income. Despite their frugality, times were still challenging economically, with periodic requests to Coolidge's father for additional funds still passing between Northampton and Plymouth.

Someone once asked Coolidge if he had any hobbies. His terse response was, "Yes. Running for office."[59] As such, it was unsurprising to see him back in another campaign just a year removed from his role in the state's House of Representatives. This time, he was focusing on local politics, tossing his hat into the ring to be the next mayor of his adopted hometown of Northampton. Coolidge spent a lot of time meeting the voters, although most encounters were exceedingly brief. Given his unconventional style, even some of his closest friends couldn't understand how he kept winning these elections. His former boss, Henry Field, who remained a strong supporter, once admitted:

> I can not see how Calvin Coolidge gets the votes. He absolutely killed every tradition we've ever had in Massachusetts as to the qualities one must have to be a successful and practical politician. So far as I know, he has wrecked them all. … I've never known him to slap a man on the back once. So far as I know he has never had a nickname in his life. People who know him call him 'Cal,' but that is as far as any of them will go. He is not what you would call a mixer. He is the quietest man I ever knew.[60]

And yet he did continue to win. Coolidge did make a handful of public speeches during the race for mayor, always trying to stay above the fray. "It is a great honor to be selected as a candidate for Mayor of Northampton," he told one gathering, "an honor which we cannot all attain. But there is a higher honor yet, for which we may all be candidates, the honor of being upright, worthy, decent citizens. I want to be a perpetual candidate on that ticket. I want my campaign run on that principle."[61] Whatever he was doing, it was working, as Coolidge edged his friend Harry Bicknell for the post by a mere 187 votes. Coolidge was true to his word on his stated approach to politics, sending the following note to Bicknell in the immediate aftermath of the race.

> My dear Harry:
>
> My most serious regret at the election is that you cannot share the entire pleasure of the result with me. I value your friendship and good opinion more than any office and I trust I have so conducted the campaign that our past close intimacy and good fellowship may be more secure than ever.
>
> Respectfully,
>
> Calvin Coolidge[62]

Like all his previous elected positions, the remuneration was not significant. The mayor of Northampton was paid only $800 a year. The position was considered part-time, so Coolidge kept his law office open, but he was so engaged in his public duties that he was able to devote very little time to his private practice. That meant more requests for cash from his father. Most of these asks were quite specific in terms of Coolidge's immediate needs. After winning the mayoral race, for example, Coolidge wrote to his father, "I have got to have an overcoat, a business suit, an evening suit, and a cutaway suit. Grace has got to have a suit, a dress, an evening dress, an evening wrap, a dress hat and a street hat. Total about $300."[63] Colonel Coolidge came through, as usual, at a time when he was also returning to government service. Coolidge's father had recently been elected to the state senate of Vermont, prompting a family visit to that state's capital, Montpelier.

Coolidge's standing as a prominent citizen of Northampton was cemented with his election as mayor. He took the role seriously, dutifully reporting for duty at City Hall just about every weekday. This was his first executive role in government, and he took the opportunity to pursue some of the policies for which he would later earn the admiration of the American people. Foremost among these accomplishments were cutting local taxes and reducing the city's debt. He accomplished these objectives while also managing to raise the salaries of the city's public school teachers. His performance earned him a second term, once again topping Harry Bicknell at the polls in the fall of 1910. Gaining the confidence of his local constituents meant a lot to Coolidge. In his post-presidential *Autobiography*, he proudly noted, "Of all the honors that have come to me I still cherish in a very high place the confidence of my friends and neighbors in making me their Mayor."[64]

The position of Northampton mayor began a string of nearly two decades of continuous government service for Coolidge. During this run, he would be elected mayor (twice), state senator (four times), Lieutenant Governor (three times), Governor (twice), Vice President of the United States (once), and President of the United States (once). He never lost a race from this point on. In the campaign of 1911, Coolidge set his sights once again on the Massachusetts General Court, this time the upper house of the state Senate. Winning the Republican nomination was the key to this post, as his district ran strongly Republican. With this victory, Coolidge found himself in a much more exclusive club than the lower house, with only 40 members from across the state. The compensation was better as well ($1000 per year) for a job that once again required weekly train trips to Boston and his small room at the Adams House for the first six months of the year. As before, Coolidge was the quietest member of this august body. Reporter William White noted that "he was not highly esteemed as a coming young man."[65] Just because he'd hit the age of 40 and was moving up the political ladder didn't mean he was inclined to change anything about his taciturn personality.

This was an awkward time for members of the Republican Party as the party itself was in the midst of fracturing on the national scene. The vibrant progressive, Theodore Roosevelt, had left the White House in 1909, turning it over to his hand-picked successor, William Taft. But Taft was proving to be far too conservative for Roosevelt's legion of progressive followers to the point where they were now urging Roosevelt to get back in the game and challenge Taft for a return to the presidency. When Roosevelt did enter the race, it led to a broken Republican Convention, in which Taft was renominated, but Roosevelt bolted across town to create a rival party of his own. By running on the Progressive ticket, Roosevelt all but ensured defeat for both him and Taft, handing the White House to Democrat Woodrow Wilson. While Coolidge had recently supported a number of progressive measures, including women's suffrage, primaries for U.S. Senate candidates, a minimum wage for female workers, and the establishment of a state income tax, he was generally aligned to the conservative wing of the party. This put him alongside the Republican Old Guard that supported Taft in 1912. "I was sorry Taft could not win," Coolidge noted, "but am glad TR made so poor a showing."[66] The Democrats surged in elections across the country as the Republicans and Progressives split their votes, but Calvin Coolidge was personally unaffected. He was re-elected and ready to take on additional responsibilities in his second term in the state senate.

Coolidge started to come out of his shell a bit during his term in 1913. He appeared more confident and, as a result, more influential. "It was in my second term in the Senate that I began to be a force in the Massachusetts Legislature," he later wrote. "I made progress because I studied subjects sufficiently to know a little more about them than anyone else on the floor. I did not often speak but talked much with the Senators personally and came in contact with many of the business men of the state. The Boston Democrats came to be my friends and were a great help to me in later times."[67] Senator Coolidge received additional responsibilities, being assigned the chairmanship of the influential Railroad Committee along with a seat on the powerful Committee on Rules. He continued to side with the conservatives. As an example, Massachusetts was home to one of the leading progressives in the country, future Supreme Court Justice Louis Brandeis. Brandeis was pushing to break up the large railroad companies, but Coolidge resisted moves along these lines. He believed the only way for the railroads to have enough capital to invest in expansion was by pooling together as larger entities. The Progressives and Republicans would spend much of the decade trying to sort through the proper roles of government, including how aggressive the push should be for these kinds of reforms. Calvin Coolidge would consistently find his place on the conservative side of that ledger.

3. State Leadership

Coolidge was ready for the next step up the political ladder in Massachusetts, but this one would require some astute maneuvering, the kind that he rarely exhibited but was in his wheelhouse when he needed it the most. Levi Greenwood had been serving as the President of the Massachusetts Senate. Early in 1913, he announced his intent to run for Lieutenant Governor. Coolidge wanted the Senate President position, which would instantly make him one of the most powerful Republicans in the state. In Massachusetts, the Senate President is chosen by the members of that body at the beginning of each new term. Coolidge's plan was to win his seat and then immediately campaign amongst his colleagues for the post. Circumstances were upended, however, as Greenwood changed his mind. At the last minute, he decided to run for his old Senate seat instead of Lieutenant Governor, potentially thwarting Coolidge's strategic plans. Fortunately for Coolidge, Greenwood unexpectedly lost his race, primarily due to strong opposition from riled-up suffragists in his district. As soon as these results became known, Coolidge jumped into action. In a rare move, he went from Northampton to Boston on the night train so he could begin to collect pledges of support in person first thing in the morning. Coolidge had the backing of Murray Crane and some of his key followers as they tracked down just about every member of the incoming Senate. Also going for him was his longstanding record of doing small favors for his colleagues, typically never asking for anything in return. Now was the time to cash in those chits, including from some Democrats. This unusual showing of political aggression on Coolidge's part paid off handsomely. Within 24 hours, he had a majority of his colleagues committed to giving him their vote for President of the Senate. According to the *Springfield Republican*, "It was nothing short of wonderful the way he walked right into the ring and took the prize before the public could realize there was a contest."[68] Coolidge had been at the political game for a while now and believed his approach had ultimately gained the respect of his peers. "My progress had been slow and toilsome," he later wrote, "with little about it that was brilliant, or spectacular, the result of persistent and painstaking work, which gave it a foundation that was solid."[69] Taking over as the President of the Massachusetts Senate was the biggest leap to date in his political career.

Coolidge was proud to have his family on-hand as he was sworn into his new office on January 7, 1914. Grace and the boys were there, along with Coolidge's father, who made the trip from Vermont. The family had recently suffered a bit of a scare with five-year-old Calvin, Jr., who had been ill most of the winter. Diagnosed with pneumonia, he needed surgery, which included the placement of a tube in his chest. He came home from the hospital on December 23 with a nurse in tow but was well enough for the trip to Boston a couple of weeks later.

Coolidge set the tone for the upcoming Senate term with an inaugural address that was one of his first speeches that was widely distributed. One of the lines from the speech would actually become the title of a collection of his addresses that would later be compiled in book form. It was called "Have Faith in Massachusetts." The new Senate President declared:

> Have faith in Massachusetts. In some unimportant detail some other States may surpass her, but in the general results, there is no place on earth where the people secure, in a larger measure, the blessings of organized government, and nowhere can those functions more properly be termed self-government.[70]

Coolidge shared some of his political philosophy in the address, including his advice to slow things down and not to be so quick to push for major reforms. "Don't hurry to legislate," he said. "Give administration a chance to catch up with legislation."[71] This expression became a common refrain for Coolidge as his conservative bona fides continued to come to the fore. Finally, Coolidge left his audience with a taste of the philosophy of Professor Charles Garman, which was clearly resident in Coolidge's psyche.

> Recognize the immortal worth and dignity of man. Let the laws of Massachusetts proclaim to her humblest citizen, performing the most menial task, the recognition of his manhood, the recognition that all men are peers, the humblest with the most exalted, the recognition that all work is glorified. Such is the path to equality before the law. Such is the foundation of liberty under the law. Such is the sublime revelation of man's relation to man – Democracy.[72]

IV-19: Coolidge as a member of the Massachusetts Senate, 1913 (age 41)

The Senate President in Massachusetts had quite a bit of authority. He set the Senate calendar, named members to their committee posts, and presided over sessions, calling on speakers and enforcing the rules of parliamentary procedure. Coolidge oversaw these sessions with discipline and efficiency. In Massachusetts, the Senate President was still a member in good standing of the body, allowed to vote on issues and speak on topics. While Coolidge rarely took advantage of this latter opportunity, when he did speak, people paid attention, partly because it was so rare but also because of the position he held.

Despite his new role, Coolidge was essentially the same person he had always been. He still lived by himself in his small room at the Adams House, still took many meals by himself, rarely socialized, and remained primarily silent. Claude Fuess, who spent six years studying Coolidge before publishing his biography of the man in 1940, provided the following description at this stage of Coolidge's career, but which could have been applied to almost any period in his life. Fuess pointed to:

> ... his passion for economy, his disgust at waste, his taciturnity, his dislike of impulsiveness, his positive hatred of ostentation. ... his habits of industry, his zeal for routine work, his apparent lack of imagination, his disinclination for sports, his obvious provincialism. His Puritan nature abhorred graft and extravagance and immorality. His tastes were simple to the point of drabness, and he cared nothing whatever for luxury. He was the very embodiment of common sense, the antithesis of what was eccentric or fantastical or irregular.[73]

This was the man now driving the legislative agenda for the state of Massachusetts.

While Murray Crane was a prominent supporter of Coolidge during his various offices in Massachusetts state government, he was not the foremost advocate in Coolidge's political career. With little effort on Coolidge's part, that role was assumed by a wealthy businessman by the name of Frank Stearns. Stearns was the heir to his father's highly successful commercial businesses in Boston, ranging from dry goods to his namesake department store (R.H. Stearns). Stearns had graduated from Amherst in 1878 and became a member of the Board of Trustees in 1908. He had no previous background in politics but had sought out Coolidge in 1912 to lobby for legislation that would allow Amherst to enlarge its sewer system. In his typical terse and cold fashion, Coolidge turned Stearns down flat, saying it was too late in the legislative session to grant his request. Stearns stewed over this affront for several months until he was caught off guard by what happened next. "The surprise of my life came the next session," Stearns later remarked. "Coolidge, who had become president of the Massachusetts Senate, made it his business at the earliest possible moment to put through our bill. He did it unsolicited. Moreover, he incorporated valuable amendments which had not occurred to us the year before. Of course this changed my attitude toward Calvin Coolidge. It interested me in the man. First, I sought his acquaintance, then his friendship."[74] When they met again, Coolidge invited Stearns to come see him at the statehouse, even welcoming him to sit on the dais with him while the Senate was in session. Stearns was impressed with how Coolidge ran that body and

IV-20: Coolidge's friend and political backer, Frank Stearns

how it was clear he had the respect of the members. While others still looked past the quiet small-town lawyer as a political lightweight, Stearns saw something in Coolidge that had the potential for greatness.

Early in Coolidge's first term as Senate President, the world was shaken by the eruption of World War I. Immediately after the assassination of Austria's Archduke Franz Ferdinand by a Serbian national, the dominoes associated with bilateral defense agreements across Europe began to fall. Coolidge was among most Americans who supported President Wilson's decision to keep the United States out of the conflict, at least for the time being. His focus was on Massachusetts and another political campaign. By the time Coolidge ran for his fourth term in the Massachusetts Senate, most people had become accustomed to his unusually quiet style of campaigning. But for those who weren't attuned to "Silent Cal," Grace hung the following lines in their living room as a reminder:

> A wise old owl lived in an oak
> The more he saw, the less he spoke
> The less he spoke, the more he heard
> Why can't we be like that old bird?[75]

Coolidge won this election easily, and this time his selection as the body's President was unanimous (including the handful of Democrats in the upper house of the legislature). Coolidge's remarks to open his second term were more typical of his public speaking, consisting of just 44 words.

> HONORABLE SENATORS:
>
> My sincerest thanks, I offer you. Conserve the firm foundations of our institutions. Do your work with the spirit of a soldier in the public service. Be loyal to the Commonwealth and to yourselves. And be brief; above all things, Be Brief.[76]

Now, that's the true Calvin Coolidge, who was becoming increasingly more comfortable speaking his mind – in as few words as possible, of course.

While Coolidge was focusing on his task at hand, Stearns was already thinking about the next rung on the political ladder. He was convinced Coolidge was ready to run for Lieutenant Governor. Initially, Coolidge did not encourage the notion, although he did consent to allow

Stearns to give a dinner at the exclusive Algonquin Club in Boston in his honor. In May 1915, 67 influential people from politics, academia, and other positions of prominence gathered for the affair. Coolidge was touched by the outpouring of appreciation for his years of service, writing his father, "I am sure you would have been proud of the character of the men who came to honor me."[77] A flamboyant progressive Republican by the name of Guy Ham had already announced his candidacy for the Republican nomination for Lieutenant Governor and was actively campaigning across the state, and Coolidge still seemed cool to Stearns's entreaties to toss his hat into the ring. That all changed as soon as the Senate session came to an end. "The Legislature was in session," Coolidge informed Stearns, "and if I had announced my candidacy, then, every word and action of mine would have been twisted. Legislation would have been in a mess. The public business would have suffered. I had to take that chance."[78] These were the kinds of selfless decisions that drew Stearns to Coolidge all the more.

Once given the go-ahead, Stearns jumped into the campaign full force, sending out letters to friends and colleagues across the state, financing the campaign out of his own pocket. When the Republican primary was held just three months later, it was a convincing win for Coolidge, who captured nearly 60% of the vote. He would be pared with gubernatorial candidate Samuel McCall, who had spent two decades in the U.S. House of Representatives. McCall and Coolidge canvassed the state together for the next couple of months, reaching as many voters as possible. Coolidge ended up giving up to 15 speeches a day over the final three weeks of the campaign. His position was clear in every address; he was there to support the top of the ticket, advocating for McCall at every turn. He also campaigned on principle. "This is not partisan," he proclaimed. "I am not criticizing individuals. I am denouncing a system. When you substitute patronage for patriotism, administration breaks down. We need more of the Office Desk and less of the Show Window in politics. Let men in office substitute the midnight oil for the limelight."[79] It turned out to be a banner year for the Republicans, reunited after the progressive split from a few years before. The party captured all the state offices and both houses of the state legislature. The largest margin of victory was for Calvin Coolidge. While McCall was elected Governor with a six-thousand vote advantage, Coolidge beat Edward Barry by more than 50,000 votes.

Coolidge was clearly now a man on the rise. The *Boston Herald* put it this way:

> The election has given the Republican Party a new leader in its Lieutenant-Governor-elect, Calvin Coolidge, of Northampton. … Going into the western hill towns where the Democrats thought they were firmly lodged through their professed interest in the farmers, Coolidge swept away their claims with his calm, business-like, persuasive argument. In gestures and flights of oratory he nowhere measured up to the picturesque Mr. [Edward] Barry, but he won the confidence of the people and won their votes. ... It is shown clearly that Coolidge has developed into a party leader of the first rank.[80]

Coolidge was grateful for this new opportunity and knew Frank Stearns had a lot to do with making it happen. "In so far as my own fortunes could be shaped by anyone but myself," he wrote to Stearns after the results were tallied in the canvass, "you are responsible for my nomination and election, above all my nomination. It was your endorsement that made my candidacy accepted at its face value. If my public services are hereafter of any value, the credit should be shared with you."[81] Stearns's attraction to Coolidge had come a bit out of nowhere, but it wasn't just his support that Coolidge welcomed, it was the selfless nature of his devotion that gave him his unique spot in Coolidge's very small inner circle. "While Mr. Stearns always overestimated me," Coolidge wrote in his *Autobiography*, "he nevertheless was a great help to me. He never obtruded or sought any favor for himself or any other person, but his whole effort was always disinterested and entirely devoted to assisting me when I indicated I wished him to do so. It is doubtful if any other public man ever had so valuable and unselfish a friend."[82] Staying within these boundaries was essential to the bond. Numerous times Stearns tried to offer expensive gifts to Coolidge, including clothes from his department store for Grace and even a better place to live, but Coolidge always turned him down. That was never his way. "I have everything we need and am able to save something," Coolidge once wrote to Stearns. "I do not think a man who cannot take care of himself is worthy of very much consideration."[83] The Coolidges and Stearnses became close friends as couples, even vacationing together at times. Frank Stearns and Grace Coolidge had a bond of their own as well. "You and I have one thing in common," Stearns once wrote to Grace. "You picked out Calvin Coolidge some years ago and gave him your endorsement; more recently I picked him out and gave him the most emphatic endorsement I knew how to. Of course, many others can claim to have picked him out, but amongst them all I think we can shake hands over the proposition that yours was the most important endorsement and mine comes next."[84] The statement was undoubtedly accurate.

Coolidge was sworn into office as the Lieutenant Governor of Massachusetts on January 6, 1916, with his wife, children, and father all on hand for the occasion. The Lieutenant Governor had specific responsibilities, including filling in for the Governor when he was unavailable. In the case of Governor McCall, that would be a fairly frequent occurrence as he took a number of trips that put Coolidge temporarily at the head of state government. McCall never had to worry about Coolidge misrepresenting him, as the Lieutenant Governor saw that his primary responsibility was to support the person elected by the people of Massachusetts at the top of the ticket. On one occasion, when Frank Stearns warned Coolidge about coming out in favor of an initiative that he knew the Lieutenant Governor opposed, Coolidge responded as follows:

> I apprehend that I was elected by the people of Massachusetts to a definite job, second in the administration, a long ways behind the first. I accepted the office and my duty is perfectly clear – to back up the administration to the limit, whether I like it or do not like it. If this position should ever be so bad that I positively cannot do this, then my duty is equally clear to keep my mouth shut. If any protests are to be made, they must be made by the rest of you.[85]

McCall vouched for Coolidge's adherence to this mantra. He wrote in his memoirs that Coolidge remained aligned with him in the state's Executive Council "even when the vote was seven to two"[86] – with McCall and Coolidge representing the 'two.' One of Coolidge's responsibilities was to chair that Executive Council, which in the state of Massachusetts was responsible for overseeing a number of commissions, providing advice and consent on gubernatorial appointments, and serving as a possible check on state expenditures by having to approve bond purchases and certain contracts, such as those for large construction projects. As before, he did a lot of his work behind the scenes, studying the relevant material for his role and being available to support the Governor wherever and whenever he was needed.

Personally, Coolidge not only kept his law practice open, but he also brought on a partner for the first time. Ralph Hemenway joined the practice, but it was somewhat of an odd arrangement since Coolidge didn't take on any clients or cases and the pair shared no revenue. Coolidge's name remained on the door, but it was basically Hemenway's practice, as Coolidge was focused almost entirely on his new role as Lieutenant Governor. His raise to $2000 a year did little to change the Coolidges' lifestyle. Grace remained home with the boys while Coolidge commuted each week, continuing to reside in his small room at the Adams House for around $1 per day. The couple did take a trip in early 1916, giving Coolidge his first glimpse at his nation's capital. In one memorable moment, Coolidge was looking out from the west front of the Capitol building, putting his eyes on the Washington Monument and the White House in the distance. Someone in the party asked, "What do you think of that?" Coolidge responded, "That is a view that would rouse the emotion of any man."[87] That was saying something coming from a man who rarely showed any emotion at all.

Frank Stearns continued to try to position Coolidge in the eyes of the public, encouraging him to speak throughout the state. He also gave another dinner for Coolidge, this time just six weeks into his term as Lieutenant Governor. The attendees for this gathering were primarily notable alums from Amherst, who assembled at Copley Plaza in Boston to celebrate their schoolmate's rise to his position of leadership. With Massachusetts politicians still operating on one-year terms, there was always another election right around the corner. These public events were intended to allow more and more people to get to know Coolidge on a personal level, although that remained difficult given his penchant to remain among the quietest at any of these gatherings.

The next election cycle coincided with a presidential campaign, with the incumbent Woodrow Wilson facing off against Republican Charles Evans Hughes. Hughes was a former Governor of New York who had stepped down from his role as an Associate Justice on the Supreme Court to accept the nomination and make the run for the White House. The critical issue was the U.S. role in the ongoing World War, with Hughes aligning with those who were ready to bring the country into the conflict while Wilson stood firmly on neutrality. It was a close contest, the result of which was not clear until three days after the polls closed. That's when California and its 13 electoral votes was called for Wilson by the tiniest margin, putting him over the top in the Electoral College. As for Massachusetts, McCall and Coolidge were both re-elected without much difficulty.

The world for all Americans dramatically changed just a month after Wilson was sworn in to start his second term as President. The Germans announced plans for unrestricted submarine warfare throughout the broad war zone in Europe, putting American commercial ships in immediate peril. The Germans had already sunk several neutral vessels, killing Americans in the process, but while President Wilson spoke out against these attacks, he had remained unwilling to take his country into the war. The new German policy changed his calculus, and Wilson asked Congress for a declaration of war on April 2, 1917. The state of Massachusetts began preparing in earnest a full month before the Federal government confirmed the national declaration. The state passed legislation appropriating $1 million for defense of the state's coastal regions against potential attacks by German submarines and for training and equipping more than 10,000 members of the State Guard. Things only accelerated once war was formally declared. Many of the state's college campuses, including Amherst, emptied out with volunteers for the fight. Thousands more were called to duty when the Federal draft was established on May 18. President Wilson led the national charge, advocating for shifting economic production to the war effort, enhancing output wherever possible while also maximizing the conservation of critical supplies and food. McCall and Coolidge were outspoken supporters of these efforts. Reflecting on these momentous times in his *Autobiography*, Coolidge recalled:

> The whole nation seemed to be endowed with a new spirit, unified and solidified and willing to make any sacrifice for the cause of liberty. I was constantly before public gatherings explaining the needs of the time for men, money and supplies. Sometimes I was urging subscriptions for war loans, sometimes contributions to the great charities, or again speaking to the workmen engaged in construction or the manufacture of munitions. The response which the people made and the organizing power of the country were all manifestations that it was wonderful to contemplate. The entire nation awoke to a new life.[88]

The 26th "Yankee Division," which consisted primarily of Massachusetts State Guard units, along with other regiments from throughout New England, was the first full U.S. Army Division to deploy to Europe. According to the Massachusetts World War I Centennial Commission, more than 189,000 men and women from the state served in the U.S. Armed Forces during the war, including 5,775 who perished as a result of their service.

Political cycles don't pause even during wartime, which put McCall and Coolidge up for re-election again in the fall of 1917. Both won easily, at which point McCall made it known that he would abide by the Massachusetts tradition to not run for a fourth term. All eyes were now centered on Calvin Coolidge as the presumptive nominee of the Republican Party to be the next Governor of the state. At the forefront of that effort was Frank Stearns, not only with his communications but also with his wallet. Over the course of the campaign, Stearns spent more than $6,000 of his own money on ads, events, transportation, and even the commissioning of a short biography to position Coolidge to move to the top spot in the state's hierarchy. Stearns made it clear to Coolidge's former Amherst classmate Dwight Morrow that the sky was the limit for the political career of Calvin Coolidge. "I do not want to be foolish about this matter and especially I do not want to do him harm by being premature in talking about bigger things for him but I do thoroughly believe that ... Calvin Coolidge is the political heir of Abraham Lincoln," Stearns wrote. "I think he has in strong development many of Lincoln's best traits and I do believe that he is better fitted even today to be President of the United States than any man, except Senator [Elihu] Root, who is mentioned." Morrow, who had made his own name in the business world as a partner at J.P. Morgan's financial enterprise, was not quite on board with Stearns's enthusiastic advocacy, but he, too, would come around in the not too distant future.

Coolidge's competition for Governor in 1918 was Democrat Richard Long, a wealthy shoe manufacturer who switched his factory production to war materials upon the U.S. entry into the conflict. While Coolidge continued to avoid personal attacks in any of his campaigns, Long was aggressive, faulting Coolidge not so much for his policies as for his personality. Coolidge kept things on a higher plane. "My conception of public duty is to face each problem as though my entire record in life were to be judged by the way I handled it, to be firm for my honesty of opinion but to recognize every man's right to an honest difference of opinion," Coolidge told the people of Massachusetts. "If chosen to be your Governor, I shall try to conduct the duties of the office so as to merit the sincere endorsement of men of fair minds in all parties. I can promise nothing more."[89] The people liked what they heard, handing the governorship to Coolidge by a difference of 51% to 47%. One week after the vote, the armistice was reached in Europe. Coolidge would not be a wartime Governor, but he would have his hands full with the aftereffects of the conflict.

Few people were better prepared to take over the top spot in the state than Calvin Coolidge. He had gained experience at every step of the political ladder in Massachusetts, from the local ranks in Northampton as a city councilman and mayor, to both houses of the state legislature (including two terms as the Senate president), and finally to three years as Lieutenant Governor. His reticent nature made him an unconventional politician, but one who had paid his dues and proved his worth to his constituents. He understood how the state functioned and was open to working across the aisle, as long as it was consistent with his core political philosophies. The main question facing him as he was sworn in as the state's 48th Governor was whether he had the leadership skills needed for the top executive position in the state. His two years as mayor represented his only previous stint in a singular position of leadership, and the state of Massachusetts, with its approximately 3.8 million residents, was on a far grander scale than anything he had faced when leading the city of Northampton a decade before.

The transfer of power in the Commonwealth of Massachusetts comes adorned with elaborate traditions. The outgoing executive follows the scripted "lone walk" through the House of Flags in the statehouse, into Doric Hall, and out the central doors of the building before crossing the street into Boston Common, where he symbolically takes his place once again among his fellow private citizens. After receiving the Butler Bible, the "Gavel," and a two-volume set of the Massachusetts General Statutes from his predecessor, the incoming Governor enters the House chamber, where he is sworn into office by the President of the Senate in a joint session of the state legislature. All of this ceremony may have been a bit uncharacteristic for the reserved inclinations of Calvin Coolidge, yet he fulfilled these ceremonial obligations without any hesitation. With his father, wife, and sons at hand, Coolidge offered a

IV-21: Coolidge being sworn in as the 48th Governor of Massachusetts, January 1919 (age 46)

31-minute address to launch his service as the chief executive of the state. He emphasized the kind of policies for which he had become well known, including the efficient transaction of the state's business while limiting government expenditures. To the state's lawmakers he suggested, "Let there be a purpose in all your legislation to recognize the right of man to be well born, well nurtured, well educated, well employed, and well paid. This is no gospel of ease and selfishness, or class distinction, but a gospel of effort and service, of universal application."[90] The philosophy of Charles Garman still had a solid hold on the conscience of Calvin Coolidge.

Coolidge's personal life would change little upon rising to the top spot in the state. Massachusetts did not provide an official residence for its Governor, so Coolidge continued to make the Adams House his home away from home. As Governor, he did upgrade from his tiny room to a two-room suite (including bath), doubling his daily rent to $2 per day. He didn't need much more since Grace still planned to spend most of her time in Northampton raising their boys. "Mr. Coolidge may be Governor of Massachusetts but I shall be first of all the mother of my sons," Grace declared at the time.[91] The boys also knew to expect few changes. William White noted that "Mr. Coolidge is the kind of a father who has the absolute respect of his sons but he does not easily become their playmate; occasionally reads to them, takes them on walks."[92] The boys understood that fulfilling his duty on behalf of his fellow citizens was going to receive his greatest attention. Grace joined her frugal husband in seeing no need for any changes in their lifestyle. "Although my husband has moved up, it makes no difference in our mode of living," she said. "Why should it? We are happy, well, content. We keep our bills paid and live like anybody else."[93] Grace occasionally made appearances in Boston, where she was universally embraced, especially when seen in contrast to her socially challenged husband, but mostly they regrouped on weekends as Coolidge continued his commute by the rails.

The entire country began welcoming soldiers back home throughout the early months of 1919, which were joyous moments but led to serious challenges. Demobilization dramatically affected the nation's economy, down to the most local levels. Women, who had entered the workforce like never before to backfill men who had gone off to fight, were now expected by many to simply return to their previous domestic stations in life, even though many were disinclined to follow that path. Economic realities were also being upended. During the war, unemployment was essentially nil, and wages were high thanks to government largesse that prioritized maximizing production almost regardless of the cost. That dynamic ended abruptly with the signing of the armistice and the more traditional economic laws of supply and demand once again took precedence. The entire country was about to face labor/management struggles as these competing factors had to find a new point of equilibrium.

These challenges would only increase as more and more soldiers arrived at the piers of Boston. But before many of those soldiers would arrive, Governor Coolidge first welcomed his nation's Commander-in-Chief, fresh from the negotiations at the Paris Peace Conference that was already underway. President Wilson decided to personally represent his nation in the gathering to determine the fate of the vanquished Central Powers, guided by his so-called Fourteen Points, including his highest priority to establish an international League of Nations as a means to prevent wars of this nature from ever happening again. A couple of months into these challenging negotiations, where the Allies seemed much more intent on punishing their enemies than establishing the foundation for a prolonged peace, Wilson returned to the States to sign legislation that was hitting his desk as the 65th Congress was coming to a close. Wilson's top adviser, Colonel Edward House, suggested that the President initially land in Boston, which was expected to be a friendly port of call compared to other possible landing spots. The political message was equally clear, with Massachusetts Senator Henry Lodge already emerging as Wilson's chief opponent when it came to his vision

IV-22: Governor Coolidge (right) is joined by Boston Mayer Andrew Peters (left) to welcome President Woodrow Wilson (center) to Boston, February 24, 1919

for the League of Nations. Wilson agreed, and was welcomed by Governor Coolidge and Boston Mayor Andrew Peters when the U.S.S. *George Washington* returned the President to American soil on February 24, 1919. Coolidge and Wilson may have represented different parties and many different views, but the Governor played no politics in welcoming his Commander-in-Chief home from the negotiations. Speaking to a large reception at the Mechanics Building in Boston, Coolidge stated, "We welcome him as the representative of a great people, as a great statesman, as one to whom we have entrusted our destinies and one whom we are sure we will support in the future in the working out of those destinies, as Massachusetts has supported him in the past."[94] President Wilson not only valued the warm welcome, but his Assistant Secretary of the Navy, Franklin Roosevelt, also appreciated the kind remarks. "I shall never forget Governor Coolidge's welcome to him," the future President later recalled. "A diffident little man whom nobody outside of Massachusetts had then heard of, the Governor had carefully prepared a very prosaic speech of welcome on three small, typewritten cards."[95] Wilson had his work cut out for him, both in Europe and with the U.S. Senate. After his one day in Boston, the President faced a much more hostile audience when he returned to Washington and began confronting the opposition presented by Lodge and a majority of Republican senators. As for Governor Coolidge, he refused to be brought into the hot debate about the League of Nations. "I am the Governor of Massachusetts," he told a reporter. "The State of Massachusetts has no foreign relations. If ever I should hold an office calling for action or opinion on this subject, I shall put my mind on it and try to arrive at the soundest conclusions within my capacity."[96] Such a time was only a couple of years away, but few outside the likes of Frank Stearns believed at this point that such a transition was even remotely possible.

Stearns, in fact, was already thinking ahead for the few rungs left for Coolidge on the political ladder. Some governors were happy to transition to the U.S. Senate, while others might set their sights on the presidency. As Coolidge was settling into his new job, Stearns was already writing letters to influential leaders far and wide to keep Coolidge in their thoughts for future advancement. At this stage, most paid virtually no attention to these entreaties. Stearns was ever-present during Coolidge's gubernatorial years, although the relationship was far different, for example, from the one that had been employed to date between President Wilson and Colonel House. Although Wilson was about to break his relations with House before the end of the negotiations in Europe, the Colonel had spent the first six years of Wilson's presidency as his alter-ego, representing his interests in Europe for years, while also providing counsel on all manner of foreign and domestic issues. Frank Stearns did virtually none of this, which is one of the main reasons Coolidge liked having him around. Stearns was well aware of the need to stay within the unwritten boundaries the pair had established. When a friend pointed out to Stearns that "you have great influence with the Governor," he replied, "Yes, perhaps more even than you think, but it will last just as long as I don't try to use it, and not one minute longer."[97] Coolidge continued to refuse any tangible tokens of generosity Stearns tried to offer. The Governor sincerely appreciated the work Stearns continued to do behind the scenes to advance his standing in various political circles, but mostly he had come to enjoy his companionship, although even that aspect of their relationship was sometimes rather odd. Coolidge didn't like to be alone, so he would often invite Stearns to meet him in the Governor's office. Sometimes they would chat, but just as often, they would simply sit together, smoke a cigar, and after a while, Coolidge would go back to work and Stearns would go about his business. This was the kind of "socializing" that the taciturn Governor welcomed, and Stearns was more than happy to comply.

One of the first bits of reality to confront Governor Coolidge was the ratification of the 18th Amendment that banned the sale and consumption of alcohol anywhere in the United States. Coolidge, who had been known to drink an occasional beer, was not a supporter of the amendment, but his personal feelings were irrelevant. Anyone familiar with Coolidge knew he would enforce the law of the land. When the Massachusetts state legislature passed a bill that sought to get around the amendment by authorizing some sales of wine and beer, he vetoed it on constitutional grounds. Coolidge as an executive was not shy about taking out his veto pen, particularly in the areas of government expenditures. He made it clear early in his tenure that he was going to guard the public purse very carefully. This included a veto that would have increased the salaries of the members of the legislature. Coolidge happily embraced a recent amendment to the Massachusetts Constitution that centralized the budget operations of the state, providing the Governor the final say on what gets sent to the legislature for annual appropriations. He used this new authority to trim approximately $4 million from the state budget in his first year as Governor.

The month of April 1919 saw the largest convoy of ships returning with soldiers from Europe back to Boston. Five other governors joined Coolidge to welcome returnees from the New England Yankee Division on April 22. They were afforded a massive celebration, including a parade that lasted five hours in temperatures that were only in the high 40s. Coolidge stood silent nearly the entire time, stoically following the proceedings, much to the astonishment of one of his colleagues. New Hampshire Governor John Bartlett noted that Coolidge uttered only a single sentence to him between the time he said hello until his departure. It was halfway through the event when Coolidge said, "Governor, I think you will find that if you put one foot on the rail and lean in my position a while and then change to the other foot, you will find it will rest you." "I tried it," Bartlett replied, "and sure enough it was a relief. But I could not, and cannot now, comprehend a man who could stand five hours and have nothing else to say."[98] Many politicians had similar experiences. Biographer Claude Fuess relates the following anecdotes:

> The tale was told of the ride which [Coolidge] took with a friend to a place thirty miles inland from Boston, where the Governor had to make a speech. Not a word was exchanged on the way out in the automobile. On the return journey there was also utter silence until they approached the seashore, when Coolidge turned and said confidentially, 'It is cooler here.'
>
> He once rode with John N. Cole from Andover to Northampton, a distance of more than a hundred miles, in the Governor's car. Mr. Cole, acquainted with Coolidge's moods, sat looking out the window at the scenery until the Governor, just as they turned to enter Massasoit Street, said, in all sincerity, 'Pleasant ride, wasn't it?'[99]

Governor or not, this side of Coolidge's personality wasn't changing. In fact, he had a pretty good comeback for those who criticized the "Silent Cal" nature of his personality. He was known to simply say, "I have never been hurt by what I have not said."[100]

Coolidge did understand the need to speak to groups as Governor, and he did so throughout the state. He crafted his own addresses and took care to be precise in his word choices. Coolidge avoided ad-libbing. It made him uncomfortable and created the risk that he might misspeak or perhaps his meaning would be misinterpreted. One of his favorite speeches in his first year as Governor took place on the campus of his alma mater. Coolidge, who had often returned to Amherst for commencement celebrations, finally had his turn to speak at one in June 1919. "I should fail in my duty and neglect my deep conviction," he told the graduates, "if I did not declare that in my day there was no better place to educate a young man."[101] The Governor would need all his education and training as he was about to confront the greatest challenge of his career to date.

4. The Boston Police Strike

The most significant source of conflict confronting Governor Coolidge in his first year in office was the clash between labor and management. It was the issue that presented the greatest risk to societal stability, not only in Massachusetts but also across large pockets of the country. The rise of the working man in the Russian Revolution struck fear in political leaders across the United States, who were anxious about any spark that might lead to a similar eruption closer to home. Within this context, it was the general strike in Seattle, Washington, in February 1919, that put the entire nation on edge. The walkout in Seattle began with shipyard workers but quickly swelled thanks to sympathy strikes that spanned more than 100 locals affiliated with the Seattle Central Labor Council. While the workers agreed to maintain services related to critical infrastructure such as sanitation, hospital laundry, and the fire department, the city was essentially shut down from all normal operations. The Russian influence was widespread, with pamphlets encouraging workers to rise up and overthrow their powerful bosses. According to one leaflet entitled *Russia Did It*, the people of Seattle were warned:

> You are doomed to wage slavery till you die unless you wake up, realize that you and the boss have nothing in common, that the employing class must be overthrown, and that you, the workers, must take over the control of your jobs, and through them, the control over your lives.[102]

RUSSIA DID IT

SHIPYARD WORKERS—You left the shipyards to enforce your demands for higher wages. Without you your employers are helpless. Without you they cannot make one cent of profit—their whole system of robbery has collapsed.

The shipyards are idle; the toilers have withdrawn even tho the owners of the yards are still there. Are your masters building ships? No. Without your labor power it would take all the shipyard employers of Seattle and Tacoma working eight hours a day the next thousand years to turn out one ship. Of what use are they in the shipyards?

It is you and you alone who build the ships; you create all the wealth of society today; you make possible the $75,000 sable coats for millionaires' wives. It is you alone who can build the ships.

They can't build the ships. You can. Why don't you?

There are the shipyards; more ships are urgently needed; you alone can build them. If the masters continue their dog-in-the-manger attitude, not able to build the ships themselves and not allowing the workers to, there is only one thing left for you to do.

IV-23: Pamphlet from the general strike in Seattle, WA, February 1919

Seattle Mayor Ole Hanson was quick to blame the Russian Bolsheviks for bringing anarchy to his city. He claimed on February 9 that the "sympathetic strike was called in the exact manner as was the revolution in Petrograd."[103] Hanson emerged defiant while his

IV-24: Seattle Mayor Ole Hansen

city went eerily silent. He told reporters, "Any man who attempts to take over the control of municipal government functions here will be shot on sight."[104] As the city ground to a halt, public opinion quickly shifted away from the workers, with the press leading the barrage of attacks on the strikers. Even some union leaders grew concerned as they feared a national backlash against their cause if things weren't settled soon. A number of the workers gave in to the pressure and began to cross the picket lines, and within a couple of more days, the sympathy strikes were all over. Hanson was widely praised for his response to the situation, but political leaders across the country were concerned that their city could be next.

Governor Coolidge had one work stoppage to deal with pretty much right out of the gate. In April 1919, the telephone operators in Boston walked out, causing an immediate impact on a city that had come to rely on this new form of communication. As the strike persisted, the governor was encouraged to intervene. Coolidge was primarily pro-business but never in a punitive way to the workers. He sought to understand their grievances and believed in the give and take of labor/management relations. In this instance, he did put his thumb on the scale, making it known that he was inquiring whether he had the authority for state employees to take over these positions. Once the striking operators were informed of this effort, the dispute ended rather quickly. Coolidge largely dodged the bullet on this one, but a far more serious walkout was right around the corner. This next incident would put the Governor to the test, ultimately focusing on a single week, and even a single sentence, that would eventually lead Calvin Coolidge to the presidency of the United States.

The American Federation of Labor (AFL) was one of the dominant unions in the United States in the first couple of decades of the 20th Century. With a surge in sign-ups in the post-war period, national membership topped four million workers. Some of this expansion came in the public sector, including some police departments for the first time in American history. By the midpoint of 1919, the AFL had signed up 37 police departments, including those in Los Angeles, Miami, and Washington, D.C. In Boston, the force of approximately 1,500 officers was disgruntled, to say the least. They were upset about wages, working conditions in dilapidated station houses, and work hours that often ran well past 10 hours per day. Management was sympathetic and had even awarded the men a raise of $200 per year (double what the rest of the city workers received), but the police rightfully argued that this increase didn't even overcome the rise in prices due to post-war inflation. The members of the Boston police were specifically prohibited in the Department Manual from unionizing. For the last several years, they had operated under an informal arrangement called the Boston Police Association, but conditions were such that they were determined to organize and fight for their rights. On August 9, they formally applied to join the AFL, and two days later their request was approved.

Based on a law passed in 1906, the Commissioner that oversaw the Boston Police Department was appointed by the Governor for a term of five years. At the same time, the Commissioner was also accountable to the mayor of Boston for all matters related to the size of the force, wages, and many elements of working conditions. The previous year, Governor McCall had tabbed Edwin Curtis, a former Boston mayor, to take on the duties of the Commissioner after his predecessor, Stephen O'Meara, suddenly died. Commissioner Curtis was crystal clear in his view of the situation. Shortly before the application was submitted to join the AFL, Curtis stated, "I desire to say to the members of the force that I am firmly of the opinion that a police officer cannot consistently belong to a union and perform his sworn duty."[105] He pointed out the inherent conflict for a police officer ordered to break up violence on a picket line while perhaps having split loyalties between the public interest and the cause of organized labor. Now that unionization had occurred, Curtis left no doubt about his position as he issued the following order: "No member of the force shall join or belong to any organization, club or body composed of present or present and past members of the force which is affiliated with or a part of any organization, club or body outside the department."[106] Boston Mayor Andrew Peters was trying to keep his police force from walking out, so he was urging cooperation. This included an initial appeal to Governor Coolidge to get involved. "I feel it is not my duty to communicate with the Commissioner on the subject,"[107] the Governor responded, offering his tacit endorsement of the policies and statements to date by Commissioner Curtis.

Curtis wasn't interested in compromise. In fact, he doubled down on his firm approach by announcing that 19 union leaders would be fired if the union was not disbanded by September 4. Union President John McInnes, a respected member of the force who had served his country in Cuba during the Spanish-American War, threatened that his men would strike if any discipline was imposed on these union leaders. In the meantime, a desperate Mayor Peters cobbled together a Citizens' Committee of Thirty-Four led by James Storrow to assess the situation and make a recommendation to him and the involved parties on how to avoid what everyone expected would be chaos if the police walked off their beats. Storrow and his colleagues met with all the stakeholders, including Commissioner Curtis and the union leadership. They tried to see all sides and quickly proposed a compromise solution. The Storrow Committee recommended that the police formally withdraw from the AFL, all the men be allowed to return to work with no discipline imposed on the leaders, and arbitration would be utilized to settle all other outstanding issues. Mayor Peters signed on immediately, telling Commissioner Curtis that, in his view, "The report [of the Storrow Committee] commends itself to me as a wise method of dealing with the subject. If acceptable to you and the men, it affords a speedy and, it seems to me, satisfactory settlement of the whole question."[108] Commissioner Curtis had a very different take, refusing to be a party to the proposed compromise. In his view, these union leaders had violated policies with which they had previously agreed to comply. He was past the point of simply letting bygones be bygones. On September 3, Peters and Storrow appealed to Coolidge to step in, but once again, the Governor stood by his police commissioner, deferring any decisions in the matter to him. After a plea from Mayor Peters, Curtis agreed to postpone any disciplinary action until September 8, but he insisted there would be no further delay after that point.

Governor Coolidge left town for the weekend of September 6-7, ironically speaking to a gathering of the AFL in another part of the state. His remarks avoided any mention of the tense happenings unfolding in the state capital. Upon his return to Boston, everything came to a head, playing out over the course of the week ahead. On Monday, September

IV-25: Governor Coolidge (left) and Boston Police Commissioner Edwin Curtis

8, Commissioner Curtis confirmed his decision that arbitration was out of the question and that the 19 union leaders were all to be terminated for violating department policy with their affiliation with the AFL. He also warned that any officer who opted to strike against the city would face punishment, including possible termination. Knowing any more appeals to Curtis were a waste of breath, Mayor Peters made one last attempt with Governor Coolidge to intervene. That plea was soundly rejected by the Governor, who never wavered in his support for Commissioner Curtis to call the shots in the dispute. "It seems plain that the duty of issuing orders and enforcing their observance lies with the Commissioner of Police and with that no one has any authority to interfere," Coolidge informed Peters. "We must all support the Commissioner in the execution of the laws."[109] When the mayor made one final push for arbitration, the Governor shut him down, replying simply, "Well, I won't do it."[110]

With the police commissioner locked into his position and no relief coming from the Governor's office, the union called for a vote of the entire force to walk off their jobs in protest over the firing of the 19 union leaders. The vote, which was held at Fay Hall, concluded around 5:45 pm on Tuesday, September 9. The tally was 1,134 to 2 to strike. A total of 1,117 policemen, representing just under 75% of the total force, immediately walked off their jobs, leaving large swaths of the city defenseless against criminal activity. The authorities now had a different problem on their hands – how to protect the safety of the people with only a quarter of the police force willing to work. Mayor Peters immediately pushed to call out the State Guard as an interim measure of protection, but Commissioner Curtis thought the move premature. He believed that the remaining officers, along with a small number of additional security personnel available and the expectation of volunteers from the public at large, would be sufficient to keep the peace. Governor Coolidge continued to support the police commissioner, and after dinner with Stearns, he retired at his usual time around 10:00 pm. Not calling out the State Guard that night was the only decision throughout the entire affair that Coolidge would later regret.

As dark fell upon the city of Boston, the citizenry awoke to the fact that the police were largely absent from their beats. The mischief began rather innocently, such as with illegal gambling out in the open. But then, some of those wandering the deserted streets saw an opportunity they couldn't resist. The first of the store windows to be smashed came shortly after midnight. By 2:00 am, the looting was becoming widespread. There was some rioting as well, with little to be done by the handful of officers still on patrol against large crowds feeling free to take advantage of the security vacuum that had been let loose by the police walkout. The newspapers chronicled the night's mischief with special editions released on the morning of Wednesday, September 10. "For the first time in the memory Boston was given over to lawlessness," screamed the coverage on page one of the *Boston Globe.*[111] "Lawlessness, disorder, looting, such as was never known in this city, ran riot last night in South Boston, the

The Boston Daily Globe EXTRA

VOL. XCVI—NO. 72 BOSTON, WEDNESDAY MORNING, SEPTEMBER 10, 1919—EIGHTEEN PAGES PRICE TWO CENTS

MOBS SMASH WINDOWS, LOOT STORES
WILD NIGHT FOLLOWS STRIKE OF POLICE

WASHINGTON ST STORES SACKED

Goods Worth Thousands of Dollars Are Stolen

Plundering Everywhere, Hoodlums Roam South Boston Streets

Lawless Throngs Surge Through Unprotected City, Demolishing Property—Members of Union Quit Stations at 5:45 in Afternoon, Leaving Only 30 Out of Usual 420 Patrolmen On Duty—Metropolitan Police Rushed to Quell Trouble in South Boston

STRIKING POLICEMEN MEET AT FAY HALL

FIFTY STUDENTS AT HARVARD ENROLLED

Will Help Protect Life and Property in Boston

SUMMARY OF THE STRIKE SITUATION

Peters Calls on Citizens to Aid Officials of the City in Preserving Order

Volunteers to Begin Duties at 8 This Morning—Coolidge

IV-26: Front page of "The Boston Globe" after the first night of looting during the Boston Police Strike, September 10, 1919

North and West ends, and the downtown sections of the municipality, following the departure of the striking policemen from their station houses," declared the *Boston Herald*.[112] The papers uniformly blamed the striking police officers for their dereliction of duty and abandonment of their community. They were also not shy about invoking the threats hanging over the country linked to the recent worker-led revolution in Russia. "Bolshevism in the United States is no longer a specter," proclaimed the Philadelphia *Public Ledger*. "Boston in chaos reveals its sinister substance." *The New York Times* labeled the walkout a "Boston essay in Bolshevism,"[113] while Massachusetts Senator Henry Lodge asserted, "If the American Federation of Labor succeeds in getting hold of the police in Boston it will go all over the country, and we shall be in measurable distance of Soviet government by labor unions."[114] From these perspectives, the police strike in Boston had very real implications for the entire nation.

The first night of the strike had indeed been a rough one for Boston, but frankly, it could have been worse. That thought was very much on the mind of the Governor as he awoke on the morning of Wednesday the 10th. Coolidge regretted the lawless destruction that he felt could have been prevented if Commissioner Curtis had agreed to call for support from the State Guard. Still standing solidly with the Commissioner on all of his other decisions, Coolidge wanted to be sure the streets would be safe while the labor conflict played itself out. An initial contingent of the State Guard was called out, but not a wholesale deployment. Things were moving rapidly, and Coolidge didn't want to be seen as overreacting to the situation. The political maneuverings then began in earnest, as Mayor Peters decided it was time for him to take charge. With his own legal advisers, Peters determined that the ultimate authority over the city's police resided with him, not the Commissioner appointed by the Governor. He was not only concerned about the immediate danger of violence and lawlessness but there were also rumblings from some of the other powerful unions in town to walk off their jobs in sympathy with the police, creating a Seattle-like situation that could bring the entire city to its knees. Mayor Peters suspended Commissioner Curtis, put himself in charge, and sought more support from the State Guard. He also welcomed 390 citizen volunteers to bolster the force. This coincided with just over a thousand applications for gun permits so that more citizens could protect themselves and their property. As for the union, its leaders were standing firm in the face of the demands to sever ties with the AFL. Union President McInnes insisted on the night of the 10th, "Nothing doing. A police union and affiliation with the American Federation of Labor is what we are striking for and what we will accept only as a settlement."[115]

Day two of the strike was indeed the most lawless. Store owners boarded up their windows, and many stood guard day and night with their own firearms prominently on display, but it wasn't enough to stop the mob mentality that had begun to permeate parts of Boston. A riot at Scollay Square turned deadly. Storekeepers were run off, and goods were ripe for the taking. Shots were occasionally fired, with four deaths reported as a result of the mayhem. As additional members of the State Guard finally arrived shortly after midnight, with bayonets fixed to their weapons as clear warnings of the fate the rioters may face if they continued their illegal activities, things finally began to calm. It was a second rough night, and Governor Coolidge was determined that it would be the last of the violence.

On Thursday the 11th, Governor Coolidge called together his own legal team. This included Acting Attorney General Henry Wyman, who had recently been placed in the position after the resignation of his predecessor Henry Atwill, as well as attorney Albert Pillsbury upon whom the Governor had come to rely for counsel. The brain trust uncovered a statute that authorized the Massachusetts Governor to call on any policeman in the state to come to his aid. In the Governor's mind, this authority trumped anything Mayor Peters could claim, so Coolidge boldly took charge of the entire situation. His first act was to immediately reinstate Commissioner Curtis. Coolidge then called out the entire State Guard, more than 5,000 troops, far more than the striking police officers and plenty to keep the peace. "The entire state guard

IV-27: Governor Coolidge inspecting troops from the Massachusetts State Guard during the Boston Police Strike, September 1919

of Massachusetts has been called out," Coolidge publicly declared. "Under the Constitution the governor is the commander in chief thereof, by an authority of which he could not, if he choose, divest himself. That command I must and will exercise."[116]

Coolidge's most controversial decision, however, was still pending. The Attorney General sided with Commissioner Curtis in the legal determination that the striking police officers had abandoned their posts, making them all subject to immediate termination. All eyes centered on Governor Coolidge and whether he would support this decision. Some of his political advisers urged caution at this drastic step, warning of political peril in his upcoming reelection campaign if he simply tossed the police out of their jobs. "Governor Coolidge, if you issue that proclamation you will defeat and probably destroy the Republican party in Massachusetts," these advisers claimed. "You will certainly make it impossible for yourself to hold another public office." Coolidge never wavered. "It is not necessary for me to hold another office," he declared in response. "It does not matter whether I am re-elected."[117] In this crucial hour, with the immediate fate of the striking officers and the citizens of Boston hanging in the balance, Governor Coolidge went public in complete alignment with his police commissioner. "The action of the police in leaving their posts of duty is not a strike. It is a desertion," the Governor declared. "There is nothing to arbitrate, nothing to compromise. In my personal opinion there are no conditions under which the men can return to the force."[118] Now there was no going back. The striking policemen were out, Curtis was to begin immediately recruiting their replacements, and the State Guard began pouring into Boston to keep the peace in the meantime.

By now, the entire nation was focused on the happenings in Boston. This was a test for the American labor movement, including how much support the people would provide when their safety was being put at risk. "We are in the eye of the nation," reported the *Herald* on Friday the 12th. "Other cities are looking on. If the Soviet theory succeeds here, it will spread to other battle grounds and become nation wide."[119] Newspapers around the country came out strongly in favor of Governor Coolidge and Commissioner Curtis, standing on the principle that public duty came first over private interests. Even President Wilson weighed in on the ongoing conflict. Wilson was in the midst of an arduous railway tour of the West, trying to drum up public support for his League of Nations, when reporters sought his views on the crisis in Boston. The Democrat Wilson was unequivocal in his support for the position of the Republican Governor of Massachusetts. Wilson blamed the striking policemen for leaving the city "at the mercy of an army of thugs," calling their actions "a crime against civilization." The President added, "In my judgment the obligation of a policeman is as sacred and direct as the obligation of a soldier. He is a public servant, not a private employee, and the whole honor of the community is in his hands."[120] This was the prevailing view throughout the country.

Governor Coolidge and Mayor Peters could both breathe a sigh of relief when the other leading unions in town voted on the 10th and 11th not to advance sympathy strikes in support of the police. By now, many of the strikers saw the writing on the wall and sought an end to the walkout, requesting reinstatement if they agreed to return to their beats. These entreaties fell on deaf ears with Commissioner Curtis. Things were too far along, and the damage could not be reversed. For the first time, Samuel Gompers, the national president of the AFL, tried to step into the fray on behalf of the policemen. He sent a telegram on Friday the 12th to Governor Coolidge, requesting a cooling down period to allow the police to return to work and await an already planned national conference set for the following month in Washington, D.C. to help adjudicate the dispute along with similar issues already on the table. Governor Coolidge was steadfast in his rejection of the idea in his response to Gompers on Saturday, the 13th. Coolidge continued to stand by Commissioner Curtis. According to the Governor, "He [Curtis] has decided that the men here abandoned their sworn duty and has accordingly declared their places vacant. I shall support the Commissioner in the execution of law and maintenance of order."[121] Gompers considered the Governor's position and then decided to try one last time to save his men from termination. "The question at issue is not one of law and order," Gompers asserted in his follow-up communique, "but the assumption of an autocratic and unwarranted position by the Commissioner of Police, who is not responsible to the people of Boston, but who is appointed by you. Whatever disorder has occurred is due to his order in which the right of the policemen has been denied, a right which has heretofore never been questioned."[122] The Governor's response, for the first time, made the name Calvin Coolidge known throughout the land.

In his telegram of Sunday, September 14, Coolidge reminded Gompers of the legal issues involved, including the authorities of the police commissioner to which the Governor had no right to overrule. He further rejected the notion of submitting the issue to the upcoming conference in Washington as not relevant to the current situation. He then got to the heart of the matter. "Your assertion that the Commissioner was wrong cannot justify the wrong of leaving the city unguarded," Coolidge wrote. "That furnished the opportunity, the criminal element furnished the action."[123] He then offered the lone sentence, the 15 words, that would eventually land him in the Oval Office, informing Gompers (and the entire country), "There is no right to strike against the public safety by anybody, anywhere, any time."[124] That was the end of it, and the people and the press ate it up. Law and order, stability – that's what the people were craving in this rather chaotic post-war environment, and Calvin Coolidge was giving it to them, not only in Boston but as a guidepost for the rest of the country.

The reactions to Governor Coolidge's bold stand on the side of public duty drew universal approbation. According to the New York *Sun*, "A plain New England gentleman, whose calm determination to uphold the law and maintain order in the situation caused by the Boston police walkout has made him a national figure."[125] The *Boston Transcript* commented, "The Governor was the Commander-in-chief, the people of the commonwealth were the invincible army, the issue was America, and in the triumph of that issue all America triumphs."[126] *The Wall Street Journal* went even further, declaring, "Governor Coolidge has shown the fibre of which presidents ought to be made."[127] Behind the scenes, Coolidge's friends were also starting to see him in a new light. Dwight Morrow sent the following note to their mutual friend, Frank Stearns:

> For the last I have been abroad dealing with all sort of government officials. Some of them have been Socialists like [Albert] Thomas, the great socialist leader in France. Some of them have been from old conservative families. … I have about come to the conclusion that the division of the people in the world is not really between conservative and radical, but people that are real people and people that are not. Calvin is one of the fellows who is real. He really wants to make things better not to pretend to make them better.[128]

As for Calvin Coolidge, what was he thinking about all this? He humbly informed his father, "This was a service that had to be done and I have been glad to do it. The result won't matter to me but it will matter a great deal to the rest of America."[129] He was wrong. It would matter to him as well, as that single sentence of defiance resonated across the American electorate, including with some of the political operatives who would have a say at the next Republican National Convention.

5. National Prominence

Frank Stearns was ready to capitalize on the new-found fame for his friend, the Governor. He quickly rushed to print a book of Coolidge's major speeches entitled *Have Faith in Massachusetts*, which was the theme from his inaugural address as the President of the state Senate back in January 1914. His statements from the recent strike were prominently featured as well. Stearns worked with publisher Houghton Mifflin to print thousands of copies that he could send not only around the state leading up to the fall elections but also to strategic political leaders across the country, thinking ahead to the presidential contest of 1920. Coolidge unanimously received his party's re-nomination for Governor just nine days after his steadfast telegram to Samuel Gompers. He would face Democratic Richard Long in a rematch from the previous year.

In the meantime, Governor Coolidge went back to work. The previous year, Massachusetts held a constitutional convention to consider the first large block of changes to that document since before the Civil War. While the progressive ideals of the Initiative and Referendum were adopted, many of the more radical proposals were rejected when put to a vote of the people. But one other significant change was approved and put Governor Coolidge in a particularly awkward position. The political apparatus of the state had become unwieldy, with more than 100 agencies and commissions responsible for a piece of the operations. The constitution required the Governor to reorganize this structure into no more than twenty agencies, getting rid of hundreds of jobs (including leadership positions) in the process. The entire mandate was fraught with political peril for the Governor, who would open himself up to personal and political condemnation for each executive post he chose to eliminate. Coolidge could have postponed the action, as it did not have to be completed for another two years, but he refused to shirk from what he believed to be his duty. He did wait to announce his decisions until after the fall election, in which he trounced his opponent to earn a second term. After beating Long the previous year by only 17,000 votes, he surged past his Democratic opponent by a margin of 125,000 votes in the rematch. The people of Massachusetts were so firmly in the Governor's corner that he nearly captured the vote of Boston, which remained overwhelmingly Democratic in its composition. Even the nation's leading Democrat seemed to be in Coolidge's corner. President Wilson sent Coolidge a telegram from the White House stating, "I congratulate you upon your election as a victory for law and order. When that is the issue all Americans stand together."[130] Shortly after the votes were counted, Governor Coolidge published the results of his reorganization decisions. Because so many state politicians were potentially affected, he performed this duty primarily by himself. Indeed, he made some political enemies in the process and likely lost a few friends, but overall, the reaction was positive. According to an editorial in the *Boston Herald*:

> Nearly all of them are good, some of them altogether admirable. There are exceedingly few, if any, of the scandalous sort which usually creep into any wholesale award of patronage. On the whole the Governor has shown intelligence and ingenuity of a high order. He has recognized the various elements of the state, and he has infused into its service some 'new blood.'[131]

Across the consolidated set of 20 state agencies, Coolidge made 64 leadership appointments, which were culled from the 144 positions under the prior construct. Like the *Herald*, the Executive Council also offered broad approval, sanctioning all but one of these selections. Only the recommendation for the Chair of the Department of Public Works failed to receive immediate consent. As for Coolidge, he offered the following perspective: "They say the police strike required executive courage; reorganizing one hundred and eighteen departments into eighteen required a good deal more."[132] In fact, the Governor concluded, "I am glad it is done! It is the worst job I ever had to do! I shall never have to do anything like that again."[133]

IV-28: Governor Coolidge, 1920 (age 48)

Coolidge carried significant momentum heading into 1920. He had received national acclaim for his resolute posture on the side of law and order during the Boston police strike, had won reelection as Governor in a landslide vote, and earned widespread praise for his deft handling of the state reorganization undertaking. To top it off, at the end of November, the Republican Club of Massachusetts took it upon itself to be the first to advocate for Coolidge as the next President of the United States. The *Boston Transcript* also began to push in this same direction. "Governor Coolidge now looms so large before the nation with his wonderful triumph and so impressive a verdict by the Massachusetts electorate behind him," wrote reporter Charles Baxter, "that he must be given serious consideration by the Republican Party in the selection of its national leaders for the presidential campaign of next year."[134] Bruce Barton offered a similar perspective in *Collier's* that same month, highlighting the essence of Coolidge's appeal to a large group of citizens he labeled the "silent majority." "The great majority of Americans," Barton wrote, "are neither radicals nor reactionaries. They are middle-of-the-road folks who own their own homes and work hard and would like to have the government get back to its old habits of meddling with their lives as little as possible. … It sometimes seems as if this great silent majority had no spokesman. But Coolidge belongs with that crowd, he lives like them, he works like them, and understands."[135] Perhaps, he should be their next President.

The prevailing sentiment for the Republican nomination at the time of the armistice was for a return to power by Wilson antagonist Theodore Roosevelt. But Roosevelt died in January 1919, leaving a wide-open field for the upcoming canvass. People like Frank Stearns were pushing to include Coolidge's name in the mix, ramping up his letter-writing campaign, which often included more copies of *Have Faith in Massachusetts* to help people get to know what Coolidge was all about. Stearns didn't stop there, however. He opened up presidential campaign headquarters in both Washington, D.C. and Chicago, the site of the Republican National Convention. He hired party stalwart James Reynolds, who had worked in the Treasury Department under Roosevelt and recently served as the Secretary to the Republican National Committee, to run the campaign. But just as quickly, Coolidge shut the whole thing down. "I do not care to express any opinion as to what should be done by men entrusted with affairs at Washington or elsewhere, in regard to matters which have been committed to their decision," Coolidge announced at the time. "I am devoting my energies to administering the affairs of Massachusetts, and that I shall continue to do so long as I am Governor."[136] Coolidge was being true to himself, focusing on the duties assigned to him by the voters of Massachusetts, but he was also playing the role of an astute politician. Coolidge knew there were others further ahead of him at this stage in the national race, and despite his recent rise in some circles, he correctly assessed that it would be nearly impossible for him to overtake the other front-runners heading into the convention. As he confided with his father, "You know there is no chance for me except when it may appear none of the leaders can get it. Then if it all my chance will come."[137] Coolidge would go about his business for the next several months, perhaps make a few speeches to continue to have his name in the mix, but his focus would be on serving the people of Massachusetts and then wait for a possible draft at the convention if a deadlock among the leaders materialized.

The Republican Party seemed to be coalescing around three leading candidates for the 1920 nomination, each with very different backgrounds. Army Chief of Staff Leonard Wood was seen as the Rooseveltian candidate, having served as TR's commander in Cuba during the Spanish-American War, his friend and ally throughout Roosevelt's presidency, and very much aligned in both style and substance with the former President. Illinois Governor Frank Lowden was also gaining momentum. Lowden was probably the closest to Coolidge among the front-runners in terms of ideological beliefs. Like Coolidge, Lowden had recently reorganized his state's government, embraced new authorities to centrally manage the Illinois budget, fought to reduce taxes in his state, favored women's suffrage, and came down hard when strikes got out of hand. Finally, there was Hiram Johnson, the U.S. Senator (and former Governor) from California, who was leading the progressive wing of the Republican Party. Johnson had broken with his party when the progressives and the Old Guard had split in 1912, but with the Progressive Party now defunct, he was back in the Republican fold, aggressively pushing the reforms that had become synonymous with the progressive movement. The primary issues in the campaign were twofold: whether or not to support President Wilson's League of Nations as negotiated in the Treaty of Versailles and the post-war economy. The latter topic spanned the areas of tariffs, taxation, rising unemployment, price stability, the plight of farmers, and the overall size of the Federal budget.

Governor Coolidge's name continued to simmer beneath the surface, but he did little to promote his own cause while many states were holding primaries to select delegates to the Republican National Convention. He did speak out occasionally, including at a campaign-like event just before the Massachusetts primary at the Home Market Club in Boston that also featured a couple of other fringe candidates, Senators Irvine Lenroot of Wisconsin and Warren Harding of Ohio. Coolidge stumbled a bit in this forum, coming off as more of a technocrat with his detailed commentary on intricate economic matters underlying his support for high tariffs and low income taxes. Senator Harding had a stronger reception for his folksy advocacy of what he called a "return to normalcy," advocating for a calmer era that would be less radical when it came to government actions and more stable for the citizenry. He also charmed the people of New England with his humor, telling the audience that "If I lived in Massachusetts I should be for Governor Coolidge for President. Coming from Ohio, I am for Harding."[138] None of the speeches at this event seemed to have much impact on the outcome of the Massachusetts primary that month. When the state's Republicans cast their ballots, Coolidge finished a distant fifth in his home state while Wood captured 70% of the vote.

With three legitimate front-runners heading into the convention, it was always going to be difficult for any candidate to emerge with a majority to seal the nomination. Plus, each of the three had baggage that might be difficult to overcome. Johnson's previous break with the party was still a sore subject for many in the Republican establishment, making it difficult to find a path for him to a majority. Wood and Lowden were being slowed by money – not that they didn't have enough, but rather the perception that they had too much behind their campaigns. Press reports led to an impromptu congressional investigation that uncovered Wood's campaign having already spent a whopping $1.8 million during the primary season, most of which was funded by a small number of millionaire backers. Governor Lowden, who had obtained personal wealth by marrying into the family that ran the Pullman Railroad Company, had spent more than $400,000, including rumors that some of that cash had been funneled directly into the pockets of some convention delegates to secure their votes. These financial disclosures were all tinged with whispers of corruption, of buying votes by candidates who would be beholden to their sponsors. Candidates like Harding and Coolidge had little to fear in this regard. Harding's campaign had spent only $113,000 to date, while Coolidge's numbers came in at a paltry $68,395, about 20% of which came from the pocket of Frank Stearns.

Stearns and Reynolds led the Coolidge contingent when the Republicans finally gathered in Chicago on June 6, 1920, to solidify the party platform and select their nominees for President and Vice President. Massachusetts Lieutenant Governor Channing Cox also made the trip, and was very much in Coolidge's corner, as were a handful of loyal Amherst alums, including Dwight Morrow, the executive in J.P. Morgan's financial empire. Morrow and Coolidge had known each other for years but had rarely been close. Nevertheless, Morrow continued his path into the Coolidge camp, gaining confidence in his quiet former classmate, particularly in these last few years. Heading into the convention in Chicago, Morrow spoke of the characteristics that set Coolidge apart from his competitors.

> He has real courage entirely free from bluster. He has faith, -- a profound faith in the fundamental soundness of democracy, and that faith has begotten, as it did in Lincoln's case, a great faith on the part of the people in him. He has tolerance, and when we think of the next four years either in our domestic or in our foreign problems, an indispensable quality is toleration. He has knowledge, and there never was a time when it was more true that knowledge is power. Finally, he has character, and not only this country, but the whole world, is hungering for a leader with character.[139]

If the front-runners stumbled, people like Coolidge and Harding and Lenroot were all waiting in the wings with their supporters on hand, ready to lobby for their man as the best dark horse alternative.

Coolidge selected Fred Gillett to place his name into nomination. Gillett was not only Coolidge's own congressman, but he was also the Speaker of the House of Representatives. Compared to several of the other nominating speeches, Gillett's remarks were relatively brief.

> Our candidate is a man of few words, and in that respect I shall imitate him. And I only wish I could imitate his effective use of words. ... We need an era of hard sense, of old freedom. We need to reinvigorate the homely, orderly virtues which have made America great. … He is as patient as Lincoln, as silent as Grant, as diplomatic as McKinley, with the political instinct of Roosevelt. His character is as

> firm as the mountains of his native state. Like them, his head is above the clouds, and he stands unshaken amid the tumult and the storm.[140]

With the 19th Amendment winding its way through state governments, women would have the constitutional right to vote in time for the 1920 election. As such, the party conventions brought a number of women onto the floor to participate in the democratic process. Only one woman was found in the Massachusetts delegation. That was Alexandra Pfeiffer, who seconded Coolidge's nomination. "If you ask what the nation most needs to-day," Pfeiffer announced, "it is the simplicity in private and in public life of Calvin Coolidge; the fidelity in public service of Calvin Coolidge; the loyalty to American institutions of Calvin Coolidge; and the humanity in public deeds of Calvin Coolidge."[141] All this advocacy aside, the applause for Coolidge's nomination quieted after less than a minute, a fraction of what was being generated for the likes of Wood, Lowden, and Johnson.

The convention broke for the night after four roll call ballots. Wood was strongly in front but well short of a majority. Lowden was a solid second, and Johnson a distant third. Coolidge was seventh, with his support almost entirely from his home state, and even that wasn't unanimous. After two previous conventions in which the Republicans were largely fractured, party leaders were concerned about a drawn-out, contentious path to selecting their nominee. Smoke-filled backroom meetings spun up across Chicago that night, the most famous of which took place in a suite at the Blackstone Hotel. This gathering represented the Old Guard of the Senate, led by the likes of Henry Lodge of Massachusetts, Charles Curtis of Kansas, Reed Smoot of Utah, and Frank Brandegee of Connecticut, along with influential newspaperman George Harvey. With other senators flowing in and out of the room all night, every conceivable combination was weighed to get to a nominee who would unify the party. Each of the three front-runners was problematic for large numbers of delegates, and since none of the three was willing to serve as the #2 to any of the others, there didn't seem to be a viable path to a ticket that centered on Wood, Lowden, or Johnson. The conversation eventually wound its way to the second tier of candidates. In this regard, Coolidge was hurt on two fronts. First, the fact that the Massachusetts delegation had not given him its unanimous support was seen as a red flag. Moreover, the most influential Republican from Massachusetts in national politics continued to be Senator Henry Lodge, who happened to be in the suite at the Blackstone Hotel. Lodge and Coolidge had had a cool relationship to date. Lodge was reluctant to concede state prominence to this country lawyer from the western part of his state. He was also leery of someone who was so closely aligned to Murray Crane, his former colleague in the Senate who was outspoken in his opposition to Lodge these days when it came to President Wilson's League of Nations. As a result, Coolidge was never seriously considered in the debates in this particular smoke-filled room.

The one name that seemed to check the most boxes, and elicited the least objections, was their Senate colleague from Ohio, Warren Harding. The gregarious Harding was hardly a leader when it came to pushing an agenda, but he was on the right side of most issues that mattered to the folks in this room. He had stayed loyal to the party's Old Guard when the Roosevelt/Taft split occurred back in 1912, he had always been a reliable party-line vote in the Senate, he supported the League of Nations but *only* if the reservations put forward by Senator Lodge and his allies were adopted, he was the opposite in temperament from the academic elitist currently sitting in the White House, and he hailed from Ohio, which had become the breeding ground for successful presidential aspirants. Importantly, Harding was someone these senators believed they could work with from the other end of Pennsylvania Avenue and perhaps could even control when it came to a legislative agenda. By 2:00 am, the decision was made. The front-runners would still be given a few ballots when the voting resumed in the morning to try to break through the logjam, but if no one emerged, then these senators would throw their weight behind Harding. And that's exactly what happened next.

IV-29: Warren Harding

When Lodge called the convention back to order on Saturday, June 12, things picked up right where they had left off the night before. By the sixth ballot, Wood and Lowden were tied at the top, Johnson remained a distant third, and Harding had inched his way into fourth. On the next ballot, Harding overtook Johnson for third and then surged to the lead on the 9th ballot. By the tenth ballot, it was over. The Lowden followers threw in the towel, handing the nomination to Harding. Harding, who was an avid card player, used a poker-themed comment to describe his rise to the top of the Republican ranks. "I feel like a man who goes in on a pair of eights and comes out with aces full," Harding said.[142]

By the time the Harding celebration subsided, the folks in the sweltering Chicago Coliseum were more than ready to catch their trains and get out of town, but there was still one important duty left to attend to – the selection of the vice presidential nominee. The same senators who had shifted their support to put Harding over the top were now advocating for another of their colleagues for the #2 spot on the ticket. The senators' candidate was Wisconsin's Irvine Lenroot, who many of the Old Guard leaders thought would be a slam dunk first ballot selection. But then something unusual in major party conventions happened, a spontaneous backlash against the party leadership. The delegates remaining in the hall (after some early departures) were not inclined to be dictated to by what was being termed the 'senate cabal,' and when a different name was tossed into the mix, the delegates responded en masse. The triggerman was Wallace McCamant, a delegate from Oregon, who had been one of the many recipients of Frank Stearns's widespread mailing of that book of Coolidge speeches entitled *Have Faith in Massachusetts*. McCamant had read the book cover-to-cover and liked what he saw from the man who had stood up to the striking Boston policemen just a few months before. Coolidge's response to Samuel Gompers that "There is no right to strike against the public safety by anybody, anywhere, any time"[143] continued to resonate and was the kind of calling card that the grass roots delegates wanted to rally around. In the midst of speeches on behalf of the Lenroot candidacy, McCamant stood on a chair in the middle of the Oregon delegation and officially tossed Coolidge's name into the mix for VP. Coolidge, he said, was a man "whose name traveled all across the country last fall when he stood for law and order and for the safety of the republic."[144] In uncharacteristic fashion, the nomination immediately caught fire across the hall. Chants of "Coolidge, Coolidge" were drowning out the names of Lenroot and the handful of other favorite sons being put forward. It was a true political stampede that was reflected in Coolidge's first ballot victory. Eighty-six-year-old Chauncey Depew of New York offered some perspective on this dramatic turn of events. "I have been present at every Republican convention beginning with 1856," Depew later told Coolidge, "and I have never seen such a spontaneous and enthusiastic tribute to a man as the vote for you for vice president."[145] Still in question, however, was whether Coolidge would even accept the nomination. Several months before, he had informed the Republican Party in South Dakota that while he appreciated their support, he declined to be considered as their nominee for the vice presidency. Now that the nomination was his for the taking, he had a decision to make. Still a bit disappointed that he hadn't emerged as the dark horse at the top of the ticket, Coolidge was with Grace at the Adams House in Boston when informed of his nomination for VP. After taking the call, Coolidge tersely told his wife, "Nominated for vice president." Grace responded, "You don't mean it." "Indeed I do," he replied. "You are not going to accept it, are you?" she inquired. "I suppose I shall have to," Coolidge concluded.[146] He then hand-crafted the following statement:

> The nomination for the Vice Presidency, coming to me unsought and unexpectedly, I accept as an honor and a duty. It will be especially pleasing to be associated with my old friend, Senator Warren G. Harding, our candidate for president. The Republican party has adopted a sound platform, chosen a wise leader, and is united. It deserves the confidence of the American people. That confidence I shall endeavor to secure.[147]

Shortly after the Republicans left for home, the Democrats gathered for the first time on the west coast, holding their convention in the city of San Francisco. They also went with a bit of a dark horse, eventually settling on Ohio Governor James Cox over the initial front-runners, former Treasury Secretary William McAdoo and the incumbent Attorney General A. Mitchell Palmer. Cox and his VP-candidate, Franklin Roosevelt of New York, were staunchly pro-Wilson, ready to campaign in favor of his beleaguered League of Nations. While Cox and Roosevelt barnstormed the country, Warren Harding went home to initiate a front porch campaign from his house in Marion, Ohio. While the quiet and reserved Coolidge was personally quite a contrast to the outgoing and convivial Harding, the two were very much aligned on the most important issues of the day.

Harding launched his front porch effort when he formally accepted his nomination on July 22. Five days later, it was Coolidge's one day during the entire canvass to stand out when all eyes centered on the VP candidate's formal acceptance of his party's nomination. All of Northampton came alive with banners and parades for the visiting dignitaries for the so-called "Notification Day." Thousands gathered at Allen Field at Smith College to hear the speeches, which featured Kentucky Governor Edwin Morgan presenting the nomination and Coolidge following with his formal acceptance.

IV-30: Campaign banner for the Republican ticket of Warren Harding and Calvin Coolidge, Notification Day in Northampton, MA, July 27, 1920

> The destiny, the greatness of America lies around the hearthstone. If thrift and industry are taught there, and the example of self-sacrifice oft appears, if honor abide there, and high ideals, if there the building of fortune be subordinate to the building of character, America will live in security, rejoicing in an abundant prosperity and good government at home and in peace, respect, and confidence abroad. If these virtues be absent there is no power that can

IV-31: Coolidge accepting the Republican nomination for Vice President at Notification Day, Northampton, MA, July 27, 1920

supply these blessings. Look well then to the hearthstone, therein all hope for America lies.[148]

These were familiar themes for Coolidge followers, and they were well-received by the hometown crowd.

Coolidge was a minor player in the 1920 election. He put himself on display in Plymouth, where national reporters were eager to learn his story, and were enamored with his small-town roots. Coolidge happily donned his familiar gear as he posed for pictures performing a variety of tasks common to the small farms

IV-32: Coolidge on the farm at Plymouth Notch, VT

of Vermont. He and Grace also made the journey to Marion, where they were graciously welcomed by Warren and Florence Harding. The candidates conferred for a while before appearing on Harding's front porch, at which point the presidential nominee spoke fondly of the #2 man on his ticket.

> The Governor and I each served as Lieutenant-Governor in our state, and we have both learned from personal experience how possible it is for a second official in a state to be a helpful part in a party administration. I think that the Vice-President should be more than a mere substitute in waiting. In establishing coördination between the executive office and the Senate the Vice-President ought to play a big part, and I have been telling Governor Coolidge how much I wish him to be not only a participant in the campaign but a helpful part of a Republican administration. The country needs the counsel and the becoming participation in government of such men as Governor Coolidge.[149]

Showing he was serious, Harding made the point that he would break tradition and invite Coolidge to sit in on all Cabinet meetings if they were sent to Washington by the American people.

While the focus remained on Harding throughout the fall campaign, Coolidge did get a little of the spotlight when he was sent by the party to make a number of speeches in the Deep South. This was the heart of the Democratic Party, so Coolidge was hardly looking forward to the trip. Nevertheless, he had made it clear from the beginning that he saw his job as doing whatever he could to support Harding's election as President. If that meant giving a bunch of speeches in politically hostile territory, then so be it. Coolidge didn't care for the old political standby of giving speeches from a platform at the back of a train, but he did engage in this kind of electioneering during his trip to the South. In all, he offered remarks to 56 different audiences over the course of six days. He never attacked his Democratic opponents, as that was never his style, but mostly he sang the praises of Harding, his policies, and his pitch to "Return to Normalcy."

Campaigning for Coolidge came to an end with the death of his long-time mentor Murray Crane on October 2, 1920, at the age of 67. It was a tough loss for Coolidge, who would later write with sadness of Crane's untimely demise, "What would I not have given to have had him by my side when I was President!"[150] The funeral led to an awkward scene with the arrival of Crane's political rival, Senator Henry Lodge. That circumstance did not sit well with Calvin Coolidge. When a reporter asked Coolidge to pose for a picture with Senator Lodge, he abruptly shut things down. "I came to bury my friend," he barked. "It is no time for photographs!"[151] Coolidge had his eyes wide open when it came to relations with people like both Crane and Lodge. "Now you ask about Lodge's friends," Coolidge said to reporter William White. "I don't think Lodge has many friends. He has a host of admirers. But there is a big difference between admirers and friends. Crane had friends and those friends will stick to Crane dead in state politics. Lodge's admirers will stick to him until he gets his first setback. When that comes you won't see many people sitting on the mourner's bench."[152] Coolidge would dearly miss his collaboration with Crane. His future engagements with Lodge would rarely feature much alignment.

Coolidge had every reason to be confident that his long-term streak of electoral triumphs would continue when voters went to the polls on November 2, 1920. There was one person who was not on the ballot but would have an outsized influence on the election. President Woodrow Wilson had increasingly grown unpopular due in part to the economic malaise beginning to envelop the country in the post-war years, but mostly for his stubborn intransigence over his all-or-nothing approach to the ratification of the Treaty of Versailles. While Wilson was trying to rally the people to his cause, he had suffered a debilitating stroke and was now cloistered behind closed doors in the White House residential quarters. Many Americans now saw him putting the welfare of the world ahead of their own country, and there was a backlash growing against him, the League, and the Democratic Party. Those sentiments were confirmed by the results of the 1920 election, which ended in a landslide victory for the ticket of Warren Harding and Calvin Coolidge. The Republicans trounced their Democratic rivals to the tune of 404 to 127 in the Electoral College. Cox won only 11 of 48 states, with no victories beyond the boundaries of the Deep South. More than 60% of the popular vote went to Harding-Coolidge, with a seven million vote margin of victory, the largest in the history of the country to date. The Republicans also locked in control of both Houses of Congress, with a nearly unprecedented 70% supermajority in the House of Representatives. The country was ready to give "normalcy" a chance.

IV-33: Vice President-elect Coolidge with his wife Grace and friends Emily and Frank Stearns on vacation during the interregnum in Asheville, NC

Coolidge immediately received countless invitations for visits and speeches. He accepted some, always staying true to his support for Harding and the Republican Platform. He and Grace did get away for a bit, relaxing with the Stearnses at Asheville, North Carolina. He also had one final ceremonial duty to perform before his term as Governor officially came to an end. On December 21, he offered the featured address celebrating the 300th anniversary of the Pilgrims' landing at Plymouth Rock. "They cared little for titles; still less for the goods of this earth; but for an idea they would die," Coolidge proclaimed. "Measured by the standards of men of their time, they were the humble of the earth. Measured by later accomplishments, they were the mighty. In appearance weak and persecuted they came – rejected, despised – an insignificant band; in reality strong and independent, a mighty host of whom the world was not worthy, destined to free mankind."[153] Two weeks later, Coolidge performed the ceremonial acts of the outgoing executive in Massachusetts, taking his "lone walk" down the steps of the statehouse and into Boston Common, where he temporarily took his place as an ordinary citizen of Massachusetts. Two months later, he was in his nation's capital for the transfer of power on a much higher plane.

On March 4, 1921, Coolidge was the first to take his oath of office, sworn in within the walls of the Senate chamber. Not surprisingly, his remarks were brief, a mere 434 words. He paid his respects to the body for which he was about to serve as presiding officer. "The great object for us to seek here," Coolidge declared, "for the Constitution identifies the vice presidency with the Senate, is to continue to make this chamber, as it was intended by the fathers, the citadel of liberty."[154] Coolidge's only constitutional duty as VP was to preside over the Senate, but he was not empowered to engage in debate and was only authorized to vote in the case of a tie, something he was never required to do in his two-and-a-half years in the seat. After the vice presidential ceremony, everyone headed to the east front of the Capitol, where Warren Harding took his oath at the hands of Chief Justice Edward White. After Harding finished his remarks, he took an unprecedented step as his first action as President of the United States. He went back inside and joined his Vice President on the dais in the Senate to personally present his Cabinet nominations for advice and consent. Harding's former colleagues in the Senate gave him exactly what he wanted, full approval of the Cabinet in a record amount of time.

The new Vice President and his wife initially looked for a home to either buy or rent in Washington, D.C., but they couldn't find anything to their liking that would fit into their admittedly tiny budget. Coolidge had scrimped and saved perhaps $25,000 over the years, but he was still renting half a duplex in Northampton which had elevated in price to $32 a month. He didn't see any reason for extravagance despite his new station in life. As he later emphasized, "There is no dignity quite so impressive, and no independence quite so important, as living within your means."[155] When outgoing VP Thomas Marshall suggested the Coolidges move into his lodgings at the New Willard Hotel right across the street from the White House, they agreed. The suite came with two bedrooms, a dining room, and a large reception room – more than enough for the couple. Coolidge chafed at the $8 per day cost, but with his new salary set at $12,000 per year, he could well afford the space.

The living situation was fine for Coolidge and his wife, but the setting was deemed inappropriate for their sons, now aged 13½ (John) and almost 12 (Calvin, Jr.). After some searching, the Coolidges decided to send their boys to Mercersburg Academy, a boarding school located just across the southern tip of Pennsylvania, about 90 miles from the

IV-34: The Coolidge Family, circa 1920
(L to R: John, Grace, Coolidge, and Calvin, Jr.)

nation's capital. The change in surroundings was perhaps the most impactful on Grace Coolidge, who, throughout her husband's lengthy tours of political duty away from the family, had generally remained with the boys in the duplex on Massasoit Street in Northampton. Washington, D.C. represented a coming out party for Grace, whose charm, poise, beauty, and friendly banter in social settings were seen in stark contrast to her extremely reserved husband. Coolidge, who continued to refrain from any engagement with his wife on matters of business or politics, relished having her by his side in these settings. Just a couple of months into his new office, he shared with his father, "She [Grace] is popular here. I don't know what I would do without her."[156]

In terms of the work, it was a difficult transition for Coolidge. He found himself in the odd role of being a heartbeat away from becoming his nation's chief executive, but he currently sat with very little to do. The folks at Amherst were undoubtedly proud to have graduates from the college running both Houses of Congress, with Fred Gillett once again elected Speaker of the House and Coolidge presiding over the Senate. But while the House Speaker had considerable authority over all aspects of that body's operations, Coolidge had little control over the upper chamber of the national legislature. "At first I intended to become a student of the Senate rules and I did learn much about them," Coolidge later wrote, "but I soon found that the Senate had but one fixed rule, subject to exceptions of course, which was to the effect that the Senate would do anything it wanted to do whenever it wanted to do it. When I had learned that, I did not waste much time on the other rules, because they were so seldom applied."[157] He quickly began to form opinions about the people who made up this august body. The reason a man has "so much trouble with the Senate," Coolidge shared with James Derieux, "is that there isn't a man in the Senate who doesn't think he is better suited to be President than the President, and thinks he might have been President except for luck."[158] If anyone was running the Senate, it was Henry Lodge, the veteran leader of the Foreign Relations Committee who had recently shepherded not one but two votes through the chamber that denied approval to Wilson's Treaty of Versailles and his League of Nations. Coolidge and Lodge may have both been Republicans from Massachusetts, but they were hardly aligned. As Coolidge noted, Lodge likely resented seeing Harding and Coolidge in their new roles, believing himself more qualified for either position. Lodge would spend the last three years of his life as a thorn in Coolidge's side.

As promised, President Harding welcomed Coolidge into the inner circle of Cabinet meetings. Harding's Cabinet was a mixture of what he called the "best minds" he could find, along with a handful of friends/cronies. The best minds included Secretary of State Charles Evans Hughes, Secretary of the Treasury Andrew Mellon, and Secretary of Commerce Herbert Hoover. The other category included close friend and political ally Harry Daugherty as Attorney General, former Senate colleague Albert Fall at the Interior Department, and Will Hays, the former head of the Republican National Committee, as Postmaster General. While Coolidge dutifully attended these sessions, not surprisingly, he rarely said a word. He sat quietly on the opposite side of the table from the President, but he did pay attention. In fact, he later concluded that these sessions were an immense help to him when the presidency was suddenly thrust upon him a couple of years later. As noted in his *Autobiography*, Coolidge came to believe that the VP "should be in the Cabinet because he might become President and ought to be informed on the policies of the administration. He will not learn of all of them. Much went on in the departments under President Harding, as it did under me, of which the Cabinet had no knowledge. But he will hear much and learn how to find out more if it ever becomes necessary. My experience in the Cabinet was of supreme value to me when I became President."[159] Given that he saw his primary role as VP was to support the agenda of the President, these insights were helpful in the short-term as well as down the road. There wasn't a single moment in his tenure as Vice President that Coolidge ever spoke out against his chief or the policies of the administration.

In some ways, this was quite natural for Coolidge, as he and Harding remained very much aligned on the policies best suited for a country that was still seeking to stabilize in the post-war environment. Harding sought and received an increase in the protective tariff, which Coolidge wholeheartedly supported. Harding worked with Secretary Mellon on tax cuts, and while they didn't get as much as they wanted, Coolidge saw this as moving in the right direction. Harding championed the Budget and Accounting Act of 1921, which centralized the Federal budget process in the executive branch within a new Bureau of the Budget, providing the President the ability to oversee all budget submissions to Congress rather than prior practices where the agencies did their own lobbying almost independent of the elected executive. Coolidge had welcomed a similar reform in Massachusetts and saw this move for the national government as a critical means to hold the reins over government expenditures. There were other policies that Harding did not support, and again Coolidge was right there with him. Congress wanted to reward veterans from the recent war with a generous financial bonus, but Harding was opposed, given that it would further increase the high debt load the country was already going to be saddled with for years because of the massive expenditures during the war. When Congress passed the measure, Harding vetoed it, with Coolidge fully in support. Similarly, Congress was inclined to give handouts to the nation's struggling farmers, to guarantee prices even when supply far-outstripped demand. Harding was opposed, once again with his Vice President firmly in his corner. When Harding convened an international disarmament conference in Washington in November of their first year in office, Coolidge watched the forging of the most comprehensive arms control agreement in the history of the world. And unlike President Wilson, who failed to get his major treaty through the Senate, Harding brought the potential opposition into the process from the very beginning and eventually had smooth sailing in gaining advice and consent. Coolidge called the pact "an epoch-making agreement for the practical limitation of naval armaments."[160] Coolidge was inclined to support Harding across the board anyway, given his views since his days as Lieutenant Governor requiring loyalty to the top of the administration, but, in this case, he didn't need to go through any political gymnastics to square his views with his chief. Coolidge remained personally as different from Harding as anyone could be, but politically and ideologically, they were almost completely aligned.

There was a side to the Harding presidency for which Calvin Coolidge scrupulously avoided, and that was the shenanigans perpetrated by the President's friends who made up the so-called "Ohio Gang." Harding loved to play golf and pal around with plenty of poker, cigars, storytelling, and illegal alcohol which still flowed regularly in Harding's White House despite the recently enacted constitutional ban. Several of Harding's cronies were not shy about their ability to provide access to administration officials if the price was right. Characters such as Jess Smith and Howard Mannington were happy to peddle influence, although none of the Ohio Gang was ever convicted of any illegal activity. One who did cross the line was Charles Forbes, a Harding friend from the west coast, who built kickbacks into many of the large contracts issued on his watch as the head of the newly established Veterans Bureau. At first, Harding denied his friend would put himself above his duty to serve the people, but when hard core evidence emerged affirming the accusations against Forbes, the President promptly dismissed his friend, who would later serve time in prison for conspiracy to defraud the Federal government. These unsavory characters seemed to surround the Harding presidency, even though no wrongdoing was ever traced directly to the President himself. Nor, for that matter, did any of these actions put a taint on the innately honest Vice President Calvin Coolidge, who had nothing to do with any of these questionable characters.

Halfway through Harding's term, Coolidge was beginning to chafe at his role, which, frankly, didn't require him to do very much of any substance. In addition to quietly presiding over the Senate and attending occasional Cabinet meetings, he had little in the way of any responsibilities. To fill the time, he and Grace accepted a lot of invitations to dinner, which often put him in the uncomfortable position of being expected to engage in idle chit-chat, a practice which he deplored. Why did he accept so many invitations? "Got to eat somewhere,"[161] he was prone to say. He did enjoy being the guest of honor, if for no other reason than making it socially acceptable to arrive late and leave early, something he did with regularity to make it home for bed by 10:00 pm. Grace was the star of these events, welcomed by the socialites of the nation's capital for her charming personality, and adored even further when placed in contrast to her tight-lipped spouse. By now, all of Washington knew about "Silent Cal," the man who had stood up to striking policemen in Boston, had been elected Vice President of the United States, and rarely said a word. "The elections of 1920 imported into the city of conversation as one of its necessary consequences perhaps the oddest and most singular apparition this vocal and articulate settlement has over known," wrote journalist Edward Lowry, "a politician who does not, who will not, who seemingly cannot talk. A well of silence. A center of stillness."[162] One socialite thought she was the one to break the spell and get the Vice President to open up. Seated next to each other at a gathering, the woman admitted that she had bet a friend that she could get Coolidge to say more than two words during the course of the evening. Coolidge's response? "You lose."[163]

Coolidge was occupied throughout much of the first two years of the Harding administration as Congress remained in session for all but a couple of months during this period. When a lengthy recess finally got underway in March 1923, everyone was ready for a break. Harding had planned an extended tour of the American West to include the first visit by a sitting President to the territory of Alaska. The Coolidges took a short trip to Burlington, Vermont, to bury Grace's father, Andrew Goodhue, who passed away on April 25. Coolidge then made his customary trip to Amherst for commencement exercises. This was an awkward visit for the Vice President, who was given the place of honor next to the President of the college, Alexander Meiklejohn, who was in the process of being ousted from that position. Coolidge accepted several other invitations to speak, including a Memorial Day address in New Hampshire, as well as a Garman-like speech at commencement ceremonies at Wheaton College in Norton, Massachusetts. Coolidge offered this audience a sense of his personal political philosophy:

> Individual initiative, in the long run, is a firmer reliance than bureaucratic supervision. When the people work out their own economic and social destiny, they generally reach sound conclusions. ... We do not need more material development, we need more spiritual development. We do not need more intellectual power, we need more moral power. We do not need more knowledge, we need more culture. We do not need more law, we need more religion.[164]

He continued his upbeat commentary in an address in Fredericksburg, Virginia, just after the Independence Day holiday. "It is not that a change is needed in our Constitution and laws so much as there is a need of living in accordance with them," Coolidge announced. "It is not our institutions that have failed, it is our execution of them that has failed. … There have been criticisms which are merited, there always have been and there always will be; but the life of the nation is dependent not on criticisms but on construction, not on tearing down but on building up, not in destroying but in preserving."[165] Coolidge refrained from most controversial topics, keeping his remarks during these various speeches to upbeat philosophical musings, in addition to his ongoing advocacy in favor of the policies of President Harding.

6. Continuing the Harding Agenda

As Warren Harding and his party traveled through Alaska in July 1923, Vice President Coolidge was ready for an extended break at his father's homestead in Plymouth Notch, Vermont. He spent most of the month relaxing with the family, enjoying the opportunity to engage in the everyday chores he had always performed on the farm. He was perfectly content to allow the reporters to snap his picture, demonstrating that the American Vice President was also a "regular" citizen, unlike the more aristocratic traditions in most countries in the world. While communications at Plymouth Notch remained rather primitive, Coolidge was aware that Harding's trip was being cut short. The President had taken ill after returning to Seattle from his Alaskan tour, and doctors recommended a period of complete rest. Harding was taken by train to San Francisco, where he checked into the Palace Hotel under the care of several physicians who were monitoring his symptoms. As for Coolidge,

IV-35: Coolidge and Grace at his father's home in Plymouth Notch

IV-36: Coolidge and Grace on the farm in Plymouth Notch, August 2, 1923 (the day before he became the President of the United States)

he saw no reason to worry, issuing a statement to the press that Harding was simply exhausted and should be fine in very short order.

Coolidge and his wife went upstairs to bed around 9:00 pm on the night of August 2. He captured in his *Autobiography* what happened next. "I was awakened by my father coming up the stairs calling my name," Coolidge wrote. "I noticed that his voice trembled. As the only times I had ever observed that before were when death had visited our family, I knew that something of the gravest nature had occurred."[166] He was right. The first to arrive at Colonel Coolidge's home in Plymouth were the Vice President's driver, Joseph McInerney, his stenographer Erwin Geisser, and reporter William Crawford, who had hitched a ride after getting the news that President Harding had died. Coolidge's father answered the late-night knock at the door since he had the downstairs bedroom. He was the one to wake his son and give him the news. "He had been the first to address me as President of the United States," Coolidge later recalled. "It was the culmination of the lifelong desire of a father for the success of his son."[167] Coolidge's first act was to dictate a note of condolence to Mrs. Harding, and then arrangements were made to string a temporary telephone line into Colonel Coolidge's home so the new President could communicate directly with the outside world. His first contact was Secretary of State Charles Evans Hughes, who advised taking the oath of office as soon as practicable. Since there wasn't a Federal judge anywhere near Plymouth Notch, Coolidge consulted both his personal copy of the Constitution and the Secretary of State, who happened to be a former Associate Justice on the U.S. Supreme Court. Coolidge wanted to know who was authorized to swear a President into office. Hughes counseled that a duly sworn notary public would be sufficient. At this point, Coolidge turned to his father, who was still a justice of the peace and had been a notary in the past, to see if his notary license was still intact. Colonel Coolidge confirmed it was, and the path was laid for the first time to have a father swear his son into the presidency. Coolidge formally dressed for the occasion, putting on a dark suit with a black tie. He got on his knees for a short prayer in which he later noted that he "asked God to bless the American people and give me power to serve them."[168] He then joined Grace to head back downstairs for the swearing-in, which took place at 2:47 am. "The oath was taken in what we always called the sitting room by the light of the kerosene lamp, which was the most modern form of lighting that had then reached the

IV-37: John Coolidge administering the presidential oath of office to his son by the light of a kerosene lamp, Plymouth Notch, VT, 2:47 am, August 3, 1919

neighborhood," Coolidge captured in his *Autobiography*. "The Bible which had belonged to my mother lay on the table at my hand. It was not officially used, as it is not the practice in Vermont or Massachusetts to use a Bible in connection with the administration of an oath."[169] There were only nine other people in the room as Calvin Coolidge became the 30th President of the United States.

People on both coasts were up all night to begin executing all the facets of the transfer of power. Warren Harding's body was prepared to be placed on a train for the slow journey back to Washington D.C., with some three million Americans showing up for an emotional outpouring to mourn a man who, at this point, had departed as a very popular leader. Plymouth Notch was alive as reporters from all over converged on the tiny hamlet, waiting for the first public appearance of the new President. As for Calvin Coolidge, he issued a statement for the public:

> Reports have reached me, which I fear are correct, that President Harding is gone. The world has lost a great and

> good man. I mourn his loss. He was my chief and my friend. It will be my purpose to carry out the policies which he has begun for the service of the American people and for meeting their responsibilities wherever they may arise.[170]

With that, he went back to bed.

He did sleep, but not for long. The new President was up early, meeting reporters around 7:20 am. Colonel Coolidge had been up all night, hosting a small gathering in his parlor, answering questions about the nation's new leader. "I think of him just as a good and honest boy, who will do his best with any job given him," Coolidge's father shared with the reporters on hand. "He always has been that way and I guess he always will be. A trusty kind of a boy who always attended to whatever he had in hand."[171] Coolidge insisted on visiting his mother's grave before being driven to the train station for the journey to the nation's capital. He had many thoughts racing through his mind, but outwardly he displayed his typical calm demeanor. He had been thrust into new challenges before, gaining confidence at each step up the political ladder as he was able to dive in and perform at every one of these levels. Some referred to these opportunities as the "Coolidge Luck," moving forward as others fell by the wayside. But Coolidge knew it was more than that. "Fate bestows its rewards on those who put themselves in the proper attitude to receive them," he wrote.[172] In one of his first letters after taking his oath, he offered some perspective to his close friend Frank Stearns. "Of course I am going to make a large number of mistakes," he wrote. "I am unable to account for the reason for it, but those things do not worry me any more. I trust that you may come into that frame of mind yourself. I am going to do what seems best for the country, and get what satisfaction I can out of that. Most everything else will take care of itself."[173] Coolidge was both humble and confident as he set out from his father's home to take on the challenges of the presidency. On the one hand, he noted in his *Autobiography*, "It is a great advantage to a President, and a major source of safety to the country, for him to know that he is not a great man. When a man begins to feel that he is the only one who can lead in this republic, he is guilty of treason to the spirit of our institutions."[174] At the same time, he was sufficiently self-assured to later share his belief with artist Charles Hopkinson that when he left his father's home as his nation's new President, he "thought I could swing it."[175]

The transition from Harding to Coolidge was at once nearly instantaneous, but from a practical standpoint, it took a couple of weeks to fully play out. The Coolidges welcomed the Harding party at Union Station, and the new President presided over memorial services at both the White House and the Capitol before escorting the deceased President's body to his hometown of Marion, Ohio. Attorney General Harry Daugherty recommended that Coolidge re-take his oath of office from a Federal judge, recognizing that while Colonel Coolidge was indeed a notary public, he was only licensed at the state level, and Daugherty believed a Federal official should be the one to administer the presidential oath. Coolidge agreed and was subsequently re-sworn in by Justice Adolph Hoehling, Jr. of the Supreme Court of the District of Columbia. Regardless of this additional step, Coolidge always maintained he became President under the unique circumstances in which the oath was administered by his father. Coolidge graciously offered Florence Harding as much time as she needed before moving out of the White House. He and Grace would remain at the New Willard Hotel for the time being. Coolidge took his first seat at the presidential desk on August 13, but didn't move into the White House until the 21st.

Coolidge told nearly everyone around him that his goal was not to upset the apple cart, that he would continue to pursue Harding's policies (with which he was strongly aligned), and wanted as many of Harding's

IV-38: President Coolidge at the presidential desk for the first time, August 1923 (age 51)

people to stay on as well, at least for the balance of Harding's term. He told Postmaster General Harry New to "continue right along in the same old way."[176] He asked Ike Hoover to remain as Chief Usher in the White House and for Elizabeth Jaffray to continue as housekeeper. "I would like, Mrs. Jaffray, for everything to go on just as it has in the past,"[177] the new First Lady said, reflecting one of her new responsibilities for overseeing the running of the executive mansion. That said, Coolidge would follow a disciplined schedule as President, which was definitely a change of pace for the White House staff. The work day would begin and end at set times, and meals would be served on a consistent schedule as well. Warren Harding went with the flow in managing his days as President. Calvin Coolidge would adhere to a much more disciplined routine.

In terms of personality, the new President was clearly very different from his predecessor, and some things reflecting the new occupant of the White House would change. The late-night poker parties, for example, were out. Coolidge informed Ike Hoover, "I don't want the public in our family rooms on the second floor so much as they have been."[178] The Washington socialite who always lived on the edge, Alice Roosevelt

IV-39: President Coolidge with his initial Cabinet on the White House lawn, 1923

(Front Row, L to R: Harry New, Postmaster General; John Weeks, Secretary of War; Charles Hughes, Secretary of State; President Coolidge; Andrew Mellon, Secretary of the Treasury; Harry Daugherty, Attorney General; and Edwin Denby, Secretary of the Navy)
(Back Row, L to R: Herbert Hoover, Secretary of Commerce; Hubert Work, Secretary of the Interior; Henry Wallace, Secretary of Agriculture; and James Davis, Secretary of Labor)

Longworth (TR's oldest daughter), remarked, "The atmosphere was as different as a New England front parlor is from a back room in a speakeasy."[179] There would be no alcohol served in the Coolidge White House, consistent with the new constitutional mandate which had been ignored by Harding. In many ways, Harding epitomized the carefree cultural aspects of the Twenties, with the rise of Jazz, innovations in fashion, and the emergence of women as norm-flouting Flappers. Calvin Coolidge embodied none of these traits, yet he oversaw a country that was experimenting far and wide in this post-war era, pushing boundaries like never before. Gamaliel Bradford noted this irony regarding the nation's 30th President. "It would be possible to make an equally effective contrast between the mad, hurrying, chattering, extravagant, self-indulgent harlotry of twentieth-century America and the grave, silent, stern, narrow, uncomprehending New England Puritanism of Calvin Coolidge," Bradford wrote.[180] All true, but none of this had much to do with Coolidge's presidential policies, which remained completely aligned with Harding and the core beliefs of their Republican Party.

While Calvin Coolidge was getting his bearings as his nation's newest chief executive, Grace Coolidge was also trying to find her way. The 44-year-old First Lady had already wowed the Washington social scene since arriving two years before as the wife of the Vice President. She continued to have no role in politics, rarely talking business with her husband, but she tended to light up any room in which she appeared and served as a great counterbalance to her highly reserved husband. On her first day in the role, she wrote a letter to a bunch of her college friends with whom she had maintained contact over the years. "There was a sense of detachment," she wrote. "This was I, and yet, not I – this was the

IV-40: First Lady Grace Coolidge (Coolidge preferred the term "Mistress of the White House")

wife of the President of the United States and she took precedence over me; my personal likes and dislikes must be subordinated to the consideration of those things which were required of her."[181] She took the role seriously and, by all accounts, performed as well as any First Lady. Edmund Starling, who was retained by Coolidge at the head of his Secret Service detail, saw the First Couple up close and personal for more than five years. He noted some advice passed along by Frank Stearns that was particularly helpful. "[Stearns] was the first to tell me that in all things Mrs. Coolidge came first, something I found to be true without exception,"[182] Starling wrote in his memoirs that reflected on his service to five presidents. Starling was frank, and at times critical, in his memoir, but had only the best things to say about Grace Coolidge. "Mrs. Coolidge was the personification of charm," Starling wrote. "She more than made up for her husband's taciturnity. Everyone liked her, and she carried off the difficult role of First Lady beautifully. Without her the little fellow [Starling's affectionate nickname for President Coolidge] would have had a difficult time at the dinners, receptions, and balls which custom forced him to attend."[183] The Secret Service nickname for Grace Coolidge was, appropriately, "Sunshine."

Helping Coolidge ease into the new job, Congress was out for its customary recess, not due back until the first week of December. Coolidge saw no reason to call for a Special Session and used the time to establish his own presidential rhythm, both out front and behind the scenes. He turned down all speaking requests to give him some time to settle in, as well as out of respect for his late predecessor. After consulting with Stearns and a few others, he brought on board C. Bascom Slemp as his secretary (what would today be called his Chief of Staff). Slemp had deep connections in the Republican Party, would be a critical liaison to Capitol Hill, and figured to play a key role assuming Coolidge planned to run for his own presidential term the following year. Slemp quickly grew to respect his new boss. "Morning, noon, and night he keeps thinking, thinking," Slemp commented. "He indulges in no distracting pleasures." He continued, "No man is harder to get an expression of opinion from than President Coolidge on a subject to which he has not applied his mental and moral processes. No man's opinion is easier to know on any subject to which he has applied it."[184] With his passion for budgets and the economy, Coolidge's closest advisers were expected to be Treasury Secretary Andrew Mellon and Budget Director

Herbert Lord. Mellon was one of the "best minds" Harding brought into government service for the first time. The former banker was one of the richest men in the world, and his views about tariffs, taxes, and the rest of the economy were very much aligned with his new boss. Coolidge would be even more forceful than Harding in backing the proposals of his Treasury Secretary. As for Mellon, he had great "confidence in the President's courage and political sense,"[185] which would be sorely tested as the two did battle with Congress over the next few years.

There were few living Americans who wanted to restrain government spending as much as Calvin Coolidge, but Herbert Lord came awfully close. Simply put, Coolidge loved budgets and reveled in the opportunity to control spending based on the recently passed Budget and Accounting law. "The budget idea, I may admit, is a sort of obsession with me," the President told a group of Jewish philanthropists.

> I believe in budgets. I want other people to believe in them. I have had a small one to run my own home; and besides that, I am the head of the organization that makes the greatest of all budgets, that of the United States government. Do you wonder, then, that at times I dream of balance sheets and sinking funds, and deficits, and tax rates, and all the rest? I regard a good budget as among the noblest monuments of virtue.[186]

His budget director would have wholeheartedly concurred with this sentiment. Herbert Lord had taken over for Charles Dawes the year before as the nation's second Director of the Budget Office, reporting directly to the President. Lord had moved up the ranks on the business side of the U.S. Army, ultimately serving as the Army's Director of Finance during World War I. He retired from the service as a brigadier general to take on the budget job for Harding. The country had accumulated massive amounts of debt to finance

IV-41: Coolidge's Budget Director Herbert Lord

the recent war, with annual spending levels topping $18 billion during the heart of the conflict. President Harding inherited a budget of more than $5 billion, and with aggressive cutting alongside Dawes and Lord, had brought that number down to $3.3 billion. Coolidge and Lord wanted to keep pushing, to get it down under $3 billion. The two began meeting every week before each Cabinet meeting to look for more ways to cut spending. In the meantime, the President was already hard at work on his first Annual Message to Congress in which he would unveil his bold economic plan.

Coolidge's parsimonious ways were nothing new to those who knew him – who knew about the duplex on Massasoit Street in Northampton and the tiny lodgings he'd had at the Adams House in Boston. The man didn't own a car or many of the other electronic items of convenience that were being scooped up by consumers across the country. In his *Autobiography*, he traced this way of life back to his own roots in Vermont.

> My fundamental idea of both private and public business came first from my father. He had the strong New England trait of great repugnance at seeing anything wasted. He was a generous and charitable man, but he regarded waste as a moral wrong. Wealth comes from industry and from the hard experience of human toil. To dissipate it in waste and extravagance is disloyalty to humanity.[187]

Despite his new $75,000 per year salary, Coolidge would micromanage the White House budget practically to the penny, to the point where Mrs. Jaffray ultimately couldn't take it anymore and resigned. Agent Starling had a front-row seat to the penny-pinching side of the President.

> One day as we passed the stand of the White House peanut vendor he sniffed at the roasting chestnuts, stopped, and put his hand into his pocket. It came out empty and he turned to me. 'Colonel,' he said, 'can you lend me ten?' 'Ten dollars?' I said, reaching for my wallet. 'No,' he said, 'Ten cents.' I gave him a dime and he bought the chestnuts. Some time after our return to the White House the elevator operator brought me an envelope. Inside it was a dime.[188]

This was the real Calvin Coolidge, and the country would soon find out there was no distance between Coolidge the private man and the public politician when it came to spending money. He would guard the people's purse as carefully as he did his own.

Agent Starling offered some of the most intimately insightful comments about Coolidge's years as President, capturing a side of the man that few saw and even fewer ever wrote about. Coolidge took to Starling right away. He was always more comfortable when Starling was around, even suggesting he relocate to the New Willard Hotel so he could be only a few minutes away at any given time. Starling agreed to make the move, and the President had a direct telephone line installed so the White House could reach him at a moment's notice. Coolidge was not much for exercise. He didn't play any sports, and other than periodic walks, he didn't engage in almost any physical activity. But with Starling by his side, he started to look forward to their walks around the White House neighborhoods each morning and often again in the afternoon. As long as Starling was on duty, these walks would occur. Sometimes, they walked in silence, as Starling knew his place and wanted to provide the President with as much time as he needed to clear his head in between the consequential meetings that filled his day. But they would talk as well, typically not about government or politics, but more so about the great outdoors – a passion for Starling that caught the President's fancy. Coolidge also liked Starling because he was a good sport. As the agent noted, Coolidge's "appetite for pranks was insatiable."[189] Coolidge loved to ring the bells for all his servants to appear at once just to watch them scramble. He planned elaborate

IV-42: President Coolidge with the head of his Secret Service detail, Edmund Starling

schemes to trick Starling on their meeting location on many mornings, just to catch him off guard and get a chuckle out of his reaction when the agent temporarily couldn't find his President. On one occasion, Starling spied Coolidge "in the basement putting a black cat in a crate with a rooster, just to see what would happen."[190] The Coolidges actually loved animals, but even they were not immune from his pranks – a side of Coolidge very few got to see.

There was one group anxious to get to know the new President that Coolidge did make time for, and that was the national press. President Harding was a newspaperman at heart and established an excellent rapport with reporters, meeting with them both formally and informally throughout his tenure in office. Coolidge picked up right where Harding left off. While reporters were still not allowed to directly quote the President as the norm for this era, Coolidge offered insights to the press on a regular basis. In fact, he held more than 500 press conferences in his five-and-a-half years in office. "I want you to know the executive offices will be open as far as possible," the President told the reporters early in his tenure, "so that you may get any information your readers will be interested to have. This is your government. You can be very helpful in the administration of it."[191] Coolidge remained his typical stoic and terse self when dealing with the press, but he believed in transparency in government and maintained an approach consistent with that belief throughout his time in office.

Coolidge enjoyed one additional change in his life during these first few months in office – he formally joined a church for the first time. As Vice President, the Coolidges had begun frequenting the First Congregational Church of Washington. He was fond of the approach of the Reverend Jason Pierce, who happened to have graduated from Amherst in 1902. Coolidge had always been a regular churchgoer but had never officially joined a congregation. That said, he welcomed the invitation when the members of First Congregational voted him in. Coolidge was not one to immerse himself in the mystical side of religion, but his personal relationship with the Supreme Being had always been an integral aspect of his character, accented by the teachings of Charles Garman in college. Coolidge's belief system provided both guidance and comfort throughout his presidency. "It would be difficult for me to conceive of anyone being able to administer the duties of a great office like the Presidency without a belief in the guidance of a divine providence," he later told reporter Bruce Barton. "Unless the President is sustained by an abiding faith in a divine power which is working for the good of humanity, I cannot understand how he would have the courage to attempt to meet the various problems that constantly pour in upon him from all parts of the earth."[192] With Congress coming back to town, the pace with which those challenges would appear on his desk was about to go into overdrive.

President Coolidge set the tone for his administration with his first Annual Message to Congress on December 6, 1923. Using concise, declarative sentences that matched his overall communication style, Coolidge stepped through his agenda, which, as he had forecasted, sought to continue many of the priorities established by President Harding. Coolidge announced that Secretary Mellon was projecting a $300 million surplus, as the Harding economy had already begun to pick up steam. The question was how to spend that money. Direct relief to discrete groups was not the path for either Harding or Coolidge. The new President eschewed a bonus payment to veterans and thought price stabilizing subsidies for the agriculture sector were not a good practice. While agreeing that tariffs should remain high to protect domestic American industries, Coolidge was emphatic that income taxes should come down and government expenditures should be decreased as the core of his economic agenda.

IV-43: President Coolidge delivering his first Annual Message to Congress, December 6, 1923

> For seven years the people have borne with uncomplaining courage the tremendous burden of national and local taxation. These must both be reduced. The taxes of the Nation must be reduced now as much as prudence will permit, and expenditures must be reduced accordingly. High taxes reach everywhere and burden everybody. They bear most heavily upon the poor. They diminish industry and commerce. They make agriculture unprofitable. They increase the rates of transportation. They are a charge on every necessary of life. Of all services which the Congress can render to the country, I have no hesitation in declaring this one to be paramount. To neglect it, to postpone it, to obstruct it by unsound proposals, is to become unworthy of public confidence and untrue to public trust. The country wants this measure to have the right of way over all others.[193]

Coolidge proposed steep cuts in the top marginal income tax rates, which had jumped during the war, particularly at the top of the scale. Coolidge and Mellon proposed dropping that top rate from 58% to 31%. They believed that lowering rates for high earners would pour money back into the economy in the form of investments and additional jobs. Mellon called this approach "scientific taxation," similar to what has become known as "supply side" or "trickle down" economics. As Mellon had observed, when railroads cut their prices, more people traveled, and revenue actually went up. The same was true for the Ford Motor Company. When Ford slashed the price of its Model-T, many more Americans could then afford what had previously been seen as purely a luxury purchase for the well-to-do. Lower prices led to sharp increases in purchasing, once again raising revenue for the company. Mellon believed that Federal taxation should be "the least burden to the people" while yielding "the most revenue to the government."[194] He and Coolidge were convinced that

IV-44: Coolidge's Treasury Secretary Andrew Mellon

by lowering tax rates, people would keep more of their own money, leading to more spending and, ultimately, more revenue for the Federal government.

While Coolidge's tax and spending plans were the highlight of his address, he touched on a number of other important issues facing the country as well. He continued the Harding mantra of not supporting American entry into the League of Nations, which had recently begun operations at its headquarters in Geneva. At the same time, he also agreed with Harding that the U.S. would be well-served by joining the World Court, which was being established as an arbitration tribunal to settle international disputes without resorting to war. Coolidge embraced the push for restrictions on immigration to help American workers have greater job security and decent wages. However, he balked at some of the specific limitations being proposed to keep all Japanese from emigrating to the U.S. Coolidge opposed formal recognition of the Bolshevik government now in control in Russia and reiterated his opposition to the veteran bonus proposal. While he supported enhanced cooperative marketing for farmers, he affirmed his opposition to outright subsidies to that industry. It was a substantive address that gave the American people the opportunity to hear from their President first-hand, as the speech was the first Annual Message carried live on the radio. The speech was generally well-received. Former President William Taft, who had recently been placed on the Supreme Court as Chief Justice by President Harding, described the speech in a letter to his daughter as "great in its comprehensiveness and style, great in the soundness of its economic statesmanship, and great in the courage that it took to say what he has said, and great in its absence of all evasiveness and in its very quiet directness."[195] There would be little ambiguity on where this new President stood on just about any issue.

There was one other topic President Coolidge touched on in his Annual Message, and that was civil rights. President Harding had called for a national anti-lynching measure to be passed by Congress, but eventually he dropped the proposal in order to get support for other parts of his agenda. Coolidge wanted to try again at a time when membership in the Ku Klux Klan was again on the rise, and not just restricted to the states of the Deep South. "The Congress ought to exercise all its powers of prevention and punishment against the hideous crime of lynching," Coolidge advocated, "of which the negroes are by no means the sole sufferers, but for which they furnish a majority of the victims."[196] Coolidge would echo this advocacy in each of his six Annual Messages, but he did little to actively push for such legislation outside of these speeches. Over the course of the next century, some 200 versions of anti-lynching legislation would be introduced in Congress, but it took that entire century to get one to pass. Lynching finally became a Federal crime, but not until President Joe Biden signed the Emmett Till Antilynching Act on March 29, 2022.

Even after some setbacks in the 1922 midterms, the Republicans maintained solid majorities in both Houses of Congress. However, things were not going to be smooth sailing for many items on the Coolidge agenda. Not only did the Democrats offer a consistent opposition, but the Republicans were often not on the same page. While many progressives had come back into the Republican fold after the split the previous decade, many in these ranks still opposed the conservative Old Guard and were willing to obstruct the President when it came to policies that didn't support their reform-minded belief system. In the case of taxes, for example, there was general support for cuts, but many of the progressives were more concerned about the lower end of the tax rates and not simply providing large windfalls to the wealthy. Progressive Senator George Norris, for example, pointed out that "Mr. Mellon himself gets a larger personal reduction than the aggregate of practically all the taxpayers in the state of Nebraska."[197] (This was a true statement, but so was the fact that Secretary Mellon paid more taxes than all the people of Nebraska as well.) Congressman Nicholas Longworth was now the House Majority Leader, and he would be on point to shepherd the Coolidge-Mellon tax plan through Congress. It would not be an easy path to maneuver.

There were two other topics hanging over the President's head as he geared up to pursue his legislative agenda. The most immediate question seemingly on everyone's mind was whether Coolidge planned to run for his own term as President in the following year's national election. While there wasn't a clear alternative to Coolidge for the Republican nomination, one name had cropped up in the presidential rumor mill, and that was business tycoon Henry Ford. Ford had started the automobile company that bore his name twenty years before, ultimately becoming a household name as the Model T found its way into driveways across the country. Ford had been a staunch ally of Democrat Woodrow Wilson and supported the League of Nations. He had previously sought the position of senator from Michigan but lost to the Republican Truman Newberry in a close race. Before the war, though, Ford had been a Republican, and some saw him as a viable alternative if Coolidge opted out. But around the time of Coolidge's Annual Message, Ford took himself out of consideration. Determining that the United States was "safe with Coolidge,"[198] Ford announced, "I would never for a moment think of running against Calvin Coolidge for president on any ticket whatever."[199] Whether Ford's decision factored into Coolidge's decision-making is unknown, but he did announce his own intent to run at the Gridiron Dinner in Washington just a couple of days after delivering his message to Congress. Coolidge had no plans to campaign for the nomination as he would let his record speak for itself. But he did agree to set up some infrastructure by bringing in a former state legislator from Massachusetts, William Butler, to run the campaign. Butler, who had been close to Coolidge's mentor Murray Crane, would work closely with Frank Stearns and Bascom Slemp to position the President for the 1924 nomination while Coolidge focused on the job at hand.

The other item that had Washington buzzing was on Capitol Hill, as the congressional hearings investigating potential malfeasance by members of the Harding administration were ramping up in intensity. In the last year of Harding's life, Charles Forbes had been fired for committing fraud at the Veterans Bureau, after which his general counsel, Charles Cramer, had committed suicide. A self-inflicted gunshot wound also ended the life of Jess Smith, one of the Harding cronies from Ohio who was believed to be the leader in some influence-peddling scams surrounding the administration. Smith had been very close to Attorney General Daugherty. Even though he was never on the government payroll, Smith had his own office in the Justice Department just down the hall from Daugherty, and many believed favors could be bought by greasing the palms of Jess Smith. Smith committed suicide shortly before President Harding left for his trip to Alaska, right after the President had informed him he was going to be arrested the next day. Many in Congress were particularly interested in Smith because they thought Daugherty was the real crook, and perhaps investigating Smith's actions would offer a path to take down the Attorney General.

The main focus of the current round of hearings had to do with the sale of oil leases that everyone referred to as "Teapot Dome." Teapot Dome was an oil preserve in Wyoming that was owned by the United

States Navy. That oil field, along with others in California by the names of Elk Hills and Buena Vista, had been set aside during the early stages of the war in Europe in case the U.S. entered the conflict and needed large amounts of oil to fuel its naval fleet. After the war, Congress authorized the executive branch to lease some of the oil fields to commercial enterprises as a way to generate revenue for the Federal government now that the military need for the reserves had been reduced. There was also a concern that some oil companies were already drilling in adjacent lands and perhaps siphoning off some of the government's oil around the edges of these fields. This was the situation inherited when Warren Harding became President of the United States. Neither Harding's Secretary of the Navy, Edwin Denby, nor any of his leadership team knew anything about leasing oil fields. That had historically been a function of the Interior Department. So, when the Secretary of the Interior Albert Fall offered to take on that role, always subject to the approval of the Navy brass, Denby welcomed the offer. President Harding, who had grown to like and trust Fall from their days together in the Senate, supported the policy. He signed out an order transferring the authority for the leases from Navy to Interior, and Fall and his team moved ahead.

The primary leases went to two oil companies, both based on no-bid contracts, which were legally permissible according to the authorizing statute passed by Congress. Fall awarded the lease at Teapot Dome to Harry Sinclair's Mammoth Oil Company, while the lease at the California sites went to Edward Doheny's Pan-American Petroleum Company. From the start, there were grumblings over the awards. First, there were charges of malfeasance due to the non-competitive awards even though no-bid contracts were legally authorized. Second, many conservationists cried foul, as they were opposed to any drilling on these lands, by either the government or commercial enterprises. Enough noise was generated to get Congress to look into the propriety of these transactions. Just a couple of months into Coolidge's presidency, these hearings were starting to heat up.

Senators Thomas Walsh from Montana and John Kendrick of Wyoming were at the forefront of the congressional investigation, and their hearings produced sensationalistic testimony regarding Teapot Dome and the other activities of the so-called "Ohio Gang." Fall, Denby, and Daugherty were all considered targets, and while no charges had emerged that directly implicated any of the three in committing any specific crimes at this stage, there was mounting pressure on Coolidge to dismiss Denby and Daugherty from his administration. (Fall had resigned the previous January after agreeing to a lucrative deal to work for Sinclair's oil company.) William Borah from Idaho was one of the leading progressive Republicans in the Senate, and he went directly to the new President to insist that he fire Daugherty. For the time being, Coolidge's answer was 'no.' "I am here to carry out the Harding policies," he told Borah. "I am here as a Republican President. Daugherty was Harding's friend. He stands high with the Republican organization. I do not see well how I can do it."[200] There was a personal aspect of this that Coolidge wasn't prepared to summarily dismiss. He posed to Republican Raymond Robins the following question: "I ask you if there is any man in the cabinet for whom – were he still living – President Harding would more surely demand his day in court, would more surely not dismiss because of popular clamor than the man who was his closest personal and political friend?"[201] Coolidge was monitoring the situation closely but would not act to force a removal from his Cabinet unless he was convinced such a move was warranted. Despite the noise being generated throughout Washington, at this stage, he felt it was not.

For the first time since taking over the presidency, Coolidge's boys came home for a visit. They spent the Christmas holiday at the White House, which included some new traditions. Coolidge ordered a giant fir from Vermont to serve as the national Christmas tree on the Ellipse next to the executive mansion. For the first time, the national tree would be covered with electric lights. The President started a new tradition when he flipped the switch on those lights on Christmas Eve. The President and First Lady (Coolidge preferred the title "Mistress of the White House") then shook hands with some 4,000 of their fellow citizens in a public reception on New Year's Day. The ever-efficient President became adept at pulling the people along with his handshake to keep the receiving line moving as quickly as possible. Right around the corner from these ceremonial duties was the fight in Congress over the President's tax plan.

Congressman Longworth was committed to the plan Mellon had put forward, but he was running into powerful opposition. Whether tax cuts for the wealthy would help the economy was secondary to many members of Congress since they weren't going to generate very many votes. Broader tax cuts might do that, as would things like a bonus for veterans or subsidies for farmers. If the administration was running a $300 million surplus, these legislators reasoned they could spread that benefit around and get a much better political windfall than by just following the Mellon Plan. The Farm Bloc in Congress was particularly powerful because it crossed party lines based on geographic interests. That group was supporting something called the McNary-Haugen Bill, which would create a $250 million fund to stabilize the prices of cotton, wheat, corn, rice, and swine. The proposed statute would guarantee the purchase of any excess production of these agricultural products that would then be sold in Europe, at a loss if necessary. Coolidge was opposed to this kind of targeted intervention in the economy. "Agriculture and banking, like all other interests, are not the business of the Government, but the business of the people," Coolidge said to an agriculture conference in February 1924. "Primarily they must assume responsibility for them."[202] Various forms of McNary-Haugen were introduced in each year of Coolidge's tenure as President, and each time he brought out his veto pen, costing him political capital but maintaining his principles.

The veterans' bonus was the other piece of legislation that was causing him angst. Coolidge continued to believe tax cuts that could benefit all Americans (either directly or indirectly) represented a sounder economic policy than doling out cash to veterans. When Congress finally passed the bonus bill in April, he vetoed it. Nevertheless, the following May, another version found its way to his desk. This time Congress had the votes to override his veto, the first of four times this happened despite the majorities his party held in the legislature. The bonus bill was going to have an immediate impact on the President's ability to get the budget below $3 billion for the year. The price tag was $132 million for the first year and $2 billion over the full 20 years covered by the statute. Coolidge and Lord would go back to the drawing board, but this made their job that much more difficult.

The President and his Budget Director had just come from their first of the semi-annual executive branch conferences on the budget. Coolidge had told the gathering very directly, "As for me, I am for economy,"[203] which meant cuts anywhere he could find them. That belt-tightening was definitely taking hold, and Lord welcomed the opportunity to spread the news of his success. In just the past few months, the administration had already eliminated nearly $100 million from current year spending. The cuts came in all shapes and sizes. Reductions in telephone and transportation bills saved $55,747 from the budget of the District of Columbia. Taking in-house the delivery of paper for the Government Printing Office saved $25,000. The budgeteers looked to repurpose used furniture equipment, including across agencies, rather than buy new. And, in one agency, government workers were allocated a single pencil at a time, knowing a new one wouldn't be distributed until the current one was practically down to the nub.[204] All these moves added up to pretty big dollars, as Lord announced that planned Federal spending for fiscal year 1924 was down to $3.053 billion. The new authorization for the bonus bill was still weighing over their heads, but they continued to search for ways to get that figure below $3 billion. That said, none of these efforts seemed to be helping the Coolidge tax plan, which was still being debated on Capitol Hill.

The President also couldn't escape the noise surrounding the Harding-era congressional investigations. In late January, he decided to get the executive branch in the game by naming two special prosecutors to oversee the investigations spawned by these congressional hearings. It was a bipartisan decision, with former Senator Atlee Pomerene, a Democrat, joining Republican Owen Roberts of Pennsylvania to try to sort out if any illegality had occurred. "Counsel will be instructed to prosecute these cases in the courts so that if there is any guilt it will be punished," Coolidge ordered. "If there is any civil liability it will be enforced; if there is any fraud it will be revealed, and if there are any contracts which are illegal they will be canceled. Every law will be enforced, and every right of the people and the government will be protected."[205] Navy Secretary Denby resigned shortly after the naming of the special counsels, but Attorney General Daugherty remained defiant despite all the accusations coming his way.

Meanwhile, Senator Burton Wheeler of Montana had stepped into a lead role in the congressional investigation, specifically going after AG Daugherty. He called several witnesses who gave dramatic testimony, much of which turned out to be false, but kept the scandal talk circulating throughout Washington. The decision that finally prompted Coolidge to act was when Daugherty not only refused to appear before Wheeler's committee, but he also declined to provide access to Justice Department records. Senators such as Borah continued to push for Daugherty's dismissal, and with these latest circumstances, the President finally asked for the Attorney General's resignation. "I am not questioning your fairness or integrity," Coolidge told Daugherty. "I am merely reciting the fact that you are placed in two positions, one your personal interest, the other your office of attorney general, which may be in conflict."[206] With that, it was time to go. The ever-combative Daugherty tried to fight for his job, but the President held firm and the Attorney General reluctantly stepped aside. Coolidge reached into his Amherst network to find the next leader of his Justice Department. Harlan Stone, who had been a year behind Coolidge in college, had eventually emerged as the Dean of Columbia Law School. Coolidge had already started seeking Stone's advice on some matters, and now with an opening at the Justice Department, he offered him the post. Step-by-step, the Harding administration was fading away, and the Coolidge presidency was coming into its own.

Domestic affairs were always front and center during Calvin Coolidge's presidency, but he did not ignore the international situation as the world was continuing to try to stabilize five years after the end of World War I. Coolidge remained in the same camp as President Harding and Senator Lodge when it came to the League of Nations, making his position crystal clear in his first Annual Message to Congress:

> Our country has definitely refused to adopt and ratify the covenant of the League of Nations. We have not felt warranted in assuming the responsibilities which its members have assumed. I am not proposing any change in this policy; neither is the Senate. The incident, so far as we are concerned, is closed. The League exists as a foreign agency. We hope it will be helpful. But the United States sees no reason to limit its own freedom and independence of action by joining it.[207]

The League, which had been up and running without U.S. participation since 1920, was part of the Treaty of Versailles, which officially ended the war for most of the combatants. But the ramifications of other elements of that treaty continued to plague international relations in Europe. The victorious Allies had not only redrawn the map of the Continent, but they also imposed onerous conditions on the vanquished Central Powers, including massive reparations that the Germans were finding nearly impossible to meet. Part of the problem was the high demand for coal and steel, whose main source was the Ruhr Valley. This territory had been traditionally part of Germany but was now under the control of the French as a result of the Treaty of Versailles. The Germans needed these materials not only for their domestic consumption but also to sell in order to raise funds to pay the reparations. When the German industrialists who still ran these production facilities started prioritizing shipments back to Germany and increasing prices to the rest of Europe, the French and Belgians stepped in with force, reoccupying the Ruhr with soldiers to compel the resumption of shipments at their preferred quantities and prices. This move was not only an affront to the Germans but also put them in even deeper financial peril.

Perhaps it is not surprising that the primary foreign policy initiative in this early stage of the Coolidge administration was fundamentally one of economics. And it wasn't just the Germans who were struggling to pay their war-related obligations. The British and French owed billions to the United States, and they were also struggling to meet these demands. Both nations were seeking to renegotiate the terms of these agreements, with a not-so-subtle hint that they believed outright forgiveness was the appropriate course of action given the much greater burden they had suffered in the war compared to the Americans. On this point, President Coolidge was adamant – repayment must still occur. "The money we furnished we had to borrow; someone must pay it," he declared. "It cannot be cancelled."[208] That said, the President was open to considering more favorable terms. In fact, the Americans took the lead in trying to smooth over the repayment challenges for both the Allies and the Central Powers.

The President tapped Commerce Secretary Herbert Hoover to appoint the U.S. members to an international commission to study the issue and quickly formulate recommendations on how to resolve this myriad of economic impasses. Charles Dawes was placed in charge of the 10-member international committee, supported by fellow American Owen Young. Dawes had excelled in a variety of public service positions after earning success in the banking industry. He had a sound financial mind, as evidenced by his commercial success as well as his prior service as the Comptroller of the Currency under Presidents McKinley and Roosevelt and Budget Director under Harding. Persevering through much of 1924, the Dawes Committee came up with a plan that was widely accepted. As a first step, foreign troops would evacuate the Ruhr to help ease tensions. Payments from the Allies to the U.S. would receive more favorable interest rates and would now stretch out over the course of 62

IV-45: Charles Dawes

years. The repayment schedule for the Germans was also relaxed and was to be financed by generous new loans from the U.S. financial sector. Firms such as J.P. Morgan and Dillon Reed would finance $200 million in debt to the Germans at favorable interest rates and repayment schedules. The bottom line of these economic musical chairs was that the booming American financial sector would loan money to Germany so it could meet its payments to Britain and France, who would then use the funds to repay the American government. Each of the parties would have something left over to stabilize their domestic economies. The Dawes Plan was universally embraced by all parties, allowing everyone to breathe a sigh of relief. The economic truce in Europe was real, thanks in large part to the leadership of the Americans. As conditions changed in the 1930s, the respite would dissipate, but stability had at least been temporarily re-established. For his efforts, Dawes was awarded the Nobel Peace Prize.

The Republican and Democratic National Conventions were scheduled for June, but there were still two major pieces of legislation related to immigration and taxes hanging in the balance before Congress would break for these events. Negotiations remained contentious, even with Republican majorities in both houses. Senator Lodge was among those who felt no duty to align with the new President. At times, in fact, he seemed to go out of his way to obstruct the efforts of the administration. The first of these bills under consideration was designed to further restrict immigration as a means to protect domestic American-born workers. Coolidge was OK with the general notion of limiting the influx of foreigners but was opposed to the exclusionary language with respect to the Japanese. Japanese immigration had been a sore issue between the two countries dating back to the Roosevelt administration. Amid a backlash growing in the American West due to a massive influx of Japanese workers who were willing to work for very low wages and did little to assimilate into U.S. culture, many Americans were pushing at that time for a ban on future Japanese immigration. The Japanese protested vigorously, leading to the so-called "gentlemen's agreement" in which the Japanese voluntarily curtailed immigration to the United States. This allowed the proud Japanese to save face by avoiding formal exclusion. That agreement still stood, but for many now in Congress, it was no longer sufficient. Coolidge lobbied to soften the new bill. "I am attempting to see if there is any way that that question can be solved so as to satisfy those that want to have restriction and at the same time prevent giving any affront to the Japanese Government,"[209] the President wrote. Nevertheless, the other end of Pennsylvania Avenue was unmoved. Coolidge opposed the measure that eventually hit his desk, but was leery about vetoing it, especially with the fate of his tax bill still to be determined. On May 26, while publicly noting his objection to the Japanese provision, he reluctantly signed the restrictive immigration measure into law. Whether this concession would help him on the tax bill was yet to be seen.

Congressman Longworth had been struggling for months to get his colleagues on board with the magnitude of the reductions in tax rates sought by President Coolidge and Secretary Mellon. In the end, he just didn't have the votes. While a tax bill was passed by Congress in June 1924, it was hardly the bill the White House wanted. The most disappointing result was the minimal reduction in the top rate, which was lowered no further than 46%. Moreover, the legislators added a significant increase to the estate tax, which would now top out at 40%. Congress also decided that individual tax returns would no longer be considered private, bringing individual finances into the open for the first time. Mellon was appalled at the resulting legislation, while Coolidge was deeply troubled. In the end, he decided to sign it, concluding that even modest rate cuts were better than none at all. "A correction of its defects may be left to the next session of the Congress," Coolidge remarked. "I trust a bill less political and more economic may be passed at that time. To that end I shall bend all my energies."[210] He would, of course, only if he remained President of the United States.

As Congress wrapped up its session, the President had a couple of additional things to attend to prior to the Republican gathering in Cleveland, Ohio. First, he welcomed his two boys home for the summer.

Due to the negotiations over the tax bill, Coolidge had missed his older son's high school graduation from Mercersburg Academy. John was preparing to attend Amherst in the fall, but he and Calvin, Jr., would first try to enjoy a few months at "home" at the White House. President Coolidge did find himself at a commencement ceremony in early June, but it was at a college campus in Washington, D.C., where he accepted the invitation to speak to the graduating class. The school was Howard University, as Coolidge became the first American President to speak at a historically Black college or university. Coolidge offered praise for the heroism shown by the Black community during World War I when more than 380,000 Blacks served in the American armed forces. "He drew no color line when patriotism made its call upon him," the President said. "He gave precisely as his white fellow citizens gave, to the limit of resources and abilities, to help the general cause. Thus the American Negro established his right to the gratitude and appreciation which the Nation has been glad to accord."[211] He then spoke directly to the graduating class of 1924, sharing his optimistic view on the value of an education and the opportunities ahead for them.

> Those of you who are fortunate enough to equip yourselves for these tasks have a special responsibility to make the best use of great opportunities. In a very special way it is incumbent upon those who are prepared to help their people to maintain the truest standards of character and unselfish purpose. The Negro community of America has already so far progressed that its members can be assured that their

IV-46: President Coolidge delivering the commencement address at Howard University, June 1924

> future is in their own hands. Racial hostility, ancient tradition, and social prejudice are not to be eliminated immediately or easily. But they will be lessened as the colored people by their own efforts and under their own leaders shall prove worthy of the fullest measure of opportunity.[212]

Calvin Coolidge wasn't just showing up at Howard to honor these graduates but was doing so as part of an agenda to support the education of Blacks at the institution's medical school. In his first Annual Message, Coolidge had called for the creation of a $500,000 fund "to help contribute to the education of 500 colored doctors needed each year."[213] Congress took him up on the proposal, appropriating $365,000 during fiscal year 1924. The fund was oversubscribed thanks to private donations on top of the Congressional funding. The following year, Congress appropriated an additional $370,000 for a new medical building at Howard.[214] Calvin Coolidge advocated each year for Congress to pass an antilynching law, but he was unsuccessful at each attempt. Nevertheless, he did manage to get significant support for expanded educational opportunities at one of the top Black colleges in the country. It was more than most of his colleagues had accomplished in the area of civil rights since the end of Reconstruction and the onset of the Jim Crow era.

The Republican National Convention of 1924 was one of the most efficient on record, emblematic of the man at the center of everyone's attention. The entire affair lasted just three days. No serious competition for Coolidge ever materialized. Early in the year, there was a little buzz about the progressive former Governor from California, Hiram Johnson, but when Coolidge beat Johnson in the primary in his home state, his chances were washed away. Frank Stearns and William Butler ran the show in Cleveland on behalf of the President. Butler, who had been running the Coolidge campaign, had recently been named the Chair of the Republican National Committee. This put him in position to keep an eye out for any surprises that might derail Coolidge's nomination, but no such challenges arose. Without any suspense or controversy, the incumbent captured 96% of the vote on the first ballot to become his party's official nominee. The only work the delegates really had to do was to pick a Vice President, which had been vacant since Coolidge assumed the presidency the previous August. Coolidge was inclined to give the position to William Borah, but the Idaho Senator thought the role was beneath him and declined. Frank Lowden, who had been in the mix for the top spot on the ticket four years before, next emerged at the top of most lists. In fact, once the vote got started, it only took two ballots to give Lowden the nomination. But when Lowden was contacted (he was not at the convention), he emphatically refused to accept the will of the party. With delegates ready to head out of town, they were told to remain in their seats as the VP roll call needed to be re-opened. Three other names were given serious consideration, including Commerce Secretary Herbert Hoover, Iowa Senator William Kenyon, and former Budget Director Charles Dawes. Dawes and Coolidge were of one mind when it came to cutting expenditures in the Federal government. It took only one ballot after Lowden declined to hand Dawes the nomination.

The Democrats were in a far different place as they dragged out the longest convention in American history before settling on its nominees. The entire affair lasted 16 days, with the presidential roll call requiring a whopping 103 ballots to select a nominee. The 1920 nominee, James Cox of Ohio, was in the mix, along with former Treasury Secretary William McAdoo and former New York Governor Al Smith. McAdoo and Smith were at the top for ballot after ballot, but neither had enough support to break through, especially with the Democrats still clinging to the requirement to reach a two-thirds supermajority to gain the nomination. Lurking in the wings throughout the voting was a former congressman from West Virginia, John Davis, who had served as the ambassador to Great Britain for the last couple of years of the Wilson administration. On the 100th ballot, Davis passed McAdoo to take over second place, still trailing Smith by 148 votes. But Smith and McAdoo both finally recognized that neither could ever attain the two-thirds threshold,

The New York Times.

DEMOCRATS NOMINATE DAVIS AND C. W. BRYAN; FORMER, ACCLAIMED, CALLS PARTY TO BATTLE; SMITH PROMISES TO WORK HARD FOR THE TICKET

IV-47: The Democratic nominees, John Davis and Charles Bryan

so, at this point, they both let their supporters choose an alternative. These concessions led to Davis's nomination on that 103rd ballot. As for the second spot on the ticket, that only took one ballot, but it did record 30 different people getting at least one vote. Emerging from the candidates was Charles Bryan, the Governor of Nebraska, and the younger brother of William Jennings Bryan, who had been the party's presidential nominee in 1896, 1900, and 1908. It was thought that Bryan could help unite the Smith and McAdoo factions to support the ticket in the fall election.

What did Calvin Coolidge think of all this? Well, not much, since he had a lot more important things on his mind, suffering the greatest tragedy of his life in the midst of the Democratic balloting. The President had continued to shy away from any campaign-related activities through this busy month of conventions. He went about doing his job, including hosting another of the semi-annual budget meetings on June 30, in which he reiterated his guiding principle: "I am for economy. After that I am for more economy. At this time and under present conditions, that is my conception of serving all the people."[215] He may not have gotten what he wanted in terms of his tax proposal to Congress, but he was bound and determined to keep reducing expenditures anywhere he and Budget Director Lord could find to cut. Grace was joined by Calvin, Jr. at Memorial Continental Hall for the budget presentation. Unbeknownst to the President, his youngest son was about to set off a chain of events that would take his life in less than a week.

IV-48: One of the last photos of Calvin Coolidge, Jr. (upper left) during the summer of 1924, with President Coolidge and Grace (seated) and John Coolidge (upper right)

Calvin, Jr. and his older brother, John, were spending their summer break at the White House. One of their favorite activities was playing tennis on the court on the White House grounds. On June 30, the same day as the budget conference, they played doubles with Dr. Joel Boone and Dr. James Coupal. Coupal had recently taken over as White House Physician, while Boone, a Medal of Honor winner, was serving as the President's physician whenever he set sail on the presidential yacht, the *Mayflower*. Noting unusual was reported at the time. But a couple of days later, Calvin, Jr. wasn't feeling well. In fact, he had some pain in his foot and was walking with a bit of a limp. Dr. Boone saw him in this state of discomfort at the White House and asked him about it. Calvin, Jr. referenced a blister he seemed to have picked up during their recent doubles match when he played without wearing socks. Dr. Boone noticed red streaks running up the boy's leg, indicating the possibility of some sort of blood infection related to the blister. His temperature was running 102 degrees.

The condition of the leg raised immediate concerns for the White House physicians, leading them to call in additional medical experts, including Dr. John Kolmer of Philadelphia's Temple University. Tests were performed, and the results came back positive for *staphylococcus aureus* – a serious staph infection. The President and First Lady spent every moment they could trying to nurture their son back to health, but things were deteriorating quickly. On July 2, vice presidential nominee Charles Dawes noted, "As I passed the door of Calvin's room I chanced to look in. He seemed to be in great distress. The president was bending over the bed. I think I have never witnessed such a look of agony and despair that was on the president's face."[216] On July 5, Calvin, Jr. was taken to nearby Walter Reed Hospital, where additional tests indicated the same diagnosis and confirmed the infection had spread to a dangerous level. Upon hearing the news, Chief Justice William Taft wrote his wife that it was as if "the boy had been bitten by a poisonous snake."[217]

The doctors started preparing the President and Mrs. Coolidge for the worst. Their boy was fading, and there didn't seem to be anything anyone could do about it. They took turns trying to provide him comfort, speaking with him and holding his hand as he moved in and out of consciousness. "In his suffering he was asking me to make him well. I could not," Coolidge wrote in his *Autobiography*.[218] By the 7th, it was over. Sixteen-year-old Calvin Coolidge, Jr. was dead. "When he went the power and the glory of the Presidency went with him," Coolidge later recalled. "The ways of Providence are often beyond our understanding.

… I do not know why such a price was exacted for occupying the White House."[219]

While the Democrats were finishing their elongated nominating process in New York, the Coolidges went into deep mourning. They brought the body of their dead son to Plymouth Notch, where he was laid to rest alongside Coolidge's mother and sister. Grace provided a written description of her thoughts of the funeral in a letter to her friend Therese Hills.

> It is a beautiful spot and it was lovely the day we left little Calvin there. Before our train got to Ludlow there had been a thunderstorm shower which had laid the dust and made everything fresh and green. As we stood beside the grave the sun was shining, throwing long, slanting shadows and the birds were singing their sleepy songs. Truly, it seemed to me God's acre. I came away filled with a 'peace which passeth understanding,' comforted and full of courage.[220]

IV-49: President Coolidge and Grace Coolidge at the burial of their son, Calvin Coolidge, Jr., at Plymouth, VT, July 1924

The Coolidges bounced back and forth between Plymouth and Northampton with nary a thought about campaigning for the presidency. Others would take care of that, with Charles Dawes leading the way on the campaign trail for the Republican ticket. A Coolidge-Dawes Caravan was launched, making its way from New York City to the West Coast, picking up cars to tag along throughout the 6,500-mile journey. But Coolidge remained deep in thought about his family, including the loved ones he would never see again.

Of course, Calvin Coolidge was not the first President to lose a child during his term in office or around the time of his presidency. John Adams lost his son Charles to alcoholism late in his term while Franklin Pierce's son Bennie died in a horrific train accident just a couple of months before taking his oath of office. But it was Abraham Lincoln's courage after losing his 11-year-old son Willie, likely from typhoid fever caused by contamination of the water supply in the nation's capital, that Coolidge primarily looked to for inspiration. Lincoln's loss came amid the Civil War, forcing him to persevere on behalf of the nation. Coolidge would also persevere, but some things would never be the same. The Coolidges decided to take a piece of Vermont back to Washington as a

IV-50: President Abraham Lincoln

IV-51: President Abraham Lincoln's son, Willie, 1862 (age 11) shortly before his death

memorial to Calvin, Jr. They uprooted a five-foot Vermont spruce and planted it on the White House grounds. Coolidge would often think of his son when he peered upon the tennis court, where a little blister had formed, and in a week's time, had taken a life. Agent Edmund Starling offered the following story in his memoirs about one way in which President Coolidge responded to his son's death.

> Very early one morning when I came to the White House I saw a small boy standing at the fence, his face pressed against the iron railings. I asked him what he was doing up so early. He looked up at me, his eyes large and round and sad. 'I thought I might see the President,' he said. 'I heard that he gets up early and takes a walk. I wanted to tell him how sorry I am that his little boy died.' 'Come with me, I'll take you to the President,' I said. He took my hand and we walked into the grounds. In a few minutes the President came out and I presented the boy to him. The youngster was overwhelmed with awe and could not deliver his message, so I did it for him. The President had a difficult time controlling his emotions. When the lad had gone and we were walking through Lafayette Park he said to me: 'Colonel, whenever a boy wants to see me always bring him in. Never turn one away or make him wait.'[221]

Grace Coolidge also tried her best to deal with the grief that would barely fade over time. Five years later, shortly after the Coolidges had left the White House, she penned a poem in remembrance of her lost son. She titled it "The Open Door."

> You, my son,
> Have shown me God.
> Your kiss upon my cheek
> Has made me feel the gentle touch
> Of Him who leads us on.
> The memory of your smile, when young
> Reveals His face,
> As mellowing years come on apace.
> And when you went before,
> You left the gate of Heaven ajar
> That I might glimpse,
> Approaching from afar,
> The glories of His grace.

Hold, son, my hand,
Guide me along the path,
That, coming,
I may stumble not
Nor roam,
Nor fail to show the way
Which leads us – Home.[222]

As the summer of 1924 wound to a close, the Coolidges waved goodbye to their other son as John began his college days at Amherst. The boys had been away from home before, but, of course, this was different. John was moving ahead with his own life, while Calvin, Jr. would never get that chance. In the meantime, the President lost a member of his Cabinet. Agriculture Secretary Henry Wallace had gone in for surgery to relieve sciatica, but developed an infection during the procedure that quickly ravaged his body and eventually took his life. President Coolidge felt grief again, telling the country that "His loss will be, indeed, a grief to the entire nation, for his fine qualities and able, untiring services had endeared him to all the people."[223]

The Coolidges did have additional friends to keep them company in the White House – four-legged friends were there in abundance. The Coolidges had more pets during his tenure in office than perhaps any President other than Theodore Roosevelt. Most of the animals primarily hung out with Grace, including the dogs (Prudence Prim, Peter Pan, Beans, Tiny Tim, Paul Pry, Blackberry, and Calamity Jane) and cats (Bounder, Climber, Tige, and Blackie). Then there were the birds (including Nip & Tuck, Snowflake, Goldy, and Do-Funny) and the ever-popular Rebecca, the raccoon. The one pet who tended to hang around the mansion with the President was a white collie

IV-52: President Coolidge with Rob Roy, October 1924

named Rob Roy. Many of these animals were given as gifts to the First Family, and while they accepted most into their home, some were a bit too exotic and sent to the zoo. These included a black bear, a wallaby, 13 ducks, an antelope, and a pair of lion cubs who were named Tax Reduction and Budget Bureau.[224]

Coolidge had little interest in the trappings of the presidency, but there was one perk that he did come to enjoy and use frequently – the presidential yacht called the *Mayflower*. After service during the Spanish-American War, the *Mayflower* was placed at the disposal of the President beginning with the Roosevelt administration. Not only during this period of extended mourning, but throughout his presidency, Coolidge looked forward to taking to the seas to clear his head and relax aboard ship. On many weekends he could be found sailing with small groups of friends and colleagues for an afternoon or even several days at a time. "The President loved the boat," wrote Agent Starling. "As soon as he walked up the gangplank he put his yachtsman's cap on. It was the symbol of his supremacy of the boat. A look of satisfaction would settle on his face, and he would prowl about the decks, inspecting things and touching them."[225] Some guests who didn't know the President well didn't realize in advance that their host might go an entire weekend with only saying a few words, but most were now prepared for their time with "Silent Cal," even in the relaxed setting on the high seas.

President Coolidge did engage in one aspect of his re-election campaign, and that was his formal acceptance of the Republican nomination. He had much to be proud of, and shared with the American people remarks that accentuated the prosperous and peaceful period the country was enjoying during what had been the Harding-Coolidge administration. "Perhaps in no peace-time period have there been more remarkable and constructive accomplishments than since March 1921," Coolidge declared.[226] He then elaborated on the core beliefs that guided his presidency.

> I believe in the American Constitution. I favor the American system of individual enterprise, and I am opposed to any general extension of government ownership and control. I believe not only in advocating economy in public expenditure, but in its practical application and actual accomplishment. I believe in a reduction and reform of taxation, and shall continue my efforts in that direction. I am

> in favor of protection. I favor the Permanent Court and further limitation of armaments. I am opposed to aggressive war. … I shall continue to strive for the economic, moral, and spiritual welfare of my country.[227]

He added his thoughts on some of the basics that made American great:

> In the commonplace things of life lies the strength of the nation. It is not in brilliant conceptions and strokes of genius that we shall find the chief reliance of our country, but in the home, in the school, and in religion. The people know the difference between pretense and reality. They want to be told the truth. They want to be trusted. They want a chance to work out their own material and spiritual salvation. The people want a government of common sense.[228]

These sentiments harkened back to the teachings of Professor Charles Garman who helped instill a belief system in Calvin Coolidge that had served him well in both his personal and political lives.

Meanwhile, there were actually two other candidates trying to get their message out to the electorate in their challenge to Coolidge. Outspoken Senator Robert La Follette decided to make a third-party run, trying to unite progressives, socialists, and farmers in a coalition to break through the dominance of the traditional leading parties. And there was the Democratic candidate, John Davis, who tried his best during the canvass to rally his supporters against the incumbent President. "I charge the Republican Party with corruption in administration; with favoritism to privileged classes in legislation," he roared. "I charge it also with division in council and impotence in action. … I indict the Republican Party in its organized capacity for having shaken public confidence to its very foundations. … An Executive who can not or will not lead a Congress that can not and will not follow – how can good government exist under such conditions?"[229] Unfortunately for Davis, this was not the reality in the United States in 1924. In fact, the "good government" of the Coolidge administration was overseeing a period in which the American citizenry had rarely had it so good.

The policies of Warren Harding and Calvin Coolidge were not solely responsible for the prosperity that was spreading across the nation, but they certainly provided positive stimuli in this direction. Harding's original "Return to Normalcy" was covered in an "America First" mindset, geared to enhancing the economic conditions of the American people. High tariffs, lower taxes, reduced Federal spending, and immigration restrictions were all intended to protect American workers and enhance their ability to gain employment at a decent wage. Those efforts were clearly paying significant dividends. Harding had taken over just as the post-war recession was bottoming out, and every economic indicator since the current presidential term began on March 4, 1921, had been on the upswing. Government expenditures had fallen by more than 40% to just under $3 billion, helping to generate a record $963 million surplus in 1924.[230] Even with marginal tax rates falling, government revenues increased, just as Secretary Mellon had predicted. Some of this excess was used to pay down the national debt, which had dropped from just over $24 billion at the start of Harding's term to just over $21 billion heading into the 1924 election.[231] As for individual workers, unemployment had fallen from nearly 9% at the outset of this presidential cycle to under 5% in 1923 and was still under 6% in 1924.[232] Wages for manufacturing workers were rising about 4% per year[233] while inflation was registering only about 1.4% per year.[234] Halfway through the decade, the Twenties hadn't begun to completely roar, but they were humming along at the kind of clip that helped secure political re-elections.

Like Harding before him, Calvin Coolidge won the presidency in a landslide. The incumbent captured 35 states to 12 for Davis (all in the South) and one for La Follette (his home state of Wisconsin). The tally in the Electoral College was a convincing 382 for Coolidge, 136 for Davis, and 13 for La Follette. Coolidge's 15.7 million votes in the national count was less than 3% shy of Harding's all-time record set four years before. Davis was a distant second with 8.4 million popular votes. The country was in a good place, the Republicans were united, and, as the campaign slogan went, the nation decided to "Keep Cool and Keep Coolidge." "I can only express my simple thanks to all those who have contributed to this result," Coolidge said in the wake of his triumph, "and plainly acknowledge that it has been brought to pass through the works of a Divine Providence, of which I am but one instrument. Such powers as I have I dedicate to the service of all my country and of all my countrymen."[235] The country knew what to expect from this unusually quiet politician and was overwhelmingly pleased to give him a full four-year term of his own.

7. The Roaring Twenties

After his election, Calvin Coolidge continued with his no-nonsense approach to his economic agenda, which remained his top priority as President of the United States. The drumbeat to reduce taxes and cut government spending continued as he welcomed Congress back to session in December 1924. "The government," he declared, "can do more to remedy the economic ills of the people [by] rigid economy in public expenditures" than by anything else. "The present method of taxation is to increase the cost of interest on productive enterprises and increase the burden of rent." To reverse that course required a tax policy that "scientifically revised [rates] downward"[236] to allow more money to remain in people's pockets for them to spend rather than for the government to potentially waste. In his mind, he saw the election as providing him with a mandate to push these policies even further in his second term. He was putting Congress on notice that that was exactly what he intended to do.

In January 1925, President Coolidge gave one of the most widely quoted speeches of his entire career, even though the key phrase was largely taken out of context. Coolidge spoke to the American Society of Newspaper Editors in the nation's capital in a speech he titled "The Press Under a Free Government." His main thesis was to address the dual responsibilities of the press, which was to serve the people with information and to run profitable businesses while not allowing either objective to interfere with the other. "The editorial and the business policies of the paper are to be conducted by strictly separate departments," he said. "Editorial policy and news policy must not be influenced by business consideration; business policies must not be affected by editorial programs."[237] Coolidge understood that newspapers existed to make money, which was perfectly fine with him. In a phrase that became synonymous with Coolidge and the era through which he presided over the country, he declared, "After all, the chief business of the American people is business."[238] But he didn't stop there. "Of course the accumulation of wealth cannot be justified as the chief end of existence," he added. "But we are compelled to recognize it as a means to well-nigh every desirable achievement. So long as wealth is made the means and not the end, we need not greatly fear it. And there never was a time when wealth was so generally regarded as a means, or so little regarded as an end, as to-day."[239] For Coolidge, however, this was only part of the equation he was looking to communicate to these newspaper editors and to the American people. "It is only those who do not understand our people who believe our national life is entirely absorbed by material motives," he noted. "We make no concealment of the fact that we want wealth, but there are many other things we want much more. We want peace and honor, and that charity which is so strong an element of all civilization." That led to the other half of his thesis: "The chief ideal of the American people is idealism." In fact, in the end, this sentiment trumped the monetary part of his message. "I cannot repeat too often that America is a nation of idealists," he declared. "That is the only motive to which they ever give any strong and lasting reaction. No newspaper can be a success which fails to appeal to that element of our national life. It is in this direction that the public press can lend its strongest support to our government."[240] So, yes, the economic-minded Calvin Coolidge did believe that the "chief business of the American people is business," which has become one of those phrases most closely associated with the nation's 30th President. But the pupil of Professor Charles Garman would not settle for that mantra without the righteous balancing act of American idealism and associated good works. That *combination* is what Coolidge saw as making America great, not just good business standing alone as the national goal.

Two months later, Coolidge gave one of his longest speeches as he faced 100,000 people from the East Front of the Capitol and millions more listening to the first inaugural address to be carried live on the radio. First, he had a little business to attend to. Congress delivered him 76 bills to sign on the last day of his first term. He signed them all, but waited until the very last minute to approve a measure that would raise the salaries of members of Congress. He then endured an awkward moment when his new Vice President surprised everyone with an aggressive speech that criticized the body over which he was about to preside. Shaking his finger and banging the desk in front of him, Charles Dawes used his inaugural remarks to rail against the undemocratic filibuster that was too frequently invoked by the Senate to thwart the legislative process. This parliamentary trick put "power in the hands of individuals to an extent, at times, subversive of the fundamental principles of free representative government," according to Dawes, and, as a result, "the rights of the Nation and of the American people have been overlooked."[241] His comments were fair, but the circumstances under which he delivered the message seemed very much out of place.

There were elements of each of Coolidge's two swearing-in ceremonies that were unprecedented. Back in 1923, Coolidge became the only person to be sworn in as President by one of his relatives when his father administered the oath in the small parlor of his home. A year-and-a-half later, Coolidge's swearing-in was the first to be conducted by a former President. William Taft had served his nation for a single term as the 27th President of the United States, but the job he always wanted was Chief Justice of the Supreme Court. When that spot opened early in Warren Harding's term, the new President fulfilled Taft's lifelong dream with the appointment. Taft, who would be a regular visitor to the White House during Coolidge's tenure in office, launched Coolidge's full term by guiding him through the constitutionally-prescribed oath taken by all U.S. Presidents.

In terms of his inaugural address, Coolidge spent 47 minutes reiterating what had become his well-known policies, buttressed by the recent vote of confidence he had recently been handed by the American people. "I favor the policy of economy, not because I wish to save money, but because I wish to save people," he declared. "Economy is idealism in its most practical form. … The wise and correct course to follow in taxation and all other economic legislation is not to destroy those who have already secured success but to create conditions under which everyone will have a better chance to be successful. The verdict of the country has been given on this question. That verdict stands. We shall do well to

IV-53: President Coolidge delivering his inaugural address, March 4, 1925

heed it."[242] The President covered many topics in the speech, all consistent with his longstanding political ideology. He ended on a high note, elevating his rhetoric to his lofty vision for his country and its people among the nations of the world. "America seeks no earthly empire built on blood and force," he proclaimed. "No ambition, no temptation, lures her to thought of foreign dominions. The legions which she sends forth are armed, not with the sword, but with the cross. The higher state to which she seeks the allegiance of all mankind is not of human, but of divine origin. She cherishes no purpose save to merit the favor of Almighty God."[243]

Coolidge's inaugural was one of 16 speeches he made as President carried on radio, a technological innovation that was changing the way people got information and various elements of entertainment. With his Vermont twang, Coolidge struggled at times with orations in front of large groups. In many cases, those unaccustomed to his speech pattern found it difficult to follow in these settings. But, on the radio, Coolidge came across crystal clear. "I am very fortunate that I came in with the radio," he once told Congressman James Watson of Indiana. "I can't make an engaging, rousing, or oratorical speech to a crowd as you can, and so all I can do is stand up and talk to them in a matter-of-fact way about the issues … but I have a good radio voice, and now I can get my messages across to them without acquainting them with my lack of oratorical ability or without making any rhetorical display in their presence."[244] This was just another example where Calvin Coolidge was the right person in the right place at the right time.

While Coolidge's policies would not change as he started his own full term as President, there would be some changes in the people around him. Charles Evans Hughes decided four years was enough as Secretary of State, stepping aside with former Minnesota Senator and Ambassador to the United Kingdom, Frank Kellogg, taking over. Also out of the Cabinet was Attorney General Harlan Stone. President Coolidge handed Stone a spot on the Supreme Court, a position he would hold for more than two decades, including the last five years of his life as Chief Justice. Finding a replacement for Stone as Attorney General represented a rare stumble for Coolidge. His choice to run the Justice Department was Charles Warren, the former ambassador to Japan. By most accounts, Warren was eminently qualified for his legal prowess, but he had run afoul of the progressives during his stint as the President of the Michigan

Sugar Company a decade and a half before. In that role, Warren had been cited by the Federal Trade Commission for illegally marketing sugar. Already a bit feisty after the tongue-lashing handed down by Dawes at the inauguration, the progressive-leaning Republicans aligned with the Democrats to yield a 40-40 tie when the vote on Warren's nomination was tallied. This should have delivered a narrow victory for the administration, except the Vice President, who should have been on hand to break the tie, had returned to his hotel for a nap. Dawes had been led to believe that the vote would not be close, and he would not be needed. When word reached him about the deadlock, he hurriedly dressed and made his way to the Capitol, but he was too late to salvage Warren's nomination. Before he arrived, one senator changed his mind, and the appointment went down to defeat 41-39. That made Charles Warren only the sixth nominee to a Cabinet post rejected by the Senate in the history of the country and the first in more than 50 years. Coolidge was frustrated and angry at the result and refused to take the outcome as the final word on the issue. Against the advice of his closest allies, he stubbornly insisted on renominating Warren, who was rejected again, this time by a slightly larger margin. Coolidge's recent landslide victory notwithstanding, his Republican majority in the Senate would remain precarious depending on the issue and the mood at the other end of Pennsylvania Avenue. Their point made in this case, the Senate quickly confirmed the President's subsequent nominee, John Sargent, one of Coolidge's oldest friends who had previously served as the Attorney General of his home state of Vermont.

IV-54: President Coolidge

Having the right people seated around the Cabinet table was important for Calvin Coolidge, partly because of his management style. He needed people he could trust because he expected his subordinates to act relatively independently based on his general policies and guidance. "In the discharge of the duties of the office there is one rule of action more important than all others," Coolidge later wrote. "It consists in never doing anything that some one else can do for you. Like many other good rules, it is proven by its exceptions. But it indicates a course that should be very strictly followed in order to prevent being so entirely devoted to trifling details that there will be little opportunity to give the necessary consideration to policies of larger importance."[245] This took some getting used to for some of his senior advisers. For example, Agent Starling related the following incident:

> One day his personal secretary, Ted Clark, came to the office and asked if he could show the President a file of papers which Secretary of Labor [James] Davis wanted him to read. 'He would like to know whether you agree with his decision,' Clark said. 'I am not going to read them,' the President said. 'You tell ol' man Davis I hired him as Secretary of Labor and if he can't do the job I'll get a new Secretary of Labor.'[246]

Davis must have learned this lesson as he ended up being just one of three Cabinet secretaries (along with Andrew Mellon and Harry New) to serve the entirety of Coolidge's presidency. Coolidge also expected his subordinates to be efficient in executing their job functions. Coolidge, for example, filled his days with work, but his desk was always clear by the end of the day. As for others, he looked with disfavor when he was informed that his original Navy Secretary Edwin Denby used to work well into many evenings. Upon hearing this news, Agent Starling remarked to the President, "He must be an excellent man for the job." "I wouldn't say that," the President replied. "I don't work at night. If a man can't finish his job in the day time he's not smart."[247] Some of the most revealing insights into Coolidge's personality can be found in the writing of the man who stood next to him more than any other throughout his presidency, often being one of the few people who actually saw the more human side of a man who typically kept his emotions in check and his comments to himself.

With Congress in recess from just after the inauguration until December 1925 was perhaps the quietest period of the Coolidge presidency. This gave the First Family the time and space to mourn over the loss of their son and ease into the new term. While Grace remained uninvolved in all things political, she was ever-present in Coolidge's life, and continued to be the standout presence at all social occasions. Commentator Will Rogers noted at the time that compared to the other

First Ladies he had met, Grace Coolidge was "the most friendly and having the most charming personality of any one of them all. She is chuck plumb full of magnetism, and you feel right at home from the minute you get near her. She has a great sense of humor, and is live and tight up and pleasant every minute, and Calvin is just setting there kinder sizing everything up."[248] Coolidge rarely shared his inner feelings with almost anyone, but occasionally he would open up about the importance of his wife in his life. "A man who has the companionship of a lovely and gracious woman enjoys the supreme blessing that life can give," the President once told his friend, the reporter Bruce Barton. "And no citizen of the United States knows the truth of this statement more than I."[249] Mary Randolph served as the First Lady's social secretary. She noted that Grace "was the sunshine and the joy in his life – his rest when tired – his solace in time of trouble. Deep, indeed, went the roots of Calvin Coolidge, and they were close bound about that wife of his."[250] They were still opposites in many ways, but they came from the same stock, were extremely compatible despite their obvious differences, and remained completely committed to each other with little change in their relationship as a result of Coolidge's election as President of the United States.

IV-55: First Lady Grace Coolidge

Frank Stearns also continued to be a reassuring presence. Stearns and his wife had a standing invitation to stay at the White House at any time, something they did on a regular basis. Stearns was occasionally thinking ahead to another campaign in 1928, but the topic wasn't one he raised directly with the President. Stearns would do anything Coolidge asked of him, which was mostly just being around to keep him company. The two would regularly be seen smoking cigars, often without saying a word for extended periods of time. This kind of "interaction" was soothing to the President, and nothing gave Stearns more pleasure than to help Coolidge in any way he could – even by just quietly hanging out.

Coolidge spent much of 1925 working with General Lord to find more ways to cut the budget, with Secretary Mellon to refine their latest tax proposal for Congress, and by making a variety of speeches to the American people. Coolidge's adherence to conservative principles was by now well known, primarily related to all things economic. But there were other aspects of his political leadership that contributed to the sense that he may have been the most conservative man ever to occupy the White House. One of those principles had to do with the topic of federalism; that is, the proper role of the federal and state governments within the constitutional system. "What we need is not more Federal government, but better local government," the President declared at a Memorial Day gathering at Arlington National Cemetery. "From every position of consistency with our system, more centralization ought to be avoided. … The individual and the local, state, and national political units ought to be permitted to assume their own responsibilities. Any other course in the end will be subversive both of character and liberty."[251] He echoed these sentiments in his next message to Congress. "The greatest solicitude should be exercised to prevent any encroachment upon the rights of the states or their various political subdivisions" he maintained. "Local self-government is one of our most precious possessions. It is the greatest contributing factor to the stability, strength, liberty, and progress of the nation."[252] These kinds of statements tend to be popular and are easy to make when times are good and relationships are calm. But Coolidge would put his money where his mouth was on this topic in times of crisis on more than one occasion later in his administration.

The Coolidges spent the summer of 1925 with the Stearnses at Swampscott, Massachusetts. The location enabled trips to Plymouth Notch to visit his father, whose body was finally starting to fail him. After undergoing prostate surgery, his recovery was slow. Coolidge continuously encouraged his father to come to Washington to stay with him at the White House, but Colonel Coolidge always declined. He knew he was dying and wanted to do so on his own terms and in his own home. After a recent a stroke, the Colonel lost the use of one leg, leaving him bedridden most of the time. While the President was unable to spend much time in Plymouth, he did have a direct telephone line installed from the White House, enabling him to speak with his father one or two times a day. Coolidge had an interesting take on this communication marvel that was spreading into homes across the country. "The president should not talk on the telephone," he once said to Bruce Barton. "In the first place, you can't be sure it is private, and, besides, it isn't in keeping with the dignity of the office."[253] He made an exception in order to communicate with his dying father.

As Congress returned to Capitol Hill in December 1925, President Coolidge and Secretary Mellon were armed and ready with a new and aggressive push for tax reform. Mellon was already optimistic based on the economic stabilization that was now underway in Europe. "With the excellent credit machinery and strong position of our Federal Reserve System," Mellon remarked, "with most nations again on the gold standard, with the reparations plan in successful operation, with the debt settlements completed or in near prospect, and with Europe every day making progress toward normality, business in America should fear few obstacles."[254] This confidence, however, didn't mitigate the need in the minds of the President and his Treasury Secretary for more tax cuts to further the prospects for American prosperity.

In his Annual Message, Coolidge lauded the efforts the House Ways and Means Committee had already made in crafting a bill in advance of the opening of the first full session of the 69th Congress that would enact many of the provisions that had been excluded from the Revenue Act of 1924. He noted the draft bill would dramatically cut the top marginal rate to 25%, cut the estate tax by 50%, cut the gift tax, and end the intrusive provision that made individual tax returns available to the public. Moreover, the exemption for the people at the lowest end of the tax rolls would be increased to $4,000, leading to a projection that approximately 40% fewer Americans would pay any Federal income tax compared to the previous year (the actual figure turned out to be 43.4% and would remain at that new level throughout the Coolidge administration).[255] For Coolidge, his cuts in spending and corresponding reductions in taxes were a means to a very important end.

> All these economic results are being sought not to benefit the rich, but to benefit the people. They are for the purpose of encouraging industry in order that employment may be plentiful. They seek to make business good in order that wages may be good. They encourage prosperity in order that poverty may be banished from the home. They seek to lay

> the foundation which, through increased production, may give the people a more bountiful supply of the necessaries of life, … by all these means attempting to strengthen the spiritual life of the Nation.[256]

This wasn't just talk. The economic moves of the Coolidge administration were making these lofty sentiments a reality. The President told Congress he wanted the bill by March 15 so that it could go into effect for the current tax year. They beat his goal by a couple of weeks, and he signed the landmark legislation into law on February 25, 1926.

IV-56: President Coolidge signing the 1926 tax bill; Treasury Secretary Andrew Mellon, who was instrumental in forging the legislation, is the third from the right

The economic situation of the United States in the 1920s would reach levels unprecedented in American history. Yes, the Coolidge tax cuts and corresponding reductions in government expenditures played a significant role in generating these positive results, but these policies were also being implemented at a time of great technological innovation in the United States, creating greater efficiencies throughout the economic value chain. Henry Ford's automated assembly line had revolutionized the manufacturing business in terms of production while also influencing massive investments in roads and construction due to the proliferation of affordable automobiles. Electronic and communication innovations could be seen in just about every household, ranging from the telephone and radio to washing machines, vacuum cleaners, electric lighting, and electric iceboxes. Each of these innovations created new industries, with good-paying jobs to produce these items that many Americans were thrilled to embrace. "Our present state of prosperity has been greatly promoted by three important causes," Coolidge said in 1926, "one of which is economy, resulting in reduction and reform in national taxation. Another is the elimination of many kinds of waste. The third is the general raising of the standards of efficiency."[257] Coolidge drove much of the first two, but the American people were largely responsible for #3, combining to create an economic wave that lasted through much of the decade (before crashing hard shortly after Coolidge left office).

The new year also brought a moment of introspection that spilled out onto the pages of a letter to Coolidge's ailing father. "I wish you were here where you could have every care and everything made easy for you, but I know you feel more content at home. Of course we wish we could be with you," Coolidge wrote before pivoting to his perception of his current lot in life. "I suppose I am the most powerful man in the world, but great power does not mean much except great limitations. I cannot have any freedom even to go and come. I am only in the clutch of forces that are greater than I am."[258] Like many Presidents, Coolidge felt extremely isolated in the role. At times he grew frustrated and even testy, which occasionally manifested in both his personal and professional lives. In the latter, for example, he would grow cold with members of his Cabinet who resisted General Lord's budget cuts or with congressmen who wanted to spend the surplus on pet projects rather than embrace the broader benefits of his tax cuts and debt reduction. On the personal front, Coolidge raised his children with the same discipline and high expectations that his own father had imposed on him. Now with just one son left, Coolidge had little tolerance for sloppiness, such as when John sent him a letter to the White House the previous summer when he knew the Coolidges were spending that time at Swampscott. "It is accuracy that counts," he reminded his son. "Shots that do not make the mark are no good. You had better remember that. The world is full of people that almost succeed, the trouble is they won't work. Many men are almost President. But only 29 have been chosen. I hope you will not be an 'almost man.'"[259] It was not easy being the son of Calvin Coolidge, and that had little to do with the fact that he was the President of the United States.

Shortly after the passage of the tax bill, Coolidge received word that his father was facing his final days. The President and First Lady immediately left for Vermont, but they were slowed by a massive snowstorm. They made the last part of the journey in a sleigh, but by the time they arrived, it was too late. John Calvin Coolidge, Sr. died on

IV-57: Coolidge's father, John Coolidge

March 18, 1826, just shy of his 81st birthday. "When I reached home he was gone," Coolidge wrote in his *Autobiography*. "It costs a great deal to be President."[260] In a simple ceremony, the Colonel was buried in the family plot at Plymouth Notch Cemetery. Unlike the sudden passing of his mother, sister, and son, Coolidge had known for months that his father's life was nearing its end, but it didn't make that ending any easier. John Coolidge had a greater influence on the man who had become the 30th President of the United States than any other human being. He embodied a core set of principles and work habits that were generations in the making and were fully embraced by Coolidge throughout his entire life. The fact that Coolidge was thrifty, faithful, honest, reticent, independent, stoic, prompt, direct, and self-reliant were all characteristics that could be traced back to the example he saw throughout his life in the form of his father. Colonel Coolidge was the one person whom he most wanted to impress and least wanted to disappoint. John Coolidge was the most important influence in his son's life, and Coolidge would miss him dearly for the rest of his days.

Congress went home for the summer the day before the nation celebrated its 150th birthday, which was also the 54th birthday of the President of the United States. Coolidge went to Philadelphia and the site of the signing of the Declaration of Independence to commemorate the occasion. He acknowledged the good times of the day but also offered some perspective for his fellow citizens. "We live in an age of science and of abounding accumulation of material things," he said. "These did not create our Declaration. Our Declaration created them. The things of the spirit come first. Unless we cling to that, all our material prosperity, overwhelming though it may appear, will turn to a barren sceptre in our grasp."[261] Coolidge wanted to go away for the summer but didn't want to head back to Vermont so soon after his father's passing. He put Agent

Starling in charge of finding some place where he could relax and enjoy the outdoors, which for Coolidge also meant no mosquitoes and no snakes. "He had a deathly fear of snakes," according to Starling.[262] The agent settled on a spot called White Pine Camp on Lake Osgood in the Adirondacks in upstate New York. After the break, he returned to Washington in time for the midterm elections. Despite the widespread prosperity and peace in the world, Coolidge's Republican Party fell to the reality that the party of the incumbent executive typically lost seats in these off-year elections. While the Republicans retained majorities in both houses, they lost seven seats in the Senate, narrowing the majority to 48-46. One loss hurt the President more than the others. William Butler, who had run Coolidge's recent re-election campaign, had been appointed to take over the Senate seat from Massachusetts when Henry Lodge died in November 1924. Butler had become Coolidge's primary ally in the Senate, but he was defeated in the '26 campaign by Democrat David Walsh. Given that a number of progressive Republicans remained aligned with the Democrats on certain issues, Coolidge could expect more challenges in certain kinds of legislation for the last two years of his term.

IV-58: President Coolidge, 1924 (age 52)

The fight with Congress that never seemed to go away was the one over agriculture policy. This was the one sector that continued to lag all the rest in terms of the economic boom the nation was generally experiencing. With a Federal surplus expected in the $800 million range for 1926, many congressmen were once again pushing for an updated version of the McNary-Haugen bill that could be used to guarantee a market for all farm production at a stable price. The Farm Bloc pushed the measure through, but once again, Coolidge vetoed it. "To expect to increase prices and then maintain them on a higher level by means of a plan which must of necessity increase production while decreasing consumption is to fly in the face of economic law as well established as any law of nature," the President proclaimed early in 1927.[263] How best to spend the surplus remained at the forefront of a contentious debate. Coolidge had already cut spending, reduced taxes, and decreased the debt by significant amounts, and still had a lot of money left over. Congress wanted to spend it, as did some members of his administration. The Navy was pushing for an investment in shipbuilding, while Commerce Secretary Hoover was advocating for a national water management plan to include new dams and sluices for at-risk locations across the country. The President remained reluctant in each of these areas. In the latter case, he was balking at both the large price tag as well as his principles related to federalism. Meanwhile, the issue of whether Federal funds should be used to address out-of-control flooding was about to be put to the test as the Mississippi Valley was about to suffer the worst floods in the nation's history.

With the grounds saturated and the rivers at capacity due to unabated rainfall throughout the latter part of 1826 and early 1827, the levees began to break, and the major waterways unleashed massive amounts of water that flooded large regions throughout the entire Mississippi Valley. Hundreds of thousands of people were left homeless as more than 27,000 square miles of land were suddenly under water. Traditionally, disasters such as this were not within the purview of the Federal government. Even something as widespread as this devastating weather event that spanned many states was still viewed by many (including the President) as the responsibility of the localities that suffered the loss. The *Washington Post* reported the President saying in the wake of the catastrophe, "The Federal departments have no funds for relief."[264] Members of Congress from the affected region were outraged at this heartless response from the national executive, especially with so much extra money sitting untouched in the Federal treasury. After some reflection, Coolidge did initiate some relief actions, but all within the bounds of his view of the Federal/state divide. He put Commerce Secretary Hoover in charge of the national response, leveraging his prior experience organizing to save the people of Belgium from starvation during World War I. Mostly, Hoover worked alongside organizations such as the Red Cross to raise funds from the private sector to fund restoration efforts. The President did make available thousands of surplus army tents, cots, and blankets for immediate use, but cash payments were not on the table from the Federal coffers. Coolidge had to absorb bitter resentment from congressmen from the South. This included Arkansas Senator Thaddeus Caraway, who implied bias against the South in the resistance by the President to provide aid to the battered region. "I venture to say that if a similar disaster had affected New England that the president would have had no hesitation in calling an extra session"[265] of Congress to consider relief legislation. In fact, Caraway misread Coolidge completely, as would become clear in the following year.

Calvin Coolidge was fascinated by airplanes. In his most recent Annual Message, he called for an investment of $3 million to regulate and promote commercial aviation. He saw this as the next great technological revolution but also had concerns about accidents, which remained too frequent for the general public to have high confidence in this new mode of transportation. Meantime, the entire world was captivated by the race to deliver the first non-stop flight from New York to Paris. To make things interesting was the establishment of the Orteig Prize, which offered $25,000 to the first person to accomplish the feat. The incentive was first announced by hotelier Raymond Orteig in 1919. Eight years later no one had yet claimed the prize, although the frequency of attempts was increasing by the month. Several of these efforts had cost the lives of the aviators, but that didn't stop others from signing up for the attempt. The most recent effort was by Charles Nangesser and François Coli, who left Paris on May 8 but were lost at sea. Next up was an American by the name of Charles Lindbergh, who had designed his "Spirit of St. Louis" monoplane specifically for this mission. The 25-year-old Lindbergh worked for the Robertson Aircraft Corporation delivering mail to the St. Louis and Chicago areas. President Coolidge was very much attuned to these attempts and wired best wishes to Lindbergh as he prepared to depart Roosevelt Field on Long Island with 450 gallons of fuel (and not much else) on the morning of May 20, 1927. Thirty-three-and-a-half hours later, Lindbergh landed safely at the Le Bourget Aerodrome in Paris. President Coolidge was thrilled with the result. "The more we learn of his accomplishment, in going from New York to Paris, the greater it seems to have been,"[266] he told reporters immediately after hearing of the successful outcome.

Coolidge anxiously awaited Lindbergh's return to the United States so he could host him in Washington. The meeting didn't take place at the

White House since the Coolidges had temporarily moved out of the residence due to some significant renovations that were now underway. Their temporary lodging was at the McKim, Mean, & White mansion on Dupont Circle, not far from the White House. It was here that the Coolidges welcomed Lindbergh and his mother on June 10, hosting him for a couple of meals and attending church together before hosting a massive celebration on the grounds of the Washington Monument. Some 300,000 people cheered as President Coolidge celebrated the unprecedented feat that had captured the imagination of the world. He followed this up by presenting the aviator with the Distinguished Flying Cross in a ceremony at the Washington Navy Yard. The following year, Coolidge added the Medal of Honor, which had rarely been bestowed on anyone who had not demonstrated extreme heroism in combat. Coolidge would come to count Charles Lindbergh as a friend and maintained contact with him for much of the rest of his life.

IV-59: President Coolidge awarding the Distinguished Flying Cross to Charles Lindbergh, June 11, 1927

Agent Starling was once again placed in charge of finding a suitable location for Coolidge's working vacation over the summer. Starling was a man of the outdoors and came up with a recommendation that would take the President and his official party more than 1,500 miles to the west, to the Black Hills of South Dakota. The President liked the idea of getting to a healthier climate for his wife. "I'm not worried about myself," he told Starling. "It's Mrs. Coolidge's health that bothers me. I don't think she can stand much more of this Washington climate and this official life."[267] In addition to the beautiful scenery and streams for fishing, the area was also home to the American monument being crafted out of the rock in a place called Mount Rushmore. Sculptor Gutzon Borglum had secured $250,000 from the Federal government to launch the project that would feature 60-foot-tall faces of Presidents George Washington, Thomas Jefferson, Abraham Lincoln, and Theodore Roosevelt. In addition to experiencing the local culture while being far away from the tumult of Washington, Coolidge would have the chance to check in on Borglum's progress to date.

The President's train made numerous stops on the way to South Dakota, allowing many to see a President in person for the first time in their lives. Governor William Bulow welcomed the Commander-in-Chief to the state capital of Pierre before Coolidge's party was taken to the State Game Lodge in Custer State Park, which was about 30 miles outside of Rapid City. The area was so remote that workers were finishing up the new road needed to get everyone to the destination about 4:00 am on the day of arrival, June 15, 1927. Fishing was a treasured pastime in the Black Hills, but the President was very much of a novice and the locals were concerned he might not catch anything. That would be a disaster in terms of their desire to increase tourism as a result of the President's visit. Just to be safe, they stocked the nearby streams and lakes with large quantities of several varieties of fish. At first, Coolidge just watched as Starling did most of the fishing, but eventually he decided to give it a try. Starling described what happened next:

> Oscar Otis, the superintendent of the estate, handled the boat. The President sat on the middle seat. I was forward. We proceeded along the shore about fifteen feet from the bank. Nothing happened for the first half hour. Then the President's spinner began to move along near the bank. His line went tight. It was a good-

IV-60: President Coolidge fishing

> sized fish. 'What'll I do with it?' he yelled at me. 'Keep a taut line with the rod tip up and let him stay in the water,' I said. … The President followed my instructions and in about twenty minutes he had his fish alongside the boat. By this time he was wild with excitement. 'Get him in the boat! Get him in the boat!' he shouted to me. 'He's still your fish,' I said, handing him the gaff. 'Lift him into the boat with this.' … I saw a beautiful Northern pike flopping on the bottom of the boat. [Coolidge] was sitting down, shaking all over. I winked at Otis and motioned him to head back to the boathouse. The pike, which weighed six pounds, I put on a fish string. When we landed I turned it over to the President, who took it in both hands and hurried up the path to the house. As he approached the cabin he called loudly for Mrs. Coolidge. She came out on the porch to see what was up. Waving the fish at her the [President] cried: 'Mama! Mama! Look what I've caught!' Thereafter we fished every day, rain or shine.[268]

Coolidge also catered to the local citizenry in ways that opened him up to ridicule but for which he had neither hesitation nor regret. For his 55th birthday, the President agreed to put on full cowboy attire for the celebration. For a man who almost always wore a business suit, even occasionally when performing chores on the farm in Vermont, it was a bit of a startling sight to see him wearing cowboy boots, chaps, a vest, and a ten-gallon hat. He was happy to pose for pictures in the outfit and rejected the notion that there was anything unseemly about being seen in the get-up. "I don't see why you object," he told a member of his traveling party. "The people here have sent me this costume, and they

IV-61: President Coolidge in a cowboy outfit during the summer of 1927

wouldn't have sent it unless they expected me to put it on. Why shouldn't I have my pictures taken with it to please them?" A month later he agreed to pose in a very different attire, but one that was also in line with the local culture. On August 17, Coolidge addressed 10,000 members of the Lakota Tribe, one of the largest subcultures of the Sioux Indians. It was the first speech given by an American President on an Indian reservation. Three years before, Coolidge had signed into law the Indian Citizenship Act. For the first time in American history, all Indians born in the United States instantly became American citizens. Coolidge, who wrote in his *Autobiography* that "his mother and her family showed marked trace of Indian blood,"[269] had previously welcomed numerous tribal leaders to meet with him at the White House. Here in the Black Hills, the Lakotas inducted Coolidge into their tribe, bestowing upon him the name Wanblee-Tokaha, or "Leading Eagle." The American President was happy to don a headdress provided by the Lakotas and pose for pictures that soon appeared in newspapers across the country.[270]

IV-62: President Coolidge in Indian attire during the summer of 1927

While the President occasionally went into Rapid City to do a little work at the office set up for him at the local high school, no one expected any major news to emanate from the Black Hills over the summer of 1927. President Coolidge, however, had something else very much on his mind. In late July, Coolidge pulled aside his secretary, Everett Sanders, and told him that he was planning to announce that he would not run for another term as President of the United States. With respect to the American tradition of limiting one's tenure in the presidency to no more than two terms, Coolidge fell somewhere in the middle. By the end of this term, he would have been in office for about five-and-a-half years, and most assumed that he would not be considered violating any norms by running one more time. While he had not spoken publicly on the topic to date, he had privately been considering the situation and had made his mind up that he would step down after his current term expired. He told Sanders that he planned to make the announcement on August 2, the fourth anniversary of his initial ascendancy to the office. Sanders was sworn to secrecy until then.

On the morning of the 2nd, Coolidge went into Rapid City and met with the press, but he had agreed ahead of time with Sanders' recommendation to wait until noon local time to make his announcement so that it wouldn't hit the wires until after the markets closed on the east coast. So, when their morning session wrapped up, he casually mentioned to the reporters, "I may have a further statement to make,"[271] and invited them to return at noon. Around 11:00 am, Coolidge took out his pencil and wrote on a single sheet of paper, "I do not choose to run for President in nineteen twenty-eight."[272] At about 11:50 am, he called for his stenographer, Erwin Geisser, gave him the handwritten note, and told him to make a number of copies, with several copies per page. When Geisser returned, the President took out some scissors and cut the pages into small strips, and then said, "I am going to hand these out myself; I am going to give them to the newspapermen, without comment, from this side of the desk. I want you to stand at the door and not permit anyone to leave until each of them has a slip, so that they may have an even chance."[273] Once the reporters were assembled, the President handed out the papers, waited for every to have a copy, and then had the door opened for the stampede to any available telephone or telegraph. One reporter

IV-63: President Coolidge's handwritten note announcing: "I do not choose to run for President in nineteen twenty eight" – August 2, 1927

asked if there was any information to add, to which the President responded, "There will be nothing more from this office today."[274]

Coolidge had made this decision entirely on his own. He hadn't even discussed it with either Frank Stearns or Grace Coolidge. Later that day, when the news was casually mentioned to the First Lady, she responded, "Isn't that just like the man! He never gave me the slightest intimation of his intention. I had no idea!"[275] While Grace was surprised at this announcement, she held no grudge for being left out of the decision-making process. That had never been her role, nor was it one she ever expected. "I am rather proud of the fact that after nearly a quarter of a century of marriage my husband feels free to make his decisions without consulting me or giving me advance information concerning them," she remarked shortly after Coolidge's presidency officially came to an end.[276] In fact, she acknowledged that if she had ever tried to intrude on her husband's professional decisions, "I feel sure that I should have been properly put in my place."[277] These diverse partners were incredibly close, yet remained comfortable in their distance when it came to Coolidge's political affairs.

As for Coolidge, the time was simply right to move on. "We draw our Presidents from the people," he captured in his *Autobiography*. "It is a wholesome thing for them to return to the people. I came from them. I wish to be one of them again."[278] With about ten months left until the Republican National Convention, he thought the timing was right in order to give the party plenty of time to find an alternate nominee. Many folks didn't take Coolidge at his word, especially with the odd phrasing ("I do not choose to run") he employed to make the announcement. Frank Stearns, for example, was shocked when he read the story in the newspaper back home in Massachusetts. There was plenty of conjecture that this was simply a ploy to avoid any campaigning but that Coolidge would be open to a draft if the party rallied around him at the Republican Convention. Perhaps his phraseology meant that while *he* didn't choose to run, he would be open to *others* choosing for him. One person who had no such doubts, however, was Agent Edmund Starling. Starling offered some insight into the peculiar phrase Coolidge had used. "To a Vermont Yankee nothing is more emphatic than, 'I do not choose,'" he later wrote. "It means, 'I ain't gonna do it and I don't give a dern what you think.' Nothing is more sacred to a New England Yankee than his privilege as an individual to make up his own mind – his freedom of choice."[279] And that choice for Calvin Coolidge was not to run in 1928.

After the announcement, Coolidge went back to relaxing in the Black Hills of South Dakota. He continued to fish with Agent Starling, go on long walks, and try to clear his head from the people who kept asking if he really meant what he said in his statement. He also decided to take the trip to Mount Rushmore to visit the early stage development of Borglum's masterpiece of Americana. The sculptor went out of his way to cheer the arrival of the incumbent President. "I am getting old," he told the crowd that day in the summer of 1927, "but I may yet live long enough to put the bust of Coolidge alongside those of Washington, Jefferson, Lincoln and Roosevelt." Borglum then made an offer that wouldn't put Coolidge's face on the monument but would capture his words. "We want your connection with it shown in some other way than by just your presence! I want the name of Coolidge on that mountain!" Borglum declared.[280] He offered the President the opportunity to craft a brief statement on American history that could be chiseled into the mountain alongside the busts of the four Presidents. Coolidge was honored by the request and indicated he would be happy to assist when the time was right. It was a nice ending to an eventful summer retreat, one which the President truly enjoyed. "You were right about these Westerners," Coolidge told Starling as they were about to leave for home. "They are hospitable, and they don't expect anything in return for it. I have had a good time."[281] That was about as strong an endorsement as one could get from Calvin Coolidge.

When the Coolidges returned to the nation's capital, they were able to move back into the newly renovated White House. The major updates were on the third floor, where attic space had been turned into new living quarters, with new bedrooms now available for additional guests. The First Lady also welcomed what she labeled her sky parlor, a space on that upper floor that was now bathed in sunshine through the newly installed skylights and windows. Meanwhile, the President was inundated with questions about his recent announcement. His general response was that the statement spoke for itself and there was nothing more to say. He did issue one formal comment on the topic when some members of the Republican National Committee came to see him at the White House in December. "My statement stands," he affirmed. "No one should be led to suppose that I have modified it. My decision will be respected. After I had been eliminated, the party began, and should continue, the serious task of selecting another candidate from among the numbers of distinguished men available."[282] Despite the President's firm stand, speculation would continue over the course of the next several months about whether anyone could get him to change his mind.

One of the reasons Coolidge's fellow Republicans couldn't understand his refusal to run was that re-election was highly likely given the fact that the American economy had truly begun to roar. All the economic indicators were solidly in positive territory. Federal revenues were up and the debt was going down. Unemployment was down and wages were up. Americans were continuing to spend the additional money in their pockets (thanks in no small measure to the cuts in the Federal income tax) on household innovations and for travel in their new cars. Heading into the fall, President Coolidge reiterated his optimistic outlook, seeing no reason that the country wouldn't continue to experience a year "of continued healthy business activity and prosperity."[283] There was also a new element to the economic prosperity that the country was experiencing that began to take hold in 1927, and that was a significant rise in the stock market. The Dow Jones Industrial Average had hovered near the 100 mark for most of the first half of the 1920s. Stocks began a noticeable uptick in 1926, ending the year at 157. The rise accelerated throughout 1927, hitting a record high of just over 200 by the end of the year.[284] Trading volume was also reaching new peaks. After eight consecutive days in which more than two million shares were traded, *The New York Times* reported, "From the standpoint of breadth and sustained strength, the present market is one of the most remarkable in the history of the Exchange."[285] While this was undoubtedly a true statement, there were some who started to worry about the overheating of this economic boom. Some were seeing the stock market as simply a new gambling fetish, in which brokers were borrowing heavily and at high interest rates in order to plunge as much money as they could into this skyrocketing market. With huge amounts of assets being used as collateral in this speculative frenzy, any serious dip in the unpredictable market was bound to have a dramatic effect on individual investors and the economy as a whole. For the time being, however, any such notes of caution were drowned out by the exuberance associated with this unprecedented rise in stock values and the outsized investment returns that came with them.

About a month before the next congressional session could get underway, another natural disaster hit a section of the United States. Senator Caraway's assertion that President Coolidge would have responded differently if the recent floods in the Mississippi Valley had hit his beloved New England was about the be put to the test. Rain fell by the bucketful throughout the Connecticut River Valley beginning on November 2. Within 48 hours, Coolidge's home state of Vermont had suffered one of the worst disasters in its history. According to *Vermont History*:

> The downpour, which went almost immediately into the river systems scattered through the state's narrow and low valets, was more than the watercourses could handle. Brooks overflowed and rivers became torrents, carrying trees and logs in their wake. Rivers reached 13 feet or more above their normal depths. Dams, bridges, and embankments were swept away. Towns and villages located along the rushing streams were engulfed. Factories submerged, farm animals drowned, and homes and barns were destroyed. As the water gradually receded, it left behind a trail of eroded farm land; layers of silt, gravel, and debris; and disorganized towns.[286]

The state's Lieutenant Governor was among the 84 people killed amid this natural disaster when he drowned trying to flee his car for safety. Damages were estimated in the millions. Many Vermonters immediately looked to their man in the White House for help.

President Coolidge had made it clear just a few months before that he did not believe the Federal government had a role to play in disaster relief. Would he, in fact, change course now that the destruction was hitting closer to home (even though Plymouth Notch was spared from the worst of the damage)? The answer was 'no.' Principles were principles, and Coolidge's view of federalism wasn't about to change, despite the clamoring for help from his neighbors to the north. Coolidge supported private fundraising and dispatched Secretary Hoover again to coordinate on relief efforts, but he would not sanction direct financial aid from the Federal government. This stance did not play well in the immediate aftermath of the disaster in Vermont. "Is not Vermont worth as much as France to the United States?" a reporter for the Boston *Globe* paraphrased a businessman as saying. "Calvin Coolidge is a Vermonter. Perhaps that boast of the state is now its chief liability," the paper concluded.[287] The

Vermont state government held a special session in which it appropriated $8.5 million for disaster relief, the equivalent of half the state's budget for the entire year. They had no choice. Their man in the White House stuck to his views on the limited role of the Federal government in the constitutional republic, even when his friends and neighbors were suffering.

A different kind of disaster – a political one – continued to unfold throughout this period, with the Harding scandals now migrating from Capitol Hill to the courthouse. The Justice Department ultimately brought charges against three people from the Harding years (beyond Charles Forbes, whose case was mentioned earlier). In separate trials, former Interior Secretary Albert Fall and oilman Edward Doheny were charged with conspiracy to defraud the Federal government. The congressional investigation had uncovered that a $100,000 cash payment had been handed to Fall in a black satchel to "encourage" him to award Doheny the oil contracts in California. Fall insisted the cash was a loan that had no bearing on his decision for the reward of the oil leases. The government characterized the payment purely and simply as an illegal bribe. The initial trials returned not-guilty verdicts, but as new evidence became available, subsequent cases would go to trial in 1929. In an odd twist, Doheny was found not guilty of bribing Fall, but Fall was found guilty in his own trial of accepting that alleged bribe. Fall became the first Cabinet secretary to go to prison for his actions in the service of a President. In a completely separate case, former Attorney General Harry Daugherty was charged with negligence in the performance of his duties under Harding related to allegedly fraudulent transactions linked to the return of enemy property captured during the war. Daugherty fought the charges and pleaded the Fifth during his two trials, both of which ended in hung juries. Despite all the sensational testimony over the course of several years of investigations, Albert Fall and Charles Forbes were the only high-ranking officials from the Harding administration to be convicted for breaking the law. No evidence ever surfaced that directly linked Harding to either these or any other crimes, yet his name was dragged through the mud for many years. Calvin Coolidge was primarily immune from any of these accusations. He had been well-served by avoiding interactions with most of the members of Harding's Ohio Gang during the early years of the administration.

As Congress returned the following month, President Coolidge remained focused on the economy in his welcoming Annual Message. He remained optimistic, with a plan to stay the course on policies that had served the country extremely well. He was prepared to play defense as well, recognizing that as the large surpluses continued, congressmen were likely going to want to spend. "I am having the usual experience with a good many members of the House and the Senate that are returning to Washington," he noted to members of the press just before the opening session. "They are all interested in some plan that calls for a considerable expenditure of public money."[288] Coolidge continued to resist these urges. When another version of the McNary-Haugen farm bill came up in 1928, he vetoed it again. "It would be difficult to conceive of a more flagrant case of the employment of all of the coercive powers of the government for the profit of a small number of specially privileged groups," he wrote as he rejected the legislation. He spoke of a "bureaucracy gone mad" and a "preposterous economic and commercial fallacy."[289] Coolidge remained committed to his narrow view of the role of the Federal government, including objections to using Federal funds as handouts to discrete industries. That said, during the course of the session, he did agree to a piece of legislation with a $500 million price tag for water management and flood control at key points across the country. The statute, which had been championed by Secretary Hoover, provided the responsibility to the Army Corps of Engineers to lead the nation's flood control programs. The law represented a significant expansion of government responsibilities that was rarely seen throughout the Coolidge presidency. Apparently, the recent disasters had convinced him that the country as a whole was at risk of future weather catastrophes, and a national program to mitigate those risks was going to be money well spent for the benefit of the entire nation.

8. Foreign Affairs

Foreign affairs had played only a minor role thus far in Coolidge's presidency, with little of note since the adoption of the Dawes Plan that restructured foreign debts left over from World War I. The international scene was not Coolidge's area of expertise, and he relied heavily on his two Secretaries of State, Charles Evans Hughes and Frank Kellogg, to guide his thinking in this arena. A couple of hot spots would gain his attention over his last couple of years in office, as would an opportunity to forge an international coalition outside the confines of the League of Nations to take a stand against using war as a method to resolve international disputes.

The most pressing foreign challenge was on the country's southern border. President Woodrow Wilson had dealt with conflicts with Mexico for years, including a brief incursion by bandits under Pancho Villa in the American border town of Columbus, New Mexico, back in 1916. As the political situation in Mexico stabilized under the leadership of Victoriano Carranza, relations with the United States also improved, even though tensions remained just below the surface. Beginning with the Carranza government, and continuing under his successor Álvaro Obregón, the Mexicans were becoming increasingly protective of their natural resources, particularly oil. Having sold land to foreign investors to exploit the country's abundant oil fields, the Mexican government began to pursue policies that would claw back those sources of potential national wealth. Foreign companies were outraged, claiming a breach of contract. No voices were louder than those from American oil companies who had the most to lose by the new policies.

President Coolidge wanted positive relations with his southern neighbor, which is why he agreed to formally recognize the Obregón government within a month of taking over the presidency from Warren Harding. When Obregón was being threatened by insurgents, the Coolidge administration agreed to sell arms to its Mexican counterpart in order to maintain order in a country that was often beset with internal strife. But the calls for President Coolidge to step in to protect American commercial interests in Mexico reached a peak after Plutaro Calles took over the presidency in 1925. After a lull in government activity on the question of these foreign-owned oil fields, the new Mexican President accelerated and expanded the volume of the property being seized on behalf of his government. By this point, Americans were not only calling for Coolidge to intervene with diplomatic pressure but also to be prepared to use force if necessary to protect these contractually valid American interests. President Coolidge was hesitant to follow this line of thinking. He offered the following perspective when confronted on the topic by Henry Stoddard, the editor of the *New York Evening Mail*:

> Now, look on the other side of the picture. Here we are the most powerful nation in the world. At this moment we have special representatives in Europe as well as all our diplomats urging reduction of armaments and preaching peace. The world of today would harshly condemn us if, despite our attitude, we should go to war with a neighbor nation not nearly our equal. What do you suppose people in years to come would say? Powerful United States crushing powerless Mexico! Don't you think it is better for us to find another way to handle the situation?[290]

The President decided to pursue an alternative approach, but first, he needed to introduce a new player into the mix.

The current American ambassador to Mexico, James Sheffield, was known to be hostile to the Calles government. Coolidge thought a change might improve the relations between the two neighbors, but he was struggling to find someone who could rise above the current strife and negotiate a settlement that would be acceptable to both countries. Frank Stearns thought he had the answer. When Stearns suggested Coolidge's old Amherst classmate, Dwight Morrow, the President immediately agreed. Morrow had achieved success in the world of finance but had mostly stayed out of politics. Earlier in his term, Coolidge had asked Morrow to serve as Chairman on a commission on the military's use of aircraft, but that had been his only official tasking. That was about to change. Once Morrow accepted the appointment to replace Sheffield in Mexico, he was

IV-64: Dwight Morrow

given one simple directive from his friend, the President. "My only instructions are to keep us out of war with Mexico,"[291] Coolidge said rather matter-of-factly.

Morrow brought a very different approach to his assignment when compared to his predecessor. He arrived in Mexico City in a conciliatory mood, using the power of personal persuasion, coupled with an unusual frankness in the world of diplomacy, to begin to make headway in the conflict over the disputed lands. After gaining the confidence of President Calles, the two were able to negotiate a compromise measure that worked for both nations. The Calles-Morrow Agreement adopted a grandfather clause to maintain the efficacy of contracts over land purchases from prior to 1917. Mexico would maintain ownership of all lands since that date, with the right to lease those lands to foreign interests while retaining actual ownership. While some of the advocates on both sides of the deal didn't feel it went far enough to protect their legitimate interests, most hailed the agreement as a landmark breakthrough for peace and stability between the two neighbors.

A little further south, the Americans were also involved in the ongoing instability in Nicaragua. President Coolidge thought things had stabilized, agreeing in 1925 to pull out the U.S. Marines who had been in the country on a peacekeeping mission for more than a decade. As soon as the American troops left, the country destabilized, erupting into a civil war. In 1926, the Coolidge administration sided with the government put forward by General Adolpho Díaz, after which Díaz immediately asked the Americans to once again send in the marines to maintain the peace while he asserted his government's authority across his country's institutions. Coolidge agreed to the request. Along with his military peacekeepers, Coolidge dispatched former Secretary of War Henry Stimson as his special envoy to negotiate a truce between the warring parties. Stimson orchestrated a cease-fire along with a return of prisoners and property that had been taken in the recent fight. Both sides agreed to new elections, which were set for the following year. When the American-backed Díaz lost in that subsequent race, all parties recognized the result, including the seating of José María Moncada as President. Stimson's service wasn't done. After helping to settle the conflict in Nicaragua, Coolidge asked him to head to the Philippines to take over as Governor-General for Leonard Wood, who had recently passed away. The Philippines remained a U.S. territory more than two decades after being acquired in the Spanish-American War, and Coolidge did not seek to change that arrangement during his term as President. In fact, independence for the Filipinos was still another two decades away. Stimson's job was essentially to maintain the status quo on the President's behalf.

Calvin Coolidge only left American soil on a couple of occasions in his entire life. One of these occurrences took place in the first week of 1928 when he agreed to participate in a Pan-American Conference in Cuba. Tens of thousands of Cubans lined the streets to greet the American President when he arrived on the USS *Texas*. The event was formally called the Sixth International Conference of American States and included representatives from 21 Latin American nations. Coolidge offered some opening remarks, including his belief in maintaining an "exact footing of equality" among nations, along with a peace-loving "admonition to beat our swords into plowshares."[292] Former Secretary of State Charles Evans Hughes led the American delegation in the meetings that followed, assisted by Dwight Morrow and Democratic Senator Oscar Underwood. The primary outcome of the event was an agreement on a multilateral treaty to utilize arbitration for all juridical questions that might arise among the members.

President Harding had negotiated a landmark arms limitation agreement in his first year in office, but that treaty only went so far. It covered several classes of naval vessels, but not all. Submarines and destroyers, for example, were excluded from that pact, and Coolidge was worried if a new agreement wasn't reached soon that covered these and other instruments of war, then a costly arms race might ensue on his watch. The British and Japanese agreed to meet in Geneva to talk arms control, but France and Italy declined to participate. The meetings themselves were not going well, with the Americans and British very much at odds. Pessimistic regarding a breakthrough, President Coolidge agreed to support a nine-year, $1 billion appropriation for U.S. naval expansion.

While the French sat out these talks, Prime Minster Aristide Briand was pushing for a more general bilateral agreement with the Americans. In April 1927, Briand proposed to an audience in the United States for the "denunciation of war as national policy."[293] A couple of months later, while the talks in Geneva were flailing, Briand formally presented this proposal to the American government. At first, there was little support for the proposition in the United States, not sure how binding the agreement would be and what ramifications either party might face if they decided to take up arms, particularly in self-defense. But the idea picked up some momentum as Senator William Borah embraced the concept as his own, becoming its champion in the U.S. While the administration generally looked askance at the bilateral proposal, Secretary of State Frank Kellogg saw value if more countries signed on. President Coolidge embraced this notion, leaving the details up to Kellogg. Kellogg and his Assistant Secretary William Castle, Jr., were concerned that negotiations with the French to expand participation in the agreement might drag on for months. With limited time left in the administration, they recommended a bold maneuver to the President. Kellogg and Castle proposed crafting the treaty language and releasing it to the world with an open invitation to sign on. On December 28, 1927, the Americans proposed the following terms:

IV-65: Secretary of State Frank Kellogg

> **Article I:** The High Contracting Parties solemnly declare in the names of their respective peoples that they condemn recourse to war for the solution of international controversies and renounce it as an instrument of national policy in their relations with one another.
>
> **Article II:** The High Contracting Parties agree that the settlement or solution of all disputes or conflicts of whatever nature or of whatever origin they may be, which may arise among them, shall never be sought except by pacific means.[294]

Briand, who was initially caught off guard by the American proposal, eventually agreed to support the globalization of the effort. President Coolidge issued a strong statement of support, making it clear that American sovereignty would remain intact regardless of signing the pact. "It is the most solemn declaration against war, the most positive adherence to peace, that it is possible for sovereign nations to make,"

Coolidge maintained. "It does not supersede our inalienable sovereign right and duty of national defense or undertake to commit us before the event to any mode of action which the Congress might decide to be wise if ever the treaty should be broken."[295] Momentum was built with other nations throughout the year, led by commitments to sign on by the powers of Britain, Italy, Japan, and even Germany. When diplomats gathered in Paris for a signing ceremony on August 27, 1928, the following nations added their concurrence with the effort: Australia, Belgium, Canada, Czechoslovakia, India, the Irish Free State, New Zealand, Poland, and South Africa. By the time the treaty went into effect in July 1929, another 30 countries had signed on.

As Americans well knew in the wake of the failure of the Treaty of Versailles in the U.S. Senate, treaties negotiated by the executive branch often faced an uncertain fate when it came to ratification. Some of the opponents of the Kellogg-Briand Pact pointed out the fact that this agreement was essentially unenforceable and, therefore, meaningless. For example, the New York *Herald Tribune* opined, "The conception of renouncing war by government fiat is inherently absurd."[296] Senator

IV-66: President Coolidge signing the Kellogg-Briand Pact, January 17, 1929; Also seated at the table is Secretary of State Frank Kellogg who negotiated the treaty

Carter Glass of Virginia was similarly skeptical of the agreement. "I am not willing that anybody in Virginia shall think I am simple enough to suppose that it is worth a postage stamp in the direction of accomplishing permanent peace," he declared.[297] But Glass voted for the popular pact anyway. In fact, with Senator Borah leading the charge, only one U.S. senator chose to oppose this commitment to favor peaceful means over war to resolve conflicts with other nations. The final vote for ratification was 85-1. The Kellogg-Briand Pact hardly eliminated war as a tool for one nation to use against another, but it was another stake in the ground in that direction as the world continued to seek to make World War I "the world to end all wars." For his efforts on behalf of President Coolidge and the American people, Frank Kellogg became the fifth American to win the Nobel Peace Prize. For a man not known for his accomplishments in foreign affairs, Coolidge is one of only two American Presidents whose administration delivered results that led to more than one such award. Only representatives of Harry Truman's administration also earned the recognition by the Nobel Peace committee on more than one occasion.[298]

9. Nothing Lasts Forever

Coolidge did his best to stay out of the election of 1928. Commerce Secretary Herbert Hoover emerged as one of the leading contenders for the Republican Nomination. On a couple of occasions, Hoover told Coolidge that he would be happy to stand aside if the incumbent changed his mind and wanted to run for another term. Coolidge had no intention of getting into the race and was getting annoyed that people kept asking him about it. The President dispatched people loyal to him to the convention in Kansas City to ensure the delegates didn't take matters into their own hands and nominate him against his will. By the time the party leaders gathered, that message had already gotten through, leaving the nomination for Hoover on the first ballot. Senate Majority Leader Charles Curtis of Kansas was handed the number two spot on the ticket.

The Coolidges were far away from these events, heading for the Brule River in northern Wisconsin for their summer getaway while the convention was being gaveled to order. Their departure was delayed by a couple of days due to an illness for the First Lady, but they were already settling in by the time the Hoover nomination became a reality. Coolidge was ready to support the party nominee, but he was in a rather foul mood when Hoover came to visit his vacation spot shortly after the convention. When the pair posed for pictures and reporters asked Coolidge for a statement, he tersely replied, "Let him talk, he's going to be President."[299]

IV-67: President Coolidge with Republican presidential nominee Herbert Hoover, at Coolidge's summer vacation home in Brule, WI, 1928

Perhaps he was just surly over his own pending departure from office, but he also seemed concerned that Hoover might not be up to the task, particularly with respect to concerns about economic headwinds that might be right around the corner. "Well, they're going to elect that superman Hoover, and he's going to have some trouble," Coolidge said at the time. "He's going to have to spend money. But he won't spend enough. Then the Democrats will come in and they'll spend money like water. But they don't know anything about money. Then they will want me to come back and save some money for them. But I won't do it."[300] In fact, Coolidge admitted that he wouldn't be the right person to lead the nation in a period of economic contraction. "I know how to save money. All my training has been in that direction," he admitted. "Perhaps the time has come when we ought to spend money. I do not feel that I am qualified to do it."[301] Given the current strength of the economy, Coolidge was confident that Hoover would win the vote of the people against the Democratic nominee Al Smith of New York. But he remained concerned about what might transpire in that subsequent administration.

Coolidge enjoyed his time away from Washington, becoming more of an outdoorsman each summer he spent with Agent Starling. He was no-nonsense when it came to fishing. "One day he lost a fish he had been playing and I heard him say, 'Damn!'" Starling later wrote. "Then he turned to me and with a shy smile said: 'Guess I'm a real fisherman now. I cussed.'"[302] In the summer of 1928, Starling convinced the President to add hunting to his repertoire of outdoor activities. He started with artificial targets, which got the President all excited, as he shared with Grace upon his return to the lodge. "Mama," he said, "Colonel Starling was shooting those things they call clay pigeons and I took the gun away from him and broke a whole lot of them."[303] Coolidge and Starling started talking about going on a grand adventure of hunting and fishing after his term as President came to an end.

At the end of the summer, Coolidge also made up with his home state of Vermont. Despite his decision not to provide relief funds in the wake of the widespread destruction from the torrential downpours earlier in the year, the President was welcomed by large cheering crowds at each of a dozen stops in his tour of the state. This included a stayover at his father's home in Plymouth, a place where he planned to spend more time once he left the White House. He was pleased to see that his fellow Vermonters had helped themselves persevere through the recent disaster, living up to the Puritan tradition of self-reliance. At the end of the tour, he spoke from the rear of his train in Bennington, expressing his heartfelt feelings for the state of his birth.

> Vermont is a state I love. ... It was here that I first saw the light of day; here I received my bride, here my dead lie, pillowed on the loving breast of our everlasting hills. I love Vermont because of her hills and valleys, her scenery and invigorating climate, but most of all because of her indomitable people. They are a race of pioneers who have almost beggared themselves to serve others. If the spirit of liberty should vanish in other parts of the union and support of our institutions should languish, it could all be replenished from the generous store held by the people of this brave little state of Vermont.[304]

By the end of this visit, any ill will some of his fellow Vermonters felt toward their President earlier in the year appeared to have faded away.

Coolidge mostly laid low when it came to the election of 1928. Secretary Hoover was proud to run on the Coolidge record, saying in a campaign address, "We in America today are nearer the final triumph over poverty than ever before in the history of any land."[305] He pledged to maintain many of the policies that had been so beneficial for Americans throughout the decade under Presidents Harding and Coolidge. Given the widespread prosperity across the United States, it was unlikely the electorate was going to change course, leading to another landslide Republican victory in the fall. Hoover trounced Smith 444 to 87 in the Electoral College, capturing 40 of the 48 states in the Union. Hoover became the first candidate to top 20 million votes in the popular tally, beating Smith 58% to 41%. This was all about the economy, what Coolidge saw as the greatest triumph of his presidency. His "policy has encouraged enterprise, made possible the highest

IV-68: President Coolidge

rate of wages which has ever existed, returned large profits, brought to the homes of the people the greatest economic benefits they ever enjoyed, and given to the country as a whole an unexampled era of prosperity," Coolidge reflected in his *Autobiography*. "This well-being of my country has given me the chief satisfaction of my administration."[306] All of this was true. The question remained, though, how long it could last.

The stock market crash that served as one of the catalysts of the Great Depression was still a year away, but the signs of instability were already causing concern among some economists. Speculation in the stock market had reached unchartered territories. Brokers were now regularly buying stocks on margin, putting down as little as 10% of the capital needed to purchase their securities, borrowing the rest while placing hard assets at risk as collateral. In 1926, call money balances were about $2 billion. By the end of 1928, they had spiked to $3.9 billion, and would reach a whopping $6.4 billion in less than another year.[307] As the market climbed, wealth accumulation seemed easy, almost automatic, justifying these risks and fueling unprecedented participation in the market. The Dow Jones Industrial Average, which started the year at 200, ended the year at 300, a 50% increase over the course of 12 months.[308] Trading volume had skyrocketed as well, with more than five million shares traded for the first time on a single day on June 12, 1928.[309] When asked to comment if he had any concerns about the stock market, particularly given all the speculative buying on margin that was occurring on the New York exchange, Coolidge declined to raise any concerns. As reported in *The New York Times*:

> Although loans to brokers and dealers held by the New York Federal Reserve member banks have reached unprecedented heights of $3,810,023,000, President Coolidge does not see any reason for unfavorable comment. … The President, it was said at the White House today, believes that the increase represents a natural expansion of business in the securities market and sees nothing unfavorable in it.[310]

Some in the market saw the President's statement as an endorsement of the behavior of buying on margin, perhaps fueling even greater degrees of speculative investment habits. And while this was an accurate portrayal of his public statements, the President's private comments were more cautious. Coolidge told his cousin H. Parker Willis, "If I were to give my own personal opinion about it, I should say that any loan made for gambling in stocks was an 'excessive loan.'"[311] Coolidge's personal investments were primarily housed in bank accounts and government bonds. Regardless of his personal concerns, however, as President he felt he had no authority to do anything with respect to the stock market, even if he were so inclined to act. When some economists, such as Professor William Ripley, met the President in the White House and urged some action to cool the market before it got completely out of control, Coolidge denied any authority to follow this recommendation. He told Judson Welliver, "Even if you and Professor Ripley are right about it, what is there I can do? The New York Stock Exchange is an affair of the state of New York, not of the federal government. I don't think I have any authority to interfere with its operations."[312] Consistent with his longstanding conservative views on the topic of federalism, Coolidge saw no role for the national executive to take action directly with respect to private markets. His presidency wound to a close with the American economy still booming and the stock market at all-time highs. An unprecedented national economic reckoning, however, was just around the corner.

Coolidge used his final Annual Message to Congress as a bit of a valedictory. He rightfully claimed to be leaving his leadership post with his nation in seemingly excellent shape in just about every area of importance.

> No Congress of the United States ever assembled, on surveying the state of the Union, has met with a more pleasing prospect than that which appears at the present time. In the domestic field there is tranquility and contentment, harmonious relations between management and wage earner, freedom from industrial strife, and the highest record of years of prosperity. In the foreign field there is peace, the good will that comes from mutual understanding, and the knowledge that the problems which a short time ago appeared so ominous are yielding to the touch of mutual friendship.[313]

For Calvin Coolidge, this was less about braggadocio and more of a statement of fact. Peace and prosperity were the watchwords of the United States as the President prepared to hand over the reins of government to Herbert Hoover.

As the President and First Lady made their final preparations to depart for their adopted home of Massachusetts, Frank Stearns was packing for home as well. Stearns had been by Coolidge's side since his rise from the state Senate to his four successive positions of executive leadership at the state and national levels. Stearns never stopped promoting Calvin Coolidge while also never pushing him to be anything but his natural self. Stearns never asked for anything for himself, rarely offered a political opinion unless directly asked for it, and could sit for hours just quietly smoking cigars until Coolidge was ready to get back to work. It was the perfect fit for a companion and ally, with high levels of mutual appreciation and esteem. Just a week before the Coolidge administration officially came to an end, Stearns wrote his Chief a final note of thanks for what had become a uniquely special relationship. He concluded his lengthy message with the following thoughts:

> For the association that has existed, in which Mrs. Coolidge, you, the boys, Mrs. Stearns, and I have had such an intimate part, I am very grateful. I hope you will not think me lacking in humility if I hug the comfort that it is sufficient to be an excuse for having lived. Wherever you are and whatever you do after March 4th, I hope and believe that you will not hesitate to call if I can be helpful in any way, big or little, to you or yours.
>
> I will conclude by signing as I have always signed my letters to you,
>
> Sincerely,
>
> FRANK W. STEARNS[314]

The President immediately responded with a note of his own, equally heartfelt but with a lot fewer words.

> MY DEAR MR. STEARNS:
>
> Your beautiful letter has been received. I shall always treasure it. It is most gratifying to know that you are still loyal to your idols. I should like to think that I was in some way worthy of the things you are always saying about me.
>
> With kindest regards, I am Cordially yours,
>
> CALVIN COOLIDGE[315]

Coolidge and Stearns both seemed to get everything they wanted out of this highly complementary association.

President Coolidge welcomed his successor to the White House and joined him for the final ride as Commander-in-Chief to the Capitol for the transfer of power. All went smoothly as Coolidge contemplated his first time in nearly 20 years as a citizen without public office. Like many of his predecessors, he wasn't quite sure what to do with himself. "I'd like to go into some kind of business," he mentioned to his friend, James Derieux, "but I can't do it with propriety. A man who has been President is not free, not for a time anyway. I wish he were. Whatever influence I might have, came to me because of the position I have held, and to use that influence in any competitive field would be unfair."[316] The ever-frugal Calvin Coolidge had saved a significant amount from his VP and presidential salaries over the past eight years, so he didn't have to work. Still, he was only 56 years old when he left the White House, and he wanted to find a way to be productive.

IV-69: President Coolidge with President-elect Herbert Hoover, on the day of Hoover's inauguration, March 4, 1929

The first stop in the Coolidges' post-presidential lives was the old duplex on Massasoit Street in Northampton, a place which, according to Grace, "fits us like a comfortable well-worn garment which has adjusted itself to our peculiarities."[317] Still only paying $36 per month in rent, the couple was content to reside in the humblest of all post-presidential surroundings. The problem was that Calvin Coolidge was no longer just a neighbor, he was the former President of the United States, which made him an attraction for all manner of his fellow citizens who wanted the chance to stop and stare at someone who had once held such a position of power. It got to the point where Coolidge could no longer sit in peace on his front porch as the gawkers tracked his every move. The invasion of privacy continued every time Coolidge wanted to take a walk down the street or head into the city for a bite to eat or to meet a friend. "Did you ever stop to think what a task it is to speak to every person you see on the streets?" he asked Derieux. "It is nice to say good morning to several persons, and to shake hands with them; but it is hard to say good morning to several hundred, and to shake hands with each one of them."[318] After a few months of this, even Coolidge realized he needed a change if he was going to be able to have any sense of privacy ever again. In the spring of 1930, the Coolidges bought the first and only home they would ever own in the more secluded Hampton Terrace area of Northampton. It was called The Beeches. "It is a modest place with a little land," Coolidge noted. "It will give my doggies a place to exercise and will enable us to entertain our occasional guests from out of town more comfortably."[319] The new home, which featured 12 rooms, was situated on nine acres of land. Importantly, it came with a gate to keep

IV-70: The Beeches, the Northampton home purchased by Coolidge after leaving the presidency; To the left is the first car owned by Coolidge. It was the car he used as President, that he purchased from the government upon leaving office.

people out and was largely shielded from view from the street. At least they'd have their privacy. The cost was $45,000, for which he paid cash out of his savings. The man who avoided debt like the plague throughout his life finally had a home, but he never had a mortgage, always living well within his means, just like he tried to do for his country as President of the United States.

As expected, Coolidge rejected nearly all of the business opportunities that were presented to him, primarily because he thought most just wanted to trade on his name and former position. He did join the board of the New York Life Insurance Company and regularly attended their monthly board meetings in New York. He also welcomed the opportunity to serve as the President of the American Antiquarian Association. Occasionally on his business trips, reporters would track him down to ask questions about current national issues. They needn't have bothered. Even as the economy went south in President Hoover's first year in office, Coolidge stuck with his standard response to the press in his post-presidential years, "Nothing whatever to say."[320] But, on many topics, Coolidge did have something to say, and he was provided a couple of outlets in which to do just that.

The first was his *Autobiography*, which was published just a few months after leaving office. Coolidge had been encouraged by Ray Long, the editor of *Cosmopolitan*, to share the story of his life with his fellow Americans. Originally released in regular installments in the magazine, the work was eventually bound and sold in book form later in 1929. The relatively brief memoir is a simple depiction of the major events in Coolidge's life, along with some context and perspective that offer a relatively rare glimpse into Coolidge's inner thoughts. It is primarily a matter-of-fact set of reflections without much depth, but given how Coolidge typically kept nearly all of his inner thoughts to himself, the book does reveal some insights that otherwise would have remained a mystery. A number of direct references have been shared throughout this text.

One area the former President expounded upon in his *Autobiography* regarded the life of a politician and the challenge associated with being the one always in the spotlight. "The political mind is the product of men in public life who have been twice spoiled," Coolidge wrote. "They have been spoiled with praise and they have been spoiled with abuse. With them nothing is natural, everything is artificial. A few rare souls escape these influences and maintain a vision and a judgment that are unimpaired."[321] He then elaborated:

> It is difficult for men in high office to avoid the malady of self-delusion. They are always surrounded by worshipers. They are constantly, and for the most part sincerely, assured of their greatness. They live in an artificial atmosphere of adulation and exaltation which sooner or later impairs their judgment. They are in grave danger of becoming careless and arrogant. The chances of having wise and faithful public service are increased by a change in the Presidential office after a moderate length of time.[322]

As a man who spent 30 years in the world of politics, Coolidge had a front row seat to come to this conclusion.

The *Autobiography* was not the only outlet for the former President to express his opinions. The folks at *McClure* offered him a syndicated column that would be featured in newspapers across the country. He would earn $3,000 a week for his daily musings along with a share of the revenue from the syndication. In total, he pocketed more than $200,000 for his one year as a newspaper columnist. Each day, Coolidge met with his secretary, Herman Beaty, to talk through possible topics for that day's column, which typically ran only 150 to 200 words. Once they settled on the topic, Coolidge took out his pencil and crafted his message by hand. He wanted his thoughts to be timely, so he didn't store up a bunch of columns in advance. A total of 60 newspapers carried "Thinking Things Over with Calvin Coolidge," which first appeared on July 1, 1930.

Coolidge used the column to engage on all manner of topics facing his country, reflecting the daily drumbeat of the nation. He largely focused on government, politics, and economics, but occasionally ventured into other areas, including ethics and overall idealism. His core beliefs of the strength of the individual, self-reliance, and the limited role of the Federal government were weaved through many of his daily offerings, all of which were shared at a time of great economic distress. The widespread prosperity that had blanketed the country for much of the Coolidge years seemed to abruptly disappear, beginning with the stock market crash of October 1929. After skyrocketing to a peak of 381.17 on September 3, 1929, the Dow Jones Industrial Average hovered for another month before "Black Thursday" witnessed a 21 percent decline in the market, falling to 299.5. Three weeks later, it was below 200, and mostly in freefall.[323] When Coolidge's first column hit the newsstands the following summer, he tried to offer encouragement despite these times of struggle. "Our country, our people, our civil and religious institutions may not be perfect, but they are what we have made them," he wrote. "They are good enough so that it has been necessary to build a high exclusion law to prevent all the world from rushing to possess them. My countrymen, it is time to stop criticizing and quarreling and begin sympathizing and helping."[324] A month later, he emphasized the power of the individual, even during difficult times.

> There are people who complain that they do not have any luck. These are the opportunists who think that their destiny is all shaped outside themselves. They are always waiting for something to happen. … Our real luck lies within ourselves. It is a question of character. It depends on whether we follow the inner light of conscience. … The man who is right makes his own luck.[325]

That was certainly his view based on his own life experiences.

As the economy continued to shrink and unemployment began to mount, the former President largely stuck to his core beliefs about the role of the Federal government on issues related to individual suffering, even if that pain was being felt across such a wide spectrum of the citizenry in terms of the current depression. "Some confusion appears to exist in the public mind as to the proper function of the national government in the relief of distress, whether caused by disaster or unemployment," Coolidge wrote. "Strictly construed, the national government has no such duties. It acts purely as a volunteer. … When the disaster is very great, federal aid has sometimes been extended. In case of unemployment, relief is entirely the province of the local government which has agencies and appropriations for that purpose."[326] Coolidge never wavered in his conservative beliefs on the limited role of the U.S. Federal government. Political ideology aside, Coolidge unveiled his own sense of depression in these difficult times, struggling to find a reason for optimism. "In other periods of depression it has always been possible to see some things which were solid and upon which you could base hope," Coolidge told his Amherst classmate Charles Andrews during a visit to The Beeches. "But as I look about I now see nothing to give ground for hope – nothing of man."[327] Nevertheless, while he occasionally used his column to weigh in on the nation's suffering, he assiduously avoided

The American Economy: 1920s to early 1930s

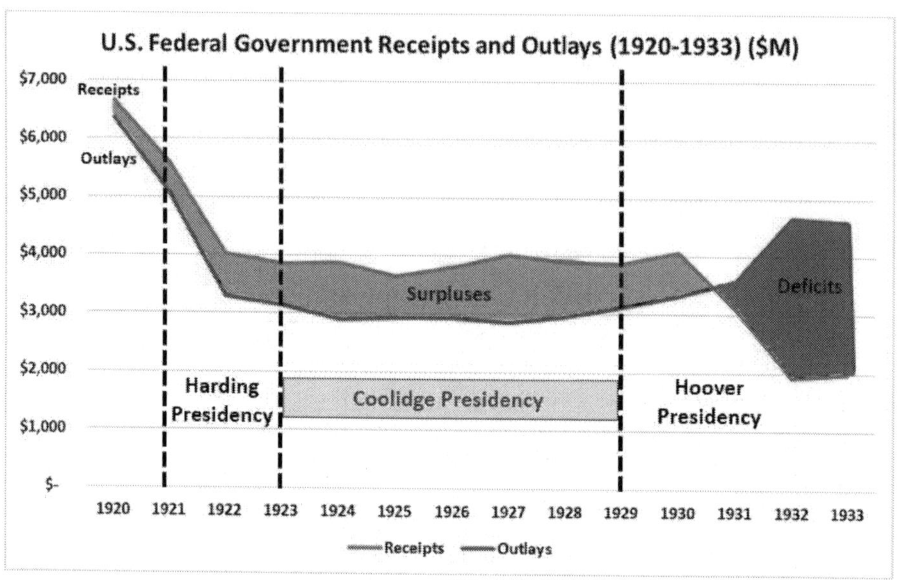

IV-71: U.S. Federal Surpluses and Deficits, 1920-1933

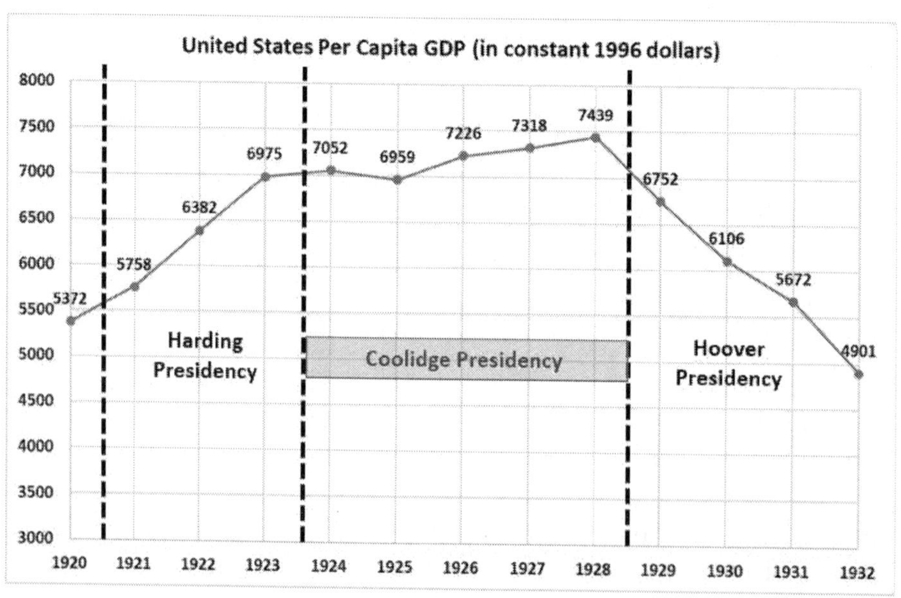

IV-72: U.S. Per Capita GDP, 1920-1932

The American Economy: 1920s to early 1930s

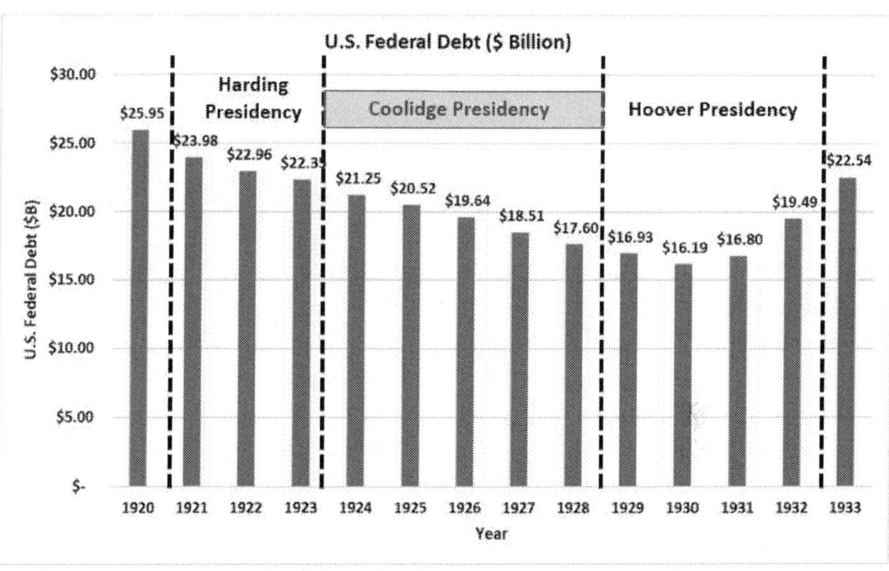

IV-73: U.S. Federal Debt: 1920-1933

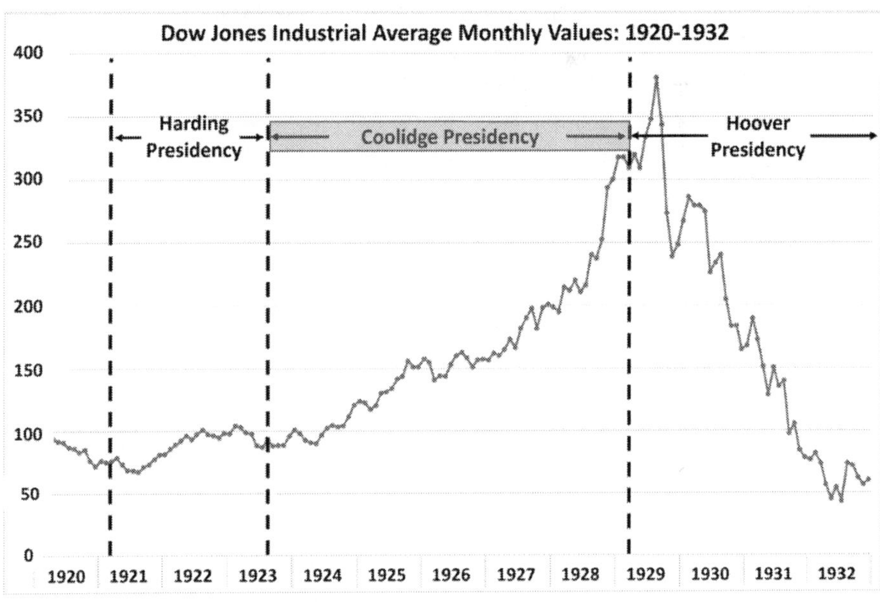

IV-74: U.S. Stock Market, 1920-1932

criticism of his successor. President Hoover had enough problems on his hand without disparaging comments from his predecessor. In the end, Hoover never asked Coolidge for his thoughts on how to respond to the Depression, and no such suggestions were ever offered directly by the former President.

Economists and historians have tried for nearly a century to pinpoint the causes of the Great Depression, as well as lay blame where it might be due. Herbert Hoover, of course, has been the primary subject of censure as he was in the seat when the crash first struck, and he was the one who struggled mightily in his attempts to return the country to a place of economic stability. It is undeniable that the seeds of the fall had begun to build during the Coolidge years, including the rampant speculation in an overheated stock market, as well as domestic spending that was fueled by easy credit for the purchase of the innovations of personal convenience that exploded during the 1920s, even for those who couldn't really afford these new luxuries. But it is difficult to pinpoint anything Calvin Coolidge could or should have done differently. Perhaps Federal policies that might have slowed the rise in broker's loans and margin purchases may have tamped down the irrational exuberance of the stock market climb during his last two years in office and may have limited the damage when the market finally came back to reality. Perhaps other regulations in the manufacturing, construction, or agricultural sectors could have better prepared the country for the inevitable correction that would have eased the downward slide the economy ultimately succumbed to. Perhaps. But, while it's easy in hindsight to identify these potential mitigating actions, it would have been very difficult to identify them, and act on them, in advance, particularly with a President in the Oval Office who did not see this kind of intervention as the role of the Federal government. Some have pointed to Coolidge's statement in 1927 that voiced no issue with the expanded use of broker's loans to buy stocks on credit as being irresponsible, perhaps adding fuel to a pattern of market behavior that proved excessively optimistic. But such blame is misplaced. First, it gives the President too much credit. Margin buying took off because buyers were chasing outsized profits, not because of a statement or two by the President. Second, Calvin Coolidge did not have a crystal ball any more than did the experts on Wall Street who continued to be bullish on the market and the economy as a whole. The policies of Warren Harding and Calvin Coolidge launched the greatest period of economic prosperity their country had ever seen. The good times lasted nearly a decade before economic reality once again took over. Perhaps Coolidge could have done something to ease the suffering that followed his departure from office, but it is hard to nail down what specifically he should have done along these lines. What followed also can't take away from the history-making economic boom experienced by the country throughout his entire time in office.

Coolidge did have one direct source of conflict during his post-presidential years, and that had to do with the inscription on U.S. history he crafted for Gutzon Borglum to use for the completion of Mount Rushmore. Coolidge carefully prepared the text but was then taken aback when Borglum decided to introduce his own edits. When the updated version made its way back to Northampton, Coolidge was no longer interested in working with the sculptor. Borglum was now on his own to complete this portion of his monument.

Even though his column was extremely popular, Coolidge decided to end the commitment after just one year. The work was challenging for him, and it had become a bit of a burden, so he decided to put his pencil and paper aside. Mostly, the Coolidges lived a quiet, private life, primarily at The Beeches, but also with stays at Plymouth Notch. Coolidge decided to finally introduce some modernization to his father's old home, adding electricity, indoor plumbing, and some other up-to-date amenities. He traveled a little, but made only one visit to the nation's capital, which was to attend a luncheon hosted by President Hoover in honor of the official activation of the Kellogg-Briand Pact. Coolidge also joined Hoover for the dedication of the tomb for Warren Harding in Marion, Ohio, in June 1931. Coolidge said only a few words at the ceremony, which had been long-delayed because of the drawn-out investigations into Harding-related scandals. Coolidge also became a Life Trustee at his alma mater, where he was active at all Board meetings. He continued to

IV-75: Coolidge, 1931 (age 59)

attend Amherst commencements but did not speak at any of these ceremonies. Invitations to speak continued to roll into The Beeches, but Coolidge declined just about every entreaty. He did agree to stump for Hoover in his re-election campaign in 1932 against the Democratic nominee Franklin Roosevelt, but his contributions were limited. At the request of Everett Sanders, the Chair of the Republican National Committee, Coolidge penned an article of support that was published in the *Saturday Evening Post*, and he also agreed to speak at a campaign event at Madison Square Garden in New York. Just before the election, he also offered a 15-minute speech that advocated for Hoover and the Republican banner that was carried on radio stations across the country. But none of this did any good. The economy had tanked, and Hoover was largely to blame in the eyes of the American people. FDR's "New Deal" provided a sense of optimism, even though the details remained largely unclear. Hoover had won 40 states in the 1928 canvass but was reduced to six states just four years later. With this massive swing in the sentiments of the electorate, even though his name wasn't on the ballot, Coolidge could see the country passing him by. He shared the following perspective with Henry Stoddard in the aftermath of Roosevelt's overwhelming victory:

> I have been out of touch so long with political activities that I feel I no longer fit in with these times. … These socialistic notions of government are not of my day. When I was in office, tax reduction, debt reduction, tariff stability and economy were the things to which I gave attention. We succeeded on those lines. It has always seemed to me that common sense is the real solvent for the nation's problems at all times – common sense and hard work. When I read of the new-fangled things that are now so popular I realize that my time in public affairs is past. I wouldn't know how to handle them if I were called upon to do so. That is why I am through with public life forever. I shall never again hold public office.[328]

For so many years, Coolidge had been the right person in the right place at the right time, but that era appeared to be gone. Coolidge would be gone in short order as well.

Coolidge did live long enough to see his lone remaining son marry his longtime sweetheart, Florence Trumbull, the daughter of the

Governor of Connecticut, John Trumbull. He did some charity work, with just about all of his energies in this regard focused on Grace's old school in Northampton, the Clarke School for the Deaf. Coolidge worked closely with Clarence Barron, the publisher of *The Wall Street Journal*, to raise $2 million for the school, which Grace continued to support by volunteering her own time. He never got around to his grand outdoor adventure with Agent Starling, who had gone on to serve President Hoover. Most days for the Coolidges included quiet time on the front porch, with Grace sewing or crocheting and Coolidge reading and smoking cigars. Over the course of their twenty-eight years together, both Coolidges had a sense of their place, both inside the home and in the outside world, and they were content with their lot. Late in life, Grace offered that her husband had "deeper sentimental feeling than most people whom I have known, but he did not reveal it in outward manifestation."[329] She and Stearns and Agent Starling may have been among the very few who ever saw that side of Calvin Coolidge.

Coolidge's health began to fade a couple of years after leaving office. He tired easily and often complained of various stomach ailments. "His was not a rugged constitution," Grace commented, "and the weight of responsibility which he had carried for many years took its toll."[330] The end came in typical quiet fashion for Coolidge. On January 5, 1933, Grace went upstairs to check on her husband, who had excused himself for a shave. When he didn't answer her call, she entered his room and found him on the floor. He had died of a heart attack at the age of 60. Also befitting his personality, Coolidge had planned for the simplest of services at the Edwards Congregational Church in Northampton. The outgoing President and Mrs. Hoover were joined by Chief Justice Charles Hughes, Associate Justice Harlan Stone, about 25 members each from the House and Senate, and the soon-to-be First Lady Eleanor Roosevelt for the simple ceremony. There was no eulogy, no speeches, and only two hymns for a service that lasted just 22 minutes. A number of the mourners then joined the family for Coolidge's burial in the family plot at Plymouth Notch Cemetery. Grace Coolidge would join him there, but not for another 24 years when she died at the age of 78.

In many ways, Calvin Coolidge was a 20th Century anomaly. Amid the rise of progressivism and the expansion of the power of the Federal government, Coolidge was a throwback to a more traditional approach to American governance. He was a simple man with deeply-ingrained beliefs that centered on the power of the self-reliant individual, where local communities represented the purest form of liberty and that a faraway national government should exercise maximum restraint in dictating to these local populations. From a practical matter, this meant a constant drive for Coolidge as President to cut government spending and reduce the national debt, all while lowering the tax burden on the American people. These efforts served to maximize the amount of money these citizens could keep in their own pockets to decide how best to spend, spreading prosperity to unprecedented levels across the American citizenry, all while ultimately increasing revenues to the Federal treasury. Coolidge's firm belief in the limited role of the Federal government surfaced even in the wake of disasters, resisting an expansion of national responsibilities to provide relief as inconsistent with the mode of federalism baked into the founding structure of the country. These conservative principles helped lead to the greatest decade of prosperity in American history. His steadfast commitment to these core tenets helped fuel a surge in economic productivity and expansion of wealth that was simply unprecedented. By every economic measure, the 1920s truly "roared" under the leadership of Warren Harding and Calvin Coolidge.

When everything collapsed shortly after Coolidge retired from public life, the laissez-faire approach to national governance seemed to go by the wayside. These true conservative beliefs were cast aside for more interventionist leadership principles, expanding the role of the Federal government on a continuous basis. A half-century later, however, along came Ronald Reagan, a former liberal Democrat who had moved to fully embrace these core conservative principles. Reagan had been inspired by Coolidge more than once. When confronted with a strike by the public sector air traffic controllers in 1981, President Reagan noted that "Governments are different from private industry. I agreed with Calvin Coolidge, who said, 'There is no right to strike against the public safety by anybody, anywhere, at any time'"[331] when he dealt with the police strike in Boston in 1919. Reagan followed Coolidge's bold stand by terminating the controllers when they insisted on striking. But Reagan's fondness for Coolidge had a broader foundation, centering on a set of fundamental principles that both saw as intrinsic to proper governance and a means to maximize the benefits to the American people. Reagan, who personally selected a portrait of Coolidge to hang in his Oval Office, wrote in his autobiography:

> I'd always thought of Coolidge as one of our most underrated presidents. He wasn't a man with flamboyant looks or style, but he got things done in a quiet way. He came into office after World War I facing a mountain of war debt, but instead of raising taxes, he cut the tax rate and government revenues increased, permitting him to eliminate the wartime debt and proving that the principle mentioned by Ibn Khaldoon [a social scientist from the Middle Ages] about lower tax rates meaning greater tax revenues still worked in the modern world.[332]

Reaganomics, which fueled economic growth and prosperity in the 1980s, was very much in the tradition of Calvin Coolidge in the 1920s.

Economists vary in their response to the legitimacy of the Coolidge and Reagan doctrines. Some sing their praises and point to reams of economic data to justify their positions. Seemingly as many refute these findings, using their own data to cast doubt on the benefits of such an approach, including the inability to sustain them over the long term. In many ways, these debates go back to the founding of the Republic, continuing to search for the proper role of the national government in this system of Federalism that was baked in from the beginning but has gone through many interpretations and evolutions over time. For Calvin Coolidge, he only knew one way to govern. It was the manner in which he was raised and had served him well personally, professionally, and politically. During the five and a half years in which he was entrusted to lead his nation, the shy, taciturn, strait-laced man from Vermont stuck to these principles and helped to deliver unprecedented prosperity to his nation. That's a record on which his legacy can stand tall, even if much of it unraveled shortly after he left the national scene.

20 Quotations from Calvin Coolidge

Date	Context and Source	Quote
Era: 1894-1895 Written: 1929	On the course taught by Charles Garman at Amherst; From his *Autobiography* (Coolidge. p. 7)	"In ethics he taught us that there is a standard of righteousness, that might does not make right, that the end does not justify the means and that expediency as a working principle is bound to fail. The only hope of perfecting human relationship is in accordance with the law of service under which men are not so solicitous about what they shall get as they are about what they shall give."
Era: 1906-1929 Written: 1929	On his simple rental home on Massasoit Street; From his *Autobiography* (Coolidge. p. 95)	"So long as I lived there, I could be independent and serve the public without ever thinking that I could not maintain my position if I lost my office. … This left me free to make my own decisions in accordance with what I thought was the public good. We lived where we did that I might better serve the people."
January 7, 1914	Elements of his personal and political philosophy; From his inaugural address as the President of the State Senate (MA), called the "Have Faith in Massachusetts" speech (Green. p. 82)	"Recognize the immortal worth and dignity of man. Let the laws of Massachusetts proclaim to her humblest citizen, performing the most menial task, the recognition of his manhood, the recognition that all men are peers, the humblest with the most exalted, the recognition that all work is glorified. Such is the path to equality before the law. Such is the foundation of liberty under the law. Such is the sublime revelation of man's relation to man – Democracy."
~ 1915	On his shyness; From remarks to R.M. Washburn (Washburn. p. 63)	"Do you know, I've never really grown up? It's a hard thing for me to play this game. In politics, one must meet people, and that's not easy for me. … It's been hard for me all my life. When I was a little fellow, as long ago as I can remember, I would go into a panic I heard stranger voices in the house. I felt I just couldn't meet the people and shake hands with them. Most of the visitors would sit with Mother and Father in the kitchen and the hardest thing in the world was to have to go through the kitchen door and give them a greeting. I was almost ten before I realized I couldn't go on that way. And by fighting hard I used to manage to get

		through that door. I'm all right with old friends, but every time I meet a stranger, I've got to go through the old kitchen-door, back home, and it's not easy."
September 11, 1919	His determination that the striking officers of the Boston Police Department had abandoned their posts and forfeited their positions; From a public statement by Governor Coolidge (Shlaes. p. 167)	"The action of the police in leaving their posts of duty is not a strike. It is a desertion. There is nothing to arbitrate, nothing to compromise. In my personal opinion there are no conditions under which the men can return to the force."
September 14, 1919	His response to AFL President Samuel Gompers regarding his position on the striking policemen; From his telegram to Gompers (Washburn. p. 137)	"Your assertion that the Commissioner was wrong cannot justify the wrong of leaving the city unguarded. That furnished the opportunity, the criminal element furnished the action. There is no right to strike against the public safety by anybody, anywhere, any time."
July 1920	On his home state of Vermont; From comments to a large gathering of his neighbors (Washburn. p. 7)	"Vermont is my birthright. Here, one gets close to nature, in the mountains, in the brooks, the waters of which hurry to the sea; in the lakes, shining like silver in their green setting; fields tilled, not by machinery but by the brain and hand of man. My folks are happy and contented. They belong to themselves, live within their income, and fear no man."
1923	On individual initiative, spiritual development, morality, culture, and religion; From the Commencement Address to Wheaton College (Norton, MA) (Ross. p. 180)	"Individual initiative, in the long run, is a firmer reliance than bureaucratic supervision. When the people work out their own economic and social destiny, they generally reach sound conclusions... We do not need more material development, we need more spiritual development. We do not need more intellectual power, we need more moral power. We do not need more knowledge, we need more culture. We do not need more law, we need more religion."
Era: 1923 Written: 1929	Self reflection on his own qualities as President of the United States; From his *Autobiography* (Coolidge. p. 173)	"It is a great advantage to a President, and a major source of safety to the country, for him to know that he is not a great man. When a man begins to feel that he is the only one who can lead in this republic, he is guilty of treason to the spirit of our institutions."

1923	On his taciturnity; From comments to a colleague at a conference of New England Governors in Maine (Washburn. p. 155)	"I have never been hurt by what I have not said."
Era: July 1923 Written: 1929	On the death of his son, Calvin Coolidge, Jr.; From his *Autobiography* (Coolidge. p. 190)	"When he went the power and the glory of the Presidency went with him. The ways of Providence are often beyond our understanding. … I do not know why such a price was exacted for occupying the White House."
December 6, 1923	His advocacy to reduce taxes; From his first Annual Message to Congress (Green. p. 247)	"For seven years the people have borne with uncomplaining courage the tremendous burden of national and local taxation. These must both be reduced. The taxes of the Nation must be reduced now as much as prudence will permit, and expenditures must be reduced accordingly. High taxes reach everywhere and burden everybody. They bear most heavily upon the poor. They diminish industry and commerce. They make agriculture unprofitable. They increase the rates of transportation. They are a charge on every necessary of life. Of all services which the Congress can render to the country, I have no hesitation in declaring this one to be paramount. To neglect it, to postpone it, to obstruct it by unsound proposals, is to become unworthy of public confidence and untrue to public trust, The country wants this measure to have the right of way over all others."
August 14, 1924	On his views on government spending; From his speech accepting the Republican nomination for President (Sobel. p. 292)	"I favor the policy of economy, not because I wish to save money, but because I wish to save people. … Economy is idealism in its most practical form. … The wise and correct course to follow in taxation and all other economic legislation is not to destroy those who have already secured success but to create conditions under which everyone will have a better chance to be successful. The verdict of the country has been given on this question. That verdict stands. We shall do well to heed it."
January 17, 1925	On the focus of the Americans people – business and idealism;	"After all, the chief business of the American people is business. … Of course the accumulation of wealth cannot be

	From a speech to the American Society of Newspaper Editors (Fuess. p. 358 and Sobel. p. 314)	justified as the chief end of existence. But we are compelled to recognize it as a means to well-nigh every desirable achievement. So long as wealth is made the means and not the end, we need not greatly fear it. And there never was a time when wealth was so generally regarded as a means, or so little regarded as an end, as to-day. … The chief ideal of the American people is idealism. I cannot repeat too often that America is a nation of idealists. That is the only motive to which they ever give any strong and lasting reaction. No newspaper can be a success which fails to appeal to that element of our national life. It is in this direction that the public press can lend its strongest support to our government."
December 8, 1925	On the topic of federalism in the American system of government; From his third Annual Message to Congress (Murray. p. 157)	"The greatest solicitude should be exercised to prevent any encroachment upon the rights of the states or their various political subdivisions. Local self-government is one of our most precious possessions. It is the greatest contributing factor to the stability, strength, liberty, and progress of the nation."
January 1, 1926	On his own limits as President of the United States; From a letter to his father (Fuess. p. 373)	"I suppose I am the most powerful man in the world, but great power does not mean much except great limitations. I cannot have any freedom even to go and come. I am only in the clutch of forces that are greater than I am."
December 7, 1926	On the causes of American prosperity during his presidency; From his fourth Annual Message to Congress (Sobel. p. 329)	"Our present state of prosperity has been greatly promoted by three important causes, one of which is economy, resulting in reduction and reform in national taxation. Another is the elimination of many kinds of waste. The third is the general raising of the standards of efficiency."
~1927-1928	His personal views on borrowing money to buy stocks (broker's loans); From remarks to his cousin H. Parker Willis, the former editor-in-chief of the *New York Journal of Commerce*	"If I were to give my own personal opinion about it, I should say that any loan made for gambling in stocks was an 'excessive loan.'"

	(White. p. 391)	
~1927-1928	On the inability of the Federal government to act on a state-based market exchange (Federalism); From remarks to Judson Welliver (Sobel. p. 362)	"The New York Stock Exchange is an affair of the state of New York, not of the federal government. I don't think I have any authority to interfere with its operations."
1931	On the role of the Federal government in disaster relief (Federalism); From one of his newspaper columns ("Thinking Things Over with Calvin Coolidge") (Sobel. p. 407)	"Some confusion appears to exist in the public mind as to the proper function of the national government in the relief of distress, whether caused by disaster or unemployment. Strictly construed, the national government has no such duties. It acts purely as a volunteer. … When the disaster is very great, federal aid has sometimes been extended. In case of unemployment, relief is entirely the province of the local government which has agencies and appropriations for that purpose."

Primary Sources

Coolidge, Cavin.

The Autobiography of Calvin Coolidge. Cosmopolitan Book Corporation. New York, NY. 1929.

Fuess, Claude.

Calvin Coolidge: The Man From Vermont. Little, Brown and Company. Boston, MA. 1940.

Green, Horace.

The Life of Calvin Coolidge. Duffield and Company. New York, NY. 1924.

Ross, Ishbel.

Grace Coolidge and Her Era: The Story of a President's Wife. Dodd, Mead, & Company. New York, NY. 1962.

Shlaes, Amity.

Coolidge. HarperCollins. New York, NY. 2013.

Sobel, Robert.

Coolidge: An American Enigma. Regnery Publishing, Inc. Washington, D.C. 1998.

Starling, Edmund and Thomas Sugrue.

Starling of the White House. Peoples Book Club. Chicago, IL. 1946.

Washburn, R.M.

Calvin Coolidge: His First Biography. Small, Maynard and Company. Boston, MA. 1923.

White, William.

A Puritan in Babylon: The Story of Calvin Coolidge. The MacMillan Company. New York, NY. 1938.

Primary Sources Specifically for Illustrations

Hennessy, M.E.

Calvin Coolidge: From a Green Mountain Farm to the White House. G.P. Putnam's Sons. The Knickerbocker Press. New York, NY. 1924.

Whiting, Edward.

President Coolidge: A Contemporary Assessment. The Atlantic Monthly Press. Boston, MA. 1923.

Illustrations and Their Sources

IV-17: **Coolidge as a State Legislator, 1908 (age 36)** (Artist: Unknown. Retrieved from "Who's Who in State Politics." Practical Politics. Boston, MA. 1908. p. 135)

IV-18: **Coolidge's political mentor, Murray Crane** (Artist: Bain News Service. Retrieved from the Library of Congress. https://www.loc.gov/pictures/item/2014680660/)

IV-19: **Coolidge as a member of the Massachusetts Senate, 1913 (age 41)** (Artist: Unknown. Washburn. p. 48)

IV-20: **Coolidge's friend and political backer, Frank Stearns** (Artist: Harris & Ewing. Green. p. 92)

IV-21: **Coolidge being sworn in as the 48th Governor of Massachusetts, January 1919 (age 46)** (Artist: Unknown. "Calvin Coolidge taking the oath of office." 1919. *Forbes Library Images from the Archives*, accessed April 15, 2023. https://images.forbeslibrary.org/items/show/2568)

IV-22: **Governor Coolidge (right) is joined by Boston Mayer Andrew Peters (left) to welcome President Woodrow Wilson (center) to Boston, February 24, 1919** (Artist: Unknown. "Massachusetts Governor Calvin Coolidge, Boston Mayor Andrew Peters, President Woodrow Wilson." February 24, 1919. *Forbes Library Images from the Archives*, accessed April 15, 2023. https://images.forbeslibrary.org/items/show/2564)

IV-23: **Pamphlet from the general strike in Seattle, WA, February 1919** (Artist: Unknown. "Russia Did It." Retrieved from Wikipedia. Attributed to Totherbarricades.tk. https://en.wikipedia.org/wiki/Seattle_General_Strike#/media/File:Russia_Did_It.jpg)

IV-24: **Seattle Mayor Ole Hanson** (Artist: Unknown. Retrieved from "Americanism versus Bolshevism" by Ole Hanson. Doubleday. Garden City, NY. 1920.)

IV-25: **Governor Coolidge (left) and Boston Police Commissioner Edwin Curtis** (Artist: *The Transcript*. Washburn. p. 88)

IV-26: **Front page of "The Boston Globe" after the first night of looting during the Boston Police Strike, September 10, 1919** (*The Boston Daily Globe*. September 10, 1919. p. 1)

IV-27: **Governor Coolidge inspecting troops from the Massachusetts State Guard during the Boston Police Strike, September 1919** (Artist: Unknown. Retrieved from Wikipedia. Original photo is at the Boston Public Library. https://en.wikipedia.org/wiki/Boston_police_strike#/media/File:Coolidge_inspects_militia.jpg)

IV-28: **Governor Coolidge, 1920 (age 48)** (Artist: John Garo. Boston, MA. 1920. Retrieved from the Library of Congress. https://www.loc.gov/resource/ds.07523/)

IV-29: **Warren Harding** (Artist: Jacques Reich. 1923. Retrieved from the National Portrait Gallery, Smithsonian Institution Gift of Oswald Reich. https://www.si.edu/object/warren-g-harding:npg_NPG.67.71)

IV-30: **Campaign banner for the Republican ticket of Warren Harding and Calvin Coolidge, Notification Day in Northampton, MA, July 27, 1920** (Artist: Herrick Foote Co., New Haven, VT. "Coolidge campaign banner." July 27, 1920. *Forbes Library Images from the Archives*, accessed April 15, 2023. https://images.forbeslibrary.org/items/show/5575)

IV-31: **Coolidge accepting the Republican nomination for Vice President at Notification Day, Northampton, MA, July 27, 1920** (Artist: Unknown. "Calvin Coolidge on speaker's platform on Notification Day." July 27, 1920. *Forbes Library Images from the Archives*, accessed April 15, 2023. https://images.forbeslibrary.org/items/show/5604)

IV-32: **Coolidge on the farm at Plymouth Notch, VT** (Artist: Bain. Washburn. p. 16)

IV-33: **Vice President-elect Coolidge with his wife Grace and friends Emily and Frank Stearns on vacation during the interregnum in Asheville, NC** (Artist: Unknown. Retrieved from "The Important of the Obvious: A Blog on the Cultural Significant of Calvin Coolidge." crackerpilgrim.com. "On 'Colonel' Stearns." Posted November 28, 2019. https://crackerpilgrim.com/2019/11/28/on-colonel-stearns/)

IV-34: **The Coolidge Family, circa 1920 (L to R: John, Grace, Coolidge, and Calvin, Jr.)** (Artist: Bain News Service. Retrieved from the Library of Congress. https://www.loc.gov/resource/ggbain.30641/)

IV-35: **Coolidge and Grace at his father's home in Plymouth Notch** (Artist: P. & A. Photos. Washburn. p. 108)

IV-36: **Coolidge and Grace on the farm in Plymouth Notch, August 2, 1923 (the day before he became the President of the United States)** (Artist: Unknown. August 2, 1923. According to Robert Sobel in "Coolidge: An American Enigma," this photo appeared in newspapers that week, placing it in the public domain. Retrieved from Fuess. p. 308)

IV-37: **John Coolidge administering the presidential oath of office to his son by the light of a kerosene lamp, Plymouth Notch, VT, 2:47 am, August 3, 1919** (Artist: Arthur Keller. The Curtis Publishing Company. circa 1924. Retrieved from the Library of Congress. https://www.loc.gov/item/93509879/)

IV-38: **President Coolidge at the presidential desk for the first time, August 1923 (age 51)** (Artist: Harris & Ewing. Green. p. 168)

IV-39: **President Coolidge with his initial Cabinet on the White House lawn, 1923 (Front Row, L to R: Harry New, Postmaster General; John Weeks, Secretary of War; Charles Hughes, Secretary of State; President Coolidge; Andrew Mellon, Secretary of the Treasury; Harry Daugherty, Attorney General; and Edwin Denby, Secretary of the Navy) (Back Row, L to R: Herbert Hoover, Secretary of Commerce; Hubert Work, Secretary of the Interior; Henry Wallace, Secretary of Agriculture; and James Davis, Secretary of Labor)** (Artist: Underwood & Underwood. Green. p. 206)

IV-40: **First Lady Grace Coolidge (Coolidge preferred the term "Mistress of the White House")** (Artist: International. Hennessy. p. 54)

IV-41: **Coolidge's Budget Director Herbert Lord** (Artist: National Photo Company. Retrieved from the Library of Congress. https://www.loc.gov/pictures/item/2016831885/)

IV-42: **President Coolidge with the head of his Secret Service detail, Edmund Starling** (Artist: National Photo Co. Retrieved from the Library of Congress. https://www.loc.gov/item/93510034/)

IV-43: **President Coolidge delivering his first Annual Message to Congress, December 6, 1923** (Artist: National Photo Company. December 1923. Retrieved from the Library of Congress. https://www.loc.gov/resource/cph.3c11906/)

IV-44: **Coolidge's Treasury Secretary Andrew Mellon** (Artist: Trinity Court Studio. 1921. Retrieved from the Library of Congress. https://www.loc.gov/pictures/item/2004680353/)

IV-45: **Charles Dawes** (Artist: Harris & Ewing. Retrieved from the Library of Congress. https://www.loc.gov/pictures/item/2016861994/)

IV-46: **President Coolidge delivering the commencement address at Howard University, June 1924** (Artist: Unknown. Retrieved from "The Bison." Howard University. C. Glenn Carrington editor-in-chief. 1925. Volume III. https://core.ac.uk/download/pdf/234737761.pdf)

IV-47: **The Democratic nominees, John Davis and Charles Bryan, Election of 1924** (Artists: Unknown and Blythe. Originally appeared in *The New York Times*. July 10, 1924. Retrieved from eBay. https://www.ebay.com/itm/374265084302)

IV-48: **One of the last photos of Calvin Coolidge, Jr. (upper left) during the summer of 1924, with President Coolidge and Grace (seated) and John Coolidge (upper right)** (Artist: National Photo Company. 1924. Retrieved from the files of the National First Ladies Library. Canton, OH)

IV-49: **President Coolidge and Grace Coolidge at the burial of their son, Calvin Coolidge, Jr., at Plymouth, VT, July 1924** (Artist: United News Pictures. New York, NY. July 1924. Retrieved from the files of the National First Ladies Library. Canton, OH)

IV-50: **President Abraham Lincoln (**Artist: Alexander Gardner. November 8, 1863. Retrieved from "The Story-Life of Lincoln" by Wayne Whipple. The John C. Winston Co. Chicago, IL. 1908. p. 679)

IV-51: **President Abraham Lincoln's son, Willie, 1862 (age 11) shortly before his death** (Artist: Unknown. From a photo in the collection of Charles McLellan. Retrieved from "The Story-Life of Lincoln" by Wayne Whipple. The John C. Winston Co. Chicago, IL. 1908. p. 437)

IV-52: **President Coolidge with Rob Roy, October 1924** (Artist: National Photo Company. October 31, 1924. Gift of Herbert French. Retrieved from the Library of Congress. https://www.loc.gov/resource/npcc.26386/)

IV-53: **President Coolidge delivering his inaugural address, March 4, 1925** (Artist: National Photo Company. March 1925. Retrieved from the Library of Congress. https://www.loc.gov/resource/cph.3c11328/)

IV-54: **President Coolidge** (Artist: Havelock Pierce. Whiting. Frontispiece)

IV-55: **First Lady Grace Coolidge** (Artist: Unknown. January 1926. Retrieved from the files of the National First Ladies Library. Canton, OH)

IV-56: **President Coolidge signing the 1926 tax bill; Treasury Secretary Andrew Mellon, who was instrumental in forging the legislation, is the third from the right** (Artist: National Photo Company. February 26, 1926. Retrieved from the Library of Congress. https://www.loc.gov/resource/cph.3c10627/)

IV-57: **Coolidge's father, John Coolidge** (Artist: Bain News Service. Retrieved from the Library of Congress. https://www.loc.gov/item/2014716673/)

IV-58: **President Coolidge, 1924 (age 52)** (Artist: National Photo Company. Gift from Herbert French. 1924. Retrieved from the Library of Congress. https://www.loc.gov/resource/npcc.25597/)

IV-59: **President Coolidge awarding the Distinguished Flying Cross to Charles Lindbergh, June 11, 1927** (Artist: Unknown. June 1927. Retrieved from picryl.com. https://picryl.com/media/lindbergh-and-coolidge-a86cd7)

IV-60: **President Coolidge fishing** (Artist: Alton Blackington. "Calvin Coolidge standing in hay with a fishing pole extended. He is wearing a suit, straw hat and fishing boots." Appeared in the *Vermont Standard* on November 13, 1975 after being discovered at Plymouth Notch, VT, by the maintenance supervisor of the Vermont Division of Historic Preservation. *Forbes Library Images from the Archives*, accessed April 15, 2023. https://archives.forbeslibrary.org/argus/final/Portal/Default.aspx?component=AAFG&record=24246ee7-695f-4b21-a46e-c302f9c17f4c)

IV-61: **President Coolidge in a cowboy outfit during the summer of 1927** (Artist: Carl Rise. Retrieved from wyomingtalesandtrails.com. http://www.wyomingtalesandtrails.com/yellowstonecoolidge.html)

IV-62: **President Coolidge in Indian attire during the summer of 1927** (Artist: Unknown. Retrieved from Wikimedia Commons. 1927. https://commons.wikimedia.org/wiki/File:President_Coolidge_being_made_Sioux_Chief_by_Henry_Standing_Bear.png)

IV-63: **President Coolidge's handwritten note announcing: "I do not choose to run for President in nineteen twenty eight" – August 2, 1927** (Artist: Calvin Coolidge. August 2, 1927. Original in the Library of Congress. Retrieved from retrocampaigns.com. https://retrocampaigns.tumblr.com/post/47628618283/president-coolidge-i-do-not-choose-to-run-for/amp)

IV-64: **Dwight Morrow** (Artist: Unknown. Retrieved from Wikipedia. https://en.wikipedia.org/wiki/Dwight_Morrow#/media/File:Dwight_Morrow.jpg)

IV-65: **Secretary of State Frank Kellogg** (Artist: Moffett. Chicago, IL. Retrieved from the Library of Congress. https://www.loc.gov/pictures/item/90709247/)

IV-66: **President Coolidge signing the Kellogg-Briand Pact, January 17, 1929; Also seated at the table is Secretary of State Frank Kellogg who negotiated the treaty** (Artist: Harris & Ewing. January 17, 1929. Retrieved from the Library of Congress. https://www.loc.gov/resource/hec.35222/)

IV-67: **President Coolidge with Republican presidential nominee Herbert Hoover, at Coolidge's summer vacation home in Brule, WI, 1928** (Artist: Unknown. Brule, WI. 1928. Retrieved from the Library of Congress. https://www.loc.gov/pictures/item/95500787/)

IV-68: **President Coolidg***e* (Artist: Bain News Service. Retrieved from the Library of Congress. https://www.loc.gov/resource/ggbain.31488/)

IV-69: **President Coolidge with President-elect Herbert Hoover, on the day of Hoover's inauguration, March 4, 1929** (Artist: National Photo Company. 1929. Retrieved from the Library of Congress. https://www.loc.gov/resource/cph.3c11327/)

IV-70: **The Beeches, the Northampton home purchased by Coolidge after leaving the presidency; To the left is the first car owned by Coolidge. It was the car he used as President, that he purchased from the government upon leaving office.** (Artist: Unknown. "The Beeches with a car in front. Car is a Lincoln and the former Presidential limo purchase by Coolidge upon leaving office in 1929. License plate MA 6979." *Forbes Library Images from the Archives*, accessed April

15, 2023. https://archives.forbeslibrary.org/argus/final/Portal/Default.aspx?component=AAFG&record=6c0f3857-421d-41bb-821d-6e6ab43bf731)

IV-71: **U.S. Federal Surpluses and Deficits, 1920-1933** (Prepared by author based on data obtained from whitehouse.gov. Office of Management and Budget. Table 1.1: Summary of Receipts, Outlays, and Surpluses or Deficits: 1789-2028. Viewed on May 14, 2023. https://www.whitehouse.gov/omb/budget/historical-tables/)

IV-72: **U.S. Per Capita GDP, 1920-1932** (Prepared by author based on data obtained from singularity.com. "Per-Capita GDP." Retrieved from singularity.com. Viewed on May 14, 2023. https://www.singularity.com/charts/page99.html)

IV-73: **U.S. Federal Debt, 1920-1933** (Prepared by author based on data obtained from thestreet.com. "Historical Debt Outstanding: Annual 1900-1949." Viewed on May 14, 2023. https://www.thestreet.com/politics/national-debt-year-by-year-14876008)

IV-74: **U.S. Stock Market, 1920-1932** (Prepared by author based on data obtained from FRED (Federal Reserve Economic Data). "Dow-Jones Industrial Stock Price Index for the United States." Not seasonally adjusted. National Bureau of Economic Research. Federal Reserve of St. Louis. https://fred.stlouisfed.org/series/M1109BUSM293NNBR)

IV-75: **Coolidge, 1931 (age 59)** (Artist: Unknown. "Ex-president Calvin Coolidge photographed in Boston, just before he presided over the semi-annual meeting of the American Antiquarian Society, of which he is president." *Forbes Library Images from the Archives*, accessed May 14, 2023. https://archives.forbeslibrary.org/argus/final/Portal/Default.aspx?lang=en-US)

Notes

[1] Washburn. 137.
[2] Washburn. 7.
[3] Fuess. 17.
[4] Fuess. 23.
[5] Coolidge. 5-6.
[6] Shlaes. 21.
[7] Green.19.
[8] Fuess. 24.
[9] Coolidge. 13.
[10] Coolidge. 25.
[11] White. 31.
[12] Coolidge. 38.
[13] Fuess. 32.
[14] Coolidge. 47.
[15] Fuess. 36.
[16] Fuess. 37.
[17] Fuess. 39.
[18] Fuess. 47.
[19] Shlaes. 36.
[20] Fuess. 50.
[21] Coolidge. 52.
[22] Shlaes. 44.
[23] Fuess. 64.
[24] Fuess. 41.
[25] White. 35.
[26] Coolidge. 59.
[27] Coolidge. 62.
[28] Coolidge. 65.
[29] Coolidge. 67.
[30] Coolidge. 65.
[31] Shlaes. 56.
[32] Green. 231.
[33] Green. 232.
[34] White. 46.
[35] White. 41.
[36] Coolidge. 71.
[37] Green. 234.
[38] Fuess. 67.
[39] Fuess. 78.
[40] Green. 38.
[41] Shlaes. 70.
[42] Coolidge. 87.
[43] Coolidge. 89.
[44] Ross. 27.
[45] Shlaes. 81.
[46] Shlaes. 83.
[47] Ross. 19.

[48] Fuess. 90.
[49] Coolidge. 95.
[50] White. 65.
[51] Ross. 30.
[52] Coolidge. 93.
[53] Shlaes. 93.
[54] Fuess. 93.
[55] Fuess. 98.
[56] Washburn. 56.
[57] Fuess. 101.
[58] Coolidge. 114.
[59] Sobel. 10.
[60] Green. 38.
[61] Fuess. 105.
[62] White. 86.
[63] Shlaes. 108.
[64] Coolidge. 101.
[65] White. 90.
[66] Shlaes. 117.
[67] Coolidge 103.
[68] Fuess. 116.
[69] Coolidge. 106.
[70] Washburn. 131.
[71] Green. 82.
[72] Green. 82.
[73] Fuess. 125.
[74] Green. 94.
[75] Shlaes. 130.
[76] Washburn. 133.
[77] Fuess. 132.
[78] Washburn. 78.
[79] Fuess. 140.
[80] Fuess. 145.
[81] Fuess. 146.
[82] Coolidge. 113.
[83] Ross. 45.
[84] Fuess. 145.
[85] Fuess. 160.
[86] White. 126.
[87] Fuess. 156.
[88] Coolidge. 121.
[89] Fuess. 169.
[90] Green. 236.
[91] Ross. 51.
[92] White. 127.
[93] Fuess. 201.
[94] Fuess. 184.

[95] White. 144.
[96] Fuess. 185.
[97] Fuess. 192.
[98] White. 142.
[99] Fuess. 197.
[100] Washburn. 155.
[101] Fuess. 43.
[102] *Russia Did It* leaflet produced during the Seattle General Strike, February 1919. Retrieved from Wikipedia. Submitted by Tothebarricades.tk. https://en.wikipedia.org/wiki/Seattle_General_Strike
[103] Hanson, Ole. Quote retrieved from Wikipedia ("Seattle General Strike"). https://en.wikipedia.org/wiki/Seattle_General_Strike#cite_ref-23
[104] White. 150.
[105] Green. 126.
[106] Washburn. 86.
[107] Fuess. 211.
[108] Green. 128.
[109] Green. 130.
[110] White. 157.
[111] Shlaes. 158.
[112] Fuess. 219.
[113] Quotes originally from *The New York Times* and *Philadelphia Ledger*. Retrieved from *The Boston Police Strike, A Harbinger for Today?* by John J. Tierney, Jr. The World Institute of Politics. Posted October 1, 2020. https://www.iwp.edu/articles/2020/10/01/the-boston-police-strike-a-harbinger-for-today/
[114] Lodge, Henry. Quote retrieved from Wikipedia ("Boston police strike"). https://en.wikipedia.org/wiki/Boston_police_strike
[115] Shlaes. 160.
[116] Shlaes. 165.
[117] Green. 149.
[118] Shlaes. 167.
[119] Fuess. 224.
[120] Fuess. 223.
[121] Washburn. 136.
[122] Fuess. 225.
[123] Washburn. 137.
[124] Washburn. 137.
[125] Shlaes. 174.
[126] Originally from the *Boston Transcript*. Retrieved from *The New York Times, Coolidge's Career Steadily Upward*. June 13, 1924. https://timesmachine.nytimes.com/timesmachine/1924/06/13/104043591.pdf
[127] Shlaes. 179.
[128] Shlaes. 179.
[129] Shlaes. 180.
[130] Fuess. 238.
[131] Fuess. 193.
[132] Green. 110.

[133] White. 174.
[134] Fuess. 240.
[135] Shlaes. 186.
[136] Fuess. 244.
[137] Shlaes. 199.
[138] Shlaes. 195.
[139] Fuess. 250.
[140] Fuess. 253.
[141] Fuess. 255.
[142] Adams, Samuel. *Incredible Era: The Life and Times of Warren Gamaliel Harding*. The Riverside Press. Houghton Mifflin Company. Boston, MA. 1939. p. 163.
[143] Washburn. 137.
[144] Shlaes. 201.
[145] Sobel. 188.
[146] Shlaes. 202.
[147] Green. 164.
[148] Sobel. 202.
[149] Fuess. 269.
[150] Coolidge. 114.
[151] White. 219.
[152] White. 219.
[153] Green. 237.
[154] Green. 243.
[155] Coolidge. 159.
[156] Fuess. 287.
[157] Coolidge. 162.
[158] White. 321.
[159] Coolidge. 164.
[160] Fuess. 291.
[161] Fuess. 300.
[162] Shlaes. 224.
[163] Shlaes. 221.
[164] Ross. 180.
[165] Fuess. 297.
[166] Coolidge. 173.
[167] Coolidge. 174.
[168] Ross. 77.
[169] Coolidge. 176.
[170] Washburn. 110.
[171] Ross. 82.
[172] Coolidge. 180.
[173] Fuess. 331.
[174] Coolidge. 173.
[175] Fuess. 311.
[176] Shlaes. 256.
[177] Shlaes. 258.
[178] White. 247.

[179] Shlaes. 263.
[180] White. 258.
[181] Ross. 87.
[182] Starling. 234.
[183] Starling. 219.
[184] White. 276.
[185] Cannadine, David. *Mellon: An American Life*. Alfred A. Knopf. New York, NY. 2006. p. 314.
[186] Shlaes. 314.
[187] Coolidge. 182.
[188] Starling. 212.
[189] Starling. 208.
[190] Starling. 227.
[191] Sobel. 239.
[192] Fuess. 27.
[193] Green. 247.
[194] Cannadine, David. *Mellon: An American Life*. Alfred A. Knopf. New York, NY. 2006. p. 316.
[195] Fuess. 334.
[196] Sobel. 250.
[197] Shlaes. 338.
[198] Shlaes. 274.
[199] Sobel. 274.
[200] White. 266.
[201] Sobel. 263.
[202] Green. 206.
[203] Shlaes. 278.
[204] Shlaes. 277.
[205] Green. 251.
[206] Sobel. 266.
[207] Coolidge, Calvin. "First Annual Message." December 6, 1923. Retrieved from The American Presidency Project, affiliated with the University of California at Santa Barbara. Gerhard Peters and John T. Woolley. https://www.presidency.ucsb.edu/node/206712
[208] White. 324.
[209] Shlaes. 285.
[210] Shlaes. 292.
[211] Coolidge, Calvin. *The Progress of a People*. Howard University commencement address. Washington, D.C. June 6, 1924. Retrieved from the Calvin Coolidge Presidential Foundation. https://coolidgefoundation.org/resources/the-progress-of-a-people/
[212] Coolidge, Calvin. *The Progress of a People*. Howard University commencement address. Washington, D.C. June 6, 1924. Retrieved from the Calvin Coolidge Presidential Foundation. https://coolidgefoundation.org/resources/the-progress-of-a-people/
[213] Coolidge, Calvin. From his Annual Message to Congress. December 6, 1923. Retrieved from the Calvin Coolidge Presidential Foundation. *Calvin Coolidge: Civil Rights Pioneer*. Posted June 16, 2016. https://coolidgefoundation.org/blog/president-calvin-coolidge-civil-rights-pioneer/

[214] Data retrieved from *The Bison*, the yearbook of Howard University, Volume III of 1925. C. Glenn Carrington editor-in-chief. https://core.ac.uk/download/pdf/234737761.pdf
[215] Fuess. 347.
[216] Sobel. 295.
[217] Shlaes. 298.
[218] Coolidge. 190.
[219] Coolidge. 190.
[220] Ross. 122.
[221] Starling. 224.
[222] Sobel. 298.
[223] *TOXEMIA KILLS WALLACE, HEAD OF AGRICULTURE. Baltimore Sun*. By the Associated Press. October 26, 1924. Retrieved from newspapers.com. https://www.newspapers.com/clip/46607454/toxemia-kills-wallace-head-of/
[224] Information on the Coolidge pets in the White House primarily comes from the Calvin Coolidge Presidential Foundation. "The Coolidge Pets" by Leah Houghton. https://coolidgefoundation.org/resources/the-coolidge-pets/
[225] Starling. 221.
[226] Sobel. 291.
[227] Sobel. 292.
[228] Fuess. 348.
[229] Fuess. 349.
[230] "Summary of Receipts, Outlays, and Surpluses or Deficits: 1789-2028." Retrieved from "Historical Tables," Office of Management and Budget (Table 1.1). https://www.whitehouse.gov/omb/budget/historical-tables/
[231] "Historical Debt Outstanding." Retrieved from the Bureau of the Fiscal Service, Department of the Treasury. https://fiscaldata.treasury.gov/datasets/historical-debt-outstanding/historical-debt-outstanding
[232] Smiley, Gene. "The U.S. Economy in the 1920s." Marquette University. Retrieved from EH.net. Figure 5: "Labor Force Growth and Unemployment, 1920 to 1930." https://eh.net/encyclopedia/the-u-s-economy-in-the-1920s/
[233] Smiley, Gene. "The U.S. Economy in the 1920s." Marquette University. Retrieved from EH.net. Table 1. "Real Average Weekly or Daily Earnings for Selected Occupations, 1920 to 1930." https://eh.net/encyclopedia/the-u-s-economy-in-the-1920s/
[234] *One hundred years of price change: the Consumer Price Index and the American inflation experience*. Monthly Labor Review. U.S. Bureau of Labor Statistics. April 2014. https://www.bls.gov/opub/mlr/2014/article/one-hundred-years-of-price-change-the-consumer-price-index-and-the-american-inflation-experience.htm#:~:text=Prices%20rose%20an%20average%20of,annually%20from%201926%20to%201929.
[235] Fuess. 354.
[236] White. 310.
[237] Coolidge, Calvin. "The Press Under a Free Government." Address to the American Society of Newspaper Editors. Washington, D.C. January 17, 1925. Retrieved from The American Presidency Project, affiliated with the University of California at Santa Barbara. Gerhard Peters and John T. Woolley. https://www.presidency.ucsb.edu/node/269410
[238] Fuess. 358.
[239] Fuess. 358.

[240] Sobel. 314.
[241] Shlaes. 327.
[242] Fuess. 361.
[243] White. 315.
[244] Sobel. 301.
[245] Coolidge. 196.
[246] Starling. 209.
[247] Starling. 209.
[248] Ross. 194.
[249] Ross. 190.
[250] Ross. 188.
[251] Fuess. 371.
[252] Starling. 272.
[253] Sobel .235.
[254] Cannadine, David. *Mellon: An American Life*. Alfred A. Knopf. New York, NY. 2006. p. 322.
[255] Hollenbeck, Scott and Maureen Keenan Kahr. "Ninety Years of Individual Income and Tax Statistics, 1916-2005." Table 1. "All Individual Income Tax Returns: Source of Income and Tax Items, Tax Years 1913-2005." p. 144. https://www.irs.gov/pub/irs-soi/16-05intax.pdf
[256] Coolidge, Calvin. "Third Annual Message," December 8, 1925. Retrieved from The American Presidency Project, affiliated with the University of California at Santa Barbara. Gerhard Peters and John T. Woolley. https://www.presidency.ucsb.edu/node/206719
[257] Sobel. 329.
[258] Fuess. 373.
[259] Shlaes. 333.
[260] Coolidge. 192.
[261] Fuess. 386.
[262] Starling. 246.
[263] Shlaes. 354.
[264] Shlaes. 358.
[265] Shlaes. 389.
[266] Shlaes. 362.
[267] Starling. 248.
[268] Starling. 241.
[269] Coolidge. 14.
[270] Shogan, Colleen. *Calvin Coolidge and Native Americans: A Complex History*. White House Historical Association. October 26, 2021. https://www.whitehousehistory.org/calvin-coolidge-and-native-americans
[271] Shlaes. 381.
[272] Starling. 258.
[273] Sobel. 370.
[274] White. 360.
[275] Fuess. 395.
[276] Ross. 222.
[277] Ross. 224.
[278] Coolidge. 242.
[279] Starling. 258.
[280] Shlaes. 384.

[281] Starling. 259.
[282] Fuess. 424.
[283] White. 332.
[284] "Monthly value of the Dow Jones Industrial Average (DJIA) from January 1920 to December 1955." Retrieved from statista. https://www.statista.com/statistics/1249670/monthly-change-value-dow-jones-depression/
[285] "Trading in Stocks Sets New Records." *The New York Times*. February 27, 1927. p. 11. https://timesmachine.nytimes.com/timesmachine/1927/02/27/96635633.html?pageNumber=77
[286] "The Flood of '27: 1927." *Vermont History*. https://vermonthistory.org/flood-of-27-1927
[287] Shlaes. 400.
[288] Shlaes. 390.
[289] Sobel .332.
[290] White. 282.
[291] Fuess. 413.
[292] Shlaes. 407.
[293] Shlaes. 411.
[294] Terms of the Kellogg-Briand Pact. Retrieved from Wikipedia. https://en.wikipedia.org/wiki/Kellogg%E2%80%93Briand_Pact
[295] Sobel. 357.
[296] Shlaes. 421.
[297] Shlaes. 431.
[298] "All Nobel Peace Prizes." The Nobel Prize. Accessed on April 28, 2023. https://www.nobelprize.org/prizes/lists/all-nobel-peace-prizes/
[299] Starling. 269.
[300] Starling. 263.
[301] Sobel. 373.
[302] Starling. 267.
[303] Starling. 268.
[304] Sobel. 384.
[305] Sobel. 384.
[306] Coolidge. 183.
[307] Snider, Jeffrey. *You Can't Judge the '30s Without Understanding the '20s*. Retrieved from RealClearMarkets. May 3, 2013. https://www.realclearmarkets.com/articles/2013/05/03/you_cant_judge_the_30s_without_addressing_the_20s_100294.html
[308] "Monthly value of the Dow Jones Industrial Average (DJIA) from January 1920 to December 1955." Retrieved from statista. https://www.statista.com/statistics/1249670/monthly-change-value-dow-jones-depression/
[309] "The Cost and Characteristics of Trades on the NYSE 1928-1929." Retrieved from ResearchGate. Table 3. Uploaded by Larry Neal. https://www.researchgate.net/figure/The-Cost-and-Characteristics-of-Trades-on-the-NYSE-1928-1929_tbl1_5186301
[310] White. 390.
[311] White. 391.
[312] Sobel. 362.
[313] Sobel. 390.
[314] Fuess. 440.

---

[315] Fuess. 440.
[316] White. 415.
[317] Shlaes. 435.
[318] White. 422.
[319] Fuess. 444.
[320] Fuess. 452.
[321] Coolidge. 229.
[322] Coolidge. 241.
[323] Bierman, Jr., Harold. *The 1929 Stock Market Crash*. Cornell University. Retrieved from EH.net. https://eh.net/encyclopedia/the-1929-stock-market-crash/
[324] Fuess. 449.
[325] Fuess. 498.
[326] Sobel. 407.
[327] Shlaes. 454.
[328] White. 439.
[329] Ross. 251.
[330] Ross. 286.
[331] Reagan, Ronald. *An American Life: The Autobiography*. Simon and Schuster. New York, NY. 1990. p. 282.
[332] Reagan, Ronald. *An American Life: The Autobiography*. Simon and Schuster. New York, NY. 1990. p. 244.

Index

About the Author

David Fisher has been studying U.S. Presidents for most of his adult life. He has lined the walls of his home with his extensive collection of more than 1,100 first edition presidential biographies, dating to the founding of the Republic. After graduating with distinction from Stanford University, he has held career positions as a radio sportscaster, a management consultant, an executive in the Federal government, and a risk management expert. His leadership positions in government spanned the Department of Defense, the Government Accountability Office, and the Internal Revenue Service. He currently resides in Bethesda, Maryland, with his wife, Helene, and their dog Chester.

Made in the USA
Columbia, SC
18 August 2024